JONAH

Volume 24B

The Anchor Bible is a fresh approach to the world's greatest classic. Its object is to make the Bible accessible to the modern reader; its method is to arrive at the meaning of biblical literature through exact translation and extended exposition, and to reconstruct the ancient setting of the biblical story, as well as the circumstances of its transcription and the characteristics of its transcribers.

The Anchor Bible is a project of international and interfaith scope. Protestant, Catholic, and Jewish scholars from many countries contribute individual volumes. The project is not sponsored by any ecclesiastical organization and is not intended to reflect any particular theological doctrine. Prepared under our joint supervision, The Anchor Bible is an effort to make available all the significant historical and linguistic knowledge which bears on the interpretation of the biblical record.

The Anchor Bible is aimed at the general reader with no special formal training in biblical studies; yet, it is written with the most exacting standards of scholarship, reflecting the highest technical accomplishment.

This project marks the beginning of a new era of cooperation among scholars in biblical research, thus forming a common body of knowledge to be shared by all.

William Foxwell Albright
David Noel Freedman
GENERAL EDITORS

THE ANCHOR BIBLE

JONAH

◆

A New Translation
with
Introduction, Commentary,
and Interpretation

Jack M. Sasson

THE ANCHOR BIBLE
DOUBLEDAY
NEW YORK LONDON TORONTO SYDNEY AUCKLAND

THE ANCHOR BIBLE
PUBLISHED BY DOUBLEDAY
a division of Bantam Doubleday Dell Publishing Group, Inc.
1540 Broadway, New York, New York 10036

THE ANCHOR BIBLE, DOUBLEDAY, and the portrayal of an anchor
with the letters AB are trademarks of Doubleday, a division of
Bantam Doubleday Dell Publishing Group, Inc.

LIBRARY OF CONGRESS CATALOGING-IN-PUBLICATION DATA

Bible. O.T. Jonah. English. Sasson. 1990.
Jonah: a new translation with introduction, commentary, and
interpretations/by Jack M. Sasson.—1st ed.
p. .cm.—(The Anchor Bible; v. 24B)
Includes bibliographical references.
1. Bible. O.T. Jonah—Commentaries. I. Sasson, Jack M.
II. Title. III. Series: Bible. English. Anchor Bible. 1964; v. 24B
BS192.2.A1 1964.G3 vol. 24B
[BS1603]
224′.92077—dc20

89-35970
CIP

ISBN 0-385-23525-9

Printed in the United States of America

October 1990

5 7 9 10 8 6

in memory of my father,
and
to my mother, in loving tribute

CONTENTS

Preface and Acknowledgments x

Abbreviations xv

The Book of Jonah: A Translation 1

INTRODUCTION 7

The Text of Jonah 9

Hebrew Text 9
Greek Translations 10
Latin Translations 10
Aramaic Translations 11
Other Translations 11

The Present Translation of Jonah 12

Jonah Among the "Twelve Prophets" 13

The Composition of Jonah 16

Components 16
Unity 19

Dating the Composition of Jonah 20

"Historical" Features 21
Literary and Linguistic Features 22
Dependence on Earlier Literature 23
Social and Theological Arguments 24
A Date for Jonah 26

Liturgical Use of Jonah 28

Judaism 28
Christianity 28

BIBLIOGRAPHY 31

NOTES AND COMMENTS 63

The Setting (1:1–3) 65

The Storm-Tossed Ship (1:4–6) 89

Storms in Ancient Lore: Introductory Remarks 90

The Singling Out of Jonah (1:7–12) 107

Lot Casting: Introductory Remarks 108

Obstinacy and Submission (1:13–16) 129

In the Fish's Belly (2:1–3a) 143

The Use of Animals in Biblical Narratives: Introductory Remarks 144

A Canticle from the Depths (2:3b–10) 159

Hebrew Poetry: Introductory Remarks 161

On Dry Land (2:11) 217

In Nineveh (3:1–4) 223

Changes of Heart, Change of Mind (3:5–10) 239

Divine Clemency: Introductory Remarks 241

Move/Countermove (4:1–6) 269

Apportioning Jonah 4: Introductory Remarks 270

Heat and Light (4:7–11) 299

CONTENTS

INTERPRETATIONS 321

Jonah as History or Fiction 327

Narrative Art and Literary Typology in Jonah 328

The Narrator 328
The Location of Jonah's "Confession" 328
Jonah as Satire, Parody, or Farce 331
The Audience 334
Jonah as Parable, "Mashal," Fable, or Didactic Fiction 335
Allegory and Jonah 337
Character Roles 340
Sailors and Ninevites 340
Jonah and "Third-Person" Prophets 342
Jonah as "Comic Dupe" 345
Jonah as "Comic Hero" 348
God 350

Looking Ahead 352

Index of Subjects 353
Index of Authors Cited 355
Index of Scriptural References 357
Index of Words 365

Preface and Acknowledgments

◆

Mention "Jonah" and most people will say "the whale." Check any recent translation of the book bearing his name and you will see that there is only a "big fish," hardly ferocious, and occupying three verses of the second chapter. Your eye scans the other episodes and you find them to be no less curious in what they have to tell about Jonah and his adventures. You make a trip to a local library or to a decent bookstore (especially a sectarian bookstore), and you look for a commentary on Jonah. You discover that publishers regularly bundle more than one "minor" prophet into a single volume in which Jonah either thickens the pages of a commentary on a more substantial prophet (Amos or Hosea) or is bunched among equally brief texts from the same collection. You notice, however, that the Anchor Bible series is devoting a volume exclusively to Jonah, and you want to know why.

Jonah is divided into four chapters; but in fewer verses than can be found in some individual psalms, the book covers much ground, geographically as well as topically. Its main personality, Jonah, faces more predicaments, in a shorter time span, than do biblical heroes accorded many more lines of narrative. In Jonah, realistic events and miraculous incidents are accorded equal space, and individuals never wait long before witnessing God's power. There is, therefore, an enormous curiosity about this book: Were Jonah's experiences regarded as true to history in ancient Israel? Or were they read comically, symbolically, allegorically, parabolically? Should modern readers assess the book anthropologically, as a quaint narrative from a distant past? Or should they examine it philosophically, as a repository of truths eternal in relevance?

In order to tackle questions such as these, I have had to devote much space to establishing what the book of Jonah says, what ancient translators understood it to say, and what contemporary authorities think it should say. The Hebrew of Jonah is not particularly difficult, though its narrative prose does differ significantly in vocabulary and texture from its hymnic verses (2:3–10). As does any language, however, Hebrew develops meanings and nuances contextually. It is therefore not always sufficient to cite dictionaries or grammars when trying to pinpoint the import of a particular word or verbal construction; nor is it enough to parallel Jonah phraseology with comparable statements in the Hebrew Bible. Such correspondences, it is true, can narrow certain choices and distance others; but to unlock the sense of a particular passage in Jonah, it is necessary to stick to the context, to follow the Hebrew text word by word and phrase by phrase. This program is not readily feasible for a good many books in Scripture—Psalms or Isaiah, for instance, would need a lifetime to write, and its publication would devastate forests. For Jonah, however, it is an ideal schedule because the complete text measures 689 (or 688) words, a length that, statisticians tell us, amounts to one-quarter of one percent of the total word count in Hebrew Scripture.

Although I do not always record it, I can assure you that I have evaluated every word, every idiom, every phrase, every clause, and every sentence within the book. I have taken nothing for granted and have left few philological opportunities open to me unexplored. The results of this painstaking process do confirm many positions of previous exegetes; but I hope you will agree that they also have led me to fresh insights and unusual results. I do not expect that my conclusions necessarily will convince all readers; but I do hope that they will stimulate them to rethink certain opinions that have acquired quasi-canonical status. I am especially keen for people to know that only superficially is Jonah a "naïve," folklike narrative. Rather, its arguments are highly nuanced and sophisticated and can accommodate many interpretations at the same time. However, while theologians may gravitate toward one explanation and humanists to another, no "big bang" solution or approach is likely to clarify the book's diverse messages, least of all the notions that Jonah exemplifies blind attachment to justice and that he serves to castigate the narrow-mindedness of Jewish repatriates.

Necessarily, the Notes are most useful to readers who can handle Hebrew; but I have sought to make them accessible to those who do not. I have tried not to stiffen my writing with grammatical jargon and I have endeavored (probably vainly at times) not to be tedious or intentionally argumentative. I could not report all opinions about an individual passage that I have examined; but those I cite (I hope fairly) are representative of what is suggested. When a current opinion has an ancient or a medieval antecedent, I give precedence its due.

Those who prefer not to follow my philological reasoning might find useful three other features of the Notes and Comments portion of the book:

1. I precede each section by quotations taken mostly from Scripture. These extracts mean to herald issues soon entertained in the respective section. Occasionally, I would like them also to reveal the intensity of theological debate in ancient Israel.

2. I open the NOTES to many sections with INTRODUCTORY REMARKS, to broaden the perspective on matters germane to their contents. Thus, in section V, which features the "big fish," I discuss various ways that animals enter into Hebrew narratives.
3. In the COMMENTS that conclude the sections, I translate the results of my philological inspections into readable prose. I also engage the narrator on how characters are made to behave and how events are plotted.

I have departed from the usual Anchor Bible format in one other important respect: I have split information the series usually reserves for the INTRODUCTION into two chapters that sandwich the NOTES and COMMENTS. In the INTRODUCTION, I discuss material basic to the study of Jonah. I use the bulk of its pages, however, to demonstrate why singling out a specific time that Jonah was written is an unrealistic, indeed unproductive, enterprise. I reserve for the INTERPRETATIONS a review of various attempts to fit Jonah into a predefined literary category. I also discuss many facets of the book's literary style by drawing together information developed in the COMMENTS. Because interpreting Jonah is by no means akin to solving its philological difficulties, however, readers should be prepared for discrepancies, even contradictions, when moving between these two divisions of the book.

Otherwise, I have stayed with the Anchor Bible pattern. I should alert you, however, to a stylistic idiosyncrasy: I use "God" when Jonah or the narrator is referring to the Hebrew deity; "god" when it is being used as a common noun or when it is invoked by non-Hebrews. I do so because it is useful for modern readers to recognize that Jonah is set in a pagan world, even if intellectual Jews, the narrative's earliest audience, acknowledged the existence of just one divine figure. One predicament I could not resolve is how to avoid gender connotation when mentioning the Hebrew God. As excuse, I could report that the Hebrew language regularly associates masculine forms when citing God; truth to tell, I simply ran out of tactics for avoiding the use of "he" or "him" and could not abide the cumbersome and wooden English my initial evasions produced.

It is remarkable how many persons have participated in the creation and production of this modest-sized book. I began researching it in Israel, when the Hebrew University's Institute for Advanced Studies invited me to join its "Bible as Literature" seminar for 1982–83. For their help and many courtesies I am indebted to its then director, Aryeh Dvoretski, as well as to Shabtay Guiron and the remarkable Bilhah Gus. With pleasure I acknowledge the valuable comments my seminar colleagues made during that wonderful year: Robert Alter, Edward Emerton, Jan Fokkelman, Menahem Haran, Bustenay Oded, Nahum Sarna, Uriel Simon, Alberto Soggin, Shemaryahu Talmon, and, *ex camera,* Moshe Greenberg and Jonas Greenfield. I had the good fortune of resuming discussions with Shemaryahu Talmon when he spent 1987–88 in Chapel Hill as fellow of the National Humanities Center. I must also recognize the generous hospitality of the École Biblique and the privileges its librarians Fathers Marcel Sigrist and Emile Puech allowed me. Avigdor Horowitz shared with me both insights and space in the Landsberger-Finkelstein Assyriological library on Mount Scopus.

I abandoned research on Jonah when I failed to locate a decent host series for it. Playing well the *shadkhan,* Kyle McCarter brought my predicament to the attention of David Noel Freedman and the Anchor Bible. The University of North Carolina and its officers, Provost Samuel Williamson and Dean Gillian Cell, awarded me a Kenan leave for 1988–89 to complete this volume. I gladly thank them all. I acknowledge gratefully the help of John Van Seters, chair of my department, in securing that leave.

A number of colleagues have helped make this volume more accurate, readable, or useful: Tamara Eskenazi has commented on the INTRODUCTION and the INTERPRETATIONS chapters; Joseph Blenkinsopp has read the NOTES and COMMENTS pages, peppering them with sharp queries; Kenneth Hoglund and Lou Silberman allowed me to cite unpublished papers; Simo Parpola wrote a note on Nineveh that I include in section XI; my colleagues David Halperin and Bart Ehrman patiently answered the many questions I had on Rabbinics, New Testament, and Septuagintal Greek. David and Noah Sasson clarified problems in the Vulgate's Latin. John Van Seters and Brian Schmidt patiently listened to my harangues.

I have a thick folder of letters from David Noel Freedman to confirm every tribute the other Anchor Bible contributors have paid to his incredible editorial feats. David's eye can spot typographical errors, isolate ungainly idioms, catch infelicitous sentences, and identify mismatched phrases. What David did most for me was to ambush me with diverse ways of treating issues, steer me to passages that must not be slighted, and tease me into considering other perspectives. He naturally pushed for his pet ideas, but he never imposed them on me; he hectored often, but complimented almost as much. I have adapted some of his insights and no doubt should have adopted more. During this correspondence I partook of a time in which letter-writing was a serious art form. I shall miss this perception most of all.

Theresa D'Orsogna cheerfully accepted the task of preparing the volume for publication. I am fortunate that Abigail Bok agreed to copy-edit *Jonah.* She has helped the final version of the book in ways I cannot begin to catalog. I am grateful to James Ashmore for preparing the indexes.

I have dedicated this volume to my parents, who have sacrificed much to bring their children to safer shores. My father rarely spoke about his boyhood in Mosul, Iraq. Once, long ago, he told me that across the river from where he grew up there used to be the center of a mighty Assyrian empire but that there remains of it only the *tell* where the prophet Jonah is buried. He quickened my imagination then, and I would like to think of this book as testimony that the spark he ignited is still glowing.

June 1989

Abbreviations

◆

AHw	W. von Soden, *Akkadisches Handwörterbuch* (Wiesbaden: Otto Harrassowitz, 1965–81)
ANET^3	J. B. Pritchard, ed., *Ancient Near Eastern Texts,* 3d ed. (Princeton: Princeton University Press, 1969)
ARM/ARM[T]	*Archives royales de Mari* (cited under individual editors)
B.C.E.	Before the Common Era (= B.C.)
BDB	F. Brown, S. R. Driver, and C. A. Briggs, eds., E. Robinson, trans., Gesenius' *A Hebrew and English Lexicon of the Old Testament,* corrected ed. (Oxford: The Clarendon Press, 1962)
BH	*Biblia Hebraica*
BH^3	R. Kittel, ed., *Biblia Hebraica,* 3d ed. (Stuttgart: Württembergische Bibelanstalt, 1962)
BHS	K. Elliger and W. Rudolph, eds., *Biblia Hebraica Stuttgartensia* (Stuttgart: Deutsche Bibelgesellschaft, 1983)
CAD	*Chicago Assyrian Dictionary* (Chicago: The Oriental Institute, 1956–)
C.E.	Common Era (= A.D.)
D(stem)	Doubled stem = *piʿel* conjugation
DB	*Dictionnaire de la Bible* (1907–12)
DBSup	*Supplément* to the *DB* (1926–)
DISO	C.-F. Jean and J. Hoftijzer, eds., *Dictionnaire des inscriptions sémitiques de l'ouest* (Leiden: E. J. Brill, 1965)
EB	*Encyclopaedia Biblica* [ʾnṣyqlwpdyh mqrʾyt] (Jerusalem: Bialik Institute, 1965–82; in Hebrew)
Enc Jud	*Encyclopaedia Judaica,* vols. 1–16 (Jerusalem: Keter Publishing House, 1972)
G(stem)	Basic stem = *qal*
GKC	*Gesenius' Hebrew Grammar,* E. Kautzsch, ed., A. E. Cowley, trans. (Oxford: The Clarendon Press, 1910)

GS	Greek version of the Minor Prophets from Naḥal Ḥever, published in Barthélemy 1963; brief description in Würthwein 1979: 180
H(stem)	*hiphʿil* conjugation
Hp(stem)	*hophʿal* conjugation
HtD(stem)	*hithpaʿel* conjugation
IDB	G. A. Buttrick, ed., *Interpreter's Dictionary of the Bible* (Nashville, Tenn.: Abingdon Press, 1962)
IDBSup	Supplementary volume to the *IDB* (1976)
JBL	*Journal of Biblical Literature*
JE	*The Jewish Encyclopedia,* vol. 7 (New York: Funk & Wagnall, 1904)
KJV	King James Version
LXX	Septuagint, the received Greek version of Hebrew Scripture
MT	Masoretic Text
Murabbaʿāt	A cave in this wadi yielded a damaged Hebrew scroll of the Minor Prophets, published in Milik 1961; brief description in Würthwein 1979: 152
N(stem)	*niphʿal* conjugation
Naḥal Ḥever	A cave in this wadi yielded fragments of a Greek version of the Minor Prophets, published in Barthélemy 1963; brief description in Würthwein 1979: 180
NEB	New English Bible
NIV	New International Version (1978)
NJPS	*Tanakh.* A New Translation of the Holy Scriptures According to the Traditional Hebrew Text (Philadelphia: Jewish Publication Society, 1985)
Radak	Acronym for Rabbi David Kimḥi, a twelfth-century Jewish grammarian
RSV	Revised Standard Version (1952)
TEV	Today's English Version (1976)
THAT	*Theologisches Handwörterbuch zum Alten Testament,* vols. 1–2 (Munich: Chr. Kaiser Verlag, 1976)
ThWAT	G. J. Botterweck and H. Ringgren, eds., *Theologisches Wörterbuch zum Alten Testament* (Stuttgart: Verlag W. Kohlhammer, 1970–)
UT	C. H. Gordon, *Ugaritic Textbook* (Rome: Pontifical Institute, 1965)
v, vv	verse(s)
W	Septuagintal ms. of Jonah in the Freer Collection of the Minor Prophets. See bibliography under Sanders and Schmidt 1927

THE BOOK OF JONAH:

A TRANSLATION

1 1When the Lord's command to Jonah the son of Amittay was, 2"Set out for
Nineveh, that large city, and declare doom upon it; the wickedness of its citizens
is obvious to me," 3Jonah, instead, sought to escape the Lord by heading toward
Tarshish. Going down to Jaffa, he found a ship that had just come from Tarshish. He paid its hire, then boarded it to accompany *the sailors*[a] toward Tarshish and away from the Lord.
4The Lord, however, hurled such furious winds toward the sea that a powerful storm raged upon it; the ship expected itself to crack up. 5Terrified, the
sailors appealed, each to his own god(s), and, to lighten their load, they flung
their equipment overboard. As for Jonah, he descended into the vessel's hold,
lay down, and fell into a trance.
6The helmsman approached him to ask, "How could you be in a trance? Up!
invoke your god; perhaps god himself[b] will intercede on our behalf so that we
may not perish." 7Turning to one another, the sailors said, "Let's get together
and cast lots to find out who is responsible for this calamity of ours." When they
cast lots and Jonah was singled out, 8they questioned him, "Tell us, you who are
responsible for this calamity of ours: What is your mission and where are you
coming from? What is your homeland and to which one of its peoples do you
belong?"
9"I am a Hebrew," he answered them, "and the Lord, God of Heaven, I
worship—he who made the sea, and the dry land as well." 10The men were filled
with the most dreadful fear and upon learning that it was the Lord he sought to
escape—now that he admitted it to them—they told him, "How could you have
done this!" 11They went on, "What must we do to you for the sea to calm its
raging against us, for the sea is becoming increasingly tempestuous?"
12"If you lift me up and cast me overboard," he informed them, "the sea will
calm its raging against you, for I personally acknowledge that this massive tempest raging against you is on my own account." 13Nonetheless, the men rowed
hard to bring the ship back to dry land; but they failed to do so, for the sea
became increasingly tempestuous around them. 14They then appealed to the

Lord, "Please, Lord, do not have us perish because of this person, and do not
assess innocent blood against us. Indeed you are the Lord, and whatever you
desire, you accomplish."

[15]No sooner did the sailors lift Jonah and cast him overboard than the sea
curbed its fury. [16]The men were seized by a powerful fear of the Lord then.
Offering sacrifices to the Lord, they made him solemn promises.

2 [1]The Lord directed a large fish to swallow Jonah. Jonah remained in the belly
of the fish three days and three nights. [2]Praying to the Lord his god from the
fish's belly, [3]Jonah said,

In my trouble, I appeal to the Lord;
he answers me.
From Sheol's belly I plead;
you hear my voice.
2:4 You cast me in the depths,
to the heart of the Sea,
while the current engulfs me;
all your billows and waves
sweep over me.
5 As for me, I ponder,
"Driven from your sight,
may I yet continue to gaze
toward your holy sanctuary?"
6 Water envelops me up to my neck,
the abyss engulfs me;
kelp clings to my head.
7 I sink to the base of the mountains.
The netherworld, its bars, about me *are there* for ever;
but you lift me up from the Pit alive,
Lord, my god.
8 Even as my life ebbs away,
it is the Lord whom I recall.
Then my prayer reaches you,
at your holy sanctuary.
9 —They who hold to empty faiths,
give up their hope for mercy.—
10 As for me, voicing gratitude,
I shall offer you sacrifices;
I shall fulfill all that I vow.

Rescue is from the Lord.

A TRANSLATION

11 The Lord spoke to the fish and made it vomit[c] Jonah upon dry land.

3 1 When once more the Lord's command to Jonah was, 2 "Set out for Nineveh, that large city, and report to it the message I tell you," 3 Jonah did set out to
Nineveh, complying with the Lord's wish. (Nineveh was a large city *for/to God,*
requiring three days to cross.) 4 Hardly had Jonah gone into town a day's journey
when he called out, "Forty more days, and Nineveh overturns."

5 Believing in God, the people of Nineveh instituted a fast and wore sackcloth, the prominent as well as the lowly. 6 When the news reached the king of
Nineveh, he rose from his throne and stripped off his royal mantle; he put on
sackcloth and sat on dirt. 7 Then, he had the following proclaimed:

In Nineveh,
On the authority of the king and his counselors:
People and beasts—herd or flock—
must taste nothing,
must not graze
and must not drink water.
3:8 They must wrap themselves in sackcloth
—people and beasts alike—and
must appeal to God with fervor.
Each person must forsake his evil conduct and
all must turn away from the
violence they plan against others.
9 Who can tell? God himself[b] may consider a change of mind and draw
away from his anger, so that we may not perish.

10 When God himself[b] examined their deeds—for they forsook their evil conduct—he renounced plans for the disaster he had threatened against them and
did not carry it out.

4 1 This *outcome* was so terribly upsetting to Jonah that he was dejected.
2 Praying to the Lord, he said,

> Please, Lord, this certainly was my opinion, while yet in my own home-
> land; accordingly, I planned to flee toward Tarshish because I realized
> then that you are a gracious and compassionate God, very patient and
> abundantly benevolent, who would also relent from bringing disaster.
> 3 Now then, Lord, take away life from me, because for me death is better
> than life.

4 The Lord said, "Are you utterly dejected?"

5 Jonah then left the city, but remained just east of it. He made himself a

shelter there and, sitting beneath it in the shade, he waited to see what would happen to the city. [6]In order to deliver him from his distress, Lord God directed a *qiqayon* plant, that then rose above Jonah to form a shade over his head. Jonah was absolutely delighted over the *qiqayon* plant.

[7]God himself[b] directed a worm, at the break of dawn, on the morrow; it attacked the *qiqayon* plant so that it withered. [8]With the rising sun, God directed a *fierce* east wind. As the sun pounded on Jonah's head, he swooned and, longing to die, he thought, "Death is better for me than life."

[9]God asked Jonah, "Are you utterly dejected over the *qiqayon* plant?" "Dejected enough to want death," he answered. [10]The Lord then said, "You yourself were fretting[c] over the *qiqayon* plant, on which you did not labor, nor did you cultivate it, a plant that came up one night and perished the next; [11]yet I myself am not to have compassion[d] on Nineveh, that large city, where there are more than twelve myriads of human beings, who cannot discern between their right and left hands, and animals galore?"

[a] Hebrew, "them."
[b] Or: "The g/God."
[c] Or: "it vomited Jonah."
[d] Same verb in Hebrew.

INTRODUCTION

The Text of Jonah

This Anchor Bible commentary is on the Hebrew text of Jonah as vocalized and punctuated by Jewish authorities (commonly labeled "Masoretes") during the second half of the first millennium C.E. To understand properly the prose and poetry of this book and to appreciate better its many possible interpretations, however, I inspect variant copies of the Hebrew text, vocalized and otherwise, and consult a select number of ancient translations. In particular I examine various recensions of Jonah in Greek, Latin, Aramaic, and Arabic. There are other translations of Jonah that deserve attention (Coptic, Ethiopic, and Armenian); but I cannot do them justice.

P. L. Trible's unpublished doctoral dissertation (1963) is still the most useful collection of various readings for Jonah; while I consult it often, I also examine its sources when appropriate. Trible's work has been mined often and by many scholars, sometimes clearly without proper acknowledgment; yet it remains a singularly sane and useful study of Jonah and I hope it gets published, even in its present shape. While not as thorough a gathering of evidence, K. Almbladh's recent study (1986) has many excellent insights.[1] É. Levine's work on the Targum of Jonah (1978) also commonly cites proposals made by other versions. The commentaries of J. A. Bewer (1912), W. Rudolph (1971), and H. W. Wolff (1977, 1986) record similar information.

Hebrew Text

The vocalized Hebrew text of Jonah I depend on is printed in the *Biblia Hebraica Stuttgartensia* (1967–68) as edited by K. Elliger. This edition is based on a manuscript now in Leningrad, and it is datable to 1008/10 C.E. Wadi Murabbaʿāt in the Dead Sea region has yielded an unvocalized text of Jonah that was

[1] On pp. 41–42, Almbladh (1986) assembles examples that she considers worthy of emendation. None of them proves necessary, however.

produced almost a millennium earlier (Milik 1961).[2] A comparison between the two documents (Milik 1961: 183–84, 205) proves that the differences are minimal and inconsequential as far as the consonants are concerned. The discovery, therefore, nicely attests to a relatively stable transmission of Jonah, at least since the destruction of the second Temple. Occasionally, however, copyists continue to enter divergences (mostly in vowels) down to the present era, and these too prove not to be significant.

Greek Translations

Jonah was translated into Greek on a number of occasions in ancient times. The earliest copy of one of these translations comes to us from the second century C.E. It was found at Naḥal Ḥever near the Dead Sea (Barthélemy 1963; a new edition is being prepared by E. Tov). I often cite as LXX ("Septuagint") the Greek of Jonah when there is relative harmony among diverse renderings on the way to present certain passages. When doing so, I rely on the edition of J. Ziegler (1967). But when various Greek translations (Aquila, Symmachus, Theodotion) record differing solutions to a specific passage, I take them from Origen's *Hexapla* as edited by F. Field (1875). I acknowledge that this is not the most precise way of handling the Greek testimony; but I trust that it will satisfy most readers.

Budde 1904: 227–28 assembles differences and discrepancies between Greek and Hebrew texts. Trible 1963: 61–64 soberly evaluates them, concluding that "the LXX of *Jonah* is a faithful translation of its Hebrew *Vorlage* (our *Textus Receptus*)." In the COMMENTS to section IX, however, I show that the Greek and the Masoretes differ radically in reporting what transpired in Nineveh once Jonah delivers God's message (chapter 3).

In writing his commentary to Jonah about 396, Jerome studies it passage by passage, giving his Latin translation of the Hebrew but also of the LXX. The last can be of interest. When I need to cite it, I do so from P. Antin's 1956 edition. (On Jerome's technique, see Antin's valuable introduction.) Finally, references to Jonah in the New Testament, in Josephus, and in the Apocrypha's Tobit can shed light on the way that certain passages were understood in Roman Palestine (see König 1906: 753; Goodenough 1953: 226, 1956: 47–49). I take these references from readily available translations.

Latin Translations

I rely most on Jerome's translation of Jonah (about 400 C.E.), taking it from Antin's 1956 edition of Jerome's commentary on Jonah. While we cannot know

[2] Parts from other copies of the Twelve Prophets have also been found in Qumran's caves IV and V; see Schneider 1979: 220–21.

how the Hebrew of Jonah was vocalized in his days, it is important to note that Jerome favors a rendering that is closer to the Masoretic than to the Greek understanding of 3:6–8. When he translates 3:9, however, he does not conform to what is implied by its Masoretic punctuation (see the COMMENTS to section IX). I occasionally cite from Trible the Old Latin, a composite translation from the Greek that precedes Jerome's work by at least two centuries.

Aramaic Translations

In pious circles, the translation of Hebrew Scripture (targum) into Aramaic is attributed to Jonathan ben Uzziel, a disciple of Hillel the Elder (first century B.C.E. and first century C.E.). The targum of Jonah is a rather free translation (occasionally a paraphrase), produced to serve the Jewish communities of the Roman period. I rely on Levine's elaborate edition, which uses a manuscript now in the Vatican. Because occasionally typographical errors have crept into Levine's work, I sometimes cite W. Wright's earlier compilation (1857) but have also consulted A. Sperber's (1962: 436–39). I should add that Levine's work is a mine of information on diverse readings and interpretations of Jonah, especially those embedded in rabbinic literature.

The Syro-Palestinian translation served the Aramaic-speaking Christian communities of western Asia, apparently from the fourth century on. I have used M. H. Goshen-Gottstein's recent edition of its many fragments (1973), which luckily includes a full text of Jonah (pp. 101–4).

Other Translations

I have occasionally turned to the Syriac and Arabic (not Saadia's) editions when their phrasings obviously betray attempts to interpret Jonah differently. Syriac studies have expanded in recent years and can now differentiate among a number of direct translations of Hebrew Scripture as well as adaptations from Greek and Aramaic renderings (see *IDBSup* 848–51). Trible (1963: 64–65) summarizes a number of features peculiar to the Syriac. A recent analysis of the Syriac of the Twelve Prophets (Gelston 1987) suggests that Jonah in Syriac may have originated among Jews familiar with the Targum.

The Arabic edition, however, seems to have addressed a Christian community and may have depended most on the Syriac and Greek versions. I found Wright's edition for both Syriac and Arabic to suit my purpose well, but also consulted the Peshiṭta Institute's recent edition of the Syriac text (Gelston 1980: 40–44).

In addition to these translations of Jonah, I have consulted a number of expositions and homilies, some destined for Jews (for example, midrash on Jonah; Jellinek 1938), others meant for Christians (bountiful overview in Y.-M.

Duval's magisterial study of 1973). L. Ginzberg (1946: 246–53, 1947: 348–52) and M. Zlotowitz (1980) assemble much information from medieval Jewish commentators.

The Present Translation of Jonah

"Anyone who translates a verse [of Scripture] literally is a liar; anyone who adds to it is a blaspheming libeler" (*Babylonian Qiddušin* 49b).[3]

I think that I can honestly say that any translation that has been undertaken for the highest and most urgent reasons (for example, translations of the Bible) or for the sheer purpose of philological study, has something absurd about it.

Yet any translation which intends to perform a transmitting function cannot transmit anything but information—hence something inessential.[4]

Persons wishing to purchase an English translation of Jonah have a variety from which to choose. They may choose the King James (or "Authorized") Version and be assured that they are reading a stylistically literal, albeit occasionally inaccurate, translation.[5] They can also select a rendering that transposes the Hebrew into a contemporary English idiom, often paraphrasing to avoid quaint formulations (for example, the Good News Bible or Today's English Version). But the majority of recent translations aim at duplicating in English what ancient Hebrews would have grasped as they read a particular passage. ("Dynamic equivalence" is the current term for this method.) To do so, translators marshal a wide variety of tools, from comparative Semitics to textual reconstruction.[6]

Yet, there are perfectly reasonable editions (for example, the Old Testament segment of the New English Bible) that do not always alert their readers when

[3] Adapted from Soncino Talmud 1936d: 246. The statement refers to translations of the Torah when read in the synagogues of ancient times. See also É. Levine 1978: 12.

[4] The two quotations are from Walter Benjamin. The first appears on p. 135 of his *Moscow Diary,* ed. Gary Smith, trans. Richard Sieburth (Cambridge, Mass.: Harvard University Press, 1986). The second is taken from p. 69 of his "The Task of the Translator," in his *Illuminations,* ed. H. Arendt (New York: Schocken Books, 1969).

[5] An exaggerated form of literal translation is Everett Fox's recent renderings of Exodus (1986), where (following Buber) he tries to duplicate the syntactic, rhetorical, and compositional styles of Hebrew.

[6] On this topic, see the recent paper of Bodine (1987). An insightful collection of opinions and reflections regarding the translation of Scripture is now available in Preminger and Greenstein 1986: 31–44.

they import a line from an ancient version or when they extensively reshuffle the original sequence. I may therefore record now that while I aim for a translation that is idiomatic rather than literal, I stay very close to the Hebrew text. This confession should give readers fair warning of what *not* to expect. I shall not depend on ancient witnesses to prune away accretions to the "original" Jonah, but shall rather aim to make sense of phrases and words in the Masoretic text even when credible textual critiques of Jonah have labeled them glosses, have assigned them to "later interpolators," or have simply deleted them. Readers should also know that the translation I offer above is not a composite created by selecting from the "better" readings available in diverse ancient translations.

I am not attached to the Masoretic text of Jonah out of religious orthodoxy or pious conviction, but because I hold that commentators serve best when clarifying what lies before them instead of explaining what they imagine to have existed. Nevertheless, I have not ignored divergent readings found in ancient translations, but register and discuss them in the NOTES. On occasions, when I am baffled by a word or a passage, I alert readers to my failure by means of italics; but I also invite them to turn to the NOTES, where I record diverse solutions.

As regards the ancient versions of Jonah and why they occasionally make better sense to us than does the Masoretic text, it is possible, as some scholars maintain, that their translators had a "better" text to work with. More likely to my mind, however, is that whenever ancient translators faced the kind of difficulty that we shall meet in Jonah, they simply offered the readers good guesses. But their goals went beyond simply translating Jonah into familiar tongues, for they also deemed themselves expositors of Holy Writ and often felt obligated to instruct and edify their Jewish and Christian contemporaries. Therefore, such translations of Jonah as those serving Aramaic speakers (the Syriac and targum) could not resist the temptation to preach occasionally to their flocks. Under such circumstances, the ancient versions of Jonah have achieved an integrity of their own and deserve to receive individual scholarly attention.[7]

JONAH AMONG THE "TWELVE PROPHETS"

We have no information on the shape or transmission of his book before it found a location among the so-called Minor Prophets (*šenêm ʿāśār*). Ben Sira

[7] I know of only two monographs devoted to an ancient translation of Jonah: É. Levine's edition of the Jonah targum (1978) and Antin's work on Jerome's commentary (1956). The various renderings in Greek particularly warrant a close treatment. Excellent articles on the problems of ancient translations are collected in Carson and Williamson 1988. Particularly useful to the issues raised above is Brock's contribution.

(early to middle second century B.C.E.) vouches for the existence of such a collection (49:10); but neither he nor any commentator of the Hellenistic or Roman periods bothers naming its contents, presumably because they were common knowledge. We can only conjecture that the roster of "minor" prophets at their disposal is duplicated in our own collection. Arguing that one, at most two, translator(s) were responsible for rendering the Minor Prophets into Greek, D. A. Schneider deduces that our own series was already in place by the third century B.C.E. (1979: 223–24).

Fortunately, however, the discovery of fragments from a long leather scroll of the Twelve Prophets gives us the information we need. This scroll apparently dates to the second century C.E. and was hidden in Wadi Murabbaʿāt (Milik 1961). Four of its fragments contain a complete Hebrew copy of Jonah, by far the earliest available to us. Although we are missing from the Murabbaʿāt fragments the books of Hosea and Malachi (the first and last prophets in our sequence), it is still possible to assert that Jonah is located fifth in the series, between Obadiah and Micah. This sequence exactly matches the order familiar to us from the "Masoretic" edition of Hebrew Scripture. Furthermore, the way the text of Jonah from Murabbaʿāt is apportioned duplicates the Masoretic division. (On this subject see the INTRODUCTORY REMARKS to section X.)

Another discovery, this time in Naḥal Ḥever, has yielded fragments of a Greek translation of diverse "minor" prophets, among them portions from Jonah (Barthélemy 1963; Würthwein 1979: 180). It is not possible to ascertain where Jonah stood in the Greek scroll; but in the Greek codices Vaticanus and Alexandrinus, Jonah is sixth in the series of prophets, which differs from what we have in Hebrew.[8] The order in the two collections is as follows:

	1	*2*	*3*	*4*	*5*	*6*	*7*	*8*	*9*	*10*	*11*	*12*
Hebrew	Hos	Joel	Amos	Obad	**Jonah**	Mic	Nah	Hab	Zeph	Hag	Zech	Mal
Greek	Hos	Amos	Mic	Joel	Obad	**Jonah**	Nah	Hab	Zeph	Hag	Zech	Mal

In these sequences, the main difference is the shift of Micah from immediately following Jonah (Hebrew sequence) to preceding it (Greek order). In both collections, however, Jonah follows Obadiah. It is possible, as some contend (Rudolph 1971: 335–36; Wolff 1986: 75), that Obadiah precedes Jonah because the former was identified with an official of Ahab, hence was regarded as being chronologically earlier than Jonah. It is also possible that Jonah succeeds Obadiah because the latter opens with "an envoy is sent among the nations"

[8] The list of prophets in 4 Ezra 1:39–40 follows the Greek order. The *Martyrdom and Ascension of Isaiah* (4:22) has its own sequence: Amos, Hosea, Micah, Joel, Nahum, *Jonah*, Obadiah, Habakkuk, Haggai, Zephaniah, Zechariah, Malachi; see Charlesworth 1985: 163.

(rabbinic tradition, picked up in König 1906: 748, probably from Delitzsch; but note Jer 49:14). But we can be wary of these and any other explanations because no single reason has satisfactorily accounted for the Hebrew or Greek sequences of prophets among the Twelve, whether it relies on the chronological priority of the prophets, on their place of origin and ministry, on their theological perspectives, on the length of their writings, or on the character of their superscriptions.[9] An interest in Assyrian matters may well explain why Micah follows Jonah in Hebrew Scripture and why Nahum takes this place in the Greek sequence (he prophesied Samaria's fall a generation after Jonah); nevertheless, were we to shift Jonah into any other slot within the sequence of prophets, I doubt that we would gain a different understanding of its contents.[10]

The consistent placement of Jonah within the Twelve (and not, say, among the Writings) demonstrates that the book was regarded as prophetic even if it differs from the others in having barely a sentence of prophecy to relate and even if, when it does so, God's words address foreigners. The fact that God and Jonah speak directly to each other in chapter 4 may have helped to ratify Jonah's prophetic credentials; and the entire book—but especially God's words of 4:10–11—comes to be the message to which Israel needs to hark (see Childs 1978: 127).

K. Budde (1904: 229) thinks that Jonah was once not included among the Minor Prophets and mentions a tradition preserved in a midrash to the book of Numbers to prove it: "There are twenty-four books in Scripture. Add to them eleven of the minor prophets, excluding Jonah which is a book by itself, the six orders and the nine chapters of Torath Kohanim, and you obtain fifty."[11] But the full context of this midrashic passage makes it clear that its author is interested in numerology more than in literary typology, manipulating all sorts of information to reach a cabalistic exegesis of the phrase "captain of fifty" from Isa 3:3.

[9] Schneider 1979 is an excellent background to the topic as well as a thorough discussion of various theories on the order of prophets in the Twelve. His own theory is ingenious; but so are most other proposals.
[10] Schneider 1979: 99 quotes Delitzsch's comments that Jonah, Micah, and Nahum share an interest in God's attributes as given in Exod 34:6–7. (See NOTES to Jon 4:2–3.)
[11] *Bammidbar rabbah* 18:21, cited from Slotki 1939: 734. The "six orders" are of the Mishna, and the "nine chapters" refer to sections of a midrashic commentary on Leviticus.

The Composition of Jonah

Components

The adventures of Jonah occupy four modest-sized chapters in Scripture and can be allocated to two contrasting settings: at sea to the west (chapters 1 and 2) and at Nineveh to the east (chapters 3 and 4). In turn, each of these settings neatly divides into two scenes, the first bustling with nameless foreigners, the second occupied only by Jonah and his God. Some scholars find detailed symmetry between the two settings, most often as paralleling the contents of chapter 1 to those of 3 and the information of chapter 2 to that of 4. In the Notes, I argue that chapters 2 and 4 cannot mirror each other and that the resemblance between chapters 1 and 3 is superficial: they gain a false likeness because 1:1–2 partially duplicates the vocabulary (but not the purpose) of 3:1–2 and because 3:9 shares the phrasing and sentiment (but not the consequence) of 1:6.

Jonah is not a homogeneous book, in style or in contents. Not only is there a difference in the vocabulary and syntax of the psalm when compared with the prose (which is not necessarily a sign of diverse authorship), but the prose of chapter 1 differs from what is found in chapter 3, and both differ from the narrative style of the fourth chapter.[12] The storm scene in the first chapter includes as complete a short story as can be conveyed in a few verses, and its contents betray a dependence either on a folktale or on a folktale pattern. It is not surprising, therefore, to find that the most persuasive studies on the literary style of Jonah cite the first chapter as especially well integrated (Pesch 1966; J. Fichman, quoted in Preminger and Greenstein 1986: 471–72). But if we append to the storm episode the prose verses of chapter 2 (1–3a and 11), we move the narrative into the realm of the fabular and may therefore regard the whole as a fairy tale. The third chapter, too, may have had an independent life, per-

[12] I quote Licht 1978: 122–23. In the Comments, however, I react differently on some of these matters:

> Usually, in the Old Testament, the three "classical" components of exposition, main piece, and resolution merge into a single uninterrupted narrative. In the Book of Jonah they are episodes, separated by clear breaks or pauses in the narrative flow. Each episode is formally treated as a complete story, making some (though partial) sense of its own; each deals with a clearly defined theme; each has a separate exposition (1, 1–3; 3, 1–3; 4, 1–4) and a proper ending. . . . The story is a unity, yet loosely structured. The effect of the loose composition is intensified by the insertion of Jonah's prayer (ch. 2), an independent psalm that functions as a poetical intermezzo, enforcing a pause in the flow of the prose.

haps as a legend or even a fable, allowing its readers to draw a moral about God's mercy (see the INTERPRETATIONS section). The moves and countermoves reported in chapter 4 are much more consciously written, setting a fine balance in words assigned to God and Jonah, embedding a thicker density of paronomasia than heretofore, and inventing expressions that are not matched elsewhere in Scripture. Unlike its predecessors, which may well have relied on orally circulating prototypes, the last chapter is more likely to be the product of a learned composer (see COMMENTS to sections X and XI).

The variety of situations Jonah encounters, the presence of a poetic psalm within a prose text, the puzzling switches from one divine name to another encourage some scholars to label Jonah a "composite."[13] Indeed, already in the Middle Ages, the Jewish exegete Kimḥi proposed that what we have of Jonah is but an extract of a more complete book now lost to us (Bickerman 1976: 61; see NOTES to 1:1). It would not be very useful to chart the various opinions on how this merging of different materials occurred, for they are many, they are not always consistent within themselves, and they rarely muster the support of scholarship either widely or for any length of time.[14] Suffice it to say that scholars discriminate among independent components on the basis of (1) differing divine names (YHWH versus Elohim)[15]; (2) variations in language and theological concerns; (3) modifications in poetic meter; (4) discrepancies that are glossed over by interpolations; (5) reduplication of incidents. Predictably, there are scholars who reject arguments for Jonah's composite nature and defend the unity of Jonah. While a majority of contemporary commentators belong to this category, they do differ among themselves on whether the "original" narrative included the psalm of chapter 2 (Landes, Magonet, Stuart, Lacocque, Allen) or not (Trible, Wolff).

In discussing the psalm, I take pains to show that if it is an insertion into the prose narrative, it is well suited to Jonah. I am careful to use this language

[13] It is interesting to compare how the midrash and al-Kisāʾī (Thackston 1978: 321–26) expand on Jonah. The former stays within the outlines of the Hebrew narrative but finds occasions to insert pious sentiments and prayers by enlarging scenes, dialogues, and descriptions. Al-Kisāʾī has much to say about Jonah's youth, inspired by what is told about Samuel in Scripture and about Muḥammad in the Ḥadīth. He reshuffles the sequence of episodes (arrival at Nineveh before escape to Tarshish) and provides his own framework (loss and recovery of Jonah's family) to contain a series of adventures that find parallels in the stories of Balaam, Abraham, and Tobias, son of Tobit.

[14] See Trible 1963: 67–91; Bewer 1912: 13–24; Allen 1976: 181–84 for reviews of a substantial number of proposals. I give only a skeletal bibliography here because most of the arguments offered in scholarship are taken up in detail in the NOTES.

[15] This has been a vexing issue in Jonah studies because we cannot easily account for the change of divine names, Yahweh (Y) and Elohim/haʾElohim (E, ₕE). I differentiate among these names as used (1) by the narrator (normal type); (2) by characters in third-person mode (*italics*); (3) by quoted characters (bold, * = Jonah).

because I recognize that narratives, biblical or otherwise, are rarely created *ex nihilo* and that they may partake of material that at one time or another circulated independently. We do know, in fact, of ancient Near Eastern narratives that achieve individuality and integrity even when they draw on materials of diverse origins.[16] It may well be, therefore, that Jonah contains the vestiges of tales that at one time circulated independently (in a written form or perhaps orally): a story about a man of God who pays for his reluctance by threat of drowning but who is saved from it by a fish (contrast it with the story of 1 Kgs 13:11–34); an account of a city that repents in the nick of time (contrast it with what happens to Sodom); an anecdote about a holy man who is taught a powerful lesson about humility (compare it with the way Balaam is treated). Scholars

---

Verse	*Chapter* I	II	III	IV
1	Y	Y	Y	
2		Y		Y, Y*
3	Y, Y	Y*	Y, E?	Y*
4	Y			Y
5			E	
6	hE			Y-E
7		Y*		hE
8		Y*	*E*	E
9	Y*		*hE*	E
10	Y	Y*	hE, hE	Y
11		Y	——	
12		——		——
13				
14	Y, Y, Y			
15				
16	Y, Y			

Various theories are offered to account for this seemingly indiscriminate usage. While most of them are credible for chapters 2 and 3 and some of them are plausible for chapter 1, they all falter when they tackle chapter 4; see Trible 1963: 82–87; Allen 1976: 232 n. 21; Wolff, 1977: 170. Magonet (1983: 33–38) offers two sets of highly sophisticated rules; but they change from one Jonah chapter to another. The only hypothesis that makes sense is one that acknowledges the lack of any recognizable overall pattern. Realism and prudence caution me from straying beyond this statement; but see also NOTES to *YHWH-'elōhîm* of Jon 4:6 in section X.

16 The Mesopotamian Gilgamesh, in both its Old Babylonian and its Neo-Assyrian versions, is an excellent specimen for investigation along those lines because we can identify in it nicely integrated fragments from Sumerian and Akkadian myths and legends; see the entry "Gilgamesh" in the forthcoming *Anchor Bible Dictionary.*

have mined comparative folklore to find tales that parallel something like the foregoing, and I cite some prototypes and analogues in the NOTES and COMMENTS (see section V). Trible gives a fuller account that includes far-fetched proposals (1963: 127–52).

Unity

(For further discussion of this topic, see G. H. Cohn 1969: 89–102.) Because Scripture is practically the sole witness to Hebrew literature before the Hellenistic period, it is not prudent to be categorical about the original form of the episodes now found in Jonah. For the same reason, it would not be judicious to assign the composition of Jonah to a single group of Hebrews. What we can say, however, is that whoever gathered its components into a single narrative did a fairly creditable job; for it is difficult to deny that Jonah does "work" as an integrated story. So much so, that if we "deconstruct" Jonah into its constituent components, the various episodes will not survive unmodified outside of their present shell.

If I do not resist the possibility that Jonah is a composite from various sources, I think it is important to mention the features that allow it to gain unity (see the NOTES for further elaboration):

1. placing Jonah in each of the four major scenes;
2. registering the voice of God at the beginning (1:1–2), middle (3:1–2), and end (4:10–11) of the entire text;
3. repeating God's injunction on two occasions (1:1–2 and 3:1–2);
4. having Jonah hark back to initial events (4:2 recalling events of 1:2–3), thus imposing a quasi-cyclical format on the complete narrative (see NOTES to 4:2 and the INTERPRETATIONS);
5. distributing marvels in each section: instant manifestation and reversal of a storm in chapter 1, protective fish in 2, remarkable turnarounds in 3, and a series of miracles in 4;
6. allocating prayers in each major change in setting: the sailors' in 1, Jonah's in 2, the Ninevites' in 3, and Jonah's again in 4;
7. harking back to information in one scene to explain otherwise puzzling events in another (the sailors' awareness of God's power is necessary to understand Nineveh's change of heart, see the INTERPRETATIONS);
8. projecting the promises of sacrifice by sailors (1:16) and by Jonah (2:9) into the future, thus establishing intangible links with subsequent events; and

9. resorting to various literary and stylistic techniques (see also Trible 1963: 239–41):
   a. distribution of thematic nouns; *raʿ*, "evil";
   b. distribution of characteristic adjectives among the four chapters (*gādôl*, "large");
   c. allocation of thematically crucial verbs to three scenes (*ʾābad*, "to perish," at 1:6, 1:14, 3:9, and 4:10); to two scenes (*niḥam*, "to relent," at 3:9–10 and 4:2; *minnâ*, "to direct, ordain, appoint," at 2:1 and 4:6–8); specialized use of *yādaʿ*, "to realize, know," at 1:10, 12 and 4:2;[17]
   d. distribution of unique or rare conjugations (*hitʿaššēt* in 1:6; *hitʿaṭṭēp* in 2:8; *hitʿallāp* in 4:8, see NOTES to the last);
   e. distribution of similar phrases in two different scenes (1:6 and 3:9; 1:14 and 4:2–3, see NOTES to 3:9 and 4:2–3); and
   f. repeated use of cognate accusatives, stressing themes of import to the tale (cited in the NOTES to *rāʿâ gedōlâ* of 4:1).

DATING THE COMPOSITION OF JONAH

(On this subject see Trible 1963: 104–16; Wolff 1986: 76–78; Schneider 1979: 104–14.) Although there is no shortage of theories and proposals regarding the date of Jonah, few scholars categorically set Jonah in a specific period of Hebrew history. Traditional Jewish exegetes and "conservative" Christians identify our protagonist with the prophet of Jeroboam II's reign (2 Kings 14). Because, however, Jonah is not a writing prophet but rather one about whom narratives are recorded, the dating of his book is not a test for religious or theological orthodoxy in the same way as is his survival in the fish's belly. Therefore, traditionalists can be free to decide whether Jonah himself or a later admirer wrote the book bearing his name, even when they do not question the historical accuracy of the activities reported in that book.

Three passages from a single tractate of the Babylonian Talmud demonstrate that this perspective was known to the rabbis (*baba bathra* 14b–15a; see Soncino Talmud 1935b: 70–71). The first has Rabbi Johanan (ben Nappaḥa, third century C.E.) listing only Isaiah, Amos, and Micah as contemporaries of Hosea. Jonah is conspicuously absent from this roster not because Rabbi Johanan doubted his existence, but more likely because he alone was not a writing prophet. In the second selection, Johanan goes on to point out that

[17] I do not list here verbs that are very common in Hebrew (*ʾāmar, ʿāśâ, hālak*).

Hosea was "written along with Haggai, Zechariah, and Malachi," a notion that is rehearsed by the third excerpt from *baba bathra:* "The Men of the Great Assembly wrote Ezekiel, the Twelve Minor Prophets, Daniel and the Scroll of Esther." We cannot pinpoint when and where the "Great Assembly" operated; but for the rabbis, it was after the Restoration, that is, in the postexilic period. Most scholars interpret the word "wrote" in the quotation as referring to "publishing," "copying," or even "canonizing" Scripture. If we stay with the basic meaning of "to write," however, the last two testimonies may give us access to rabbinic opinions that did not necessarily synchronize a prophet with the writings attributed to him.

In current scholarship, the very features that remove the dating of Jonah from being a single-solution issue also create problems for the nonorthodox exegete: the book of Jonah has no superscription that tells when or where Jonah receives his commission, and it cites by name no other person but Jonah. The earliest date assigned to it is, naturally enough, Jeroboam II's reign (early to middle eighth century B.C.E.), when Jonah prophesied. The latest it could be dated seems to be about the third century B.C.E., the probable period in which Tobit, a book that mentions Jonah, was written (see the COMMENTS to section I). Because this leaves us with as much as five centuries of Israelite and Judean history, scholars follow various means to narrow the span meaningfully.

"Historical" Features

Jonah's involvement with Nineveh has elicited opposite reactions on the matter of dating his book. On the one hand, Kaufmann argues that the story makes most sense before Sennacherib, that is, before Nineveh became "a symbol of the heathendom despised by postexilic Judaism, but a legendary 'great city' with its own king."[18] But this view would miss a main thrust of the story that requires Nineveh to be a logical choice for divine sanction and an absurd choice for God's change of mind. Other scholars opt for the period in which Nineveh was an active metropolis (list in Trible 1963: 104–5); they therefore posit that Jonah must have circulated before (but certainly not much after) the fall of Nineveh in 612 B.C.E.

On the other hand, some commentators judge the statement, "Nineveh was a large city *for/to God,* requiring three days to cross" (3:3) and the reference to the "king of Nineveh" (3:6) as strong evidence that Nineveh was distant from the narrator's (and audience's) memory. Many estimate that the postexilic period makes best sense for the composition of Jonah, as some time must have

[18] Kaufmann 1960: 83. On Kaufmann's attempt to date Jonah to the eighth century, see Bickerman 1976: 55 n. 71.

passed for accurate historical knowledge about Nineveh to turn anecdotal. (See Allen 1976: 185–86.)[19]

In my NOTES to 3:3 and 3:6, I raise doubts about turning to these passages to draw any historical conclusion. The statement in 3:3 is not about Nineveh's past, but about how large a metropolis it is, a point that is crucial to God's final argument in 4:11. In fact, Nineveh looms huge in sheer size, second in the ancient world only to Babylon, and it is not surprising that, of all Mesopotamian cities, Scripture accords these two anecdotal treatment. "King of Nineveh" is not a slip of an ignorant narrator, but may actually be a subtle guide to interpreting the story. Beyond the aforementioned features, nothing of historical value remains in the book to help us in dating the book of Jonah.[20]

Literary and Linguistic Features

(See especially Landes 1982.) When scholars turn to Jonah's language to secure a date for the book, they invariably assess idioms and terminology that are judged typical of "late" Hebrew and assemble evidence for Aramaic influence on it. Often discussed are the following:

1. nouns such as *mallāḥ* ("sailor," 1:5), *sepînâ* ("ship," 1:5), *zaʿap* ("fury," 1:15), *qerîʾâ* ("message," 3:2), *ṭaʿam* ("authority," 3:7), or *ribbô* ("myriad," 4:11);
2. verbs such as *ʿāšat (hithpaʿel,* "to intercede," 1:6), *šātaq* ("to calm down," 1:11), *minnâ* ("to direct, ordain, appoint," 2:1, 4:6–8), *qiddēm* ("to plan," 4:2), or *ʿāmal* ("to labor over," 4:10);
3. verbs and constructions, albeit unique to Jonah, such as *ḥāšab* (1:4, with an inanimate object), *šātaq* and *zaʿap* (1:15, when applied to sea), *ḥātar* (1:13, when applied to rowing), *yēraʿ ʾel-* (4:1), or *ḥûs* with inanimate as object (4:10);
4. expressions such as *ʾelōhê haššāmayim* ("God of Heaven," 1:9) and *mâlle-* (1:6);

[19] As far as I know, no one in this century has placed the writing of Jonah in the exilic period, though it might make sense that Judean exiles would choose as an object lesson of God's mercy another of Babylon's victims.

[20] The same conclusion can be applied to that other scriptural composition which features Nineveh: the book of Nahum. As far as I know, no one has noted how close in genre Nahum is to the *Curse of Agade* (J. S. Cooper 1983), a Sumerian composition that allegedly is a witness to the destruction of a major capital city. Both texts include vivid, often figurative descriptions of the fortification and fall of cities, divine curses against them, and laments over their demise.

5. reversal of well-known formulas, such as *ḥannûn weraḥûm* (4:2, for *raḥûm weḥannûn*);
6. diverse particles such as the relative *š* • (1:7, 12; 4:10), the compound prepositions in which it is embedded (*bešell-*, 1:12; *bešellemî*, 1:7);
7. frequent confusion between *ʾel* and *ʿal*.

Almbladh 1986: 43–46 opens up an interesting issue regarding authors consciously adopting various styles of writing (for example, many Persian words in Esther but not in Nehemiah, whose theme is restoration). As she can find no stylistic reason for Jonah's author to adopt a late language, Almbladh agrees with many to locate Jonah in the postexilic period. Landes (1982) has meticulously evaluated this evidence, and it allows him to conclude that linguistics does not offer a sure guide for deciding when Jonah was composed. Landes shows, in fact, that in some cases the author writes good preexilic Hebrew.[21]

Dependence on Earlier Literature

(Sources are discussed especially in Feuillet 1949: 1122–24; and Trible 1963: 107–8, 110–12.) Arguments are offered to show that the language of Jonah emulates what is found in other prophetic books. Feuillet (1949; critique by Trépanier 1951) gives the most elaborate accounting: Jonah's sea narrative depends on Ezekiel 27; his prayer is a pastiche from Psalms; his involvement with Nineveh copies from the Elijah cycle; and his theological sentiments draw on Jeremiah and Joel. In the COMMENTS to section VI (Jonah's psalm) and in the NOTES to sections X and XI (with regards allusion to 1 Kings 19), I try to show that such comparisons are often superficial and do not adequately recognize how ideas and phraseology are transmitted in an ancient Israel.

Jonah, other scholars argue, cannot have appeared before the dissemination of Joel's writings, on which it depends. But it makes little sense to solve a difficult problem (the dating of Jonah) by relying on an intractable issue (the dating of Joel). It used to be that the composition of Joel was placed in the preexilic period (as early as Jehoash's reign, late ninth century). Although there is no agreement on the matter now, Joel is generally placed in the mid-fourth century B.C.E. Nevertheless, scholars who recognize the fluidity of Israel's theological diction find it prudent to resist crediting the invention of a particular religious expression to a single prophet. (Joel, in fact, is a veritable anthology of venerable thoughts and sentiments.) More within our power to elucidate (and sometimes also to evaluate) is the effectiveness with which a prophet harnesses an inherited idea. In the NOTES to Jon 3:9, and particularly in those to 4:2, I try

[21] In the use of unassimilated *min-* (3:8; 4:5) and in the phrasing of *way(ye)hî kizrōaḥ haššemeš* (4:8); Landes 1982: 162*–63*.

to show that whenever Joel and Jonah use similar notions, Joel places them in their conventional hymnic setting while Jonah gives them a plot function.

Social and Theological Arguments

(These points are presented in Clements 1975; Orlinsky 1970; and Landes 1976: 490.) To establish Jonah's date of composition, many scholars find it necessary to place it in the development of Hebrew theological consciousness or to treat it as a document in Israel's struggle for ethnic integrity. On the one hand, Jonah is seen as instructing pagans on the truth of Israel's God. On the other hand, it is said to illustrate the universalistic creed adopted in prophetic circles within Israel. In either case, Jonah is regarded as an excellent intermediate for a change in Israel's theology and thus reflects a broadening of its intellectual vision.

Although these two contentions can be argued separately and on diverse grounds, I treat them together because they are strongly affected by how broadly one casts for evidence. If the book is evaluated from a New Testament perspective (perhaps because it cites Jonah and his "sign"), Jonah's mission to Nineveh can be seen as endorsing the transport of God's word to foreign nations. But Hebrew Scripture gives such an assessment scant support. Thus, while Elijah and Elisha are known to have visited Phoenicia and Aram, their business there (whether true to history or otherwise) is not to win souls or to preach repentance. (See also INTERPRETATIONS.)

Another manifestation of Gospel exegesis (Orlinsky would call it "eisegesis") is a tendency to report on the "conversion" of the sailors and especially of the Ninevites. As the term is used in our days, conversion implies a move from one faith to another. In Jonah, neither the sailors nor the Ninevites are expected to drop their religious activities in favor of Mosaic law and practices. The sailors merely offer sacrifices to a powerful god, an act that any civilized pagan would gladly fulfill when grateful for divine interference.[22] The Ninevites promise to behave; but for how long?

In Scripture, in fact, only persons who are already Israelites are urged (or reported) to "turn" or "return" (*šûb*) to the faith of their fathers. Thus, the widow of Zareptah's acknowledgment of the power of Elijah and of his God (1 Kings 17 and v 24) is no testimony for conversion, because polytheists are under no obligation to recognize the greatness of just one deity. Likewise, Ruth's allegiance to Naomi's God is hardly an expression of conversion; rather, it must be seen as part of a complete pledge (1:16–17) wherein, upon her husband's death, Ruth willingly gives up her freedom of movement to attach herself to Naomi. While married to Mahlon, Ruth shared his life; so presumably she was

[22] When first-millennium Jewish exegetes describe the sailors' conversion, they have them undergo circumcision.

also under the protection of her husband's god. As a widow with no (male) offspring, Ruth could have gone back to her parents' house, but she chose instead to remain with Naomi. In ancient Israel, there were no synagogues or churches to attend and, for wives, worship mostly meant partaking of sacrifices offered by the husband to his family's god.[23]

There is only the case of Naaman who, though foreign born, accepts the supremacy of the Hebrew God. The narrative in 2 Kings 5, however, is at pains to link the land of Israel with Naaman's newly found faith (v 17) and to excuse his involvement with pagan worship (v 18).

Likewise developed from New Testament premises is the notion that Jonah is a "genuine Old Testament witness against a misunderstanding of the election of Israel" (Childs 1978: 127). Jonah's reactions are said by many scholars to reflect a tension in Israel between a universalistic and a parochial view of God. The thesis, however, is by no means evident. To begin with, God's opinion of Nineveh shifts from strongly condemnatory (1:3) to barely contemptuous (4:11), nowhere clearly demonstrating the boundless love of God that allegedly is the book's central idea. (In this regard, see Clements 1975: 18.) Furthermore, there is much debate whether universalistic sentiments were ever available to ancient Israel. I offer as example the opinion of H. M. Orlinsky, who, though willing to place Jonah's composition in the postexilic period, nevertheless argues forcefully for a relatively stable theology throughout Israel's scriptural history. Israel, he maintains, writes about a God who shows interest solely in its own history and fate (1970: 213): "the *natural* God of biblical Israel is a *universal* God, but not an *international* God."[24]

There is also an oft-repeated argument for dating Jonah to postexilic times that distinguishes between views attributed to the narrator and those of Jonah himself. Whereas the former is thought to espouse universalistic or missionary beliefs, Jonah is made to hold a particularly unlovely attitude: he is an exclusivist who refuses to allow the Ninevites the benefit of divine grace, which he covets for himself when in trouble. Jonah, therefore, is said to embody a mentality that is best known to us from the books of Ezra and Nehemiah. There, powerful leaders among repatriated exiles urge their compatriots to drive away their foreign wives and the children they bore them (Ezra 9–10; Neh 9:1–5).

[23] It was otherwise in Mesopotamia, where women did have direct access to the gods. On Balaam as a mouthpiece of the Hebrew God, see the INTERPRETATIONS.

[24] In Orlinsky's view, Israel has no changing theology with regard to foreign nations, whether the evidence comes from Jonah or from any other prophetic book; there are only differences in settings due to changing historical conditions (1970: 230–31; also Miles 1974–75: 178–79 n. 12; G. H. Cohn 1969: 99–100 n. 4). Orlinsky's study of 1967 treats phraseology generally accepted as universalistic (Jer 1:5; Isa 42:6, 49:6). I may add here that one can arrive at similar conclusions when studying Near Eastern theologies regarding major gods such as Amon, Marduk, and Baal; see S. D. Sperling 1986.

Whether the exiles' call can be considered a xenophobic drive toward exclusion rather than a perfectionist (and probably unsuccessful) program to maintain *religious* identity is a problem for specialists in those particular books.[25] As it pertains to Jonah, however, the reasoning presented earlier proves to be not always cogent. To begin with, it relies too much on splitting the book's hypothetical positions into opposite postures. While this is not impossible as a device in literary analysis, it can easily distort the narrative's intent.[26] Second, this reasoning underplays some passages (4:2, for example) and dismisses others (the psalm in chapter 2, for example) where Jonah openly affirms God's redemptive power. Finally, in the COMMENTS to sections X and XI, I will argue that the confrontation between Jonah and God as detailed in Jonah 4 is only tangentially due to Nineveh's survival; rather, its brunt is to engage an issue infinitely more complex: is God godly when acting beyond the comprehension of prophets, let alone ordinary human beings?

A Date for Jonah

Despite its length, this report on the dating of Jonah is but a sample from a large literature on the topic. It must be evident that instead of helping us to pinpoint a definite date for Jonah, the survey leaves us with contestable clues about placing Jonah on either side of that great divide in Israel's history: the Exile–Restoration period (586–438). None of the arguments offered above, whether assessed singly or in tandem, is conclusive. Yet, if I am swayed by any of

[25] See the good comments in Blenkinsopp 1988: 173–200, 348–52. He discusses how comparatively few were those affected by Ezra's call and how Judaism remained open to proselytes at least through the Roman period. An indication that the dissolution of marriages with foreign women is to resolve religious (not necessarily theological) problems is the fact that an issue is never made about foreign husbands. An interesting explanation for the measures taken by Ezra and Nehemiah is K. Hoglund's (in press). He speculates,

> The new rules against intermarriage promulgated, and presumably enforced, by Ezra and Nehemiah may be reflective of the larger imperial concerns over security in the region signalled by the intensive militarizing of the entire Levant in the mid-fifth century. As such, the effort to ethnically circumscribe the postexilic community may have been necessary to insure the continued physical survival of the socioeconomic cohesiveness of the "assembly of the Exile." If so, the insistence by imperial officials [Ezra and Nehemiah] on the community's ethnic separation from surrounding groups generated a self-definition that has become the lasting legacy of the Achaemenid empire on the descendants of that community.

[26] In the INTERPRETATIONS, I shall come back to this point, for Jonah is assigned to a number of literary categories on this basis.

them, it is by the cumulative evidence collected above under the rubric "Literary and Linguistic Features." It suggests that a final editing or composing of Jonah took place during the exilic, but more likely during the postexilic, period. At the same time, however, I acknowledge how little this admission contributes to a fuller understanding of this particular book. To begin with, aside from the skewed glimpses Haggai, Zechariah, Ezra, and Nehemiah allow us into Judea in the first half of the Persian period (that is, until about 430 B.C.E.), the intellectual and political histories of the Jewish people are almost totally open to conjecture. We do not begin to recover useful information about these subjects until the Hasmonean period; by then we are in the second century B.C.E.

"To date" a particular document to a specific period, however, should fulfill at least two reciprocal functions: first, the intellectual positions of the period to which it is assigned ought to clarify the text; and second, the text should inform us about the period in which it is created. In the case of Jonah, whether we place it in the early fifth century or in late third century B.C.E., we gain little insight either into the text or into the selected period. For this reason, we may find it a reasonable tactic when, within a couple of sentences, Wolff (1986: 78) moves Jonah's historical niche from "the last third of the fourth century" to "the third century." (Fuller listing of proposals is found in Trible 1963: 105–7.)

In fact, to render more meaningful Jonah's historical context, it is not enough to hang a date on its final composition, for other considerations beg to be entertained. For example, can we establish a time in which narratives *about* a Jonahlike prophetic character first circulated orally or in a written form? Because Jonah's adventures (indeed even his words) will occasionally remind us of those attributed to Elijah and Elisha, we may wonder whether they imitate these prototypes (hence produced later) or share their auspices and circumstances (hence contemporaneous).

Another question to consider is whether we can posit a date when a composition resembling our own version of Jonah was first penned down or last edited. Here the connection with the Jonah ben Amittay of 2 Kings 14 becomes intriguing. We may speculate that a collection of narratives was given unity and focus by importing the name of this prophet from its context in Kings and inserting it rather frequently (eighteen times) into the resulting text. (For possible reasons, see INTERPRETATIONS.)

Finally, can we fix the era in which the complete composition we call "Jonah" entered Israel's religious literature? It is reasonable to suppose that Israel's storytellers and bards launched a greater number of accounts regarding the patriarchs, kings, and prophets than is preserved for us in Hebrew Scripture. Some of these tales may have found place eventually in the Apocrypha, Pseudepigrapha, and in midrashic literature; no doubt many more are now lost to us.

It is possible, of course, that all of these steps occurred at the same time; more likely, however, is that they took place independently. If so, then the process of assigning a date for Jonah may be less useful an enterprise than is generally assumed, for centuries may separate the invention and oral circulation of stories about errant holy men from the artfully narrated and theologically sophisticated book we now call "Jonah."

Liturgical Use of Jonah

Judaism

Acts 13:15 states that Paul went to the synagogue at Pisidian Antioch and, after hearing the reading of the Law and the Prophets, rose to give a speech. This passage is the earliest witness to the practice of supplementing Sabbath readings from the Torah with portions extracted from the prophets (*hafṭarôt*, sing. *hafṭarâ*). Luke 4:16–20, in which Jesus gives a Sabbath lesson from Isaiah to a Nazareth synagogue, is sometimes taken as supportive evidence for a regularized, fixed harmony between selections from the Law and those from the prophets (see *Enc Jud* 16.1342–45). If so, then a liturgical practice, which still obtains among today's Jews, may already have existed before the destruction of the Temple.

We cannot tell, therefore, how far back in Jewish history the book of Jonah began to serve as *haftarah* for the afternoon of Yom Kippur, the Day of Atonement; it is certainly in force when the Babylonian Talmud states, "On the day of Atonement we read *After the death* [Leviticus 16] and for *haftarah, For thus saith the high and lofty one* [Isa 57:15–]. At *minḥah* [afternoon service] we read the section of forbidden marriages [Leviticus 18] and for *haftarah* the book of Jonah."[27] By Philo's days (early first century C.E.), it had come to be customary among Jews to spend the Day of Atonement in a synagogue, fasting and beseeching God (*Special Laws* 2.193–203; Colson 1937: 427–35). Today, prayers run seamlessly into prayers until late in the afternoon. A few minutes after reading the full text of Jonah, worshipers reach the "Closing of the Gates" devotional just as God seals the fate of individuals for the coming year. The surcease that God allots sinful Nineveh gives worshipers hope that they too will partake of divine mercy.

Christianity

Until the Second Vatican Ecumenical Council, Roman Catholics drew on the book of Jonah for the liturgy of Holy Saturday of Easter Week, the last week of

[27] *B. megillah* 31a, trans. Soncino Talmud 1938e: 188. Gaster (quoted by Trible 1963: 248 n. 1) may be correct that the practice was known in the second century C.E., but incorrectly cites the Tosefta to the *mishna megillah* as proof. See Halperin 1980: 55–56.

Lent. After the blessings of the new fire, the grain of incense, the paschal candle, and preceding baptism, a number of Old Testament lessons (varies from seven to eighteen) are read. In one series that features twelve such lessons, six are extracted from the Pentateuch (Genesis 1, 5, 22; Exodus 14, 12; Deuteronomy 31), four from the prophets (Isaiah 54, 3; Ezekiel 38; Jonah 3), one from the Writings (Daniel 3), and one from the Apocrypha (Baruch 3). In the Greek Orthodox liturgy for the same day, the entire book of Jonah is read.[28]

Since the Second Ecumenical Council, Jonah is no longer read on Holy Saturday. Its third chapter, however, is still read on Wednesdays of the first week of Lent (Ember Day), as well as on Tuesdays of the twenty-seventh week in alternate years. On Mondays of this last mentioned week, Jonah 1–2 is read.

Anglicans and Lutherans read portions of Jonah during their three-year lectionary cycles. Anglicans and Episcopalians recite Jonah 3–4 on the Sunday closest to September 21, when the Gospel lessons are drawn from Matt 20:1–16 ("Parable of God's Reward") and Phil 1:21–27. Lutherans refer to Jon 2:2–9 on Easter evening and quote Jon 3:1–5 and 10 on the Third Sunday after the Epiphany.[29]

[28] According to the Ambrosian Rite, the complete book of Jonah was read during Vespers on Maundy Thursday. For the history of readings for Holy Week, see Tyrer 1932, especially pp. 85–86, 94–95, and 156–60. Fáj 1974: 340–45 interprets the meaning and purpose of the liturgy.

[29] I am grateful to P. Byron, R. W. Pfaff, and L. Hartsell (all of Chapel Hill) for the information I give in this paragraph.

Bibliography

◆

Aalders, G. C.,

1948: *The Problem of the Book of Jonah.* London: Tyndale House.

Ackerman, J. S.,

1981: "Satire and Symbolism in the Song of Jonah," pp. 213–46 in Halpern and Levinson 1981.

1987: "Jonah," pp. 234–43 in Alter and Kermode 1987.

Ackroyd, P. R.,

1968: *Exile and Restoration: A Study in Hebrew Thought of the Sixth Century B.C.* Philadelphia: Westminster Press.

Aejmelaeus, A.,

1986: *The Traditional Prayer in the Psalms.* [*Zeitschrift für die alttestamentliche Wissenschaft* Beiheft 167:1–117.] Berlin: Walter de Gruyter.

Albrektson, B.,

1981: *Remembering All the Way: A Collection of Old Testament Studies.* [Oudtestamentische Studiën XXI.] Leiden: E. J. Brill.

Alexander, T. D.,

1985: "Jonah and Genre," *Tyndale Bulletin* 36: 35–59.

Allen, L. C.,

1976: *The Books of Joel, Obadiah, Jonah and Micah.* [The New International Commentary on the Old Testament.] Grand Rapids, Mich.: W. B. Eerdmans.

Almbladh, K.,

1986: *Studies in the Book of Jonah.* [Studia Semitica Upsaliensis 7.] Stockholm: Almqvist & Wiksell International.

Alster, B., ed.,

1980: *Death in Mesopotamia.* [XXVI[e] Rencontre Assyriologique Internationale. *Mesopotamia* 8.] Copenhagen: Akademisk Forlag.

Alter, R.,

1981: *The Art of Biblical Narrative.* New York: Basic Books.

1985: *The Art of Biblical Poetry.* New York: Basic Books.

Alter, R., and Kermode, F., eds.,

1987: *The Literary Guide to the Bible.* London: Collins.

BIBLIOGRAPHY

Andersen, F. I., and Forbes, A. D.,

1983: " 'Prose Particle' Count in the Hebrew Bible," pp. 165–83 in Meyers and O'Connor 1983.

1986: *Spelling in the Hebrew Bible.* [Biblica et Orientalia 41.] Rome: Pontifical Biblical Institute.

Andersen, F. I., and Freedman, D. N.,

1980: *Hosea. A New Translation, with Introduction and Commentary.* [Anchor Bible 24.] Garden City, N.Y.: Doubleday & Company.

1989: *Amos. A New Translation, with Introduction and Commentary.* [Anchor Bible 24A.] New York, N.Y.: Doubleday.

Anderson, H.,

1985: "3 Maccabees (First Century B.C.)," pp. 509–29 in Charlesworth 1985.

Anderson, W. S.,

1966: "Horace *Carm.* 1.14: What Kind of Ship?" *Classical Philology* 61: 84–98.

(Anonymous)

1979: "An Approach to the Book of Jonah: Suggestions and Questions. By a Group of Rennes, France," pp. 85–96 in Culley 1979.

Antin, P., ed.,

1956: St. Jerome's *In Ionam.* [Sources Chrétiennes 43.] Paris: Les Editions du Cerf.

Archer, Jr., G. L.,

1964: *A Survey of Old Testament Introduction.* Chicago: Moody Press.

Auffret, P.,

1978: " 'Pivot Pattern': Nouveaux exemples (Jon. ii 10; Ps. xxxi 13; Is. xxiii 7)," *Vetus Testamentum* 28: 103–10.

Avishur, Y., and Blau, J., eds.,

1978: *Studies in Bible and the Ancient Near East Presented to Samuel E. Loewenstamm on His Seventieth Birthday.* Jerusalem: E. Rubinstein's Publishing House.

Barnett, R. D.,

1968: "Nineveh," pp. 832–37 in *EB,* vol. 5.

Barnham, H. D.,

1924: *The Khoja.* New York: D. Appleton and Co.

Barr, J.,

1961: *The Semantics of Biblical Language.* Oxford: Oxford University Press.

1968: *Comparative Philology and the Text of the Old Testament.* Oxford: The Clarendon Press.

1983: *Holy Scripture: Canon, Authority, Criticism.* Philadelphia: Westminster Press.

BIBLIOGRAPHY

Barthélemy, D.,
1953: "Redécouverte d'un chainon manquant de l'histoire de la Septante," *Revue Biblique* 60: 18–29 [= pp. 38–50 in Barthélemy 1978].
1963: *Les Devanciers d'Aquila.* [Supplement to *Vetus Testamentum* X.] Leiden: E. J. Brill.
1978: *Études d'histoire du texte de l'Ancien Testament.* [Orbis Biblicus et Orientalis 21.] Göttingen: Vandenhoeck & Ruprecht.
Bass, G.,
1967: "Cape Galedonia: A Bronze Age Shipwreck," *Transactions of the American Philosophical Society* 57: part 8.
1972: *A History of Seafaring, based on Underwater Archaeology.* New York: Walker and Company.
1973: "Cape Galedoniya and Bronze Age Maritime Trade," pp. 29–38 in Hoffner 1973.
Batto, B.,
1983: "The Reed Sea: *Requiescat in Pace,*" *Journal of Biblical Literature* 102: 27–35.
Becker, P. J.,
1973: "Einige Hyperbata im Alten Testament," *Biblische Zeitschrift* 17: 257–63.
Ben-Menahem, E.,
1973: "Sefer Yona," *Trei ʿaśar,* I. Jerusalem: Daʿat Miqraʾ.
Ben-Yosef, I. A.,
1980: "Jonah and the Fish as a Folk Motif," *Semitics* 7: 102–17.
Bendavid, A.,
1972: *Parallels in the Bible.* Jerusalem: Carta.
Benoit, P., et al., eds.,
1961: *Les Grottes de Murabbaʿât.* [Discoveries in the Judaean Desert II.] Texte. Oxford: The Clarendon Press.
Bérard, V.,
1927: *Les Phéniciens et l'Odyssée,* vol. 2: *Mer Rouge et Méditerranée.* Paris: Armand Colin.
Berlin, A.,
1976: "A Rejoinder to John A. Miles, Jr., With Some Observations on the Nature of Prophecy," *Jewish Quarterly Review* 66: 227–35.
1987: *The Dynamics of Biblical Parallelism.* Bloomington: Indiana University Press.
Bewer, J. A.,
1912: *Jonah.* [The International Critical Commentary.] Edinburgh: T. & T. Clark.
Bickerman, E. J.,
1967: *Four Strange Books of the Bible: Jonah, Daniel, Koheleth, Esther.* New York: Schocken Books.

1976: "Les Deux Erreurs du prophète Jonas," pp. 33–71 in *Studies in Jewish and Christian History,* vol. 1. Leiden: E. J. Brill. [First published in *Revue d'histoire et de philosophie religieuses* 45 (1965): 232–64.]

Birot, M.,

1974: *Lettres de Yaqqim-Addu, gouverneur de Sagarâtum.* [= *Archives royales de Mari* XIV, 1976.] Paris: Paul Geuthner.

Blank, S. H.,

1955: " 'Doest Thou Well to Be Angry?' A Study in Self-Pity," *Hebrew Union College Annual* 26: 29–41.

1974: "The Prophet as Paradigm," pp. 111–30 in Crenshaw and Willis 1974.

Blenkinsopp, J.,

1988: *Ezra-Nehemiah.* [The Old Testament Library.] Philadelphia: Westminster Press.

Bodine, W. R.,

1987: "Linguistics and Philology in the Study of Ancient Near Eastern Languages," pp. 39–54 in Golomb 1987.

Böhme, W.,

1887: "Die Composition des Buches Jona," *Zeitschrift für die alttestamentliche Wissenschaft* 7: 224–84.

Borger, R.,

1967: *Die Inschriften Asarhaddons Königs von Assyrien.* [*Archiv für Orientforschung,* Beiheft 9.] Osnabrück: Biblio-Verlag [reprint of 1956 edition].

Bowers, R. H.,

1971: *The Legend of Jonah.* The Hague: Martinus Nijhoff.

Braude, G., and Kapstein, I. J., trans.,

1975: *Pesiḳta de-Rab Kahana. R. Kahana's Compilation of Discourses for Sabbaths and Festal Days.* Philadelphia: Jewish Publication Society of America.

Brekelmans, H. W.,

1970: "Some Translation Problems," *Oudtestamentische Studiën* 15: 170–76.

Brenner, A.,

1979: *"lšwnw šl sfr ywnh kmdd lqbyʿy zmn ḥybwrw," Beth Miqra* 29: 396–405.

Brenot, A., ed.,

1924: Phèdre, *Fables.* [Collection Budé.] Paris: Les Belles-lettres.

Briend, J.,

1981: "Jeroboam II, sauveur d'Israël," pp. 41–49, in Caquot and Delcor 1981.

Brinkman, J. A.,

1983: "Through a Glass Darkly: Esarhaddon's Retrospects on the Downfall

of Babylon," *Journal of the American Oriental Society* 103 [= J. M. Sasson 1984b]: 35–42.
Brock, S. P.,
1988: "Translating the Old Testament," pp. 87–98 in Carson and Williamson 1988.
Brongers, H. A.,
1981: "Some Remarks on the Biblical Particle *h^alōʾ*," pp. 177–89 in Albrektson 1981.
Broshi, M.,
1974: "The Expansion of Jerusalem in the Reigns of Hezekiah and Menasseh," *Israel Exploration Journal* 24: 21–26.
Bruns, G. L.,
1987: "Midrash and Allegory: The Beginnings of Scriptural Interpretation," pp. 625–46 in Alter and Kermode 1987.
Bühlmann, W., and Scherer, K.,
1973: *Stilfiguren der Bibel. Ein kleines Nachschlagewerk.* [Biblische Beiträge 10.] Fribourg: Verlag Schweizerisches Katholisches Bibelwerk.
Budde, K.,
1892: "Vermutungen zum 'Midrasch des Büches der Könige,'" *Zeitschrift für die alttestamentliche Wissenschaft* 11: 37–51.
1904: "Jonah, Book of," pp. 227–30 in *JE.*
Burrows, M.,
1970: "The Literary Category of the Book of Jonah," pp. 80–107 in Frank and Reed 1970.
Butterworth, G. M.,
1978: "You Pity the Plant: A Misunderstanding," *Indian Journal of Theology* 27: 32–34.
Calvin, J.,
1847: *Jonah, Micah and Nahum.* [A Commentary on the Twelve Minor Prophets, vol. 3.] Trans. by John Owen. Edinburgh: The Calvin Translation Society. [First published in Latin in 1559.]
Caquot A., and Delcor M., eds.,
1981: *Mélanges bibliques et orientaux en l'honneur de M. Henri Cazelles.* [Alter Orient und Altes Testament 212.] Neukirchen-Vluyn: Verlag Butzon & Bercker Kevelaer.
Carrez, M., Doré, J., and Grelot, P., eds.,
1981: *De la Tôrah au Messie.* Paris: Desclée.
Carrière, J., ed.,
1975: *Théognis. Poèmes élegiaques.* [Collection Budé.] Paris: Les Belles-lettres.
Carson, D. A., and Williamson, H. G. M., eds.,
1988: *It Is Written: Essays in Honour of Barnabas Lindars, SSF.* Cambridge: Cambridge University Press.

BIBLIOGRAPHY

Casson, L.,

1959: *The Ancient Mariners.* New York: Macmillan.

1971: *Ships and Seamanship in the Ancient World.* Princeton: Princeton University Press.

Cassuto, U.,

1973: "The Book of Jonah," pp. 299–306 in *Biblical and Oriental Studies,* vol. 1. Jerusalem: The Magnes Press.

Castillo, C.,

1983: "Jonas en la leyenda musulmana," *Al-Qantara* 4: 89–100.

Charlesworth, J. H., ed.,

1983: *The Old Testament Pseudepigrapha,* vol. 1: *Apocalyptic Literature and Testaments.* Garden City, N.Y.: Doubleday & Co.

1985: *The Old Testament Pseudepigrapha,* vol. 2: *Expansions of the "Old Testament" and Legends, Wisdom and Philosophical Literature, Prayers, Psalms, and Odes, Fragments of Lost Judeo-Hellenistic Works.* Garden City, N.Y.: Doubleday & Co.

Childs, B. S.,

1978: "The Canonical Shape of the Book of Jonah," pp. 122–28 in Tuttle 1978.

1979: *Introduction to the Old Testament as Scripture.* Philadelphia: Fortress Press.

Chotzner, J.,

1883: *Humour and Irony of the Hebrew Bible.* Harrow: J. C. Wilbee.

1905: *Hebrew Humour and Other Essays.* London: Luzac & Co.

Christensen, D. L.,

1985: "The Song of Jonah: A Metrical Analysis," *Journal of Biblical Literature* 104: 217–31.

1987: "Narrative Poetics and the Interpretation of the Book of Jonah," pp. 29–48 in Follis 1987.

Clements, R. E.,

1975: "The Purpose of the Book of Jonah," *Supplement to the Vetus Testamentum* 28: 16–28.

Cohen, A., trans.,

1939: *Lamentations.* [*Midrash Rabbah.*] London: The Soncino Press.

Cohen, A. D.,

1972: "The Tragedy of Jonah," *Judaism* 21: 164–75.

Cohen, C.,

1982: "*ʿdwywt ʾkdywt ḥdšwt lgby hmwbn whʾṭymwlwgyh šl hmwnh* <*mšl*> *bmqrʾ* (Some Overlooked Akkadian Evidence Concerning the Etymology and Meaning of the Biblical Term *māšāl*)," pp. 315–24 in Uffenheimer 1982.

BIBLIOGRAPHY

Cohn, G. H.,

1969: *Das Buch Jona im Lichte der biblischen Erzählkunst.* [Studia Semitica Neerlandica 12.] Assen: Van Gorcum.

Cohn, L.,

1984: "Motifs bibliques dans l'oeuvre d'Albert Camus," pp. 105–14 in Hirsch and Aschkenasy 1984.

Colson, F. H., ed.,

1937: *Philo,* vol 7. [Loeb Classical Library.] Cambridge, Mass.: Harvard University Press.

Cooper, A.,

1983: "Ps 24:7–10: Mythology and Exegesis," *Journal of Biblical Literature* 102: 37–60.

Cooper, J. S.,

1983: *The Curse of Agade.* [The Johns Hopkins Near Eastern Studies.] Baltimore: The Johns Hopkins University Press.

Cornelius, J.,

1981: "A Bird's Eye View of Trade in Ancient Ugarit," *Journal of Northwest Semitic Languages* 9: 13–31.

Correns, D.,

1980: "Jona und Salomo," pp. 86–94 in Hanbeck and Bachman 1980.

Crenshaw, J. L.,

1971: *Prophetic Conflict: Its Effect Upon Israelite Religion.* [*Zeitschrift für die alttestamentliche Wissenschaft,* Beiheft 124.] Berlin: Walter de Gruyter.

1983: *Theodicy in the Old Testament.* [Issues in Religion and Theology 4.] Philadelphia: Fortress Press.

1986: "The Expression *mî yôdēaᶜ* in the Hebrew Bible," *Vetus Testamentum* 3: 274–88.

Crenshaw, J. L., and Willis J. T., eds.,

1974: *Essays in Old Testament Ethics* (*J. Philip Hyatt, In Memoriam*). New York: Ktav Publishing House, Inc.

Cross, F. M.,

1983a: "Studies in the Prosody of Hebrew Verse: The Prosody of the Psalm of Jonah," pp. 159–67 in Huffmon 1983.

1983b: "Studies in the Structure of Hebrew Verse: The Prosody of Lamentations 1:1–22," pp. 129–55 in Meyers and O'Connor 1983.

Culley, R. C.,

1979: *Perspectives on Old Testament Narrative.* [*Semeia* 15.] Missoula, Mont.: Scholars Press.

Curtis, A. D., and Madsen, A. A.,

1910: *The Books of Chronicles.* International Critical Commentary. Edinburgh: T. & T. Clark.

BIBLIOGRAPHY

Culley, R. C.,

1967: *Oral Formulaic Language in the Biblical Psalms.* Toronto: The University of Toronto Press.

Dahood, M.,

1969: "Hebrew-Ugaritic Lexicography, VII," *Biblica* 50: 337–56.

1970a: *Psalms III: 101–150.* [Anchor Bible 17A.] Garden City, N.Y.: Doubleday & Co.

1970b: "The Independent Personal Pronoun in the Oblique Case in Hebrew," *The Catholic Biblical Quarterly* 32: 86–90.

Daube, D.,

1962: "Death as a Release in the Bible," *Novum Testamentum* 5: 82–104. [Published also as *Donum Gratulatorium Ethelbert Stauffer.* Leiden: E. J. Brill.]

Davies, G. I.,

1977: "The Uses of *R*ʿʿ Qal and the Meaning of Jonah IV 1," *Vetus Testamentum* 27: 105–11.

Davies, P. R.,

1987: "Potter, Prophet and People: Jeremiah 18 as Parable," *Hebrew Annual Review* 11: 23–33.

1991: *Sociology of the Second Temple Period.* [*Journal for the Study of the Old Testament,* Supplement.] Sheffield: JSOT Press. [In press.]

Day, J.,

1988: "Prophecy," pp. 39–55 in Carson and Williamson 1988.

Delcor, J.,

1976: *Religion d'Israël et du Proche Orient ancien: des Phéniciens aux Esséniens.* Leiden: E. J. Brill.

1979: "Des Diverses Manières d'écrire le tétragramme sacré dans les anciens documents hébraïques," pp. 1–29 in his *Études bibliques et orientales de religions comparées.* Leiden: E. J. Brill.

Delekat, L.,

1964: "Zum hebräischen Wörterbuch," *Vetus Testamentum* 14: 7–66.

Dorssen, J. C. C. van,

1951: *De derivata van de stam* ʾmn *in het hebreeuwsch van het Oude Testament.* Amsterdam: Amsterdam Drukkerij.

Dover, K. J.,

1974: *Greek Popular Morality in the Time of Plato and Aristotle.* Oxford: Basil Blackwell.

Driver, G. R.,

1934: "Studies in the Vocabulary of the Old Testament, VII," *Journal of Theological Studies* 35: 380–93.

1950: "Studies in Old Testament Prophets," pp. 52–72 in Rowley 1950.

BIBLIOGRAPHY

Driver, G. R., and Miles, J. C.,

1952: *The Babylonian Laws,* vol. 1: *Legal Commentary.* Oxford: The Clarendon Press.

Driver, S. R.,

1892: *A Treatise on the Use of the Tenses in Hebrew.* Oxford: The Clarendon Press.

1896: *Deuteronomy.* [International Critical Commentary.] Edinburgh: T. & T. Clark.

Dubarle, A. M.,

1966: *Judith: Formes et sense des diverses traditions,* vols. 1–2. Rome: Institut Biblique Pontifical.

Dundes, A.,

1965: *The Study of Folklore.* Englewood Cliffs, N.J.: Prentice Hall.

Durand, J.-M.,

1984: "À Propos du Nombre 10 000, à Mari," *MARI* 3: 278–79.

Durand, J.-M., and Charpin, D.,

1986: "Fils de Sim'al," *Revue d'Assyriologie* 80: 141–83.

Durham, J. I.,

1987: *Exodus.* [Word Biblical Commentary 3]. Waco, Tex.: Word Books.

Duval, Y.-M.,

1966: "Les Sources Grecques de l'exégèse de Jonas chez Zénon de Vérone," *Vigiliae Christianae* 20: 98–115.

1973: *Le Livre de Jonas dans la littérature chrétienne grecque et latine,* vols. 1–2. Paris: Études Augustiniennes.

Ebach, J.,

1987: *Kassandra und Jona, gegen die Macht des Schiksals.* Frankfurt-am-Main: Athenäum.

Eerdmans, B. D.,

1947: *The Hebrew Book of Psalms.* [Oudtestamentische Studiën 4.] Leiden: E. J. Brill.

Ehrlich, A. B.,

1912: *Randglossen zur Hebraïschen Bibel,* vol. 5: *Ezechiel und die Kleinen Propheten.* Leipzig: J. C. Heinrichs'sche Buchhandlung.

Eissfeldt, O.,

1964: "Amos und Jona in volkstümlicher Überlieferung," pp. 9–13 in *. . . und fragten nach Jesus. Festschrift für Ernst Barnikol zum 70. Geburtstag.* Berlin: Evangelische Verlagsanstalt. [Reprinted as pp. 137–52 of *Kleine Schriften,* vol. 4. Tübingen: Mohr, 1965.]

Elat, M.,

1982: "Tarshish and the Problem of Phoenician Colonisation in the Western Mediterranean," *Orientalia Lovaniensia Periodica* 13: 55–69.

BIBLIOGRAPHY

Ellison, H. L.,

1985: "Jonah," pp. 361–91 in *The Expositor's Bible Commentary,* vol. 7. Grand Rapids, Mich.: Zondervan Publishing House.

Emerton, J. A., ed.,

1980: *Prophecy: Essays Presented to Georg Fohrer on His Seventy-fifth Birthday.* Berlin: Walter de Gruyter.

Emerton, J. A., and Reif, S. C., eds.,

1982: *Interpreting The Hebrew Bible. Essays in Honour of E. I. J. Rosenthal.* Cambridge: Cambridge University Press.

Even-Shoshan, A.,

1982: *A New Concordance to the Torah, Prophets, and Writings.* 4th ed. Jerusalem: Qiryat-Sepher.

Fáj, A.,

1974: "The Stoic Features of the *Book of Jonah,*" *Istituto Orientale di Napoli, Annali* 34 [n.s. 24]: 309–45.

Feuillet, A.,

1947a: "Les sources du livre de Jonas," *Revue Biblique* 54: 161–86.

1947b: "Le sens du livre de Jonas," *Revue Biblique* 54: 340–61.

1949: "Jonas (le livre de)," pp. 1104–31 in *DBSup,* vol. 4.

1975: *Études d'exégèse et de théologie biblique.* Paris: Editions Gabalda. [Slightly modified reprint of 1949 on pp. 395–433.]

Field, F., ed.,

1875: *Origenis Hexaplorum quae supersunt,* vol. 2. Oxford: The Clarendon Press. [Reprinted Hildesheim: Georg Olms Verlag, 1964.]

Fingert, H. H.,

1954: "Psychoanalytic Study of the Minor Prophet, Jonah," *Psychoanalytic Review* 16: 55–65.

Fisch, H.,

1986: "The Hermeneutic Quest in *Robinson Crusoe,*" pp. 213–35 in Hartman and Budick 1986.

Fishbane, M.,

1985: *Biblical Interpretation in Ancient Israel.* Oxford: The Clarendon Press.

Fisher, L. R.,

1972: *Ras Shamra Parallels,* vol. 1. [Analecta Orientalia 49.] Rome: Pontifical Biblical Institute.

Fitzgerald, A., ed.,

1926: *The Letters of Synesius of Cyrene.* Oxford: Humphrey Milford.

Fitzmyer, J. A., and Harrington, D. J.,

1978: *A Manual of Palestinian Aramaic Texts.* [Bibbia et Orientalia 34.] Rome: Pontifical Biblical Institute.

Flacelière, R.,
1965: *Devins et oracles grecs.* ["Que sais-je?" 939.] Paris. Presses Universitaires de France.
Follis, E. R., ed.,
1987: *Directions in Biblical Hebrew Poetry.* [*Journal for the Study of the Old Testament,* Supplement Series 40.] Sheffield: JSOT Press.
Fox, E.,
1986: *Now These Are the Names; A New English Rendition of the Book of Exodus.* Translated with Commentary and Notes. New York: Schocken Books.
Fox, M. V.,
1980: "The Identification of Quotations in Biblical Literature," *Zeitschrift für die alttestamentliche Wissenschaft,* 92: 416–31.
Fränkel, W.,
1967: *"wrḥmyw ʿl kl mʿśyw," Maʿyānôt* 9: 193–207.
Frank, T. H., and Reed, W. L., eds.,
1970: *Translating and Understanding the Old Testament. Essays in Honor of Herbert Gordon May.* Nashville, Tenn.: Abingdon Press.
Frankena, R.,
1966: "Einige Bemerkungen zum Gebrauch des adverbs *ʿal-ken* im Hebräischen," pp. 94–99 in van Unnik and van der Woude 1966.
Freedman, D. N.,
1958: "Jonah 1,4b," *Journal of Biblical Literature* 77: 161–62.
1980: *Pottery, Poetry and Prophecy: Collected Essays on Hebrew Poetry.* Winona Lake, Ind.: Eisenbrauns.
1985: "Prose Particles in the Poetry of the Primary History," pp. 49–61 in Kort and Morschauser 1985.
Fretheim, T. E.,
1978: "Jonah and Theodicy," *Zeitschrift für die alttestamentliche Wissenschaft* 90: 227–37.
1977: *The Message of Jonah: A Theological Commentary.* Minneapolis: Augsburg Publishing Co.
1987: "The Repentance of God: A Study of Jeremiah 18:7–10," *Hebrew Annual Review* 11: 81–92.
Friedlander, G.,
1981: *Pirḳê de Rabbi Eliezer.* 4th ed. New York: Sepher-Hermon Press. [1st ed. 1916.]
Friedrich, J., et al.,
1940: *Die Inschriften vom Tell Halaf. Keilschrifttexte und aramäische Urkunden aus einer assyrischen Provinzhauptstadt.* [*Archiv für Orientforschung,* Beiheft 6.] Berlin: E. F. Weidner.

Gammie, J. G., et al., eds.,
1978: *Israelite Wisdom: Theological and Literary Essays in Honor of Samuel Terrien.* Missoula, Mont.: Scholars Press.
Garr, W. R.,
1983: "The Qinah: A Study of Poetic Meter, Syntax and Style," *Zeitschrift für die alttestamentliche Wissenschaft,* 95: 54–75.
Gaster, T. H.,
1969: *Myth, Legend, and Custom in the Old Testament,* New York: Harper & Row.
1976: *The Dead Sea Scriptures.* 2d ed. Garden City, N.Y.: Doubleday/Anchor Books.
Gelston, A.,
1980: *Dodekapropheton—Daniel-Bel-Draco.* [The Old Testament in Syriac According to the Peshiṭta Version 3.4.] Leiden: E. J. Brill.
1987: *The Peshiṭta of the Twelve Prophets.* Oxford: The Clarendon Press.
Gernet, L., ed.,
1923: Antiphon, *Discours, suivis des fragments d'Antiphon le Sophiste.* [Collection Budé.] Paris: Les Belles-lettres.
Ginsberg, H. L.,
1967: "Lexicographical Note," pp. 71–82 in *Hebräische Wortforschung* (Festschrift Baumgartner). [*Vetus Testamentum,* Supplement 16.] Leiden: E. J. Brill.
Ginzberg, L.,
Legends of the Jews. Philadelphia: Jewish Publication Society.
1946: vol. 6.
1947: vol. 4.
Godfrey, J. H., ed.,
1944: *Iraq and the Persian Gulf.* [Geographical Handbook Series. B.R. 524 (Restricted).] London: Naval Intelligence Division.
Goedicke, H.,
1968: "The Capture of Joppa," *Chronique d'Égypte* 86: 219–32.
Goitein, S. D.,
1937: "Some Observations on Jonah," *Journal of the Palestinian Oriental Society* 17: 63–77.
Golomb, D. M., ed.,
1987: *"Working with No Data": Semitic and Egyptian Studies Presented to Thomas O. Lambdin.* Winona Lake, Ind.: Eisenbrauns.
Good, E. M.,
1981: *Irony in the Old Testament.* 2d ed. Sheffield: Almond Press. (First published in 1965.)
Goodenough, E. R.,
Jewish Symbols in the Greco-Roman Period. [Bollingen Series 37.] Princeton: Princeton University Press.

1953: vol. 2: *The Archaeological Evidence from the Diaspora.*
1956: vol. 5: *Fish, Bread, and Wine.*
Goodman, P.,
1965: *Three Plays: The Young Disciple, Faustina, Jonah.* New York: Random House.
Gordis, R.,
1971: *Poets, Prophets, and Sages: Essays in Biblical Interpretation.* Bloomington: Indiana University Press.
1976: *The Word and the Book: Studies in Biblical Language and Literature.* New York: Ktav Publishing House.
Gordon, C. H.,
1978a: "The Wine-Dark Sea," *Journal of Near Eastern Studies* 37: 51–52.
1978b: "Build-up and Climax," pp. 29–34 in Avishur and Blau 1978.
Goshen-Gottstein, M. H.,
1958: "Linguistic Structure and Tradition in the Qumran Documents," pp. 101–37 in Rabin and Yadin 1958.
1965: *The Book of Isaiah: Sample Edition with Introduction.* Jerusalem: The Magnes Press.
1973: *The Bible in the Syropalestinian Version,* vol. 1: *Pentateuch and Prophets.* Jerusalem: The Magnes Press.
Graeve, M.-C. de,
1981: *The Ships of the Ancient Near East.* [Orientalia Lovaniensia, Annual 7.] Leuven: Department of Oriental Studies.
Grayson, A. K.,
1976: *Assyrian Royal Inscriptions,* vol. 2. [Records of the Ancient Near East.] Wiesbaden: Otto Harrassowitz.
Green, A., ed.,
1986: *Jewish Spirituality: From the Bible Through the Middle Ages.* [World Spirituality: An Encyclopedic History of the Religious Quest 13.] New York: Crossroad Publishing Company.
Greenberg, M.,
1983: *Biblical Prose Prayer as a Window to the Popular Religion of Ancient Israel.* Berkeley: University of California Press.
Grether, O.,
1934: *Name und Wort Gottes im alten Testament.* [*Zeitschrift für die alttestamentliche Wissenschaft,* Beiheft 64.] Giessen: Alfred Töppelman.
Grigson, G.,
1959: *The Cherry-Tree.* London: Phoenix House.
Grossouw, W.,
1938: *The Coptic Versions of the Minor Prophets: A Contribution to the Study of the Septuagint.* [Monumenta Biblica et Ecclesiastica 3.] Rome: Pontifical Biblical Institute.

BIBLIOGRAPHY

Gruber, M. I.,
1980: *Aspects of Nonverbal Communication in the Ancient Near East.* [Studia Pohl 12.] Rome: Pontifical Biblical Institute.

Hackett, J. A.,
1986: "Some Observations on the Balaam Tradition at Deir ʿAllā," *The Biblical Archaeologist* 49: 216–22.

Hadas, M., and Smith, M.,
1965: *Heroes and Gods: Spiritual Biographies in Antiquity.* [Religious Perspectives 13.] London: Routledge & Kegan Paul.

Halperin, D. J.,
1980: *The Merkabah in Rabbinic Literature.* [American Oriental Series 62.] New Haven: American Oriental Society.

Halpern, B., and Friedman, R. E.,
1980: "Composition and Paronomasia in the Book of Jonah," *Hebrew Annual Review* 4: 79–92.

Halpern, B., and Levinson, J. D., eds.,
1981: *Tradition and Transformation.* Winona Lake, Ind.: Eisenbrauns.

Hanbeck, W., and Bachmann, M., eds.,
1980: *Wort in der Zeit* (Festschrift K. H. Rengstorf). Leiden: E. J. Brill.

Handford, S. A.,
1954: *The Fables of Aesop: A New Translation.* Baltimore: Penguin.

Haran, M.,
1967: "The Rise and Fall of the Empire of Jeroboam ben Joash," *Vetus Testamentum* 17: 266–97.

Harper, W. R.,
1905: *A Critical and Exegetical Commentary on Amos and Hosea.* [International Critical Commentary.] Edinburgh: T. & T. Clark.

Hartman, G. H., and Budick, S., eds.,
1986: *Midrash and Literature.* New Haven: Yale University Press.

Harviainen, T.,
1988: "Why Were the Sailors Not Afraid of the Lord Before Verse Jonah 1,10?" *Studia Orientalia* 64: 77–81.

Haupt, P.,
1907: "Jonah's Whale," *Proceedings of the American Philosophical Society* 46: 151–64.

Hauser, A.,
1985: "Jonah: In Pursuit of the Dove," *Journal of Biblical Literature* 104: 21–37.

Helck, W.,
1980: "Joppe," *Lexikon der Egyptologie* III: 269–70.

Held, M.,
1973: "Pit and Pitfalls in Akkadian and Biblical Hebrew," pp. 173–90 in Marcus 1973.

Herzog, Z., et al., eds.,
1989: *Excavations at Tel Michal, Israel* [Publications of the Institute of Archaeology 8.] Minneapolis: University of Minnesota Press.
Hesseling, D. C.,
1901: "Le livre de Jonas," *Byzantinische Zeitschrift* 10: 208–17.
Hill, D.,
1967: *Greek Words and Hebrew Meanings: Studies in the Semantics of Soteriological Terms.* Cambridge: Cambridge University Press.
Hirsch, D. H., and Aschkenasy, N., eds.,
1984: *Biblical Patterns in Modern Literature.* [Brown Judaic Studies 77.] Chico, Calif.: Scholars Press.
Hirsch, E. G.,
1904: "Jonah," pp. 225–27 in *JE.*
Hoffner, Jr., H. A., ed.,
1973: *Orient and Occident* (Festschrift C. H. Gordon). [Alter Orient und Altes Testament 22.] Neukirchen-Vluyn: Verlag Butzon & Bercker Kevelaer.
Hoglund, K. G.,
1991: "Sociology of the Second Temple Period: The Achaemenid Imperial Context," in P. R. Davies. [In press.]
Holbert, J. C.,
1981: " 'Deliverance Belongs to Yahweh!' Satire in the Book of Jonah," *Journal for the Study of the Old Testament* 21: 59–81.
Holman, C. H.,
1980: *A Handbook to Literature.* 4th ed. Indianapolis: Bobbs-Merrill.
Holm-Nielsen, S.,
1960: *Hodayot: Psalms from Qumran.* Aarhus: Universitetsforlaget.
Horwitz, W. J.,
1973: "Another Interpretation of Jonah I 12," *Vetus Testamentum* 23: 370–72.
Hüsing, G.,
1907: "Taršiš und die Jona-Legende," *Memnon* 1: 70–79.
Huffmon, H. B., et al.,
1983: *The Quest for the Kingdom of God: Studies in Honor of George E. Mendenhall.* Winona Lake, Ind.: Eisenbrauns.
Hummel, H.,
1957: "Enclitic *Mem* in Early Northwest Semitic, Especially Hebrew," *Journal of Biblical Literature* 76: 85–107
Hurvitz, A.,
1985: "Originals and Imitations in Biblical Poetry: A Comparative Examination of 1 Sam 2: 1–10 and Ps 113: 5–9," pp. 115–21 in Kort and Morschauser 1985.

Immerwahr, H. R.,

1966: *Form and Thought in Herodotus.* [American Philological Association, Chapel Hill, N.C.; Philological Monograph 23.] Cleveland: Western Reserve University.

In der Smitten, W. Th.,

1972: "Zu Jona 1: 2," *Zeitschrift für die alttestamentliche Wissenschaft* 84: 95.

Irvin, D.,

1978: *Mytharion: The Comparison of Tales from the Old Testament and the Ancient Near East.* [Alter Orient und Altes Testament 32.] Neukirchen-Vluyn: Verlag Butzon & Bercker Kevelaer.

Jacobsen, T.,

1987: *The Harps That Once . . . : Sumerian Poetry in Translation.* New Haven: Yale University Press.

Jastrow, M.,

1950: *Dictionary of Talmud Babli, Yerushalmi, Midrashic Literature and Targumim.* New York: Pardes Publishing Co.

Jirku, A.,

1969: "Ugaritische Eigennamen als Quelle des Ugaritischen Lexicons," *Archiv Orientálni* 37: 8–11.

Jean, C.,

1950: *Lettres diverses, transcrites et traduites.* [*Archives royales de Mari,* vol. 2.] Paris: Imprimerie Nationale.

Jellicoe, S.,

1968: *The Septuagint and Modern Studies.* Oxford: Oxford University Press.

Jellinek, A.,

1938: *Bet ha-Midrasch Sammlung: Kleiner Midraschim und vermischter Abhandlungen aus der ältern jüdischen Literatur,* part 1. 2d ed. Jerusalem: Bamberger & Wahrman. [1st ed., 1853.]

Jepsen, A.,

1970: "Anmerkungen zum Buche Jona," pp. 297–305 in *Wort—Gebot—Glaube.* [Festschrift W. Eichrodt.] Zürich: Zwingli Verlag.

1978: *Der Herr ist Gott.* Berlin: Evangelische Verlagsanstalt.

Jerome, St.,

see Antin, 1956.

Johnson, A. R.,

1950: "Jonah II. 3–10: A Study in Cultic Phantasy," pp. 82–102 in Rowley 1950.

Jones, A. H. M.,

1964: *The Late Roman Empire,* vol. 2. Oxford: Basil Blackwell.

Joslin, M. C.,

1986: *The Heard Word: A Moralized History. The Genesis Section of the*

"Histoire Ancienne" in a Text from Saint-Jean d'Acre. [Romance Monographs 45.] University, Miss.: Romance Monographs.

Joüon, P. P.,
1947: *Grammaire de l'Hébreu Biblique.* Rome: Pontifical Biblical Institute. [Reprint of 1st ed., 1923.]

Kahlmeyer, J.,
1934: *Seesturm und Schiffsbruch als Bild im antiken Schrifttum.* Hildesheim: Gebr. Fikuart.

Kaplan, J.,
1972: "The Archaeology and History of Tel Aviv—Jaffa," *Biblical Archaeologist* 35: 66–95.

Kaplan, J. [with H. Kaplan],
1976: "Jaffa," pp. 532–41 in *Encyclopedia of Archaeological Excavations in the Holy Land,* vol. 2. London: Oxford University Press.

Kaufmann, Y.,
1960: *The Religion of Israel.* Abridged version, trans. by M. Greenberg. Chicago: University of Chicago Press.

Keel, O.,
1977: *Vögel als Boten.* [Orbis Biblicus et Orientalis 14.] Göttingen: Vandenhoeck & Ruprecht.

Keil, C. F., and Delitzsch, F.,
1900: *The Twelve Minor Prophets,* vol. 1. [Biblical Commentary to the Old Testament.] Edinburgh: T. & T. Clark.

Keller, C.-A.,
1982: *Jonas.* [Commentaire de l'Ancien Testament XIa.] Genève: Labor et Fides.

Kirk, E. P.,
1980: *Menippean Satire. An Annotated Catalogue of Texts and Criticism.* New York: Garland Publishing.

Kisāʾī, al-,
see Thackston 1978.

Kittel, B. P.,
1981: *The Hymns of Qumran: Translation and Commentary.* [SBL Dissertation Series 50.] Chico, Calif.: Scholars Press.

Koehler, L.,
1953: "Syntactica IV," *Vetus Testamentum* 3: 299–305.

König, E.,
1900: *Stilistik, Rhetorik, Poetik in Bezug auf die biblische Litteratur.* Leipzig: Theodor Weicher.
1906: "Jonah," pp. 744–53 in *Dictionary of the Bible,* vol. 2. New York: Charles Scribner's Sons.

BIBLIOGRAPHY

Komlós, O.,

1950: "Jonah Legends," pp. 41–61 in *Études Orientales à la Mémoire de Paul Hirschler.* Budapest: Allamosított Kertész-nyomda.

Kort, A., and Morschauser, S., eds.,

1985: *Biblical and Related Studies Presented to Samuel Iwry.* Winona Lake, Ind.: Eisenbrauns.

Kraeling, E. G.,

1971: "The Evolution of the Story of Jonah," pp. 305–16 in *Hommages à A. Dupont-Sommer.* Paris: Adrien-Maisonneuve.

Krantz, E. S.,

1982: *Des Schiffes Weg Mitten im Meer.* [Coniectanea Biblica, Old Testament Series 19.] Lund: C. W. K. Gleerup.

Krašovec, J.,

1984: *Antithetic Structure in Biblical Hebrew Poetry.* [*Vetus Testamentum,* Supplements 35.] Leiden: E. J. Brill.

Kraus, H.-J.,

1988: *Psalms 1–59. A Commentary.* [Translation of the 5th ed. of *Psalmen,* 1978.] Minneapolis: Augsburg Publishing Co.

Kugel, J.,

1981: *The Idea of Biblical Poetry: Parallelism and Its History.* New Haven: Yale University Press.

Kuyper, L. J.,

1963: "The Meaning of *ḥsdw* Isa. xl 6," *Vetus Testamentum* 13: 489–92.

Lacocque, A.,

1986: "Jonah as a Satire, the Bearing of Genre on Date," p. 187 in *AAR-SBL Annual Meetings. Abstract.* Atlanta: Scholars Press.

Lacocque, A., and Lacocque, P.-E.,

1981: *The Jonah Complex.* Atlanta: John Knox Press.

Lambdin, T. O.,

1971: *Introduction to Biblical Hebrew.* New York: Charles Scribner's Sons.

Landes, G. M.,

1967a: "The Kerygma of the Book of Jonah," *Interpretation* 21: 3–31.

1967b: "The 'Three Days and Three Nights' Motif in Jonah 2 1," *Journal of Biblical Literature* 86: 446–50.

1976: "Jonah," pp. 488–91 in *IDBSup.*

1978: "Jonah: A *Māšāl?*" pp. 137–58 in Gammie et al. 1978.

1982: "Linguistic Criteria and the Date of the Book of Jonah," *Eretz Israel* (The Orlinsky Volume) 16: 147–70.

1983: "Matthew 12: 40 as an Interpretation of the 'Sign of Jonah' Against Its Biblical Background," pp. 665–84 in Meyers and O'Connor 1983.

Lange, N. R. M. de,

1982: "Two Genizah Fragments in Hebrew and Greek," pp. 61–83 in Emerton and Reif 1981.

Lasswell, H. D., et al., ed.,
1979: *Propaganda and Communications in World History*, vol. 1: *The Symbolic Instruments in Early Times.* Honolulu: University Press of Hawaii.
Lawrence, P. J. N.,
1986: "Assyrian Nobles and the Book of Jonah," *Tyndale Bulletin* 17: 121–32.
Lettinga, J. P.,
1980: *Grammaire de l'Hebrue Biblique.* Leiden: E. J. Brill.
Levine, B., and de Tarragon, J.-M.,
1984: "Dead Kings and Rephaim," *Journal of the American Oriental Society* 104: 649–59.
Levine, É.,
1978: *The Aramaic Version of Jonah.* 2d ed. New York: Sepher-Hermon Press.
1984: "Jonah as a Philosophical Book," *Zeitschrift für die alttestamentliche Wissenschaft* 96: 235–45.
Lewis, C.,
1972: "Jonah—A Parable for Our Time," *Judaism* 21: 159–63.
Licht, J.,
1957: *Megîl(l)at hāhôdayôt mimmegîl(l)ôt midbar Yehûdâ.* Jerusalem: The Bialik Insitute.
1978: *Story Telling in the Bible.* Jerusalem: The Magnes Press.
Lichtheim, M.,
1973: *Ancient Egyptian Literature,* vol. 1: The Old and Middle Kingdoms. Berkeley: University of California Press.
Lindblom, J.,
1962: "Lot-Casting in the Old Testament," *Vetus Testamentum* 12: 164–78.
Lindström, F.,
1983: *God and the Origin of Evil. A Contextual Analysis of Alleged Monistic Evidence in the Old Testament.* [Coniectanea Biblica, Old Testament Series 21.] Lund: C. W. K. Gleerup.
Link-Salinger, R.,
1982: *Jewish Law in Our Time.* Denver: University of Colorado Press.
Lipiński, E.,
1973: "La Colombe du Ps. LXVIII: 14," *Vetus Testamentum* 23: 365–68.
1988: "Carthage et Tarshish," *Bibliotheca Orientalis* 45: 59–81.
Loewe, R. J.,
1982: "The Bible in Medieval Hebrew Poetry," pp. 133–57 in Emerton and Reif 1982.
Lohfink, N.,
1961: "Jona ging zur Stadt hinaus (Jon 4,5)," *Biblische Zeitschrift* 5: 185–203.
Longman III, T.,
1982: "A Critique of Two Recent Metrical Systems," *Biblica* 63: 230–54.

Loretz, O.,

1960: "Herkunft und Sinn der Jonaerzählung," *Biblische Zeitschrift* 5: 18–29.

1984: *Habiru-Hebräer: Eine sozio-linguistische Studie über die Herkunft des Gentiliziums* ʿibrî *vom Appelativum* ḫabiru. [*Zeitschrift für die alttestamentliche Wissenschaft*, Beiheft 160.] Berlin: Walter de Gruyter.

Magonet, J. D.,

1976: *Form and Meaning: Studies in Literary Techniques in the Book of Jonah.* [Beiträge zur biblischen Exegese und Theologie 2.] Bern and Frankfurt-am-Main: Herbert Lang, Peter Lang.

1983: 2d ed. of the same, with supplement. Sheffield: The Almond Press.

Maidment, K. J.,

1941: *Minor Attic Orators*, vol. 1. [Loeb Classical Library.] Cambridge, Mass.: Harvard University Press.

Maillot, A.,

1977: *Jonas, ou les farces de Dieu; Sophonie, ou l'erreur de Dieu.* Paris: Delachaux et Niestlé Éditeurs.

Marcus, D., ed.,

1973: *The Gaster Festschrift.* [= *The Journal of the Ancient Near Eastern Society of Columbia University* 5.] New York: ANE Society.

Marti, K.,

1904: *Das Dodekapropheton.* Tübingen: J. C. B. Mohr.

Masing, H.,

1938: *The Word of Yahweh.* [Acta et Commentationes Universitates Tartuensis (Dorpatensis)—B. Humanoria, 39.4] Tartu (Estonia): The University of Tartu.

Mather, J.,

1982: "The Comic Art of the Book of Jonah," *Soundings* 65: 280–91.

McAlpine, T. H.,

1984: "Human and Divine Sleep in the Old Testament." Ph.D. diss., Yale University. Ann Arbor, Mich.: University Microfilms International, order no. 8509742. [Published in 1987 as *Sleep, Divine and Human, in the Old Testament.* Sheffield: JSOT Press.]

McCarter, P. K.,

1973: "The River Ordeal in Israelite Literature," *Harvard Theological Review* 66: 403–12.

1980: *I Samuel.* [Anchor Bible 8.] Garden City, N.Y.: Doubleday & Co.

1984: *II Samuel.* [Anchor Bible 9.] Garden City, N.Y.: Doubleday & Co.

McKane, W.,

1986: *Jeremiah*, I, I–XXV. [The International Critical Commentary.] Edinburgh: T. & T. Clark.

BIBLIOGRAPHY

Melville, H.,

1851: *Moby Dick; Or, The Whale.* [Modern Library Edition.] New York: W. W. Norton (1950 printing).

Meschonnic, H.,

1981: *Jona et le signifiant errant.* Paris: Gallimard.

1984: "Translating Biblical Rhythm," pp. 227–40 in Hirsch and Aschkenasy 1984.

Meyers, C. L., and O'Connor M., eds.,

1983: *The Word of the Lord Shall Go Forth. Essays in Honor of David Noel Freedman in Celebration of His Sixtieth Birthday.* [American Schools of Oriental Research, Special Volume Series 1.] Winona Lake, Ind.: Eisenbrauns.

Michaels, L.,

1987: "Jonah," pp. 232–37 in D. Rosenberg 1987.

Midrash Rabbah

Numbers, see Slotki 1939.

Lamentations, see Cohen 1939.

Miles, G. B., and Trompf, G.,

1976: "Luke and Antiphon: The Theology of Acts 27–28 in the Light of Pagan Beliefs About Divine Retribution, Pollution, and Shipwreck," *Harvard Theological Review* 69: 259–67.

Miles, Jr., J. A.,

1974–75: "Laughing at the Bible: Jonah as Parody," *Jewish Quarterly Review* 65: 168–81.

Milik, J. T.,

1961: "Textes hébreux et araméens," pp. 67–205 in Benoit 1961.

Miller, Jr., P. D.,

1980: "El, the Creator of Earth," *Bulletin of the American Schools of Oriental Research* 239: 43–46.

1982: *Sin and Judgment in the Prophets.* [Society for Biblical Literature, Monograph Series 27.] Chico, Calif.: Scholars Press.

Mitchell, S.,

1989: "Five Parables," *Tikkun* 4: 31.

Montefiore, C. G., and Loewe, H.,

1974: *A Rabbinic Anthology,* with a *Prolegomenon* by R. Loewe. New York: Schocken Books. [Reprint of 1938 ed.]

More, J.,

1970: "The Prophet Jonah: The Story of an Intrapsychic Process," *American Imago* 27: 3–11.

Morrison, J. S., and Williams, R. T.,

1968: *Greek Oared Ships (900–322 B.C.).* Cambridge: Cambridge University Press.

BIBLIOGRAPHY

Muecke, D. C.,

1970: *Irony.* [The Critical Idiom.] London: Methuen & Co.

Muraoka, T.,

1985: *Emphatic Words and Structures in Biblical Hebrew.* Jerusalem: The Magnes Press.

Murphy-O'Connor, J.,

1985: "On the Road and on the Sea with St. Paul," *Bible Review* 1: 38–47.

Negev, A.,

1986: *The Archaeological Encyclopedia of the Holy Land.* Revised ed. Nashville: Thomas Nelson Publishers.

Neil, W.,

1962: "Jonah, Book of," pp. 964–67 in *IDB,* vol. 2.

Nielsen, E.,

1979: "Le message primitif du livre de Jonas," *Revue d'histoire et de philosophie religieuses* [= *Mélanges E. Jacob*] 59: 499–507.

Noth, M.,

1928: *Die Israelitischen Personennamen im Rahmen der gemeinsemitischen Namengebung.* [Beiträge zur Wissenschaft vom Alten und Neuen Testament, 3d ser. 10.] Stuttgart: Kohlhammer.

O'Connor, M.,

1980: *Hebrew Verse Structures.* Winona Lake, Ind.: Eisenbrauns.

Oppenheim, A. L.,

1954: "The Seafaring Merchants of Ur," *Journal of the American Oriental Society* 74: 6–17.

1964: *Ancient Mesopotamia: Portrait of a Dead Civilization.* Chicago: University of Chicago Press.

1970: *Glass and Glassmaking in Ancient Mesopotamia.* [The Corning Museum of Glass, Monographs 3.] New York: Corning Museum of Glass.

1979: "Neo-Assyrian and Neo-Babylonian Empires," pp. 111–44 in Lasswell et al., 1979.

Orlinsky, H. M.,

1967: *The So-Called "Servant of the Lord" and "Suffering Servant" in Second Isaiah.* [*Vetus Testamentum* Supplement 14.] Leiden: E. J. Brill.

1969: ed., *Notes on the New Translation of the Torah.* Philadelphia: Jewish Publication Society.

1970: "Nationalism-Universalism and Internationalism in Ancient Israel," pp. 206–36 in Frank 1970 [= pp. 78–116 in Orlinsky 1974].

1974: *Essays in Biblical Culture and Bible Translation.* New York: Ktav Publishing House.

Ovadiah, R.,

1974: "Jonah in a Mosaic Pavement at Beth Guvrin," *Israel Exploration Journal* 24: 214–15; plate 46.

BIBLIOGRAPHY

Page, D.,

1955: *Sappho and Alcaeus. An Introduction to the Study of Ancient Lesbian Poetry.* Oxford: The Clarendon Press.

Paine, T.,

1834: *The Theological Works of Thomas Paine.* Boston: The Advocates of Common Sense.

Pardee, D.,

1975: "The Ugaritic Text 2106: 10–18: A Bottomry Loan?," *Journal of the American Oriental Society* 95: 612–19.

1981: "Ugaritic and Hebrew Metrics," pp. 113–30 in G. D. Young 1981.

Parpola, S.,

1980: "The Murderer of Sennacherib," pp. 171–82 in Alster 1980.

1983: *Letters from Assyrian Scholars to the Kings Esarhaddon and Assurbanipal,* II: *Commentary and Appendices.* [Alter Orient und Altes Testament 5/2.] Neukirchen-Vluyn: Verlag Butzon & Bercker Kevelaer.

Parrot, A.,

1961: *The Arts of Assyria,* trans. S. Gilbert and J. Emmons. New York: Golden Press.

Patai, R.,

1941: "Jewish Seafaring in Ancient Times," *Jewish Quarterly Review* 32: 1–26.

Payne, D. F.,

1979: "Jonah from the Perspective of Its Audience," *Journal for the Study of the Old Testament* 13: 3–12.

Payne, R.,

1989: "The Prophet Jonah: Reluctant Messenger and Intercessor," *The Expository Times* 100: 131–34.

Peiro, A. N., and Castro, F. P.,

1977: *Biblia Babilonica. Profetas Menores.* Madrid: Instituto "Arias Montano," C.S.I.C.

Perowne, T. T.,

1905: *Obadiah and Jonah.* [The Cambridge Bible for Schools and Colleges.] Cambridge: Cambridge University Press. [Reprint of 1883 ed.]

Pesch, R.,

1966: "Zur konzentrischen Struktur von Jona 1," *Biblica* 47: 577–81.

Pitard, W. T.,

1987: *Ancient Damascus: A Historical Survey of the Syrian City-State from the Earliest Times Until Its Fall to the Assyrians in 732 B.C.E.* Winona Lake, Ind.: Eisenbrauns.

Pollard, A.,

1970: *Satire.* [The Critical Idiom.] London: Methuen & Co.

BIBLIOGRAPHY

Porten, B.,

1968: *Archives from Elephantine: The Life of an Ancient Jewish Military Colony.* Berkeley: University of California Press.

1981: "Baalshamem and the Date of the Book of Jonah," pp. 237–44 in Carrez, 1981.

Porter, J. R.,

1962: "Samson's Riddle: Judges xiv, 18," *Journal of Theological Studies* 13: 106–9.

Preminger, A., and Greenstein, E. L., eds.,

1986: *The Hebrew Bible in Literary Criticism.* New York: The Ungar Publishing Co.

Price, B. F., and Nida, E. A.,

1978: *A Translators Handbook on the Book of Jonah.* New York: United Bible Societies.

Qimron, E.,

1986: *The Hebrew of the Dead Sea Scrolls.* [Harvard Semitic Studies 29.] Atlanta: Scholars Press.

Rabin, C., and Yadin, Y.,

1958: *Aspects of the Dead Sea Scrolls.* [Scripta Hierosolymitana 4.] Jerusalem: The Magnes Press.

Radermacher, L.,

1906: "Walfischmythen," *Archiv für Religionswissenschaft* 9: 248–52.

Rainey, A.,

1989: "The 'Lord of Heaven' at Tel Michal," pp. 381–82 in Herzog, et al., 1989.

Ratner, R.,

1987: "*Derek:* Morpho-syntactical Considerations," *Journal of the American Oriental Society* 107: 471–73.

Rauber, D. F.,

1970: "Jonah—The Prophet as Schlemiel," *The Bible Today* 49: 29–38.

Redford, D. B.,

1970: *A Study of the Biblical Story of Joseph* (*Genesis 37–50*). [*Vetus Testamentum* Supplement 20.] Leiden: E. J. Brill.

Reiner, E.,

1985: *Your Thwarts in Pieces, Your Mooring Rope Cut: Poetry from Babylonia and Assyria.* [Michigan Studies in the Humanities 5.] Ann Arbor, Mich.: University of Michigan Press.

Robertson, D. A.,

1972: *Linguistic Evidence in Dating Early Hebrew Poetry.* [Society for Biblical Literature, Dissertation Series 3.] Missoula, Mont.: The Society of Biblical Literature.

BIBLIOGRAPHY

Robinson, B. P.,

1985: "Jonah's Qiqayon Plant," *Zeitschrift für die alttestamentliche Wissenschaft* 97: 390–403.

Röllig, W.,

1980: "Joppe," *Reallexikon der Assyriologie* 5: 281–82.

Rofé, A.,

1982: *Sippûrê hannevî'îm.* Jerusalem: The Magnes Press.

1988: *The Prophetical Stories.* [English ed. of the above.] Jerusalem: The Magnes Press.

Rosen, N.,

1987: "Jonah," pp. 222–31 in D. Rosenberg, 1987.

Rosenberg, D., ed.,

1987: *Congregation: Contemporary Writers Read the Jewish Bible.* New York: Harcourt Brace Jovanovich.

Rosenberg, J.,

1986: *King and Kin. Political Allegory in the Hebrew Bible.* [Indiana Studies in Biblical Literature.] Bloomington, Ind.: Indiana University Press.

1987: "Jonah and the Nakedness of Deeds," *Tikkun* 2: 36–38.

Rougé, J.,

1981: *Ships and Fleets of the Ancient Mediterranean.* Middleton, Conn.: Wesleyan University Press.

Rouillard, H.,

1985: *La Péricope de Balaam* (Nombres 22–34): *La Prose et les Oracles.* [Études Bibliques n.s. 4.] Paris: J. Gabalda.

Rowley, H. H.,

1950: *Studies in Old Testament Prophecy* (Festschrift T. H. Robinson). Edinburgh: T. & T. Clark.

Rudolph, W.,

1971: "Joel-Amos-Obadja-Jona," pp. 323–71 in *Kommentar zum alten Testament,* 13.2. Gütersloh: Gerd Mohn.

Ruether, R. R., and Ruether, H. J.,

1989: *The Wrath of Jonah.* New York: Harper & Row.

Ruppert, L., et al., eds.,

1982: *Künder des Wortes: Beiträge zur Theologie der Propheten.* Würzberg: Echter Verlag.

Sanders, J. A.,

1965: *The Psalms Scroll of Qumrân Cave 11* (11QPs[a]). [Discoveries in the Judaean Desert of Jordan 4.] Oxford: The Clarendon Press.

Sanders, H. A., and Schmidt, C.,

1927: *The Minor Prophets in the Freer Collection and the Berlin Fragment of Genesis.* New York: The Macmillan Press.

BIBLIOGRAPHY

Sasson, J. M.,

1966: "Canaanite Maritime Involvement in the Second Millennium B.C.," *Journal of the American Oriental Society* 86: 126–38.

1972: "Flora, Fauna and Minerals," pp. 383–452 in Fisher 1972.

1979: "On M. H. Pope's *Song of Songs* [AB 7c]," *Maarav* 1: 177–96.

1981: "Literary Criticism, Folklore Scholarship, and Ugaritic Literature," pp. 81–98 in G. D. Young 1981.

1983: *"Reḥōvōt ʿîr," Revue Biblique* 90: 94–96.

1984a: "On Jonah's Two Missions," *Henoch* 6: 23–30.

1984b: ed., *Studies in Literature from the Ancient Near East by Members of the American Oriental Society Dedicated to Samuel Noah Kramer.* [American Oriental Series 65=*Journal of the American Oriental Society* 103.1.] New Haven: American Oriental Society.

1984c: "Mari Dreams," pp. 283–93 in J. M. Sasson, 1984b.

1985a: "Unlocking the Poetry of Love in the Song of Songs," *Biblical Review* 1: 10–19.

1985b: *"wᵉlōʾ yitbōšāšû* (Gen 2,25) and Its Implications," *Biblica* 66: 418–21.

1987: "Esther," pp. 335–42 in Alter and Kermode 1987.

Sasson, V.,

1985: "The Book of Oracular Visions of Balaam from Deir ʿAlla," *Ugarit Forschungen* 17: 283–309.

Schäfer, P.,

1981: *Synopse zur Hekhalot-Literatur.* [Texte und Studien zum antiken Judentum 2.] Tübingen: J. C. B. Mohr.

Schmidt, L.,

1976: *"De Deo." Studien zur literarkritik und Theologie des Buches Jona, des Gesprächs zwischen Abraham und Jahwe in Gen 18:22ff. und von Hi. 1.* [*Zeitschrift für die alttestamentliche Wissenschaft,* Beiheft 143.] Berlin: Walter de Gruyter.

Schneider, D. A.,

1979: "The Unity of the Book of the Twelve." Ph.D. diss., Yale University. Ann Arbor, Mich.: University Microfilm International, order no. 79-26847.

Schoors, A.,

1981: "The Particle *ky,*" pp. 240–76 in Albrektson 1981.

Schuller, E. M.,

1986: *Non-Canonical Psalms from Qumran: A Pseudepigraphic Collection.* [Harvard Semitic Studies 28.] Atlanta: Scholars Press.

Schwartzbaum, H.,

1966: "The Jewish and Moslem Versions of Some Theodicy Legends," *Fabula* 3: 119–69.

Scott, R. B. Y.,

1965: "The Sign of Jonah," *Interpretation* 19: 16–25.

BIBLIOGRAPHY

Segert, S.,

1980: "Syntax and Style in the Book of Jonah: Six Simple Approaches to Their Analysis," pp. 121–30 in Emerton 1980.

Sellin, E.,

1922: *Das Zwölfprophetenbuch.* Leipzig: Werner Scholl.

Siegert, F.,

1980: *Drei hellenistisch-jüdische Predigten.* [Wissenschaftliche Untersuchungen zum Neuen Testament 20.] Tübingen: J. C. B. Mohr.

Silberman, L. H.,

"On Understanding a Midrashic Text: The Case of the Inhabitants of Nineveh," (author's manuscript).

Simon, E.,

1953: "Flight from God—and Return," *Commentary* 16: 214–18.

Simon, M., and Levertoff, P. P., trans.,

1949: *The Zohar,* vol. 4. London: The Soncino Press.

Simon, U.,

1983: *"spr ywnh—mbnh wmšmᶜt,"* pp. 291–317 Zakovitch and Rofé 1983.

Slotki, J. J.,

1939: *Numbers.* [*Midrash Rabbah.*] London: The Soncino Press.

Smith, W.,

1857: *Dictionary of Greek and Roman Geography.* Boston: Little, Brown, and Company.

Snaith, N. H.,

1945: *Notes on the Hebrew Text of Jonah.* London: The Epworth Press.

Soncino Talmud,

I. Epstein, ed., *The Babylonian Talmud.* London: The Soncino Press.

1935a: H. Freedman, ed. and trans., *Sanhedrin,* vol. 2.

1935b: M. Simon and I. W. Slotski, eds. and trans., *Babba bathra,* vol. 1.

1936a: I. W. Slotski, ed. and trans., *Yebamoth,* vol. 2.

1936b: M. Simon, ed. and trans., *Giṭṭin.*

1936c: H. Freedman, ed. and trans., *Nedarim.*

1936d: I. Epstein, ed. and trans., *Kiddushin.*

1938a: L. Jung, ed. and trans., *Yoma.*

1938b: I. W. Slotski, ed. and trans., *ᶜErubin.*

1938c: J. Rabbinowitz, ed. and trans., *Taᶜanith.*

1938d: M. Simon, ed. and trans., *Rosh Hashanah.*

1938e: M. Simon, ed. and trans., *Megillah.*

1948a: L. Miller, ed. and trans., *Temurah.*

1948b: I. Porusch, ed. and trans., *Kerithoth.*

Sperber, A.,

1962: *The Latter Prophets According to Targum Jonathan.* [The Bible in Aramaic 3.] Leiden: E. J. Brill.

BIBLIOGRAPHY

Sperling, H., and Simon, M., trans.,

1949: *The Zohar.* Volume I. London: The Soncino Press.

Sperling, S. D.,

1982: "Bloodguilt in the Bible and in Ancient Near Eastern Sources," pp. 19–25 in Link-Salinger 1982.

1986: "Israel's Religion in the Ancient Near East," pp. 5–31 in Green 1986.

Stadelmann, L. I. J.,

1970: *The Hebrew Conception of the World: A Philological and Literary Study.* [Analecta Biblica 39.] Rome: Pontifical Biblical Institute.

Stamm, J. J.,

1939: *Die akkadischen Namengebung.* [Mitteilungen der Deutschen Orient-Gesellschaft 44.] Leipzig: J. C. Heinrichs Verlag.

Steffen, U.,

1982: *Jona und der Fisch: Der Mythos von Tod und der Wiedergeburt.* Berlin: Kreuz Verlag.

Stek, J. H.,

1969: "The Message of the Book of Jonah," *Calvin Theological Journal* 4: 23–50.

Stenzel, M.,

1952: "Zum Vulgatatext des Canticum Jonas," *Biblica* 33: 356–65.

Sternberg, M.,

1987: *The Poetics of Biblical Narrative: Ideological Literature and the Drama of Reading.* Bloomington, Ind.: Indiana University Press.

Stol, M.,

1987: "The Cucurbitaceae in the Cuneiform Texts," *Bulletin on Sumerian Agriculture* 3: 81–92.

Stuhlmueller, C.,

1970: *Creative Redemption in Deutero-Isaiah.* [Analecta Biblica 43.] Rome: Pontifical Biblical Institute.

Stuart, D.,

1987: *Hosea-Jonah.* [Word Biblical Commentary 31]. Waco, Tex.: Word Books.

Szermach, P. E.,

1972: "Three Versions of the Jonah Story: An Investigation of Narrative Technique in Old English Homilies," *Anglo-Saxon England* 1: 183–92.

Talbert, C. H.,

1978: "Biographies of Philosophers and Rulers as Instruments of Religious Propaganda in Mediterranean Antiquity," pp. 1619–51 in *Aufstieg und Niedergang der Römisches Welt,* vol. 2, 16.2. Berlin: Walter de Gruyter.

Talmon, S., and Fields, W. W.,

1989: "The Collocation *mštyn bqyr wʿṣwr wʿzwb* and Its Meaning," *Zeitschrift für die alttestamentliche Wissenschaft* 101: 85–112.

Thackston, Jr., W. M.,
1978: *The Tales of the Prophets of al-Kisa'i.* Boston: Twayne Publishing.
Theognis,
see Carrière, 1975.
Thomas, D. W.,
1953: "A Consideration of Some Unusual Ways of Expressing the Superlative in Hebrew," *Vetus Testamentum* 3: 209–24.
Thompson, S.,
1955–58: *Motif-Index of Folk Literature.* Bloomington, Ind.: Indiana University Press.
Thomson, J. G. S. S.,
1955: "Sleep: An Aspect of Jewish Anthropology," *Vetus Testamentum* 5: 421–33.
Tigay, J. H.,
1985–86: "The Book of Jonah and the Days of Awe," *Conservative Judaism* 38: 67–76.
Toorn, K. van der,
1986: "Ḥrem-Bethel and Elephantine Oath Procedure," *Zeitschrift für die alttestamentliche Wissenschaft* 98: 282–85.
Torrance, R. M.,
1978: *The Comic Hero.* Cambridge, Mass.: Harvard University Press.
Torrey, C. C.,
1922: " 'Nineveh' in the Book of Tobit," *Journal of Biblical Literature* 41: 237–45.
Tov, E.,
1986: "The David and Goliath Story," *Bible Review* 2: 34–41.
Trépanier, B.,
1951: "The Story of Jonah," *Catholic Biblical Quarterly* 13: 8–16.
Trible, P. L.,
1963: "Studies in the Book of Jonah." Ph.D. diss., Columbia University. Ann Arbor, Mich.: University Microfilm International, order no. 65–7479.
Tromp, N. J.,
1969: *Primitive Conceptions of Death and the Netherworld in the Old Testament.* [Biblica et Orientalia 21] Rome: Pontifical Biblical Institute.
Trumbull, H. C.,
1892: "Jonah in Nineveh," *Journal of Biblical Literature* 11: 53–60.
Tsumura, D. T.,
1988: "A 'Hyponymous' Word Pair: *ʾrṣ* and *thm(t)* in Hebrew and Ugaritic," *Biblica* 69: 258–69.
Tuttle, G. A., ed.,
1978: *Biblical and Near Eastern Studies: Essays in Honor of William Sanford LaSor.* Grand Rapids, Mich.: Eerdmans.

BIBLIOGRAPHY

Tyrer, J. W.,
1932: *Historical Survey of Holy Week, Its Services and Ceremonial.* London: Oxford University Press.

Uffenheimer, B.,
1982: *Iyunim ba-Miqra: Sefer Zikaron li-Yehoshua Meʾir Grintz* (Joshua Grintz Memorial Volume.) Tel Aviv: University of Tel Aviv Press.

Unnik, W. C. van, and Woude, A. S. van der,
1966: *Studia Biblica et Semitica Theodoro Christiano Vriezen . . . Dedicata.* Wageningen: H. Veenman & Zonen.

Urbach, E. E.,
1979: *The Sages: Their Concepts and Beliefs.* 2 vols. [Publication of the Perry Foundation.] Jerusalem: The Hebrew University.

Vanoni, G.,
1978: *Das Buch Jona.* [Münchener Universitätsschriften, Arbeiten zu Text und Sprache im Alten Testament 7.] St. Ottilien: Eos Verlag.

Vattioni, F.,
1968: *Ecclesiastico: Testo ebraico con apparato critico e versioni greca, latina e siriaca.* [Pubblicazioni del seminario di semitistica, Testi 1.] Napoli: Istituto Orientale di Napoli.

Vaux, R. de,
1961: *Ancient Israel: Its Life and Institutions.* New York: McGraw-Hill Book Co.

Vawter, B.,
1983: *Job and Jonah: Questioning the Hidden God.* Ramsey, N.J.: Paulist Press.

Veenhof, K. R.,
1982: "Observations on Some Letters from Mari (ARM 2, 124; 10, 4; 43; 84; 114) with a Note on *tillatum,*" *Revue d'Assyriologie* 76: 119–40.

Vermes, G.,
1975: *The Dead Sea Scrolls in English.* 2d ed., New York: Penguin Books.

Versnel, H. S.,
1981: *Faith, Hope, and Worship: Aspects of Religious Mentality in the Ancient World.* [Studies in Greek and Roman Religion 2.] Leiden: E. J. Brill.

Vogt, J.,
1970: "Synesios auf Seefahrt," pp. 400–8 in *Kyriakon* (*Festschrift Johannes Quasten*). vol. 1. Münster: Verlag Aschendorff.

Walsh, J. T.,
1982: "Jonah 2,3–10: A Rhetorical Critical Study," *Biblica* 63: 219–29.

Watson, W. G. E.,
1984: *Classical Hebrew Poetry. A Guide to Its Techniques.* [*Journal for the Study of the Old Testament,* Supplement Series 26.] Sheffield: JSOT Press.

Weidner, E. F.,
1940: "Des Archiv des Mannu-kî Aššur," pp. 8–46 in Friedrich, et al., 1940.

BIBLIOGRAPHY

Weimar, P.,

1982: "Beobachtungen zur Entstehung der Jonaerzählung," *Biblische Notizen* 18: 86–109.

1982b: "Literarische Kritik und Literarkritik: Unzeitgemässe Beobachtungen zu Jon 1,4–16," pp. 217–35 in Ruppert, et al., 1982.

Weiser, A.,

1967: *Das Buch der zwölf kleinen Propheten, vol. 1: Die Propheten Hosea, Joel, Amos, Obadja, Jona, Micha.* Göttingen: Vandenhoeck & Ruprecht.

Wesselski, A.,

1911: *Der Hodscha Nasreddin.* 2 vols. Weimar: A. Duncker.

West, M.,

1984: "Irony in the Book of Jonah: Audience Identification with the Hero," *Perspectives in Religious Studies* 11: 233–42.

Westermann, C.,

1974: *Genesis.* [Biblischer Kommentar Altes Testament 1.1.] Neukirchen-Vluyn: Verlag Butzon & Bercker Kevelaer.

Wiesel, E.,

1981: *Five Biblical Portraits.* South Bend, Ind.: University of Notre Dame Press.

Wilson, A. J.,

1927: "The Sign of the Prophet Jonah and Its Modern Confirmation," *Princeton Theological Review* 25: 630–42.

Wilson, R. D.,

1918: "The Authenticity of Jonah," *Princeton Theological Review* 16: 280–98, 430–56.

1918b: "*mnh,* 'To Appoint,' in the Old Testament," *Princeton Theological Review* 16: 645–54.

Winckler, H.,

1900: "Zum Buche Jona," *Altorientalische Forschungen* 2: 260–65.

Wischmeyer, W.,

1981: "Die Vorkonstantinische christliche Kunst in neuem Lichte: Die Clevelands-Statuetten," *Vigiliae Christianae* 35: 253–87.

Wiseman, D. J.,

1979: "Jonah's Nineveh," *Tyndale Bulletin* 30: 29–51.

Witzenrath, H.,

1978: *Das Buch Jona.* [Münchener Universitätsschriften, Arbeiten zu Text und Sprache im Alten Testament 6.] St. Ottilien: Eos Verlag.

Wolff, H. W.,

1977: *Dodekapropheton 3, Obadja und Jona.* [Biblischer Kommentar Altes Testament 14.3.] Neukirchen-Vluyn: Verlag Butzon & Bercker Kevelaer.

1986: *Obadiah and Jonah: A Commentary.* [English trans. of the above.] Minneapolis: Augsburg Publishing Co.

Woude, A. S. van der,
1981: "Bemerkungen zu einigen umstrittenen Stellen im Zwölfprophetenbuch," pp. 483–99 in Caquot 1981.
Wright, W.,
1857: *The Book of Jonah in Four Oriental Versions, Namely Chaldee, Syriac, Aethiopic, and Arabic, with Glossaries.* London: Williams and Norgate.
Wünsche, A.,
1907: *Aus Israels Lehrhallen. Kleine Midraschim zur späteren legendarischen Literatur des Alten Testaments.* II. Band. Leipzig: Eduard Pfeiffer.
Würthwein, E.,
1979: *The Text of the Old Testament:* An Introduction to the *Biblia Hebraica.* Grand Rapids, Mich.: W. B. Eerdmans. [Reprinted 1987.]
Young, E. J.,
1960: *An Introduction to the Old Testament.* Grand Rapids, Mich.: W. B. Eerdmans.
Young, G. D.,
1981: *Ugarit in Retrospect. Fifty Years of Ugarit and Ugaritic.* Winona Lake, Ind.: Eisenbrauns.
Yountie, J.,
1945: "A Codex of Jonah," *Harvard Theological Studies* 38: 195–97.
Zakovitch, Y., and Rofé, A., eds.,
1983: *Sefer Yitsḥaq Aryeh Seeligmann,* vol. 2. (*Y. A. Seeligmann Memorial Volume: Studies on the Bible and the Ancient Near East.*) Jerusalem: Elḥanan Rubinstein Publishing House.
Ziegler, J.,
1967: *Septuaginta. Vetus Testamentum Graecum,* vol. 13. *Duodecim prophetae.* 2d ed. Göttingen: Vandenhoeck & Ruprecht.
Ziskind, J. A.,
1974: "Sea Loans at Ugarit," *Journal of the American Oriental Society* 94: 134–37.
Zlotowitz, M.,
1980: *Yonah/Jonah: A New Translation with a Commentary Anthologized from Midrashic and Rabbinic Sources.* Brooklyn, N.Y.: Mesorah Publishing.
Zmudi, J.,
1982: *"haqqîqāyôn šel yōnâ," Beth Miqra* 92: 44–48.
The *Zohar,*
Sperling and Simon, 1949 (vol. I).
Simon and Levertoff, 1949 (vol. IV).
Zorell, F.,
1933: "Gibt es im Hebraïschen ein *'kî* recitativum'?," *Biblica* 14: 465–69.

NOTES AND COMMENTS

I. The Setting (Jonah 1:1–3)

◆

Then, as the Lord stretched out his hand to touch my mouth, the Lord told me, "There, I am placing my words into your mouth. As of this moment, I appoint you over nations and over kingdoms, to uproot and knock down, to destroy and overthrow, to build and plant." (Jer 1:9–10)

Shipmates, this book, containing only four chapters—four yarns—is one of the smallest strands in the mighty cable of the Scriptures. Yet what depths of the soul Jonah's deep sealine sound! what a pregnant lesson to us is this prophet! What a noble thing is that canticle in the fish's belly! How billow-like and boisterously grand! We feel the floods surging over us, we sound with him to the kelpy bottom of the waters, sea-weed and all the slime of the sea is about us! But *what* is this lesson that the book of Jonah teaches? Shipmates, it is a two-stranded lesson; a lesson to us all sinful men, and a lesson to me as a pilot of the living God. (Father Mapple, in Herman Melville's *Moby Dick*)

Who hath not heard the story of Jonas? Jonas was in the whale's belly: the place was very dark: the waves beat on every side: he was drowned, yet touched no water; he was swallowed up, yet not consumed; he lived without any sense of life; the fish was death, the sea was death, and the tempest was death; yet he died not; but lived in the midst of death, he could not see, he could not hear, he knew not to whom he might call for help; he was taken and carried away, he knew not whither. Let us mark well this story: it is a true pattern of our estate, and sheweth what our Life is in this world. (John Jewel, Bishop of Salisbury)[1]

[1] From his *A treatise of the Holy Scriptures* (1570). Quoted from Bowers 1971: 75.

I. THE SETTING (1:1–3)

1 [1]When the Lord's command to Jonah the son of Amittay was, [2]"Set out for Nineveh, that large city, and declare doom upon it; the wickedness of its citizens is obvious to me," [3]Jonah, instead, sought to escape the Lord by heading toward Tarshish. Going down to Jaffa, he found a ship that had just come from Tarshish. He paid its hire, then boarded it to accompany *the sailors*[a] toward Tarshish and away from the Lord.

[a] Hebrew, "them."

NOTES

1:1. *way(ye)hî debar-YHWH ʾel-yônâ ben-ʾamittay lēʾmōr.* This opening is by no means without significant consequences for an understanding of Jonah. We need therefore to inspect it carefully. The various translations of Jonah into the languages of antiquity (Greek, Latin, Aramaic, and so on) render this opening rather slavishly. The Targum, however, makes it clear that prophecy was at stake in this narrative by expanding the sentence into *whwh p[y]tgm nbwʾh mn qdm YY ʿm ywnh br ʾmty lmymr,* "A prophetic message from God came to be with Jonah as follows . . ." (Levine 1978: 55).

The root *hāyâ* in the *G*-imperfect with a *waw*-conversive is very common in the Hebrew Scripture. Of interest here are two matters: (1) its use in opening individual books of Hebrew Scripture, and (2) the consequences of such usage for the book of Jonah.

1. The word *way(ye)hî* opens a number of books with narratives that the Hebrew deemed to be history. In such cases, the verb *hāyâ* bears a weakened sense and is treated as a stative, with an impersonal subject; Joüon 1947: 293–94 [§ 111.h]. Koehler 1953: 304 labels this usage "hypertrophic." In such cases, either a temporal or a circumstantial clause provides the needed context. A verb launches the main activity, and it is most often given in the imperfect with a *waw*-conversive, but sometimes also in the perfect, with or without a conjunction; GKC 327 [§ 11.f]. A few examples will suffice:

a. Temporal clauses: *way(ye)hî ʾaḥarê môt mōšeh . . . wayyōʾmer YHWH* (Josh 1:1; see also Judg 1:1);

b. Circumstantial clauses: *way(ye)hî ʾîš ʾeḥād . . .* [v 3] *weʿālâ hāʾîš . . .* (1 Sam 1:1–3);

c. Temporal + circumstantial clauses (commonly in this sequence):

i. (expressed as *way(ye)hî . . . we . . .): way(ye)hî ʾaḥarê môt šāʾûl wedāwid šāb mē- . . . wayyēšeb dāwid . . .* (2 Sam 1:1);

ii. (expressed as *way(ye)hî . . . way(ye)hî): way(ye)hî bimê šepôṭ haššōpeṭîm way(ye)hî rāʿāb bāʾāreṣ wayyēlek ʾîš . . .* (Ruth 1:1);

iii. (with multiple digressions): *way(ye)hî bimê ʾaḥašwērôš . . . bayyāmîm hāhēm . . . ʿāśâ mišteh . . .* (Esth 1:1).

Only two prophetic books open with *way(ye)hî.* In the complex introduction to Ezekiel, this *way(ye)hî* is used in a manner similar to the example offered under c.iii, thus forcing immediate focus on the prophet, his call, and his vision rather than on the content of his divine message. The other example occurs in Jonah.

2. As introduction to the prophetic books, it is much more common to find the verb *hāyâ* in the perfect with *debar-YHWH* as its subject. Grether 1934: 63–76 studied this expression thoroughly and concluded that *debar-YHWH* is nearly everywhere *the* technical terminology for the opening of prophetic message, before and after the exilic periods. Subtle differences, however, can be recognized:

a. Hosea, Joel, Micah, and Zephaniah have *debar-YHWH ʾašer hāyâ ʾel* + name of prophet. Here the relative pronoun *ʾašer* allows the clause to act as a superscript, thus emphasizing *debar-YHWH,* "(This is) God's message that came to such and such prophet." This formula therefore sharpens our awareness of the message instead of informing us about the prophet who carries it. Except in the case of Joel, such a formula is regularly succeeded by a clause to situate the prophecy in a specific period. Once it makes its initial appearance, however, this formula does not return in any one of the above-mentioned prophetic books.

b. Haggai and Zechariah, by contrast, open with temporal clauses before proceeding with the *hāyâ* formulation. Thus Zech 1:1 has "time" + *hāyâ debar-YHWH ʾel* [prophet] . . . *lēʾmōr.* This rather abrupt statement is repeated in 1:7 where it (awkwardly) introduces visionary material. All subsequent reappearances of *debar-YHWH* (at 4:8; 6:9; 7:1; 8:1, 18), however, are cast in a form that is familiar to us in Jonah: *way(ye)hî debar-YHWH ʾel. . . .*

This observation is relevant, for a check into any Hebrew concordance will show that the expression *way(ye)hî debar-YHWH ʾel . . .* is found only when contexts and circumstances regarding the prophet and his mission are already established in previous statements. Thus, in the Book of Kings, once Elijah enters the stage *way(ye)hî debar-YHWH ʾel ʾēliyyāhû* becomes the standard formula by which he receives all subsequent divine messages. The same can be said about many occasions in Jeremiah. Bewer (1912: 28) reached the same conclusion, albeit through faulty reasoning. Rudolph (1971: 335–36) offers the farfetched opinion that the *waw* in *way(ye)hî* is meant to connect with the Jonah narrative of 2 Kings and/or to make editorial linkings with the last verse of Obadiah.

The compound *debar-YHWH* appears often in Scripture, and O. Grether's work (1934) offers an exhaustive classification of its usage; see also BDB 182 (2.a). There is also a brief overview of the same in Schmidt's article for *ThWAT* 1.118–22 (iv.1.a, c). An eccentric but very insightful analysis of the same formula is available in the neglected work of H. Masing (1938), who claims that "the only way to understand a prophet's soul, even a little, is to understand the expression *daβar iahwe,* because it is the very essence of the matter for a prophet" (p. 3).

Despite the commonly held opinion that the use of *debar-YHWH* betrays Deuteronomistic popularization (Stuhlmueller 1970: 175—with statistics), this term cannot be restricted to a specific period of biblical prophecy; indeed, in view of the simplicity of the construction—*debar,* "word (of)" + divine name or epithet—and the wide attestation of semantic equivalent(s) of this formula at all periods and in many areas of the ancient Near East, the Hebrew is not likely to have awaited a specific time in order to invent it.

The divine message that is given in v 2 is not addressed through Jonah to a people who are to benefit from its contents; on the contrary, it is meant solely for his ear. For in other prophetic texts, whenever God's word is to reach people, either a *kōh ʾāmar YHWH* ("This is what God is saying") or a similar formula usually succeeds a brief order to the prophet (for example, a 2 Sam 7:5 [Nathan]; 24:11 [Gad]; 1 Kgs 13:21 [Bethel prophet]). One may also find a verb in the imperative ordering the prophet to convey a message (for example, 1 Kgs 12:24 [Shemaya]). The few cases in which *debar-YHWH* does not introduce an oracle can be found in the narratives regarding Samuel (1 Sam 15:10) or those regarding Elijah (1 Kgs 17:2, 8; 18:1; 21:17). It can also be noted that in these latter examples, the prophet's order is for him to "go" (*lēk,* the first three attestations) or to "go down" (*qûm rēd*).

yônâ ben-ʾamittay. I have avoided rendering, "Jonah, ben-Amittay," which would be closer to how Hebrews "heard" such conjunctions of names and patronyms, lest today's audiences presume that "ben-Amittay" is a family name in the style that is now common in modern Israel.

The versions have preserved differing transcriptions of the prophet's name (LXX, *Iōnas* [undeclined in W, *Iōna*]; Vulgate, *Ionas;* Arabic, *Yûnis*). The meaning of *yônâ* is "dove," though the Zohar connects it with (*hāʿîr hay)yônâ,* the "oppressive city" of Zeph 3:1. (I give a full quotation of the Zohar passage in the INTERPRETATIONS.) There is nothing exceptional about a name derived from the animal world, whether in Hebrew or in other ancient languages: for Mesopotamia, see Stamm 1939: 254–55; for Ugarit, see Jirku 1969: 8–9. The same situation obtains in the classical world. In fact, Hebrew knows of other personal names derived from the same family of birds (*columbianae): yemîmâ* (Jemima), *gôzāl* (Gozal), and *tôr* (Tor); see *ThWAT* 3.586–94 for a discussion and full listing. Other etymologies for "Jonah," whether based on roots such as **ynh,* "to be strong," **ywn,* "Greece," or perceived as by-forms of *Yehonatan,* "Jonathan," are unnecessary and often philologically not plausible (partial bibliography in Rudolph 1971: 335).

Although "Dove" is a perfectly legitimate choice for Hebrew parents to bestow upon a male son—in modern Israel the name is held by women as well—many scholars have sought symbolic or even esoteric reasons for its assignment to a prophet. For example, König 1906: 747b finds it significant that the Northern Kingdom prophet Hosea twice alludes to a "dove" that runs to and from Assyria (Nineveh): 7:11, "Ephrayim [Israel] is becoming a silly, aimless dove: its people appeal to Egypt, but run to Assyria." The simile is completed in 11:11, with the return of the dove from Assyria.

Recently A. Hauser (1985) has spun a whole reading of the text by exploiting the symbolism of the prophet's name, and I shall treat such an approach in the INTERPRETATIONS. At this stage, it could be noted that the Bible frequently alludes to doves: in listings for sacrificial offerings, as a term of endearment, and as an inspiration for similes and metaphors; see, conveniently, McCullough in *IDB* 1.866–67. There are instances in which doves bring good tidings: in the famous ending for Noah's confinement in the ark, as well as in a difficult psalm passage (Ps 68:14; for which see Keel 1977: 34; Lipiński 1973; Eerdmans 1947: 328).

The name *ʾamittay* (LXX: Amathi, with vocalic variations in other Greek versions; Peshitta and Arabic omit the first syllable; see Trible 1963: 11) is ultimately based on the root *ʾmn* but is more immediately constructed on the word *ʾemet* (Jepsen, in *ThWAT* 1.333 [VI.1]). The *yod* at the end of the word can be regarded as a hypocoristicon, allowing the name to mean something like "Yahweh is steadfast." The closest etymological equivalents would be names likewise based on *ʾmn,* but this time from one of its derivatives, *ʾemûnâ* (Amnon, Amon, etc).

As to Jonah's background, because he was identified with the Jonah from Gath Hepher of 2 Kings 14, he was believed to belong to the tribe of Zebulun (see Josh 19:13). But other tribal affiliations are known to tradition, most prominent of which is Asher, because Jonah is identified with the resurrected (resuscitated?) son of the Zareptah widow and because Zareptah lies in Asher Territory (Zlotowitz 1980: 78). In the COMMENTS to section XI, I quote Jonah's *vita* as given in the *Lives of the Prophets.*

1:2. *qûm lēk ʾel-nînewēh hāʿîr haggedôlâ ûqrāʾ ʿālêhā kî-ʿāletâ rāʿātām lepānāy.* The verb *qûm* is often used as auxiliary in Hebrew when the main activity is reserved for the succeeding verb; see Orlinsky 1969: 34–35; GKC 33–37

[§ 120.g]; Amsler, in *THAT* 2.638 [3.c]. This syntactic feature is not appreciated enough by modern commentators on Jonah, who therefore often make unwarranted evaluations, treating *qûm* as an active verb. In turn, the verb that is affected by the auxiliary, in our case *hālak*, "to go," no longer maintains its primal meaning, but is attenuated to convey volition rather than direction. Vanoni (1978: 126–27) lists nine occasions for this construction in the Hebrew Bible, of which seven involve commands to prophets. Magonet's exposition on "movement and counter-movement," which relies on undifferentiated usage of *hālak* in Jonah, is often quite forced (1976: 29–30). For idiomatic reasons, LXX and the Vulgate insert a conjunction between the two verbs; see Trible 1963: 11.

ʾel-nînewēh. To the prophets of Israel, even to those who lived after Assyria's fall, the name Nineveh was enough to prompt memory of a bitter and long-lasting yoke. Zephaniah (2:13) foresees the day that God "will stretch out his arm against the north and destroy Assyria; he will make Nineveh a desolation, arid as the desert." When the prophet Nahum asked (2:12), "What has become of that lion's den?" he was sardonically exulting over the fall of Nineveh, "a city of crime, utterly treacherous, full of violence, where killing never stops" (3:1).

The few other references to Nineveh likewise are unflattering. According to 2 Kgs 19:36–37 (paralleling Isa 37:37–38), one of Nineveh's temples is the scene of Sennacherib's assassination (see Parpola 1980). The sixth-century B.C.E. Greek gnomic poet Phocylides is credited with coining a maxim that betrays contempt: "A prudent city riding a rock is better than stupid Nineveh that has been destroyed" (cited by Oppenheim 1979: 139 n. 8). An Egyptian demotic tale tells how Egyptian gods triumphed when brought into Nineveh's temples; Bickerman 1976: 68.

Nineveh's reputation as a center of savage power is reason enough for Jonah to have made out of it a paradigm for utter wickedness reprieved by utter mercy. But because Scripture gives it prestige as mankind's first city after the Flood, the book of Jonah might have deemed it particularly worthy of reprieve. In Genesis's Table of Nations, Nineveh is recalled as the first city founded by Nimrod, son of Kush, as he extended his power northward from Babylon (vv 8–12; verses ignored in Chronicles):

> Kush fathered Nimrod, who strove to be a tyrant on earth. In fact, he was a mighty hunter, facing the Lord.[2] Therefore, when people say, "Like Nimrod," (it means) "a mighty hunter, facing the Lord."
>
> Now [Nimrod's] power bases were Babylon, Uruk and Akkad—all of which are in the land of Shinʿar. From this region, [Nimrod] sallied forth toward Assyria [read: *ʾaššûrâ*], founding Nineveh, the broadest city, Ca-

[2] Possibly "measuring up to God," that is, extraordinary, almost divine, in size, as were the Nephilim of old. See Kraeling, cited by Thomas 1953: 263 n. 4.

lah and Resen—(the last), between Nineveh and Calah, the mightiest city.[3]

Nineveh lies now across the Tigris River from the modern Iraqi town of Mosul. Archaeology and cuneiform evidence tell us that Nineveh endured for thousands of years, but that its great moments took place in the early first millennium, beginning with Shalmaneser I and Ashurnasirpal II (ninth century). During the reign of the same Jeroboam (II) in whose reign a Jonah son of Amittay prophesied (see the COMMENTS below), Nineveh was yet to reach the full glory that it experienced under Sennacherib (704–681). It was then that the town achieved massive constructions, with trapezoidal-shaped fortifications running eight miles around the perimeters. (See further below, under 3:3.) A combined Babylonian and Median force destroyed the city in the summer of 612 B.C.E., and its population was taken captive. Upon its site on the left bank of the Tigris river no other city was founded until Mongol times (Qoyunjik, a suburb of Mosul), though two Jewish romances of the Hellenistic period, Tobit and Judith, spoke of it as a viable town (Torrey 1922). When Xenophon visited Nineveh two hundred years after its fall, he marveled at its remains, yet could find no one who remembered its past glories with any accuracy (*Anabasis* 3.4.10–12). Classical sources hesitated about its locations, some placing it on the Tigris (Herodotus, Arrian, Strabo), others locating it on the Euphrates (Diodorus, Ctesias).[4]

Today, the ruins of a palace built by Esarhaddon (681–669) within the ramparts of Nineveh are given the name Tell Nabi Yunis, "Tell of the Prophet Jonah," and its site is commonly honored as holding Jonah's tomb (*tell al-tawba,* "Penitence Hill," Wolff 1986: 147 n. 1). But three other places are similarly honored, most prominently one near Nazareth (Mesh'hed); see Marti 1904: 241.

One curiosity with regard to Nineveh is the cuneiform writing of its name. The sumerogram NINA could look like the sign ÈŠ (which could mean "temple, house") within which is placed the sign HA (which could mean "fish"). This writing of Nineveh's name is no doubt based on Assyrian folk etymology, and although we really do not know much about its origin and meaning, it has not deterred some fanciful reconstruction by those who make connection with Jonah's own sojourn in the fish's belly.

hāʿîr haggedôlâ. The accents, conjunctive under *hāʿîr* and disjunctive under *haggedôlâ,* bind the two vocables and set them slightly apart from the rest of the words in the sentence. Indeed, the accents are not alone in highlighting "the large city," for the articles are used here in their capacity as weak demonstratives

[3] On rendering the last verses, see Sasson 1983.

[4] A handy, albeit dated, citation of the classical evidence is available in Smith 1857: 2. 437–39.

(Joüon 1965: 422 [§ 137f.I.3]) as if to insist that everyone is aware of Nineveh's reputation as that large city. The LXX, but not the Targum or the Peshitta, translates with similar emphasis (Trible 1963: 12). We shall soon note that this vocabulary will act as a leitmotif in the prose chapters of Jonah (at 3:2, 3 and 4:11). But subtle differences registered by accents and contexts will distinguish among the various occurrences. Just once, in Jer 22:8, *hāʿîr haggedôlâ* is applied to Jerusalem; the remaining attestations of the phrase describe foreign (for example, Gibeon in Josh 10:2), but more commonly Assyrian, cities. In Gen 10:2 it is applied to Calah (present-day Nimrud). I have elsewhere argued (Sasson 1983) that in the Table of Nations of Genesis 10 Nineveh is also provided with its own appellative, "Broadest of cities," *reḥōbōt ʿîr.* But one more citation for *hāʿîr haggedôlâ* as applied to Nineveh should be mentioned here, though the full import of this observation will be clearer later: in some manuscripts of Jdt 1:11 Nineveh is called *hē polis hē megalē,* "the large city," and this is but one of a number of contacts between Judith and Jonah (see, for now, Delcor 1976: 273–74; Dubarle 1966: 152–53).

ûqrāʾ ʿālêhā. To translate adequately a phrase that contains the verb *qārāʾ, careful attention has to be paid to the substantives that it regulates, as well as to the prepositions with which it is construed. In Jonah, we meet with the following occurrences:*

1. *qārāʾ ʿal*	a.	Imperative: *(qûm lēk . . .) ûqrāʾ ʿalêhā* . . . (1:2);
2. *qārāʾ ʾel*	b.	Imperative: *(qûm) qerāʾ ʾel-ʾelōhêkā* . . . (1:6);
	c.	Imperative: *(qûm lēk . . .) ûqrāʾ ʾelêhā ʾet-haqqerîʾâ* (3:1);
	d.	Perfect: *qārāʾtî (miṣṣarâ lî) ʾel-YHWH* (2:3);
	e.	Conversive imperfect: *wayyiqreʾû ʾel-YHWH (wayyōʾmerû)* . . . (1:14);
	f.	Jussive: *weyiqreʾû ʾel-ʾelōhîm (beḥozqâ)* . . . (3:8).

One can immediately note that the examples with *qārāʾ* in the imperative are addressed to Jonah, with a more immediate injunction to attend to this act when coming from the *rab haḥōbēl* (2.b: *qûm ûqrāʾ*) than when it comes from God (1.a, 2.c: *qûm lēk . . . ûqrāʾ*). And *qārāʾ* is in the perfect when the subject is Jonah (2.d) and in the imperfect (conversive, jussive) when the subjects are sailors and Ninevites (2.e, f).

But our main task here is not to assess meanings and gauge nuances for the various idioms in which *qārāʾ ʾel* occurs; we merely note now that the idea of "praying, appealing to someone" is borne by *liqrōʾ ʾel,* with the construction not requiring a noun as direct object (but see 2.c at 3:1, where a cognate accusative occurs). If the words of a specific prayer are to be recorded, they are usually introduced by a verb referring to speaking (as in 2.e, at 1:14).

THE SETTING (1:1–3)

We need to ascertain here whether grammar requires us to offer perceptibly differing translations for the two clauses (1.a and 2.c) in which the verb *qārāʾ* is construed with different prepositions. The LXX's translation for 1:2 has an order for the prophet to enter the city in order to proclaim a specific message (*kai kērukson en autē*). It uses pretty much the same language in rendering 3:2 and thus implies continuity in the two missions, adding "according to the previous message I gave you." (Duval [1973: 54 n. 199; 73] recounts the consequences that emerged among Christian interpreters through this lack of distinctions.) Similarly, the Targum made no distinctions between the two occurrences of *qārāʾ ʿal/ʾel* (Levine 1978: 55, 83; for the remaining versions, see Trible 1963: 12). Unfortunately, the Murabbaʿât fragments from the Dead Sea concerned with Jonah are not preserved for 3:2, and we cannot tell whether that community discriminated between the two passages.

Modern exegetes generally take their cue from these ancient versions and note that the Hebrew text, in all manuscripts, consistently distinguishes between *ʿal* in 1:2 and *ʾel* in 3:2. Most scholars, however, follow the LXX in sensing no perceptible difference and argue that *ʾel* and *ʿal* are basically interchangeable, especially in "late" Hebrew (see, lately, Brenner 1979: 400). A few scholars do offer different translations, but, as far as I can gather, do not draw markedly distinct conclusions. Thus, Keil and Delitzsch (1900: 389) object to the oft-stated harmonization in meanings but conclude only that in chapter 1 Jonah is to warn of the need to do penance while in chapter 3 he carries a more detailed program to the Ninevites. Magonet (1976: 25–26) suggests that a change in Jonah's prophetic status might be at stake: in the first case, at 1:2, Jonah is given a free hand to preach as he will, while in 3:2 he carries a specific message. Similar notions are offered by Levine (1975: 56), basing himself on the Targum. In der Smitten (1972: 94) translates "und schreie zu ihr hin," relying on a faulty understanding of God's objection to the Ninevites' activities; he is criticized for it by Wolff (1986: 95). Almbladh (1986: 17) thinks that "*ʿlyh* is probably used for stylistic reasons to make an alliteration [with] *ʿlyh* . . . *ʿlth rʿtm*."

Most often, however, those who object to making no distinction between the two usages write in a vein that is decidedly equivocal. Landes (1982: 158*) reasons as follows:

> The fact that in 3:2 the author of Jonah employs *qrʾ ʾl* in a verse that is consciously molded after 1:2 possibly suggests that no difference in meaning was intended between the two phrases, and *qrʾ ʾl* is . . . simply a stylistic variant of *qrʾ ʿl*. . . . On the other hand, the possibility should perhaps not be ruled out that the author intended a somewhat stronger expression with *ʿl* in 1:2 than with *ʾl* in 3:2, because of the different content that follows each of these constructions. Thus, in 1:2,

*qr*ʾ *ʿl* may have the sense of "denounce" which *qr*ʾ *ʾl* in 3:2 clearly does not have.

While Hebrew may well interchange *ʾel* and *ʿal* in many passages, the issue is not simply a matter of two prepositions used promiscuously; rather, it needs to be established that the idioms *qārāʾ ʾel* and *qārāʾ ʿal* are interchangeable. We therefore need to look at the usage for *qārāʾ ʿal*, in order to judge whether the idiom (or phrase) bears a specific meaning as it is found in Hebrew Scripture and whether this idiom (or phrase) has equivalents in which *qārāʾ ʾel* is substituted.

A. *qārāʾ ʿal* with no noun modifiers:

1. 1 Kgs 13:2: (a prophet comes) *wayyiqrāʾ ʿal-hammizbēaḥ bidbar YHWH wayyōʾmer* . . . ("He condemned the altar of Bethel on God's order, saying . . ."). Note intended consequences in v 3: ("This altar shall be broken up and the ashes upon it spilled"; see also 1 Kgs 13:4, 32);
2. Deut 15:9: (a rejected kinsman in need) *weqārāʾ ʿālêkā ʾel-YHWH* "so that he condemns you to God." Note the consequence: "and you will incur guilt." (Similarly Deut 24:15.) See also Exod 22:22–23, where God's response to a similar appeal is registered: "I will put you to the sword, and your own wives will become widows and your children orphans."

This usage, which has *qārāʾ ʿal* + pronominal suffix + *ʾel* + divine name, does have a parallel in an Aramaic text from Elephantine, one that, moreover, seems to register a substitution *ʿal* for *ʾel*. In Cowley 7 (see, conveniently, Porten 1968: 314–17, 156; *contra:* Toorn 1986), a man protests his innocence in a burglary case and is forced to invoke the God: *ʾnk mlkyh ʾqr ʾlk ʿl ḥrmbytʾl*, "I, Malchiyah, do inform? you before Ḥerembethel . . . (the god among four avengers, as follows: I did not enter your house by force)." While this particular usage in preposition may be attributable to Aramaic syntax, it ought to be assessed in conjunction with example 2.c, above, where *qārāʾ ʾel* + pronominal suffix + verb for speaking introduces an appeal.

B. *qārāʾ ʿal* with the meaning modified by a noun:

1. *magôr.* Jer 49:29: *weqāreʾû ʿalêhem māgôr missābîb,* "And they subject them [Kedar's inhabitants] to all-encompassing terror"; see also Lam 2:22;
2. *môʿēd.* Lam 1:15: *qārāʾ ʿālay môʿēd,* "God has called a convocation [or: set a time] against me (in which to crush my elite personnel)";

3. *ḥereb.* Jer 25:29: *kî ḥereb ʾanî qōrēʾ ʿal-kol-yōšebê hāʾāreṣ,* "For I have imposed the sword against the earth's population." Note play on *qārāʾ* (in the N stem) *ʿal* in the same verse;
4. *rāʿāb.* Ps 105:16: *wayyiqrāʾ rāʿāb ʿal-hāʾāreṣ,* "He set famine upon the land (destroying every staff of bread)."

In the preceding examples, *qārāʾ ʿal* can be further nuanced; what obtains, however, is the notion of "imposing an (unpleasant) fate upon something." In none of the citations offered above would a similar meaning obtain were we to substitute *ʾel* for *ʿal!*

kî-ʿāletâ rāʿātām lepānāy. The versions (LXX, Vulgate, Targum, and Peshitta) use ambiguous elements to render *kî;* see Trible 1963: 12. It is not always possible to distinguish, on purely syntactical grounds, among *kî*'s various functions. It can act as an asseverative/emphatic particle or as a subordinating conjunction. (On all of these possibilities, see most recently the fine study of Schoors 1981.) I acknowledge that *kî* might here introduce a causal clause, "*since/because* the wickedness of its citizens." It cannot, as it seems to do in some accounts, introduce direct speech: "declare against it *that* its citizens' wickedness . . ." In fact, this last way of translating *kî* is not available to Hebrew and should be deleted from the dictionaries.

By rendering *kî* as an emphatic particle in the translation given above, I have sought to underscore the limited role assigned to Jonah in God's decision. According to this understanding, God is not consulting his prophet; nor is this prophet advised of God's reasoning. Jonah is merely informed of a decision, and no opportunity is given him to debate the matter. This situation stands in sharp contrast to the occasions in which God shares with Moses (Exodus 32, Numbers 14) and Abraham (Genesis 18) an intent to unleash destructive forces from above.[5]

The word *rāʿātām* needs an observation and a few comments. I treat the third-person masculine plural possessive *-ām* metonymically, that is, as referring to the citizens within Nineveh. A more cavalier approach would be to regard the *mem* as an enclitic and to regard the form as **rāʿātâ* ("her [Nineveh's] wickedness"), to which is appended the enclitic *mem.* All Hebrew copies of Jonah have this plural suffix, as do the Targum, Peshitta, and a few Greek manuscripts. The LXX and the Vulgate, however, have a singular suffix (Trible 1963: 13). Arabic goes its own way and has "your evil," *šurûrakum,* thus (wrongly) rendering the whole as a quotation to be communicated to the Ninevite (Wright 1857: 109). In any case, one wonders whether a particularly clever narrator chose to sand-

[5] Although they differ syntactically, it might well be that *kî-ʿāletâ rāʿātām lepānāy* of Jon 1:2 is influenced by what is found in Gen 18:20: *zaʿaqat sedōm waʿamōrâ kî-rabbâ weḥaṭṭāʾtām kî kābedâ meʾōd,* "The outrage of Sodom and Gomorrah is so great, and their sin so grave!" (NJPS).

wich seven cases of *rāʿâ* in the absolute form (at 1:7, 8; 3:8, 10 [twice]; 4:1, 2) between the two examples of the noun constructed with pronominal suffixes (at 1:2 and 4:6, *rāʿātô*). If not coincidental, this condition can be labeled "grammatical inclusio."

Less speculative is the observation of Magonet (1976: 22–25) regarding the use of *rāʿâ* in Jonah. He points out that the word is employed in conjunction with the main "characters" of the narrative: there is *rāʿâ* of the Ninevites (at 1:2; 3:8, 10), the *rāʿâ* that befalls the sailors (at 1:7, 8), the one that comes from God (at 3:10), and the one felt by Jonah (at 4:1, 6). It should be added, however, that at each one of its occurrences *rāʿâ* bears a distinguishing nuance. For example, at 4:1 and at its first of two occurrences of 3:10, *rāʿâ* helps to smooth the transition between different objects of focus. In its other occurrence in the same verse, however, the word allows a theosophical pun as it contrasts the evil acts of men with the evil punishment they deserve.

The projection of a theological concern by means of paronomasia is, of course, well documented in Hebrew literature. A recent monograph by P. D. Miller (1982) is a rich collection of material on the subject. One may turn to his selection (p. 116) of examples that contain this particular homily on *rāʿâ,* evil acts result in evil punishment (2 Sam 12:7–15; 1 Kgs 21:17–19, 20–24; Isa 31:1–3; Mic 2:1–5). One occurrence, not cited by Miller, deserves a new translation because it also shares a vocabulary with our passage in Jonah: Lam 1:21–22 reads,

They rejoiced, all my enemies who learned of my plight
Because it is you who did it,
When you brought on the threatened day.
May they then become like me!
When all their wickedness reaches you,
Deal with them,
As you have treated me for all my sins.

The idiom *laʿalôt . . . lipnê* + personal name/pronoun is poorly attested in Hebrew Scripture, where there seems to be a preference for *lābōʾ . . lipnê.* Goitein (1937: 72–73) finds a parallel to this idiom in Gen 6:13, which has *qēṣ kol-bāśār bāʾ lepānay,* rendering it as "I decided to put an end to all mankind," a singularly premature understanding of the narrative's flow, for it anticipates God's decision which does not come until the end of the verse. For our Jonah passage, Goitein offers, "and inform them that I intend to do them evil," but, as already pointed out by Wolff (1986: 95) and Rudolph (1971: 335), this translation also does not commend itself, not only because it misses the counterpoint inherent in *rāʿātām,* but also because it treats *kî* in a manner that is unacceptable (see above). The Greek versions offer paraphrases (for example, LXX: "for the cry of its wickedness has come up to me"), some of which are obviously influenced by the Sodom narrative of Genesis 18; see Trible 1963: 13–14.

1:3. *wayyāqom yônâ librōaḥ taršîšâ millipnê YHWH wayyēred yāpô wayyimṣāʾ ʾonîyâ bāʾâ taršîš wayyittēn śekārāh wayyēred bāh lābôʾ ʿimmāhem taršîšâ millipnê YHWH.* This intricately worked-out verse contains two sets of activities involving Jonah and connected by the mention of a ship upon which a thrilling drama will unfold. Moreover, as is well attested in biblical narratives, each set of activities is cast in triplets, featuring three verbs to communicate three facets of the events:

	First Set	*Second Set*
1. intent:	(*wayyāqom*) *librōaḥ*	*wayyittēn*
	(he sought) to escape	he paid (its hire)
2. activity:	*wayyēred*	*wayyēred*
	he went down (to Jaffa)	he boarded (the ship)
3. goal:	*wayyimṣāʾ*	*lābôʾ ʿimmāhem*
	he found (a ship)	to accompany them

In each set, the crucial *taršîšâ* and *millipnê YHWH* act as framing devices. Additionally, each of Jonah's two series of movements flanks a "static" middle one, where a moored ship awaits Jonah's initiative. Finally, infinitive constructions (*librōaḥ/lābôʾ*) can be found at either end of the series (disregarding the tense of the auxiliary verb *qûm*).

N. Lohfink (1961: 201) finds a concentric structure for this verse but is criticized by Rudolph (1971: 338 n. 5) for doing so. Lohfink's layout of this particular structure, however, is convincing, even if his other examples drawn from Jonah are clearly too forced and facile.

wayyāqom yônâ librōaḥ taršîšâ. While *qûm* as an auxiliary verb is unexceptional (see above), here it serves to accentuate Jonah's contradictory act. One Hebrew manuscript (cited by Trible 1963: 14) has the imperfect *wayyibraḥ,* thus beginning here the series of actions that leads Jonah to board a Tarshish-bound ship. The infinitive, however, is a better form for the context.

As regards the verb *bāraḥ* when it is construed with the partitive *min-*, the emphasis is not just on the direction of the escape or the manner in which it occurs—hurried, sneaky, or the like—it is also on the object that is being abandoned (see Job 20:24; Isa 45:20). If Hebrew wishes to focus on the person or the place that is left behind, however, it consistently links the compound preposition *mippenê* to *bāraḥ.* Ibn Ezra had noted this point long ago: "When I searched the whole Bible, I never found a word about flight except in connection with the word *pny.* . . . And I did not find in regard to Jonah's prophecy that he fled *mpny* God, but only *mlpny* God."

The phrase *librōaḥ millipnê YHWH* appears also in 1:10 (but note its glaring absence from 4:2). The compound preposition, which is formed out of *min* + *le* + *penê* + indirect object, invests Jonah's flight with direction and goal not available to it had *mippenê* been used alone here. Ibn Ezra has compared this clause to Gen 4:16. Realizing how difficult it is to remain close to a displeased God (Gen 4:14), Cain is said to have "left the Lord's presence" (*wayyēṣēʾ qayin millipnê YHWH*). To account for Cain's startlingly innocent notion about the limits of God's reach, Ibn Ezra espouses a figurative interpretation in which Cain is merely trying to escape serving God spiritually (Zlotowitz 1980: 84). Israel's ancient poets, however, knew better and affirmed God's omnipresence in passages such as Ps 139:7–10:

Where can I escape your will?
Where can I flee your presence?
If I climb Heaven, there you are!
If I penetrate Sheol, here you are!
If I test the Dawn's wings,
Settling at the furthermost Sea,
Even there will your hand control me,
Will your right hand grasp me!

Magonet (1976: 82–84) is impressed by the vocabulary shared by these psalm verses and by Jonah 1:3 and finds a "mirror image" structure to the two extremities mentioned in v 7 (Heaven // Sheol). These psalm verses, however, actually refer to four (not two) compass points and, paradoxically, convey an immobility due to a situation acknowledged as hopeless: whether fleeing heavenward, or to Sheol (Hades); whether escaping toward the East, or toward the West—the poet acknowledges—there is no escape (Dahood 1970a: 287). For our purpose, let it be noted how economically the poet realizes the futility of spurning God by merely leaving out *-le-* from the compound preposition.

One final remark on the consequences of using *millipnê* rather than *mippenê:* Jonah's ear has picked up only on *lepānāy* from God's statement. We shall return to this observation when we consider Jonah's own explanation for his response: *qiddamtî librōaḥ taršîšâ* (4:2).

taršîšâ. On the forms of the place-name with the locative *-â,* see Trible 1963: 14. Targum consistently has *ymʾ*, "sea," in place of Tarshish (Levine 1978: 57). Because of the threefold repetition of *taršîš(â)* in close proximity, scribes have (inadvertently) omitted phrases with similar endings (*homoeoteleuton*) after its first occurrence through the second (Greek W manuscript) or after the second occurrence through the third (Greek Sinaiticus codex); see Trible 1963: 15, 16.

Recent overviews offer fine updating of the discussions on Tarshish, its etymology, and its location (Lipiński 1988; Elat 1982; Krantz 1982: 48 n. 44; see also Hüsing 1907). The place-name has been explained through Semitic roots, for example, by Gesenius: from *ršš*, "to break into pieces"; by Albright: from Akkadian *rašāšum*, allegedly meaning "to melt metals" (correct meaning: "to turn [glass compound] red," cf. Oppenheim 1970: 93); and by Gordon (1978a): from *trš* "wine dark (said of the sea)." Non-Semitic etymologies have also been suggested, for example, as a derivative of Greek *tarsos*, "oar."

Tarshish has been located at practically every important Mediterranean trading station known to present-day scholars: Phoenicia, Asia Minor's southern coastline, Etruria in Italy, Sardinia, even Tartessos in Spain (see Lipiński 1988). One can even allude to an inscription of Esarhaddon, king of Assyria (*ANET*³ 290a), which seems to regard *Tar-si-si* as somewhere to the west of Cyprus and Greece. To these suggestions, collected by M. Elat, one could add patristic notions that identified Tarshish with Rhodes or Carthage (Duval 1973: 724; index, Tharsis). Locating Tarshish is complicated by the ancient translations, which either ignored it (for example, the Targum, which merely speaks of "the sea"; Levine 1978: 57 n. 1) or linked it to contemporaneous geographical sites that superficially sounded like the Hebrew name (see Duval 1973: 74, 364). Some exegetes, such as Rashi, understood the term as referring to the *sea* of Tarshish, claiming that Jonah just wanted to be floating as long as possible in the mistaken notion that prophecy does not come to sea travelers (Zlotowitz 1980: 82). John Calvin (1847: 30), who believes it to be in Cilicia, collects many other suggestions he deems mistaken; "but men are very bold in dreaming" is his terse judgment.

Although it was certainly not an invented place (as are Eldorado or Shangrila), *taršîš* seems always to lie just beyond the geographic knowledge of those who try to pinpoint its location. In this way, it might be the Hebrew equivalent to the Melukhah and Magan of cuneiform documents and to the *ḥꜣt·nbw* of Egyptian inscriptions. It is not probable, however, that Tarshish was a name applied to more than one locality at the same time.

As it concerns Jonah, Tarshish is obviously chosen for its location as the geographical and directional opposite of Nineveh, lying to the east of Jerusalem; on this venerable interpretation, see Wolff 1986: 100–101. It is also well worth remembering that Isa 66:19, which is quoting God, places Tarshish among faraway places that "have not heard of my reputation or witnessed my glorious presence." There, former sinners will be sent to spread God's fame. Jonah, therefore, is doubly foolish to think he could escape there.

On the assumption that Jonah could not have known where to escape until he reached Jaffa and found a Tarshish-bound ship, some scholars would delete this first mention of Tarshish. Rudolph 1971: 337 (and n. 11) rightly rejects this severely rational suggestion. Not only would such a step remove a contrast in direction to Nineveh, it would also ruin a nicely balanced threefold repetition of the locality (*taršîšâ—taršîš—taršîšâ*) within a single sentence structure. Moreover, such a deletion would convey, falsely, that Jonah's choice of Tarshish as a place to escape God was fortuitous and dependent on pure chance. On the contrary, as we shall see, if there is hazard at all, it is that Jonah, who *intended* to go to Tarshish, lost no time whatsoever in finding the proper transport! Ruth 2:3 and Gen 24:12 are other passages in which the element of chance cannot be divorced from a predesired end (Sasson 1979: 45).

wayyēred yāpô. There is nothing exceptional about the verb *yārad* to connote a movement toward a city. One should not, therefore, depend on its use to speculate on Jonah's whereabouts when God first addressed him. It is likewise too pedantic to observe that Jonah needed to negotiate a steep descent to reach Jaffa, a port that is surrounded by a chain of rocks; Hebrew simply speaks of "sailing" by means of the idiom "to descend into the sea" (for example, at Ps 107:27 and Isa 42:10). We should, however, draw attention to this verb *yārad* because at its future recurrences, at 1:3 and 5 and especially at 2:7, it will progressively become invested with a psychological dimension (see Magonet 1976: 17).

Jaffa and five millennia of its history are recently surveyed by J. Kaplan (1972 and especially 1976). The town was known in documents from Egypt (*ya-pu;* see Helck 1980), Mesopotamia (*yappu;* see Röllig 1980), the Bible (see *IDB* 2.970–77; for the spelling *yāpôʾ*, see König 1906: 347), and Greek sources (Ioppē, named after the daughter of Aeolus). Jaffa attracted early attention as a setting for historicizing tales. We have two Egyptian Ramesside (Late Bronze Age) texts, one a nationalistic tale that reveals how Jaffa was captured by means of clever military strategies, the other a satire on the life of scribes and messengers that tells how easy it was to seduce Jaffa's fair damsels (translation: Wilson, in *ANET*[3]: 22–23, 475–79; discussion of military strategies and elaborate paronomasia, Goedicke 1968). Classical tales regarding Perseus and Andromeda are cited by Wolff (1986: 102).

As far as can be ascertained from historical records (Josh 19:46), Jaffa always remained outside Hebrew control. During the Assyrian period, Jaffa is listed as belonging to Askelon, a Philistine power (*ANET*[3]287), and it fell into Jewish hands apparently only during the rule of Simeon Maccabeus (1 Macc 12:34). The narrator of Jonah, therefore, must have chosen it knowing well its status, very likely intending to have the prophet seek escape from God's control even before boarding the Tarshish-bound ship. This aim was recognized and shrewdly developed by Jewish medieval exegetes; see Zlotowitz 1980: 82–83.[6]

wayyimṣāʾ ʾonîyâ (bāʾâ taršîš). The word *ʾonîyâ,* the masculine form of which collectively refers to a fleet, has gathered comments because of three factors: (1) its vocalization; (2) its etymology; and (3) its relation, if any, to the word *sepînâ.* (1) I have no explanation for the fact that most Hebrew manuscripts preserve a *qameṣ* under the first *aleph,* whereas a *qameṣ-ḥatûp* is found in each of the other attestations (at 1:4 and 5). At any rate the accent on the last syllable explains

[6] This point is lost on Wolff (1986: 102), who regards Jonah's mention of Jaffa as a misinformed historicizing feature.

why this shortened vowel is to be found here. (2) Whether the term is derived from Semitic, Indo-European, or Egyptian vocabulary; and whether it is to be regarded as a *Kulturwort* or as a loanword that was borrowed from foreign merchants are points fully developed and discussed in Krantz 1982: 32. Her opinion is that *ʾonîyâ* was a general term for a seagoing ship. (3) See below, at 1:5.

It is needless to speculate on the size of the ship taken by Jonah. As evidence from the Early Bronze Age down to modern times shows, Mediterranean ships varied enormously in size, construction, equipment, and company, as well as in cargo and passenger capabilities. (On all of these matters, consult Casson 1971: 157–218, as well as Murphy-O'Connor 1985.) I shall make more specific comments presently on some of these matters. My own notion, which cannot be proved, is that the author of Jonah could have had in mind a ship that differed little from the Syrian vessel shipwrecked off Cape Galedonia (Bass 1967: 162–67; idem 1973). For that matter, I imagine Jonah taking a ship similar to the one Bishop Synesius of Cyrenaica boarded in Alexandria about the fourth century C.E. I quote a relevant passage from one of the bishop's letters (Epistle 4, latest edition, Vogt 1970: 401–6; Fitzgerald 1926: 80–91):

> The Captain longed for death, so deep was he in debt. There were twelve sailors in all, the thirteenth was the captain. Over half the crew and the captain were Jews, an untrustworthy people, convinced that to send Greeks to their death is to do good. Most were average persons, peasants, who have never previously handled a rudder. In one way or another, they were all bodily deformed. Whenever we were not in danger, they made jokes by calling each other not by personal names but by the deformity: "Lame," "Goitrous," "Lefty," "Squinty."

The verb *māṣāʾ* (BDB 593), often involves an unexpected discovery or good fortune. From Jonah's perspective, as contrasted to the reader's or the author's, the fact that he found a ship going to the earth's other extremity must have promised a successful flight from God. The collusion of a series of events that seem to bode well at the beginning of a long venture, yet prove to be otherwise —sometimes disastrously so—is not an unknown motif to the ancient world. Suffice it to note that in one other great sea voyage recounted in the Bible, that of Paul toward Rome as preserved in Acts 27, sailors who are forewarned of disaster nevertheless venture into the sea when the south wind unseasonably blows softly into their sails, thus giving them false hopes for an uneventful voyage (v 13).

The better to appreciate Jonah's good fortune in locating a ship with which to make his escape, we need to survey briefly the maritime practices of ancient days.

According to the fourth–fifth-century C.E. tractate of Vegetius, *Epitoma rei militaris* (4.39), the sailing season for the Mediterranean is limited to four months during the year, from the end of May through the middle of September. By taking risks, one could stretch this period by as much as two months at either end.[7] The ship that takes Paul on one of his sea voyages is doomed, at least because it sails after the *fast*, presumed to be Yom Kippur, that most commonly occurs in late September to mid-October (Acts 27:9). This notion is recalled in a proverb that urges, "when you bind your *lulav*, bind your ship."[8] During the bulk of the year, however, the ports of antiquity hibernated; and if harsh winds or lack of visibility stymied navigation, stricken ships could not expect help from nearby ports.

Wherever Tarshish was to be found, it obviously lay far from Jaffa, which allows us to make our second observation. Travels between major ports took much time when vessels averaged two to four knots. Gaza to Byzantium, for example, required three weeks in each direction (approximately 850 nautical miles). Alexandria to Marseilles, almost twice as far, required a full month one way (on this see Casson 1971: 281–96). According to *baba bathra* 38a–39a (cited in Rudolph 1971: 338 n. 14), it took a full year to travel between Spain and Israel. Solomon's Tarshish ships returned home once every three years (2 Chr 9:21).

These details about navigation are not needed, of course, to analyze Jonah's theological import; but they must certainly have been common knowledge to ancient audiences who, very much like modern readers of science-fiction space sagas, recognized the difficulties that distant travels entailed and therefore appreciated the literary value in the accumulation of fortuitous events.

bāʾâ taršîš. More than any other, this phrase reinforces the series of chance occurrences that give Jonah false hope. The Masoretic accent on the verb's last syllable has allowed scholars to parse *bāʾâ* as an active *G* stem feminine participle with future (or permanent) intent. The phrase, therefore, is commonly taken to mean either that the ship was heading toward Tarshish or that it was a ship that regularly plied the Tarshish route. But there are difficulties in such understandings. Bewer (1912: 31–32) realizes that the verb *bôʾ* directs the movement toward the narrator or speaker and refers to BDB (evidently, 98 sub 4) where are collected some examples of the opposite sense, that is, away from the speaker. Except for one very difficult and ambiguous citation in Isa 47:5, however, all of these BDB attestations have *bôʾ* depending on the imperative of the auxiliary verb *hālak* and should be understood to mean something like "go to enter," that is, "proceed in order to reach." To indicate a direction that is away from the

[7] Bérard 1927: 171 has wonderfully evocative passages on the winds off Syria and the havoc they wreak on unseasonable shipping. For convenience's sake, however, consult Casson 1971: 270ff.

[8] Patai 1941: 10. The *lulav* is a ritual object made of fastened branches that is used during the autumn festival of Sukkot.

reader, Hebrew normally employs the verb *hālak.* That *bôʾ* and *hālak* (without prepositions) establish maritime movement in opposite directions is clearly demonstrable from 2 Chr 9:21: "The king's fleet would travel to Tarshish [*hōlekôt, G* stem participle] with Huram's officers. But once every three years, the Tarshish ships would come back [*tābôʾnâ, G* stem imperfect], loaded with gold, silver, ivory, monkeys and peacocks (or: baboons)."

A shift of accent to the first syllable would turn the participle *bāʾâ* into the past tense. This is not necessary, however, for the participle often conveys past sense. I consider the phrase *bāʾâ taršîš* as implying the ship's *return* from a distant port. Such an understanding actually underscores Jonah's haste in escaping God, for the sailors are given little time to recover from their voyage before they set sail to Tarshish.

wayyittēn śekārāh. A Jewish exegetical tradition has it that Jonah hired the whole ship in his haste to escape God, and this notion permitted speculations on Jonah's wealth. *Babylonian nedarim* 38a reads, "R. Yohanan observed: He paid for the hire of the whole ship. R. Romanus said: The hire of the ship was four thousand gold *denarii* [an incredible sum!]"; Soncino Talmud 1936c: 120. Yalkut, quoted in Bewer 1912: 37, is understated: "Jonah was rich." Another equally venerable opinion attributes to Jonah the suffix attached to "wages," thus having Jonah merely purchase a ticket as a passenger. Note Targum: *wyhb ʾgrh;* LXX: *kai edōke to naulon autou,* "paid *his* fare," Vulgate: *naulum eius,* on which see Levine 1978: 58; Trible 1963: 16. Almbladh (1986: 17) thinks that the LXX treated as *mater lectionis* the suffixed consonant *h.* The wording in the Arabic rendering neatly straddles the issue: *faʾaʿṭa ʾalmallāḥa ʾajrahu,* "He paid the sailors his own wage" (as passenger or for hire?).

Recent commentators are likewise divided over the matter, though the second opinion, that Jonah purchased his fare, seems more prevalent. There is even disagreement on establishing a referent for the feminine suffix on *śekārāh.* Wolff, for example (1986: 102), is sure that Jonah secured the whole ship and finds it a delicious irony that the prophet had to do so. Rudolph, by contrast, thinks it implausible that Jonah would undertake the expense. The feminine suffix, he asserts (1971: 334), should not be linked to the ship, but is to be understood in a neuter sense.

Without entering the debate over Jonah's personal wealth, I nevertheless support the contention that Jonah hired the ship and its crew, for the following reasons. First of all, the narrative in chapter 1 speaks only of Jonah and the crew. As a matter of fact, the narrative would become too cluttered, and certainly off-focus, were there other passengers on board. Think how complicated the lots-casting scene would have become, for one example! Rudolph meets this objection by suggesting that this was a cargo-laden ship; but such a distinction between passenger and cargo transports did not obtain in the ancient world. Second, the vocable *śākār* is worthy of attention. As used in Scripture, it clearly means wages, for hire of services. (An extended Hebrew sense allows it even to mean "a reward.") A similar range of meanings is available to the root *śkr* in other West Semitic languages *(DISO* 299–300), as well as to the vocables *idū* and *igrum* in East Semitic texts (see *AHw* and *CAD,* s.v.). As far as I can research the matter, until Roman times (Jones 1964: 866–72) the ancient world did not have a specific word for "a fare," a charge for the purchase of space in an expedition, seagoing or otherwise. The information available to me suggests that the person who hired a ship and its captain had the right to change its destination and, in some cases, its specific function; see Driver and Miles 1952: 473–75.

While there is really no definitive rendering for *wayyittēn śekārāh,* it is plausible to reconstruct a situation in which Jonah, hasty as he was, hired the whole vessel and requested that anchors be lifted promptly! Such a reading can yet be bolstered by the vocabulary that follows.

wayyēred bāh. We note here that the LXX distinguishes between different occasions on which *yārad* is used, by translating here *anebē* and previously *katebē.*

lābôʾ ʿimmāhem (*taršîšâ*). At stake here is not the verb *bôʾ*, but rather the idiom *lābōʾ ʿim,* which is substantially different in meaning, as is clear from Ps 26:4–5:

> I have neither fraternized with the vain,
>   Nor *associated with* the deceivers,
> I have shunned the evil-doers' company,
>   And have not fraternized with the wicked.[9]

I therefore translate the verb *bōʾ* here differently from its previous appearance, despite the repetition of *taršîšâ* in both contexts and despite the strong temptation to find a parallel in usage at Lachish 3:14–16, *yrd. šr. hṣbh . . . . lbʾ ./ mṣrymh,* "General [PN] has moved south in order to enter Egypt" (Pardee 1981: 3.25).

The phrase *lābōʾ ʿimmāhem taršîšâ* allows us to speculate that far from being a mere passenger, Jonah became a member of the crew during that voyage and thus tried to escape from God's vision by joining a crowd. The LXX might have had similar notions when it offered *tou pleusai met autōn,* "to sail with them." The irony will be fully explored, of course, when Jonah remains starkly distinguishable from the rest.

As to the third-person plural suffix on *ʿimmāhem,* it is, as in the case of *rāʿātām* of 1:2, metonymic for the ship's sailors (König 1906: 457 [§ 346.q]).

[9] *lōʾ-yāšabtî ʿim-metê-šāwʾ*
  weʿim naʿalāmîm lōʾ ʾābôʾ
śānēʾtî qehal merēʿîm
  weʿim-rešāʿîm lōʾ ʾēšēb.

COMMENTS

God sent Jonah to Ninevy land.
Jonah disobey my God command
Paid his fare and he got on board.
Children, don't do that!
Don't you do that!
Don't you do that!
God got his eye on you!
Don't you do that!
Don't you do that!
Don't you idle your time away!
(*Slave song from All Saints Parish, Ga.*)[10]

In any piece of literature, the opening lines are crucial, for they give clues to the way the narrative will unfold and establish the tone and mood that will control the relationship among author, characters, and audience. In the case of Jonah, the first three verses are rich with hints that might be overlooked by a modern reader, especially one who is unfamiliar with the Hebrew narrative art. In the NOTES I have focused on the vocabulary in these verses; here I draw the conclusions that it suggests.

The way Jonah begins, *way(ye)hî debar-YHWH ʾel yônâ . . . lēʾmōr,* is typical of prophetic narratives in which a *series* of divine messages are being communicated to a prophet. This prophet is himself introduced earlier in such narratives by means of an appreciably different language. Therefore, whatever sources were available to the narrator of Jonah (a term that is loosely used at this stage), what we now have of the book are episodes plucked from many Jonah adventures that apparently circulated in ancient Israel.

Another observation can be made from the use of *way(ye)hî debar-YHWH ʾel yônâ . . . lēʾmōr.* This language is used most commonly when the adventures of a prophet are of more immediate interest than the words that God communicates through him. If there are to be divine messages, these tend to be terse, undeveloped, often ambiguous, serving mostly as a backdrop for the prophet's reaction to God's directives. This is certainly the case in Jonah 1 where, as my grammatical notes on *debar-YHWH* show, Jonah had nothing to communicate to the Ninevites. In fact, God's statement to Jonah in 1:2 serves mainly to launch the narrative toward the misadventures of Jonah.

Because Jonah invites readers to draw lessons from the way God deals with

[10] Quoted from Charles Joyner, *Down by the Riverside* (Urbana: University of Illinois Press, 1984), pp. 163–64.

his prophet rather than from the wordings of God's message, the instruction is never bound to one moment in the past. The occasion on which Jonah sought to escape God's summons becomes less important than the way the two react to each other at different turns of the narrative. To be sure, this occasion is bound to history by mention of Nineveh; but the involvement of any other superpower of the time—say Egypt or Babylon—could have led to similar results, though perhaps not as pregnantly so.

This opinion can be bolstered by yet another observation. Jonah, the son of Amittay, remains the only character in the whole book to be given a name, and it is surely significant that even the king of Nineveh is left anonymous.[11] Moreover, in the book named after him, Jonah is never termed *nābîʾ*, but his intimate association and easy familiarity with God are characteristic of other prophets who likewise experience multiple adventures in the service of God, most notably Elijah and Elisha. It is not surprising therefore that ancient exegetes linked Elijah to Jonah through homiletics on the name of his father, Amittay. They searched Scripture for a candidate who would be suitable as a father to the prophet Jonah and settled on the story of the widow from Zareptah (1 Kgs 17:24). It might be recalled that when Elijah resuscitated this widow's son, she said: "God's word is truth in your mouth" (*ûdebar-YHWH bepîkā ʾemet*). Hence, these exegetes reasoned, the child was known as *ben-ʾamittay*, "Child of Truth."

This extrabiblical invention might have been spurred by a desire to span the period of a century or so that separated the reigns of Ahab (ca. 874–853 B.C.E.), when Elijah prophesied, and of Jeroboam II (ca. 793–753). During the latter's reign, a Jonah son of Amittay brought God's message (2 Kgs 14:23–27):

> In the fifteenth year of Amaziah son of Joash, king of Judah, Jeroboam son of Joash, king of Israel began to reign in Samaria, and he reigned forty-one years. He was sinful in the sight of God, departing not at all from the sins of Jeroboam the son of Nebat who had made Israel sin. Yet, it was he who restored Israel's frontiers from Hamath's vicinity as far as the Dead Sea; this, according to the word of the Lord, Israel's god, who spoke through his servant, Jonah the son of Amittay, *the* prophet from Gath Hefer ["Sunken winepress"]. For the Lord observed how very bitter was Israel's plight, with absolutely no ruler, no one to help rescue Israel. The Lord did not seek to wipe out the name of Israel from

[11] It may be equally significant, however, that Jonah's name is repeated eighteen times, a number with paronomastic potential (see Sasson 1979: 223). Segert 1980: 127 contrasts this condition with another brief narrative, that of Ruth, in which eight persons are given names, excluding the genealogy. By contrast, Jonah contains a rather high frequency of place-names, and these three—Jaffa, Tarshish, and Nineveh—are cited one, three, and nine times, respectively.

beneath heaven; rather, he rescued them through Jeroboam son of Joash. (See Talmon and Fields, 1989.)

We need not reconstruct the historical contexts for Jeroboam II or evaluate his success as king of Israel; elaborate accounts that often go beyond our sources are available in Haran 1967 and Briend 1981. We can, instead, reason why tradition as well as some responsible scholars have linked the Jonahs of Kings and of the Minor Prophets. This last topic, however, is best entertained in the INTERPRETATIONS section.

Two more observations are elicited by the philological remarks given in the preceding NOTES. Our long annotation to *qārāʾ ʿal* has shown that God did not want Jonah to warn the Ninevites into repentance; rather, God wants him only to announce their impending doom. In this instance, Jonah's mission cannot be differentiated from that of the angels who went to Sodom.[12] Unlike the Sodom occasion, however, Jonah had no one to save from the impending destruction. No wonder that Jonah refused his charge, probably fearing the anger of the Ninevites.

We have testimony that this particular perception of Jonah's mission was shared by some Jewish exegetes of the Roman period. Josephus summarized the situation in *Antiquities of the Jews* 9.10.2 as follows: "Having received an order to proceed to the kingdom of Ninos and to proclaim, at his arrival to the city, that it would lose its hegemony [over Asia, see end of passage], [Jonah] got scared and instead of going there, he escaped God's presence into Jaffa." That Josephus was not alone to share this reading of Jonah's motivation can be surmised from Tob 14:3–4 where, as it is preserved in some manuscripts, the protagonist's son is to make his escape from Nineveh because of its imminent demise, "as it was announced by Jonah [other manuscripts: Nahum] who had proclaimed its destruction." Jerome too shared this understanding of events (Duval 1973: 82–86 and in particular 84 n. 75).

My last observation deals with the way that Jonah meant to escape from God. Jonah headed to a port not within Israel's sphere of influence, hired a ship that was headed in a direction away from Nineveh, and tried to meld with its sailors. The annotations show how fortunate Jonah was to have fulfilled his wishes so easily, which should raise expectations that reversal will not too be long in coming. This, I think, is precisely what the ninth-century homily on Jonah, the *Pirke* of Rabbi Eliezer, has in mind when it fleshes out details in the following way:

[12] It is interesting that the LXX had some notions in this regard, for it has *hoti anebē hē kraugē tēs kakias autēs pros me,* "for the cry of its wickedness is come up to me," thus betraying obvious connection with Gen 18:20, *weḥaṭṭaʾtām kî kābedâ meʾōd.* See above, NOTES to 1:2.

JONAH

Jonah went down to Joppa, but he did not find there a ship in which he could embark, for the ship in which Jonah might have embarked was two days' journey away from Joppa. In order to test Jonah, what did the Holy One, blessed be He, do? He sent against it a mighty tempest on the sea and brought it back to Joppa. Then Jonah saw and rejoiced in his heart, saying, Now I know that my ways will prosper before me.[13]

[13] Friedlander 1981: 66, incorporating the remark of note 6. The same expansion is given in the Midrash Yona (Jellinek 1938: 97).

II. The Storm-Tossed Ship (Jonah 1:4–6)

◆

How could Jonah "flee from the presence of the Lord?" Does it not say, "whither shall I flee from thy presence, etc." (Ps. cxxxix)? But Jonah said, "I will go beyond Palestine to a land where the Shechinah [God's presence] has not revealed itself, for the nations are near to repentance, and I will not make Israel guilty." It is like the slave of a priest who ran away from his master. He said, "I will go to a country where my master cannot follow me." His master said, "I have substitutes to fill your place." So when Jonah said, "I will go beyond Palestine to a land where the Shechinah has not revealed itself," God said, "I have messengers to act in thy place," as it is said, "And the Lord sent out a great tempest upon the Sea."

R. Jonathan said that Jonah had intended to destroy himself [for the sake of Israel], as it says, "Take me up and cast me forth into the sea."[1]

II. THE STORM-TOSSED SHIP (1:4–6)

1 [4]The Lord, however, hurled such furious winds toward the sea that a powerful storm raged upon it; the ship expected itself to crack up. [5]Terrified, the sailors appealed, each to his own god(s), and, to lighten their load, they flung their equipment overboard. As for Jonah, he descended into the vessel's hold, lay down, and fell into a trance.

[6]The helmsman approached him to ask, "How could you be in a trance? Up! invoke your god; perhaps god himself[a] will intercede on our behalf so that we may not perish."

[a] Or: "The g/God."

[1] From *Mekilta, Pisḥa,* Bo, §1, p. 3; cited in Montefiore and Loewe 1974: 17, 560–61.

STORMS IN ANCIENT LORE: INTRODUCTORY REMARKS

Storms over the seas, awesome and beyond human control, fascinated the literary mind of antiquity; for, beyond finding in them excellent opportunity to use language dramatically, storms permitted the writer to ponder the cosmic significance behind such cataclysms by singly or successively contrasting the benevolence accorded the survivor to the punishment meted out to the shipwrecked. The storm scene in Jonah requires a few introductory words in order to permit better focus on the ensuing discussion. From a huge lore preserved from ancient times I have selected samplings, but more examples will be involved at appropriate junctures.

Survivors of storms, it was universally acknowledged in antiquity, felt themselves graced by the gods. In some cases, their experience was recalled for purely personal gains. We have testimony, repeated widely in the classical world, that mariners sketched pictures of their experiences on wooden plates that, when worn around the neck, elicited both wonder and coins from passersby (for example, Juvenal, *Satires* 14.301; Phaedrus, *Fables* 4.22; Horace, *Art. Poet.* 20; see Carrière 1975: 167 and compare to *Aggada Bereshit* 34, for which see Patai 1941: 5).

But others saw in their survival signs of divine election to higher call. Thus, in his autobiography (*Vita* 14–16), Josephus recalls how a storm interrupted his youthful journey to Rome when on a mission to save fellow priests from an unjust prefect. That he survived—one of eighty to do so from a ship carrying six hundred passengers—that he succeeded in arguing his case, and that he had an audience before a sympathetic Poppaea proved to be major moments in his career.

Perhaps more directly relevant to us are the occasions on which characters either fictional or drawn from real life were set within raging seas. The most ancient storm scene of all, preserved on an Egyptian papyrus from the Middle Kingdom (early second millennium B.C.E.) is embedded in a structurally sophisticated and thematically elaborate fantasy that broods over personal destiny and divine tyranny. In this tale, the foundering of the ship takes place immediately after its sailors are praised: "Looked they at sky, looked they at land, their hearts were stouter than lions. They could foretell a storm before it came, a tempest before it broke" (Lichtheim 1973: 212).

The lesson to be drawn from shipwrecks can be derived from a fictitious storm even when it includes historical personalities. For example, Phaedrus, the Roman fabulist of the first century mentioned above, made Aeschylus's contemporary, Simonedos of Keos, a hero in a raging tempest in order to drive home a moral lesson: "One's whole fortune lay in one's head" (*Fables* 4.22; See Brenot 1924: 72–73).

The Apostle Paul makes manifest his dedication to his ministry as well as his special election to the task by referring to the three times he came to be shipwrecked on God's service (2 Cor 11:25–27; see Murphy-O'Connor 1985). By contrast, Luke's recreation of one of Paul's journeys (Acts 27:1–28) is highly embellished with elements from Hellenistic romances, albeit based on a historical event. Paul's calm amidst the danger, his ability to predict the fate of the passengers, his survival of both storm and viper's bites, all are elements that have allowed many to find in Paul's voyage echoes of Jonah's experience.

I cite the chapter in Acts because it allows me to shift to another of the lessons that can be drawn from tales regarding storms: that those who do not survive are merely paying for guilts earned long before setting foot on a ship's deck. Such is Homer's opinion on the fate awaiting Odysseus's brazen crew (*The Odyssey* 12.127–41, 249–446); and such is the opinion of ancient authorities who investigated actual cases of sailors lost at sea (Glotz, mentioned by Gernet 1923: 131 n. 2; see further, Levine 1978: 62 n. 6). G. B. Miles and G. Trompf (1976) mention a case that deserves attention. About 419 B.C.E., a man sailed with a companion who later disappeared when the ship docked at port. Accused by the companion's family of murder, the man defended himself by offering an argument that is quoted by the Attic orator Antiphon (translations: Maidment 1941: 262 and Miles and Trompf 1976: 262):

> And now, let's look at the signs sent by the gods; in such matters, they must weigh more heavily in sentencing. . . . I think you know that before now many men whose hands are unclean and who have some other pollution have boarded ship with others and along with their own lives have destroyed those who are pure in matters relating to the gods, and that others who are pure, while they have not perished, have experienced the most extreme dangers on account of such [polluted] men. And in addition, many in attendance at sacred rites have been revealed to be impure and to be hindrances to the performance of the proper ceremonies. But in my case the opposite is true on every count. For all those with whom I have sailed have enjoyed good voyages. And wherever I attended sacred rites they have always turned out excellently. I claim all this as great proof of the charge that the plaintiffs have accused me falsely.

Finally, I allude to two instances in which tempest over the sea and shipwreck of fleet were used by writers to comment on the course of human affairs. The most elaborate example is found in Herodotus's account regarding the Persian Wars. At books 7 (188) and 8 (10–13), tempests wreck Xerxes' fleet (see also 6.44 regarding Mardonius's discomfiture). These two storms allow Herodotus to illustrate a favorite theme by locating them at junctures crucial to his narrative: "All this [storms and consequent havoc upon the Persian fleet] was the work of heaven's providence, that so the Persian's power might be more equally matched with the Greeks, and not much greater than it" (7.12). Immerwahr (1966: 72, 263–67) comments that whether there were in fact two storms or just one that Herodotus duplicated for didactic purposes (264 n. 77), Herodotus's construction is absolutely logical. We shall soon have occasion to quote yet another storm from book 8 (118–20), one that shed light upon Xerxes' character as perceived by Herodotus.

The other example comes from the Hebrew Scripture and is preserved in two versions found in 1 Kings and 2 Chronicles. By focusing on the activities of Jehosaphat, a king who invited ambiguous feelings, the incident shows how storms reflected God's judgment on human schemes.

1 Kgs 22:49–50	2 Chr 20:35–37
Jehosaphat constructed Tarshish ships to sail to Ophir for gold. But he did not sail, because the ships were wrecked [*qere: nišberû; ketib: nšbrh*] at Ezion-Geber. Ahaziah son of Ahab [king of Israel] then proposed to Jehosaphat: "Let my officers sail on the ships with your own officers." But Jehosaphat would not agree.	King Jehosaphat of Judah entered into partnership with King Ahaziah of Israel, thereby acting wickedly. He joined with him in constructing ships to sail to Tarshish (*lāleket taršîš*), making them in Ezion-Geber. Eliezer son of Dodavahu, of Mareshet, prophesied against Jehosaphat, "Since you have made a partnership with Ahaziah, the Lord will shatter your work." The ships were wrecked (*wayyiššāberû*) and therefore were not able to sail to Tarshish.

In comparing the two versions, I first note that the account in Kings has Jehosaphat readying Tarshish-type ships to retrieve the gold of Ophir. By the Chronicler's time, however, the destination has become Tarshish, a land that in Scripture comes to symbolize goals doomed to fail. Second, the relationship of the kings of the divided kingdoms is timed differently within each version. In Kings, Ahaziah proposes to equip a new fleet when Jehosaphat's original venture fails. That Jehosaphat turns Ahaziah down is deemed a virtue, allowing Jehosaphat to end his reign on a relatively positive note. In Chronicles, an odious partnership with the wicked Ahaziah compromises Jehosaphat's rectitude. An otherwise unknown prophet, Eliezer, communicates God's displeasure. As a result, the destruction of the fleet becomes a sinister omen regarding the fate of Judah.

NOTES

1:4. *waYHWH hēṭîl rûaḥ-gedôlâ ʾel-hayyām way(ye)hî saʿar-gādôl bayyām wehāʾoniyyâ ḥiššebâ lehiššābēr.* In sentences within continuous narratives, special emphasis is placed on the subject by modifying the usual order of the Hebrew sentence, which is verb, subject, object/complement. In this verse we find a construction in which the subject is introduced by a *waw*-conjunctive. The verb, in past tense, is given next, with the complement following it. Such a construction, which shifts the focus from the activity to the actor, is more common to poetic or legalistic writing and therefore in Jonah will be encountered in the psalm of chapter 2 and in the royal proclamations registered in 3:4 and 3:7. In the narrative, however, the construction is found only here and in two other passages, where it draws attention to matters of special significance (at 3:3 and 4:11).

What is worthy of annotation here is the fact that three examples of such a construction are clustered within a few words of one another: (1) applied to God as he hurls the stormy winds; (2) applied to the ship as it recognizes its plight; and (3) applied to Jonah as he reacts to the storm.

waYHWH hēṭîl (rûaḥ-gedôlâ) ʾel-hayyām. The Vulgate recognizes this emphatic construction by translating *Dominus autem* . . . (Trible 1963: 17). When referring to the Hebrew god, the book of Jonah uses both YHWH and Elohim. Once, at 4:6, we find YHWH-Elohim (see there). Elohim, unlike YHWH, need not be a name, for it is merely the plural form of the Hebrew word for "deity"; *ʾelōhîm,* therefore, can stand for "God" or for "gods," with a lowercase initial consonant. Because of this difference in employment two separate issues confront the reader of Jonah: first, how to recognize the instances in which *ʾelōhîm* is used as a common noun rather than as the name of God, on which see below, at 1:5; and, second, how to assess the narrator's choices in using either term to refer to God, a topic to be broached on another occasion.

The verbal form, *hēṭîl,* is derived from the causative conjugation (*H* stem) of the verb *ṭwl.* But both the LXX (*kai kurios eksēgeire pneuma* [*mega*] *epi tēn thalassan*) and the Targum (*wYY ʾrym rwḥ-rb ʿl-ymʾ*) translate with "the Lord raised up a great wind," suggesting that they presumed **hiṭṭîl* to be a (nonattested) *H* stem perfect of *nāṭal,* "to lift"; see Almbladh 1986: 18.

All occurrences of the verb *ṭwl* (in the *H* stem), construed with the preposition *ʾel,* are to be found in this unit of Jonah. (One occurrence in Job 41:1 is difficult to assess.) Magonet (1976: 16–17) finds a "causal relationship" among all four occurrences in Jonah (at 1:4, 5, 12 [twice]), and refers to this verb as exemplifying activities that "are revealed not merely on the level of the narrative itself, but also on the 'subliminal' level of the word that repeats and repeats itself through the episode." We can buttress such a remark by first recalling that in other biblical passages, the preposition *ʿal* serves our verb to indicate the direction to which an object is hurled (1 Sam 20:33; Jer 16:13; 22:26, 28; Ezek 32:4). When the preposition *ʾel* is used, however, the narrative focuses on the intention behind the act of hurling rather than on the consequence and direction of that act. About these subtle divergences in usage, a number of observations can be made. First of all, when the verb *ṭwl* is linked with *ʾel* rather than with *ʿal,* as it is in v 4, it is obvious that God's anger is not directed at the sea, as is found in other biblical passages. Rabbinic literature might have been sensitive to this particular possibility, for it contains remarks to the effect that God limited the storm only to the area of Jonah's ship.[2]

Second, when the verb *ṭwl* is linked with *ʾel* rather than with *ʿal,* as it is in v 5, it suggests that the sailors did not cast their load overboard to lighten the ship only, but that they sought to appease the sea with offerings. That such a response to the sea's raging waves is not farfetched is suggested by classical writers who speak of libations poured over the ship's stern (Morrison and Williams 1968: 120, quoting Hipponax). I shall have more to say on sacrifices aboard ship at 1:16.

Last, especially after Jonah's declaration regarding his role in inviting the storm, recourse to *ʾel* rather than *ʿal* in the idiom duplicates (in v 12) and completes (in v 14) the series of activities inaugurated in v 4 (see further at 1:14). This particular observation will be sharpened as I annotate the next phrase, *rûaḥ gedôlâ.*

With the above in mind, it becomes fairly obvious why Goitein's opinion (1937: 67 n. 8) that 1:4a "could have been eliminated without affecting the narratives" misses the point; if tolerated, this step would remove the initial line in a complex narratological counterpoint.

The words *rûaḥ gedôlâ,* which I render here by "furious winds," are said always to come from God (Job 1:19). The attributive *gedôlâ* (omitted by the LXX, but not by the Greek of Symmachus) refers here to the volume of the wind that is generated rather than to its velocity or strength. To evoke the latter characteristics for a divinely dispatched east wind (*rûaḥ-yām*), Exod 10:19 uses *ḥāzāq meʾōd* as adjective. (Note, too, that in this passage God's injection of a storm to remove the locust is conveyed by *hāpak,* "to stir up," a verb that will concern us also in 3:4.) Belonging to God's storehouse (*ʾôṣār,* consult BDB 70a [sub 3 d]), winds may themselves serve as messengers, a motif available also to Akkadian literature (see Reiner 1985: 65–66). For our purpose it is worth noting that a wind, said to be *gedôlâ* as well as *ḥāzāq,* can forecast God's desire to address his prophet (1 Kgs 19:11). I find unnecessary and unuseful the attempts to link the conjunction of God, wind, and sea to the creation narrative of Genesis 1. (See also below at 4:8.)

[2] To buttress the same point, midrashic literature cites also the prefixing of an article to the word "ship" in 1:5; Zlotowitz 1980: 87.

way(ye)hî saʿar-gādôl bayyām. The *saʿar/seʿārâ,* which can indicate God's own presence (Job 38:1; 40:6; Ezek 1:4; Zech 9:14), is deemed a sign of God's anger against nations (BDB 704). In this note, I want to focus on the way the root **sʿr* is treated in its four Jonah occurrences.

The verb *sāʿar,* "to storm, rage," is found in two passages that view the storm from the sailor's perspective (at 1:11 and 1:13). It is very clever on the narrator's part to make the sea the subject of this verb, for the sailors do not know why the storm broke over them. Conversely, the narrator uses the noun *saʿar* when he (1:4) and Jonah (1:12), aware of God's plan, need to refer to the raging tempest. This clear-cut distinction might, of course, be fortuitous. But if otherwise, it may provide a subtle reinforcement to a point that is important to the narrator: the sailors were pagans and could well have regarded the sea, *yām,* as the source of their woe (see, conveniently, Ringgren in *ThWAT* 3.645–57). That this contrast might have been nurtured by the author can be bolstered by examining *way(ye)hî* in this phrase.

way(ye)hî may be taken as a verb with an impersonal subject, or it could have *saʿar* as its subject. Either understanding is possible, for the issue is not really a grammatical one but one of philology and interpretation. Were we to render it impersonally, "and there was a great storm upon the sea," then God's activity would not be limited to hurling the winds but would include raising the storm. This perspective could in fact be promoted by "linking" the two clauses through duplication of *gedôlâ/gādôl* as adjectives for *rûaḥ/saʿar.* But to render the phrase "and the tempest (that is, the great storm) raged upon the sea" would give the storm its own creative force once the wind quickened upon the sea.

We can note a similar dichotomy in meaning as we gather references and previous suggestions regarding *yām,* "the sea." Its eleven attestations are all located within this particular sequence in Jonah 1. While the narrator (at 1:4 [twice]) and Jonah (at 1:9) know who is controlling the upsurgings of the sea, the sailors do not; and they can only try to mollify the sea's anger (at 1:5; see above). Even when Jonah makes it clear that the sea is within God's domain, the sailors stubbornly attribute to it an independence that is natural in pagan mythology (see at 1:11, 13, 15 [twice]). Consequently, Jonah can only respond to them by using their own vocabulary (at 1:12 [twice]).

This philological inspection yields a surprising result, for it would indicate that to the end, the sailors have not given up their cosmological view; it would seem, in fact, that they have merely enlarged their pantheon to include one more deity that needs to be cajoled: Jonah's God, YHWH. Too, this inspection gives reason to understand why, when Jonah utters his psalm from within the fish's bowel, he avoids using *yām,* potentially the name of the Canaanite sea god, preferring the less ambiguous, albeit more poetic, *yammîm* (2:4). Such an observation will be picked up and enlarged when we discuss the way the psalm is tailored to fit only Jonah.

wehāʾonîyâ ḥiššebâ lehiššābēr. This clause brings the drama initiated in heaven swiftly and neatly down to earth. It does so on a number of levels:

1. *Syntactically.* The syntax of the phrase, with *waw* + subject + verb + object/complement, forces the attention on the subject, as it did at the beginning of this verse and, as we shall see, as it will do when Jonah regains the audience's attention (v 5).
2. *Paronomastically,* or more precisely *onomatopoeically, ḥiššebâ lehiššābēr* captures the sound of planks cracking when tortured by raging waters. Such aural bravura must have pleased a listening audience that also included all who sounded their words as they read.
3. *Psychologically.* In all biblical attestations but this one, the subject of *ḥāšab* is animate. This problem has led commentators:
   a. to depend on non-Hebraic usage in order to capture a translation (for example, RSV; NEB: "The ship/boat threatened to break up"; see Targum: "sought to break in pieces"; Calvin: "cogitabit frangi" [1847: 33]);
   b. to fudge on the basic meaning of this verb in the *D* stem, *ḥiššēb* (for example, NJPS: "the ship was in danger of breaking up");
   c. to guess from content (for example, LXX: *ekinduneuen [tou] suntribēnai,* "was in danger of being broken"; similarly Vulgate: *periclitabatur conteri*); see Trible 1963: 17;
   d. to revocalize (for example, *ḥuššebâ* [G. R. Driver 1950: 69–70], meaning "and the ship was reckoned to be breaking up"; *ḥašābûhā* [Ehrlich, following D. Kimḥi 1912: 264], meaning "they (the sailors) reckoned it (the ship) to break up"; and
   e. to emend the verb (for example, from *ḥāšâ,* "to hurry" [Sellin 1922: 244]; from *ḥwb,* "be in danger": Freedman 1958; criticized in Rudolph 1971: 339).

Such suggestions, however, do not reckon with the fact that Hebrew is full of vocabulary in which inanimates are the subjects of verbs that are logically acted upon only by animates, and in particular by human beings, for example, the land that sins (Ezek 14:13) or vomits its inhabitants (Lev 18:25). This usage was recognized even by ancient rhetoricians, who labeled it "prosopopoeia" or "personification." The prophetic books are stocked with such instances, and it might be sufficient here just to mention Isa 23:1, where Tarshish ships are (onomatopoeically) commanded to "howl" (*hêlîlû ʾonîyôt taršîš*). The reverse, that is, individuals becoming subject of verbs ordinarily reserved for inanimate conditions, is also known, and examples were collected long ago by Adrian of

Tyre, who lived about the second century C.E.; on these matters, see König 1900: 105–6.

The preceding examples are all embedded in poetry; it therefore needs to be explained why the prose of Jonah employs such a verb as *ḥiššēb*. One answer must surely be that in many languages ships commonly attract anthropomorphic vocabulary. In a late thirteenth-century B.C.E. letter the king of Byblos sent to the king of Ugarit, a ship caught in "heavy rain" (*gšm ʾadr*) is said to have "died" (*mtt*); Sasson 1966: 137. (The same expression is applied to a ship-wrecked sailor's unfortunate boat; Lichtheim 1975: 212.) Ships of the rabbinic period are said to "desire" (*mbqšt*) nice winds (*Esther Rab.* 1, cited by Patai 1941: 10 n. 35).

But there is yet a better reason why Jonah's ship is granted the faculty to think. Normally suited only to the animate world, *ḥiššeb* is singularly well placed in a story that easily shifts toward the fabulous. Its usage jolts readers, albeit temporarily, preparing them to expect the occurrence of the unexpected.

1:5. *wayyîreʾû hammallāḥîm wayyizʿaqû ʾîš ʾel-ʾelōhāyw wayyāṭilû ʾet-hakkēlîm ʾăšer bāʾonîyâ ʾel-hayyām lehāqēl mēʿalêhem weyônâ yārad ʾel-yarketê hassepînâ wayyiškab wayyērādam.* Verse 5 divides neatly into two spheres of activities: the sailors' and Jonah's. In each, the final verbal forms are bunched into sequences of three, repeating the pattern for v 3.

wayyîreʾû hammallāḥîm. The term for the profession, *mallāḥ*, has been studied most recently by Krantz 1982: 182–84. It is commonly found in other Semitic languages but, as is the case of almost all words in Hebrew that refer to professions, it is ultimately derived from Sumerian, in this case má.lah$_4$, referring to ship handling. (The term, therefore, has nothing to do with Hebrew *melaḥ*, "salt," as is commonly stated in the commentaries.) It is a "general" term, applied to sailors of all specialities. As the narrative progresses, the author merely uses *ʾanāšîm*, "men," when speaking of the crew.

Depending on Fränkel 1967: 195 (and on G. H. Cohn 1969: 53), Magonet (1976: 31–32) discusses the verb *yārēʾ*, "to fear," and shows how fear progressively sinks deeper into the the sailors' hearts. I have only a few observations to add here. As it is used in Hebrew, the verb *yārēʾ* allows for many subtle shadings: there is the fear of death that one experiences when engaged in violent acts; there is the awe that one feels when before majesty; there is the apprehension that one senses when facing the mysterious; there is the anxiety that sets in when one is planning evil (Prov 14:16); and there is even the respect and solicitude with which one responds to parents (cf. BDB 431). In order to allow precision within this range of meaning, Hebrew links an accusative or complement to *yārēʾ*. In 1:5, the possibility of shipwreck is by itself enough to suggest that sailors felt nothing less than total panic. But when the *yārēʾ* has *ʾet-YHWH* as the direct object (in Jonah's confession of 1:9), the verb acquires a theological significance and fear is replaced by reverence. It could be observed, however, that despite the frequent reference to "fear," both as verb and as noun (*yirʾâ*, uniquely enough qualified by "great"), very little of the dread experienced by the sailors is shared by an audience because it knows the source of their troubles.

wayyizʿaqû ʾîš ʾel-ʾelōhāyw. The idiom *zaʿaq ʾel-* (someone), "to call upon (someone) for help," which can scarcely be distinguished in meaning when the verb *ṣāʿaq* is substituted, has been nicely studied by Hasel in *ThWAT* 2.628–39. It belongs to a theological vocabulary, for it is often God (but also a foreign deity) who is entreated. The verb will manifest a thoroughly secular sense when it reappears in 3:7 (*H* stem).

The problem of deciding whether to translate *ʾelōhîm* as "God" or "gods" has been broached above, at 1:4. Ordinarily, we can discriminate between these radically different usages by the contexts, most clearly when *ʾelōhîm* is subject of a verb conjugated in the singular (therefore "God"), or in the plural (therefore "gods"). In this context, *ʾelōhîm* is the (indirect) object of the verb and could ostensibly be translated "gods." Even though *wayyizʿaqû* is in the plural, *ʾîš* individualizes the appeal and therefore may encourage the translation "god [that is, of each sailor]"; see Berlin 1976: 228. The versions faced this quandary and resolved it differently: the LXX has them appealing individually to a god; the Vulgate has them appealing to many (Trible 1963: 18). The Targum went its own way. Because the soon-to-be-"converted" sailors could not be too attached to false gods, it reshuffled the text, replacing "god(s)" with "fear," and developed the sentence to make the sailors aware of their own impotence when facing the Hebrew God: *wdḥylw spnyʾ wbʿw gbr mn-dḥltyh wḥzw ʾry-lyt bhwn ṣrwk,* "The sailors became frightened and they prayed, each man according to his fear. But when they realized there was no hope . . ." (see, further, Levine 1978: 59–60).

I have rendered *ʾelōhāyw* by the inelegant "god(s)" because I too cannot judge whether the sailors were praying to an individual national god or were invoking as many deities as each could recall. Although there is no correct choice for the making, it is nevertheless worth noting that by inserting *ʾîš ʾel-* (*ʾelōhāyw*), and thereby individualizing the fright of the sailors, the narrator subtly reminds the reader of Jonah's personal plight. The focus on an individual in the midst of a storm is a motif common to seafaring literature (for example, Theognis, *Elegy* 670–82; Xenophon, *Anabasis* 5.8.20); it will be discussed more thoroughly in the INTERPRETATIONS section.

wayyāṭilû ʾet-hakkēlîm. The all-purpose word *kelîm* refers to material objects, finished products, utensils, or tools. In order to become more specific on the object, Hebrew enters *kelîm* in a compound construction. Hebrew is rich in vocabulary to express merchandise or cargo (for example, *maśśāʾ, hôn, maʿarāb,* and various derivatives of the root *sḥr*), but Jonah mentions none of these. A venerable notion is that the sailors dumped their idols once they realized how utterly worthless they were (Zlotowitz 1980: 88).

Lightening a ship's cargo to avoid shipwreck was common enough in antiquity that it was regulated by Jewish laws:

> If a boat was sailing on the sea and a gale arose threatening to sink it so that it became necessary to lighten the cargo, the apportionment (of the loss of each passenger) will have to be made according to the weight of the cargo . . . and not according to the value of the cargo, though they should not deviate from the general customs of mariners.[3]

The sailors of Jonah, however, obviously kept enough on board with which to make offerings when their ordeal came to an end (1:16).

lehāqēl mēʿalêhem. Ehrlich suggests (1912: 264) emending the second word to *mēʿalêhā,* "from her (the ship)"; but this is not necessary because, when it is construed with *mēʿal, lehāqēl* usually treats persons as indirect objects (BDB 886b). Targum, LXX, and Vulgate translate as if Hebrew had *mhm* rather than *mʿlyhm.* In this way, the Targum recreates a scene in which the sailors drop one idol after another into the seas in an effort to single out the one true god; Levine 1978: 60 n. 5. One Greek manuscript inserts here "And there was a great storm upon the sea"; see Trible 1963: 18.

weyônâ yārad ʾel-yarketê hassepînâ. This clause is commonly translated with a pluperfect verbal form, "But Jonah *had gone* down into the inner part of the ship and *had lain* down, and was fast asleep" (RSV; my italics). The justification for such a translation is given by Bewer (1912: 34; cf. Wolff 1986: 106): "lest we get the unjustifiable meaning that [Jonah] went down at the time of the storm when the others were doing all they could to save the ship. This is most improbable." Similar exegesis is held in rabbinic literature: Zlotowitz 1980: 88.

Such an understanding is not necessary, however. To begin with, Hebrew has no grammatical indicators to signal the use of a pluperfect construction, that is, to introduce information anterior to what is being stated. Modern translations that use it to render a past tense are really interpreting what ought to be happening in a narrative. I do not deny that pluperfect renderings can be defended, especially in the few passages in which the Hebrew perfect is used (see Driver 1892: 22, 84–89 [§§ 16, 76]); but I think that the cases so treated in Jonah (most prominently at 2:4, 3:6, and 4:5) are misguided.

[3] Quoted from Patai 1941: 13. See also the article "Maritime Law" in *Enc Jud* 11.996–97. During Paul's sea voyage, the following is recorded in Acts 27:15ff.: "The ship was caught and could not be turned head-on to the wind, so we had to give way to it and let ourselves be driven. . . . As we were making very heavy weather of it, the next day they began to jettison the cargo, and the third day they threw the ship's gear overboard with their own hands. For a number of days both the sun and the stars were invisible and the storm raged unabated until at last we gave up all hope of surviving." The situation became so desperate that the sailors later had to cast their own food to the waves (v 38).

The syntax of this phrase is the same as in *waYHWH hēṭîl rûaḥ-gedôlâ ʾel-hayyām* and *wehāʾonîyâ ḥiššebâ lehiššābēr* of v 4. The conjunction precedes the subject, and both precede the verb with a past conjugation. This thrice-repeated phraseology is significant, and it urges us to regard the three events as occurring in a sequence: God hurls the storm on the ship; the ship expects to crack up; *then* Jonah goes down to the ship's bowel. The sequence itself seems similar to an episode recorded in Matt 8:23–27, where Jesus and his disciples board a boat. When a storm breaks and the ship is swamped by the waves, Jesus falls asleep. Whereas both stories give the appearance of insouciance in the face of disaster, they use the protagonist's sleep for different purposes. In Matthew, the disciples know who is among them and apparently lose faith in him before they are shown his power and rebuked for their inconstancy. In our text, however, the sailors do not know who Jonah is and, more importantly, Jonah himself does not know how to react to the impending disaster. How he learns what is expected of him is discussed in the next note.

The noun *yerēkâ,* a feminine form of *yārēk,* is rarely used in the singular (see Gen 49:13) and commonly occurs in the dual. When attached to another word (GKC 279 [§ 95.i]), *yerēkâ* pinpoints the joining of two angles belonging to the word in question. Most commonly, it refers to the recesses of a cove, a house, or a geographic area. But the direction to be taken for reaching this recess depends on the particular object that is at stake. Thus, if one is destined to reach the *yarkātayim* of the *bôr,* "the Pit (Netherworld)" (Ezek 32:23; Isa 14:15), the direction is downward; if it is to those of a building (for example, as in Exod 26:22 [see BDB 438 for more examples]), then one needs to go toward the back.

We do not have, as yet, adequate knowledge about the inner construction of the upper levels in Phoenician merchantmen: was there a railing? A central superstructure? An overall decking? (See Graeve 1981: 132–34, who opts for the last choice.) It is not clear whether there was a special kiosk for the owners, let alone a shelter for the crew. The unfortunate Herodes, whose death and presumed murder were recounted by Antiphon (see above), met his end when rain forced him to exchange his undecked ship for one with such a shelter. In *Philoctetes* (481–82), Sophocles tells us that passengers could find themselves in the bowels, the bow, or the stern of the ship depending on their wealth or status. The stern definitely offered the choicest area, for a cabin was generally mounted in the poop (Casson 1971: 180–81).

To decide where Jonah slept on the basis of ancient shipbuilding techniques, therefore, remains an imaginative undertaking. Krantz (1982: 146) places him aft, depending on an (inadequately studied!) reference to *arkat eleppi* in an Akkadian literary text, though *araktu* in fact is not the etymological equivalent to *yārēk!* It is better, therefore, to choose a location at the ship's rounded bottom by simply following Jonah as he descends (verb: *yārad*) progressively to the lower depths, both physically and psychologically. This is the understanding of the ancient versions, and it seems to me the likeliest. The Targum tries to be more specific on the location, claiming that Jonah went to the base of the mast (*l'r'yt šydh d'ylp'* [with variations among manuscripts]), see Levine 1978: 59–61.

As to *sepînâ,* a word occurring only here, frequent studies have addressed two main issues (Krantz 1982: 69–70). The first is its etymology: although the term is a *hapax legomenon,* it is known to a number of Semitic languages and is found in texts from Mesopotamia and Egypt. A root "*spn,*" to cover" (1 Kgs 7:3, 7), is often discussed to explain *sepînâ.* Because this root is available to Hebrew and (through derivatives) to Phoenician, it is not necessary to derive the word from Aramaic. Whatever its origin and etymology, the word is first found in a seventh-century Assyrian document, if not earlier;[4] hence any attempt to regard Jonah (or portions thereof) as a postexilic text should not use *sepînâ* as evidence.

The second issue is its use in Jonah. Why should Jonah turn to *sepînâ* when *'onîyâ* is the more frequent term in the book? This is a matter of an author's style and cannot be used to conjecture the synthesis of separate versions of the same story. (A pun between *'nyh* and *ynh*?) The author of Jonah does have a propensity to use synonyms; see above. Halpern and Friedman 1980: 84 n. 1 and Ackerman 1981: 229–30 think that Jonah's author uses *sepînâ* here because his audience enjoyed the pun with the better-known phrase *yarketê ṣāpôn,* "the edge of Saphon." This intriguing (apparently Harvardian) suggestion is beyond evaluation, but it seems to me a trifle too learned. For a possible connection with *beṭen še'ôl,* see below at 2:3.

wayyiškab wayyērādam. According to the LXX, once he witnessed the storm Jonah went down to the ship's bowel, lay down to sleep, and promptly began to snore (*kai eregche* [*erregchen*]; so also [Pseudo]-Philo: König 1906: 745). Harmonizing the two readings by reconstructing a plausible common text for both is unnecessary, for the LXX is simply introducing humor that will sharpen when the helmsman frantically turns to Jonah for help. In his oration on Jonah, Philo depends on the LXX but regards snoring as a plot device to bring Jonah to the helmsman's attention (cited in König 1906: 745a). Josephus (*Antiquities* 9.10.2) expands by stating that "Jonah lay still and covered, without imitating anything that the others did." The church fathers commented on this act as betraying evil conscience and deep remorse (cf. Keil and Delitzsch 1900: 393–94).

The Hebrew vocabulary for Jonah's act, however, is less jocose than the LXX's, and its reading does not support the fathers' speculations. In fact, the verb *rādam* has frequently caused problems to translators of Hebrew Scripture into Greek (Thomson 1955). It occurs in the *N* stem and has as its closest synonym the verbs *yšn* and *nwm,* respectively, meaning "to sleep" and "to doze." Those who comment on *rādam,* and on its derivative *tardemâ,* generally refer to how much more intense it is than mere sleep (Magonet 1976: 679). In wisdom literature, we do have a citation or two in which *rādam* and *tardemâ*

[4] Loretz 1961: 23 reports the opinion of B. Landsberger that the Akkadian term *sapinatum* stood for Sumerian giš.má.

refer to the sleep of the irresponsible. Thus, Prov 19:15a warns that "Laziness induces (deep) sleep," while 10:5b advises that "He who sleeps during the harvest is an incompetent." In stories about prophets, however, "deep sleep" is said to overtake a prophet only *after* signs and wonders of God's presence become manifest (Ps 76:7; Dan 10:9—but only superficially similar to 1 Kgs 19:5, cited in comparison by Magonet [1976: 68]). Prophets come to be *nirdāmîm* when, upon recognizing signs of God's presence, they make themselves ready to receive the divine message.[5] In this way, they readily accept divine control over their future behavior. Jonah's situation is not, however, similar to the abandoned prophets upon whom an angry God pours deep sleep (cf. Isa 29:10); rather, his condition is that of a prophet who realizes that there is no escaping God. It is at this juncture in our narrative, therefore, that Jonah capitulates and runs away no more.

1:6. *wayyiqrab ʾēlāyw rab haḥōbēl wayyōʾmer lô mah-llekā nirdām qûm qerāʾ ʾel-ʾelōhêkā ʾûlay yitʿaššēt hāʾelōhîm lānû welōʾ nōʾbēd.* This particular verse does not bear new information on the ship and its survival amidst the storm, it does not offer more details on the pandemonium that reigned on board, and it does not dwell on Jonah's reaction to the situation. The narrative slows down, and all movement seems to freeze while we all pay heed to the words of one officer aboard ship. For a brief moment, this officer appears to recognize that he and his shipmates are but pawns in a test of will between an unknown man and his powerful God.

wayyiqrab ʾēlāyw rab haḥōbēl. A few Hebrew manuscripts have *wyqrʾ*, "(the helmsman) called to him, saying," a reading paralleling some Greek versions: Trible 1963: 19–20.

The easiest way to translate *rab haḥōbēl* is to be literal. *ḥōbēl* means "ropes"; *rb* means "chief, foreman" (Jer 39:3, 13, Esth 1:8, Dan 1:3, etc.); hence the whole can be translated as "chief of those who handle the ropes." In Ezek 27:29, however, *kol topśê māšôṭ mallāḥîm,* "oarsmen and mariners," seem to parallel *kol ḥōbelê hayyām,* "sea pilots"; it thus suggests that some poets regarded the term as generic for all knowledgeable in ship craft.

The versions' renderings for *rab haḥōbēl* are not especially illuminating on the specific function of this individual. The LXX has *prōreus,* meaning, according to classical sources, a "first mate," the "key assistant in the running of the ship and the one who assumed command if anything happened to his superior" (Casson 1971: 319). Other Greek versions have *kubernētēs,* "captain," and this reading is followed by the Vulgate's *gubernator.* The Targum has *rb spnyʾ,* by which it probably means to suggest that he was the owner of the boat (Levine

[5] See also Job 33:14–17. In a recent Yale dissertation, McAlpine recognizes this usage for the verb *rādam,* but fails to apply it to Jonah and hence misses its implication (1984: 200). So too Vawter 1983: 91.

1978: 51). Josephus (*Antiquities* 9.10.2) resolves the problem by splitting the position into that of a master and that of a pilot.

Our knowledge of the hierarchy aboard Levantine ships is little (see Krantz 1982: 187–88). Cuneiform sources, from Mesopotamia as well as Ugarit, speak of a *rab malāḫi* (CAD M/1, 152), but we really do not know the specific duties of such an officer. The Ugaritic alphabetic documents know of a *bʿl ʾany*, a term that might refer to the owner of a ship but for the fact that the person so labeled is himself said to "belong" to yet another person (*UT* 2123). We also know of a *rb br* (same text) and a *rb tmtt* (*UT* 2059), but we cannot be precise on the meaning of the word *tmtt*, let alone its relationship to its *rb*, "chief." He might well have been the chief officer.

It is only from surveying artistic depictions of ships of a later period that I can offer the following suggestion: a prominent figure upon a ship's deck is the helmsman, that is, the one in charge of navigating the ship by means of a steering oar. This oar was commonly attached to the stern by means of ropes, and it is this last detail that has stirred me into the translation I offer above.

I have one more reason why I chose to render *rab haḥōbēl* by "helmsman," and it will be detailed in the INTERPRETATIONS section.

mah-llekā nirdām. The compound *mah-llekā/llākem* is most commonly construed with *kî*, which is then followed by a present or past tense in the second person, singular or plural (Joüon: 1947 [§ 161.i]).[6] Only in Ezek 18:2 and in our passage is it construed with a verbal noun, a coincidence that has led some scholars to treat the construction as evidence of Late Hebrew (Brenner 1979: 403, nicely refuted by Landes 1982: 162*–63*). The word *nirdām* itself is grammatically ambiguous. It is a participle and is acting here as an accusative of state (GKC 385 [§ 120.b]); hence it suggests something like, "what's with you being in a trance?" My translation has understood it as such. It can also be regarded as a vocative, even without an article (Joüon: 1947 [§ 137.g]), and hence can be translated "What's with you, entranced man?" The versions tend to be literal except for the Vulgate, which has *quid tu sopore deprimeris?* "Why are you depressed by sleep?" Rudolph (1971: 339) needlessly suggests emending the form to the infinitive absolute.

qûm qerāʾ ʾel-ʾelōhêkā. As pointed out above (v 2), this clause only superficially resembles the language with which God addressed Jonah. With regard to *ʾelōhêkā*, unlike the occasion in v 5 on which it could be taken as singular or plural, it is clear from the verbal form in the following clause that the helmsman means for Jonah to appeal to one god only.

ʾûlay yitʿaššēt hāʾelōhîm lānû. The adverb *ʾûlay* is most often found with imperfect conjugations and expresses a wish or a hope, but also doubt (BDB 19). The verb, *yitʿaššēt*, is in the singular, and its subject, *hāʾelōhîm*, must be taken as

[6] Vanoni (1978: 130) is most impressed by its usage in an episode regarding Elijah: 1 Kgs 19:9, *mah-llekā pōh ʾēlîyāhû.*

such. Because an overwhelming number of such constructions (plural subjects, yet singular verbal forms) refer to Israel's God, it is possible that the helmsman is doing the same here. But similar constructions have foreign gods as subjects (Judg 11:24, featuring Chemosh), so it may be best to render "god." The article can be regarded as a mild demonstrative, "that god," meaning, "of yours"; GKC 404 (§ 126.a, b). "God himself" gives a smoother rendering, especially in the other occasions of its occurrence in Jonah (3:10 [twice], 4:7), and I adopt it despite my qualms about its gender implication.

Although the context makes obvious what the helmsman is trying to tell Jonah, the verb *ʿšt occurs here only in the *HtD* stem, hence a precise translation cannot be established. Landes (1982: 155*–56*) reviews the discussion and suggests something like "to have favorable thought towards someone; to be gracious to someone." In this he agrees with an earlier evaluation by Ginsberg (1967: 81–82) who comes to this rendering via an Aramaic usage (cf. Dan 6:4; but see *DISO* 223–24, where *ʿšt ʾl* and *ʿšt ʿl* are distinct in meaning). The versions translate interpretively: LXX, *hopōs diasōsē ho theos hēmas,* "that God may save us"; Targum, "perhaps there will be mercy upon us from before the Lord"; Vulgate, "If God could think of us (we will not perish)." Jewish medieval exegetes generally translated with "pay us heed" or the like, basing their understanding on *ʿeštōnōtāyw* of Ps 146:4; Zlotowitz 1980: 91. Calvin (1847: 42–43) understands it as "God's face appear bright [= to favor]" on the basis of Jer 5:28.

I have translated the verb in Jonah by means of "intercede" in order to make full allowance for the causative and reflexive elements inherent in the *HtD* conjugation. I have done so, having a fanciful notion that the helmsman, a pagan, expects Jonah's god to plead the crew's cause before a divine assembly.

welōʾ nōʾbēd. The verb *ʾābad* can refer to a death delivered by human brutality as well as by divine punishment. The clause's syntax and its connection to the previous phrase (with a negative preceded by a conjunction, modulating an imperfect; cf. GKC 323 [§ 109.g]; 503–4 [§ 165]) allow us to think of two alternative understandings. One way is for the helmsman's words to be wishful: your god might intercede, and we will therefore not die. The other is in my opinion more appropriate to the context; it judges the helmsman's tone as more anxious and desperate: your god will perhaps intercede [meaning, he *ought* to intercede], *lest* we die. For this understanding see Gen 14:23, which likewise poses a hypothetical situation before stating the unwelcome consequence: "[May I be punished] should I take anything of yours, lest you say (*welōʾ tōʾmar*), 'I have enriched Abram.' " The helmsman, therefore, is acknowledging that only Jonah's god can effectively ward off punishment for the entire crew.

COMMENTS

The textual notes permit us to chart a course for Jonah's escape. When he embarked on the ship and headed for Tarshish, Jonah saw signs to make him believe that his getaway would be successful. Jaffa lay outside of Israel, and presumably outside its god's effective control; a ship that plied the Tarshish route had just come in; he was able to engage its services and to join its crew. Faster than imagined, the expedition was out of port.

But God had other plans for Jonah. How soon after his ship sailed out of port before God hurled mighty winds against it cannot be established. The ship was obviously in open sea, but not so distant that its crew could abandon thought of rowing ashore (but see below at v 13). In fact, hugging the littoral just within the bluest edge of the sea was the common pattern for ancient seafaring.

The scene that then unfolded aboard is brilliantly conceived, with a thrice-repeated grammatical construction controlling the rhythm of events. The winds that God unleashes churn the waters and play with the ship as with a toy. The ship is first to realize the brutality of the storm, and its own terror at breaking up is quickly communicated to the sailors. Pandemonium occurs, and at first the mariners call to their many gods, each a protector of an individual sailor. When this fails to quiet the winds, the sailors heave everything but oars and food overboard.

Jonah's own activities are simultaneous. He hears the winds and feels their effect on the ship. These are signs from above, and the man of God knows what is expected of him. He goes to an isolated place, to the bottom of the ship in fact, and awaits God's words. Whether or not he hears what the helmsman tells him cannot be assessed; the sailors themselves, we soon discover, were paying no heed to that exchange as they searched for one more avenue by which to still the storm.

We, by contrast, can read in these words of the helmsman a foreshadowing of the sailors' eventual recognition that only Jonah's God has the power to give them peace.

III. The Singling Out of Jonah (Jonah 1:7–12)

◆

Those who go to the sea in ships,
  who do business upon vast waters,
Are indeed people who see the Lord's works,
  his remarkable feats upon deep brine:
The Lord speaks, and raises a wind storm,
  that lifts the waves high.
They are flung to Heaven,
  and plunged into the depth,
  their courage melts at the danger.
They reel about, staggering like sots,
  their skill at sea useless.
In their anguish, they appeal to the Lord,
  who retrieves them from peril.
The Lord lulls the storm into gentle murmur,
  its waves become hushed.
People are elated that all is still;
  The Lord then guides them to their desired harbor.

(Ps 107:23–30)

III. THE SINGLING OUT OF JONAH (1:7–12)

1 7Turning to one another, the sailors said, "Let's get together and cast lots to
find out who is responsible for this calamity of ours." When they cast lots and
Jonah was singled out, 8they questioned him, "Tell us, you who are responsible
for this calamity of ours: What is your mission and where are you coming from?
What is your homeland and to which one of its peoples do you belong?"

[9]"I am a Hebrew," he answered them, "and the Lord, God of Heaven, I worship—he who made the sea, and the dry land as well." [10]The men were filled with the most dreadful fear and upon learning that it was the Lord he sought to escape—now that he admitted it to them—they told him, "How could you have done this!" [11]They went on, "What must we do to you for the sea to calm its raging against us, for the sea is becoming increasingly tempestuous?"

[12]"If you lift me up and cast me overboard," he informed them, "the sea will calm its raging against you, for I personally acknowledge that this massive tempest raging against you is on my own account."

LOT CASTING: INTRODUCTORY REMARKS

In antiquity, lot casting (cleromancy, a term derived from Greek) was one of many divinatory practices by which to solicit an immediate and unambiguous response from a deity. While Hebrew laws and customs severely condemned any activity that smacked of fortune-telling or witchcraft, Israel resorted to lot casting quite commonly, reasoning that the results could only be directed by God. Thus, Prov 16:33 reminds us that "the lot might well be cast from/into the lap, but judgment must come from God."[1] Among its many uses (well covered in BDB 174; a full listing in Lindblom 1962), the technique of lot casting led to

1. *selecting:* Israel's first king (1 Sam 10:19); warriors for military expedition (Judg 20:9); individuals to live in postexilic Jerusalem (Neh 11:1); sacrifice for the Day of Atonement (Lev 16:8–10); apostle to replace Judas (Acts 1:23–26);[2]
2. *assigning:* specific burdens for the upkeep of the Temple (Neh 10:35); tribes to various areas in Canaan (Judg 20);
3. *distributing:* booty (for example, Nah 3:10); or
4. *settling disputes* (Prov 18:8).

Most interesting for us are the moments that lot casting is a plot device in narratives. In addition to the Jonah episode at hand, we meet with the proce-

[1] Read, perhaps, *ḥôq* rather than *ḥêq* (that is, *ḤWQ* rather than *ḤYQ*) and translate, "The lot might well be cast in legal matters, but the judgment must come from God." We often find *ḥôq* and *mišpāṭ* paired. An emendation in the opposite direction (i.e., to read *ḥêq* for *ḥôq*) has been proposed for Job 23:12 on the basis of readings in many manuscripts.

[2] This method of choosing Matthias bothered Jerome: "We should not put faith in lot casting because of this example [in Jonah] nor connect it with the [New Testament] instance, since privilege granted to individuals cannot make a rule common" (Antin 1956: 67).

dure in three other instances, the best known of which occurs in the Esther scroll. Haman's notorious casting of lots to determine a date for the destruction of Mordecai's folk gave Judaism its Purim festival, of course; but it also taught it the Babylonian word for "lot" (*pūr*) and gave Jews an excellent opportunity to witness the reversal of fortune when hope had faded.

In Joshua 7, lots identify Achan as guilty of *knowingly* scorning God's ban on retaining spoils forbidden to Israel. We can note that Achan, along with his family, paid the ultimate price; and possibly because he was of the tribe of Judah, the city in which the trespass occurred was ultimately allotted to Benjamin.

The casting of lots is once more called upon to identify another person guilty of breaking a ban. In this case, it is Jonathan who *unknowingly* trespasses against a needless vow foolishly imposed by his father (1 Sam 14:24). That in his drive to gain victory Saul places a burdensome condition upon Israel foreshadows future examples of Saul's lack of balanced judgment; and this assessment remains true even when the people stop Saul from executing Jonathan, whom the lots identify as the guilty party (1 Sam 14:43–46). Eventually, of course, Jonathan (like Jephthah's daughter) does pay with his life for his father's intemperance; furthermore, Jonathan's seed never comes to rule Israel.

The biblical testimony on the way the Hebrews proceeded with lot casting is not very revealing, for in the majority of cases in which the practice is cited in the Bible, we are not told what Israel used for lots. Comparison with evidence from neighboring lands, however, allows us to suppose the use of bones, stones, sun-dried and fired clay, shafts of arrows, sticks of wood, and the still mysterious Urim and Thummim. Because the substance of the lot and its physical shape differed, the way to read the answer differed; it is likely, therefore, that individuals appealing to the lot established their own regulations and made solemn declaration before deities and witnesses to obey its results.

Albeit etymologically obscure, in Israel the word *gôrāl* generically stood for any of the various types of materials used in determining lot. For this reason, the terminology associated with *gôrāl* varied. Most commonly, however, the *gôrālôt* are said to be "dropped" from something into something: people "cast" (*H* of *šālap;* of *ṭûl; yādad*), "drop" (*H* of *nāpal*), "shoot" (*yārâ*), or simply "gave" them. Lots were said to be "be" (*hāyâ*), to "occur" (*nāpal*), or to "come out" (*ʿālâ* or *yāṣāʾ*); they can "bring (quarrels) to an end" (*H* of *šābat*) and can lead men to "be picked" (*N* of *lākad*). Proverb 16:33 suggests that the lots were dropped from the lap, but, as noted above, the sentence yields better sense when the crucial word *ḥêq* is emended.

Haman does not tell us how he singled out the fateful day on which to destroy the Jews. From the Achan incident in Joshua, we can only surmise that the procedure to identify the culprit was elaborate (vv 13–19), no doubt taking up the better part of a week. Only the passage in Samuel 14 gives hint of the procedure. Saul established two camps: one for himself and his son Jonathan, the other for the rest of the population. "Saul asks the Lord, god of Israel, 'Give what is right'; Jonathan and Saul were picked (by lot) while the people were cleared. Then Saul asked, 'Cast between me and Jonathan my son'; Jonathan was picked." The LXX to this passage, however, preserves a more elaborate version of the procedure (quoted from the NEB; cf. also RSV):[3]

> Saul said to the Lord the God of Israel, "Why hast thou not answered thy servant today? If this guilt lie in me or in my son Jonathan, O Lord God of Israel, let the lot be Urim; if it lie in thy people Israel, let it be Thummim." Jonathan and Saul were taken, and the people were cleared. Then Saul said, "Cast lots between me and my son Jonathan"; and Jonathan was taken.

NOTES

1:7. *wayyōʾmerû ʾîš ʾel-rēʿēhû lekû wenappîlâ gôrālôt wenēdeʿâ bešellemî hārāʿâ hazzōʾt lānû wayyappilû gôrālôt wayyipōl haggôrāl ʿal-yônâ.* The versions simplified this phrase, which has a plural verb and a singular subject; Trible 1963: 21. The spelling of *rēʿēhû* is more common than *rēʿêhû* (consonantal *rʿyhw;* cf. Job 42:10; 1 Sam 30:26), for Hebrew scribes often choose to drop the first in a sequence of two pure-long *i-* or *u*-vowel indicators.

While unexceptional to Hebrew, the vocabulary in this phrase, nevertheless, affords comparison with a similar one that occurs in v 5, *wayyizʿaqû ʾîš ʾel-ʾelōhāyw.* At an aural level, the similarity recalls and reinforces the pandemo-

[3] Lindblom 1962: 173–78 has a full account of the discrepancy and the various scholarly opinions that it has fostered. His opinion (p. 177) is that "the Greek translators give a confused picture of what really occurred. Their text must be regarded as a valueless product of fancy." This must certainly be too harsh a judgment. In fact, McCarter's treatment of the passage for the Anchor Bible (1980) supports a venerable opinion that the reverse is at stake here: the LXX is closer than is the Hebrew version to the original reading. I hold to a minority opinion that we are not dealing here with an event that can be authenticated by confronting differing literary traditions: Saul's vow and its consequences are beyond our capacity to prove or re-create historically. Rather, we are dealing with an account that manipulates various traditions to advance reasons for the fall of the house of Saul. Therefore, neither the LXX nor the Masoretic version can be said to contain one reading that is more "authentic" than the other, but each offers its own plausible detailing. From this perspective, about all that we can say is that the LXX's rendering of the incident preserves a more sharply drawn version on the way to invoke God's response when an issue is beyond human solution. (A good and accessible discussion of the difficulty of reconstructing "original" readings is E. Tov's 1986 paper.)

nium that broke out all over the ship. More crucial, however, is what it reveals of the sailors' state of mind. In v 5 we are told that their first reaction to the storm was to seek help, each from his own god. In taking that avenue, each man was of course not only exaggerating the power of the god to whom he was appealing, but also presuming himself capable of interceding before a deity from whom he wished to obtain relief. In fact, each of the sailors was exaggerating his own power as well. Only when these measures taken by individuals on board miserably failed to calm the waves did the sailors realize that they were not suited to assume a prophet's role. Appreciating the virtues of humility, they then changed tactics. Acting as one body, the seamen sought to identify who among them was the "defiler" (to use the terminology of Antiphon [see remarks to section I]). To do so, they resorted to lot casting.

lekû wenappîlâ gôrālôt. The imperative of the verb *hālak* is here merely introductory to the main act, which is conveyed by the cohortative of *nāpal;* on this construction, see BDB 234 (I.5.f [22]). Some scholars consider the use of *gôrāl* in the plural (where the singular would be perfectly suitable) an indicator of Late Hebrew prose; see Landes 1982: 162*. This might well be so; but, as is suggested by other biblical citations (for example, Lev 16:8; 1 Chronicles 24–26), it could also tell us that the sailors do not repeat the same query until the choice eventually whittles down to Jonah (as was the case in the Joshua and Samuel passages cited above). The sailors, rather, probably plucked the one shard that bore Jonah's name from among the others similarly inscribed. This was definitely the quicker measure and, in time of stress, no doubt the most appealing. The same approach seems to have guided the unfortunate victims of zealotry at Masada, as the ostraca uncovered by Yadin amply testify (conveniently, see *Enc Jud* 11.1089–90). The Targum makes it clear that the sailors were using something that could be rolled on the ground (*ʿdbʾ*), that is, dice; see Levine 1978: 63. The Muslim embellishments to the legend merely string two separate approaches: "They cast lots, and they fell on [Jonah]; but they said, 'The lots fall and may be mistaken. Let us cast names upon the sea.' So each one wrote his name on a lead ball and threw it into the sea. The ball of each except Jonah sank, but his name appeared on the surface of the water"; al-Kisāʾī, see Thackston 1978: 323.

Commentators such as Bewer 1912: 35, König 1906: 745a, and Perowne 1905: 63 present Buddhist and other "parallels" to the incident aboard Jonah's ship. Modern sea and air lore teems with stories, usually set on a raft or an airplane full of famished survivors, in which the lot singles out victims for cannibalism.[4]

wenēdeʿâ bešellemî hārāʿâ hazzōʾt lānû. The feminine noun *rāʿâ* makes the second of seven appearances in Jonah. I have discussed it above, at Jon 1:2, and indicated that, together with its third occurrence in the next verse, they are *rāʿôt*

[4] Almost always, a ship appears at the nick of time to solve the problem!

that affect the sailors, albeit temporarily. They are God-sent and are meant to complicate Jonah's flight from his responsibility. Ironically enough, this mission is to make the Ninevites face the true *rā'â* that endangers their wicked lives.

The vocabulary used by the narrator to bring the sailors to the moment of truth is deceptively cluttered, leading even ancient exegetes to lighten the phraseology of the succeeding verse. Thus, the LXX (Sinaiticus, Vaticanus), the Soncino prophets, and some Hebrew manuscripts excise the second occurrence of the phrase; Trible 1963: 22. The Targum paraphrases to sharpen the sailor's request: "Tell us, for what reason (*bdyl mn*) is this evil upon us"; Levine 1978: 63. One manuscript (codex 384), however, places the repetition in a margin, which has led some modern scholars to think it a gloss (see Keil and Delitzsch 1900: 394–95). It should not be surprising, therefore, that there is stark division in opinion among commentators about the integrity of the phrase, especially in its second manifestation. Some merely excise the phrase (for example, Rudolph 1971: 338; Bewer 1912: 35–37); others would keep it, offering reasons that are often guided by homiletics rather than grammar. Wolff (1986: 107) retains it in his translation but agrees that it is secondary. Joüon (cited by Rudolph 1971: 340) emends *lemî* of v 8 to *lammâ,* but this is unnecessary.

The two phrases in v 7 and v 8 almost match:

v 7: *bešellemî hārā'â hazzō't lānû*
v 8: *ba'ašer lemî-hārā'â hazzō't lānû*

but we should note that the phrases are alluding to two dissimilar situations. *Before* casting lots, the sailors wanted to force heaven to single out the guilty. By contrast, *after* the lots had singled Jonah out, the sailors turned to him and began to ask different sets of questions.

In v 7, *bešellemî* is a compound made up of the following four elements: the preposition *b*(*e*), the relative particle *še*(*l*), the preposition *l*(*e*), and the interrogative pronoun *mî.* We cannot know how it functions, however, merely by stringing meanings for each one of its elements. While *beše(l)-* can either be a pronoun, "that which," or a conjunction, "because," it acts solely as a pronoun when combined with another distinct morpheme, the interrogative pronoun (*le*)*mî,* "for whom." Thus the compound *bešellemî* is not likely to mean anything else but "on whose account."

In v 8, these four elements combine to form two distinct vocables because, unlike the relative particle *šel* which must be attached to other particles, *'ašer* cannot have anything suffixed to it.[5] In the twenty or so cases in which it appears in Scripture, *ba'ašer* is always followed immediately by the phrase it

[5] It is immaterial for us that a number of grammarians judge *še*(*l*) to be an abbreviation of *'ašer* and that others regard it as an originally distinct demonstrative particle that became synonymous with *'ašer* in later Hebrew usage; the two compounds eventually

modifies. Thus, when confronted with it, the Masoretes felt constrained to insert a *maqqeph,* effectively binding *lemî* to *hārāʿâ.* Irrespective of the way that particular phrase functioned when Jonah circulated in its earliest form, the punctuation as we have it now suggests a rendering that makes a subtle distinction between the two occurrences and that can be reproduced by a literal (if inelegant) English:

v 7: (for us to find out) "on-account-of-whom this evil is ours"
v 8: (tell us) "because (or: inasmuch as) to-whom—this evil is ours"

This distinction is noted by Kimḥi (cited by Levine 1978: 63–64), who treats the phrase as a relative clause: "Tell us, you who are bringing this calamity upon us. . . ." It may be best, however, to understand the phrase's intent as "because it is you who are bringing this calamity upon us."

1:8. *mah-mmelaʾkteka ûmēʾayin tābôʾ mâ ʾarṣekā weʾē-mizzeh ʿam ʾāttâ.* It is important to note that the sailors pose four questions, aiming to elicit distinct and separate answers. These four questions can be arranged into two sets of double questions: (1a) what is your mission? (1b) where are you coming from? (2a) what is your homeland? (2b) to which one of its peoples do you belong? The Masoretic punctuation, however, suggests an alternate organization into three unequal portions: (1a) what is your mission? (1b) whence are you coming? (2) what is your homeland? (3) to which one of its people do you belong?"[6]

However arranged, the questions seem to reverse logical order because the mariners ask Jonah about his origins *after* they inquire about his mission. To the audience, this arrangement makes much sense, for it has been interested in Jonah's mission (and his neglect of duty) all along and already knows the answer to the other queries. But to the sailors as well there is coherence to the priority given the four questions; for, as they turn to Jonah, they know about him only that he boards a Tarshish-bound ship in Jaffa; that he falls into a trance when everyone else is frantic about the ship's survival; and that he is designated by the lots (that is, by the gods) as responsible for a danger that still menaces. In order to find a solution to their problem, therefore, the sailors need above all to hear

---

functioned differently enough that we can find them linked in Eccl 8:17, *bešel ʾašer,* "because of the fact that . . ." (see Gordis 1976: 107).

[6] The narrative expects us to believe that Jonah was never quizzed when he boarded ship. When the sailors are finally moved to do so, they do not ask Jonah his name, a question that in our culture is likely to be posed first. It may be that they failed to do so because they only wanted answers to their pressing situation; but in Hebrew narratives people rarely ask a visitor's name unless there is a lesson to be derived from the exercise. For example, after wrestling all night with Jacob, the angel asks him his name, a prelude to altering it into "Israel."

Jonah tell, not about his origins, but about the infraction that has made the sea heave up over them. They therefore ask about his *melāʾkâ.*

This word is derived from *lʾk,* a root that conveys the idea of "sending"; but this root works as a full-fledged verb only in Ugaritic, Ethiopic, and in exotic Arabic. To convey the same notion, Hebrew most commonly uses *šālaḥ*. The form *melāʾkâ* bears an anomalous vocalization (for **malʾākâ;* see GKC 80 [§ 23.c]), and what we usually translate as "angel," *malʾāk,* is a masculine form of the same word. In most of its occurrences, *melāʾkâ* refers to human occupation or trade. In order to convey an activity that is spiritual or religious, this word is normally linked to another such as "holy," "temple," or "God" (BDB 522 [6.b]).

Whether the sailors were trying to learn from Jonah about his "trade" or his "mission" is for each of us to decide, and I admit that there are merits to each rendering. On the one hand, we can support the translation "trade, business" by noting how the sea passage of Psalm 107, quoted as epigraph to this section, uses the word *melāʾkâ* (v 23): "Those who go to the sea in ships, who do business (*ʿōśê melāʾkâ*) upon vast waters." Furthermore, it is reasonable to argue that from the sailors' perspective anyone going to faraway Tarshish would be a merchant. If the narrative had told us something about the cargo (or the lack of it) that Jonah had loaded on board, we might have gauged how early on his shipmates began to suspect him of a purpose other than trading; but the narrative says not a word about this subject, and on this issue we are left at the mercy of speculations. Finally, there is merit in translating *melāʾkâ* by means of "profession, trade," for it retains suspense about Jonah's identity at least through v 10.

Despite these cogent arguments, I have chosen to translate *melāʾkâ* "mission" simply because, once the lots fall upon Jonah, the sailors must suspect him of pursuing a vocation beyond merchandising. I am encouraged to follow this line of thinking by noting that in other contexts in which the inquiry is specific about someone's work (for example, Gen 46:33; 47:3), Hebrew poses the question as *mah-mmaʿaśeh* (+ pronominal suffixes), using language that is appreciably different from what the sailors use in our passage.

The sailors next want to know whence Jonah came. Of course they know that Jaffa is a harbor city and that Jonah was merely in transit there until boarding a ship. While the Vulgate omits the question, it is nevertheless not redundant. In fact, an inspection of other biblical passages reveals that (*û*)*mēʾayin* + *bôʾ* is posed to learn what impelled a person to travel (reason and goal; so, for example, in Judg 17:9; 19:17).[7] If the question tries to localize the origins of a traveler, it is done for exceptional reasons (Jacob trying to find out whether he had reached his mother's homeland, Gen 29:4; Joshua making sure that the travelers are not from the promised land, Josh 9:8ff.). In our case,

[7] With an exception at Gen 42:7, the phrase is commonly construed with the imperfect even when referring to the past.

therefore, we should presume that the sailors are expanding on their inquiry regarding Jonah's mission by trying to find out what had set him on his travels. It is left up to the next set of questions to pinpoint Jonah's origins.

The term *ʾereṣ* is very broad, for it can have cosmological ("Earth"), physical ("ground"), political ("country"), and geographical ("district, province") connotations. The sailors obviously can have only the last two meanings in mind. Because ancient Near Eastern powers rarely harbored just one ethnically identifiable group within their constantly shifting frontiers, it is natural for the sailors to probe deeper into Jonah's background. In fact, *weʾê-mizzeh ʿam ʾāttâ* is the most significant question within the last set, for what the sailors are seeking to do is to tie Jonah to a specific "folk," *ʿam* (usually distinguished from *gôy*, "nation"; see A. Hulst, in *ThWAT* 2.290–325). The manuscript from Murabbaʿāt (Milik 1961: 190:14) makes no separation between *wʾy* and *mzh.*

1:9. *wayyōʾmer ʾalêhem ʿibrî ʾānōkî weʾet-YHWH ʾelōhê haššāmayim ʾanî yārēʾ ʾašer-ʿāśâ ʾet-hayyām weʾet-hayyabbāšâ.* In consonance with Hebrew narrative techniques, the last in a series of questions is the one that a respondent commonly first addresses. Calvin records this example as an instance of *husteron proteron* ("last first"), 1847: 50. Jonah's "I am a Hebrew" consists of only two Hebrew words; but he evidently thought them enough to satisfy fully everything that the sailors wanted to know about his homeland and people.

When persons of Hebrew stock wish to identify themselves to others of similar background, they would naturally mention the tribes to which they belong. But if they wish to convey their origins to foreigners, they call on a broader terminology. Scripture recognizes three terms: Israelite, Hebrew, and Jew.

The expression (*benê*) *yiśrāʾēl* is used when referring to members of the Israelite "nation." The etymology of this expression is obscure, but tradition has linked it eponymously with Jacob. Although (*benê*) *yiśrāʾēl* occurs during all periods of Hebrew literature, we do not know when it first came into common usage, for the only extrabiblical witnesses to it are found on the Mesha Stone (ninth century) and in Late Assyrian documents.[8] By then, however, the Northern Kingdom had come to bear this name, and it might well be that the traditions linking it to the premonarchical period were anachronistic and, perhaps, evocative of a unity for early Israel that probably never existed. All of these matters are the subject of legitimate controversy, but they need not detain us here.

Likewise etymologically cryptic, *yehûdâ* is a tribal and territorial name that Scripture firmly links with the third son of Jacob, who is also David's ancestor. It is applied to the Southern Kingdom, citizens of which came to be known as

[8] I do not believe that it necessarily occurs in the so-called "Israel" stela of Merneptah, for the Egyptian syllabic consonants for this word can render a number of West Asiatic tribal and place-names.

yehûdîm and, eventually, as God's people, the Jews. If we presume that the storyteller (or whoever was last to edit Jonah into its present shape) was not totally ignorant of his people's history, it becomes obvious why he would not have used either of these terms. *yiśreʾēlî* was not favored as a gentilic to refer to an Israelite, and all of its Hebrew attestations (in both genders) can be found in the very peculiar legal episode in Lev 24:10–11.[9] Nor would the storyteller have used *yehûdî,* "Jew," for it is likely that he was aware of Jonah, the prophet who appeared before Jeroboam of Israel. Moreover, to label Jonah a *yehûdî* might have confused an ancient audience, who doubtless knew that Gath Hepher of Zebulun, whence Jonah hailed, could in no way be located in Judea. We can be fairly sure that even into the third century B.C.E. there was linkage between the two prophets because, instead of having Jonah label himself a "Hebrew," the LXX has him admitting, *doulos kuriou egō eimi,* "the Lord's servant am I." This statement could only have resulted from a paraphrase of 2 Kgs 14:25 (see above), where we are told that Jeroboam II succeeded in enlarging Israel "according to the word of the Lord, Israel's god, who spoke through his servant [*ʿabdô*] Jonah the son of Amittay, *the* prophet who hailed from Gath Hepher." We need not suppose that the LXX is the "original" reading from which the Hebrew swerved, because the versions as well as all of the Hebrew copies consistently presume or preserve *ʿbry* (Trible 1963: 23–24). In truth, it is doubtful that there ever was a single, pristine, "original" Jonah text that the LXX translators could learnedly improve. Rather, during their time, there probably were many Jonah copies, some of which apparently read **ʿbdy* where Hebrew now has *ʿbry.* The LXX's copy was one with **ʿbdy,* and this reading was treated as an apocopated form of *ʿbd y<hwh>*.[10]

So *ʿibrî* could be the only ethnic term really available to a discerning storyteller. We need to find out what such a designation meant for an ancient audience listening to the story of Jonah and how that audience assessed the sailors' understanding of the term. If Hebrews were aware of their own traditions, they would know that *ʿibrî* is derived from the root *ʿbr,* "to cross (over)," likely referring to those who lived in the *ʿēber,* the land across the (Euphrates?) River; but they would more likely recall that the term acquired such an ethnic label because of an eponymous ancestor, Eber, who was fourteen (twice seven) generations removed from Creation and who, according to the Sethite genealogy, was the seventh descendant since Enoch.[11] They might also know of a

[9] The only other occasion for its usage, at 2 Sam 17:25, was judged so odd that even in ancient times Ithra the "Israelite" was given other ethnic appellatives ("Jezreelite" in the LXX's version of the passage; "Ishmaelite" in 1 Chr 2:17).

[10] Delcor (1979: 11–12) collects similar examples of differences between the MT and the LXX.

[11] Modern scholars do not take such a tradition at face value and constantly debate the validity of linking the Hebrews with the Hapiru of the second millennium B.C.E.

number of stories in which *ʿibrî* was attached to ancestors (Abraham, Joseph, Moses) in order to distinguish them from foreigners (see simply GKC 8–9 [§ 8.b]). Therefore, when a storyteller quotes Jonah as labeling himself a *ʿibrî*, he aims to distance his protagonist from the heathen sailors. Too, the sailors are expected to recognize in *ʿibrî* a discriminating ethnicon. In this common realization of the vast gulf that separates Jonah from those on board, the storyteller conveys a certain pride at the pedigree of Jonah, the single character in the story who is of immediate interest to heaven.

There might be more to this usage, however. From the mid-seventh century B.C.E. at least until Roman times, the "land of the Hebrew" had come to represent what is now modern Israel, the west bank of the Jordan River, eastern sections of Transjordan, and the regions south of Syria (Redford 1970: 201–3). We cannot tell how soon it was after Jonah began circulating that readers began to ignore the storyteller's discriminative use of *ʿibrî* and to believe that foreigners made no distinction between Judeans and anyone else living in the land of the Hebrews.[12] Be that as it may, by the time the Targum of Jonah was prepared (around the second century C.E.), readers of Jonah imagined that the prophet was revealing more than his nationality to the sailors. "I am a Jew," *yhwdʾh ʾnʾ*, Jonah says in the Aramaic version, and he thus confesses his religion even as he reveals his nationality (Levine 1978: 65–66). In the Hebrew version, however, this confession of faith does not come until Jonah responds to the sailors' first and most important set of queries.

The word *ʾānōkî* is the independent personal pronoun, "I." Hebrew has also an alternate form, *ʾanî*, and grammarians have not yet offered a convincing explanation of why and when they are used: some think they come from successive periods, with *ʾānōkî* the more archaic of the two; others suggest they betray rhetorical options, with *ʾanî* a lighter choice when appended to verbs. I do not know why Almbladh (1986: 22) connects the usage of each with a supposed "elevated style," but I give here a table for the appearance of each form:

	Prose	*Poetry*
ʾānōkî	1:9 [Jonah]; 3:2 [God]	—
ʾanî	1:9, 12 [Jonah]; 4:11 [God]	2:5, 10 ["Jonah"]

"Hapiru" seems to be not an ethnicon but a term that was most likely applied to persons who have attachment neither to a specific city-state nor to a distinctive tribe. Fortunately, this debate is not relevant to the problem of *ʿibrî* in Jonah. Loretz 1984 is a hefty volume that discusses the issue exhaustively.

12 How to use the mention of *ʿibrî* in Jonah to extract information on postexilic Jewish historiography as well as on dating the book is discussed by Loretz 1984: 179–81.

The sentence *we' et-YHWH 'elōhê haššāmayim 'anî yārē'* has been shaped in such a manner (direct object + subject + verbal adjective) as to stress the name of Jonah's god, YHWH. Here, of course, we are expected to think that as soon as the Tetragrammaton—the four-consonant personal name of the Hebrew god—is pronounced, the sailors would instantly recognize the source of their misfortune; but this in fact does not happen, as will soon be seen. Nevertheless, because the same verbal root *yārē'* has just been used to report the mariners' first reaction to the storm, an audience is in better position to appreciate the storyteller's brilliance. Jonah's words effectively contrast the moods aboard ship: while the pagans panic and blindly grope for answers, Jonah has faith in God only, and calmly confesses it. Recent commentators have similar opinions of the situation; see above at 1:5.

It is unfortunate that the Targum (as well as some of the Greek versions; see Trible 1963: 24) did not fully appreciate the potential within this repetition of the verbal root, for its awkward translation ("I fear from before the Lord," *wmn-qdm YY . . . 'n' dḥyl*) obviously superimposes a notion derived from the next verse; see Levine 1978: 65. Some modern commentators (for example Bewer 1912: 36–37; 38, citing others), prefer this misguided reading.

The appellative *'elōhê haššāmayim,*[13] as has been pointed out by many commentators, is well attested in Hebrew Scripture (and the Elephantine Papyri), especially in writings that are commonly set in the Persian period; see Wolff 1986: 115; *DISO* 310. Israel knew of other appellatives of God that are similar in their sentiments, "builder/rider/maker of heaven." Why Jonah chose to cite first this attribute of God might have more to do with the context than with any theological intent. Jonah recognizes that the sailors are looking toward heaven as the source of their calamity; after all, any sea tempest (see v 4) must include heavy black clouds, lightning, and thunder: one and all weapons of a storm god. That Jonah's words could have carried bite is also plausible, for the sailors were likely Phoenicians and as such would have worshiped Baal Shamem, "Baal (is) Heaven," as their main god; Porten 1981: 240–43; Almbladh 1986: 21; Rainey 1989 [at Tell Michal!]. This god's propensity for shipwrecking those he despises is explicitly cited in the "curses" segment of a treaty between Assyria's Esarhaddon and the king of Tyre, "May Baal-sameme, Baal-malage and Baal-saphon raise an evil wind against your ships, to undo their moorings, tear out their mooring pole, may a strong wave sink them in the sea . . ." (cited from *ANET*[3] 534).

The sailors might be satisfied to know of God's power over the skies (the source the winds); but Jonah intends his message to declare God's omnipotence, and he carries the argument further by means of *'ašer-'āśâ 'et-hayyām we'et-hayyabbāšâ.* The verb in this phrase, *'āśâ,* will soon allow the narrator to develop homilies (v 14, and to a lesser extent v 10). By contrast, *yām* and *yabbāšâ,* "sea

[13] Also once *'ēl haššāmayim* and many times in Aramaic *'elāh šemayyā'*.

and dry land," can merismatically refer to all that is found on this planet because they refer to opposites. With this clause, therefore, Jonah is telling the sailors that God is not solely the Lord of heaven, but also the creator of all that is found beneath the firmament; in effect, the ruler over the whole universe.

The sequence of the vocabulary in Jonah's panegyric to God is itself interesting. Hebrew knows many passages that combine the three major components of the cosmos: heaven (*šāmayim*), earth (*ʾereṣ/ʾadāmâ/yabbāšâ*), and waters (*yām, mayim*).[14] Most commonly the progression is either heaven–earth–water or its reverse. It is worth noting that this passage in Jonah is unusual in having the sequence heaven–waters–earth. This is hardly accidental. Jonah is not relying simply on words to convey God's omnipotence; rather, he is cleverly using these terms in order to appeal to the less sophisticated instincts of the sailors. The God of heaven, who can bring a storm to a dead halt, will also guide their future travel upon the seas and will continue to monitor their lives once they reach dry land. One Greek manuscript has not fully appreciated this point, for it gives "the *heaven* and the sea" (Trible 1963: 24).

Jonah's language is also unusual here in its use of *yabbāšâ* instead of the more common *ʾereṣ*.[15] The word *yabbāšâ* is not commonly used as a synonym for "earth" in the geographical or physical sense; rather, it emphasizes the dryness of a piece of land, *terra firma* itself. Thus, in the majority of biblical occurrences of this word, the Hebrews are said to step over *yabbāšâ* when crossing the Re(e)d Sea or the Jordan (five times; see BDB 387a). Indeed, God as creator of the *yabbāšâ* is a notion that is known from the first chapter of Genesis (vv 9, 10), but it is a moot point whether the storyteller chose this vocabulary (Magonet 1976: 65–66 cites Ps 95:5 as well) to recall how God created the nonliquid portions of Earth. As a cue word (German: *Leitwort*), however, *yabbāšâ* will soon be featured twice more in Jonah (see below at 1:13 and 2:11).

1:10. *wayyîreʾû hāʾanāšîm yirʾâ gedôlâ wayyōʾmerû ʾēlāyw mah-zzōʾt ʿāśîtā kî-yādeʿû hāʾanāšîm kî-millipnê YHWH hûʾ bōrēaḥ kî higgîd lāhem.* This and the next two verses feature subordinated clauses introduced by *kî* (see the Comments above under 1:2). This uniformity, however, by no means simplifies the way to interpret the function of each occurrence. Jonah's dignified acknowledgment of his veneration for God includes the participle *yārēʾ*. As it transfers to the sailors, however, the verbal root *yārēʾ* is transformed in both its meaning and its intensity. It does reacquire the nuance of "fear" that it had when the storm first broke (v 5); but the emotion is now sharpened because "a great dread" (*yirʾâ*

[14] To these a fourth, *Sheol* or Netherworld, may occasionally be added or given as substitute.

[15] For *ʾel qōnēh ʾereṣ,* "El (God), creator of Earth," in an inscription from Jerusalem, see Miller 1980.

gedôlâ) is construed as direct object of the verb to "fear."[16] The LXX tries to convey the same feeling by translating literally; but other non-Semitic versions (Aquila, Symmachus) found means by which to highlight the phrase by construing it either as a dative or as an ablative; Trible 1963: 25.

"Great dread" is a phrase unique to this chapter of Jonah, where it occurs again in v 16. The two occurrences thus bracket the sailors' distraught reactions to Jonah's revelations. Much more common to Hebrew Scripture, however, is the phrase *yirʾat YHWH/ʾelōhîm,* "reverence for God," an expression that the storyteller does not apply to the sailors (see below at 1:16).

It will be noticed that the next clause, *wayyōʾmerû ʾēlāyw,* "They told him," is repeated at the beginning of the next verse (v 11), even though Jonah gives the sailors no response in the interval. This is a sandwiching device that is fairly common in Hebrew. By resorting to it, the narrator makes the sailors utter only one statement even when separated by explanatory information. I have not fully allowed for this technique in my translation because it would force a radical reshifting of material, as the next comments will explain.

The linking of the interrogative pronoun to the feminine demonstrative results in a sharply drawn question consistently construed with the perfect of *ʿāśâ,* "to act." The phrase occurs about ten times in Hebrew Scripture (see GKC 471 [§ 148.b]; 442 [136.b]; BDB 261b [4.d]) and, depending on whether one treats *zōʾt* as a pronoun or as an enclitic, one may pose the question rhetorically ("What is this that you have done!"), searchingly ("What, then, have you done?"), or accusingly ("Whatever have you done?"). An overview of the passages in which *mah-zzôʾt* plus forms of *ʿāśâ* occurs allows two observations: first, as an inquiry, it can stand alone or within a series of queries (usually at the end); and second, as an inquiry, it is as likely to meet with silence (Gen 26:10; 42:28; Exod 14:5, Judg 2:2) as to prompt replies (Gen 3:13; 12:18; 29:25; Exod 14:11; Judg 15:11; some of these answers, however, could be lame or could convey no new information).

Precisely because *mah-zzōʾt ʿāśîtā* can elicit a response, we wonder whether Jonah's answer of v 9 satisfied the sailors. Did they really understand everything about their situation merely because Jonah had revealed himself to be God's worshiper? Hellenistic and medieval exegetes generally thought otherwise, and they took the query to be shorthand for a full trial at sea in which Jonah eventually confessed his guilt to all on board. Such a notion is paralleled in some manuscripts of the Targum in which we find the following italicized brief expansion: "For the men knew that he was fleeing before *he would prophesy in the name* of the Lord" (see Levine 1978: 65–66).

Modern commentators, however, are almost unanimous in assessing *mah-zzōʾt ʿāśîtā* as an exclamation—of shock, of horror—rather than as a query. The

[16] GKC 367 (117q). As we shall see, this type of cognate or internal accusative is much favored in Jonah.

reason is that terror should be emphasized when the sailors recognize the source of their calamity.[17] The phrases that follow the exclamation are treated either as later insertions or as marginal glosses, probably because there are very few Scriptural occasions where *mah-zzōʾt ʿāśîtā* is bound to *kî* clauses (Bewer 1912: 37; Trible 1963: 25, with more amplification in 88–89; but see Wolff 1986: 107).[18] Exodus 14:5, for example, has "(*mah-zzōʾt ʿāśînû*), that we have let Israel leave our service?" Here the *kî* clause does not offer an answer but is consecutive to the phrase preceding it. In order to evaluate properly how *mah-zzōʾt ʿāśîtā* functions in the present context, we need to inspect the three instances of *kî* clauses within v 10.

When a sentence includes a verb such as "to know, feel, believe, remember," it is common for Hebrew to link an object clause to it by means of the conjunction *kî;* GKC 491 (§ 157); *kî-millipnê YHWH hûʾ bōrēaḥ* follows this rule. The third clause, *kî higgîd lāhem,* however, stands parallel to the two just preceding it and should, indeed, be regarded as likewise directly causal to "The men were filled with the most dreadful fear." We should recall that the verb in this clause, *lehaggîd,* "to relate, reveal, inform," normally presumes that a full retelling is unfolding, albeit not recorded in a text. This verb thus differs from the ubiquitous *ʾāmar,* which means "to say, state" when followed by a full and definite statement.[19]

The phrase *kî higgîd lāhem* explains why the men were afraid. By no means, therefore, should one follow the many commentators who regard the last clause of v 10 (if not even the two preceding it!) as a gloss.[20] Rather, we ought to reconstruct the following steps for the events given in vv 9–11: (a) Jonah's revelations of v 9 are (b) followed by lengthy elaborations on why he is aboard

[17] As one example of the posture, I quote the succinct reason offered by Keil and Delitzsch (1900: 395–96): "*What hast thou done!* is not a question as to the nature of sin, but an exclamation of horror at his flight from Jehovah . . . as the following explanatory clauses . . . clearly show." The NEB is in the minority when it renders "What can you have done wrong?" To translate so, however, NEB is forced to render the rest of v 10 in the pluperfect and even to ignore (delete?) the first of the three instances of *kî* within it.

[18] The *kî* clause in Gen 12:18 is consecutive to another inquiry introduced by *lāmmâ.*

[19] There are exceptions to this observation (for example, at Exod 19:25, Judg 17:2, and the difficult Gen 4:8). Moreover, when the verb *ʾāmar* means "to mention," in some cases a report may not follow (see BDB 56 [right column, top]).

[20] Blenkinsopp has privately suggested to me that "the author forgot to allow Jonah to state the purpose of his travel, and then rather naïvely stuck it in subsequently." T. Harviainen (1988) proposes that the sailors had at one time misunderstood Jonah to be escaping his master, having heard him say *ʾadonî,* when he was thinking of YHWH. This suggestion is flawed not only because it presumes that the Tetragrammaton was pronounced differently than is written when this portion of the story was achieving a final form, but also because it retrojects Jonah's explanation into the moment when he first boarded ship rather than after the luck of the draw forced him to confess his flight.

ship (summarized by *kî higgîd lāhem*), (c) leading to the sailors' understanding of the situation (reflected in *kî-yādeʿû hāʾanāšîm kî-millipnê YHWH hûʾ bōrēaḥ*), (d) that steers them to utter the exclamation (*mah-zzōʾt ʿāśîtā*) (e) and to follow it with a question that is to be found in v 11. It is worth noting that the Arabic version arrives at a partially similar resolution of the last clause, but through radical means. It attaches this clause to v 11 through *falammā,* "when," rendering, "When Jonah informed them, they said, 'So what should we do to you . . .' " (Wright 1857: 110).

1:11. *wayyōʾmerû ʾēlāyw mah-nnaʿaśê llāk weyištōq hayyām mēʿālênû kî hayyām hôlēk wesōʿēr.* As noted in the preceding discussion, this verse continues the line of query that the sailors aimed at Jonah. The main issue here is whether the last clause, *kî hayyām hôlēk wesōʿēr,* forms part of the sailors' address or is to be placed outside of the quotation marks.

The clause *mah-nnaʿaśê llāk*[21] is couched as a question; but its vocabulary encourages the audience to hark back to the previous verse. What Jonah did (verb: *ʿāśâ*) in running away from God's commission now sharply contrasts with what the sailors must try to do (verb: *ʿāśâ*). The irony, of course, is that when Jonah tells them what must be done, they find it just as difficult to accomplish their own commission. Playfulness with the verbal root will not cease until the sailors acknowledge God's omnipotence (v 14).

The question is linked to the next phrase by means of the conjunction, thus establishing a purpose for the inquiry: the sailors want to know how to stop the sea from raging. The LXX and the Vulgate translate slavishly by means of conjunction even when idiomatic usage would have required other particles (Trible 1963: 26). The Arabic version, instead, boldly uses *ḥatta,* "in order that"; Wright 1857: 110.

The verb *šātaq* will occur once more, in v 12. Because the clause here is consecutive, the verbal form is a jussive, albeit found in one of the rare occasions that it follows an indicative (GKC 504 [§ 166.a]; Joüon 1923: 316 [§ 116.e]).This particular verb is not heavily used in Scripture (BDB 1060), but this circumstance hardly makes it "late" in Hebrew usage. Nor does the fact that it is well represented in Aramaic make this verb necessarily an Aramaic loanword (*DISO* 322). Equally misguided are the attempts to regard the verb as "early," by (impossibly) linking it to an alleged derivative from Ugaritic (collected in Wolff 1986: 117). We simply do not have enough evidence to make such categorical judgments. What we can note is that the verb is found in two other passages. While the sentiments of Prov 26:20 were undoubtedly penned after the Exile, no criterion on dating Ps 107:30, either "early" or "late," is

[21] On the doubling of the "lamed" by means of a *dagesh euphonicum* to compensate for the loss of accent on the previous word, see GKC 72 (§ 20c).

convincing.[22] I quote a long passage from Psalm 107 as this section's epigraph because it too depicts sailors hoping for divine deliverance, calm seas, and prosperous voyages. The verb *šātaq* occurs in v 30, and despite some claims that it refers to the sailors, it more likely has as subject *gallîm,* "waves," very much like what obtains in Jonah.

In *hôlēk wesōʿēr* the verb *hālak* fulfills an auxiliary function, as it does in the related construction, *hālôk we-.* The two verbs here are participles—literally, "going and storming"—and form a hendiadys to convey both repetition and increasing intensity; GKC 344 (113.u) offers three other examples for the same construction. Almbladh 1986: 22 indicates that most attestations of the construction come from preexilic texts.

As noted above, however, the major issue that is raised in this verse is whether the last clause, *kî hayyām hôlēk wesōʿēr,* belongs within or outside the sailors' remarks. Grammar is not at stake here, and the decision is purely interpretive. The versions could well have been influenced by the last phrase of v 13, where essentially the same vocabulary (with only the addition of *ʿalêhem*) continues the narrator's comment on the sailors' reaction to Jonah's drastic advice. This is clear in the case of the Syriac version, which says, "for the sea was becoming increasingly boisterous, and it came to be boisterous *over them.*" The other versions either hew close to the Hebrew's ambiguity (Targum) or dramatize a bit "for the sea went (rose?), and increasingly lifting up its waves" (LXX); "the sea went and did swell" (Jerome); see Trible 1963: 25–26; Levine 1978: 66. Modern translations and commentaries are unanimous in following this line of interpretation.

The Arabic version, however, adopts an alternate understanding in which the sailors turn to Jonah—who no doubt appears to them much too nonchalant in the crisis—and advise him of the worsening situation. In order to do so, however, the Arabic combines the last two clauses into one: *liʾanna-lbaḥra huwa ḏā munṭaliqun yazḫaru ʿalaynā,* "for the sea is now cut loose, surging upon us."[23]

In my translation, I too have placed this clause within the quotation; but I have done so not because I am adopting the Arabic version's approach but because of the next verse, where Jonah also refers to the tempest. I think it potentially more dramatic that Jonah should practically borrow the mariners' vocabulary as he acknowledges his own responsibility. In assuring them in this

[22] The fusion of disparate segments with similar themes and under one heading (vv 2–3) may, however, have come to completion after the Exile. The psalm praises God's goodness: travelers in the desert (vv 4–9) and in the seas (23–32)—in fact, those who operate outside of Zion—are redeemed, as are those who are imprisoned within it, either by the state (17–22) or by ill health (23–32). The structure of these passages is also worth noting, for the "outsiders" (desert and sea) sandwich the "insiders" (prisoners and sick).

[23] Note that the Arabic is less independent in treating the same phrase in v 13.

manner that he is fully alert to their dilemma, Jonah is also subtly urging them to follow his advice if they expect to survive the stormy seas.

1:12. *wayyōʾmer ʾalêhem śāʾûnî wahaṭîlunî ʾel-hayyām weyištōq hayyām mēʿalêkem kî yôdēaʿ ʾānî kî bešellî hassaʿar haggādôl hazzeh ʿalêkem.* Some versions (LXX, Syriac) add Jonah's name at the opening of the verse. Jonah asks the sailors to lift him and pitch him into the sea. The verbs he uses are two, the second of which, *ṭwl,* we have already met at 1:4 (see above) and will presently feature it again 1:15. The first verb, *nāśāʾ*, seems hardly necessary here, for Jonah did not need to tell the sailors how to go about dropping him into the sea. Yet a number of benefits accrue by its usage.

First of all, on the *narrative level* the verb *nāśāʾ* allows us to appreciate Jonah's assured control as he gives the sailors detailed instructions for carrying out his request. Genesis 29 has a passage that uses similar means to enter a character's personality. Jacob has fled to Aram Naharayim and has run into Laban's shepherds. Contrary to Near Eastern etiquette, which requires the stranger to await his hosts' solicitous interrogation, it is Jacob who bombards the shepherds with questions. The intent here is for the reader to appreciate Jacob's pluck and temerity, in marked contrast to his dealings with Esau on the one hand, and Laban on the other.[24]

A second advantage is that, on the *psychological level,* the use of *nāśāʾ* must surely have given the sailors pause, for it forces them to contemplate a horrifying prospect. Jerome has a touching paragraph about Jonah's willingness to accept his punishment.[25] But Jonah is not making it easy on his shipmates! He is not about to throw himself into the sea just because he recognizes his own culpability.[26] Rather, he wants the sailors to bear full responsibility for what must happen.

Finally, it might be here that we locate the third, *semantic,* level on which this word operates: *nāśāʾ* is a verb that seldom refers to lifting up an individual. It is constructed, rather, with nouns such as "sin" and "evil" when Scripture wants to speak of guilt and the many ways in which human beings sustain it (BDB 671 [2]; Stolz in *THAT* 2.113–14 [3.d–e]). Such a connotation, therefore, could have penetrated the sailors' minds. That the Targum, LXX, and Vulgate

[24] Note the plucky use of *ʾaḥay* in his first question, "My brethren, where are you from?"

[25] *In Ionam* 1.12 (Antin 1956: 72): "We should note at this point the magnanimity of our fugitive. He does not evade, he does not hide, he does not deny; rather, upon admitting his escape, he openly accepts his punishment. He wants to die, so that others might not perish because of him and to avoid adding murder to desertion. This, then, is the story."

[26] The medieval exegetes who thought Jonah was contemplating suicide are way off the mark on this; Levine 1978: 67. (Pseudo)-Philo's decision to have Jonah jump into the sea is mentioned below at 1:15.

never operated on this level is clear from the rather innocuous verb, "to take," by which they chose to render *nāśā*ʾ.

weyištōq hayyām mēʿalêkem. In promising the sailors an end to their terror, Jonah turns to the same vocabulary that they used when questioning him (v 11). He assures them that no less (and no more) than what they wish will occur if only they follow his guidance. Prophets normally do not tell people what they want to hear; but the response here is just right, in view of the dismal and stressful situation. Good (1981: 45) wonders whether "a touch of sympathetic magic may be implied here. If Jonah be 'hurled to the sea' . . . it may offset and nullify the storm, that Yahweh had 'hurled to the sea' [v 4]" (so too Freedman, privately).

The sentence ends with two phrases featuring *kî* clauses, the second of which has been amply discussed in previous pages (at 1:10 and 1:11). We need to add here that Jonah is responding to the sailors' initial search for the responsible man, for he refers to previous vocabulary; compare *wenēdeʿâ* bešellemî *hārāʿâ hazzôt lānû* of 1:7 with our *kî* bešellî *hassaʿar haggādôl hazzeh ʿalêkem.* The versions have various particles to render *bešellî,* with the Syriac enlarging negligibly on the phrase; Trible 1963: 26–27.

What is exceptional here is that the first clause, *kî yôdēaʿ ʾānî,* is accorded special attention. Snaith (1945: 20) points out that by reversing the more normal phraseology, *ʾanî yôdēaʿ*, the narrator stresses Jonah's awareness of his role. The Masoretes recognized this emphasis and sharpened it by placing the pausal accent *zaqeph qaton* over *ʾanî.* Furthermore, as has been amply recognized in recent years, the verb *yādaʿ* can carry a legal sense, "to recognize, to know, to admit," when accepting or entertaining a legal decision (Sasson 1979: 118; with bibliography). With these words, therefore, Jonah goes beyond admission of his own guilt and actually freely gives the sailors leave to throw him into the sea. Should they do so, he is informing them, they will incur no blame at all.[27]

The sailors, we shall soon find out, are not convinced by Jonah's directives.

COMMENTS

The narrative we follow in this section opens on confusion and clamor reigning aboard a storm-tossed ship but closes upon a single voice giving chilling advice on how to escape a dire fate. How this remarkable change takes place within the brief span of five verses is discussed in the NOTES. This particular scene, however, also gives us a good opportunity to feature the conflict between the narrator's wish to develop a story with coherence and consistency and his need to provide occasions that will please the audience.

[27] For these reasons, as well as for the arguments presented in Wolff (1986: 118), we should reject W. J. Horwitz's proposed revocalization of *ʾanî* into *ʾonî,* "fleet" (1973).

The sailors have exhausted their skills, both practical and spiritual, in trying to discover why they are in such a dangerous predicament. They have, to no avail, dumped everything overboard, and each has sought the intercession of a favorite god. Now they find themselves driven to unpleasant measures: they must identify the person who brought calamity upon them and, thereafter, press him into revealing his trespass against one of the many gods with control over the waves.

The casting of lots is a standard measure by which to force heaven into giving an unequivocal answer. As the sailors scrutinize the lots for the predestined answer, we can imagine Jonah rising from his trance and approaching his shipmates. The questions that the sailors have for him are many; yet, with their careful balance and with their intricately developed program of inquiry, these questions are much too calmly posed, considering the dangerous circumstances. We may legitimately wonder whether panicked sailors can really be interested in all of these details about Jonah's life, occupation, and background when what they should really be soliciting are answers to a twofold query: who is your god, and how have you offended him?

In truth, the narrator is here responding to demands other than those required to develop his story. He could be following normal conventions that obtain in Near Eastern storytelling: whenever a protagonist is on alien soil (here: waters), those who meet him bombard him with questions as soon as they dispose of the preliminary niceties (washing the feet of a distant traveler; placing food before the famished). We can observe, however, that the narrator attributes to the sailors an interrogation that cannot be meant for Jonah's ears only. The narrator knows that his public would not mind temporarily embarrassing Jonah, as heathens remind him of his mission, of the land and of the people he left behind in his rush to avoid his duty.

The narrator knows too that, once posed, the sailors' questions will not rate of equal importance to his audience. Much too skillful to burden the tale with unnecessary detail, the narrator does not waste ink on formal and sequential responses to the sailors' inquisition. Do Israelites need to learn what ought to be the *melāʾkâ* of a prophet? Where else but from among the Hebrews could a true prophet arise? For all of these reasons, Jonah's explanation of why he boarded the ship in Jaffa, as well as his reply to the sailors' remaining queries, are brusquely relegated to passages attributed to Jonah but not quoted (see NOTES on v 10).

The narrator allots Jonah a direct response only to the last of the sailors' series of queries. Moreover, he has Jonah offer them an explanation that seems unsolicited. Jonah is made to state his allegiance to God by using a highly panegyric vocabulary that, albeit a trifle overblown if meant only for the sailors, is just right when addressing a Hebrew audience. "I am a Hebrew and the Lord, God of Heaven, I worship," therefore, remain as the only quoted words that the sailors really needed to hear.

THE SINGLING OUT OF JONAH (1:7–12)

In the Notes above (at 1:9), I searched tradition and history in order to offer plausible reasons for the use of *ʿibrî* in Jonah. I stated that a Hebrew narrator wishing to place a label on a compatriot would be limited in choice to this ethnicon. Here too, it should be noted, the narrator is appealing to his audience's pride; for *ʿibrî* can operate as a device to alert it to the extraordinary nature of a Hebrew's character. In Scripture, at least two other contexts have a similar purpose: when Mordecai confesses to the Persians that he is a Jew (Esth 3:4, using "Jew") and when Joseph tells the high officers in Pharaoh's jail that he was stolen from Hebrew territory (Gen 40:15).

The sailors are stunned by the news, but they now understand perfectly why they are facing danger. In view of their situation, it is rather surprising that they would ask Jonah's opinion on how to rid themselves of the evil aboard their ship. Once they have identified the guilty and singled out the god to whom he is responsible, the mariners should, of course, have launched more prayers to this particular deity and begun a new series of lot casting in order to establish the best avenue for deliverance. But the narrator is once more operating on another level than mere storytelling. His hero is, after all, a prophet, a man with direct access to God, and it would be unthinkable that such a person would not know what must be done. The narrator, therefore, casts the sailors not so much as independent souls who would pluck out the guilty from their midst, but rather as children who must listen attentively to a prophet's instruction.

Jonah solemnly absolves the sailors of any blame incurred if the sailors follow his counsel. Good (1981: 45) needlessly questions Jonah's sincerity: "perhaps we must see Jonah's offer not as a sudden burst of generosity but as his perception that death might yet be a way out of his frightful mission." I think we best reject such an insidious notion, for whatever faults Jonah displays in this story, they do not include passivity or playing the sacrificial goat. In fact, the advice Jonah is proposing will seem perfectly understandable to a Hebrew audience; after all, it would not be the only occasion on which God forced seemingly baroque choices upon Israel and its prophets. To the men aboard ship, however, this advice does not plausibly resolve an acute problem, and they refuse to heed it. We shall soon learn why.

IV. Obstinacy and Submission (Jonah 1:13–16)

◆

As to the foreigner also; he may not belong to your people Israel, but when he comes from a distant land because of your fame—for your powerful reputation, your power, and your wide reach will surely become known—; so when he comes to this Temple to pray, do listen in your heavenly abode and fulfill whatever appeal the foreigner makes to you. In this way, all the people of the earth will recognize your fame and will come to worship you and to know that your name is bestowed upon the Temple that I have just built—just as does your people Israel. (Prayer of King Solomon, 1 Kgs 8:41–43)

On that very day, there will be an altar to the Lord within the land of Egypt and a pillar to the Lord at its border that will serve Egypt as an emblem and witness to the Lord of Hosts. When they appeal to the Lord because of oppressors, he will send them a forceful savior to deliver them. The Lord will be revealed to Egypt so that, on that very day, its people will acknowledge and offer the Lord animal and grain sacrifice; they also will make vows to the Lord and fulfill them. (Isa 19:19–22)

Have mercy, Lord, our God, on the righteous, on the pious, on Israel's elders, on its remaining sages, on sincere converts, and on us.[1]

[1] From the thirteenth benediction of the *Amidah.* The *Amidah* (*Shmoneh Esreh*), the core prayer in Jewish daily service, gathers eighteen (later nineteen) benedictions, many of which date to the period just after the destruction of the Second Temple. This particular benediction addresses God as the "Support and Trust of the Righteous." The Jonah midrash and the ninth-century *Pirke* of Rabbi Eliezer (Friedlander 1981: 72–73) regard this prayer as particularly relevant to the sailors after their conversion.

IV. OBSTINACY AND SUBMISSION (1:13–16)

1 [13]Nonetheless, the men rowed hard to bring the ship back to dry land; but they failed to do so, for the sea became increasingly tempestuous around them. [14]They then appealed to the Lord, "Please, Lord, do not have us perish because of this person, and do not assess innocent blood against us. Indeed you are the Lord, and whatever you desire, you accomplish."

[15]No sooner did the sailors lift Jonah and cast him overboard than the sea curbed its fury. [16]The men were seized by a powerful fear of the Lord then. Offering sacrifices to the Lord, they made him solemn promises.

NOTES

1:13. *wayyaḥterû hāʾanāšîm lehāšîb ʾel-hayyabbāšâ welōʾ yākōlû kî hayyām hôlēk wesōʿēr ʿalêhem.* I translate the verbal form *wayyaḥterû* by means of "rowing hard"; but this meaning is an extension of the verb's basic implication. The root **ḥtr* apparently means "to burrow, hollow out, dig" and is used mostly in constructing similes, referring to the making of holes in a wall (Ezek 8:8; 12:5ff.) and to the tunneling into a house (Job 24:16). In Amos 9:2 the same verbal form is applied to men who burrow into Sheol (Hades), seeking to escape God's wrath. The imagery is obviously that of people who desperately and feverishly drive an instrument into the earth in order to escape their own world. In Jonah, a parallel atmosphere is evoked. Here, the mariners try to break through the waves, to master and overcome them; Keil and Delitzsch 1900: 396. The versions strive to parallel the notion; but not all of them are slavish to the Hebrew. While the Vulgate and the Targum refer to the rowing that the men needed to do, the LXX (the Syriac and Arabic as well) only says that "The men tried hard (*parebiazonto*) to return to the land." See Trible 1963: 27 and Levine 1978: 67.

Imprecisely rendered though it may be, *wayyaḥterû* does allow us to gauge the terror that drives the sailors' oars anxiously, smartly, and repeatedly into the waters. The practical measure that they end up taking—that of maneuvering their ship toward dry land—is conveyed by *lehāšîb.* This verbal form is based on the causative (*H*) stem of the verb *šûb,* with the subject (the sailors) causing another (the ship) "to turn back." This refocusing on the ship draws attention back to v 5, where the ship is the first to suffer the powerful storm God hurls upon the waters. As the sailors try to evade the order that God delivers through Jonah, the ship is once more central to the action.

One more observation is in order. The verb *šûb* in the causative stem is rarely used as in this Jonah verse (BDB 999 [10]). It is much more common to find it imbued with theological connotation (Soggin, in *THAT* 2.886–91). This observation need not be significant, except that this usage comes rather quickly after we have noted a similar semantic extension in the case of the verb *nāśâ* (v 12). It is also arresting that, in telling us of the sailors' vain efforts to steer to safety, the narrator chose a word that Jonah had just used: *hayyabbāšâ.* That this choice of vocabulary allowed playful soundings of consonants shared by *hšyb* and *hybš* might be intentional also; Halpern and Friedman 1980: 83. All four Greek versions translate *hayyabbāšâ* by means of "earth" (*pros/eis tēn gēn,* Trible 1963: 27). While such a rendering is accurate enough in telling us where the sailors sought to go, it misses the narrator's subtle comment on the futility of the enterprise. For how could the sailors hope to reach a destination that, as Jonah has just finished telling them, is God's to create and control?

They obviously could not. The Hebrew tersely states *welōʾ yākōlû,* "but they failed to do so," a phrase that is given finality by the Masoretes, who placed a pausal accent under the last word. The Vulgate, too, emphasizes this failure by choosing a verb that focuses on the weakness of the sailors, *et non valebant,* "and they could not manage it"; Trible 1963: 27.

1:14. *wayyiqreʾû ʾel-YHWH wayyōʾmerû ʾānnâ YHWH ʾal-nāʾ nōʾbedâ benepeš hāʾîš hazzeh weʾal-tittēn ʿālênû dām nāqîʾ kî-ʾattâ YHWH kaʾašer ḥāpaṣtā ʿāśîtā.* This verse is the heart of Jonah's first chapter, for it catches the moment in which illumination finally strikes the sailors. The sailors utter the name of the Hebrew God for the first time, recognizing—as they did not in v 11—that mercy must be obtained not from the sea, but from that very God. The narrator here uses *qārâ ʾel-(YHWH),* a phrase that is idiomatic for "appealing to a deity" (see above, at vv 2 and 6). By resorting to this vocabulary, the narrator shows preference for an idiom he had assigned to Jonah (v 6; 2:3) over one used by the sailors in v 5 when they appealed to their own gods (*wayyizʿaqû ʾîš ʾel ʾelōhāyw*). Conscious of this subtle change, the versions offer "shouted, pleaded" (LXX, Vulgate), or "prayed" (Targum); see Trible 1963: 28.

The supplication itself is couched in the pattern of the simple Hebrew prose prayer, which consists of three parts: (1) an *address,* (2) a *petition,* and (3) a *motivation* for the petition (Greenberg 1983: 1–18).[2]

[2] M. Greenberg's collection of evidence on prose prayers among Israel's neighbors is appreciated. Nevertheless, it is not necessary to follow his theories on the use of the Hebrew prayer style by Jonah's "heathen" sailors (Greenberg 1983: 61 n. 7). To begin with, Jonah does not exactly belong to *verismo* literature, in which authenticity is a major feature. Moreover, it would be a totally foreign experience for ancient narrators to transpose the style, structure, and mood of another culture's oral expressions. If they were seeking such a degree of verisimilitude, narrators occasionally would (mis)quote a full phrase, as in the case of the Ramesside papyri, which include Semitic sentences. More

(1) The *address* draws attention to the body of the appeal itself, which usually consists of an interjection (*ʾānnâ;* also: *ʾānnaʾ*) and can be followed by the vocative—as it is here. When presented as a quotation (see NOTES to 4:2), this appeal most often uses an imperative when the request is for a positive act; but it uses a jussive when it aims to withhold or to cancel a threatened action (BDB 58; GKC 307 [105.b]). In the present passage, the Syriac has simply an "Oh!" while the Arabic similarly gives "Oh, you God." The other versions, however, acknowledge this interjection through a variety of circumlocutions. The LXX gives *mēdamōs Kurie,* something like "By no means, O Lord."[3] The Vulgate has *quaesumus Domine,* "We beseech you, O Lord." Somewhat similar is the Targum's *qbyl bʿwtnʾ*, "Accept our pleas." See Trible 1963: 28; Levine 1978: 68.

(2) The *appeal* is a double entreaty for fairness as God judges the sailors. The two pleas are juxtaposed; but they are by no means repetitive. The seamen are bewildered, for they see themselves in a no-win situation: they are suffering because of Jonah's guilt; yet sending him to his death might well bring his god's wrath upon their heads. To overcome this double predicament, therefore, they shape separate appeals.[4] The first, *ʾal-nāʾ nōʾbedâ benepeš hāʾîš hazzeh,* harks back to past actions and the guilt that has accumulated against the sailors because of the obduracy of one man; the second segment, *weʾal-tittēn ʿālênû dām nāqîʾ*, concentrates on the immediate future and begs God not to charge them with a crime because of what they are about to do.

The verb used in the first of the sailors' supplications, *ʾābad,* recalls the helmsman's appeal to an entranced Jonah (v 6). The conjugation here, however, is different and includes the particle *nāʾ*. Hebrew uses this ventive (energic) particle rather frequently (Even-Shoshan 1982: 61), and when the negated volitive (cohortative or jussive) is at stake, it is inserted between the negative adverb *ʾal* and the conjugated verb (Joüon 1923: 308–9 [114.f]). The *nāʾ*, however, came to be vestigial by the time most Hebrew literature was penned and, despite the opinion of many grammarians, we cannot really sense much difference between the forms in which it occurs and those in which it is absent. Most versions, therefore, practically ignore its presence; only the Targum allows for it with *kʿn,* which can be rendered by "now" or the like; see Trible 1963: 28. Vestigial though it may be, the particle *nāʾ* does have its impact on the audience, for it makes the phrase reverberate with the sound of repeated labials (*beth* and *pe*) and sonants (*nun* and *lamed*), thus imitating hushed pleading.

---

often, when they were moved to impart a foreign flavor to a narrative, storytellers found it enough merely to insert an alien word or two into the text.

[3] See Acts 10:14.

[4] Completely misunderstanding what is at stake here, the Arabic version transposes both entreaties, "Do not reckon innocent blood against us so that (or: and) we should not perish because of this man's life"; Wright 1857: 110. A number of modern commentators (for example Bewer 1912: 39–40) sympathize with this approach.

OBSTINACY AND SUBMISSION (1:13–16)

What the sailors want is for God not to blame and punish them because of Jonah's grave delinquency. The LXX and the Vulgate use vocabulary that hews close enough to the Hebrew's language. The Targum sought to unclutter the mariners' reasoning and therefore expanded on our text, here as well as in the next clause, by inserting the word *ḥwbt* (*npšyh*), "sin, guilt": "Do not have us perish because of this person's guilt." See Levine 1978: 68–69. But this addition is hardly necessary.

In the word *benepeš,* the preposition *be-* is not to be understood as "together with," for this reading would place a sentiment in the mouth of the sailors that would definitely be out of place: the sailors are not begging to be spared from sinking with Jonah, for they have just resolved to throw him overboard. Rather, the preposition functions here as a causal preposition and finds its best cluster of parallels in Gen 18:23–33 (so also Wolff 1986: 119). At issue there is God's readiness to save the many because of the virtue of the few: "What if there are five righteous individuals short of the needed fifty," Abraham asks God, "would you devastate a whole town because of the lack of five?" (*hattašḥît baḥamiššâ*). (Further citations for this usage are given in BDB 90 [III.5].) The noun *nepeš* itself is one of Hebrew Scripture's most versatile; see the dictionaries and Westermann in *THAT* 2.71–96. We arrive at a specific meaning for it either through context or by evaluating its association with other words. The phrase *nepeš ʾîš* is not common in biblical Hebrew, occurring elsewhere only in a brief saying (Prov 13:8), "A person's wealth could well provide for his ransom; but a pauper will not even hear rebuke." More common are examples of *nepeš* (*hā*)*ʾādām,* which in most of its ten attestations, can be rendered by "living human" or more idiomatic to English "human being, person" (Num 19:11 and other legal contexts; Ezek 27:13)—hence the translation that I offer.

The sailors next launch a prayer designed to neutralize potential blame for murder.[5] The versions understand what is at stake, but give more or less literal translations for the crucial *dām,* "blood"; Trible 1963: 29. The Targum, as in the preceding clause, inserts "sin, guilt"; Levine 1978: 69. The verb *nātan* is here construed with the preposition *ʿal* + pronominal suffixes to mean "to set or impose (something) against/upon someone"; BDB 680 (2.c). That "something" is the *dām nāqîʾ*, and it deserves some attention.[6]

The word *nāqîʾ* is written with a final aleph, here and in Joel 4:19; scribal tradition, however, suggests that it should not be taken into consideration when

[5] A. Sperber totally misunderstands what is at stake here when he suggests that scribes emended an original *ʾal-tittēn ʿalêKA* ("and do not assess innocent blood against yourself!") in order to remove potential blame on God; this opinion is mentioned with approval by Almbladh 1986: 23.

[6] Here, and in the Jeremiah passage quoted in the following NOTE, I sharpen its effect by giving it a legal significance when I render "assess against us."

reading.[7] In fact, many Jonah manuscripts, including an early one from Murabbaʿāt, merely drop it. It could either be a scribe's confusion with the Aramaic spelling (Dan 7:9) or the result of a mistaken association with the verb *qîʾ* that will occur at 2:11 in the form *wayyāqēʾ*.[8]

Hebrew Scripture knows of two different ways in which the words "blood" and "pure, clean, innocent" are bound to each other. In the case of *dām nāqîʾ*, "innocent" is simply an adjective to "blood," with each word receiving its own accent; I translate this phrase simply by "innocent blood." In the other case, "blood" loses its accent and enters into construct with the nominalized adjective "innocent person," leading to a phrase (*dam [han]nāqî/neqîyîm*) that can be rendered with "blood of the innocent person(s)." (See simply BDB 196 [2.d] or 667 [1]; exhaustive listing in Vanoni 1978: 131–32.) The difference between the two constructions is subtle and is available to the eye rather than to the ear, for we cannot hear any difference when either is pronounced. "Innocent blood" focuses on the *act* of shedding blood, regardless of who is the victim, while "blood of an innocent person" dwells on the *blamelessness of a victim.*[9]

In this light, "innocent blood" in our verse permits one more perspective by which to appraise the sailors' prayer: they are begging God's understanding, not for judging a prophet guilty, but for a crime they are about to commit. In other words, the sailors are not completely convinced of the truth conveyed by Jonah even as they make ready to heave him overboard. Despite their prayer, therefore, the sailors have not yet completely and obediently yielded to God's will.

(3) The *motivation* for the appeal is likewise given in two segments because it addresses the two components of the sailors' prayers. The first segment, *kî-ʾattâ YHWH,* is separated from the second through the strong disjunctive ac-

[7] On the issue, see Andersen and Forbes 1986: 81–90; Goshen-Gottstein 1958: 111–13.
[8] It is not likely to be a pun, as Halpern and Friedman suggest (1980: 85).
[9] Vocabulary parallel to Jonah's is found Jer 26:15. Despite the soothing words of the other prophets, Jeremiah insists on predicting calamity and destruction to the unreconstructed. Angered officials seek his death, to which Jeremiah responds, "I am, now, at your disposal; do with me as you deem it right and proper. However, do realize that if you put me to death, innocent blood will be assessed against you (*kî-dām nāqî ʾattem nōtenîm ʿalêkem*), and upon this city and its inhabitants. God has indeed empowered me to deliver these words to you individually." Jeremiah does not hope to frighten his enemies by warning about hurting God's messenger (they are too callous for that), but to alarm them about the crime of shedding any individual's blood. The vocabulary in the Jonah and Jeremiah passages can be compared to that found in Deut 21:1–9, where a crime has been committed, but the criminal cannot be identified. Levites will break the neck of an unworked (and unmated?) heifer and elders will pledge, "We are not personally responsible for this crime, nor have we witnessed it. Accept expiation, Lord, for your folk Israel, whom you have redeemed; do not impose the guilt of innocent blood upon your folk Israel (*weʾal-tittēn dām nāqî beqereb ʿammekā yiśrāʾēl*). May this bloodshed be expiated for them."

cent *zaqeph qāton.* This pause, possibly not known by the versions and unfortunately often ignored by modern renderings, forces attention on the name of the Hebrew God, turning us back to the opening of the sailors' petition, *ʾannâ YHWH.* "We are in the midst of storm because there was a crime against you, by your own man, Lord" is what this terse statement implies. But it is left to the second member of the *motivation* to carry the mariners' deepest anxiety.

In *kaʾašer ḥāpaṣtā ʿāśîtā,* two verbs are juxtaposed, both conjugated in the perfect. The phrase has created difficulties because the first of these verbs can leave us with the impression that God harbors vindictiveness. Alert to such a possible interpretation, the versions linked contrasting verbal forms. The LXX offers *hon tropon eboulou pepoiēkas,* "as you were wishing, you have done," and, by allocating God's anger to Jonah's *past* action, it avoids the implication that God enjoys tormenting blameless sailors; Trible 1963: 29–30. The Targum, instead, has a rendering that looks forward to God stilling the seas: "For you, Lord, have done it as it is pleasing before you" (*ʾry ʾt YY kmʾ drʿwʾ qdmk ʿbdtʾ*). It therefore looks forward to what will happen *after* Jonah is thrown overboard; Levine 1978: 68–69. The Arabic adopts an imperfect that is timeless: "You are doing what you are wishing" (*taṣnaʿu mâ tašâʾu*); Wright 1857: 110.

It is not necessary to be so circumspect, however. To begin with, the verb *ḥāpēṣ* is realistic to the circumstances in which the sailors uttered it. Trying to survive a merciless storm, the men cannot but think God vindictive for placing so many in danger because of the error of so few. At this stage, too, they cannot be certain that God will be satisfied with the punishment of one man. Would they not be blamed once Jonah sinks into the waves? As they stand ready to bring death to Jonah, therefore, the sailors want God to know that just as he was responsible for singling out Jonah through lot casting, he is likewise liable for what is about to happen.

There is another reason why *ḥāpēṣ* should not be weakened by translation, and I introduce it by quoting two other prayers from Scripture:

Why would foreigners say, "Where then is their god?," when our God is in heaven, *having done what he wished.* Their own idols, however, are of silver and gold, the work of human beings. They have a mouth, yet cannot speak; eyes, yet cannot see; ears, yet cannot hear; a nose, yet cannot smell; hands, yet cannot feel; legs, yet cannot move. With their throats, they cannot make a sound.

May their makers become just as they are; so too, those who trust them. (Ps 115:2–8)

I myself know how great is the Lord; how much greater is our lord than all other deities. *What the Lord has wished, he has done,* in heaven as in earth, on the seas as in the nethermost depths. Raising mists from the earth's extremities, He makes lightnings for the rain. He releases the winds from his stockpiles. (Ps 135:5–7)

We observe how these two prayers in Psalms share themes encountered in Jonah.[10] In all three occasions, the speaker praises God for his dominion over nature and his superiority over other deities. "God is doing what he wished" is a notion that functions similarly even when the three contexts differ. The verbs themselves are juxtaposed and are always couched in the perfect; yet on all of the occasions *k(l-)ʾšr ḥpṣ(t) ʿśh/ʿśyt* hardly restricts God's action to a single time frame, whether past or future: God has been doing whatever he wished in the past and will continue to do as he pleases in the future. The expression, therefore, looks very much as if it could be used at any time that a Hebrew wanted to compare God's limitless freedom of action to the pagan gods' more restricted movements.

This observation has interesting consequences for the assessment of the sailors' prayer in Jonah. It allows us, first, to sidestep the issue of vindictiveness, for what God is fulfilling need not be confined to the terrible events on Jonah's ship. Furthermore, we appreciate the cleverness of the storyteller in alloting so Hebraic an expression to the sailors, just as they are to witness the most stunning of God's miracles over the elements. The phrase thus becomes a perfect vehicle by which to prepare the audience for the "conversion" that is soon to take place. Finally, and perhaps most importantly, as we once more review its vocabulary and idioms, we come to recognize that the sailors' perfectly couched prayer is almost a miniature *cento;* that is, it is a composition that draws together, if not always known biblical passages, at least perfectly recognizable Hebraic sentiments. As such, therefore, it prepares us to confront and understand the touching prayer that Jonah will soon utter from the fish's belly.

1:15. *wayyiśśeʾû ʾet-yônâ wayyeṭiluhû ʾel-hayyām wayyaʿamōd hayyām mizzaʿpô.* Finally, coming to terms with what they must do, the sailors fling Jonah into the sea. The vocabulary for their action follows very closely the word in Jonah's instruction (v 12). More importantly, it closes a scene that opened long ago, when God hurled mighty winds upon the sea (see NOTES at 1:4). Because of the duplication of idiomatic language in both passages, we are encouraged to imagine that the sailors' tribulations with the stormy sea stop the instant Jonah touches the waters.

The versions allow themselves minor and inconsequential freedom in rendering the preposition in *ʾel-hayyām* either as "in" or "to(ward)"; Trible 1963: 30. It is interesting to note here that the late Hellenistic homily of (Pseudo)-Philo has the prophet throwing himself into the waters, Duval 1973: 79.

The verb *ʿāmad* of v 15 can refer to "(physically) standing up"—said mostly

[10] In Ps 135:7 one may read *b(ā)rāqîyaʿ*, which would nicely balance *miqṣê hāʾāreṣ* and would allow us to render, "He raises vapors from the earth's extremities, turning them into rain in heaven." As a meteorological explanation for the source of rain, however, this may be too advanced a concept; Stadelmann 1970: 120–26.

of human beings—or merely to the act of "being in a position" to do something. In Gen 29:35 and 30:9, the verb, used in the latter sense, is construed with the preposition *min* to tell us that the matriarch Leah "*stopped from* bearing," an event obviously unwilled on her part.[11] A similar usage occurs in our passage. What does happen upon the waves now is described differently here than the way Jonah had foretold it, and the difference in the choice of vocabulary is instructive. In v 11 the seamen imagine it to be the sea that is endangering them as they seek to know how "the sea will calm its raging against us" (*weyištōq hayyām mēʿālênû*). Responding in v 12, Jonah is careful to soothe their feelings by borrowing their language. In v 15, however, the idiom reflects an involuntary and unwilled action. The sea is still personified; it is even majestic, to judge from its control of *zaʿap*, a noun that elsewhere in Hebrew denotes emotions attributed to kings and to God. Its movements, however, are now restricted, thus assuring Jonah's audience that it is God, not the sea, who controls the waves. As their reactions will soon testify, the sailors too are about to draw the same conclusion.

1:16. *wayyîreʾû hāʾanāšîm yirʾâ gedôlâ ʾet-YHWH wayyizbeḥû-zebaḥ laYHWH wayyidderû nedārîm.* The verse tells of three reactions on board ship, as the sailors witness a stunning reversal of fate. A potentially murderous act gives the sailors unpredicted calm and peace. The point in this rapidly unfolding sequence of events at which the sailors come to believe in Jonah's God cannot be recovered; but because Hebrew prose style allows nonsequential episodes to occur simultaneously, we could conjure a scene in which this reversal occurs just as the seafarers watch Jonah disappear into the fish's gullet.[12]

In v 16, the verb *yārēʾ* is unique here in having two direct objects: *ʾet-YHWH,* along with the cognate accusative, "a great fear." Because there is a tendency on the part of Hebrew to place cognate accusatives as close as possible to the verb of similar root, *ʾet-YHWH* is left dangling at the end of the clause. The versions found this phrase awkward and offered minor stylistic changes, mostly turning the plural nouns into singulars (Trible 1963: 30–31). The Targum simply turns *ʾet-YHWH* into an indirect object, *qdm YY,* "The men feared greatly before the Lord"; Levine 1978: 69–70. Syriac and Arabic seem to follow

[11] The idiom differs radically when *ʿāmad* is construed with the prepositional expressions *mēʿal* or *minneged.*

[12] Curiously enough, many medieval Jonah illustrations show the sailors lowering the prophet directly into the open mouth of the fish; Steffen 1982: 49, 64. There is a talmudic legend preserved in tractate *berakhot* (9.1) that is obviously dependent on Jonah. It tells of a little Jewish boy whose prayers saved a ship caught in a tempest. The gentile voyagers, who vainly appealed to their gods, end up by recognizing God's superiority without, however, committing themselves or their property to the worship of the Hebrew god.

suit; Wright 1857: 110–11. The LXX and the Vulgate are more adventurous: they make the phrase dative, suggesting "The men feared the Lord very greatly." A very few modern commentators suggest simply to delete *ʾet-YHWH;* see Bewer 1912: 40. This deletion, however, is gratuitous and betrays a lack of appreciation of the narrator's art. As has often been noted (for example, by Magonet 1983: 92), the narrator visually displays the rising fear aboard ship by placing *ʾet-YHWH* at the end of the clause:

v 5: *wayyîreʾû hammallāḥîm*
v 10: *wayyîreʾû hāʾanāšîm yirʾâ gedôlâ*
v 16: *wayyîreʾû hāʾanāšîm yirʾâ gedôlâ ʾet-YHWH*

But there is yet another point to be made. We recall that when Jonah confesses his error to the horrified sailors, he tells them that "the Lord, god of Heaven, is whom I worship" (v 9), *weʾet-YHWH ʾelōhê haššāmayim ʾanî yārēʾ.* In annotating that statement above, I pointed out that locating *ʾet-YHWH* at the *head* of the clause gives God's name special attention. Despite this rhetorical flourish, the sailors did not seem totally convinced then by Jonah's words. Now, however, an eerily instantaneous calm follows Jonah's seaward plunge. By shaping the clause this time to *end* in *ʾet-YHWH,* the narrator is finally granting the sailors their own recognition of God's greatness.

The sailors now understand everything about God and divine power. They demonstrate this recognition by two activities, a sacrifice and a vow.[13] The first of these measures troubled ancient exegetes, who were aware that, except in a couple of instances in which it is read metaphorically or ironically (BDB 257 [III]), the *G* of the verb *zābaḥ* always refers to the slaughter of animals. Where did the sailors get the victims, especially after they had denuded the ship to keep it afloat? Moreover, could sailors so recently "converted" to the true God risk losing it all by offering sacrifices outside of the Jerusalem Temple? Jerome resolves such difficulties with the comment (Antin 1956: 75–76),

> They offered animal sacrifices that, certainly to take matters literally, they could not do in mid-waters; but it is that the sacrifice to God is a humble spirit. Elsewhere, it is said "Offer God a thanksgiving sacrifice, pay your vows to the Most High [Ps 50:14]." Again, "We shall repay our vows that we have promised [Hos 14:3]."[14] This is how, at sea, they

[13] Josephus thought it best to transfer the sacrifice and vow scene to before the lot casting. It is not clear to me why he did so. It is a fact that he was very troubled by the whole story of Jonah—and especially by Jonah's survival in the fish's belly—and that he omits any information on the sailors once they fling Jonah into the sea. He may not have wanted to force upon his pagan audience a much too obvious conversion episode.

[14] The Hosea passage is very difficult. I quote here Jerome's rendering.

slaughter animals and they spontaneously offer thereby others, vowing never to distance themselves from him whom they have begun to worship.

Some of the versions reconciled the concerns mentioned previously by regarding the "sacrifice" and the "vow" clauses as referring to simultaneous and incremental acts. In accordance with rhetorical tenets available to Hebrew (*hysteron proteron;* see Bühlmann 1973: 46–47), the second clause can control the first, resulting in something like "they vowed to sacrifice to the Lord." The Targum found a way to retain such an understanding by inserting a verb and a preposition into the second clause, thus expanding into "They *promised* to present sacrifices *before* the Lord" (*w'mrw ldbḥ' dbḥ-qdm YY*). By appending *wndrw ndryn,* "and they made vows," however, the Targum remained true to the Hebrew original, but at the cost of becoming redundant.

Admirable though they are, these resolutions need not be supported. To begin with, testimony from ancient sea narratives makes it clear that sacrifice could indeed take place aboard ship; *during* sea voyages, and not just before and after. I quote from Rougé's easily accessible volume on ancient seafaring (1981: 199–200):

> Routine ceremonies [for sea voyages] were of two kinds, those for departures and those for arrivals. When a departure was to be made, those who were about to sail would first make a pilgrimage to a nearby temple to obtain divine protection. Then, once on board ship, there would be a ceremony, not in port when the ship weighed anchor, but rather when the open sea was reached. The ceremony consisted of a sacrifice and prayers to the ship's god and to the divinities of the sea. Likewise, when a ship was about to put into port, before it actually entered the port, there was another ceremony, this time one of thanksgiving. . . . During the course of the sailing other sacrifices took place whenever an especially famous sanctuary was passed, or in the face of danger serious enough to require recourse to the gods. This is why certain figurative representations of ships show an altar located at the stern, an altar that must have been portable.[15]

Were animals carried on board ships, as cargo or as food resource? While some of the more sumptuous ships of the Hellenistic period had fully equipped stables on board (Casson 1971: 197), we cannot easily know whether flock

[15] More detailed information and a copious bibliography can be had from Casson 1971: 181–82. Levine 1978: 70 n. 1 refers to Judaica bibliography on this topic.

animals were loaded on smaller ships.[16] We have tales, however, that suggest that animals could indeed be taken on board (Patai 1941: 24, quoting *Ecclesiastes rabbah* 11.1).

This last observation does not, of course, imply that the sailors sharpened their knives as soon as Jonah disappeared from their view. It does suggest, however, that the narrator, who doubtless knew of legal provisions for the acceptance of offerings from a non-Hebrew (Lev 22:25), was giving the sailors instant opportunity to demonstrate their veneration. Had not King Solomon himself offered a prayer at the inauguration of the Temple that was concerned precisely with this topic (1 Kgs 8:41–43)? Had not the prophet Isaiah echoed the same sentiment about Israel's former taskmasters (Isa 19:19–22)? And are these predictions not finding close fulfillment aboard a small Mediterranean ship?[17]

There is yet another reason to regard the "sacrifice" and "vow" clauses as successive rather than linked as one act: in Hebrew Scripture, *zābaḥ, nādar* and their congeners are sometimes bound sequentially; see, conveniently, Keller, in *THAT* 2.41. In view of our context, the Isaiah prophecy quoted above as an epigram is particularly relevant, "[Egyptians] will acknowledge and offer the Lord animal and grain sacrifice; they also will make vows to the Lord and fulfill them" (Isa 19:21).

Vows are normally entered when facing a danger or when making a request from God. They may consist of a promise to perform a specifically stated deed in the future (sacrifice or the distribution of goods), or they may involve placing a limitation on one's projected actions. With the calming of the seas, the sailors are obviously entering into a pledge not under duress but more in thanksgiving. We have one other biblical narrative that suggests that a vow is occasionally taken for just such a purpose, and it involves Samuel's father (1 Sam 1:21–22): "When the man Elkana and his whole household went up to offer God his annual sacrifice and [to fulfill] his vow, Hannah did not join them." Some psalm passages (65:2; 116:14–18) can likewise be interpreted as evidence for vows freely entered by those feeling blessed by God. Later I shall inspect the pairing of these terms in Jon 2:10.

As to how the sailors chose to fulfill their vows, the rabbis were sure that it included circumcision; for how else, they speculated, could the sailors enter the covenant (Levine 1978: 70 n. 5; Duval 1973: 102)? So dramatic a display of gratitude is not necessary, however. We know that in the Hellenistic period, sailors could offer the god who rescued them votive testimonials of their good fortune.[18]

[16] Underwater archaeology, which has revolutionized our knowledge of ancient seafaring (Bass 1972), cannot be relied on to give us evidence on the topic.
[17] See the quotations offered as epigraph to this section.
[18] They could also present models of ships in recognition of divine protection during a voyage, which explains why we find numerous models of ships even inland; Rougé 1981: 199, 213 n. 5. See also the classical dictionaries under *euploia*.

COMMENTS

The mariners hear Jonah's admission of culpability and listen to his exhortation on what they must do to still the raging seas. Notwithstanding the precarious situation, Midrash Yona found it an occasion for humorously describing how the sailors tested Jonah's veracity (quoted from Levine 1978: 68–69):

> They took him and placed him into the sea up to his knees, and the storm abated. They lifted him back on board, and the sea became agitated against them. They placed him back up to his neck, and the sea-storm abated. Once again they lifted him back among them, and the sea again agitated against them. Finally they cast him in entirely, and immediately the sea-storm abated.

Whatever scene we recreate in our minds, the mariners must no doubt have had much on which to ponder. While certainly relieved when Jonah accepts full responsibility for his act, thus absolving them from any future blame, yet they must have harbored grave doubts about the counsel they were receiving; for it came from the very person who did not volunteer information, but confessed his guilt only when singled out by the lots! The mariners had other worries: could Jonah's god, who seemed willing to endanger a whole ship because of a single sinner, be satisfied with the sacrifice of just one person? What if Jonah's advice were ill informed? What if throwing him into the sea merely prompted that god to reckon yet another crime against them?

In the face of all of this uncertainty, the sailors chose to ignore Jonah's recommendation and tried to find another resolution to their plight. They could, of course, resolve their doubts through further lot casting and omen taking. But because of their dire condition and the lack of time in which to analyze their options calmly, this choice could not be pursued.

The sailors hit upon another stratagem by which to save their skin. They chose to row ashore. In steering the whole ship toward "dry land," they hoped to drop Jonah off at the closest shore. This, instead of veering the vessel into a safe harbor, is what *lehāšîb ʾel-hayyabbāšâ* suggests. They failed to achieve their purpose, as could be expected, for there is no alternative to accepting God's instruction even when it seems unreasonable.

Now if we believe that the author of Jonah was totally ignorant of proper sailing procedures, we could agree with the usual interpretation given this act: by trying to row ashore, the sailors were merely demonstrating their humanity beyond normal expectations. Jerome, for example, has this to say on the situation: "They refused to spill blood, choosing rather to die than to lose. What a change! . . . They are ordered to kill, the sea is in turmoil, the storm is overwhelming, and here they are forgetting their own danger and only think of saving another."[19]

But, as centuries of nautical common sense taught, steering a ship to shore when in the midst of a storm is a foolish, even suicidal enterprise! To the contrary, a ship must at all costs not be driven to the coastline where it will surely wreck.[20] It could be, of course, that the difficult circumstances led the sailors to lose their cunning, skill, and knowledge (see Ps 107:27, quoted above). The sailors, however, could have been reasoning that if they steered ashore in the midst of a storm, it should prove them no longer willing to shelter God's errant prophet. Surely this powerful deity would not allow them harm as they rowed ashore! With faith in divine mercy and justice, the sailors were betting their lives on the success of this measure.

It was well for them that God frustrated their plan, for had the sailors succeeded in taking Jonah ashore, they no doubt would have expressed amazement and shouted their gratitude. The story of yet another miraculous deliverance by yet one more local god would have begun to circulate as soon as the sailors, minus Jonah, reached Tarshish.

But the contest aboard ship was no longer just between Jonah and his God. The sailors were discovering the hard way that the events aboard ship were by no means a drama about wayward individuals and divine vengeance; nor were they about testing human compassion under impossible circumstances. Rather, they were about learning a lesson wherever and whenever a prophet of God appeared—willingly or otherwise. The lesson itself is one that Israel has been taught repeatedly, but one that Israel must be made to recall throughout its history: that the God who apportions death can also grant life and that unconditional submission to divine will can, in fact, turn fate around. When learned under stressful conditions, such difficult lessons are especially prone to long-lasting retention.

[19] Jerome (Antin 1956: 73). Similar sentiments are expressed by most commentators. As one example, I quote Greenberg's particularly felicitous rendering (1983: 16): "Their prayer climaxes their service to the story as a spiritually sensitive foil to the unresponsive, finally lethargic, prophet. While he slept in the teeth of the storm, they prayed each to his God; while he refused to warn Nineveh away from disaster, these heathen sailors risked their lives to save his; whereas he was in rebellion against his God, they acknowledged his sovereignty in their prayer to him." Medieval Jewish commentators saw another angle to the sailors' efforts: they wanted to make sure that Jonah fulfilled his duty to go to Nineveh; Ben-Menahem 1973: 7.

[20] This procedure is commonly advised in ancient manuals on sea travels. A most delightful narrative, which brings this point out well, is available in Bishop Synesius's letter to his brother (404 C.E.), in which a ship with a Jewish captain and crew unaccountably veers off into open sea, to the distress of the voyagers. It later ensues that the shrewd captain had predicted the arrival of a storm and decided to avoid the danger of wrecking on reefs. See Fitzgerald 1926: 80–91 (letter no. 4); for treatment, see Vogt 1970.

V. In the Fish's Belly (Jonah 2:1–3a)

◆

A cream of phosphorescent light
Floats on the wash that to and fro
Slides round his feet—enough to show
Many a pendulous stalactite
Of naked mucus, whorls and wreaths
And huge festoons of mottled tripes
And smaller palpitating pipes
Through which a yeasty liquor seethes

Seated upon the convex mounds
Of one vast kidney, Jonah prays
And sings his canticles and hymns,
Making the hollow vault resound
God's goodness and mysterious ways,
Till the great fish spouts music as he swims.[1]

They say Jonah was swallowed by a whale
But I say there is no truth to that tale
I know Jonah
Was swallowed by a song.[2]

[1] Aldous Huxley, "Jonah," quoted from Grigson's anthology (1959). Mitchell's brief parable on Jonah (1989) seems to me strongly influenced by this poem.
[2] Paul Simon, "Jonah," from the album *One Trick Pony,* Warner Bros. LP record, HS 3472. Copyright © 1978 by Paul Simon. Used by permission of the publisher.

V. IN THE FISH'S BELLY (2:1–3a)

2 [1]The Lord directed a large fish to swallow Jonah. Jonah remained in the
belly of the fish three days and three nights. [2]Praying to the Lord his god from
the fish's belly, [3]Jonah said. . . .

THE USE OF ANIMALS IN BIBLICAL NARRATIVES: INTRODUCTORY REMARKS

Animals are commonly mentioned in the Bible, in realistic as well as in imaginative contexts. Domestic animals are mentioned for their value as property and for their use in travel. In establishing regulations about animals available for sacrifice and human consumption, the Laws painstakingly distinguish between permissible and forbidden animals. The Pentateuch also codifies measures to protect animals from human abuse.

Poetry and proverbs often allude to the attributes and characteristics of particular animals symbolically, as when lions are cited to convey strength and nobility or when ants are mentioned to denote steady hard work. Such allusions give insight into the ways that ancient Hebrews reacted to the fauna familiar to them.[3] Scripture also turns to animals in constructing fables (for example, Ezek 17:3–10) and parables (for example, 2 Sam 12:1–4). It invents (or appropriates from neighboring cultures) a whole panoply of marvelous creatures when illustrating God's power and omniscience: for example, Leviathan, Behemoth, Tannin, Rahab, Tehom.

Beyond such usage, animals are featured in narratives, but they fulfill differing purposes, enumerated below.

(1) *Animals as characters in a scene.* Beyond its common manifestation in fables and proverbs, this trait is also known to Near Eastern literature: for example, the eagle in the Babylonian Etana fantasy, the snake in the Egyptian Shipwrecked Sailor parable, the cow in the Hittite Sun God and the Cow myth.[4] There is only one certain example of an animal with a major role in biblical narratives. The snake in the famous seduction episode of Genesis 3 is given such a subtly shaded and multisided role that it could be played diabolic (as is commonly done in Christian theology) or promethean (as is done in Milton's *Paradise Lost*). For more on this topic, see J. M. Sasson 1985a and 1985b.

[3] A convenient compilation of symbolic references to animals is found in the *Universal Jewish Encyclopedia* (1939), 1.321–26.

[4] For details and bibliography on the Near Eastern examples cited, see Irvin 1978.

(2) *Animals as a focusing device.* This too is available to Near Eastern literature, for example, the bee in the Hittite Telepinu myth and Semel, a vulture, in the Ugaritic Aqhat drama. I know of two biblical examples of such a manifestation:

(a) Numbers 22:22–35 tells how the famous talking jenny of Balaam teaches him that seers can be blinder than dumb animals.[5] When the donkey opens its mouth to speak and when Balaam fails to recognize the miraculous element in such a wondrous act, the animal teaches her master another moral: obedience and loyalty are virtues that a prophet of God might well neglect; see further Rouillard 1985: 115–21. As I shall develop it in the INTERPRETATIONS, some of these lessons are also relevant to Jonah.

(b) We are told in Judges 14 that once Samson made up his mind to marry a Philistine woman, he hectored his parents into accompanying him to Timnah for the needed bridal negotiations. On the way there, and presumably when momentarily alone, Samson kills an attacking lion and shoves aside its carcass. Within a year, a swarm of bees fills the carcass with honey, and the circumstance inspires Samson to formulate a pun by which to best his opponents.

The lion episode of Judges 14, however, is not told just to regale us with Samson's strength (this particular lion was not fully grown, *kepîr ʾarāyôt*); in fact, its verses (5–9) disrupt the narrative's flow and inhibit the coordination of movements among Samson and his parents. The incident does, however, give a solution (v 18) for a riddle (v 14) that, as Bauer showed long ago, could originally have depended on a pun no longer recognized between the word for "lion" (*ʾry*) and that for "honey" (*ʾr*); see Porter 1962.[6]

(3) *Animals with cameo appearances.* I mention five biblical episodes that reflect this phenomenon:

(a) Straying donkeys belonging to Kish force his son to seek help from a seer. This is how Saul gets to meet Samuel, who later anoints him as Israel's first king (1 Samuel 9).

[5] Many commentators have compared this episode to the *Iliad* 19.406–22, wherein the steed Xanthe predicts the death of her master Achilles.

[6] The Ugaritic connection between the Arabic and Hebrew words at stake is very flimsy, however. Note how the repeated sounding of the labial *mem* allows the lips to smack as if with pleasure from eating honey. This particular segment concocts a number of allusions to a previous Samson episode. (1) The cub's remains (*mappelâ*, v 8) remind readers of an attribute of God, *YHWH maplīʾ laʿaśôt*, "The Lord, Working Wonders" (13:19). (2) Samson's rending of the lion as a "kid" recalls the sacrifice the parents offered God's messenger. (3) Above all, when Samson's mother eats honey drawn from a corpse, she apparently contravenes, albeit unknowingly, an injunction not to partake of the unclean (13:9ff.), which likely remains in force even beyond Samson's birth. (The same can be said about Samson who, as a lifelong Nazirite, ought to have known better.) These features allow the reader to locate the episode at a critical junction in Samson's fortunes, as he progressively becomes entangled with the Philistines.

(b) First Kings 13 tells the story of the Man of God, his condemnation of Jeroboam's house, his encounter with a deceiving prophet, his unmeditated betrayal of his God's command, and his subsequent death from the attack of a lion. From this point on (vv 23–32), a miracle unfolds as the slaying lion stands guard over the Man of God's corpse, protecting him—and his donkey for that matter—until the prophet gathers his body for burial. (See further the INTERPRETATIONS.)

(c) Explosively making his debut in Scripture, Elijah declares drought on Ahab's land. God orders the prophet toward the Wadi Cherith and commands ravens to supply him with bread and meat (1 Kgs 17:1–6).[7] The miraculous element here is threefold: the ravens must first avoid carrion, which is their normal diet; second, they must surrender their food when it is scarce; third, they must deliver it to a particular human being, who, were it not for their interference, might have turned into excellent carrion. The birds are therefore acting throughout against their instinct.

(d) In a bizarre and obscure episode from the life of the prophet Elisha, she-bears obey his call to maul forty-two children who dared taunt him (2 Kgs 2:23–24).

(e) When Daniel survived the ordeal in a den of lions because of his continued worship of Israel's god, his slanderers and their families were forced into it. The lions "overpowered them, crushing all their bones" (Dan 6:24). That the lions behaved naturally in this last case serves to stress the miraculous in Daniel's delivery, and it is recognized as such by Darius himself (v 28).

Examples 3.a–e include animals not as full-fledged participants in narratives but as devices by which to reveal characteristics of the main actors: because riding donkeys was a sign of kingship (*IDBSup* 73–74), there could be a hidden agenda on the narrator's part in having Saul chase donkeys rather than sheep, goats, or cattle; in 1 Kings 13 and in 2 Kings 2, a lion's protection and a bear's attack are indication of divine care for the dignity of a prophet, even when the prophet does neglect God's command; in 1 Kings 18, God keeps alive his obedient prophet. (On the last two cases, see the INTERPRETATIONS.) These animals are paraded into the tale neither to resolve a particularly difficult sequence (that is, as a *deus ex machina*) nor to bestow their own characteristics upon the protagonists. Rather, such beasts have no will of their own and should simply be considered as useful in linking consecutive episodes.

By contrast, in the story of Jonah, a fish, albeit uncommonly large, breaks out of this pattern to become inextricably linked with the protagonist of the whole tale. This situation is unusual, and we shall have to investigate the details and consequences in the next two sections.

[7] I do not think it valid to revocalize *ʿōrebîm*, "ravens," to obtain either "merchants" or "Arabs," an avenue widely shared in scholarship, for example in *EB* 4.4017.

NOTES

The Qumran scroll of the Twelve Prophets does not recognize any boundary between the sailors' prayers and the arrival of the fish. Only after the fish spews Jonah forth does its scribe leave a vacant space to indicate the beginning of a new episode (Milik 1961: 190). Numbering for chapters is a relatively recent phenomenon, taking place in medieval times. New chapters normally give a story occasion to head in a new or in a radically differing direction. The second chapter of Jonah opens with the fish ingesting Jonah. But other (mostly Protestant) editions of this book attach 2:1 to the previous chapter, numbering it as 1:17. The discrepancy is useful because it invites us to observe how a story develops from subtly differing yet equally exemplary perspectives.

Unlike the episode on board ship (or at Nineveh, for that matter), Jonah's adventure in the fish's belly is not dependent on a developing chronology. We are not told exactly when after entering the fish's jaws Jonah settled down to compose his prayer, how long it took him to finish it, or when he began to intone it. We simply learn that his experience lasted three full days.

The editions that reckon this verse as 1:17 exploit the situation well. Because of its location at the close of chapter 1, the verse that tells of the fish's arrival harks back to the activities on board ship and freezes into focus two simultaneous events: the dumping of Jonah overboard and his disappearance into the fish's belly. What is sandwiched comes into very sharp focus: v 16, with its comments on the sailor's acceptance of the one true God.

When the Hebrew edition places the fish's appearance and the psalm within the same chapter, it gives the two segments unity, integrity, and coherence. Additionally, it encourages readers to treat the whole as different (perhaps even as separate) from the surrounding episodes: aboard ship, at Nineveh, and in a tent.

2:1. *wayyeman YHWH dāg gādôl liblōaʿ ʾet-yônâ way(ye)hî yônâ bimʿê haddāg šelōšâ yāmîm ûšlōšâ lêlôt.* The verb at stake in the opening phrase of chapter 2 is *mānâ,* which in the *G* covers a broad spectrum of meanings, "to count, enumerate, assign, reckon." On its occurrence in Jonah as evidence for the book's composition date, see Landes 1982: 149*–50*. In this verse, the verb is conjugated as a *D* stem (*piʿel*) imperfect with a *waw*-consecutive, with YHWH as subject and a "big fish" as object. In chapter 4, this verbal form will make three more appearances. Although I await these separate occasions to give a fuller description or a more refined calibration for each, I can make three observations now:

1. At each of *wayyeman*'s appearances, there is a differing invocation of God's name:
   a. at 2:1, with *YHWH* as subject;
   b. at 4:6, with *YHWH-ʾelōhîm* as subject;
   c. at 4:7, with *hāʾelōhîm* as subject;
   d. at 4:8, with *ʾelōhîm* as subject.
2. At each of *wayyeman*'s appearances, the object of God's control belongs to a different order in nature:
   a. at 2:1, with the *dāg*, a fish, as object;
   b. at 4:6, with the *qîqāyôn*, a plant, as object;
   c. at 4:7, with the *tôlaʿat*, an insect('s larva), as object;
   d. at 4:8, with the *rûaḥ qādîm ḥarîšît*, an eastern scorching wind, as object.
3. At each of *wayyeman*'s appearances, a play on words follows:
   a. at 2:1, with consonant reversal, *DG GD(wl)*;
   b. at 4:6, with *ṢL . . . lhṢL* (perhaps also *wyʿL mʿL*);
   c. at 4:7, with *tWLʿT bʿLT;*
   d. at 4:8, with *RWḤ . . . ḤRšt.*

The versions offer two widely diverging renderings: LXX and Old Latin "to command"; Vulgate, Arabic, Syriac, and Targum "to prepare" (see Trible 1963: 31). This difference is informed by separate notions on when the fish reached Jonah's boat: either arriving there as Jonah plunges into the foaming waters, or lying in wait for that occasion. Scholars are still split on this issue, with those favoring the latter position either resorting to pluperfect construction ("Meanwhile, Yahweh had appointed a great fish"—Wolff 1986: 125; see Levine 1978: 72 n. 6) or expanding on the language ("But the Lord ordained that a great fish should swallow Jonah"—NEB). My own translation ("The Lord directed a large fish to swallow Jonah") means to avoid the issue, at least because I do not deem the prehistory of Jonah's fish as relevant to the narrative. I want it rather to emphasize the fortuitous—yet God-directed—nature of the event, just as major moments in the previous narrative have also depended on seemingly chance occurrences and split-time arrivals: the appearance of a Tarshish-bound ship just as Jonah gets to Jaffa; the sudden outbreak of the huge storm, and its sudden end as well.

The verbal form at stake in the phrases listed above, the *D* (*piʿel*) of *mānâ*, commonly appears in Scripture. In Daniel 1 it occurs twice (vv 5, 10), referring to Nebuchadnezzar favoring Jewish youths by *allotting* them provisions; and once (v 11), alluding to a Babylonian officer *entrusting* the same men to a guard. In Job 7:3 the verbal form is parallel to the *Hp* (*hophʿal*) of *nāḥal,* with both segments indefinite in their subject, "I am dealt fruitless months/I am *allotted* anxious nights." Aside from the Jonah references, however, only in Ps 21:8 is God also the subject, with "constant mercy" as object; but the passage is difficult and the verbal form there is often removed to achieve a smoother rendering.[8]

What these attestations suggest is that *minnâ* is an act that generally needs a medium through which to be fulfilled. Applying this insight to Jonah 2:1, we can say that God is not so much keen to appoint a "big fish" (nor, for that matter, in bringing forth plants, worms, or hot winds) than to set the most appropriate conditions for teaching Jonah the desired lessons. This philological point, therefore, complements the conclusion of the survey given above that in such narratives animals are introduced that can most economically achieve a desired end. The specific genus of the animal is not at issue nor, as held in a venerable Jewish homiletic tradition, is its primordial nature (Levine 1978: 71). This point is further reinforced by the next comment.

dāg gādôl. Some of the versions try to be more precise on the identity of this "large fish." The LXX uses *to kētos,* and it is recalled as such in Matt 12:40, in Josephus, and in the Arabic version's *ḥût.* In Greek literature, however, the *kētos* is an aquatic animal that, as we follow its attestations chronogically, exhibits a progressively larger size, changing from Homer's "seal" to Pliny's "whale." It is a fact, moreover, that Scripture has preserved no specific names for the many types of salt- or sweet-water fish known to the eastern Mediterranean.[9] This does not mean, of course, that the ancient Hebrews were not able to distinguish among the area's wide varieties of fish; it simply suggests that no biblical context seems to require a specific vocabulary for fish.[10] This observation holds true even in the listing of animals deemed suitable for sacrifice or consumption; Scripture merely distinguishes between fish with scales and gills (acceptable) or those without (unacceptable), making no judgment on any aquatic animal with no vertebrae (Lev 11:9; Deut 14:9).[11]

The text merely states that the fish was "large." We have seen that the adjective *gādôl* permits a play on the consonants it shares with *dāg* (see above); but it also maintains an interest in aggrandizing objects (Nineveh and its evil,

[8] The form possibly occurs also in Ps 68:24. That the *D* of *mānâ* is a conjugation that belongs to the "later" stages of Hebrew is a notion that has been adequately refuted by R. D. Wilson 1918b.

[9] A handy overview, albeit slightly out of date, on fish and fishery in the Hebrew Bible is in *EB* 2.1525–32.

[10] Wolff's opinion (1986: 132) that "landlubbers like the Israelites were unable to define the beast any more closely" is ludicrous.

[11] Moreover, any fish with lungs—which includes sea mammals—is apparently treated as a "creeping thing" and is therefore prohibited. The *Enc Jud* 6.35–36 provides a handy discussion of these issues as developed in the Bible and in the Talmud.

the wind, the storm, the sailors' fear). For those who read Jonah on its most realistic level, the adjective "great" no doubt makes Jonah's sojourn within the fish more plausible. It has to be said, however, that the miraculous in Jonah's experience is also basic to the story (see NOTES to chapter 4), and a guppy would have perfectly suited (if not sharpened) this element. In fact, in another Jewish tale that features a "big fish" (and that, interestingly enough, has Nineveh among its settings), the size of the fish turns out not to be all that significant a feature. When a "huge fish . . . leaped out of the water and tried to swallow [Tobias's] foot," only its internal organs proved useful: to ward off the attacks of evil demons and to cure blindness (Tob 6:2).

In view of the type of literature to which Tobit belongs, it would not be necessary to appeal to medical evidence in order to confirm the suitability of fish organs for curing ills. Similarly, it would not be very profitable to comb medical opinions on how reasonable, or how many times duplicated, is Jonah's survival within the fish. In the rabbinic period, when stories of remarkable sea survivals were not unknown, Jonah's lodging in the fish's belly was deemed a factual, but also miraculous, event and hence not usefully measured by how close it adheres to reality.[12] Most religious commentators, be they Jewish rabbis or church fathers, searched Scripture for the identity of the animal in question and suggested that it was either Leviathan or another enormous fish that eventually gets swallowed by Leviathan just before the apocalyptic Feast of the Just.[13]

Contemporary Jonah literature, which sometimes collects testimony on men (usually sailors) surviving Jonahlike ordeals, invariably tries to locate an aquatic animal that could swallow human beings whole. A choice is usually made among species of whale or shark (see Keil and Delitzsch 1900: 398 n. 1; *Enc Jud* 11.90). Some scholars give this literature credence, generally in order to defend the authenticity of Jonah's experience (for example, Keil and Delitzsch 1900: 398–99; A. J. Wilson 1927; Aalders 1948; Archer 1964: 302–3 n. 8, who defends his position more vehemently in later editions). Others try to explain it away. An interpretation that resurfaces now and then (traceable to Ibn Ezra) has Jonah dreaming the whole episode while sleeping aboard ship. Another theory rationalizes that a drowning Jonah was once rescued by the crew of a ship called *The*

[12] For rabbinic-period sea tales, see Patai 1941. (Pseudo)-Philo (probably third century C.E.), followed by the ninth-century *Pirke* of Rabbi Eliezer, treats the whole incident as an occasion for God to teach Jonah the mysteries of the oceans; see Duval 1973: 78–80; 100–102. Josephus is obviously uncomfortable with the whole tale, inserting "It is also related" just before he briefly mentions the incident. Josephus makes sure, further, that Jonah prays only after he reaches land! Bickerman (1976: 34 n. 1) says that Luther was probably the first Christian to read Jonah as a fable.

[13] Ibn Gabirol connected Jonah's fish with the zodiac's pisces; Loewe 1982: 152–53. In a medieval Greek translation of Jonah preserved in Hebrew characters, the term for the fish is *psari*; Lange 1982: 70 n. 15.

Big Fish. Subsequently, he spent three nights in a tavern called "At the Sign of the Whale." Eventually these details got totally misconstrued by repeated storytelling until they were preserved in the version known to us (see Bickerman 1976: 34–35). Many more scholars do not read the incident historically at all, and they occasionally use a sarcastic tone (for example, Bewer 1912:5) to debunk the elaborate explanations offered by those who do.

It is not necessary to enter the dispute here. Suffice it to say that stories of wondrous escapes from the giant gulps of a fish have survived into our own days, and they are not necessarily promulgated or believed merely to sustain fundamentalist convictions.[14] Such stories simply make the news in the same way as do reports of travel in an alien flying saucer, and they ask us to suspend disbelief in order to stretch our sense of wonder and amazement. If the incident is treated as a problem in folklore research, however, we do well to recognize that the incident in Jonah clusters three motifs, each of which can be found in other tales. Only in the Bible, however, are they reported in the following sequence:[15] (1) The swallowing of individuals (almost always male) by an aquatic animal *in order to save them from drowning;* (2) the survival of individuals in the fish's belly; and (3) the disgorging of *living* individuals by a fish.

liblōaʿ ʾet-yônâ. It is not necessary for us to follow A. B. Ehrlich (1912: 266) in emending the construct infinitive (here as well as in 4:7) in order to obtain conversive imperfect forms (as in 4:6). Curiously enough, there are rare scriptural examples in which the verb *bālaʿ*, "to swallow, gulp down," speaks of human or animal ingestion of food.[16] Possibly because of its onomatopoeic potential, however, this verb allows either for the construction of sensually evocative metaphors or for the creation of imaginative scenes—for example, at Gen 41:7, 24, where lean ears of grain consume others that are swollen; or at Ex 6:12, where Aaron's rod swallows those of others. In the *G* (*qal*), *bālaʿ* can have "greed," "violence," or "calamity" as subjects (BDB 118 [2]). Worth citing here because of the vocabulary and features it shares with Jonah is Job 20:15. Zophar suggests that the wicked's prosperity is short-lived, *ḥayil bālaʿ wayyeqiʾennû mibbiṭnô yōrišennû ʾēl,* "The riches he swallows he vomits; God empties it out of his stomach" (NJPS). But *bālaʿ* does not always depend on abstract terminology with which to construct metaphors; it can also use concrete vocabulary. Thus in Jer 51:34 we have, "Nebuchadnezzar king of Babylon devoured me and humili-

[14] I limit myself to an example published while I worked on this commentary. A banner headline in the *Weekly World News* of June 16, 1987, reports: "Shark swallows fisherman —then spits him out alive!" In this instance the lucky escapee, a Mikado Nakamura, even gives an interview from his hospital bed in Kanazawa, Japan.

[15] Folktales with similar motifs are commonly cited in Jonah literature; but the largest collection of variants is in Ben-Yosef 1980; see also Komlós 1950, Gaster 1969: 653; and Radermacher 1906.

[16] The same observations apply to the verb *qîʾ* in most of its occurrences.

ated me, setting me aside, an empty dish; Like a sea monster (*tannîn*) he gulped me down, filled his stomach (*kerēšô*) with my flesh as dainty, then spewed me forth."[17] These examples permit us to observe that when Jonah turns to a vocabulary that includes verbs such as *bālaʿ*, "to swallow," and *qîʾ*, "to vomit," the narrative is striving for an imaginative, perhaps even metaphoric, setting. Moreover, the poetic and lyrical effects these verbs achieve in other scriptural passages also encourage readers to recognize that the same hand has worked both the poetry of Jonah 2 and its sandwiching narrative verses.

way(ye)hî yônâ bimʿê haddāg. This phrase follows a strong pausal accent, an *atnaḥ*, that effectively arrests the movement of the narrative. The arrest is momentary, of course, long enough for the fish's maw to snap shut, for its throat to carry its victim down to a cavernous haunt. Although other writers have written novels around such split-second events (for example, William Golding's *Pincher Martin*), our narrator leaves all reconstructions to our imagination. When he brings Jonah into focus once more, he simply states that Jonah "remained in [*way(ye)hî be-*] the fish's belly for three days and three nights."

Where Jonah settled is said to be in the fish's *mēʿîm*, a term that does not refer to any specific bodily organ or anatomical feature. Hebrew employs this word loosely, referring to any internal (once: external) organ, be it of digestion or procreation; it is only our imagination (to judge from numerous cartoons, also our sense of humor) that finds for Jonah a specific niche within the fish. All that we can be certain about is that the narrator means for Jonah to sink one level deeper than he previously had: after going down to Jaffa, away from God, Jonah had descended to the ship, slumped down in its bowels, and dropped into the churning waters. For the narrator, even when Jonah lodges in the fish's innards he has yet to complete his plunge; for, as we shall see, there is yet one more downward rung for Jonah to negotiate—albeit only in his conscience.

šelōšâ yāmîm ûšlōšâ lêlôt. When a cardinal number between three and ten modifies an indefinite noun, it precedes that noun, which is given in the plural but differs from it in gender. At 3:3, we have an alternative construction, which is likewise perfectly proper grammatically and in fact much more common to Hebrew. There, the cardinal number is given in the construct form, *šelōšet yāmîm.* Most of the versions follow the Hebrew phrase in 2:1 slavishly, except for the Old Latin and for some Coptic translations, which excise "three days," presumably because there could only be nights in the stomach of a fish; Wolff 1986: 126. The LXX and the Old Latin invoke the same number of days when

[17] Throughout this Jeremiah quotation, the *ketiv* has "us" while the *qere* has "me." Because this passage shares with Jonah references to the verbs for swallowing and regurgitating, some scholars have read Jonah as an allegory. (See further the INTERPRETATIONS segment.) I shall have more to say about Ps 69:16, which tells of the progressively dire situation of a God-forsaken poet: "May streaming waters not overwhelm me; may the deep not *swallow* me; may the grave not shut its mouth over me" (NJPS).

Jonah informs Nineveh of its doom (see the COMMENTS at 3:4 regarding "forty days").

Hebrew literature is especially fond of the number three, resorting to it only slightly less than to the number seven.[18] An act is repeated three times to enhance it or to bring it to full effect: Elijah stretches himself three times upon a child to bring him back to life (1 Kgs 17:21); Daniel is said to pray three times a day (Dan 6:11). Noteworthy for the present context are the instances in which "three days" is cited: Joseph jails his brothers for three days (Gen 42:17); Ezra waits three days for a vision finally to come to him (2 Esdr 14:1); Holofernes' troops march three days to cover the distance between Nineveh and Bectileh in Upper Cilicia (Jdt 2:21). We note that in 2 Kgs 20:8 (but not in the parallel passage at Isa 38:22) Hezekiah hopes to heal from festering wounds "by the third day." In the last case, the phrase is equivalent to "a brief period."

In Jonah, however, the significance of the time span "three days (and three nights)" is difficult to ascertain. Hebrew uses such spans not only to measure how long it took for a certain act to come to completion, but also to indicate distances. (In this matter it differs neither from other Semitic cultures nor from ours; "a couple of hours' walk/drive from here" is one way we estimate time as well as distance.) When in 3:4 Jonah goes "one day's journey" in Nineveh, the noun *mahalak* makes it clear how we should assess the word "day." Here, however, the solution is not as explicitly charted.

Landes 1967b (also 1967a: 10–12) has an extensive treatment of the phrase. The only other full citation of it in Scripture occurs at 1 Sam 30:12–15. The passage tells of an Egyptian slave abandoned by his master for "three days and three nights" (*šelōšâ yāmîm ûšlōšâ lêlôt*) when he became sick and could not ride with Amalekite raiders. The datum is given us there not so much to dwell on the slave's famished state (so Landes) as to explain why David was able to overtake the Amalekites: after sacking Ziqlag and presuming themselves beyond catch, they unwisely took time to celebrate. In the Samuel passage, therefore, the phrase is meant to convey a distance of some significance and matches well other citations wherein "three days" yields a similar effect.[19] Nevertheless, because there are many references in which the phrase "three days" is equivalent to a substantial time span (Vaux 1961: 180–83), it would be stretching the intent of the phrase (if not credulity) to conclude that "the fish is assigned [this] time span to return Jonah from Sheol to the dry land" (Landes 1967b: 449). What about the time the fish took to get him there? There are, to be sure, good reasons to cement the vocabulary of the poetic psalm to that of the prose narrative of Jonah, but we can hardly use (as does Landes) 2:1 as commentary to

[18] Consult any good biblical dictionary (BDB) or encyclopedia (*EB, Enc Jud, IDB*) under the entry "Number."

[19] Landes 1967b: 448. Despite his arguments to the contrary, the phrase "three days and three nights" in a Sumerian myth denotes a time span rather than a distance.

2:7; such an approach risks turning the psalm into a travel guide to hell and back![20]

Does the expression "three days and three nights" cover the whole period of Jonah's ordeal? Commentators who think the phrase is an exact stretch of time rather than an approximation generally seek either to have it match the interval between Christ's death and resurrection (so already Jerome, who admits to speculating) or to establish it as a reasonable period in which an individual can survive gastric juices (for example, Ellison 1985: 375).

Is "three days and three nights" a measure of how long it took Jonah to begin praying? Josephus apparently places v 11 before v 2 (editing *mimmeʿê haddāgâ* out), for he puts Jonah on dry land before the latter utters a word. A number of medieval commentators argue that if Jonah had spent three days in prayer within the fish, v 2 should have read *bimmeʿê haddāgâ,* "in the fish's belly," rather than *mimmeʿê haddāgâ.* They therefore read the psalm as a hymn of gratitude and treat the verbs in vv 3b–10 as expressing past events. (See Notes to the next section). Ibn Ezra, a powerful rationalist, nevertheless criticizes this approach. He cites evidence from within the psalm to indicate that Jonah was in desperate condition when he prayed and reminds readers that the "prophetic perfect" often reflects present tense (Magonet 1976: 127 n. 5; Zlotowitz 1980: 106–7).[21] In fact, the text of Jonah does not support this shuffle in chronology, for *meʿê haddāg(â)* of v 1 and its repetition in v 2 obviously act as a device to synchronize Jonah's stay within the fish with his composition of the psalm.

2:2–3a. *wayyitpallēl yônâ ʾel-YHWH ʾelōhāyw mimmeʿê haddāgâ wayyōʾmer. . . .* Hebrew *lehitpallēl ʾel/lipnê* (followed by a divine appellative) is a common idiom for "praying." Although it can refer to petitioning foreign gods (for example, Isa 44:17; 45:20), it is usually reserved for entreaties made to God. If a prayer is immediately quoted (frequently introduced by *lēʾmōr/wayyōʾmar;* less often, as here, by *wayyōʾmer*), it can be couched in poetry (as is the case in Jon 2:3ff.) or in prose (as in Jon 4:2). I should note—albeit without offering a good explanation for the phenomenon—that up to now, Jonah has used two other idioms, *zāʿaq ʾel* (a deity) and *qāraʾ ʾel* (a deity) when alluding to prayers, and that it will soon use additional idioms (*šiwwaʿ*, 2:3; perhaps also *zākar,* 2:8). Outside of Jonah, there are at least a dozen more terms, similarly referring to

[20] Ackerman, who favors a quasi-Jungian understanding for the episode in the fish's belly (1981: 235–36), accepts Landes's analysis but reverses the goal of the journey: Jonah is being carried to death (221 n. 11).

[21] Luther took a mediating position: "[Jonah] did not actually utter these very words with his mouth, and arrange them in this orderly manner, in the belly of the fish; but that he here shows what the state of the mind was, and what thoughts he had when he engaged in this conflict with death" (quoted from Keil and Delitzsch 1900: 399).

worship, for which scholars have tried with uneven success to fix a more precise meaning and usage (see Stähli, in *ThWAT* 2.431 [4.d]; *IDB, EB, Enc Jud,* etc., under "Prayer"). Suffice it to say that resorting to etymology or studying comparative religion to reach such ends often leads to irrelevant, if not preposterous, results. Thus, some argue that the "basic" meaning of the root *pll,* from which *lehitpallēl* is derived, is "to cut the hair or gash the skin" (see *EB* 3.3823–24).

As to why Jonah is said to pray to the Lord, "his god" *ʾelōhāyw* (a circumstance that has elicited some lovely Jewish homilies on Jonah's attachment to God), I need only mention that similar expansions are frequent in Hebrew, especially when major personalities are brought into intimate colloquy with God: Moses, when he tries to placate God (Ex 32:11); a potential king (Deut 17:19); David (1 Sam 30:6; 1 Kgs 5:17; 15:4); Solomon (1 Kgs 11:4); Elisha (2 Kgs 5:11); King Ahaz (2 Kgs 16:2); sinning notables (Lev 4:22; but note its absence from v 27!); a Levite (Deut 18:7); and Israel (Jer 7:28; Micah 5:3); further references may be found in Even-Shoshan 1982: 73.

The noun *dāgâ,* "fish," is a feminine form, thus contrasting in gender with the way the animal is twice mentioned in v 1 and once in v 11. This condition has led to a number of suggestions and explanations. The most radical, if also the simplest, is to remove the fish's second occurrence from the text. This *might* be the solution guiding the anonymous and undatable Hekhalot fragment I will shortly discuss (see COMMENTS to section VI). Another approach to the problem of *dāg/dāgâ* is to use the gender difference as an obvious focusing device. In a recent analysis, Ackerman thinks the change of gender helps to parallel Jonah's experiences on ship and in the fish: "The prophet rejoices in the fish's belly because it provides him with the same false, death-like security he had sought out in the *yarketê hassefînâ. And this is why what should have been Jonah's lament-appeal becomes a song of thanks"* (1981: 235–36; the italics are Ackerman's; see my comments in the INTERPRETATIONS).

A third approach is followed by some medieval exegetes. They simply invent two different vehicles for Jonah's delivery: because the first fish, masculine in gender, affords Jonah much too comfortable a sanctuary, God transfers him to a pregnant female fish, her belly chock full of babies! Bothered by the tight quarters and by the nipping of baby fish, Jonah finally comes to terms with his situation and utters his touching psalm.[22]

More mundane are the solutions based on grammar. While *dāg/dāgâ* does not fit the category of "double gendered" words that Hebrew treats either as masculine or as feminine,[23] it does belong to a small collection of words of

[22] This anecdote is cited by Levine 1978: 71–72 and by Zlotowitz 1980: 108, who offers variations on it. Bewer 1912: 43, unimaginatively terms such stories "grotesque." S. Talmon informs me of an illustration on a manuscript at his disposal wherein a mermaid awaits Jonah's splash into the waters.

[23] Ibn Ezra (*ad loc*) wrongly gives *ṣedeq/ṣedaqâ* as a parallel example.

which the feminine form actually refers to a *group*—in the case of *dāgâ,* to a shoal of fish (as in Gen 1:26, 28; Isa 50:2, Ezek 47:10; see BDB 185). Hebrew also knows of occasions on which the feminine forms allow exactly the opposite pattern from what we have just described: the masculine refers to a group, but the feminine addresses single items.[24] Obviously neither of these grammatical features is at stake in the case of Jonah's *dāg/dāgâ.* Therefore, some scholars suggest that the feminine ending on *dāg* (the consonant *-h* in texts without vowels) could have mistakenly crept into an early copy of Jonah. Such a proposal is unlikely, however, for the feminine form is consistent in both the Hebrew and the earliest Targum manuscripts; Levine 1978: 71–72; Trible 1963: 31–33.

In view of this impasse, I would like cautiously to introduce yet another explanation. In isolated cases, when *number* is not the main point of a biblical passage, Hebrew can use the singular rather than the plural form of a word (for examples, see GKC 395 [§ 123.b]). The same condition occasionally obtains when *gender* is involved; but the examples cited by grammars are of masculine supplanting feminine words (for example, "donkey" is used instead of "jenny"; see GKC 390 [§ 122.f]). I do not think that such blurring of gender is really a grammatical issue; more likely it is a vernacular or a narratological one. A storyteller could simply use either gender for an animal—or both at once—when the sex of the animal was of no importance to the tale. To illustrate the phenomenon, I give translations of two Akkadian letters from Mari of about 1765 B.C.E. These letters apparently treat the same incident; but more importantly they involve lions, animals whose gender cannot be missed because of their starkly differing physiognomies. The writer, Yaqqim-Addu, is a governor of a province under the control of the king of Mari, to whom he writes. He first sends him ARM[T] 2.106 (Jean 1950: 184). Then, realizing that he has written with much more finality and confidence than is warranted, Yaqqim-Addu is forced to follow it with a second letter, ARM[T] 14.1 (Birot 1974: 21).

I have italicized the occurrences of either "lion" or "lioness." The way the second letter switches the animal's gender between masculine and feminine invites obvious comparison with the situation in Jonah.

Previously, I had sent the following message to my lord, saying, "A *lion* was caught in a loft at Bit-Akkaka. My lord should write me whether this *lion* is to remain in the loft until my lord's arrival or whether I should have it conveyed to my lord."

A *lioness* was caught at night in a loft at Bit-Akkaka. The next day, when they notified me, I made my way (there). In order not to allow striking this *lion,* I am remaining in Bit-Akkaka all day. I thought to myself, "I want to have it reach my

[24] Jonah contains an example of this phenomenon, in which the feminine (*ʾonîyâ*) means "one ship" while the masculine (*ʾonî*) has to be translated "a fleet" (1 Kgs 9:26). On all of these points, see GKC 394 [§ 122.s, t].

Now then, since my lord's letter is slow to come to me and the *lion* has been stuck within the loft for five days now—a dog and pig were thrown to him, but he refused to eat —, I thought, "The *lion* might yet become depressed."

Fearing this, I have forced the *lion* into a wooden cage, loaded it on a boat, and had it conveyed to my lord. (ARM 2.106)

lord in full health." So I threw him a [dog and] a pig, and he killed them. I left them (there), but he would not take them for food.

I have myself written to Bida to bring (me) a wooden cage. While they were transferring the cage, on the day following, the *lion* died. I inspected this *lioness:* she was old and sickly.

My lord may want to say, "they have willfully killed this *lion!*" If anyone had even touched this *lion,* (may I be treated) as if I have transgressed my lord's ban!

Now then, since this *lion* died, I have had his skin flayed, handing it over for tanning. This *lion* was old, it died from depression. (ARM 14.1)

COMMENTS

Like a general marshaling his troops on familiar terrain, God directs another of his creations to intrude into human affairs. Having previously roused the winds into churning the sea, this time he summons a creature from the watery depths and moves it into instant obedience. Soon enough, there will likewise be plants, insects, and hot winds to obey his call unhesitatingly. This parade of objects that are guided by the will of God is made to authenticate and confirm what Jonah had told the sailors when on board ship: that the Lord is indeed the god of heaven, the maker of the sea and of the dry land as well (1:9).

Unlike the previous chapter, in which activities spawn other activities, this chapter features just one movement and one countermovement. Gone are the frequent and nervous shifts in scenery: a quick passage toward Jaffa, a descent into its quay and exit from its harbor, a gathering storm, a groaning ship with panicking sailors, a tense hovering over cast lots, an anxious interrogation with calm answers from a Hebrew, a frightening choice, a mad attempt at steering ashore, a fateful decision to heave overboard . . . followed by a total and eerie peace, punctuated occasionally by murmurs of gratitude and promises. In this chapter, once Jonah plunges into the waters, further events turn strangely limp, with only the novelty of an enwombed human to occupy an audience's attention and to stir its curiosity. The action is about to come to a full halt in order to leave Jonah alone with his God.

When we first meet "three days and three nights," it startles us because of its incongruous location: we do not normally expect such long sojourns within a fish. We then quickly become alert to the fact that we have had no reference to time in any verse of the first chapter, even when they reported one frenetic scene after another. We begin to realize, therefore, that this expression of time is not meant to test our credulity about its length or about its setting—although many may feel so tested; to the contrary, it effectively neutralizes the series of questions that comes to mind as soon as Jonah settles down to pray: How long does it take for Jonah to begin praying, and how long to finish it? When does he sink toward the depths, and how soon afterward does God raise him from them? Response to such questions—and many more inspired by the psalm—can now be subsumed under the three days and three nights during which Jonah lodges in the fish's belly.

Unlike the previous chapter, in which the pagan sailors are featured as novices who have much to learn about Israel's God, this segment focuses on a Hebrew who knew much about his deity, but who now needs to be reminded of what it means to be committed to God. Jonah therefore receives our undivided attention as he formulates his response to him. The setting is unusual, but the Hebrew vocabulary subtly aims to overcome features that some may easily deem baroque. We read that God directs a fish to swallow Jonah; we are never told that the fish hears God's command, evaluates it, then acts upon it. The text resists dwelling on the fish as it maneuvers to slurp a large prey; rather, it chooses only to tell us that "The Lord readied a fish to swallow Jonah." This reticence on the part of the narrator is costly for all of the missed opportunities to embellish, to astonish, and to provoke speculation. (In fact, neither rabbinic sources nor medieval commentaries will prove to be as laconic.) The narrator, however, realizes that to enlarge on the fish's activity could lead us to grant the beast its own will. Such a possibility must be avoided, for animals—for that matter, plants, insects, and winds too—are but instruments to carry out divine instructions. None is allowed to complicate the confrontation of wills between God and his elect, a confrontation that is progressively proving to be a major theme in Jonah.

VI. A Canticle from the Depths (Jonah 2:3b–10)

◆

God who answered Elijah at Mount Carmel,
  May answer you and listen to your loud cry today.
  May you be blessed, Lord, who answers at time of need.
God who answered Jonah from the fish's belly,
  May answer you and listen to your loud cry today.
  May you be blessed, Lord, who answers at time of need.
God who answered David and Solomon his son in Jerusalem,
  May answer you and listen to your loud cry today.
  May you be blessed, Lord, who answers at time of need.[1]

And as to others' souls I preached Thy word,
Be this my text, my sermon to my own,
Therefore that He may raise, the Lord throws down.
  (John Donne, "Hymn to God my God, in my Sickness")

Recall how Dhul-Nūn went away angry, hoping that we have no control over him. When in the darkness he called, "There is no God but you—praise upon you; I am indeed a sinner," we answered and delivered him from the gloom. In the same way, we can deliver those who believe.[2]

[1] This traditional Jewish prayer of the High Holy Days is studied by Correns 1980. The appeal to Jonah's experience is preceded by reminders of the virtues of Abraham, Israel at the Re(e)d Sea, Joshua, and Samuel. Talmudic rabbis observed that listing David and Solomon after Jonah, which is chronologically inaccurate, serves to end the prayer on a plea for universal mercy; *Babylonian Taʿanit* 17a (Soncino Talmud, 1938c: 80). The same passage, however, adds, "A Tanna taught: It was reported in the name of Symmachos [second–third century C.E.], [that the prayers were concluded] with, Blessed are thou who humblest the proud." If it applies to Jonah, the blessing indicates that Hellenistic Jews were ambivalent about his character. Correns's article may explain why Jesus made seemingly unconnected references to Jonah and Solomon in Matt 12:38–41 and Luke 11:29–32 (cited as epigraph to section VII).

[2] Koran 21:87–88. Jonah is the only biblical prophet who is cited by his own name in the Koran. He is often mentioned there, either by his name Yunus, ultimately coined on

VI. A CANTICLE FROM THE DEPTHS (2:3b–10)

2:3 In my trouble, I appeal to the Lord;
he answers me.
From Sheol's belly I plead;
you hear my voice.
4 You cast me in the depths,
to the heart of the Sea,
while the current engulfs me;
all your billows and waves
sweep over me.
5 As for me, I ponder,
"Driven from your sight,
may I yet continue to gaze
toward your holy sanctuary?"
6 Water envelops me up to my neck,
the abyss engulfs me;
kelp clings to my head.
7 I sink to the base of the mountains.
The netherworld, its bars, about me *are there* for ever;
but you lift me up from the Pit alive,
Lord, my god.
8 Even as my life ebbs away,
it is the Lord whom I recall.
Then my prayer reaches you,
at your holy sanctuary.
9 —They who hold to empty faiths,
give up their hope for mercy.—
10 As for me, voicing gratitude,
I shall offer you sacrifices;
I shall fulfill all that I vow.

Rescue is from the Lord.

Greek Ionas, or by the sobriquets Dhul-Nūn, "He-of-Nūn," and *ṣāḥib ʾal ḥût*, "companion of the whale." Sura 10 is named after him. Conveniently, see the *Encyclopaedia of Islam* under the entry "Yūnus, ibn Mattay." Muslim legends expand on the Koranic material, occasionally adapting material from Jewish lore. Al-Kisāʾī's work is one such collection of Muslim lore. Jonah is a favorite subject of Islamic art, where are depicted episodes mostly familiar to us.

HEBREW POETRY: INTRODUCTORY REMARKS

Languages accommodate diverse vehicles by which to express thought; among them are poetry and prose. Hebrew is no different in this respect, so that when Israel's poets versify, they depart from the norms and conventions controlling spoken or written Hebrew. As far as we can judge, however, scribes relatively rarely lined up poetic lines distinctively from prose when copying Scripture. The method (if there was one) that they followed in deciding which poetry received a distinctive treatment is still obscure to us. By Talmudic times, however, the rules that controlled Torah copying had come to be codified, and these rules are followed today only in editions of Scripture destined for synagogue use.[3] From our perspective, the "received text" (that is, a version of Hebrew Scripture generally regarded as authoritative) does not seem consistent in displaying poetry embedded in prose texts. Thus the songs of the Sea (Exodus 15), of Moses (Deuteronomy 32), of Deborah (Judges 5), as well as one of David's psalms (2 Samuel 22; hence also Psalm 18) receive special treatment; but neither the testaments of Jacob and Moses (Genesis 49, Deuteronomy 33) nor the oracles of Balaam (Numbers 23–24) are distinguished from prose. None of the poetry within the Twelve Prophets (which includes Jonah's psalm) is presented in a manner that distinguishes it from prose.

Even if Hebrew manuscripts continue to apportion the text of Jonah in the same format as before, it is nevertheless universally recognized by students of Scripture that within 2:3b–10, language and vocabulary shifts dramatically from prose to poetry. Accordingly, I arrange the translation of these verses to reflect this shift. Nevertheless, because contemporary biblical scholarship is currently reassessing the language, meaning, and purpose of Hebrew poetics, it may be useful to preface the analysis of Jonah's psalm with a few comments on Hebrew poetry and how its language differs from that of prose.[4]

[3] On this code, see *Enc Jud* 14.1100–1104. The editors of modern critical editions of the Hebrew Bible (for example, BH^3 and BHS) make their own decisions on how to present the Hebrew texts on a printed page. It is possible, therefore, to find one edition with acres of Hebrew lined up as poetry and another to be relatively reticent to display it as such.

[4] The subject has received widespread scholarly attention lately, and my brief account only restates basic information. Brief and general expositions can be found in biblical dictionaries such as *IDB* and *Enc Jud.* For more detailed study, I recommend the following: Watson 1984, which is a good general guide to the techniques; O'Connor 1980, which is a brilliant and original effort to establish new measures and criteria toward understanding the poetic idiom; Kugel 1981, which overviews the way western scholarship came to better appreciate biblical poetry; and Alter 1985, which has interesting

Parallelism

Hebrew specialists have long ago recognized that parallelism is the essential ingredient of Hebrew poetry. A line is divisible into two, sometimes three segments, each containing material of import to the other(s). The way the information in one segment bears on the contents of another can be very complex. They may "parallel" each other synonymously, antithetically (see Krašovec 1984), or expansively, obeying versatile rules by which they combine, whether for comparison or contrast (see Berlin 1987).

Beyond agreeing that poetry features parallelism as a major element, scholars spiritedly debate whether it also exhibits other components.

Meter

There are scholars who deny that Hebrews used meter to regulate poetry. But those who regard meter as a significant component of Hebrew poetry most commonly conceive it as a pattern of *stresses* (emphasis by accenting). There are currently a number of hypotheses regarding ways to measure this pattern of stresses (Watson 1984: 103–11), and some of these theories will be broached in this section's COMMENTS.

"Prose Particles"

In an attempt to find a pragmatic criterion by which to distinguish prose from poetry, two recent studies have measured the density of three particles within Hebrew Scripture, *ʾet* (an indicator of a definite direct object), *ʾašer* (a relative pronoun, but also a conjunction), and *ha-* (a definite article); Andersen and Forbes 1983; Freedman 1985. Their statistics suggest that poets relied less on these particles than did prose writers. The density of prose particles in a narrative remains relatively constant whether they incorporate poetry or not, which suggests that throughout its history, Hebrew literature discriminated noticeably between two modes of communicating information.

In the case that immediately interests us, Jonah's psalm, there are 3 such particles in a poem of 81 words (3.7 percent), while there are 93 such particles in the 608 words of narrative (15.3 percent).[5] These percentages compare favorably with what obtains in other segments of Scripture.

---

chapters on diverse types of biblical poetry. Rich insights can be had from D. N. Freedman's many essays, collected in 1980. I want to acknowledge here that I have benefited much from a lively correspondence we have had on this topic, especially as he edited my COMMENTS to chapter 2.

[5] The figures are kindly supplied by Freedman. Another counting method gives 688 as the total number of words in Jonah.

Oral effects

When striving for specific effects, Hebrew reciters very likely altered the volume and quality of their voice as well as changed the pitch and duration with which they uttered individual syllables. They may have found hints in the written poetry to do so; unfortunately, it is practically impossible for us to devise ways of classifying these features.

Stylistics

Hebrew poetry is especially alert to the possibility of playing on words (paronomasia), whether such play is visual, that is, accessible only to a reading audience, or aural, that is, meant for a listening public. Hebrew poetry employs a wide selection of technical devices by which to (de)emphasize or anchor certain notions (repetition, brackets, onomatopoeia, refrains, and the like). It can use imagery and similes when it needs to project certain ideas and impressions; it easily turns to metaphors of all varieties to expand the vision of the poet.

Tense

In prayers, appeals, and vows, the speaker is not normally concerned with a meticulous and accurate rehearsal of past deeds. In fact, in such poetry the language tends to be hyperbolic and metaphoric because the poet is striving for a sharp contrast between the condition of a sinner who is sinking to sordid depths and that of a penitent who is achieving extraordinary triumphs. There is an abiding and timeless quality to these statements that can be compromised by a servile attachment to the verbal forms of the Hebrew.

Consequently, I commonly use the English general present to translate Jonah's psalm where the Hebrew has the perfect, but also imperfect, tense forms. This decision in no way contravenes Hebrew grammar, for grammarians commonly recognize that in Hebrew poetry (and in legal expression) the perfect tense often conveys information without significant attachment to time as long as the poet is establishing a solid context or point of view. Thus, prophets and poets may use the perfect when in fact they are alluding to an event that either is taking place as they speak or is meant to occur in the future.

I use the English present not merely to arrive at a more elegant ("less complicated," critics may charge) rendering for Jonah's psalm, but also to approach exegetical problems that have distorted the study of Jonah. These follow at least two separate paths. Josephus and a few other ancient readers of Jonah judged the occurrence of the past tense as proof that Jonah must have written his psalm after he was disgorged by the fish, that is, after 2:10. They reasoned further that God in any case would not save a Jonah who had not completed uttering penance. Many modern commentators, who argue that in gulping Jonah the fish rescued him from death, similarly seek to explain the past tense: Jonah's psalm gratefully acknowledges God's interference in his behalf; lastly Stuart 1987: 479–80. We shall see Greek-speaking interpreters taking another path to resolve the issue. Some modern scholars have raised the issue of single versus multiple authorship for Jonah because events related in the poem do not match easily those in the prose narrative—for instance, the psalm never talks of ships and storms, while the prose has nothing about kelp and holy sanctuaries. The poem is regarded, therefore, either as an insert by another (and later) hand or as an imperfect adaption of poetic material by the same author. We shall have more to say about this topic in the COMMENTS.

Inner Biblical Comparisons

Hebrew poets operated within a tradition in which it was perfectly proper to appropriate specific ideas and imagery from other sources. Poets might choose to alter the language of an appropriated thought or merely to pluck snippets from within it the better to suit their own poem's purpose. Even so, it is often possible to find poetic lines embedded in radically different types of literature that nevertheless have the same meaning regardless of the setting. In such cases, the wholesale importation of a line and its insertion in a different context may be intentional, for the poet may be ironic, mocking, pedagogic, or the like. It may, however, betray an impoverished poetic inspiration. In modern scholarship, it is possible to find opposing opinions on why and how the shuffle of phrases and lines occurs. In such cases, the ensuing discussion usually considers the type of literature in which are embedded the lines under consideration; the date of the poems from which they come; differences in the language used for each; whether the poet or a (later) editor/redactor is responsible for the appropriation or insertion. These issues are all relevant to a consideration of Jonah's psalm, for it contains many lines that are met elsewhere in Scripture. For this reason, I offer a *selection* of lines that most strikingly parallel the sentiments Jonah expresses and briefly state the literary category to which belongs the text from which these lines are derived.

Voice

Hebrew poetry commonly exhibits a radical shift in the subject of a sentence, and poets may have differing reasons for choosing to make this shift. The famous song of Hannah (1 Sam 2:1–10), a poem that is likewise embedded within narrative (see COMMENTS), is even more ambitious in this regard. The poet reminisces on divine intercession before addressing God directly (second-person singular suffix). Then the poet quickly turns to the audience and, inviting it to appreciate a common God (first-person plural suffix), warns against irreverence (second-person plural):

A CANTICLE FROM THE DEPTHS (2:3B–10)

1 My heart glories in the Lord
my pride soars because of the Lord
I boast widely over my enemies;
for I delight in your deliverance.
2 No god is holy like the Lord
—none beside you;
indeed, no rock is like our God.
3 Do not increase your words,
inflating them enormously,
your mouth pouring out insolence;
The Lord is a fully informed god,
by whom human acts are measured.

"Poet" and "Jonah"

In the NOTES and COMMENTS to the poem, I shall use "Jonah" as often as the term "the poet," not because I am insisting that Jonah is the psalm's author, but because I want it kept in mind that the ancient Hebrew deemed him to be so. For stylistic reasons, however, I will occasionally make Jonah obey the whims of the "poet." (Although I recognize that in ancient Israel poetry may be crafted by women and that the Hebrews attributed some of their finest poetry to women—Deborah, Hannah, Miriam—I nevertheless retain the form "poet," because for us "poetess" is a moribund term.)

Terminology and Structure

Students of Hebrew verses are not yet settled on a standard terminology. Commonly used is a vocabulary that is derived from classical rhetoric, and I adapt it here, by way of Watson 1984. I divide Jonah's psalm into stanzas, strophes, lines, and versets. While some biblical poetic units fall into neat subdivisions (for example, Psalms 67, 107, 119), many (if not most) do not; and charting the structure of some compositions can be a private and artificial enterprise, guided solely by taste and experience. Therefore, while I sincerely hope that readers will find convincing and helpful my annotations to the language and vocabulary of the psalm, I would not want them to be unduly awed by the divisions I make within it. Others have offered equally valid apportionments.

Jonah's poem begins in v 3 right after *wayyōʾmer,* and the verse numbering I follow for it ignores that word. I have taken the moments that the poet refers to making personal utterances as indicative of major shifts in the poem. I with the initial *wayyōʾmer* set outside the contents of the poem, I locate stanzas in the poem, at vv 3a, 5, and 10. I assign two strophes to the first four (including an observation) to the second, and one to the last:

STANZA I: (vv 3a–4; *qārā'tî* . . .)

strophe i: (v 3a–d)

strophe ii: (v 4)

STANZA II: (vv 5–9; *wa'anî 'āmartî* . . .)

strophe iii: (v 5; . . . *'el-hêkal qodšekā*)

strophe iv: (vv 6–7; . . . *YHWH 'elōhay*)

strophe v: (v 8; . . . *'el-hêkal qodšekā*)

strophe vi: (v 9; observation)

STANZA III

strophe vii: (v 10; *wa'anî beqôl tôdâ* . . .)

In the annotations, I will argue that v 3 (I.i) and v 10 (III) form an envelope for the entire poem; that its focal center is located at vv 6–7 (II.iv); that v 5 (II.iii) and v 8 (II.v) balance by repetition of the phrase "holy sanctuary"; and that v 9 (II.vi) may be an aside. In order to permit a quick view of the way ideas are mapped in the poem, I reprint it in light of the previous observations, positioning the copy sideways to allow it to fit on the page:

A CANTICLE FROM THE DEPTHS (2:3B–10)

3 In my trouble, I appeal to the Lord; he answers me. From Sheol's belly I plead; you hear my voice.
4 You cast me in the depths, to the heart of the Sea, while the current engulfs me;
all your billows and waves sweep over me.
5 As for me, I ponder, "Driven from your sight, may I yet continue to gaze toward your holy sanctuary?"
6 Water envelops me up to my neck, the abyss engulfs me; *kelp* clings to my head.
7 I sink to the base of the mountains. The netherworld, its bars, about me *are there* for ever;
but you lift me up from the Pit alive, Lord, my god.
8 Even as my life ebbs away, it is the Lord whom I recall.
Then my prayer reaches you, at your holy sanctuary.
9 [They who hold to empty faiths, give up their hope for mercy.]
10 As for me, voicing gratitude, I shall offer you sacrifices; I shall fulfill all that I vow.
Rescue is from the Lord.

NOTES

I.i (v 3a–d). This strophe includes two lines, each of which consists of two versets, unequal in length. Jonah opens with the argument for the whole psalm: when in distress, he appeals to God, who listens to him. Appropriate to the situation, the first line is cast as a first-person appeal. The second line, however, is so only in the first verset; the second segment addresses God directly.

Although parallelistic lines in Hebrew poetry are not normally concerned with detailing chronology of activities or of events, it is worth noting that the logical sequence is here reversed; for we are told that God "answers" Jonah's plea and then "hears his voice" when we expect the reverse: God should hear his voice *before* he answers his appeal. It may be that the setting of the psalm demanded some sort of transition, which was achieved by the inversion: the first line assuring us that all will be well with Jonah, coaxing us away from unnecessary fixation with fish and their bellies. The second line can then steer us toward "Sheol," where the latest drama will unfold.

qārāʾtî miṣṣārâ lî ʾel-YHWH *wayyaʿănēnî*
mibbeṭen šeʾôl šiwwaʿtî *šāmaʿtā qôlî*

Illustrative Passages

A. Ps 18:7 [= 2 Sam 22:7], a historicizing potpourri:[6]
baṣṣar-lî ʾeqrāʾ YHWH
weʾel-ʾĕlōhay ʾăšawwēaʿ [/*ʾeqrāʾ*]
[*way*]*yišmaʿ mēhêkālô qôlî*
wešawʿātî {*lepānāyw tābōʾ*} *beʾoznāyw*
In my distress, I call my Lord,
To my god I plead [/appeal]
From his holy sanctuary, he hears my voice,
[Ps:] My appeal comes before him, at his ear[7]
[2 Sam:] My appeal is at his ear.

B. Ps 120:1, a personal appeal:
ʾel-YHWH baṣṣārātâ llî qārāʾtî *wayyaʿănēnî*
To the Lord, in my distress, I pray; he answers me.

[6] The Psalm redaction avoids repetition of verbs in *b* and inserts a verb in *d* to avoid incongruity of subject and verb. Opinions differ on which of the two versions of this long composition is the "original."
[7] The rendering of Ps 18:7d in NJPS ignores Masoretic accentuation, "my cry to him reached his ear."

C. Ps 130:1–2a, a personal (or communal) appeal:
mimmaʿamaqqîm qerāʾtîkā YHWH *ʾadōnay šimʿâ beqôlî*
Out of the depths, I call you, Lord; heed my voice, my lord.

D. Lam 3:55–56:
qārāʾtî šimkā YHWH mibbôr taḥtîyôt *qôlî šamāʿtā*
I shout your name, Lord, from the deepest Pit; you hear my voice.

E. Ps 116:3, individual thanksgiving:
ʾapāpûnî ḥeblê-māwet *ûmṣārê šeʾôl meṣāʾûnî* *ṣārâ weyāgôn ʾemṣāʾ*

With the ropes of Death round me, Sheol's clutches reaching me, I find misery and torment (and invoke the Lord by name).

qārāʾtî miṣṣārâ lî ʾel-YHWH. In this poem, Jonah registers his activities through the perfect tense (seven times) or the cohortative (twice). (The *ʾôsîp* of v 5, an imperfect, acts as auxiliary to the infinitive.) He begins his appeal to God by using an idiom that is conspicuous in Jonah: *qārāʾ ʾel* (+ a deity). This being so, we should not divorce God's name from the idiom, turning it into a vocative (for example, "In my distress, O LORD": Today's English Version); nor should we allocate *ʾel-YHWH* to the lines' second verset to obtain metrical balance (implicit in BH³ and BHS). In this connection, note how example B treats the various parts of the sentence. It stresses the addressed instead of dwelling on the situation that the poet is seeking to escape (see below).

Above, at 1:2, I have noted that the narrator is able to nuance meaning by manipulating the conjugation of the verb *qārāʾ* and by attaching to the preposition *ʾel* diverse divine names. It may be of importance therefore that, in the only other context in which "YHWH" is at stake, the sailors finally come to terms with the omnipotence of God. At 1:14, the sailors offer a beautifully conceived prayer in which they surrender body and soul to the Hebrew God.

The LXX and the Old Latin add the phrase, "my god," probably to parallel information from the previous verse, "Jonah prayed to the Lord, his god." Trible (1963: 33) refers to a Hebrew manuscript that has "to my lord, the Lord" (*ʾdny* YHWH).

Jonah is said to appeal *miṣṣārâ lî,* literally, "from an affliction that is mine." Wolff (1986: 134) may be correct in thinking that this construction intentionally aims to coordinate the vocabulary of Jonah's plea with the observation in v 2 that Jonah prayed when "in the fish's belly, *mimmeʿê haddāgâ.*" The noun employed here, *ṣārâ,* is feminine, but its masculine equivalent, *ṣar,* has a similar meaning. Poets attach to nouns diverse prepositions when seeking to control the intensity of a stressful situation. The association of two prepositions *min-* and *le-* with either gender of the noun is unique to Jonah and gives the sentiment a poignancy and intimacy that is hard to parallel in English.[8] Other passages approximate the intent either by using *min-* alone, attaching a pronoun directly to the noun (Isa 46:7; 2 Chr 20:9 [prose]), or more commonly by substituting the preposition *be-* for *min-*.[9] We thus have occasions on which poets pray to God while simply "in distress" (Ps 81:8) or while "in personal distress"; examples A (using the masculine noun) and B (using a poetic form of the feminine noun). In example C the poet prays to God from "the depths," even though Psalm 130 nowhere refers to sinking into waters. The term "depths" is therefore conventional in this sort of danger (Ps 69:1ff.) and is figurative for the distress that sin causes.

wayyaʿanēnî. The use of *ʿānâ* is common when God's answers positively to a plea. The verb *šāmaʿ* (+ voice), while meaning "to hear, listen," often intimates that God is similarly disposed (as in examples A, C, and D). The two verbs, moreover, may be paired in parallel lines, and they are so here. It is worth noting that the poet, as is rather common in Hebrew poetry, has also switched tenses, from the perfect to the *waw*-conversive imperfect.[10] This pattern will recur at crucial junctures throughout the poem, announcing either a major shift in Jonah's fortunes or an important change in action sequence (italics signal the *waw*-conversive imperfects):

2:3, I appeal (perf.) . . . he *answers* me

2:4, You *cast* me . . . the current engulfs me (imperf.)

2:7, I sink (perf.) . . . you *lift* me *up*

2:8, (the Lord) I recall (perf.) . . . my prayer *reaches* you.

mibbeṭen šeʾôl šiwwaʿtî. Before the second Temple period, when Babylonian theology and especially Persian dualism had not yet heavily influenced Israel's eschatology, the Hebrews generally distinguished among three separate realms: Heaven, where dwelled the immortals (God and a celestial entourage); Earth,

[8] That *lî* does not have the expected *dagesh* has been noted by medieval grammarians. The same anomaly occurs in 4:4 and 9; see Trible 1963: 32. In some cases the use of the *dagesh* seems optional; see for example 1 Sam 1:26 (reference courtesy of J. Blenkinsopp).

[9] In fact, the LXX seems to treat the passage as if it uses *be-* rather than *min, eboēsa en thlipsei mou,* "I cried in my affliction."

[10] The switch is common in lines of prayers that feature a plea in the first verset and a response in the second; Joüon 1947: 235 n. 2. Some scholars consider it to be characteristic of later Hebrew poetry. There are exceptions, however; an example of which is Ps 34:5. Although it is a brief poem, Jonah is a remarkable smorgasbord of verbal sequences: (1) perf. . . . conv. imperf. in 3a, b; 7a, c; 8b, c; (2) perf. . . . perf. in 3c, d; (3) conv. imperf. . . . imperf. in 4a, b [note conj. in 4b!]; and (4) imperf. . . . imperf. in 6a, b [no conj. in 6b!].

where mortals lived out their allotted time; and Sheol, where they removed upon death.

Much has been written about Sheol, and the very meaning, etymology, and origin of the term are still under dispute. Because our information on the Hebraic concept of the afterlife comes mostly from poetry, a medium in which imagination normally triumphs over realism (Sheol is cited as a voracious monster), we have imprecise and sometimes contradictory knowledge on exactly what the Hebrew believed occurred after death. For the present purpose, I merely note that the Hebrew language is rich in synonyms for Sheol and that Israel's poets generally locate this other world somewhere below *terra firma* or even below the oceans; occasionally they place it beyond God's control and assign to it the dead, no matter what may have been their earthly social status or spiritual condition.[11]

Hebrew poets intensify the level of despair the pleader experiences by attaching to "Sheol" a vocabulary (anatomical or otherwise) that progressively advances the reader toward Sheol's inner core: gates and mouths (Isa 38:10, Ps 141:7); paths and hands (Prov 7:27, Pss 49:16 and 89:49); ropes and snares (Ps 18:6 [2 Sam 22:6], 116:3); bars and valleys (Job 17:16, Prov 9:18). Psalm 88:2–14 nicely illustrates how Sheol serves the Hebrew poet to shape a prayer where hope abandoned becomes hope restored:[12]

2 Lord, god of my liberation,
daily, I pray; at night, near you—
3 may my prayer reach you,
pay attention to my shout.
4 I am truly engorged with woe,
and my life is nearing Sheol.
5 I am reckoned among plungers into the Pit,
a person without vigor,

[11] *General bibliography:* Useful compilations on Sheol and on the concept of death and the afterlife are available in Stadelmann 1970: 165–76; *Enc Jud* 12.996–98; *EB* 4.4453–54; Gerleman, in *ThWAT* 2.837–41. Tromp's monograph of 1969 is devoted entirely to this topic. *Synonymous terminology:* I mention here only *ʾabaddôn*, "place for the annihilated," *qeber*, "Grave," *šaḥat*, "Pit," *bôr*, "Cavity," *ʾereṣ*, "Earth." For a fuller listing, giving the nouns as they occur in synonymous parallelism, see Held 1973. It is worth noting that most of these terms retain their power to quicken the imagination of the Qumran poets; see below and Kittel 1981: 175–79. *On God's control of Sheol:* While there is evidence for Sheol's independence from God's control, occasionally the opposite holds true; see Psalm 139; Job 26:6.

[12] Note how v 14 not only is paired with v 2 as a bracket for vv 3–13, but also serves to introduce another prayer (vv 15–19) that is not quoted here. Notice, too, how in the series of rhetorical questions the benefits that are from God are repeatedly set against various manifestations of Sheol.

6 left among the dead,
as are corpses that lie flat in the Grave,
whom you no longer consider,
who are kept away from your care.
7 You place me at the lowest Pit,
in pitch darkness,
in deepest water.
8 Your anger bears down on me,
with your waves you torment me. *Selah*
9 You are distancing my friends from me,
making me repugnant to them.
I am stuck and cannot go out;
10 my eye is dimming from pain.
Yet I call to you, daily, Lord,
stretching toward you my palms in prayer.
11 Will you do miracles for the dead?
Can specters rise to glorify you? *Selah*
12 Is your benevolence praised in the Grave,
your reliability in Abaddon?
13 Are your marvels recognized in the Gloom,
your impartiality in a Land without memory?
14 Yet I plead with you, Lord,
each morning, my prayer meets you.

The metaphor "belly of Sheol" is unique to Jonah and conveys despair of the darkest hue. The poet probably found it particularly appropriate to the context because *beṭen,* "belly," allows yet another connection with the "fish's belly" of 2:1 (but using other internal organs, the *mēʿîm*) and possibly also with the "ship's hold" of 1:5 (using *yārēk,* occasionally a synonym for *beṭen,* Num 5:21ff.). This use of corresponding vocabulary to bridge prose and poetry is not adequately realized by some of the versions; the Targum, for example, has *mʾrʿyt* (*thwmʾ*), "from the bottom (of the Deep [Tehom])"; Levine 1978: 72. By substituting "Tehom" for "Sheol," however, the Targum misses a pithy lesson; for the poet is here exploiting a commonly accepted notion within Israel: Sheol holds tightly to its denizens, permitting them no communication with the other realms, Earth and Heaven (Isa 38:18; Ps 30:10). Therefore, while others do escape Sheol's grasp when God shows them mercy, none is as deeply entombed in its core as is Jonah.

From Sheol's belly, Jonah pleads. Here there may be irony, for Jonah, who had sought to escape God by reaching the furthest land of the known earth, Tarshish, recovers his senses and begins to plead with his maker upon reaching the nethermost side of the cosmos. The Hebrew verbal form is *šiwwaʿ* (*D* stem), which biblical poetry often pairs with *šāmaʿ,* "to hear, listen" (for example, Ps

18:42; Job 19:7; Hab 1:2). The LXX (but not Symmachus), the Old Latin, and some Targumic versions read this form as if vocalized **šawʿātî*, "my plea" (*kraugēs mou*); Trible 1963: 33; Levine 1978: 73. Arabic adds "to him," an expansion made necessary because it retains the last clause in the third person, *wamin baṭni (ʾi)ljaḥîm taḍarraʿtu ʾilayhi wasamiʿa ṣawṭî*, "and [conjunction also in Syriac] when from the belly of Hell I humbled myself to him, he heard my voice"; Wright 1857: 111.

šāmaʿtā qôlî. The switch to the second person gives more immediacy to heaven's response upon appeal. As mentioned in the INTRODUCTORY REMARKS to this section (under "Voice"), this shift in voice is part of the poet's arsenal and does not necessarily reflect the psalm's "use in actual worship situation at one time" (Ackerman 1981: 215). The Arabic continues in the third-person mode until 2:4b, where the second-person suffix to "billows and waves" make the shift unavoidable. The other versions stay with the Hebrew in switching to the second person. The Targum, however, understands the clause as a summary of what will unfold for it translates, "you fulfilled my prayer," *ʿbdtʾ bʿwty;* Levine 1978: 72–73. Syriac translates as if the preposition *b-* were prefixed to *qôlî*, a reading known to some Hebrew manuscripts; see Trible 1963: 33.

I.ii (v 4). Two lines are found here, again unequal in length. The poet reports on God's punishing acts (first verset in each line) and rehearses how they affected the poet (second verset in each line). This strophe foreshadows imagery that will be more fully developed in the second stanza.

wattašlîkēnî meṣûlâ bilbab yammîm *wenāhār yesōbebēnî*
kol-mišbārêkā wegallêkā *ʿālay ʿābārû*

Illustrative Passages

A. Ps 88:7, a lament (see above):
šattanî bebôr taḥtîyôt *bemaḥašakkîm bimṣōlôt*
ʿālay sāmekâ ḥamātekā *wekol-mišbārêkâ ʿinnîtā*
You place me at the lowest Cavity,
in pitch darkness,
in deepest water.
Your anger bears down on me;
with your waves, you torment me.

B. Ps 18:5–6 [= 2 Sam 22:5–6], see above:
ʾapāp{û}nî ḥeblê-[*/mišberê-*] *māwet*
{*we*}*naḥalê belîyaʿal yebaʿat*{*û*}*nî*
ḥeblê šeʾôl sebābûnî [*sabbunî*]
qiddem{*û*}*nî mô*[*/ō*]*qšê*[*/-*] *māwēt*

Deadly ropes bind me [Perilous billows encircle me],
  streams of demise also terrify me.
Hellish ropes surround me,
  deadly snares confront me.

C. Ps 42:8, a hymn of trust and thanksgiving:
(My God, when I am deeply depressed, I then speak of you. From Jordan to Harmon to Mount Mizar, throughout the land; where,)
tehôm-ʾel-tehôm qôrēʾ leqôl ṣinnôrêkā
  kol-mišbārêkā wegallêkā ʿālay ʿābārû
Deep calls to Deep, echoing your cascading roars.
All your billows and waves sweep over me.

D. Mic 7:19:
yāšûb yeraḥamēnû yikbôš ʿawōnōtênû
wetašlîk bimṣûlôt yām kol-ḥaṭṭōʾtām
Once again [God] will be compassionate with us,
  containing our sins.
You will hurl into the deepest sea
  all their trespasses.

The word *meṣûlâ,* "watery Deep," is a feminine noun that poets may personify and thus place as subject of a verb, as they do in Ps 69:16, "Flood should not sweep over me, the Deep swallow me (*ʾal-tiblāʿēnî meṣûlâ*), the Cavity shut its mouth on me." In Jonah, "the Deep" may be regarded as the subject of *tašlîkenî* if the verbal form is parsed as a third-person feminine singular; indeed, M. Buber (cited in Wolff 1986: 126) does translate it as such: "the Deep has thrown me into the heart of the seas." But the verb *šālak* (*H* stem), whether construed with or without a preposition, normally has human beings or God as subject (F. Stolz, in *THAT* 2.916–19). A *meṣûlâ* is commonly a place in which God displays wonders (Ps 107:24), sinking within it Israel's enemies (Neh 9:11; see Exod 15:5), sinners (our passage), and, in a playful reversal of expectation, sins (example D). God can keep sinners mired in the "Deep" (Ps 88:9), but can also bring them out (Ps 68:23). These observations suggest that Jonah's distress is not the result of the sailors' action, nor is it caused by an engulfing Sea, a powerful god in the Canaanite pantheon (Yam); rather, it expressly comes from God.[13]

bilbab yammîm. Despite many attempts to do so, usage for *lēb* and *lēbāb* cannot easily be assigned to different time periods, though it is apparent that some texts and writers preferred one over the other; see BDB 523–25, but

[13] Notice how the poet resisted calling on a synonym for *hišlîk* that had been powerfully featured in the first chapter: *hēṭîl.* The reason may be that *hēṭîl* had God (1:4) as well as sailors as subjects (1:5, 12, 15).

contrast to Stolz, in *THAT* 1.861–67. It seems that *lēbāb* is rarely used when referring to the inside of inanimate objects, and our example in which it is in construct with "waters" is unique to Scripture. (It is probably for this reason that Ehrlich 1912: 267, proposes emending into *lēb.*) By contrast, *lēb yammîm* is favored by Ezekiel in the "Ship Tyre" allegory (six times, at 27:4–28:8) and it is known to the Psalms (46:3). The construct *leb-yām* occurs in Exod 15:8; and in Prov 23:34 and 30:19. In prose texts, these last expressions are equivalent to English "open sea(s)." In poetry, however, these phrases convey an unfathomable and unchartable expanse that can swallow mountains whole and even contain the congealed Deep (Ps 46:3; Exod 15:8). Therefore, if *meṣûlâ* is where God places the unrepentants, *bilbab yammîm* tells us how hopeless is their situation. The two sets of images are therefore complementary, and not necessarily equivalent, formulas. Notice how Ps 88:6–7 (cited above) evokes a similar condition by also juxtaposing two images of "darkness" and "depth." There is little justification, therefore, to prune either *meṣûlâ* (for example Johnson 1950: 84 n. 9) or *bilbab* (Landes 1967a: 6 n. 13; Cross 1983a: 162). Stuart's notion (1987: 469) that "either one or the other, but not both, was actually sung on any one occasion when the song was heard" has no parallel elsewhere in Scripture.[14] These attempts at ameliorating the passage in Jonah have really little to do with grammatical needs (Johnson 1950: 84 n. 9, recording the opinions of other exegetes); they are almost completely motivated by metrical adjustments.

In fact, all of the versions follow the Hebrew in preserving both expressions; see the chart in Trible 1963: 34–35. Where they differ, it is in two relatively inconsequential adjustments of Hebrew vocabulary: (1) *yammîm* is occasionally given as singular (for example LXX, Targum; but not Aquila or Theodotion), thus setting up a condition wherein the Sea, and not God, is the immediate cause of Jonah's despair; see below and Levine 1978: 73–74.[15] (2) The Greek renditions differ in translating *meṣûlâ;* the LXX and GS offer *bathē* and Aquila, *buthō.* Theodotion, however, is not reluctant to use *abussos,* which the other Greek translations of Jonah are careful to reserve for rendering *tehôm* of v 6.

When prosaically used, *nāhār* refers to a large stream, be it natural (river) or artificial (canal). Depending on the geographical context, the term may even refer to a specific river (most often the Euphrates, but also the Nile or the Tigris). In poetry, however, *nāhār* may be attached to an article and thus can

[14] Freedman has privately suggested to me that Stuart may be speaking of another phenomenon, the conflation of text, with alternative phrases retained by scribes, adding, "[this is] certainly a possibility, but I agree that there is no compelling evidence for it." If so, Stuart would be following Cross 1983a: 162, who is "inclined to see [in their preservation] a conflation of ancient variants, both stock phrases."

[15] Batto's decision (1983: 32 n. 21) to treat the last *mem* of *yammîm* as enclitic has little merit, if only because the plural form is known to other Scriptural passages. Moreover, it would leave an overhanging *yod* with no particular function.

refer to a large body of (primordial) water that does not always flow on earth. For this reason, I have used a generic term to render *nāhār,* rather than the more precise "river," "torrent," "flood," or the like.[16] In GS the noun also appears in the singular ([*pota*]*mos periekuklōsen m*[*e*]); Barthélemy 1963: 170. In its plural form, however, *nehārôt* can be equated with "seas" (Ps 24:2). It may be to parallel *yammîm* that the LXX, Old Latin, and Arabic make *nāhār* plural (*kai potamoi ekuklōsan me; et flumina me circumiirunt; walʾanhār ʾaḥāṭat bî*).

We shall soon see (at v 6) that the poet will lament his fate by using another set of commonly paired words, *mayim* and *tehôm,* as well as a repetition of *yesōbebēnî.* In the G stem (*qal*) the verb *sābab* can express a threatening condition, as a passage from example B shows (*ḥeblê šeʾôl sebābûnî* [*sabbunî*]). The form in Jonah, however, is an imperfect of the *poʿel* conjugation. Scriptural attestations indicate that this verbal conjugation conveys a *protective* rather than a threatening act. Thus, when Israel is aimlessly roaming the desert, God "embraces and tutors him" (Deut 32:10). Similarly, Ps 32:10 says that "good things will envelop" those whose faith is in God.[17] We may dare imagine, therefore, that even as Jonah drowns, God is warding death away from him. If we do so, we must admire the poet's particularly clever manipulation of conventional imagery.

When the poet says that *kol-mišbārêkā wegallêkā ʿālay ʿābārû,* he gives us the only line in Jonah's psalm that finds an *exact* duplicate elsewhere in Scripture (example C). In the Psalm passage, however, the statement that "your waves and billows sweep over me" does not easily follow a context in which the poet's utterances are picked up, amplified, and turned into a symphony for nature. We may appreciate both applications but rightly decide that it is Jonah's poet who found the most compatible and harmonious location for it.

The Greek versions give different renderings for the Hebrew *mišbārîm* (Trible 1963: 35); the LXX has *meteōrismoi,* "billows," while Aquila gives *suntrimmoi,* "crashings" (used in the LXX for Zeph 1:10's *šeber gādôl*), and *gnophoi,* "gloom" (Symmachus). The Arabic version lumps the two threats into one, *wajamîʿu ʾamwājika,* "all your waves"; Wright 1857: 111. I have noted above that the Targum radically alters the intent of the Hebrew by reading *kl*

[16] I have consciously avoided translating by "River" (with a capital *R*) because I do not agree that the poet is emulating a trial by river ordeal, as suggested by McCarter 1973.
[17] Jeremiah (31:22) sarcastically alludes to a future time in which "women embrace men," that is, when the natural order is reversed. It may be, however, that Jeremiah is being metaphorical here, playing on a royal motif obtaining in the ancient Near East whereby goddesses embrace their favored kings. There is also the possibility that the *poʿel* of *sābab* may take the pronominal suffix as direct object, allowing us to translate the Jeremiah passage as "women will whirl men around," that is, they will run their husbands' lives. In the opinion of M. Hirsch, quoted in Zlotowitz 1980: 111, the same grammatical condition obtains in Jonah, "currents whirl me around."

nḥšwlwhy dymʾ wglwhy ʿly ʿdw. It thus inserts *ymʾ*, "sea," and gives third-person (rather than second-person) suffixes to *nḥšwl,* "gale," and to *gl,* "waves." In harking back to a word, *nḥšwl,* that was obtrusively used in 1:13, the Targum not only reminds the reader of the tempestuous scene of chapter 1, but also faults the sea, rather than God, for nearly drowning the prophet; see Levine 1978: 73–74. The change, however, is misguided for, as we shall soon see, the poet is blaming his lack of rapport with God on his hopeless situation (v 5). In acknowledging that alienation from God is the core of Jonah's difficulty, the poet prepares us better for the reversal of fortunes that God alone can bestow (v 7c–d).

The strophes of stanza II are bound as a unit by the poet's twofold recall of *ʾel-hêkal qodšekā,* at 5d and 8d. As we sink with Jonah and then are raised with him to God's grace, we are reminded of the path Jonah took in his adventure aboard ship.

II.iii (v 5). The poet's impossible situation is described in terms of psychological anguish:

waʾanî ʾāmartî
nigraštî minneged ʿênêkā
ʾak ʾôsîp lehabbîṭ ʾel-hêkal qodšekā

Illustrative Passages

A. Ps 31:23, a lamentation followed by thanksgiving:
waʾanî ʾāmartî beḥopzî
nigraztî minneged ʿênêkā
ʾākēn šāmaʿtā qôl taḥanûnay
bešawweʿî ʾelêkā
As for me, anxiously I reason,
"I am cut off from your sight;
yet you hear my loud entreaty,
when I plead with you."

B. Lam 3:54:
ṣāpû-mayim ʿal-rōʾšî ʾāmartî nigzārtî
With water flowing over my head, I think, "it is over for me."

waʾanî ʾāmartî. In Jonah and in example A, the Masoretic punctuation divides the line into two versets, one containing the verb *ʾāmar,* the other *gāraš/z.* In A, however, an adverb gives bulk to the first verset. For this reason, I would retain this division, preferring it over what is found in BH^3 and BHS, where, for metrical reasons, these editions unappealingly pile up the verbs: *waʾanî ʾāmartî nigraštî minneged ʿênêkā.*

When individuals are speaking to no one in particular, the verb *ʾāmar,* "to say, to speak," is best translated, "to think, ponder." (To achieve the same sense, Hebrew writers often link this verb with variations on the expression, "in the heart.") We will find *waʾanî* (conjunction + independent first-person pronoun) again in v 10, opening a clause that tells of the poet's vow and pledge to God. These two attestations of the independent pronoun therefore sandwich two sets of emotions and perceptions: despair then salvation; gratitude then illumination. Worth observing, too, is the contrast in the mood of a poet who in v 5 ponders quietly his predicament, but because of God's intervention ends up with loud thanksgiving.

The phrase *nigraštî minneged ʿênêkā* finds its closest analogue in *nigraztî minneged ʿênêkā* (example A). The difference between them is the verbs, *gāraš* in Jonah, *gāraz* in the psalm, both of which are in the *N* stem. Because the verb *gāraz* occurs only once in Scripture—and doubtless attracted by the reference in Lam 3:54 (example B)—commentators suggest that it be emended to the more common *gāzar,* which, when in the *N* stem and construed with *min,* refers to separation from God's bounties. This procedure is defensible; nonetheless, I would retain the verb *gāraz* in example A, reasoning that if in two phrases only the quality of the third sibilant of the verbal roots differs, it may be due simply to dialect variations. Furthermore, it is not necessary to suppose that Jonah's line depended on the passage in the psalm (Delekat 1964: 11–13). In fact, the phrase does not fit very well in the psalm, where the psalmist is already singing God's praises and hardly needs to lament his condition.

Because Hebrew uses anatomical features to form abstract ideas or to discuss the emotions, "eyes of God" need not become evidence for an anthropomorphic God in ancient Israel. The phrase "eye(s) of the Lord/God" is very frequent in Scripture. It refers to God's constant vigil over mankind or it is found embedded in the idiom, "good/bad in the sight (i.e., opinion) of God." Interesting for our purpose is Ps 34:16–17, where divine features express benevolence as well as wrath: "The Lord's eyes are on the just; his ears alert to their appeal. The Lord's face is set on the evil doers, resolving to wipe their memory from Earth."[18]

The Targum, however, is uncomfortable with anthropomorphic vocabulary, and therefore substitutes *mymrʾ*, God's hypostatized Word, for *ʿênêka,* "your eyes." The verb it uses, *ʾtrṣyt,* is difficult; but some manuscripts read *ʾtrkyt,* "I was expelled" (note Peshitta's *dʾtrḥqt,* "I was distanced"); see Levine 1978: 43; 74–75. The Vulgate may too be softening the anthropomorphism with *abiectus sum a[/e] conspectu oculorum tuorum,* "I am rejected from the sight of your eyes." The Greek versions read differently, with the LXX closest to the Hebrew:

[18] For "God's face" as a sign of anger, see also Lam 4:16, quoted below.

apōsmai [Aquila: *eksebēn*] *eks ophthalmōn sou,* "I am cast away from your sight." GS tries to be more precise with *apōsmai eks enantias ophthalmōn sou,* "I am cast away from across your sight"; Barthélemy 1963: 170.[19] Symmachus uses different language to arrive at a similar meaning, *ekseblēthēn apenanti tōn ophthalmōn sou.*

The verset *ʾak ʾôsîp lehabbîṭ ʾel-hêkal qodšekā* begins with one of the most contested readings in Jonah. The particle *ʾak* normally functions in three different ways: temporal ("just as, no sooner"), emphatic/asseverative ("truly, surely"), and restrictive/adversative ("nevertheless, for all that"); see BDB 36. The last two modes are not often mutually compatible, and there are cases in which the choice depends on individual judgment. (The two possibilities are discussed by Muraoka [1985: 130], who also gives a relevant bibliography.[20]) In Jonah's case, readers choose a meaning to accord with the way they empathize with Jonah's circumstances. Having just acknowledged his hopeless situation, is Jonah (or the poet) meekly begging God to permit him to achieve that goal ("Truly, I want to continue gazing upon your holy sanctuary")? Or is he defiantly stating his resolve to seek God's shrine ("Nevertheless, I continue to gaze upon your holy sanctuary")? The Renaissance rabbi Sforno is closer to the first interpretation, rendering, "I ask only that I be permitted to gaze upon your holy temple"; quoted in Zlotowitz 1980: 112. The Targum sides with the latter interpretation, using the adversative *brm,* "nevertheless," and so does the LXX (followed by Arabic) when it frames the sentence as a rhetorical question: "Do you think that I may yet see your holy temple?"

Translating v 5c–d, however, is complicated because the Greek rendering of Theodotion uses *pōs,* "how," equivalent to *ʾêk* (*ʾyk*) rather than the *ʾak* in our Hebrew text. Although his reading is not sustained by any of the other ancient versions, it has nevertheless led some modern scholars to suppose that Theodotion had before him a Hebrew manuscript of Jonah that actually read *ʾêk* rather than *ʾak.* Because an interrogative pronoun does make sense here ("How may I continue to gaze upon your holy sanctuary?"), there has been a heated debate about its "original" presence in Jonah. Bewer (1912: 45) regards any expression of hope as premature to the context and therefore adopts Theodotion's reading. Wolff (1986: 127) is one of many to choose this alternative on the ground that a humble question "is more probable than an expression of tenacious defiance or longing." Wolff explains the "misreading" as "due to the similarity between v. 5a . . . and Ps. 31:22a [example A] and its continuation with the adversative *ʾākēn* in v. 22b." Cross (1983a: 164), who finds any expression of hope and trust

[19] The preposition *neged* is rendered differently in various Greek recensions; see Barthélemy 1963: 80, 200.

[20] In some cases, *ʾak* carries with it so slight an adversative sense that in parallel passages the ubiquitous conjunction *waw* may replace it; compare, for example, Jer 30:11 with 46:28.

inappropriate at this juncture of the poem, offers a different reason: "The frequent use of *ʾak* in laments, to introduce an affirmation of confidence, may have triggered the misreading."

Because variations on the preceding opinions are commonly met in Jonah literature of the nineteenth century and because many reliable Bible translations adopt the emendation based on Theodotion—a list is offered in Price and Nida 1978: 41—many scholars have felt it necessary to defend their attachment to the "Masoretic" reading. Van der Woude (1981: 490) points out that there are attestations of "I/you ponder" (*ʾanî ʾāmartî*/*ʾattâ ʾāmartā*) followed by *ʾak* (for example, Isa 14:13–15 and Jer 5:4–5), and even more citations with the similarly adversative *ʾākēn*. A. R. Johnson (1950: 84 n. 11) protests that poets need not be so logical as to worry about the proper sequence for their expressions of gratitude. Nevertheless, Johnson finds it necessary to suggest that the unemended Hebrew contains "an emotional content wholly in keeping with the situation which the psalmist contemplates." Landes (1967a: 6 n. 15) is another scholar who affirms the value of the unemended Hebrew, arguing that Jonah is not proclaiming a desire for a future visit to God's temple, but that "in his derelict and nearly hopeless situation in the Deep, [Jonah] resolves to turn to Yahweh in prayer" (p. 22).

None of the positions offered above is so convincing that it must carry the day. Because of the absence of a *yod* among this particle's consonants, the Masoretes could not have vocalized it in any other way but *ʾak*. Additionally, Johnson's protest against expecting poets to follow "logical" narrative sequences is worth retaining; otherwise we may be forced into wholesale reshuffling of dozens of psalms. Moreover, emending the Hebrew of Jonah because of a variant reading located in an ancient translation is not a useful approach, especially because we have repeatedly observed how translators adapt whenever it suits their (or their audience's) theology. The rendering I offer follows an unemended Hebrew because it makes pretty good sense in the context; not because I base it on the trite notion that "the more difficult reading is to be preferred" (Ellison 1985: 377 n. 4). ("'More difficult' for whom?" I can protest.) Had I been translating Theodotion's version of Jonah, I would have stuck to his choice of particles or adverbs and then tried to justify his *interpretation* of Jonah's thought.

I have couched *ʾôsîp lehabbîṭ ʾel-hêkal qodšekā* as a rhetorical question expressing a wish. This solution is quite in conformity with the rules of Hebrew grammar, wherein a question can be posed without an interrogative particle and a wish can be expressed by means of the simple imperfect (GKC 473 [§ 150.ab]; 317 [§ 107.n]). A more direct rendering is possible, for example, "I nevertheless want to continue to gaze upon your holy sanctuary." Imprecise, however, are translations that do not recognize that in the *H* stem the verb *yāsap* (with or without the adverb *ʿôd*) serves as auxiliary, giving continuity to an act expressed by a verb following; André, in *ThWAT* 3.687. Thus, NEB's "(I thought . . .)

[I] should never see thy holy temple again" does not communicate Jonah's fear of interrupting his rapport with God. The same criticism is applicable to the translation of Johnson 1950: 84, "I can gaze once more . . ." and that of Rudolph 1971: 345, "Yet I should like once more to gaze toward your holy temple."[21]

We are told that the poet wants to keep sight of God's "holy sanctuary." There is a reversal of roles and expectations in another Scriptural verse (Lam 4:16), which tells that "The Lord's face has split [the sinful]; he shall not continue to stare at them (*lōʾ yôsîp lehabbîṭṭām*)." The choice of vocabulary in Jonah is interesting. Eyes and sight are setting a contrast between Jonah's fear of being distanced from God and his resolve to remain near his presence. The verb *hibbîṭ* (*H* stem of *nābaṭ*) belongs to a group that in Hebrew prayers serves to draw God's attention to the petitioner (Aejmelaeus 1986: 26–29). When used in a reverse fashion, it can refer to human beings trying to stare at God (for example, at Exod 3:6) or at his "form" (Num 12:8).[22] It also has them scrutinizing either various manifestations of divine power (commands, Ps 119:6; brass snake, Num 21:9; plans and future deeds, Isa 5:12) or, as is our case (*hêkal qodšô*), where God's authority is enshrined.

The word *hêkāl* is ultimately derived from Sumerian *é.gal*, literally meaning, "imposing residence." In Hebrew, the word refers to the dwelling of a king or of God. It refers as well to the midsection of the Jerusalem Temple, where religious rituals took place. Occasionally, our sources speak of the *hêkāl* simply as *qōdeš*, "the Holy Space," while they label as "the Holiest Space" the *debîr* where rested the ark. The phrase *hêkal qodšekā*, "your holy sanctuary," may seem redundant; but it is common to Scripture and serves to bolster the notion that God's presence is what makes the sanctuary a place for worship (Pss 5:8, 138:2). When it is located on earth, God's holy sanctuary can be Jerusalem (Ps 79:1); but it can also be found in Heaven (Ps 11:4; Mic 1:2; and probably also Hab 2:20). Therefore, the poet may not necessarily be thinking of Jerusalem's Temple when Jonah laments his fate. In view of his proximity to Sheol, it makes sense for the prophet to grieve over his separation from God's power; so too Landes 1967a: 21. Another point may be made here. It has been argued that if the psalmist wants a Jonah to keep sight of God's holy *hêkāl*, it could not be the prophet Jonah of 2 Kgs 14:25, for the latter operated in the Northern Kingdom; see Levine 1978: 75. We may note, however, that another psalmist creates a similar scene for David (Ps 138:1–2) even when everyone knew that the king did not build the temple.[23]

[21] Wolff 1986: 127 levels the same criticism against Rudolph's rendering.
[22] In other contexts, human beings are said to dream of a divine form or shape (Job 4:16) and "to have a vision" of God's face (Ps 17:15). The verb *lehabbîṭ* is not used then.
[23] Some Greek copies of the LXX add Haggai and/or Zechariah to the David ascription; this is not immediately relevant to this issue.

The versions differ from the Hebrew in minor ways. The Targum wants to make it clear that Jonah hopes to gaze upon rather than *toward* the holy sanctuary. The Vulgate and the Syriac are similarly motivated when making the phrase a direct object of "seeing." Codex B, however, reads *laon*, "people," where other Greek texts have *naon*, "sanctuary"; see Trible 1963: 36.

II.iv (vv 6–7). Together, these two lines bring Jonah into and out of a threatening condition. As shall be seen in the COMMENTS below, each of them recalls material previously set out by the poet. In v 6, the poet turns once more to expressing his distress. The line is divisible into three versets, which match v 4 in recounting the progressive deterioration of the poet's condition:

4a You cast me in the depths, to the heart of the Sea,	6a *Water envelops me up to my neck,*
4b while the current engulfs me;	6b *the abyss engulfs me;*
4c all your billows and waves sweep over me.	6c kelp *clings to my head.*

This parallelism is accentuated by the middle versets, which share the same verbal form, *yesōbebēnî*, as well as nouns that share words that are commonly paired in Hebrew poetry, *nāhār* and *tehôm*. But because the poet has just admitted that God's displeasure is the reason for Jonah's predicament (v 5), the second description need no longer include reference to divine management of the punishing instruments. Conversely, whereas in v 4 the poet had featured God-directed surges and swells of a mighty sea, in v 6 he has us focus on the almost fully submerged Jonah, suffocating under clinging seaweed. There can only be one deeper level of sorrow; but the poet will not reach it until the next line.

Verse 7 is the psychological center of the psalm. Just as Jonah's perilous descent brings him almost beyond return, God rescues him from beyond the grave. This line's critical role is greater when appraised within the full narrative concerning Jonah. Miserly in its supply of verbs (see below), this line is conspicuous in having just two, sharply contrasting, ones: *yārad*, "to descend," and *heʿelâ*, "to raise, lift up."[24] We have seen how the second verb (in the G stem)

[24] When Ezek 26:19–21 similarly constructs an image of the netherworld, but reverses the sequence of these verbs, a stark contrast with Jonah obtains: "Lord God has said this, 'When I turn you into a desolate city, the uninhabited kind, when I hoist the Deep upon you (*behaʿalôt ʿālayik ʾet-tehôm*) so that its immense waters cover you, then I make you join those who go down into the Pit (*wehôradtîk ʾet-yôredê bôr*), an unchanging people.' " The last phrase's *ʿam ʿôlām* hardly means "nation of old"; for, as it is clear in many passages, *ʿôlām*'s basic meaning, "eternal," occasionally refers to the netherworld; see Tromp 1969: 72–73 and especially A. Cooper 1983: 42–43.

was called upon to "explain" God's initial resolve to send his prophet toward Nineveh; see at 1:2 and soon also at 4:6. We have also seen how crucial the first of these two verbs has been in detailing Jonah's inexorable descent ever since he turned a deaf ear to God's request.[25]

I make yet one more preliminary observation as we inspect these two lines: *nepeš* and *ḥayyîm,* which Scripture often places in proximity, either as complements or as pairs, are here assigned to vv 6 and 7, respectively. Yet the difference in mood as the poet calls upon these terms is staggering: in v 6, *nepeš* tells us of the prophet's dire situation; in v 7, *ḥayyîm* announces his triumphant delivery.

ʾapāpûnî mayim ʿad-nepeš
tehōm yesōbebēnî
sûp ḥābûš lerōʾšî
leqiṣbê hārîm yāradtî
hāʾāreṣ beriḥêhā baʿadî leʿôlām
wattaʿal miššaḥat ḥayyay *YHWH ʾelōhāy*

Illustrative Passages

A. Lam 3:54:
ṣāpû-mayim ʿal-rōʾšî *ʾāmartî nigzārtî*
With water flowing over my head, I think, "it is over for me."

B. Ps 69:2, an individual lament:
hôšîʿēnî ʾelōhîm *kî bāʾû mayim ʿad-nāpeš*
Save me, God, the waters are reaching my neck.

C. Ps 18:5 (fuller quotation at I.ii, example B):
ʾapāpûnî ḥeblê-māwet *wenaḥalê belîyaʿal yebaʿatûnî*
Deadly ropes bind me, streams of demise also terrify me.

D. Ps 30:4, a psalm of gratitude:
YHWH heʿelîtā min-šeʾôl napšî
ḥiyyîtanî mywrdy [qere: *miyyāredî*]-*bôr*
Lord, you have raised me from Sheol,
[*qere:*] Giving me life, when I go down to the Pit.
[*ketib:*] Giving me life among those descending into the Pit.

E. Ps 103:4, a psalm of gratitude:
haggôʾēl miššaḥat ḥayyāyekî
[Bless God, my soul,] who redeems you alive from the Pit

25 Wolff 1986: 137 labels this observation "improbable." See also above, at 1:3, 5; Magonet 1976: 17; Landes 1967a: 25.

ʾapāpûnî mayim ʿad-nepeš. Scriptural occurrences of the verb *ʾāpap* are few, but unanimous in conveying sinister situations, whether they are reached by means of deadly ropes, perilous billows (see example C), water (this passage), or (generically) through "troubles" (Ps 40:13). The verb is highly poetic and in equivalent pronouncements is replaced by "to flow over" or simply by "to reach" (see examples A and B).

Greek renderings usually give the plural of "water"; but the LXX and the Old Latin give it in the singular; Trible 1963: 36. The Targum understands *ʿad-nepeš* as *ʿd mwtʾ*, "until death"; but as far as Jonah is concerned this sentiment may be premature. Most of the versions translate *nepeš* with words that refer to the spiritual aspect of Jonah (*psuchē, anima, nafsun,* or the like). This need not be; for it has become increasingly clear that *nepeš* also refers to the neck (as part of the upper respiratory system) in such passages as Isa 5:14 ("gullet" rather than "appetite"); Pss 69:2 (example B) and 105:18 ("iron around the neck"); Dahood 1970a: 56; Landes 1967a: 7 n. 16. Indeed, there is here a progression from neck to head that very likely parallels the heightened danger Jonah is experiencing. Something similar occurs in Ps 40:13, which shares interesting vocabulary with our passage, "Troubles without count bunch up against me (*ʾāpepû-ʿalay rāʿôt ʿad-ʾên mispār*); my faults overtake me, and I can no longer see; they are more numerous than my head hair, and I have given up hope."

We need not evaluate the various scholarly proposals regarding the etymology and derivation of *tehôm* to recognize that in Scripture it serves as a poetic term for a (primordial) body of water. *Tehôm* is commonly paired with liquid masses such as *māyim,* "waters," *yām,* "sea," *ṣūlâ/meṣōlâ/meṣūlâ/maʿamaqqîm* "(ocean) depths." (For citations and basic information, see Westermann, in *THAT* 2.1026–31.) It is therefore not surprising that Symmachus uses *thalassa,* "sea," when translating our passage. Normally, however, Greek Scripture translates *tehôm* with *abussos,* "abyss," a term likely derived from Sumerian that meant "bottomless, unfathomable" to writers such as Herodotus and Sophocles. (See, however, above under *meṣûlâ* of v 4.) Arabic uses a general word for "terror," *ʾahwāl,* but actually ignores *sûp,* "Terror surrounds me at the lower depth of the sea, and my head was caught"; Wright 1857: 111.

sûp ḥābûš lerōʾšî gives us an image that is not easily paralleled in Scripture. The verb *ḥābaš* occasionally speaks of tightening cloth to make headgear (BDB 289.1.a); but often it tells of binding a wound or of placing a medicinal poultice on the human body. It occasionally (for example, Job 40:13) alludes to veiling in darkness the face of the proud (that is, death); see Münderlein, in *ThWAT* 2.726–30). The amphibolous application of this verb is intriguing, for it makes it possible to think of Jonah's punishment as also potentially redemptive. But we cannot be sure what is truly at stake as long as the word *sûp* remains difficult to translate.

Three attestations of *sûp*—vocalized with a *šureq* (a long *u*-vowel)—refer to some sort of cane or rush that grows on the banks of Egyptian waters (Exod 2:3,

5; Isa 19:6). Jonah translations that give "seaweed, kelp," or the like generally infer that the term must also refer to a sea plant, though it is difficult to find cane or rushes in seawater.[26] More common in Scripture are the attestations in which *sûp* is attached to *yām,* yielding a phrase for the "Re(e)d Sea," *yam-sûp.*[27] The versions had a very difficult time with what stuck to Jonah's head. They treated the crucial term in a radically different way than is done by modern translators, and thereby made Jonah continue to experience exotic travails.[28] Probably influenced by *sûp* of Deut 1:1, which apparently is an abbreviation (or corruption) of *yam-sûp,* Aquila gives *eruthra* (*thalassa*), "Red Sea." Theodotion's *to pelagos* and the Vulgate's *pelagus,* "ocean," reflect a similar understanding of *sûp.* The Targum translates, "The Red Sea was wrapped around my head," reflecting (or creating) all sorts of fabulous traditions in which the fish took Jonah on a tour of the region; Levine 1978: 75–76.[29] Treating the middle vowel of **swp* as a *ḥolem-waw,* a number of ancient translations offered "last, extreme, limitless" for a presumed reading, *sôp* (LXX, *eschatē;* Old Latin, *postremo;* Symmachus, *aperantos* [note the LXX's Job 36:26 for *welōʾ ḥēqer*]). Syriac expanded into "bottom of the sea."

I have italicized "kelp" in my translation because I am not sure how to render *sûp* properly in this verset. I have followed modern renderings in picturing a Jonah who is choking under clinging marine plants. Still, mindful that the psalm's ancient readers saw no connection with Egyptian flora, whether they read *sûp* or **sôp,* I find appealing Batto's argument (1983: 32–35) that we are dealing here with one more expression for a primordial body of water. I am also struck by a reversal in the sequence of imagery as embedded in a passage from the Song of the Sea, Exod 15:4–5. There we have *yām/yam-sûp* → *tehōmōt* →*meṣôlōt,* which we may contrast with our *sûp* ← *tehôm* ← [*nāhār*] ← *meṣûlâ* (*bilbab yammîm*). Perhaps we do not need to arrive at a consistent translation for *sûp,* but we may modify the meaning to suit changing moods or occasions.

leqiṣbê hārîm yāradtî. While the GS seems to agree with the Hebrew in allocating the various segments of the verset (*hē* [*gē mochlo*]*i autēs kat emou,* Barthélemy 1963: 229–30), the LXX and the Old Latin (followed by the

[26] Highly imaginative is Wolff's observation, "Here we have to think of huge algae growing in the depth of the sea" (1986: 136).

[27] A connection between *sûp* and the Egyptian word for papyrus, "*ṯwf,*" seems very unlikely to me. Similarly implausible is the identification of the *yam-sûp* with an alleged "Re(e)d Sea"; see the arguments presented by Batto 1983.

[28] The Greek version from Qumran neatly spans the two different understandings of **swp, helos perieschen tēn kephalēn mou,* "marsh(y ground) surrounded my head"; Barthélemy 1963: 170. See also his discussion on the treatment of the word in Coptic renderings, 229–30.

[29] Because Jonah was inside the fish when he uttered his psalm, medieval exegetes felt it necessary to explain that he was actually referring to the fish's head, whose eyes served him as windows from which to view a bottomless sea; Zlotowitz 1980: 113.

Arabic) reapportion differently, which leads to an appreciably different understanding of what Jonah is expressing:

6b *abussos ekuklōse[n] me eschatē*
6c *edu hē kephalē mou eis schismas oreōn*
7a *katebēn eis gēn*
7b *hēs hoi mochloi autēs katochoi aiōnioi*

The last/furthest abyss encompassed me,
my head sank to the clefts of the mountains;
I went down into the earth,
whose bars are the everlasting barriers.

It can be noted that the LXX (1) attaches **swp* to what in Hebrew is 6b; (2) treats the verb in 6c in a manner compatible neither lexically nor syntactically with Hebrew *ḥābûš le-* (see Rudolph 1971: 346–47); and (3) links what in Hebrew are the first two words of 7a to the preceding verset. Many modern translations (NEB) and an impressive cavalcade of exegetes also attach the first two words of Hebrew 7a to the preceding verset; but even when citing the LXX as authority, they do so often to regularize the poetic meter (see, recently, Rudolph 1971: 346–47; Landes 1967a: 7; Cross 1983a: 164; Wolff 1986: 127). They would thus read:

sûp ḥābûš lerōʾšî *leqiṣbê hārîm*
yāradtî hāʾāreṣ *beriḥêhā baʿadî leʿōlām*

Such a reading is no improvement on the Masoretic accentuation and draws little sustenance from the testimony of ancient exegeses, which as we saw above, sharply moved from its sense when they differed at all from the Hebrew text. Worth noting is the fact that some Hebrew manuscripts (as well as the Targum) attach a conjunction to *hāʾāreṣ,* thus preventing its connection with the preceding verb; Trible 1963: 38 n. 2. I shall soon discuss why it is not prudent to recapture a more "original" Hebrew text on the basis of Hebrew metrics. I have two objections to apportioning the vocabulary according to this suggestion. First, while it may be plausible for *the same verset* to accommodate differing applications of the preposition *le-* (one indicating direction, the other location[30]), it is not clear to me what the poet would be implying if Jonah laments, "Seaweed was twisted round my head at the root of the mountains."[31] Is *what* is choking Jonah the reason for his despair? Or is *where* he is choking that is making him lose hope? Other lines of Hebrew poetry may well furnish us with

[30] I do not understand why Almbladh refers to Judg 5:16–17 in this context (1986: 28).
[31] The quotation I give as example is Wolff's (1986: 126).

examples of similarly bifurcated sources of sorrow; but I doubt that Hebrew poets would choose to cram them into the selfsame verset. It may therefore be prudent of us not to force them into doing so here.

The second objection has to do with the reconstructed phrase **yāradtî hāʾāreṣ*. It is simply not idiomatic to Hebrew. If Israel's poets wanted to say "I descended into the netherworld," they had the following choices:[32] (a) attach the noun to a preposition, as in Ezek 32:24, "(slain Elamites) who went down, uncircumcised, deepest into the netherworld, *ʾăšer-yārēdû ʿărēlîm ʾel-ʾereṣ taḥtîyôt*" (see also 26:20); (b) remove the article from the relevant noun, as in the following idioms: *yārad bôr/šeʾôl/ʿāpār/šaḥat;*[33] (c) end the noun with a locative, as in *yāradtî ʾarṣâ.*[34]

Jonah, then, sinks to the *qiṣbê hārîm.* Because in its two other attestations (1 Kgs 6:25; 7:37) the noun *qeṣeb* vaguely refers to the shape of manufactured cultic objects, and because the phrase is unique to our passage, many emendations have been proposed during the nineteenth century to suit the context better. We need not rehearse them here, however, for the suitability of the Hebrew has been manifest for a long time now; see Bewer 1912: 48–49. Nor need we seek an Arabic etymology for *qeṣeb* (Driver, cited approvingly by Jellicoe 1968: 325), because the phrase itself shows up in Ben Sira 16:19, *ʾp qṣby hrym wyswdy tbl bhbyṭw ʾlyhm rʿš yrʿšw*, "The base of the mountains and the foundation of the earth shake terribly when [God] looks at them."[35] The LXX, which seems aware of the occasions on which the verb *qāṣab* refers to cutting and shearing, renders by *schismas,* "crags, clefts." The remaining ancient versions emulate the poet by choosing a vocabulary that is similarly cosmological—Targum, Vulgate, "to the roots of the mountains"; Arabic, "bases of the mountains"—for they shared a cosmological concept in which, upon an axis formed by primordial mountains, there joined three components of the universe: the earth, the seas, and the underworld (see Talmon, in *ThWAT* 2.473–75). It is possible, as Cross suggests (1983a: 165), that the poet chose the first word ("roots of") because it is immediately antithetical to *rōʾšî,* "my head."

I have just noted that the verbs in this line may have been purposely limited

[32] See the listing in Tromp 1969: 32–35; Held 1973: 173 n. 2.

[33] Relying on the Greek, which he regards as "original" [but note GS, *hē gē*], Cross removes the article on *hāʾāreṣ* (1983a: 160–61).

[34] Despite many examples of *ʾarṣâ*, **hāʾārṣâ*—that is, *ʾereṣ* with the article *and* a locative ending—is unknown to Scripture. Note Ugaritic *yrdm ʾrṣ,* cited by Ottosson in *ThWAT* 1.427.

[35] Vattioni 1968: 81. Note the proximity of Ben Sira's *wyswdy tbl* to Jonah's phrase. While this last expression is itself unknown to Scripture, it is more or less equivalent to *môsedôt tēbēl,* "foundations of the (inhabited) world," of Ps 18:16 [= 2 Sam 22:16] and of *qeṣat tēbēl,* "extremity of the cosmos," of Ps 19:5. To make the circle complete, Deut 32:22 speaks of *môsedê hārîm* while Job 28:9 refers to overturning "the mountains by the roots."

to a strongly contrastive set, *yārad* and *ʿālâ.* Consequently, *hāʾāreṣ beriḥêhā baʿadî leʿôlām* remains a verbless clause that the Masoretes punctuated into three segments. The first one (*hāʾāreṣ,* "the land") is lightly drawn to a two-word segment (*beriḥêhā baʿadî,* "its bolts, about me"), which itself is kept separate from the last segment, *leʿôlām,* "eternally, for ever." To emulate this stagger in English, I have inserted "are there" between the second and third segments. As far as I know Gaster (1969: 723) is alone in providing a verbal form to the clause when he emends *leʿôlām* to the passive participle *neʿûlîm* ("Earth's bars *were bolted* against me"). While interesting, even plausible, this suggestion eliminates a brilliant effect, which will be detailed presently.

Among the versions, only the LXX (see above), Old Latin ("whose bolts are eternal barriers," *cuius vectes sunt continentes aeternae*) and Arabic ("its bars are before me forever," *ʾaǵlāquhā* [*ʾaʿlāquhā*] *fî wajhî ʾila* [*ʾad*]*dahri*) do not supply a verb. The Targum instead expands on it, "and the earth pulled [var.: locked] with its power over me forever," *wʾrʿʾ ngdt* [*ngrt*] *btwqphʾ ʿyl-mny lʿlm* [(*l*)*ʿlmyn*] (Levine 1978: 77; Wright 1857: 2). The Vulgate shortened one phrase and supplied a verb to the clause, "The bolts of the earth have locked me in forever," *terrae vectes concluserunt me in aeternum.*

In poetic reconstructions, the dead lead an eternal but dull existence, where the hurt is due to an unbridgeable separation from the loved left on earth. It is now recognized that Hebrew poets called upon these components when speaking of life away from God.[36] In Hebrew, one of the many meanings of the word *ʾereṣ* is "netherworld," and I give a few illustrations for its occurrence as such, chosen also because they contain themes of interest to our Jonah passage:

1. Isa 26:19, "May your dead revive, may corpses rise. Awake and cheer, dwellers in the dust, for your dew is the dew of tender herbs, and the *Land* shall cast out the shades."[37]
2. Jer 17:12–13, "Throne of glory, exalted from yore; our Holy Sanctuary; Israel's hope; Lord! Those who forsake you will come to shame—may they be reckoned among those who turn toward the *Land* [Targum: *bghynm!*]—for they have forsaken the Lord, the source of life-giving water."[38]

[36] Overviews of the subject as well as bibliography can be found in Stadelmann 1970: 128–29; 166–68; Ottosson, in *ThWAT* 1.426–27; Schmid, in *THAT* 1.230; Dahood 1969: 337.

[37] For the difficult *nebēlātî,* it may be necessary to read *nebēlôt,* by transposing the last two letters and reading the *yod* as *waw.* In this and the next verse, Isaiah is making a powerful contrast between God's mercy for the dead in one "Land" (that is, the "Netherworld") and his anger against those living in this "Land."

[38] This too is a very difficult passage, about which much has been written; see McKane 1986: 398–408. Regarding the *mayim-ḥayyîm,* I am reminded of the "water of life" that, according to Sumero-Akkadian myths, is needed to revive the dead Inanna-Ishtar.

3. Ps 22:30, "Imposing men of the *Land* shall eat and worship; those who go downward to the dust, each of whom is not alive, shall bend the knee before him."[39]
4. Ps 71:20 (reading the *ketib* throughout), "You who make us experience many and terrible ordeals, once again you will revive us, from the core of the *Land,* once again you will raise us."
5. Eccl 3:21 (ironic?), "Who knows whether the human soul goes upward, while that of beasts goes downward into the *Land?*"
6. Sir 51:19, "I raise my voice from the *Land,* my plea from the gates of Sheol."
7. Jer 15:7, "I will scatter them as with a winnowing fork within the gates of the *Land.* I will bereave, I will destroy my folk, for they do not turn back from their habits."[40]

The last two examples speak of "gates," of Sheol and of the "land."[41] These "gates," seven in all, are secured by "bars" (for which the more common term is

[39] For *napšô lōʾ ḥiyyâ,* we may render, "he [God] did not revive him." The full verse itself is very difficult and has received a variety of interpretations (see Tromp 1969: 32–35) as well as merciless emendations (for example, Kraus 1988: 292). Actually, this verse, which speaks of shades invited to partake of a meal (after which to worship God), reminds me of rituals recovered from Babylon (see, most recently, Durand and Charpin 1986) and from Ugarit (see, most recently, B. Levine and Tarragon 1984), in which the living invite the ghosts of kings and high officials to partake of a meal. The verse is also contrasting the poor on *this earth,* who nevertheless can come into God's presence, and the well fed of the *other earth* (that is, the afterlife), who cannot do so, except by the poet's invitation; see vv 27–28, "May the lowly eat and be satisfied; may those who seek [the Lord] praise him; may you always be vigorous. The confines of the Earth shall recall the Lord and turn to him, while kinsmen of the nations shall worship you; because kingship is the Lord's and he rules the nations."

[40] Scholars do not usually regard this passage as referring to the underworld; see most recently McKane 1986: 338–40. Because winnowing does not take place at the city gate but at a relatively distant threshing floor, I connect this passage to a mythological scene in which an avenging Anat treats Mot, the god of the Netherworld, as grain, "She seizes the Godly Mot— / With sword she doth cleave him. / With fan she does winnow him — / With fire she does burn him. / With hand mill she grinds him— / In the field she doth sow him" (Ginsberg in *ANET*³ 140: 31–36). Another echo of this motif is found in Exod 32:20, paralleled by Deut 8:21.

[41] These portals are cited in the plural, but "Netherworld" can also be replaced by epithets or synonyms, for example, by Death (Mot): Pss 9:14, 107:18; Job 38:17 (paralleled with Death's Shadow); and Matt 16:18. The most impressive allusion to these infernal gates, however, may be in Psalm 24, where the poet instructs them to open wide for God's entrance, a possible prelude to his triumphal conquest of the realm of the dead; see A. Cooper 1983.

term is *berîaḥ*), cited in the singular or in the plural.[42] In the Jonah passage, the poet has chosen to give a highly distilled formulation of a phrase fully cited elsewhere in Scripture, *sāgar haddelet beʿad* + (someone); Gen 7:16; 2 Kgs 4:4–5, 23; and Isa 26:20. Keil and Delitzsch (1900: 402) refer to a wonderful passage in Job 38:8–10 in which God forces the waters to stand behind bars and gates.

Here *leʿôlām* is a temporal adverb, but, as I have noted previously, in some scriptural passages one of the noun's basic meanings, "eternity," can be metonymous for the netherworld; A. Cooper 1983: 43 n. 34. In the present clause, therefore, we may find two figures for the cruel beyond (*ʾereṣ . . . ʿôlām, "the* [under]world eternal") sandwiching the hapless Jonah.

We are told by *wattaʿal miššaḥat ḥayyay* that Jonah's rescue comes in the nick of time. That God may spare human beings from the netherworld is a notion known to Israel (see BDB, under *ḥāśak,* 362). Commonly expressed, too, is the concept that God may even rescue the dead from that realm; Hebrew uses then the verbs *ḥāyâ* (*D* stem, example D), "to revive"; *pādâ,* "to rescue, ransom"; *gāʾal* (example E), to "redeem"; *hēšîb,* "to retrieve"; as well as our own *heʿelâ,* "to raise."[43] God, who gives life, can also revive (Deut 32:39; 1 Sam 2:6; 2 Kgs 5:7). Such ideologies partake of commonly shared Near Eastern beliefs that by divine grace individuals may occasionally be resuscitated (1 Kgs 17:17–24; 2 Kgs 4:18–37), renewed (Naaman, 2 Kgs 5:1–14), rejuvenated (Adam and Eve, when they had access to the Tree of Life), immortalized (Enoch, Elijah), or even resurrected (Israel: in Hos 6:2; in Ezekiel's vision 37:1–14).[44] They are not necessarily to be equated with the elaborate messianic doctrine of mass resurrection in eschatological times (already in Isa 26:19; Dan 12:2–3).[45]

The word *wattaʿal* can be rendered in one of four ways, differing in subject (second-person masculine singular or third-person feminine singular) and in stem (*G:* "go up, climb, ascend" or *H:* "bring up, raise"). As vocalized by the

[42] Job 17:13–19, "If I expect Sheol to be my home, to make my bed in darkness, to say to the Pit, 'you are my father,' to the maggot, 'you are my mother (or sister)'—Where then can my hope be? Who can determine what is my hope? Can they descend with me behind Sheol's barriers (*baddê šeʾôl*), if we are to lie together upon dust?" In Jonah, the choice of vocabulary for "barrier" may well be intentional, for *berîaḥ* has the same consonants as a verb featured in the first chapter (at vv 3 and 10), *bāraḥ,* "to escape (God)." Kimḥi (cited by Levine 1978: 78) might have had this connection in mind when he rendered the noun as a verb, thus suggesting that the land is now escaping from Jonah!

[43] For listing, see Held 1973: 175 nn. 21–25.

[44] Apparently unknown to ancient Israel were reincarnation, metempsychosis, and transmigration of the soul, doctrines discussed in medieval Jewish philosophy (see "Gilgul" in *Enc Jud* 7.573–77).

[45] M. Greenberg (*Enc Jud* 14.96–98) disputes Dahood's retrojection of this concept into the psalms.

Masoretes, however, the subject can only be in the second person, for the other components of the clause are either indirect objects (*miššaḥat*) or masculine plural (*ḥayyîm* + first-person possessive suffix). In view of this narrow choice, the identity of the subject becomes manifest: the poet is obviously addressing God, whom he invokes in the vocative at the end of the line, "Lord, my god." The verb can then only be transitive and thus must be construed as a causative (*H* stem).

All of this may seem obvious, except that some of the versions apparently treated the passage differently. To begin with, there seems to have been a concerted effort not to have Jonah rising from "the Pit," possibly because the prophet should not *presume* the certainty of his rescue when God had not yet ordered the fish to vomit him. Therefore, the noun *šaḥat* is derived from the verb *šāḥat*, "to go to ruin," allowing renderings connected with "corruption, perdition."[46] The Targum simply turns the whole passage into a prophetic vision of rescue, "And it is revealed before you to raise my life from destruction," *wʾtgly* [var.: *wʾt qryb; wʾtqryb*] *qdmk lʾsqʾ mḥblʾ-ḥyy;* Levine 1978: 77–78. The Vulgate regards the verbal form as an imperfect with a simple conjunction *waw* (instead of with the conversive *waw* + *dagesh* forte; perhaps **wetaʿal*[*eh*]). Thus the Vulgate has "And you will make my life rise up from corruption," *et sublevabis de corruptione vitam meam.* Greek versions, however, treated the verb as a precative and equated *ḥayyay* with a word that is feminine singular; see Hill 1967: 163–75. Thus we have the LXX's Vaticanus and Sinaiticus, "yet may my corrupt life be restored," *kai anabētō phthora zōēs mou* and the LXX's Symmachus and Theodotion (cf. C. Alexandrinus and W), "and from corruption, may my life be restored," *kai anabētō* [*ek*] *phthoras zōēs mou.* The Old Latin has *šaḥat* as subject, also with a precative verb, "may the corruption of my life rise toward you," *et ascendat corruptio vitae meae ad te.*

"Lord, my god" (v 7d) is common to Hebrew prayers (for example, Pss 7:2, 4; 13:4; 18:29), whether it opens or closes petitions. Here it is an obvious device by which to link Jonah's prayerful words to what is said about Jonah's activity when in the fish's belly; see at 2:2. In the next two lines, the poet shows that Jonah's rescue did not come unsolicited, but that God acted after hearing his plea.

II.v (v 8). It may be accidental that the book of Jonah reaches its halfway mark in verse count just as it comes to the very strophe in which Jonah and God are in their closest proximity.[47] Here, the poet is not renewing his lament but is recalling how during his travail his rescue was effected as soon as lips uttered prayers to God. Therefore, the sentiments of 8a–b reflect all of the agony

[46] A correct etymology for the term is not yet established. Held (1973) has shown that *šaḥat* cannot be derived from *šwḥ*, "to sink down," which may well be a nonexistent verb.
[47] In 2:4, *yesōbebēnî* marks the center of the book in word count.

experienced in vv 5 and 7. To make this assessment perfectly transparent, the poet sandwiches his fall and rise within two verbs for the uttering of words (*ʾāmartî*, at v 5a; *zākartî*, at v 8b) as well as two repetitions of *ʾel-hêkal qodšekā*, at vv 5d and 8d).

behitʿaṭṭēp ʿālay napšî *ʾet-YHWH zākārtî*
wattābôʾ ʾēlêkā tepillātî *ʾel-hêkal qodšekā*

Illustrative Passages

A. Ps 142:4, a psalm of lament and supplication:
behitʿaṭṭēp ʿālay rûḥî
weʾattâ yādaʿtā netîbātî . . . (v 6, *zāʿaqtî ʾēlêkā*)
Even as my spirit is ebbing away from me,
you yet know my direction . . . (I then call to you).

B. Ps 77:4, a psalm of lament and of praise:
ʾezkerâ ʾelōhîm weʾehemāyâ
ʾāśîḥâ wetitʿaṭṭēp rûḥî
I want to recall God, but only groan;
I want to complain, but only faint.

C. Ps 143:4–5, a psalm of lament and prayer:
wattitʿaṭṭēp ʿālay rûḥî . . .
zākartî yāmîm miqqedem[48]
As my spirit ebbs away from me . . .
I recall past moments (and stretch my hands in prayer).

D. Ps 107:5–6 (see 13, 19, 28), a thanksgiving psalm:
reʿēbîm gam-ṣemēʾîm *napšām bāhem titʿaṭṭāp*
wayyiṣʿaqû/wayyizʿaqû ʾel-YHWH baṣṣar lāhem
Hungry and thirsty, their spirit dwindling within them,
in their anguish, they call on the Lord
(who saves them from their predicament).

E. Ps 88:3:
tābôʾ lepānêkā tepillātî haṭṭēh-ʾoznekā lerinnātî
May my prayer reach you, pay attention to my shout.

F. Ps 102:2 [cf. Ps 39:13], a psalm of lament and praise:
YHWH šimʿâ tepillātî *wešawʿātî ʾelêkā tābôʾ*
Lord, listen to my prayer; may my appeal reach you.

[48] Note that Ps 77:6 parallels this verset by substituting the verbal form *ḥiššabtî*, "I consider, review," for *zākartî*.

G. Ps 18:7 [= 2 Sam 22:7] (see above, I.i, example A):
wešawʿātî {lepānāyw tābōʾ} beʾoznāyw
[Ps:] My appeal comes before him, at his ear.
[2 Sam:] My appeal is at his ear.

H. 2 Chr 30:27 (prose text):
(When the priest and the Levites began to bless the people, their voice was heard,)
wattābôʾ tepillātām limʿôn qodšô laššamayim
their prayer going heavenward to his holy abode.

behitʿaṭṭēp ʿālay napšî. To capture an image of a person about to give up hope, Hebrew poetry links a word for the human vital force, either *nepeš* (examples D and Jon 2:8) or *rûaḥ* (examples A, B, and C), to the *HtD* stems of *ʿāṭap.*[49] It is not surprising, therefore, that some Hebrew manuscripts read *rûḥî* in place of *napšî;* Trible 1963: 38 n. 6. As to the verb, the dictionaries distinguish between three different words *ʿṭp,* suggesting that they originally (that is, in their "proto-Semitic" phase) differed in some of their root consonants. It is not necessary to do so. Although it is difficult for us to conceive how the idiom arose—the spirit curling upon itself?—all three verbs semantically share the notion of something turning either aside or on itself. (See further the notes to *wayyitʿallāp* at 4:8.) The versions are pretty close to the Hebrew, finding idioms to express the same notion.[50]

ʾet-YHWH zākārtî. Once poets recognize how hopeless is their situation, they turn to God. The verbs relevant to the response vary, and in the example above we have instances of *zākar* (B, C) and of *z/ṣāʿaq ʾel-* (A, D). In example B, the more common sequence (despair leading to appeal) is reversed: so benumbed is the poet that the words simply cannot come out right. The verb *zākar* merges the notions of "remembering" and "orally invoking" something or someone; Schotroff, in *THAT* 1.507–18. This fusion is illustrated in a famous line from Ps 137:5–6, "If I forget you, Jerusalem, may my right hand wither [or: lose its skill]; may my tongue stick to my palate if I do not *recall* you (*ʾezkerēkî*), if I do not prefer Jerusalem over my sweetest pleasure." For our *zākārtî,* I have tried to approximate this convergence of activities through the English "recall"; other translations usually offer "think," "remember," "mention," or the like, to suit the context. When it is YHWH whom individuals are "recalling," Hebrew

[49] The idiom does not mean "to lose consciousness" (so Allen 1976: 214 and Stuart 1987: 469). Jonah must be aware of what is happening to him when he calls on God's mercy.

[50] The idiom may or may not (example B) need an indirect object: examples A and C use *ʿal;* example D uses *be-*. J. Rosenberg's rendering (1987: 37), "My life wrapped like a prayer shawl over me," owes more to Chagall or to Jewish devotional activities than to Semitic philology.

sets the Tetragrammaton off by means of the particle *ʾet* (for example, Deut 8:18; Judg 8:34).[51] This observation is reason enough to reject Dahood's revocalizing the particle *ʾet* into *ʾattâ* (1970b: 86).

wattābôʾ ʾēlêkā tepillātî. The versions generally parallel the Hebrew. Consistent with the position that Jonah cannot presume on God's mercy, the LXX and the Vulgate treat the consonants of the verbal form (*wtbwʾ*) as a jussive ("may my prayer reach you"; **wetābôʾ*). The Hebrew text, however, opens up an interesting issue.

Seeking a favorable divine judgment for themselves, people utter a *tepillâ* to appeal to God's mercy. A petition, which plays a major role in psalmody, commonly requires the worshiper to address God with requests that in Hebrew are couched normally as imperative or jussive verbal forms.[52] The word *tepillâ* obviously recalls the narrator's observation (at 2:2–3a) that "Jonah prayed (*wayyitpallēl*) to the Lord, his god . . . saying" (and also looks forward to 4:2); but, in fact, nowhere in the psalm does Jonah ask of God specific measures to counteract his misery. I doubt that Jonah fears losing contact with God because he is no longer in downtown Jerusalem for, unstated though it may be, we nevertheless know that Jonah's appeal does reach (idiom: *bôʾ* + *ʾel-*, *le-*, or *lipnê*) God.

Jonah's particular wishes are not difficult to imagine; yet the poet is reticent about revealing more than what is implied by the phrase *ʾet-YHWH zākārtî.* This terse treatment (not to say elimination) of Jonah's petition may leave us wanting, however, for we do after all relish listening to the cant and grovel of the powerful and the privileged. Nevertheless, the poet, who is sensitive to Jonah's despair of ever returning to God's confidence (v 5), harks back to a more positive moment when the prophet obtained God's mercy (v 3). (The sequence, "hearing a [pleading] voice . . . reaching God," is paralleled in examples F and H.) In this way, the poet is free to describe (rather than to judge) the calamities that befell the prophet (vv 4–7b). We need not be as restrained as the poet, and we can devise an appropriate prayer for Jonah by quoting Ps 9:14–15: "Have mercy on me, Lord. Look how I am hurt by my enemies, you who can pull me from the gates of death. I shall then recite all your praise at Fair Zion's gates and find joy in your deliverance."

II.vi (v 9). This very brief line of just two versets is not likely to carry Jonah's prayer, for it contains neither the language nor the construction of a petition. It holds nicely contrasting ideas, with two antithetical verbs at the outer edges and two opposing concepts facing each other. (Walsh 1982: 224 is sharpest on the contrast.) We may note, however, that the Masoretes have accented it into four individual thoughts, a pattern that is difficult to emulate in English; see Mes-

[51] This rule does not always obtain when *ʾelōhîm* is the direct object, as example B shows.
[52] Aejmelaeus 1986, and Greenberg 1983, offer illustrations and further explanations. I have adopted Greenberg's definition for *tepillâ* (21–22; bibliography, 62–63 n. 2).

chonnic 1984: 238–39. Although I call it "a strophe," it may better be ranged among *cris de coeur,* of the type occasionally found, for example at Gen 49:18 (perhaps also at example E, below). Or it may be placed among observations that are occasionally inserted into longer poetic texts (example C; Ps 106:3), but that are more thickly embedded in didactic psalms such as 37, 49, and 73. That the line may be an interpolation is plausible; more likely to me, however, is that the poet found in it a particularly opportune occasion by which to arrest and thus accent starkly the stages in Jonah's shift from heartfelt contrition to firm resolve.

Medieval exegetes generally regarded this line as Jonah's comment on the sailors and on their failure to understand truly what God requires of human beings; Zlotowitz 1980: 115–16. It may be remembered that according to midrashic embellishments, only after the fish vomits Jonah do the sailors, erstwhile pagans, turn back to land, proceed to Jerusalem, and undergo circumcision (Hirsch 1904: 227). Modern commentators who parallel motifs between the psalm and chapter 1 (for example, Landes 1967a: 16–17; Stuart 1987: 471–72) implicitly agree that the verse is meant to censure the sailors.

mešammerîm hablê-šāwʾ *ḥasdām yaʿazōbû*

Illustrative Passages

A. Ps 31:7, a psalm of petition and praise:
śānēʾtî haššōmerîm hablê-šāwʾ
waʾanî ʾel-YHWH bāṭāḥtî
ʾāgîlâ weʾeśmeḥâ beḥasdekā
I detest those who keep empty faiths;
I want only to trust in the Lord,
exhuberantly rejoicing in your mercy,
(that you notice my distress, recognize my many anxieties).

B. Zech 10:2:
kî hatterāpîm dibberû-ʾāwen *wehaqqôsemîm ḥāzû šeqer*
waḥalōmôt haššāwʾ yedabberû *hebel yenaḥēmûn*
For idols speak deceit, diviners conjure lies;
dreams tell fantasy, comforting deceptively.

C. Ps 16:4, a difficult passage in a psalm of praise:
yirbû ʿaṣṣebôtām *ʾaḥēr māhārû*
They multiply their sorrow, those who pursue another [god].

D. Deut 32:21 (cf. 16), Moses' testament:
hēm qinneʾûnî belōʾ-ʾēl *kiʿasûnî behablêhem*
They make me jealous of non-gods,
anger me with their trifles.

(I shall make them jealous of non-entities,
anger them through foolish folk.)

E. Jer 8:19, possibly an interjection (see McKane 1986: 193–94):
(Now I hear the loud plea of my people, from distant lands: Is the Lord not in Zion? Is her king not with her?)
maddûaʿ hikʿisûnî bipsilêhem *behablê nēkār*
Why must they anger me with their idols, with alien trifles?

F. Hos 4:10:
(They eat but are not sated; are promiscuous, but remain sterile,)
kî-ʾet-YHWH ʿāzebû lišmōr
since they abandon worshipping God.[53]

G. Ps 71:9, a psalm of praise and supplication:
ʾal-tašlîkēnî leʿēt ziqnâ *kiklôt kōḥî ʾal-taʿazbēnî*
Do not cast me away when I age abandon me, when powerless.

mešammerîm hablê-šāwʾ. It is clear that the first word is a *D* stem participle of *šāmar.* Because Scripture has no other example for this conjugation of the verb, many commentators suggest alternative readings. Because Aquila gives *apō phulassontōn mataiotēta eikē,* "from keepers of trivial images," some scholars think that he pronounced consonantal *mšmrm* as **miššomērîm* (that is, as *min* + *šōmerîm*), which would suggest that *mem* was prefixed to the word in Aquila's text (Wolff 1986: 127); and, indeed, this insight is corroborated by the reading found in the slightly earlier Murabbaʿât (Qumran) scrolls (Milik 1961: 191). Ehrlich, instead, presumes that the text in question read **ʿim šōmerîm* (1912: 267).

As to the conjugation of the verbal form, because Mishnaic Hebrew knows the *piʿel* of the verb *šāmar* and has many occasions to use the *D* stem participle (Jastrow 1950: 1600–1601), it could be that the scriptural form is not aberrant. Indeed, biblical Hebrew knows of a few verbal forms that, though similarly rare in Scripture, find common attestation in literature from later periods. It might not be necessary, therefore, to invoke comparative lexicography to vouch for the

[53] It is a difficult passage. Many commentators attach the first word from the next verse to the same line. Harper simply deletes *lišmōr* (1905: 259). G. R. Driver (1934: 384–85) emends into a *D* stem, thinking of Jon 2:9 (on which see below). Andersen and Freedman (1980: 363–64), who prefer to follow Dahood in discovering yet another emphatic *l,* finally "fall back on the MT" and settle on the more probable exegesis. Nevertheless, Hebrew sentences can end in infinitives, as for example in Gen 2:3, *ʾašer bārāʾ ʾelōhîm laʿaśôt,* "that God had planned to create." (More examples of such a construction are given in GKC 351 104o.) Moreover, in the Hosea passage, "the Lord" is direct object to both verbs, "abandon" and "keep, revere." Because, as is clear from v 12, Israel's fault includes lechery and drunkenness, *zenût,* "whore-mongering," introduces well the remaining words in v 11.

verb's validity (as does Allen 1976: 215 n. 6, who depends on G. R. Driver 1934: 384–85). In biblical Hebrew, there are a few participial forms such that, when they are available in both G and D stems, the latter confers a regular or habitual routine to the act: *zābaḥ, rāṣaḥ, 'āhēb*; a fuller listing of such verbs in GKC 141 § 52.f. If this is the case here, we may then render 2:9a as "They who *maintain* empty faiths."

There is one more consideration, however. Bothered by the lack of a construct ending to *mešammerîm*, some scholars want to treat its last consonant as an enclitic *mem* (Hummel 1957: 99; Batto 1983: 32 n. 21). It is not necessary to do so, for the participle in the absolute state may also control dependent nouns (best examples in Joüon 1923: 343 [§ 121l]; see also Almbladh 1986: 30).

People, then, are keeping hold of *hablê-šāw'*. Individually, the words in this phrase can abstractly connote "foolishness, futility, vanity," while concretely it can refer to "idol, (false) gods" (example E). The range of meanings is well brought out in example B, where the two words complement each other and are found within a sequence of negative words. Because in our passage *hebel* and *šāw'* are linked by the plural construct, Joüon (1923: 437 [§ 141.m]) suggests for them a superlative nuance, "extreme vanity" (or the like). The versions treated the phrase differently. Although the LXX (*mataia kai pseudē*) and the Old Latin (*vana et falsa*) inserted a conjunction between the words, hendiadys merges them into one concept, "false vanities." Aquila (see above) and Symmachus (*atmous mataious*) approximated the Hebrew, while the Vulgate (*qui custodiunt vanitates frustra*) became more interested in the nature of the act and therefore treated *šāw'* as an adverbial accusative, "they who pointlessly retain vanities." Worrying lest the reader attach nefarious deeds to Israel, the Targum supplied two words and unabashedly paraphrased the rest of the line, "Not as the nations, worshipers of idols (who do not understand the source of their well-being)." (On all of these matters, see Trible 1963: 39 and Levine 1978: 79–80.)

I have treated the phrase neither as a superlative nor as a hendiadys, but as a formation in which the adjective appears in the plural construct state before the noun it modifies. Thus, *'ebyônê 'ādām* does not mean "humanity's poor persons," but simply "poor folk" (more citations in GKC 428 [§ 132.c]). I have purposely rendered *šāw'* by "faiths," because our words "idol, statue, image," and the like do not fully convey what cultic figurines meant to the ancient world. The statue of the god was a tangible way by which a deity communicated with worshipers. Coming into its presence, the ancients were as full of awe, fear, and hope; as conscious of the deity's power to heal or hurt bodily and psychologically; as cognizant of the god's capacity to end or lengthen life as would be today's believers when nearing a church or synagogue sanctuary. By using this word "faith"—for which *'emûnâ* is the better equivalent—I want to stress that it was not easy for ancients to shake their attachment to a god they had worshiped since childhood. At the same time, by resorting to "faith," I seek to clarify why a Hebrew poet found Jonah's psalm a perfect vehicle by which to urge allegiance to Israel's God.

The poet tells us what the insensitive idolaters are risking: they are about to *ḥasdām yaʿazōbû*. The verb *ʿāzab* refers to the act of leaving (something or someone) and is used figuratively of human beings forsaking God (or vice versa). It is thus a good opposite to *šāmar* (*D* stem) of the first verset and may well stimulate the memory toward *šālak* (*H* stem) of v 4, a verb that it can parallel (example G). The form can be a jussive and is so taken by Keller 1982: 279 ("may they give up on their devotion"). But it is difficult to be precise about the consequences of idolatry because of the breadth of meaning of the word *ḥesed*, because human beings as well as God can display *ḥesed*, and because there is uncertainty about the relation between *ḥesed* and the third-person personal suffix attached to it. (Good discussion on these matters is in Price and Nida 1978: 46–48.) We shall meet with the term once more in 4:2.

An enormous amount of scholarly attention has been devoted to *ḥesed*, which has prompted the invention of quaint nouns ("lovingkindness," already in the KJV); but it has yet to be pinned down satisfactorily; bibliography and overview in *THAT* 1.600–621. For the present purpose, it may loosely be defined as the potential (as well as its fulfillment) for a person in a higher position (god, king, husband, or father) to act favorably and benevolently to another person or entity in a lower position (nation, subject, wife, or child). Because it is not likely that the poet is warning idolaters that they may lose their capacity to shower favors on others, scholars have had to propose more plausible threats. Possibly encouraged by the Syriac version, which simply changes the suffix into a second-person singular ("they abandon *your* [God's] kindness"), some exegetes presume that *ḥasdām* refers metonymically to God, conveying the notion that idolaters will no longer enjoy the favors of the true god.[54] But as this expansion of the word *ḥesed* is only dubiously supported by the relevant passages, Bewer (1912: 49) cites Marti as authority for emending the word into *maḥasēhem*, "their refuge" (thus also Moffatt, probably inspired by Ps 91:2). Most Jonah commentators, however, refer to Ps 144:1–2 (*bārûk YHWH . . . ḥasdî ûmeṣûdātî*, "Blessed is the Lord . . . my *ḥesed* and bulwark"), but then proceed with a rendering that suits Jonah's condition.[55] Differing radically is Radak who, after Ibn Janah, cites Lev 20:17 (also Prov 14:34), where a homonym of *ḥesed* actually means "shame." He therefore suggests that the culprits "have

[54] BDB 737 (2.c), 339 (II); Keil and Delitzsch 1900: 403; Rashi, "the fear of God," Zlotowitz 1980: 115. Landes (1967a: 7) essentially agrees but finds a more circuitous way of doing so, "the One [sic] who loves them."

[55] Thus, Kuyper (1963: 491) offers "strength" and is followed by Rudolph 1971: 347. In the NEB, RSV, and Holbert (1981: 73) we find "loyalty." The KJV gives "mercy," and Cross (1983a: 166) expands it into "(source of) mercy." Johnson (1950: 85) unsuccessfully defends the ambiguous "devotion," yet manages to persuade Keller 1982: 279.

abandoned their shame," a notion that can be very equivocal (cited in Zlotowitz 1980: 115–16).

I have listed more prior suggestions than I normally do because I cannot promote a defensible solution. In offering my translation, I have reasoned that v 9b is consequential to 9a; that the verb in 9b is chosen to contrast with 9a; and that *ḥesed* is a gratification that is not available to individuals attached to *hablê-šāwʾ*, whether it be for them to receive or dispense it.

Caveat emptor.

III.vii (v 10). We may separate the sentiments expressed in the first two versets (10a–b) from that of the last (10c) because the final two words amount to a doxology. As it stands, two of this line's verbs are in the cohortative mood, suggesting that Jonah's promises cannot be realized right away. Nonetheless, the line does fulfill the expectations we have harbored ever since learning that God has responded to Jonah's anguished appeals (v 3). Therefore these two verses, 3 and 10, envelop and enclose the powerful portrait of a soul about to lose touch with its creator.

waʾanî beqôl tôdâ ʾezbeḥâ-llak
ʾašer nādartî ʾašallēmâ
yešûʿātâ laYHWH

Illustrative Passages

A. Ps 116: 17–18, 19, a psalm of gratitude and praise:
lekā-ʾezbaḥ zebaḥ tôdâ *ûbšēm YHWH ʾeqrāʾ*
nedāray laYHWH ʾašallēm *negdâ-nnāʾ lekol-ʿammô*
. . . *hal(l)elû-yāh*
I shall offer sacrifice in gratitude to you,
invoking the Lord's name;
I shall fulfill my vow to the Lord,
facing all his people (at the Temple, in Jerusalem).
. . . Hallelujah!

B. Ps 26:7, a confession:
(I wash my hands in innocence, and walk around your altar, Lord,)
lašmiaʿ beqôl tôdâ *ûlesappēr kol-nipleʾôtêkā*
loudly proclaiming gratitude and recounting all your feats.

C. Ps 50:14, a liturgical and didactic psalm:
zebaḥ lēʾlōhîm tôdâ *wešallēm leʿelyôn nedārêka*
Sacrifice to God in gratitude; fulfill your vow to the Most High.

D. Ps 50:23 (as above):
zōbēaḥ tôdâ yekabbedānenî
weśām derek ʾarʾennû beyēšaʿ ʾelōhîm
One who sacrifices in gratitude, honors me;
to the one *who makes it possible,*
I will disclose God's salvation.

E. Ps 56:13, a psalm of lament and affirmation of faith:
ʿālay ʾelōhîm nedārêkā *ʾašallēm tôdôt lāk*
On me, God, are your vows; I will render you thank offerings.

F. Isa 19:21, a prose text:
(The Lord shall come to be known to Egypt, and Egypt shall acknowledge the Lord on that very day)
weʿābedû zebaḥ ûminḥâ wenāderû-neder laYHWH wešillemû
They shall worship with all kinds of sacrifice [literally, animal and grain]; they shall make vows to the Lord and fulfill them.

G. Ps 3:3, 9, a morning prayer (see also Ps 37:39):
rabbîm ʾōmerîm lenapšî *ʾên yešûʿātâ llô*
Many say to my face, . . . "there is no rescue for him."
laYHWH hayyešûʿâ *ʿal-ʿammekā birkāteka*
Rescue is from God; your blessing should be on your folk.

waʾanî beqôl tôdâ ʾezbeḥâ-llak. I give as one clause what most modern editors and commentators separate into two, mostly to arrive at a suitable meter. The noun *tôdâ* (singular or plural) refers either to songs or to sacrifices presented by an individual grateful to God's benevolence. When animal sacrifice accompanies such a worshiper's devotion, the noun *zebaḥ* and the verb *zābaḥ,* either singly or together, can be attached to the term. It is noteworthy, however, that when the noun *tôdâ* is in proximity to *zābaḥ,* they share the same poetic verset, as is exemplified by examples A, C, and D. Greek and Old Latin give two words separated by a conjunction to approximate Hebrew *tôdâ: aineseōs* [W: *deēseōs*] *kai eksomologēseōs* and *laudis et confessionis,* both phrases meaning "praise [W: supplication] and acknowledgment"; Trible 1963: 39. Origen suggests excising the second word in the Greek; but this may not be necessary, as the two words may be read as one unit of thought. The Targum becomes prolix: "As for me, I will make an offering before you with praise of thanksgiving (*btwšbḥt ʾwdʾh*)."

Some scholars have emended the verb into **ʾazammerâ* (cited by Bewer 1912: 49); but this reading is taking *qôl* too literally. The noun functions here almost as an adverb to *zābaḥ,* as it does also in example B, and we should avoid the cumbersome "voice of thanksgiving" or "voice of the song of gratitude," both of which are commonly met in renderings.

ʾašer nādartî ʾašallēmâ. Hebrew uses a number of verbs when vows are being taken (*nādar,* see at 1:16), imposed, confirmed, or reversed; but *šillam* is the verb that speaks of its fulfillment. Constructing an object clause to the verb *šillam* by means of *ʾašer* plus the verb *nādar* is pretty common to Scripture; Even-Shoshan 1982: 744. I therefore cannot see how Auffret (1978: 103) reshuffles v 10 in order to give *ʾašer* (*nādartî*) a pivotal role within the line.

I have avoided the English "pay," commonly used in translations (for example, NJPS), lest it be presumed that monetary restitution must always be involved. What is noteworthy in the poem is Jonah's stated intention to discharge his obligation, which has been contrasted by various exegetes with the sailors' vague formulation, "they took vows." We do not know what Jonah vowed to God. It may not have gone beyond the last verset's promise to sacrifice.

yešûʿātâ laYHWH. This verset was linked by ancient and by some medieval exegetes to the preceding clause. The Targum judged it as explanation to Jonah's vow: "(what I have vowed, I shall fulfill:) redemption price for my life, in prayer, before the Lord," *pwrqn-npšy bṣlw qdm YY;* Levine 1978: 65–66. The LXX is less obvious in turning the phrase into a lesson: *hosa ēuksamēn apodōsō soi sōtēriou tō Kuriō,* "all that I vowed, I shall discharge to you, Lord, for salvation (obtained)." Similar is the Vulgate, *quaecumque vovi reddam pro salute Domino,* "the vows that I made, I shall fulfill them to the Lord, for (received or future) salvation." (See Trible 1963: 39.) Arabic simply cuts out the first of the two words: *wamā nadārtu ʾawfîhi lirrab,* "I shall fulfill what I have vowed to God"; Wright 1857: 111. Rashi reads the verset as if it were preceded by a preposition, "for (because) salvation is from God." By contrast, David Kimḥi thinks it emphasizes that God alone is responsible for Jonah's deliverance; Zlotowitz 1980: 116.

In meaning, *yešûʿātâ* does not seem to differ from the more common *yešûʿâ,* "deliverance, salvation." It belongs to a small group of feminine nouns with an extra but unaccented *-ātâ.* Such words (collected in GKC 251 [§ 90.f(b)]) are embedded in poetic passages (example G). Because they can occur at any point in the poem, these nouns defy a simple explanation. In this last verset of Jonah's poem, however, the pulling back of the accent may have served to brake the poet's declamation (note the disjunctive accent under *-ʿā-*) as well as to isolate and thereby to accentuate the name of God upon which the poem ends. The audience readily recognizes that such a sharply chiseled ending is "at once a confession and praise, a Creed and a *Te Deum*" (Perowne 1905: 73).

Thus ends Jonah's fine poem. The Murabbaʿāt scroll leaves an empty line before resuming with the prose text. Some of the manuscripts recognize the difficulty of immediate transition by placing at this juncture the consonant *samekh* (for *perāšâ setûmâ/setûmāʾ,* "closed unit of Scripture readings"), instructing scribes to leave a space vacant.

COMMENTS

I will use this space to take up a number of topics about the psalm of Jonah that scholarly literature commonly addresses. We have seen that when quoting the terrified sailors' plea to God (1:14), the narrator fashions it out of pious tenets known to Hebrew entreaties. That particular prayer, lyrical though not poetic, suits the context perfectly, with language and conviction naturally emerging from the unfolding narrative where awe and dread predominate. I will address Jonah's prayer of 4:2–3 when we get to it.

Language

The psalm of chapter 2, however, is quite different in this respect, and many commentators rehearse the contrasts between the psalm and the surrounding narrative, pointing out that they differ in the use vocabulary (words are particular to each, or are conspicuously absent from either),[56] tense (narrative past versus poetic/prophetic present-future), setting ("natural" versus surrealistic), as well as in the attitude Jonah displays (disobeying versus submissive).[57] I have treated a number of these features in the preceding NOTES, where I suggest that these disparities are organic to the distinctive dictions obtaining in poetry and prose. Therefore, once we realize that the language of poetry does not demand an attachment to a specific time frame, we need not be puzzled by Jonah's thanking God in 2:2 for acts not delivered until 2:11. Moreover, once we appreciate the hyperbolic flavor of poetry, we would not expect Jonah to fear the fish's gastric juices more than flooding waters. (Drowning is, in any case, a favored theme in biblical psalmody, where it is merely figurative for death; see Psalm 69.) Nor would we fault Jonah for setting his sight firmly on Jerusalem's temple rather than on *terra firma.*

Typology

Some scholars are disturbed by the category of the psalm because it is about gratitude when the narrative context needs it to be about penitence. (The usual defense is that the fish's belly rather than dry land is the instrument of salvation.) I have noted that the distinction is deceptive, for the psalm contains elements of both, though it may be said that penitence is understated while

[56] Note for instance how the word *gādôl,* which occurs fourteen times (*sic*) in the narrative, is absent from the psalm.
[57] Among recent commentators, Ackerman 1981: 213–17 and Stuart 1987: 469–74 give the latest rundown of these issues. Vanoni 1978: 28–35 reviews the positions of Landes, Crüsemann, Rudolph, and Feuillet. Trible 1963: 67–82 assesses mostly earlier theories.

gratitude is brought to the foreground, as befits Jonah's mounting recognition of God's mercy. This illumination on the part of Jonah sets the stage for the subsequent dramatic acts, wherein Jonah wants God to accord him as much compassion as he showered on the Ninevites.

Symmetry

Scholars also debate whether the psalm aids or damages a potential symmetry between Jonah's second and fourth chapters. The hidden agenda here is that if there is symmetry, it would help establish that the psalm partakes of the book's original scheme. Just why books display better symmetry when they are original to individual writers is rarely argued by commentators. I imagine that the opposite case can also be defended, because interpolators also have strong stakes in neatly balanced books.[58] Needless to say, opinions on this matter differ. Trible, who devotes many pages to proving symmetry between the odd-numbered chapters, finds no symmetry between those even numbered (1963: 184–202; 76–77). Moreover, she finds it possible to obtain a terrific story even if the psalm is cut from its present location. Young (cited by Trible 1963: 76 n. 2) has tried to parallel the even-numbered chapters; but it is Landes who has established the most thorough comparison (1967a: 16–17). Here is an extract from the latter's effort:

Jonah 2		*Jonah 4*	
6b–7	[Jonah] asserts God's merciful deliverance	2a	[Jonah] draws an inference from the thought God may save Nineveh: he must flee Tarshish
8	He draws an insight from this deliverance: idolators forsake the One who loves them	2b	He asserts the mercy of God that leads to deliverance
9	Jonah's response to Yahweh: worship with sacrifices and vows	3	Jonah's response to Yahweh: a plea for death
10	Yahweh's response to Jonah: he acts so that the prophet may respond favorably to the divine mission (still to be accomplished)	4–11	Yahweh's response to Jonah: he acts so that the prophet may respond favorably to divine missions (already accomplished)

[58] Trible, who makes an eloquent case for symmetry between chapters 1 and 3, is nevertheless forced to extol the virtues of authors whose Oriental "symmetrophobic" mentality forced imperfections into their schemes; Trible 1963: 199–202.

Even those most sympathetic to spotting symmetry in biblical literature are likely to find these correspondences farfetched and much too dependent on a highly accommodating analytic language.[59] Not much more successful are the more recent schemes, examples of which are Magonet's discovery of a "stepwise, mirror-image structure" for chapters 2 and 3 (1976: 60–63) and Stuart's attempt to parallel the psalm with the book as a whole (1987: 471–72).

Aramaism

Another issue widely discussed in Jonah literature is the influence of Aramaic on the book's Hebrew. During the nineteenth century, when scholarship sought to calibrate and date securely the incursion of Aramaic into Hebrew, it was common to locate in the prose of Jonah numerous Aramaic words as well as verbal forms and idioms morphologically and syntactically affected by Aramaic ("aramaisms"). One scholar found in Jonah almost half of the total number of aramaisms in the remaining Minor Prophets (Feuillet 1949: 1106, citing H. Schmidt). Jonah's psalm, however, was deemed to be free of such contaminations. These discoveries have encouraged some scholars to assign the narrative to a period in which Aramaic culture and tongue became prevalent in Judah, and to consider the psalm as predating it. We now know, however, that Hebrew and Aramaic had the potential to influence each other's *vocabulary* at practically all periods of the Hebrew kingdoms (tenth to sixth centuries B.C.E.). We are also now more aware how difficult it is to filter aramaisms from pristine Hebrew constructions. Furthermore, we are careful not to depend automatically on the presence (or absence) or aramaisms when dating the *creation* of a text: first because any biblical text remained potentially revisable right through the second Temple period, when Aramaic was more influential in Israel's daily life; second, because antiquarians of that late period were always capable of emulating archaic, relatively Aramaic-free, diction. In fact, Hebrew poetry reasonably free of aramaisms was being composed in Hellenistic Judea, comparable in this respect to the better examples drawn from the psalter! (See Kittel 1981: 168–69; Qimron 1986: 116–17.) It may not be surprising, therefore, that in a recent study Landes manages not only to whittle down a long list of alleged Jonah aramaisms to just two words and two constructions, but also to show how often Jonah's language accords perfectly with normal classical tenets:

> The complete lack of Persian or Greek loan words [in Jonah], together with the paucity of characteristics distinctive of L[ate] B[iblical] H[ebrew], including Aramaisms, suggests not only that the traditional dating of Jonah in the time of Ezra and Nehamiah [*sic*] or later is in error, but also that it is quite unlikely that our author, while writing in this period,

[59] See also the valid criticism of Vanoni 1978: 30 n. 146.

> was deliberately archaizing the language of his story to bring it into conformity with its obvious pre-exilic setting. (Landes 1982: 163*)

Setting in the Book of Jonah

How the psalm got to nest within the book of Jonah is another matter, which has also attracted much comment. For some scholars, the most prominent issues about the book are its sources, their transmission, and the way they were entered into the composition we now know so well. Nineteenth-century critics developed an elaborate scheme to explain how, just after the return from the Exile, separate prose pieces were sewn into a whole. But many of their arguments for multiple sources belong to an age in which biblical criticism sliced Scripture into the thinnest cuts. We need not be concerned with the many hypotheses that were promoted then, some more outlandish than others.[60] It is only useful for us to keep track of their insistence that poem and narrative were originally separate entities, combined into their present shape not by the storyteller, but by a later editor. They therefore debate whether this editor trimmed an existing psalm to suit the tale's purpose or created one by copying a type familiar from the psalter. In either case, the (re)invented psalm is likely to postdate the prose.

During the past two decades a number of scholars have sought to uncover how Jonah "works" as a piece of literature instead of charting its redactional history. They argue that poetry and prose in Jonah are the products of the same pen.[61] Consequently, they choose whether the author of Jonah created the psalm or merely made room in his story for an existing psalm. If the latter is the case, then the psalm should predate Jonah.

Poetry Within Prose

These concerns and inclinations are by no means limited to Jonah's prayer, for they regularly surface whenever poetry interrupts prose narrative. This prose-embedded poetry can be generated by information located in the narrative just preceding it. An example is the famous series of "fates" God imposes on the snake, Woman, and Man in the garden of Eden story (Gen 3:14–19).[62] Poetry can also retell a narrative, allowing readers to hold distinct perspectives from which to observe the same incident as well as to deepen their appreciation of it

[60] Bewer (1912: 13–21) and Feuillet 1949: 1108–10 review many of them nicely. Trible 1963: 65–75 and Budde 1904 give more illustrations. An unusual solution to the relationship between the poem and the tale is Gaster's (1969: xlvii, 655). He considers the psalm to be a *cante-fable,* a concoction of well-known psalm passages that are recited by an *audience* during an intermission as a tale is about to take its second wind.
[61] Christensen 1985: 217–18 n. 1 lists scholars who adopt this position.
[62] We will not be concerned here with the question of whether the "fates" or the story should be regarded as primary.

through contrasting emphases. An example of this phenomenon is the Jael and Sisera confrontation preserved in the book of Judges, as prose (4:15–22) and as poetry (5:24–31).[63]

Poetic Utterances by Prose Personalities

In Scripture there are occasions on which protagonists in a narrative are credited with poetic statements. Again, such verses may depend on the circumstances detailed in the story, as do the cases in which Deborah boasts of victory (Judg 5), in which David composes a stunning dirge for Saul and Jonathan (2 Sam 1:19–27), and in which he creates lesser verses on Abner's behalf (2 Sam 3:33–34).

It is not uncommon, however, that the poetry uttered by a major character finds no (or superficial) reference in the immediately surrounding narratives. This is what occurs in Jonah, as well as in the Testament of Jacob (Genesis 49), in the Song and Testament of Moses (Deuteronomy 32–33), in the Song of Hannah (1 Sam 2:1–10), in the penitential Psalm of Hezekiah (Isa 38:10–20; but absent from 2 Kings 20) and in much of Balaam's panegyrics (Numbers 23–24). In most cases, were we to remove the poetic lines, the surrounding prose verses would dovetail nicely into each other (as is also the situation in Jonah). A major reason is that Israel's poetic imagination is rarely attracted to themes and topics that require a chronological expansion. (Such undertakings are left to prose smiths, who can apply a formidable array of techniques to the task. Because we know so little about Israel's intellectual atmosphere, however, we cannot be certain that its masterful [hi]storytellers were not also its brilliant poets.) By inspecting the occasions on which poets do recount Hebrew history (for example, Psalms 78, 106), we may easily note that they are more minded to hammer away at moral and theological truths than to transmit an accurate rehearsal of past events. That events within narratives need no rehearsal or confirmation within adjacent poetry—or vice versa—can be corroborated by the many instances in which certain psalms are attributed to well-known ancestors, are precisely located within their past, yet have contents that are generic, universal, or sweeping.[64] I can suggest, therefore, that the transformation of one form

[63] The comparison is nicely handled in Alter 1985: 43–59.

[64] Despite frequent assertions to the contrary, it is often impossible to assign titles and contents to separate hands. A few examples drawn from psalms with David as the protagonist may suffice to illustrate the point: Psalm 3 ("when David fled from his son Absalom") is a plea for help in time of need; Psalm 7 ("concerning Cush the Benjaminite") is an appeal for God's judgment; Psalm 18 ("after the Lord saved him . . . from Saul") contains a variety of sentiments; Psalm 34 ("when he feigned madness before Abimelech") is an acrostic pastiche; Psalm 51 ("when Nathan the prophet came to him after he had slept with Bathsheba") is a confession to an unspecified sin; Psalm 57 ("when he fled from Saul in a cave") is a beautiful statement of faith; Psalm 63 ("when he was in the

of reality (history and history-telling) into another (theology, conviction, creed) need not be due only to poets who witness the activities of past heroes; nor must it presuppose a single school of poets active at one specific period of Israel's history. Rather, it can be accomplished by any of Israel's poets, at any time, even long after the passing of a quoted protagonist.

Poetic Sentiments

Inspecting the poems attributed to protagonists allows me to make another observation: the convictions, triumphs, travails, hopes, and fears of these speakers are couched in a language that easily switches themes and topics. Whether whole or piecemeal, these words transport easily across centuries and can be recalled under diverse conditions. The poetry that Israel admires typically invokes time-tested imageries, idioms, and allusions; its great poets are not only those relishing the quaint and the unusual. Rather, they also include those who can marshal an abundance of metaphors, who can easily manipulate conventions, who can revitalize worn similes by an unexpected setting, who can split a beloved phrase into opposite lines, who can interrupt an expected cadence to stimulate attention. In brief, Israel's most beloved bards are also those who creatively exploit the familiar before a savvy audience.[65]

In the NOTES to the psalm, I insert a small sampling of illustrative passages just before tackling each of its strophes. I do so to show that one can easily locate comparable sentiments in other segments of Scripture; but I also want them to illustrate how these sentiments differ from each other in minor but crucial ways. Had there been space (and will on my part), I might have indicated how each of these divergences fulfills the requirements of its own setting. I can bolster the lessons I want learned by delving into the many ways in which scriptural verses inspired each other.[66] It may be sufficient to note here that

---

Judean wilderness") is a hymn of gratitude; and so on. We may note also that Israel could sing Psalm 114 at any time during and after its exit from Egypt and that the LXX attributes Psalm 137 (a lament by Babylonian exiles) to Jeremiah on David's behalf, neither of whom of course "sat by the rivers of Babylon." The condition is not unique to biblical hymnology; see Schuller 1986: 25–32.

[65] This style of poetic invention continues to be exploited in the Hellenistic period, in the poetry of Ben Sira and that of the Qumran sectarians; for the latter, see the good pages of Kittel 1981: 48–55 and of Schuller 1986: 32–38.

[66] This can be easily ascertained by looking into Bendavid's harmony of Hebrew texts (1972, especially pp. 200–19, where are paralleled quotes and paraphrases from diverse poets and prophets). The topic needs a thorough treatment, and it would be a fine contribution to biblical inner-exegesis. I give here a few illustrations. (1) A psalm that is attributed to David (1 Chr 16:8–36) is created by joining, pruning, and slightly altering materials drawn from the psalter. (Some scholars imagine a similar genesis for Jonah's psalm.) Verses 8–22 = Ps 105:1–15 (unattributed), cf. Isa 12:4; vv 23–36 = Ps 96:1–13

because of their floating nature, the expressions and imagery of Jonah's poem cannot be securely assigned to a specific school of poetry; indeed, they may be available at all periods of Israel's literary history, and for this reason alone scholars have been able to suggest dates half a millennium apart for a single psalm's creation.

Verse Structure and Meter

We have seen that Hebrew poetry is distinguished from prose by its miserly distribution of certain particles, by the freedom of its syntax, by its propensity to parallel versets, by the density of its plays on words (paronomasia), and by the timeless quality of its verbal tenses. The texture of the psalm may be analyzed further by examining how its words fit a pattern of recurring rhythmic sequences (conveniently termed "meter").

There are now a number of theories on ways to measure this meter, by counting accents, syllables (accented or otherwise), vowel lengths (morae), consonants, words—even by combining some of these elements. There are specialists who categorically deny that Hebrew poetry was controlled by meter (for example, M. O'Connor), and they do so partly because they do not find in it regularity, consistency, or stability over an extended stretch of lines. Others regard its principles as constantly permutating, resulting in what in effect is a free rhythm (for example, R. Alter, following Hrushovski). There are also scholars who withhold judgment on ways to plot and tabulate the meter of Hebrew poetry but who have yet found it useful to establish a mechanism by which to amass a large amount of data (for example, D. N. Freedman). There is also a resurrected notion that finds prose and poetry obeying the same measurable rhythm (D. L. Christensen).[67]

(unattributed), cf. Ps 48:2; *vv 31–32 = Ps 98:7 (unattributed); *v 34 = Ps 106/107:1 (unattributed); *vv 34–36 = Ps 106:47–48 (unattributed doxology). (2) Certain psalm expressions are assigned to various individuals: Ps 105:1 (unattributed) = Josh 12:4 = 1 Chr 16:8 (attributed to David); Ps 68:2 (attributed to David) = Num 10:35 (attributed to Moses); Ps 68:8–9 (attributed to David) = Judg 5:4 (attributed to Deborah); Ps 135:14 (unattributed) = Deut 32:36 (attributed to Moses); Ps 113:7–8 (unattributed) = 1 Sam 2:8 (attributed to Hannah); Ps 118:14 (unattributed) = Isa 12:2 = Ex 15:2 (attributed to Moses). (3) I shall soon comment extensively (NOTES to 4:2) on the adaptation of a well-known and obviously beloved conviction—that God is sympathetically merciful, patient, full of benevolence (etc.). I mention here that as this statement moves across theological, hymnic, and prophetic documents, it is attributed to diverse leaders: Ex 34:6 (attributed to Moses or God); Num 14:18 (attributed to Moses); Ps 86:15 (attributed to Korahites); Pss 103:8; 145:8 (attributed to David); Joel 2:13 (attributed to Joel); Jonah 4:2 (attributed to Jonah); Neh 9:17 (attributed to Nehemiah).

[67] O'Connor 1980: 29–54 has a clear discussion and critique of the issues and positions taken by modern prosodists. O'Connor has developed complicated rules of "constraints" that are said to control Hebrew.

The "Qinah" Meter

For more than a century now, the poetic features of a *qînâ* (a term Scripture attaches to dirges or elegies intoned in ancient Israel) have been said to control Jonah's psalm. They include the cluster of five-stress sequences, with three stresses separated from the other two by means of a caesura. We now know that the *qinah* "meter" was imperfectly understood by the prosodists who first charted it, that it controlled many differing types of poetry, and that its stress sequences can be irregular. Its most distinctive feature, however, remains relevant: a sequence of unequal parts, the first of which is normally longer than the second; see Garr 1983.

Representative Treatments of Jonah's Psalm

Because Jonah's psalm does not smoothly and consistently observe this minimal criterion, scholars promote many solutions to make it do so. My own effort, charted above, is representative of other analyses that do not regard meter and proportional symmetry as dominant or controlling factors. Instead of turning these pages into a repository for conjectures, I focus on two syntheses that I regard as paradigmatic of approaches to assess the psalm within a metric framework. I have chosen them also because they have different purposes in mind: the first is primarily a contribution to the study of Jonah; the second is principally a study in poetic structure.[68]

The first, Bewer's effort (1912: 43–44), is fairly typical of an approach that in modified form still obtains in most commentaries. He divides the psalm into three stanzas. The first two end in "toward/into Thy holy temple" (vv 3–5, 6–8). Each of them contains three strophes, with a total of twelve *qinah* versets. Although he approves of it, he resists injecting into his rendering a line in order to provide length and balance for v 9. The third stanza (v 10) has only one strophe. To obtain a consistent series of 3 + 2 stress sequences, Bewer follows a program of (1) minimal deletions of words; at 4, *meṣûlâ* is trimmed of an inordinately long line; (2) a major reapportioning of words, largely following the Greek texts; v 7a is hooked to 6c in order to attain strophic symmetry within the stanzas; and (3) splitting and allocating components of idioms to separate versets; at v 3a–b (*qārā'tî . . . // 'el-YHWH*), at v 5a–b (*nigraštî // min +*), and to a lesser extent at v 10 (*beqôl tôdâ // 'ezbeḥâ-llāk*).

Bewer finds it necessary to emend the text on two occasions: at v 6, where, with Theodotion, he reads *'êk;* and at v 9, where, with Ps 31:7, he reads *haš-*

[68] I do not feature Christensen's approach (1985). While I can follow his method of scanning the psalm, I do not grasp how he interprets his evidence. I also do not find any justification in his system for granting the psalm a separate analysis from the surrounding narratives.

šōmerîm. In doing so Bewer is not motivated by metrical exigencies; rather, he only wants to clarify the psalm's meaning for his readers.

In the NOTES, I suggest that most of these modifications are not necessary, basing my reasoning on grammatical and idiomatic grounds. Although I am fairly attached to the received Hebrew text upon which we all rely, I nevertheless do bear in mind that it passed through many hands during a fairly long stretch of time, that its vowels and accents were assigned hundreds of years after its initial circulation, and that the Masoretes could not always recognize forms that were moribund in later times. I also realize that no one yet has uttered the last word on Hebrew poetry and that *qinah* specifications may well have obtained in ancient Israel. I acknowledge that idioms can be much more free in verse than in prose; hence Bewer and others may well be justified in spanning a phrase across two versets (*enjambment*). I can even imagine Israel's poets occasionally defying the dictates of grammar (but do balk when scholars impose upon them ungrammatical or unidiomatic emendations). For the above reasons —and because his suggestions minimally alter the received Hebrew—I can appreciate Bewer's effort as representative of a defensible realization of Jonah's poem.

The second synthesis is that of F. M. Cross, who focuses on Jonah's psalm in a recent study (1983a), the methodology for which is more fully conveyed in a companion article published in the same year (1983b). In the latter essay, Cross maintains that establishing a sound text and reconstructing the original early Hebrew language are activities that must accompany poetic analysis. Once attended to, these indispensable tasks can demonstrate the regularity of Hebrew verses. To measure poetic sequences, Cross relies on a syllable count by which to obtain a bicolon; he names *l*(*ongum*) the colon of higher count, and *b*(*reve*) the shorter one. His conclusion is that Jonah's poem is divisible into two major sections, vv 3–7 and vv 8–10, which were composed by different poets. Cross does not speculate on who linked the psalm's two entities or on how they came to be in Jonah; he simply notes that neither portion fits better or worse within the narrative about the prophet.

For vv 3–4, Cross (1983a: 163) obtains "a pair of couplets in interlocking structure *b* : *l*: : *l* : *b*—*l* : *b* : : *b* : *l*." This chiastic and cyclic arrangement allows him to comment on diverse aspects of the poet's artistry. But this design can easily be challenged. To begin with, Cross is rather indulgent in categorizing 3a–b as *b* : *l*, where in fact the two bicola are by his own count equivalent in length.[69] Despite his major alteration for v 4a and the minor one in 4b, the resulting count (8!/7) cannot be comfortably assigned to an *l* : *b* pattern, especially because it relies on elision of a conjunction in 4b when other opportunities to do the same are passed over. Finally, he splits *mišbārêkā wegallêkā* between

[69] To arrive at a *b* : *l* measure, Cross "suspects that the original reading of the first colon was *ʾqrʾ mṣrh ly*" (1983a: 161). Such reasoning is circular.

two cola in order to obtain a *b : l* sequence, where the reverse order (*l : b*) is more natural, is universally accepted, and is easily secured by someone very sympathetic to his approach. Therefore, the "nicely interlocking structure" that Cross develops, and from which he generates observations on the poet's artistry, can easily be modified to suit other tastes and arguments. I can record similar objections to Cross's analysis of v 5 and vv 6–7. Instead of dwelling on what seems to me a capricious method, however, I want to focus on a few points relevant to an appreciation of Jonah's psalm.[70]

It is clear (to me, at least) that Cross is more interested in the "archaic" portion of Jonah's psalm (vv 3–7) than in its "late Hebrew" segment (vv 8–10), devoting more than five pages to the former, but hardly two paragraphs to the latter. He uses transparently preferential vocabulary ("dramatic," "exquisite") when explaining how this "archaic" and "traditional" poetry is inspired by oral formulations. By contrast, he terms vv 8–10 "monotonous" and repetitive, full of elements he attributes to later Hebrew poetics: oral formulas are missing, prosaic elements are difficult to expunge, chiastic structuring is faint, and "pseudo-cohortatives" abound.

These distinctions are artificial. Not everyone will find the phrases within vv 3–7 to be more (or less) "formulaic" than those in vv 8–10. To appreciate how broadly based and widely replayed are the phrases of the entire psalm, one may simply review the small samples I have gathered in the NOTES under the heading "illustrative passages." Moreover, because "formulaic" sentiments can be transmitted in written forms no less commonly than by mouth, it is not essential to agree that vv 3–7 stem from a period in which "traditional-oral skills were flourishing" (167). (I read somewhere beyond my ability to locate now a study that shows a higher percentage of formulas in Lucretius than in Homer.)[71]

Cross finds that vv 3–7 evidence "archaic material" because they deal richly with the theme of death and with its imagery. This is hardly credible because far from being "perhaps vague and forgotten in later Israel," such material is constant in biblical literature and is indeed a major component of Qumran hymnology. (It is recalled to good effect even in medieval Jewish poetry.) His effort with regard to the psalm is informed by a desire not only to realize its poetic structure, but also to recover the "original" form in which it circulated. To me, this is a valiant but nevertheless a misguided enterprise. Short of discovering a cache of poetic sketches from monarchic Israel, there is no reason why one scholar's reconstruction of a poetic line should be preferable to another's. The various Hebrew manuscripts (from Qumran, etc.) come much too late in Israel's history to be better witnesses than what we now have to the "original" form of any

[70] Other scholars have voiced similar criticism of the methodology; see Longman 1982; O'Connor 1980: 30–35; Pardee 1981.
[71] See also O'Connor's good comments on the issues, 1980: 42–47.

biblical poem. Moreover, while the translations of Scripture into Greek, Aramaic, and Latin do occasionally give us variant readings that are very interesting, the discrepancies can be internally motivated. Therefore, when we use these versions as tools to recover the "original" form of any poem, we risk perpetuating the distortions of bygone translators, well meaning though they may be.

To my mind, there is no reason that ancient Israel, especially preexilic Israel, should want to keep totally unchanged a piece of poetry. Perfect balance, uniform regularity, beautiful symmetry, chiastic and cyclical structures are certainly not the sole artistic yardsticks guiding ancient poets; and for us to recast their poetry to fulfill such ideals seems to me to hold too narrow an appreciation of Hebrew aesthetics. There is no doubt that Israel's poets can, and sometimes do, fulfill these criteria; but jaggedness, imbalance, asymmetry, and discord, in proper dosage, can be equally attractive. In the case of vv 8–10, the repetitive patterns of which are found "monotonous," I can urge on the readers a more appreciative series of adjectives, "haunting," "comforting," "serene," "purposeful," or the like.

I think it would be worth our while occasionally to step back and ponder the consequence of manipulating what we have into something that can never be proved and of applying rules developed from one poem to reframe another. Where does it all lead, after all, this reconstruction of texts by maneuvering this or that element and by modifying metrical counts through the exchange of this or that syllable? Are we resurrecting thereby an "original" text as it looked when it was first written? When it was edited in its most perfect form? And if Israel's poets once spouted only regular, balanced verses, why and when did their efforts lose favor in Israel? Are copyists and scribes alone to blame for the metrical irregularities in our received Hebrew text? If not, should we identify then the ancient critics who so ruined inherited poems? Is it insensitivity, mischief, or perversion on their part that drove them to do so? Finally, it must also be asked whether courage of conviction should not compel us to replace corrupted poems in our *Biblia Hebraica* with those we restore to pristine beauty?

It may also be opportune to reflect on an obvious partiality commonly shared in contemporary scholarship for poetry produced in early Israel. I do not think that there is anything intrinsically "better" about a Hebrew poem launched about 1200 B.C.E. than one first surfacing seven hundred years later. Quality, we might all agree, depends on the genius of poets and not on the antiquity of their production. In the case of Israel, there is no reason to believe that the truths that so inflamed its prophets were any different in the time of Moses or in that of Second Isaiah; that the inspiration which moved its poets to versify was less in Josiah's court than in David's.[72] Nor is a poem more "honest," more true to a

[72] We can come to such a conclusion by inspecting the long-lived but clearly datable Akkadian literature in which, to some tastes at least, some of the finest poetry (Poem of Erra; long stretches in Neo-Assyrian Gilgamesh, etc.) appear relatively late in its long

nation's heritage and imagination when it lives by word of mouth than by symbols formed on leather, papyrus, or clay. After all, how else but in a written form has Jonah's psalm come to move so many generations toward piety and aesthetic pleasure—perhaps also toward scholarly exertion?

Qumran and Jonah's Psalm

Jonah imagery (and its scriptural parallels) was harvested by Hebrew poets for centuries, among whom are Ben Sira (51:1–12) and the anonymous composers of Qumran's Hodayot (Thanksgiving) hymnology.[73]

Jon	*Hymn*	*Transliteration*	*Translation*
2:4	6:23	[L 116]	[V 170–71]
			[I am] as a sailor in a ship amid furious seas;
		glyhm wkwl mšbryhm ʿly hmw	Their waves and all their billows roar against me.
2:6	5:39	[L 108]	[V 168]
		[wnḥly b]lyʿl ʾppw npšy	[The torrents of Satan] have encompassed my soul
		l[ʾyn plṭ]	[leaving me without deliverance]
2:7	3:18	[L 82]	[V 158]
			And the Gates [of Hell] shall open [on all] the works of Vanity; and the doors of the Pit shall close on the conceivers of wickedness;
		wbryḥy ʿlm	and the everlasting bars shall be bolted
		bʿd kwl rwḥy ʾpʿh	on all the spirits of Naught.
2:7–8	8:29–30	[L 138]	[V 178]
		wʿm mtym yḥpš rwḥy	My spirit is imprisoned with the dead
		ky hgyʿw lšḥt ḥyy	for [my life] has reached the Pit;
		wgm ttʿṭp npšy	My soul languishes [within me]
		ywmm wlylh lʾyn mnwḥ	day and night without rest.

history. The same can be said of Egypt's output. In the case of the deservedly admired Ugarit's poetry, it is perhaps unnecessary to point out that it is all "late," for we have nothing from Ugarit's earlier phases.

73 The examples I give are among the more obvious. See also my NOTES to Jon 4:8 (under *ḥarîšît*). I cite the Hebrew from [L]icht 1957, and quote the English from [V]ermes 1975. See also Duval 1973: 87.

We may notice by these examples how the Qumran poets did not actually quote Jonah but merely appropriated from its psalm enough vocabulary to bring the book to mind. This notion is particularly plausible for the last example. There the Qumran poets juxtaposed two phrases (*šḥt ḥyy . . . ttʿṭp npšy*) that are similarly connected in Jonah. Finally, the Qumran poet sharpened the association with Jonah by setting these allusions within material that is thematically similar to the context in Jonah.

A Magical Reformulation of Jonah's Psalm

A particularly striking witness to the manipulation of biblical poetry is the remarkable talisman or amulet created out of Jonah's psalm.[74] Although the result can hardly be regarded as great poetry, it nicely illustrates how new poems can easily be made from older material. I give the text and its equivalent Jonah references:

wytpll ywnh ʾl YHWH	(2:2; quoted accurately)
ʾlyw qrʾty mṣrh ly	(2:3a; see next note)
ʾl YHWH mbṭn šʾwl šywʿty	(2:3b–c)[75]
šmʿt qwly	(2:3d; quoted accurately)
ʾbyṭ ʾl hykl qdšk	(2:5c–d; verb turned into imperfect)[76]
wtʿl mšḥt ḥyy	(2:7d; quoted accurately)
YHWH ʾlqy yśrʾl	(2:7e; pious spelling of *ʾlhy* + expansion)
ʾzbḥh lk	(2:10b)
zkrty wbqwl tḥyyh . . .[77]	(2:10a; rewriting of *beqôl tôdâ?*)

[74] The text is published in Schäfer 1981: 144–45 (§ 343.60–62). My colleague David Halperin, who kindly discussed this text with me, points out that the passage is embedded in a long section that is unique to one manuscript in New York. It may be conflating materials about Moses at the Red Sea with those derived from Jonah. There is no adequate way to date this particular segment.

[75] Because the fish is no longer relevant to such a context, the compiler made two changes in verse 2:3: (1) *ʾelōhāyw*, "to his God," of the prose text in 2:2 is turned into *ʾlyw*, "to him," which now functions as the first word of the new poem; and (2) *wayyaʿanēnî*, "He answers me," of 2:3b is deleted, allowing "ʾel-YHWH" to balance *ʾlw*. (Not consequential is the insertion of a "yod" in *šywʿty*.)

[76] Halperin thinks that *hykl* (*qdšk*) is of central concern here, for Hekhalot literature tends to interpret *hykl* mystically.

[77] The rest of the paragraph is difficult, appealing to God in the name of Michael, the angel.

A CANTICLE FROM THE DEPTHS (2:3B–10)

Jonah prayed to the Lord:
To him I appeal in my trouble;
To the Lord, I plead from Sheol's belly,
You hear my voice.
I gaze upon your holy shrine.
You raise me from the grave alive,
Lord, god of Israel.
I sacrifice to you
and recall [?]
And with the *sound of resurrection*. . . .

The last line is apparently referring to the Resurrection Day. It allows us to link this poem to the Gospel's reading of Jonah's adventure (see below), as well as to the Koranic and Zohar assessments of Jonah's plight that I quote when introducing the NOTES to the psalm.

VII. On Dry Land (Jonah 2:11)

At this some of the doctors of the law and the Pharisees said, "Master, we should like you to show us a sign." [Jesus] answered: "It is a wicked, godless generation that asks for a sign; and the only sign that will be given it is the sign of the prophet Jonah. Jonah was in the sea-monster's belly for three days and three nights, and in the same way the Son of Man will be three days and three nights in the bowels of the earth. At the Judgement, when this generation is on trial, the men of Nineveh will appear against it [*or:* will rise again together with it] and ensure its condemnation, for they repented at the preaching of Jonah; and what is here is greater than Jonah. The Queen of the South will appear at the Judgement when this generation is on trial, and ensure its condemnation, for she came from the ends of the earth to hear the wisdom of Solomon; and what is here is greater than Solomon. (Matt 12:38–42)

With the crowds swarming round him he went on to say: "This is a wicked generation. It demands a sign, and the only sign that will be given it is the sign of Jonah. For just as Jonah was a sign to the Ninevites, so will the Son of Man be to this generation. At the Judgement, when the men of this generation are on trial, the Queen of the South will appear against [*or:* will be raised to life together with] them and ensure their condemnation, for she came from the ends of the earth to hear the wisdom of Solomon; and what is here is greater than Solomon. The men of Nineveh will appear at the Judgement when this generation is on trial, and ensure its condemnation, for they repented at the preaching of Jonah; and what is here is greater than Jonah. (Luke 11:29–32)[1]

[1] The translations are from the NEB; see also Matt 16:4. In Mark 8:11–13 neither Jonah nor the Ninevites is mentioned. Luke does not refer to Jonah's sojourn in the whale's

When Jonah was pining away unpitied in the belly of the monster of the deep, you, Father, restored him uninjured to all his household."[2]

Wait patiently for your God's judgment. Be not like him of the whale, who appealed *only* when in trouble. Had his God's mercy not reached him, he would have been cast upon barren land. But his God answered him and reckoned him among the righteous. (Koran 68:48–49)

If Jonah had not praised God, he would have stayed in the fish's belly until Resurrection Day. (Koran 37:145–46)

. . . until the time when the Holy One, blessed be He, will awaken the dead. . . . It is of that occasion that it is written: "And the Lord spoke unto the fish, and it vomited out Jonah upon the dry land"; for as soon as that voice will resound among the graves they will all cast out the dead bodies that they contain.[3]

VII. ON DRY LAND (2:11)

2 [11]The Lord spoke to the fish and made it vomit[a] Jonah upon dry land.

[a] *Or: "it vomited Jonah" (see* NOTES).

---

belly. Much has been written on the "sign of Jonah," and I refer to the following studies on its connection with Jonah; A. J. Wilson 1927; Scott 1965; Landes 1983. With regard to the Ninevites, they are witness to the power of repentance, responding to the exhortation of a foreign prophet, and the argument presented is typically rabbinic *qal wāḥōmer* (*a fortiori*): if the Ninevites believe a *foreign* prophet without any accompanying signs, how much more should Jews believe when Jesus preaches to them. (On this hermeneutic principle, see below at 4:10–11.) For the relation between Solomon and Jonah, see Correns 1980 and above, note 1 of section VI. On the midrashic disputation with the gospel's understanding of Jonah's motives, see Urbach 1979: 558–59.

[2] Prayer of Eleazar the Priest, 3 Macc 6:8; see H. Anderson 1985: 526.

[3] The Zohar (*wayyaqhēl* 199b): comments to a passage from *wayyaqhēl* (Exod 35:5), cited from M. Simon and Levertoff 1949: 175. This passage is taken from an extended allegory on the soul and its judgment based on the first two chapters of Jonah. In this reading, the sea is the accuser, the shipmaster is the conscience, the sailors are advocates, and the fish is the grave (Sheol) from which the justified soul arises after three days. I quote an earlier passage from this text in the INTERPRETATIONS. In this context, recall how the New Testament discusses "the sign of Jonah" (quoted above) and then turn back to the passage from Melville's *Moby Dick* (itself a grand allegory) that I quote as epigraph to section I.

NOTES

With the last words of the psalm proclaiming God's power to deliver even the disobedient, the prose narrative of Jonah resumes. Immediately God's control over the elements is once more displayed as the fish receives divine instruction. A strong disjunctive accent, an *atnah,* splits the verse into two major segments, each one of which, moreover, divides into two subsections to realize effectively two sets of activities: God speaks, to the fish; it spews Jonah, toward dry land.

2:11. *wayyōʾmer YHWH laddāg wayyāqēʾ ʾet-yônâ ʾel hayyabbāšâ.* The versions had difficulty with the verb *ʾāmar,* which is normally followed by a quotation and which, in any case, seems much too trite and plain for the occasion. While the Targum, the Vulgate, and some Greek manuscripts (Aquila, Theodotion, Symmachus) follow the Hebrew slavishly, other LXX manuscripts as well as the Syriac (*wpqd*) and Arabic (*ʾamara*) use much more forceful language, "to order," or the like; Trible 1963: 40. Such renderings might well be striving to emulate the verb *mānâ,* "to direct, appoint," of v 1 (so Levine 1978: 1).[4] But the ancient translators might have assessed *ʾāmar* as equivalent to a well-documented Hebrew meaning "to order, assign, appoint"; BDB 56 (4) and Landes 1982: 150*–51*. There are, though, Greek manuscripts (and the Old Latin as well) that resort to a passive construction, "The whale was commanded by the Lord (*kai prosetagē apo Kuriou tō kētei*), and it cast up Jonah on the dry land."[5] In doing so, however, such renderings weaken the power of the Hebrew phrase by focusing on the fish rather than on God.

There is only one other scriptural passage that says that God "speaks" to creatures other than human beings; in Gen 3:14, God utters a curse against the snake of Paradise (*wayyōʾmer YHWH ʾelōhîm ʾel-hannāḥaš*). For this reason, some Jewish exegetes thought that God is merely imparting to the fish the desire to disgorge Jonah (so Kimḥi); this way, they avoided conferring on it the

[4] Freedman privately suggests to me that together the verbs *mānâ* (at 2:1) and *ʾāmar* (at 2:11) create an "envelope construction" that depends on a minimum of words. "In v 1, God presumably commands the fish to swallow Jonah, but we are not told explicitly that the fish swallowed him, only that Jonah ended up inside the fish. I believe that this is not normal procedure, but in this case, the action of the fish is assumed or subsumed. Then at the end of the [episode], we get the reverse: God speaks to the fish, but we are not told what he says. We can infer that from the action of the fish, which is spelled out. In the first part we get the instructions from Yahweh to the fish, and in the second part we get the response of the fish to the instruction."

[5] In some Greek manuscripts that adopt the passive construction, the divine name is also omitted, *kai prosetagē . . . tō kētei.*

power to react as prophets do when commanded by God (so Rambam). Other exegetes, to the contrary, found in God's order to the fish an excellent occasion to indicate that even the dumbest animals unquestioningly obey God (David Cohen). (For these opinions, see Zlotowitz 1980: 117.)

wayyāqēʾ ʾet-yônâ. The verb *qîʾ* means "to vomit, regurgitate." To translate with "to disgorge, spew out" (as do most translations into English) is to be delicate, discreet, and polite; but certainly not fully appreciative of the narrator's effort. With other Hebrew verbs to convey ejection (*hôṣîʾ, pālaṭ*) at the teller's disposal, the loathsome *qîʾ* must have seemed just the right term with which to heap upon Jonah one more indignity. The LXX chose to render with the more innocuous "to cast out" (*kai eksebale*). Other Greek translations favored a more forceful vocabulary, by using verbs either for vomiting up, *kai eksemese* (Aquila; said of Charybdis, in the Odyssey 12.235ff.) or for spitting forth, *hina apemesē* (Symmachus). Jerome similarly translated by *et evomuit Ionam,* "vomited up Jonah"; he added, "as to the expression 'vomited up,' we must regard it as an *emphatikōteron* [conveying more by using less], to mean that life triumphant is emerging from the deepest life-core of death."

How to analyze the form *wayyāqēʾ* is yet another interesting problem. The construction is an imperfect of either the *G* or the *H* stem. In fact, BDB 883 cites this Jonah passage under both derivations.[6] Of the nine attestations of this verb, only one can safely be assigned to the *G* stem (at Lev 18:28, probably to be read as a perfect), and only one can be regarded as an *H* stem (at Prov 25:16). Because all of the verbal nouns based on this root are derivatives of the *G* stem, and because *haddāg* is the most immediate antecedent for the verb, *wayyāqēʾ* is usually treated as *G* stem (Snaith 1945: 30). Even so, it may also be possible, and indeed very instructive, to analyze the form as belonging to the *H* stem.

Hebrew grammar has it that if the *H* stem possesses only one object (rather than the two that transitive verbs allow), and if the object of the verbal idea is missing, then using an English passive form is the best way to make sense of certain Hebrew sentences. (This process is explained best in Lambdin 1971: 211–13.) Therefore, we can render our phrase, "[God] made Jonah be vomited [by the fish]." In my translation, however, an asterisk refers to a note in which I give the other possible rendering for *wayyāqēʾ*. (On the significance of this observation, see the COMMENTS.)

ʾel-hayyabbāšâ. Although the tale is never precise on where Jonah landed, speculations abound. Traditional commentators naturally think of a place near Jaffa, thus allowing Jonah a fresh start, both spatially and psychologically, when he finally obeys God. H. C. Trumbull (1892) lands him on the Phoenician coast, a few kilometers to the north of Jaffa because, he thinks, it was there that a fish

[6] Joüon 1923: 175 (§ 81.c) regards the *H* forms of verbs such as *qîʾ* as pseudo-*hiphʿîls,* secondarily constructed on a misinterpreted *G.* I am very skeptical of this suggestion.

god would find strongest attachment.[7] Haupt, however, has him on the Syrian coast, presuming that Alexandretta (Lattakiye) led fastest to Nineveh (1907). Josephus placed Jonah somewhere at the Euxine (= Black Sea), either because this is where he located the nearest path to Nineveh or because he was aware that "inhospitable" was an etymology for that sea. (For more suggestions, see Ellison 1985: 378.)

The book of Jonah has a monopoly on the scriptural citations of cases in which the preposition *ʾel* precedes *yabbāšâ*. Even if this restriction proves accidental, it should nevertheless be significant that *ʾel hayyabbāšâ* is precisely the direction to which the sailors unsuccessfully steered their boat (1:13). How pregnant in symbolism, therefore, is the narrator's use of the preposition *ʾel* (which might easily be *ʿal*, as in Isa 44:3)! A lesson that Jonah had tried to inculcate into the sailors (1:9), but which had fallen on undiscerning ears (see Comments at 1:13), is now the audience's to appreciate fully.

COMMENTS

The psalm emanates from the troubled heart of a prophet who knows no way out of his prison in the heart of a fish. The circumstances are so fantastic that generations of Jews, Christians, and Muslims took them literally. Modern readers, however, do have choices when confronting this narrative. They too could take them at face value, precisely because miracles, if they are to be judged as such, must have us suspend doubts that events are real only when tested by human capability.[8] Or they could continue to enjoy the narrative, reading it either as a fable, as an allegory, or simply as an extravagant tale, purposely shaped as such by a Hebrew wishing to match the context of Jonah's prayer with the literal meaning of his words.

Whoever told us the story of Jonah, however, did not find it possible to leave ends loose. Jonah needs to come out from the fish; and, lest our sustained focus on the psalm makes us lose sight of that goal, we must be reminded that the fish's deference to God's command is total. Verse 11 neatly fulfills this twofold agenda. It informs us that the fish surrenders its hostage to dry land where, as Jonah had acknowledged (1:9), God is also dominant. It also tells us that the fish

[7] The Philistine god Dagon was commonly understood in the nineteenth century to be a deity worshiped in the form of a fish because of a presumed dependence on the word *dāg*, "fish," even when Phylo Byblius had offered a correct interpretation based on *dāgān*, "grain."

[8] Ridicule of the way Jonah survived his ordeal and of those who believe in its validity can already be found in antiquity. Josephus, as we have seen, neatly skips over the fish and over the series of miraculous incidents reported in chapter 4. Augustine reports that the episodes elicited great laughter among the pagan audiences; cited in Keil and Delitzsch 1900: 382 n. 1.

does not do so of its own volition, but under God's guidance. We should not be surprised, however, if the language of Jonah's return to reality means also to stimulate our sense of humor. Whatever we decide is the narrator's real aim in rehearsing Jonah's return to his task, his fastidious attention to details has its consequences: like their homonyms Cetus ("Whale") and Columba ("Dove" = "Jonah" in Hebrew), two constellations that are forever locked within the same quadrangle of the Southern Hemisphere, Jonah and his whale cannot easily distance themselves, from each other and from our recall as well.

VIII. In Nineveh (Jonah 3:1–4)

Before they implore, I answer; even as they speak, I respond. (Isa 65:24)

The Lord's word reached me, "Mortal! Now they are saying in the House of Israel, 'What he sees is for a distant morrow; what he prophesies is for a remote future.' Tell them, therefore, 'Thus says my Lord God: not one of my words will be postponed any longer; whatever word I utter, it will be done' "—oracle of my Lord God. (Ezek 12:27–28)

If a ram's horn is sounded in town, are people not anxious? If disaster befalls a town, is the Lord not its source? Yet my Lord God does nothing without disclosing his design to his servants, the prophets. (Amos 3:6–7)

The Master [Rabbi Akiva] said, *"And the word of the Lord came to Jonah a second time, saying,* only *a second time* did the *Shechinah* speak unto him; a third time the *Shechinah* did not speak to him." But surely it is written in Scripture, *He restored the border of Israel from the entrance of Hamath* [quoting 2 Kgs 14:25]. . . . R. Nahman b Isaac replied . . . "[this means:] as [God's] intention towards Nineveh was turned from evil to good, so was his intention towards Israel, in the days of Jeroboam the son of Joash, turned from evil to good.[1]

Segnors, de ceste cité que fundée e faite fu en la terre d'Asire est il drois que je vos die la noblece. Uns des fluns de Paradis, Euphratés, plentivos de totes creatures, li corroit joste les murs devers l'une partie. E la citez estoit assise sor le flum e si duroit .iii. jornees, e grans e plenieres. E mains n'avoit ele mie de largece en totes costés qui le voussist bien

[1] *Babylonian Yebamot* 98b; quoted from Soncino Talmud 1936a: 673.

sarcher tote e avironier, si com Jonas li prophetes dist e testimoine. Devers le flum, dont l'aigue est grans e large, estoient fait un fundé li riche palais et les hautes sales. Et d'autre part estoient li mur haut e plenier, e les grans tors hautes quarrees sus asises. Cent portes i avoit d'araint e de cuevre quant hon voloit, qui clooient e ovroient e devers orient en avoit .iiii. e devers occident .iiii. que plus maistres estoient. Sor celes avoit riches tors espesses e grandes amont vers le ciel estendues. Dedens les murs de la cité e dedens la forterece estoient li grand vigoble e li riche jardin ou on trovoit fruis de toute manieres. La cités estoit orguoillouse e riche d'avoirs e de haus homes enforcee.[2]

VIII. IN NINEVEH (3:1–4)

3 [1]When once more the Lord's command to Jonah was, [2]"Set out for Nineveh, that large city, and report to it the message I tell you," [3]Jonah did set out to Nineveh, complying with the Lord's wish. (Nineveh was a large city *for/to God,* requiring three days to cross.) [4]Hardly had Jonah gone into town a day's journey when he called out, "Forty more days, and Nineveh overturns."

[2] Section cxxviii; cited from Joslin 1986: 124. The extract is from a Crusader copy of a widely reproduced moralized history of the world prepared for Rogier, Chastelain de Lisle about 1210 C.E. The *Histoire ancienne* is essentially an adaptation of Genesis within which are inserted various anecdotes known from classical or homiletic sources. The text reproduced here is a composite from a number of copies of the *Histoire* produced for the Crusaders at Saint-Jean d'Acre (Akko). I adapt a translation Joslin was kind enough to prepare for my use: "My lords, it is appropriate for me to tell you of the nobility of this city that was founded and built in the land of Assyria. One of the rivers of Paradise, the Euphrates, full of all sorts of creatures, ran along the walls at one side. The city was set on the river and it therefore took three long, full days (to traverse it). It did not have less size on all (remaining) sides, were one to go and make the turn round it; exactly as the prophet Jonas says and testifies. On the side of the river, whose flow is great and broad, were founded the sumptuous palace and the tall halls. On another section were the tall and broad wall and the large towers, high and square, that rested upon it. There were one hundred gates, of bronze and copper, which shut and opened whenever one wished, four to the east and four to the west that were more imposing. On these were elaborate towers, thick and great, extending upwards toward the sky. A large vineyard and a beautiful garden with fruits of all sorts were within the walls of the city and the fortress. The city was proud and rich in possessions, sustained by noble men."

NOTES

The Murabbaʿât scroll of Jonah leaves a small space empty after 2:11, before it proceeds with what in our texts is labeled chapter 3; Milik 1961: 191. In some Hebrew manuscripts this gap is recognized by the insertion of the consonant *pê* (for *perāšâ petûḥâ/petûḥāʾ*, "open unit [of Scripture readings])," instructing scribes to leave a space vacant. This feature is important because it tells us that at least in the Roman period, if not earlier, those who read Jonah recognized that they had reached a juncture in the narrative. For this reason, and because there will be an almost verbatim repetition of Jonah's initial words in 3:1, we must judge that the story had come to a sudden stop at 2:11. When God calls Jonah a second time, the story, in fact, is renewing itself, and our hero has a new chance by which to fill the prophet's role better. I therefore advise against following current commentators (for example, Wolff 1986: 126) who run 2:11 into 3:1, thus effortlessly transporting Jonah from dry land to Nineveh's outskirts.

3:1. *way(ye)hî debar-YHWH ʾel-yônâ šēnît lēʾmōr.* This verse is essentially the same as the book's opener (1:1), with two exceptions. First, the Masoretes divide it into two phrases, instead of the three of 1:1, and omit the *dagesh lene* from *debar.* They thus give prominence to the adverbial element, "When the Lord's command to Jonah, once more was. . . ." Second, *šēnît* replaces the prophet's patronym. Normally a feminine ordinal adjective, *šēnît* acts as an adverb here and may well reflect the narrator's relatively skillful patch by which to join two originally separate narratives into one.[3] C. H. Gordon (1978b: 30) suggests that it alerts readers that a narrative has reached its high point. Trible (1963: 185) claims that *šēnît* points to a deliberate paralleling of chapters 1 and 3. This purpose is too heavy a burden for an adverb, and she misses the way that it actually functions. As it happens, we have constructions in Haggai that are reminiscent of Jonah's. That book opens with "time setting" + *hāyâ debar-YHWH* + *beyad-ḥaggay hannābîʾ* + *ʾel* (Zerubbabel). Subsequent occurrences (at 2:1 and 10) drop the *ʾel* clause and address the message directly. But at 2:20, the book's introductory sentence is reformulated as follows, *way(ye)hî debar-YHWH šēnît ʾel-ḥaggay . . . lēʾmōr.* Here, *šēnît* does not necessarily imply repetition of the previously received message; rather, it emphasizes that this particular message is the second one to be delivered on that same day.

When *šēnît* is featured where activities are duplicated, they may do so after a long time passes: Gen 41:5, 1 Kgs 9:3 (dreaming); Lev 13:6–7 (outbreak of

[3] Another scriptural example in which *šēnît* brings together disparate segments may be 1 Chr 29:22; see Curtis and Madsen 1910: 307.

skin rash), 13:58 (washing); Josh 5:2 (circumcising); Mal 2:13 (acting offensively); Esth 2:19 (gathering of maidens[4]). Certain activities may also be renewed on the same day: 1 Kgs 19:7 (awakening Elijah); Isa 11:11 (redeeming Israel). What is curious is that whenever Scripture uses *šēnît* to replay divine messages, only a brief interval separates the two occasions (Gen 22:15; Jer 1:13, 13:3; probably also Jer 33:1 and Zech 4:12). Unless this observation is purely coincidental, it has interesting implications. The storm scene and three-day psalmodizing within the fish make it difficult, of course, to believe that God is entrusting Jonah with two messages on the selfsame day. We could, therefore, surmise that the narrator has knowingly used *šēnît* to belittle the passage of time as a dominant factor in this tale, possibly to have us concentrate on the renewal of opportunity for Jonah.

We may note the talmudic exegesis, quoted in this chapter's opening, wherein *šēnît* separates two errands assigned to Jonah, one to Nineveh, the other to Jeroboam. This suggests that to Nahman ben Isaac (fourth century C.E.), Jonah was sent to Nineveh twice on the same mission.

3:2. *qûm lēk ʾel-nîneweh hāʿîr haggedôlâ ûqrāʾ ʾēlêhā ʾet-haqqerîʾâ ʾašer ʾānōkî dōbēr ʾēlêkā.* The sentence duplicates 1:2 in vocabulary until it reaches the preposition *ʾel-*, which here replaces *ʿal.* In the COMMENTS to 1:2, I have shown that two different idioms are at stake in the two contexts. The first time around, Nineveh is simply being served with a death warrant. In this case, however, God commissions Jonah with a *qerîʾâ;* Nineveh, therefore, will receive a specific message from Israel's god.

The word *qerîʾâ* is obviously formed from the consonants of the controlling verb, *qārāʾ*. While it occurs only here in Scripture, it is frequent in rabbinic literature (Jastrow 1950: 1419), leading some scholars to assign it to postexilic Hebrew vocabulary. Landes (1982: 150*) and Almbladh (1986: 31) have rightly questioned this position, and we need not rehearse their arguments here.[5] The word is neutral ("something uttered"), and I have rendered it "message" (rather than, say, "warning," "condemnation," "admonition") because how to categorize Jonah's actual speech of v 4 is itself an issue in Jonah.

The versions translate interpretively. The Arabic simply ignores all changes in the language, duplicating 1:2 up to this point; Wright 1857: 112. The Targum minces no words; because it uses "to prophesy" as the controlling verb, it simply gives its cognate, *nbwʾtʾ* ("prophecy"), in place of *qerîʾâ.* The LXX speaks of *kērugma,* "proclamation," probably because it derives from *kērussō,* a verb

[4] In the last example, it is better to read *šōnôt,* "when various young women were gathered," allowing 2:19–20 to synchronize with 2:12–15.

[5] The same can be said for *miqrāʾ*, "reading," as used in Neh 8:8. In a passage that parallels ours, Jer 19:2, the noun is simply *haddebārîm,* "the statement."

the LXX prefers when rendering Hebrew *qārā*ʾ.[6] But the LXX (followed by some Latin texts) adds, "according to the former proclamation," *kata to kērugma to emprosthen,* and Budde is one of many scholars who regard this reading as more "authentic" (1904: 297). Such a reading, however, would require wholesale alteration in our consonantal text (**bqrʾh hrʾšnh ʾšr dbrty ʾlyk*) when it is obvious that the LXX is simply seeking to give constancy to God's plans for Nineveh; see also Rudolph 1971: 354. The issue whether God is sending Jonah on the same or a different errand continues to be debated in Judaism; see Zlotowitz 1980: 119.

ʾašer ʾānōkî dōbēr ʾēlêkā. The clause stands in apposition to the noun *qerîʾâ.* It contains a participle of the verb *dābar,* "to speak, tell," which in the *G* stem appears only in verbal nouns (infinitives and participles). Diverse prepositions readily bind with *dōbēr* to create idioms such as we have here, and *dōbēr ʾel-* can refer to instructions about to be given (Exod 6:29; Dan 10:11) as well as to information already communicated (Jer 48:20).[7] We therefore cannot be certain whether God's message had been, is being, or will be delivered.

3:3. *wayyāqom yônâ wayyēlek ʾel-nînewēh kidbar YHWH wenînewēh hāyetâ ʿîr-gedôlâ lēʾlōhîm mahalak šelōšet yāmîm.* Syntax sharpens the contrast in the two ways Jonah responds to God's requests at 1:3 and 3:3. In the first instance, the verb sequence includes an infinitive that accents Jonah's willful escape from duty (*wayyāqom . . . librōaḥ . . . wayyēred,* "Jonah sought to escape . . . and went down to Jaffa"). Here, however, conversive imperfects are strung together to emphasize his obedience, *wayyāqom . . . wayyēlek . . .* [4]*wayyāḥel (lābôʾ),* "Jonah did set out to Nineveh . . . and began to enter it."

The words *kidbar YHWH* could be rendered more literally, "in accordance with the Lord's command." The phrase is commonly attributed to Deuteronomists and in fact may be purposefully placed here to sharpen recall of that other narrative about Jonah in 2 Kgs 14:25: "[Jeroboam II] restored Israel's frontiers; . . . this, according to the word of the Lord (*kidbar YHWH*), Israel's god, who spoke through his servant, Jonah the son of Amittay, *the* prophet who hailed from Gath Hepher"; (so also Vanoni 1978: 134). I have purposely used imprecise vocabulary ("Lord's wish") to translate the phrase here because I want it to distinguish between Jonah's strikingly contrasting attitudes.

Persisting in locating God's message in Jonah's preflight past, the LXX has a full verbal clause here, *kathōs* [*katha*] *ʾelalēse*[*n*] Kurios, "as the Lord had spoken." The Old Latin, but not the Vulgate, follows suit; Trible 1963: 42.

The second half of v 3, *wenînewēh hāyetâ ʿîr-gedôlâ lēʾlōhîm mahalak šelōšet*

[6] In the LXX of 1 Chr 30:5 it renders Hebrew *qôl.* Trible (1963: 41 n. 2) cites some Greek manuscripts that have *rēma,* a word normally translating Hebrew *dābār,* "word, matter," and *pitgām,* "decree."

[7] The same can be said of the synonymous *ʾōmēr ʾel-;* see GKC 359–60 (§ 116.m–r).

yāmîm, is a two-part circumstantial clause that is cut into the narrative to provide relevant background information. The technique is frequent in Scripture (Num 13:22; Ruth 4:7; 1 Sam 9:9), and we can best reproduce its intended effect by displaying such clauses between brackets, parentheses, or the like. Therefore, when some commentaries (Wolff 1977: 143; Stuart 1987: 483) initiate a major section of Jonah with this statement, they actually arrest and disturb a sequence of activities, spanning vv 2–4, that exposes an insight into Jonah's new relationship with God. The NEB needlessly shifts the whole clause into the next verse.

As one of the quotations opening this section illustrates, two millennia after Nineveh's destruction a St. Jean d'Acres Crusader can yet be inspired richly to embellish Jonah's description of the Assyrian city. "Nineveh," Jonah says, "was (*hāyetâ*) a large city." The narrator uses the verb *hāyâ* in the perfect tense; but the conjugation is not necessarily attached to past time (so also Stuart 1987: 484). In fact, if time is an essential component in such inserted clauses, Hebrew frequently adds *lepānîm,* "previously," *bāʿēt hāhî,* "at that time," or the like. So *hāyetâ* is not meant to push Nineveh's greatness into "time immemorial" (Wolff 1977: 147), nor does it imply that Nineveh was no longer a power when the story of Jonah first circulated (Bewer 1912: 53). Rather, it is the *size* of Nineveh that draws the narrator's attention; and it is not surprising that God singles out this very feature when teaching Jonah one of his many lessons (4:11).

The words *ʿîr-gedôlâ lēʾlōhîm* include a familiar phrase (at 1:2, 3:2, and soon also at 4:11), but here shorn of articles because it functions as object to the verb. It is the addition of *lēʾlōhîm* that obscures what the entire clause is after. There are three possibilities: (1) *lēʾlōhîm* turns the whole into a superlative phrase: "The most enormous city." Kimḥi long ago promoted this interpretation (Zlotowitz 1980: 120); it has been occasionally adopted ever since (Fáj 1974: 312 n. 18), and has gathered nearly universal critical accolades since Thomas revived it (1953: 210, 216). We may nevertheless note that if this is indeed the meaning of the construction in Jonah, it would be unique to Scripture, for such superlatives have a noun in construct with *ʾelōhîm/ʾēl.* We should, therefore, expect to have **ʿîr ʾelōhîm* or even **ʿîr-ʾelōhîm gedôlâ* if we retain the superfluous *gedôlâ* in deference to its formulaic usage in Jonah. In any case, the ancient translations apparently failed to recognize a superlative construction because, except for the Vulgate and the Arabic, they are unanimous in taking *lēʾlōhîm* literally; Trible 1963: 42. Moreover, for the Targum and some Greek texts, a superlative is out of the question because their translations do not reflect *ʾelōhîm,* but the divine name YHWH with which superlatives cannot be constructed; Levine 1978: 84; H. A. Sanders and Schmidt 1927: 186.

(2) If we take *lēʾlōhîm* literally, we can pursue two separate analyses. We can translate the full statement either as "a large city to the gods," or "a large city to/for God." Should we choose the former possibility, then we are stating either that Nineveh is important to the many gods of the Assyrian empire or that it

contains many shrines. Certainly Assyrians praised Nineveh as the pride and joy of Mesopotamian gods and proudly cataloged its many shrines. But why should Jonah's author care to tell us this fact? The story, after all, is not about divine confrontations (as is the Carmel encounter between God and Baal). To the contrary, Nineveh will hardly bat an eye before following God's commands. Otherwise, we are left with "Nineveh was a large (or great) city to/for God." Rashbam (Rashi's grandson, twelfth century), citing Gen 10:9, thinks of Nineveh as *the* big city in God's creation. Possibly influenced by the Targum's *qdm YY,* Ibn Ezra finds in the clause proof that at one time Nineveh worshiped God. Baḥya ben Asher (thirteenth century) explains it to mean that Nineveh's greatness is due to God. (On all of these readings, see Zlotowitz 1980: 120.) Luther is of the opinion that God loved Nineveh and was bound to save it (cited by Fáj 1974: 312). Some modern scholars suggest that *ʿîr-gedôlâ lēʾlōhîm* reveals Nineveh as "great (even) for God" (Bewer 1912: 53), or, when "measured by the incomparable yardstick of God" (Wolff 1977: 148). Such understandings depend on comparative folklore and do not easily find support in Scripture.[8] Keil and Delitzsch (1900: 404) think that God placed Nineveh among great cities. Relying on NIV's translation of Josh 10:2, where *ʿîr-gedôlâ* refers to Gibeon, Stuart renders "Nineveh was a city important to God." But this reading misunderstands the function of the phrase in Joshua. Archaeological remains notwithstanding, Josh 10:2 is not assessing Gibeon's status among contemporaneous city-states; rather, it is comparing Gibeon's *size* to Ai's, permitting the former to raise a larger warrior population than the latter.

(3) In my translation, I give the phrase literally because I can neither pin down its meaning nor offer a clear argument why it was coined. Nevertheless, I do favor treating *ʿîr-gedôlâ lēʾlōhîm* as a circumlocution whereby "the large city" is said to "belong" to God. Such a construction, in which the preposition *le-* introduces the genitive, is fairly common to Hebrew sentences; GKC 419–20 (§ 129.a–d). It may be superfluous for us (and very likely for the ancient Hebrews) to be reminded of God's dominion over the staunchest of Israel's foes.[9] Nevertheless, it is an important notion to keep in mind as the narrative unfolds, for it explains why the Ninevites readily follow Jonah's directives and why Nineveh is made the object of God's grace. We shall see, furthermore, that it also plays a major role in multiplying possible explanations for Jonah's self-defense of 4:2. A more immediate advantage to my interpretation, however, is that it invests the statement with a spiritual dimension missing from the next

[8] *Contra* Allen 1976, who cites Isa 40:22, where, however, the proportions are distorted by distance and not by God's measure.

[9] Isaiah 19:24 certainly adopts this notion when stating, "On that very day, Israel, being a third partner to Egypt and Assyria, becomes a source of blessing upon Earth because the Lord of Hosts has blessed thus the triad, 'Blessed be my people Egypt, my handiwork Assyria, and my heritage Israel.' "

clause. A final observation: In the COMMENTS to the first chapter (especially at 1:16), I have noted how the narrator progressively sharpens the focus on the sailors' fears, crowning a series of citations with, "The men were seized by a powerful fear of the Lord." There too the narrator resorts to an awkward (albeit grammatically defensible) divine-name construction in order to communicate a message about God's power over the sea. We may therefore have here a continuation of Jonah's old argument (1:9), that God is dominant everywhere on earth as well.

mahalak šelōšet yāmîm. Scripture ordinarily bases units of length on the human anatomy. For larger spans and distances, the criteria and terminology become vague and apply only roughly to various lengths: "bowshot" (Gen 21:16); "some distance" (calque from Akkadian; Gen 35:16, 48:7; 2 Kgs 5:19); "Sabbath-day journey" (Acts 1:12); "day's journey" (one day [Num 11:31]; three days [Gen 30:36; Exod 3:18; Num 10:33]; seven days [Gen 31:23]); on this subject see Vaux 1961: 196–99. The term *mahalak* is one of two (the other being *derek,* "road, way") used in such circumstances; but it can also be used to define other proportions; BDB 237. Literally, a "walk, march, hike," *mahalak* is not a standard linear measure, so that when King Artaxerxes asks of Nehemiah, "How long will your journeying be and when do you return?" (*ʿad mātay yihyê mahalākekā ûmātay tāšûb*), his twofold question means only to ascertain when Nehemiah expects to be back on his job (Neh 2:6).

The versions are faithful to our clause's Hebrew, though the LXX expands somewhat: *hōsei poreias hodou triōn hēmerōn,* "of about a journey of three days." There is no merit to Stuart's translation, "requiring a three-day visit," which depends on Wiseman's incongruous weaving of Assyrian evidence regarding diplomatic visits to royal cities (1987: 483, 487–88); Jonah is hardly sent to Nineveh to negotiate treaties or the like.

About Nineveh's size, Bewer (1912: 50–52) gives ample citations from classical sources, most of which accentuate its inordinate size. R. D. Barnett (1968) and L. C. Allen (1976: 221–22) refer to archaeological and cuneiform sources showing that at its zenith Nineveh was about three miles on its widest axis, almost eight miles in circumference, and occupied about 1,850 acres.[10] Because in a three-day march individuals normally cover thirty to forty miles, some scholars imagine that the narrator is referring to "greater" Nineveh, that is, the city and its outlying territory. Be that as it may, we are not likely to gain much

[10] The last figure comes from Oppenheim 1964: 140. In comparison, Babylon, the largest Mesopotamian city, covered 2,500 acres (see Herodotus 1.178, who gives about 8,000 acres); the Athens of Themistocles was about 550 acres. Jerusalem grew from 10 acres in David's time to 40 acres in the eighth century; after the fall of Samaria, it almost quadrupled its size, to about 150 acres. (The figures on Jerusalem come from Broshi 1974: 23–24; slightly different figures [respectively, 15, 37, and 137½ acres] are given in Negev 1986: 197.) On Nineveh's population, see NOTES to 4:11.

by testing the validity of Jonah's "three-day walk/journey" against Nineveh's actual dimensions. "Three-day" merely establishes that a large space separates two positions (see especially Gen 30:36 and Exod 3:18). Strikingly similar in vocabulary and spirit is the way the Greeks remembered Babylon's size. Herodotus tells us (1.191) that it took a long time before news reached the town's center that the Persians had captured Babylon's fortifications. Aristotle apparently embellishes the same tradition by specifying that the city "had been taken for *three days* before some part of the inhabitants became aware of the fact."[11] In Jonah, the phrase also prepares us to learn about Nineveh's immense population (4:11). More immediately, however, "three-day walk" sets up an obvious contrast with the "one-day walk" of the next.

I may sum up the comments about Nineveh's proportions by claiming that in two separate, but mutually reinforcing, segments, the narrator first attends to the city's prominence in God's scheme, then to its physical size. Another passage, at the end of the book, will corroborate the second point from yet another perspective.

3:4. *wayyāḥel yônâ lābôʾ bāʿîr mahalak yôm ʾeḥād wayyiqrāʾ wayyōʾmar ʿôd ʾarbāʿîm yôm wenîneweh nehpāket.* Up to this point in the verse, the versions have followed the Hebrew. The Syriac, however, substituted *lnynwʾ*, "to Nineveh," for *bāʿ îr,* "into the town," perhaps implying that Jonah was yet within a day's march of the city when he delivered God's message; the intention was probably to avoid complicating his exit that is reported in 4:5. In the Masoretic Hebrew, an *atnah* splits the sentence into two portions: the first describes Jonah's activity on reaching Nineveh while the second contains the only prophecy of the book. The Hebrew takes pains to achieve a time frame for this message. The word *ḥālal* occurs only in the *H* stem, and when it is linked to an infinitive of another verb, the combination evokes an ongoing act.[12] If there is a completion to that act, Hebrew usually places the verb *kālâ* (*D* stem) in close proximity. The point then is not that Jonah is idle a full day before beginning his oration on the morrow (Bewer 1912: 52 and many other commentators), but that sometime within this first day, he breaks the bad news to the Ninevites. To convey this notion, I rely on "hardly" in my translation. In the COMMENTS I

[11] *Politics* 3.5.1276a. I cite B. Jowett's translation (Oxford: Clarendon Press, 1938 reprint) but also italicize "three days."

[12] This verb is to be separated from another, with the same consonants, occurring in the *G* stem. There is a third homonym that appears in the *N* and *D* stems, and also at least twice in the *H* stem (Ezek 39:7; Num 30:3, vocalized in the imperfect with a *pataḥ* under the preformative!). The imperfect forms, which carry the meaning "to begin," are vocalized with a *qameṣ* under the preformative. BDB 319–21 is confusing here; better see Even-Shoshan 1982: 372–73.

will consider why the story needs to tell us that Jonah makes his declaration within one day's walk into the city.

Jonah is finally relaying a message to the Ninevites. The Hebrew juxtaposes two verbs, *wayyiqrā᾽ wayyō᾽mar,* either one of which would be enough. But the first of them reminds us of God's injunction in 1:2 and 2:2, while the second is frequent as a second verb when Hebrew introduces a quote; see below, v 6. While in 1:2 and 3:2 the Targum translates the verb *qārā᾽* with forms of *htnb᾽*, "to prophesy," here it turns to *᾽kryz,* "to announce"; Levine 1978: 84. (It will use it again in v 7 to render Hebrew *hizᶜîq.*)

How does Jonah expect to be understood? Does he speak the local Nineveh patois of Assyrian, which Isaiah once called a "stammering jargon of an alien tongue" (28:11; see 33:19)? Or, to the contrary, do Ninevites understand Hebrew? The issue is raised in a scriptural passage in which God tells Ezekiel (3:4–7),

> Mortal, make way toward the House of Israel and relay my words to them, for you are sent to the House of Israel—not to a people of obscure speech and dense language; not to the many people of obscure speech and dense language, whose talk you cannot understand. Had I sent you to them, however, they would certainly have understood you! Yet, the House of Israel refuses to listen to you, since they refuse to listen to me.

Foreigners will be able to understand a prophet whatever their tongue. For the Hebrew, therefore, the problem is not in grasping the meaning of God's message, but in obeying it. This point is sharpened in the way the prophet uses the selfsame verb *šāmaᶜ*, "to hear," when setting up the distinction.

The issue, however, continues to exercise some modern interpreters, a few of whom even analyze alleged Akkadian equivalents to Jonah's speech (Wiseman, cited approvingly by Stuart 1987: 489). In truth, the Ezekiel resolution of the problem is uncommon to Scripture. Hebrew narrative art hardly ever pauses to recognize language distinctions, and it does so only when it is important to the plot, for example, when Joseph is said to speak through interpreters so that his brothers cannot identify Hebrew as his native tongue; or when Sennacherib's chamberlain, who otherwise speaks Hebrew, is urged toward Aramaic, lest the Judeans understand what he says (Isa 36:4–11). Otherwise, everyone speaks perfectly gorgeous Hebrew: Pharaohs and Philistine kings turn to it when conversing with patriarchs; Babylonian and Persian dignitaries do so similarly when they address exiled Jews.[13]

Although it nearly duplicates the brevity of Belshazzar's MENE MENE TEKEL

[13] J. Blenkinsopp reminds me of Ezra 4, written in imitation of the style then current in diplomacy, which mentions letters translated into and from Aramaic (see vv 7, 18). In the second citation, however, the Aramaic verbal form, *mepāraš,* may or may not refer to

UPHARSIN (Dan 5:25), Jonah's message, *ʿôd ʾarbāʿîm yôm wenînewēh nehpāket,* is much more intricately assembled. The pattern is well attested in Scripture, with two segments linked by a conjunction. Haggai 2:6 similarly includes a participle in the second segment, "In just a short while longer, I shall shake heaven and earth, sea and dry land" (*ʿôd ʾaḥat meʿaṭ hîʾ waʾanî marʿîš ʾet-haššāmayim*). Finite verbs may also be found in the same position without appreciably affecting a future timing for the consequent act. Isaiah is particularly rich in apt examples.[14]

In the first half of the clause, Jonah threatens dire happenings in "forty days," *ʿôd ʾarbāʿîm yôm.* The number Jonah quotes is likely conventional for, whether it refers to days or years, a major change generally comes at the end of this interval, be it physical, social, or spiritual.[15] One Hebrew manuscript (663) gives "thirty" rather than "forty" days; but the biggest discrepancy is in the LXX and Old Latin versions, where the Ninevites are to have only a "three-day" respite. This difference from what the Hebrew text now has could be due to an effort to synchronize Nineveh's change of heart with the completion of Jonah's three-day march through a wide city. That it also quickens the story's tempo and therefore gives Jonah much less time to wait outside the city (see at 4:5) is also a potential advantage. Philo has this reading, and church fathers try either to

---

translations, as is also the case of the Hebrew *mepōrāš* of Neh 8:8. See the discussion in his commentary, 1988: 114–15; 287–88.

[14] Isa 21:16: "One more year . . . the glory of Kebar shall vanish" (*beʿôd šānâ . . . wekālâ kol-kebôd qēdār*); this passage is in wonderful contrast to Isa 65:24, a text I quote as preface to this section (*wehāyâ ṭerem yiqrāʾû waʾanî ʾeʿeneh ʿôd hēm medabberîm waʾanî ʾešmāʿ*). See also Isa 10:25.

[15] Without citing all instances in which multiples of forty are invoked (fuller listing in *Enc Jud* 12.1258), I mention only the following: (1) *years.* The trek in the wilderness on exiting Egypt (Exod 16:35); peace in Israel upon God's election of a judge (Judg 3:11). "Forty years" can signify a period within which there is a major change in attitude. It is therefore not necessary to emend 2 Sam 15:7. (2) *days.* Moses at Sinai (Exod 24:18); spies take forty days to reconnoiter the promised land (Num 13:25); Elijah's fast (1 Kgs 19:8); Jesus' fast (Matt 4:2) and postcrucifixion theophany (Acts 1:3). (3) *days symbolizing years* (courtesy Freedman). Ezekiel must lie on his side forty days (4:6). Many of the same scriptural passages are cited by Jerome and other early exegetes, indicating that the symbolism of the number forty was appreciated already in ancient times. Islamic legends merely transfer the same number to Jonah's stay in the fish's belly; Thackston 1978: 324. Some Jewish *midrashim* imagine that Jonah's prophecy was fulfilled, but after forty *years;* Ginzberg 1946: 351. n 37. This notion may well be ancient and may explain Tob 14:14–15 [NEB]: "Tobias [son of Tobit] died greatly respected at the age of one hundred and seventeen. He lived long enough to hear of the destruction of Nineveh [his native city] by Ahasuerus king of Media and to see his prisoners of war brought from there into Media. So he praised God for all that he had done to the people of Nineveh and Asshur; and before he died he rejoiced over the fate of Nineveh and praised the Lord God who lives for ever and ever. Amen."

blend the different numbers (hence Justin Martyr's "forty-three days") or to harmonize them (hence Augustine, who matched three-day as well as forty-day experiences of Jesus). Josephus avoids all such ambiguities, including the issue of God's mercy to the brutal Ninevites, by turning Jonah's message into a prophecy on Nineveh's eventual loss of its Asiatic strongholds. (On these points, see Levine 1978: 85; Barthélemy 1963: 209–10; Duval 1973: 72–74; Bickerman 1976: 58–62.)

Despite the "forty days," the language of *ʿôd ʾarbāʿîm yôm wenînewēh nehpāket* does not precisely time the cataclysm. Is it to happen at the end of forty days or within them? The versions therefore try to help. The Targum makes the timing clear by adding *bswp* to *ʾrbʿyn ywmyn,* "at the *end* of forty days." The LXX and the Vulgate, however, use respectively *eti* and *adhuc,* "as yet, yet, still," suggesting that the Ninevites are granted a surcease before the world collapses on them (so Wolff 1977: 149, following Fáj 1974: 313).

Nineveh is to become *nehpāket.* We need to dwell on this word because it is crucial to the development of the plot. The verb *hāpak* is well represented in Scripture in the *G, N,* and *HtD* stems. In the *G,* and in noun forms probably based on the *G* (*hapēkâ, mahpēkâ*), there are several attestations to the destruction of Sodom and/or Gomorrah (Gen 19:21, 25, 29; Deut 29:22; Amos 4:11; Lam 4:6; probably also Jer 20:16; 2 Sam 10:3 and 1 Chr 19:3 speak of Ammon's demise). This circumstance has naturally compelled many to treat Jonah's *nehpāket* as simply a participle of the *N* (hence "Forty more days, Nineveh will be undone"). Indeed, this notion underlies all of the early translations (LXX, *katastraphēsetai;* Vulgate, *subvertetur;* Targum, *mthpkʾ*). Some exegetes even insist that this must be the only correct understanding of the verbal form; Wolff 1986: 149.

Nevertheless, because the *N* stem applies to cities only in Jonah and because a great number of these forms bear a reflexive sense, already in rabbinic times Jewish exegetes argued that the passage ought to be rendered, "Forty more days, Nineveh is to turn over [meaning: re(-)form]." Philo (Augustine as well) thinks that God is not interested in overturning stones, but in turning hearts around; Bickerman 1976: 60–61; Fáj 1974: 313. Such an interpretation would resolve a problem about God changing his mind when Scripture frequently insists on the constancy of divine pronouncements (see opening quotes). Moreover, it would avoid confronting (as does Origen) the problem of a deity who purposely tests (Genesis 22, the Akedah; 1 Kgs 13:11–32, the man of God), provokes (Exod 7:13, hardening Pharaoh's heart), misleads (Judg 14:4, Samson choosing a Philistine bride), or deceives (1 Kgs 22:19–23, Ahab warring against Aram; 2 Sam 17:14, Ahitophel's good advice ignored). (See INTERPRETATIONS.)

There is yet a third position, that *nehpāket* is deliberately ambiguous. This too is apparently an ancient notion, for the talmudic tractate *Sanhedrin* (89b) dwells on this point: "Jonah was originally told that Nineveh would be turned, but did not know whether for good or evil."[16] This line of reasoning was picked up by many medieval Jewish commentators, as cited by Zlotowitz 1980: 122. In modern times, the suggestion is offered by B. Wolf (1897; unfavorably cited by König 1906: 745) and has found repetition in recent work (Clements 1975: 24; Halpern and Friedman 1980: 87; Stuart 1987: 489). I shall come back to this proposal in the COMMENTS to this and the following sections, as well as in the INTERPRETATIONS.

COMMENTS

> When I looked among them for a person who might mend the wall and stand in the breach before me in this land's behalf, to avert its destruction, I found none. (Ezek 22:30)

Chapter 18 of Genesis tells us that, though wishing to obliterate Sodom and Gomorrah from the face of Earth, God shares his plan with Abraham. Lot notwithstanding, Sodom means little to Abraham who, earlier, had disdained accepting its king's gifts (Gen 14:21–24). Nevertheless, instead of piously embracing the decrees from on high, Abraham forces God to distinguish between a geographical entity called Sodom and the numerous souls, some less sinful than others, who live within it. Abraham eventually fails to change God's verdict; but in pressing heaven to acknowledge the merits of righteousness, Abraham personifies the moral courage to question authority when the lives of fellow human beings are at stake. Midrash and Jewish homiletic embellishments consider this moment—and not when his blade rises over Isaac—to be the patriarch's noblest.[17]

We shall never really know why Jonah chooses escaping to Tarshish over fulfilling God's request. In the NOTES above, I cite a number of opinions on the subject, and I shall soon attend to Jonah's less than satisfying explanation (4:2). It may well be that Jonah's escape, in its own way, is equivalent to Abraham's better argued and more eloquent challenge to God's decision: by shirking his duty to God, Jonah finds a way to arrest the terrible event. Jonah had no way of realizing that by boarding ship, he was merely postponing Nineveh's calamity. Eventually Jonah pays dearly for his response, as rabbinic Judaism ranks him among those whom God punishes for suppressing prophecy, disregarding true

[16] Cited from the Soncino Talmud 1935a: 594.

[17] Abraham, of course, is not alone in Hebrew tradition to intercede for a condemned folk. But unlike Moses, who repeatedly intercedes in behalf of Israel as it wanders through the wilderness, Abraham speaks in defense of even the most odious of folks. In Gen 20:17, Abraham prays to restore Abimelech of Gerar's health.

prophecy, transgressing their own prophecy, or prophesying in the name of idols; Soncino Talmud 1935a: 590–95.

Humbled and wiser because of his adventures on the high seas, Jonah is now ready to follow God's dictates. Although the narrative in the third chapter risks escaping Jonah's immediate control, his experiences of chapter 1 are background to what ensues in Nineveh. Thus, it is only from 1:2 that we know why Jonah is being sent to Nineveh: God has had enough of its wickedness. More importantly, it is in chapter 1 that God's awesome power is sampled and confirmed. There too, God is shown to be ready to test Gentiles as well as Hebrews, the guilty as well as the innocent. Chapter 1, therefore, allows us to penetrate the minds of pagans as they listen to Jonah's pithy sermon on the effectiveness of God's control beyond the confines of Israel and as they behold convincing evidence of divine mastery over the elements. All of these testimonies and evidence are necessary as background to chapter 3; otherwise, we may be stunned by the ease with which Jonah's message convinces Assyrians to forsake their evil way.

Jonah himself is still not quite able to react normally to God's directives. In chapter 1, he escapes rather than face their demand. Here he does the opposite: he assiduously fulfills God's request. This is my explanation for the text's references to Nineveh's three-day measure and Jonah's one-day journey into it. It is not that he was too tired to proceed farther into the city (Allen 1976: 222); that he was still reluctant to carry God's message (Hauser 1985: 32); that he wanted to be in the heart of the city by the second day (Bewer 1912: 52; Wolff 1977: 148–49; most medieval Jewish exegetes, Zlotowitz 1980: 121); or that he was purposely defying diplomatic protocol (Stuart 1987: 487–88). No; the contrast in number means to sharpen our perception of a prophet who is very much in a hurry to do what God asks of him, whether earnestly and enthusiastically or just to get it over with. That the king of Nineveh forfeits his chance of being first to react to the prophetic message may be one practical effect of Jonah's alacrity; it is more germane to note, however, that this eagerness on Jonah's part prepares us well for his sulky despair, which is a feature of the next chapter. As days pass without fulfillment of his prophecy, Jonah must certainly feel insignificant; for whether he rejects or embraces God's commands, Jonah can find in them neither release nor gratification.

I am certain that to the end of his days, Jonah keeps to the following understanding of God's message: within a specific period of time—whether it be three days, forty, or any span in between—Nineveh is to become *nehpāket.* Jonah might have remembered the dire punishments God inflicted on Sodom, Gomorrah, and their allied city-states; he could also have recalled how an angry God almost wiped out the earth's population when confronted by unacceptable behavior; he may even share the insights expressed by Amos and Isaiah (quotes opening this section) about God's obligation to fulfill prophecies. For these and similar reasons, therefore, the only meaning of this verbal form that registers in

Jonah's mind is the one partaking of a passive sense: Nineveh will soon disappear from the Assyrian landscape. God, Jonah feels, is entrusting him with a *declaration of doom,* no different in this respect from when God first charged him to tell Nineveh that its fate has already been sealed (*qerāʾ ʿaleyhā*).

Shortly, events will disabuse Jonah of such expectations. Mortified, he will openly reflect his dismay at what seems to him an exploitation of prophets, and he will dread the resulting humiliation and derision. Better be dead than submit to such a future. But, as the next episode unfolds, we shall find that there can indeed be another meaning and understanding of *nehpāket.*

IX. Changes of Heart, Change of Mind (Jonah 3:5–10)

◆

> At one point, I may sentence a people and kingdom for reversal, humiliation, and destruction; but if this people whom I have sentenced turns away from its iniquity, I may change my mind from the destruction I planned against it. At another, I may order rebuilding and planting for a people and kingdom; but if I deem it is acting contemptibly by ignoring my wishes, I may change my mind from bestowing the benefits I planned for it. (Jer 18:7–10)[1]

> I am ready to respond to those who do not ask; I am available to those who do not seek me. I tell a nation that does not invoke my name, "Here I am; here I am." I am forever stretching hands toward a disloyal people that tread an unworthy path, pursuing their own plans. (Isa 65:1–2)

> In fact, Israel's Glory does not deceive and does not change course, for God is no human being for whom there is change of course. (1 Sam 15:29)[2]

> God is not human to mislead,
> Or mortal to feel regret.
> Does he speak but not act?
> Does he promise but not fulfill it? (Num 23:19)

> O brethren! It is not said of the men of Nineveh that "God *saw* their sackcloth and their fasting", but "And God *saw their works* that they

[1] These verses have been much discussed in scholarly literature because they do not naturally fit the parable of potter and clay that precedes them (1–6). Two recent studies in the same volume try to explain the connection between the two sections: P. R. Davies 1987 and Fretheim 1987.

[2] This statement stands in sharp contrast to 1 Sam 15:11.

turned from their evil way" (Jonah iii 10), and in the Prophets it is enjoined "Rend your heart and not your garments" (Joel ii 13).[3]

R. Isaac [second century C.E.] further said: Four things cancel the doom of a man, namely, charity, supplication, change of name, and change of conduct. . . . Change of conduct (*šinnûy hammaʿaśeh*), as it is written, *And God saw their works,* and it continues, *and God repented of the evil which he said he would do unto them and he did not.*[4]

They queried Wisdom, "what is the sinner's punishment?" and it told them, "Misfortune pursues sinners [Prov 13:21]."

They queried Prophecy, "what is the sinner's punishment?" and it told them, "The sinful being alone shall die [Ezek 18:20]."

They queried the Torah, "what is the sinner's punishment?" and it told them, "He shall be forgiven upon presenting a guilt-offering."

They asked God, "what is the sinner's punishment?" and he told them, "He shall be forgiven upon repenting."[5]

IX. CHANGES OF HEART, CHANGE OF MIND (3:5–10)

3 [5]Believing in God, the people of Nineveh instituted a fast and wore sackcloth, the prominent as well as the lowly. [6]When the news reached the king of
Nineveh, he rose from his throne and stripped off his royal mantle; he put on
sackcloth and sat on dirt. [7]Then, he had the following proclaimed:

In Nineveh;
On the authority of the king and his counselors:
People and beasts—herd or flock
must taste nothing,
must not graze
and must not drink water.
8 They must wrap themselves in sackcloth—people and
beasts alike—and must appeal to God with fervor.
Each person must forsake his evil conduct and all
must turn away from the violence they plan against others.
9 Who can tell? God himself[a] may consider a change of mind and
draw away from his anger, so that we may not perish.

[3] Elder's admonition on fast days, *Mishna Taʿanit* 2:1; quoted from Urbach 1979: 464.
[4] *Babylonian Roš Haššana, Moʿed,* 16b; quoted from the Soncino Talmud 1938d.
[5] *Jerusalem Makkot* 2:6; adapted from Zlotowitz 1980: xx.

10When God himself[a] examined their deeds—for they forsook their evil conduct —he renounced plans for the disaster he had threatened against them and did not carry it out.

[a] Or: "The g/God"; see NOTES to 1:6 and below, at 3:9.

DIVINE CLEMENCY: INTRODUCTORY REMARKS

When, at the beginning of the reign of Jehoiakim, the priests and prophets at the Temple sought Jeremiah's death for daring to prophesy against Jerusalem, a few elders rose to say (Jer 26:18–19),

> Micah the Morashite, who prophesied in the time of King Hezekiah of Judah, once told everyone in Judah,
>
> The Lord of Hosts says,
> Zion will be plowed as a field,
> Jerusalem will become ruins,
> The Temple Mount, brushwood heights.
>
> Did King Hezekiah of Judah and the whole nation put [Micah] to death? Rather, did [Hezekiah] not fear the Lord, and did he not implore the Lord so that the Lord renounced the punishment that he planned for them? We may be doing ourselves a great harm [in punishing Jeremiah].

The elders who cite Micah's words (3:12) are very likely recalling Sennacherib's threat against Jerusalem. Second Kings 19 tells us that Hezekiah's penitential acts and extraordinary entreaties within the Holy of Holies effectively led to the retreat of the Assyrians.[6] The Chronicler makes even more of Hezekiah's reforms, his many penitential acts, and their calming effect on God (2 Chronicles 29–30). For the present purpose, it is worth noticing how one leader's penance wards off a divinely directed threat *against a whole nation.* Variations on this theme are known from elsewhere in Scripture: for example, Moses repeatedly deflects God's anger against the whole of Israel by punishing only the guilty parties (Exodus 32; Exod 34:6–7; Num 11:1–3; 14:10–28; 16; 21:4–9,

[6] We do not know, indeed do not need to know, how Micah reacts when his prophecy proves false (at least during his own lifetime). In Jonah, however, his response to being so used becomes a major feature of the book bearing his name. For textual differences in the Micah and Jeremiah quotations, see Fishbane 1985: 458–60. For further remarks on prophecies that are not immediately fulfilled, see the COMMENTS to section X.

details differ in each episode); Samuel intercedes with God when the Philistines march against Israel (1 Samuel 7); and Ezra grieves in order to deflect God's anger (Ezra 10). That the contrition of one leader may only postpone destruction to a dynasty and the people it rules, is also known from experiences credited to Ahab (1 Kings 21), Hezekiah (2 Kgs 20:12–19) and Josiah (2 Kings 22–23). In turn, these successful entreaties may be contrasted with the activities of Jehoiakim who, in addition to his personal depravity (2 Kgs 24:4), remains deaf to Jeremiah's appeal and thereby forfeits a chance to save Israel from Nebuchadnezzar's clutches.

A variation on this theme is also exploited in cuneiform lore. When a city is destroyed, appeals to a potent god reverse the condemnation, thus allowing it to be restored to full glory.[7] Thus, in a reminiscence attributed to Nabonidus's mother, but written entirely to affirm her son's legitimacy, Adad-guppi tells how, upon Sin's abandonment of Harran, she mortified herself, body and soul:[8]

> In order to appease my personal God and Goddess, I did not permit apparel made of fine wool, gold and silver jewelry, any new garment, perfumes and scented oil to touch my body. I was clad in a torn garment, and when I departed, it was in silence. I constantly pronounced benedictions for them, the praise of my personal God and Goddess was in my thoughts and I performed the services for them. (*ANET*[3] 561; slightly modified.)

Sin relents, and by raising her son to the throne of Babylon, proves that his affection for Harran and its citizens was only temporarily deflected.

Biblical narratives also assign contrition and acts of penance to foreign leaders who come to realize God's power, even if their fear is for their own rather than their nation's safety. Thus, in an evident foreshadowing of the Exodus and its motifs, a Pharaoh learns not to abuse Abram's wife when plagues hit his household (Genesis 12); Abimelech of Gerar is threatened with death for acting in the same way toward Abraham (Genesis 20). When the Philistines are painfully disciplined for capturing God's ark, "the town's outcry reaches heaven" (1 Sam 5:12). The diviners among the Philistines finally advise loading the ark with

[7] An oft-cited example is drawn from Esarhaddon's inscriptions recalling his father's destruction of Babylon. Originally, Babylon was to remain barren for seventy years (written in cuneiform with a vertical sign [= sixty] and a pressed wedge [= ten]), but Marduk turned the numbers upside down and restored it after eleven years (when inverted the same signs would read ten + one); Borger 1967: 15, episode 10. On the circumstances, see Brinkman 1983. The theme is also known in Scripture; see Jer 25:12, 29:10, and the consequence as cited in 2 Chr 36:21; Dan 9:2.

[8] On Mesopotamian fasting, see the remarks by Parpola 1983: 194–95.

(admittedly quaint) guilt offerings. In such stories and, in fact, as is likely the case for Nineveh, the repentance is hardly ever long-lasting.

A modified version of the repentance theme has it that a chosen few save a whole nation from harm. This is the lesson derived from Abraham's dialogue with God about Sodom: had there been no more than ten righteous individuals within the city, it would be spared calamity (Gen 18:22–33). Jehoiakim the priest, son of Hilkiah, is commissioned to intercede with God, lest Israel be stuck in Babylon (Bar 1:10–13). The same idea is fairly well represented among the prophets (Isaiah, Micah, Joel, Jeremiah, Obadiah), who speak of a "remnant" in Israel that eventually secures permanence for a people (see *IDB* 4.32–33, and for terminology, *IDBS* 735–36).

A third and final elaboration of the theme has a whole nation participating in penitential activities in order to deflect potential disaster (Joel 2:15–17). Ezra and the returning exiles pray and fast lest God, who may still be angry against his people, impede their voyage (Ezra 8:21–23). While Ezra mortifies himself to avert potential disaster against Israel (see above), all of Israel participates in acts of atonement (Nehemiah 9).

In the COMMENTS, I will come back to these three separate models by which sinful people escape divine retribution.

NOTES

3:5. *wayyaʾamînû ʾanšê nînewēh bēʾlōhîm wayyiqreʾû-ṣôm wayyilbešû śaqqîm miggedôlām weʿad-qeṭannām.* The first to react to Jonah's call are Nineveh's citizens. The verbal root *ʾāman,* from which is coined the name of Jonah's father Amittay, is conjugated just this once in Jonah. In the storm scene, the narrator did not use this verb at all when speaking of the sailors, choosing instead a vocabulary that allows play on the verb *yārēʾ,* "to fear" (at 1:5, 9, 10, 16). In the *H* stem, the verb allows various meanings: when construed with the preposition *le-, heʾemîn* means "to trust" or "to rely on" someone or something, but "believe in" or "have faith in" someone or something when it is linked to the preposition *be-*.[9] Scripture often cites this sentiment, sometimes in the wake of awe (Exod 14:31); and when it is brought out positively, it foreshadows good things to come from heaven (Gen 15:6; 2 Chr 20:20). Alternatively, when individuals or nations "do not put their trust" in God, only unhappy consequences follow (Num 14:11; 20:12). Therefore, when the narrator uses this particular vocabulary as an opening to the scene in Nineveh, a knowledgeable audience can anticipate a radical shift from what is supposed to happen.

Scripture has many more attestations of individuals who believe "in

[9] "Having faith in a god," *ʾemûnâ,* is an abstraction that is remarkably Hebraic; in the cuneiform world, for example, the language of devotion tends to be more concrete.

YHWH," than "in *'elōhîm*." Aside from the present passage, the latter occurs just one other time, at Ps 78:22. Bewer (1912: 53–54) is one of many who think it is significant that the Ninevites have faith in *'elōhîm* rather than in *YHWH*; indeed, *'elōhîm* is retained throughout this episode. In contrast, Jonah expressly refers to *YHWH* when seeking to convince the sailors of God's power and omnipresence; the narrator also uses *YHWH* when the context for Jonah's mission is reestablished (3:1–3). Despite the prevalence of *'elōhîm* in chapter 3, however, the text wants the Ninevites to be wholeheartedly moved, not by the power of a divine being, but by the might of the unique God of Israel. The Targum underscores this notion by simply observing that the Ninevites were affected *bmymr' dYY*, "by the Lord's word."

Commentators frequently ponder why Nineveh responds so readily to Jonah's message. Israel itself had to witness a stunning miracle at the edge of the Re(e)d Sea before it believed in God and in Moses (Exod 14:31). The Ninevites' transformation is judged by Bewer (1912: 54) as too swift "even if we take into account the emotional nature of the orientals." Ibn Ezra and Kimḥi imagined that the sailors recounted their miraculous experience before the Ninevites. One interpretation, reflected in medieval illustrations for this particular scene, posits that Jonah's flesh was made so ghastly by the fish's gastric juices that the awed Ninevites were ready to believe his message (Ginzberg 1947: 252). Abravanel (twelfth century) proposed that the Ninevites are so stunned by a foreigner's gutsy condemnation that they quickly believe him. This is essentially the position of Stuart (following Wiseman), albeit generated by a fanciful recreation of the Assyrian context (1987: 490).

While Luther thought that "none but saints inhabited the city" (cited by Wolff 1977: 151), Jewish exegetes debated the Ninevites' sincerity. There were those who confirmed it for, among other reasons, it would not do for God to be tricked by clever stratagems (Silberman, in press). Nevertheless, a number of Jewish commentators either regarded it as "deceptive" (Urbach 1979: 468) or fault the depth of the Ninevites' commitment by suggesting that they obeyed the Hebrew God as they would any other deity that they served; Zlotowitz 1980: 123. Jerome (Antin 1956: 95) found in the Ninevites' conversion a pungent lesson that has influenced Christian exegesis ever since (with unfortunate consequences for Jews): "the foreskin believes; but circumcision remains faithless" (*credidit praeputium et circumcisio permanet infidelis*). D. F. Rauber (1970: 33) reads the whole scene as exaggerated reaction bordering on buffoonery.

wayyiqre'û-ṣôm wayyilbešû śaqqîm. Instituting fasting and wearing tatters are the Ninevites' practical measures. These are just two of a series of penitential activities recorded in Scripture, which may also include prayers, sacrifice, weeping, languishing in ashes or dirt, shaving, and tearing parts of a garment. The goal is to return (verb: *šûb*) to God's favor by obtaining forgiveness.[10] But the

[10] See "Forgiveness" and "Repentance," in *Enc Jud* 6.1433–35 and 14.73–74.

prophets declare these motions as worthless in themselves if they are not accompanied by heartfelt contrition and pledges to discontinue evil activities (see Isa 58:1–7; Jer 14:11–12; Zech 7:4–7; Joel 2:13 [figuratively]).

"Fasting" (*ṣwm*) can be paired with "personal affliction" (*ʿinnâ nepeš*); when combined, these two hardships realize the goal of complete mortification. "Fast" (*ṣôm*) is most commonly a direct object to the verb *qārāʾ*, "to institute, schedule, proclaim"; Joel uniquely uses the verb *qiddaš*, "to observe solemnly."[11] Individuals may fast to ward off God's anger against themselves (Ahab, to avert his own downfall, 1 Kgs 21:27f.), or against a (ultimately false!) friend (Ps 35:13). They may do so also to propitiate God before undertaking a journey (Ezra 8:21), to obtain his support (Esther, to survive an unannounced visit with the king, Est 4:16), or simply to protest an unhappy condition (Neh 1:14). Unusually frank is David's breaking his fast when it fails to keep alive his ill-begotten child (2 Sam 12:22), and unusually sordid is the occasion on which Jezebel tells elders to fast as prelude to falsely convicting Naboth (1 Kgs 21:9).

We are interested most, however, in circumstances in which communities band together in public fasting and other symbolic displays of humiliation. Trible collects representative incidents in which potential disasters are averted by communal penitence (1963: 221–24). Relevant are the following incidents: when the Philistines threaten Israel with destruction (1 Sam 7:3–14); when pestilence breaks out upon David's census taking (2 Sam 24); when Holofernes is about to destroy Bethuliah (Jdt 4:9–15). We may add the interesting situation in which Israel, twice defeated in its war against Benjamin, approaches God with fasting and sacrifice when previously it had only wept (Judg 20:14–37). As far as I can tell, Jonah is unique to Scripture in featuring foreigners who fast for penance.

Nationwide participation in penitential acts is by no means limited to Hebrew culture, however, and we know of similar procedures as early as Sumerian times. Some scholars have introduced Neo-Assyrian testimony to give plausibility to (if not confer historicity upon) the events in Nineveh. Most often cited is a document uncovered at Tell Halaf, the biblical Gozan (Weidner 1940: 13–14). An Assyrian king of the ninth–eighth centuries (we are not sure which one) writes to a provincial governor:

> A Royal message. To Mannu-ki-Assur: Over a three-day period, you and your district's citizens should pray and perform a public weeping before the god Adad. Purge all your land and fields, and offer many burnt-sacrifices. The purification of the *nakarkānu*-house should be undertaken within one full day, so that you may bring about the reconciliation of Adad.

[11] To indicate clearly that the Ninevites fast in order to absolve themselves of guilt, the Targum chooses a verb (*gzr*) that carries a strong negative connotation; Levine 1978: 86.

Landes (1982: 156*–58*) speculates that knowledge of such rituals may have reached Judah after Sargon resettled captives from defeated Samaria around Gozan (2 Kgs 17:6; 18:11; 1 Chr 5:26). Wiseman (1979: 493) offers a translation designed to accentuate the text's connection with Jonah. Stuart (1987: 493–94) follows Wiseman in hinting at an Assur-dan dating for this letter order (not a decree!); but he also worries about the length of time penitents can abstain from water.

The word *śaq* refers to a type of cloth, coarsely woven from inferior material, usually goat's hair, and crudely dyed. It can be worn on the body, spread out as bedding, or used for both purposes. The word is used in Hebrew exclusively to denote humiliation, mourning, or penitence—so much so, that the removal of *śaq* from the body can be equated with happiness: "You have turned my lament into dancing; loosened my sackcloth to dress me in joy (Ps 30:12)." It is normally and correctly rendered in English by "sackcloth" ("hair shirt" may do as well), though for us "rags, tatters" would be less antiquarian and would more readily approximate what the custom is meant to achieve.

The two acts of penance, fasting and wearing sackcloth, form a single unit in which organic suffering is mirrored by a public exhibition of a humiliated body. In Jon 3:5, this integration of internal and external forms of self-denial introduces another merging of opposites, albeit from another category. The phrase *miggedôlām weʿad-qeṭannām* is a merismus, referring to the whole population, prominent and humble, old and young, tall and short. The expression occurs frequently in Scripture, either in the same or in the reverse order (respectively, seven and twenty-four times, according to Vanoni 1978: 85 n. 167). Landes (1982: 159*–60*) has looked into the suggestion that the pattern obtaining in Jonah typifies postexilic stylistics, while the reverse (young/humble/strong . . . old/prominent/weak) allegedly exemplifies preexilic formulations. He offers illustrations to spoil this observation, which, in any case, is much too neat and categorical. Almbladh 1986: 32–33 cites a number of studies that suggest that the more common (and frequently shorter) of the two words is placed first in the sequence. To my mind, if there is any principle guiding the sequence of the words (and I am not certain that there is), it may be that in Jonah *gādôl* occurs first because the narrator will soon pick it up when alluding to the king and his entourage.

The versions generally find literal equivalents to the individual words in the expression. But Duval (1973: 414 n. 104) collects evidence for a lively patristic debate on whether "great to small" refers to social classes (Cyril) or to age groups (Jerome).

3:6. *wayyiggaʿ haddābār ʾel-melek nînewēh wayyāqom mikkisʾô wayyaʿabēr ʾaddartô mēʿālāyw wayyekas śaq wayyēšeb ʿal-hāʾēper.* How does the information in this verse relate to the contents of the edict that the king will soon promulgate? Ibn Ezra thinks that the proclamation of vv 7–9 precedes the people's penitence; Zlotowitz 1980: 125. The English Authorized Version reads 3:6, "For word came unto the king of Nineveh . . ." and implies that v 5 is a *general* overview of what will be specifically detailed later (see Perowne 1905: 77; similarly Landes 1982: 160*). Wolff (1986: 145) regards vv 6–9 as a "flashback explanation, which catches up with events that have already taken place." In order to make his point, Wolff uses the pluperfect throughout the Nineveh portion in Jonah.[12] Thus he awkwardly opens v 6 with "[For] the saying had (meanwhile) reached the king of Nineveh. . . ." But Wolff relies much too often on the pluperfect to elucidate the narrative (he does so also at 1:5, 10; 2:1; and 4:5). I rather imagine that the reactions of Nineveh's citizens and of its king are simply following a sequential order. Thus, in v 5, the response is individual and probably spontaneous, albeit repeated widely among the citizenry. Only after tidings reach the palace is there a more formal and official response that is extended over animals as well.

We may be able to bolster this interpretation by reviewing how in Jeremiah 36 a divine message is said to reach the king. God reveals a warning to Jeremiah, who dictates it to his scribe Baruch. *Almost a year later,* Baruch reads the warning in Gemariah's chamber (within the Temple), during a fast day when a large population was sure to gather. When Gemariah's son hears God's words, he reports them to the nobles within the royal palace. Upon receiving confirmation from Baruch himself, the nobles transmit the divine message to the king. It is only then that Jehoiakim asks for and is read the full report as recorded on a scroll. (Subsequently, Jehoiakim treats the whole matter contemptuously.)

There is of course much difference between the effects the narratives in Jeremiah and in Jonah want to achieve. In Jeremiah 36, the warning travels a circuitous route, probably reflecting the strained relations between God and those who ruled Israel. The jagged path may also epitomize a real chasm between differing social classes and opposing spheres of powers. In Jonah 3, however, this is not at all at stake; and nothing comes to separate the message from those it means to influence. It is also possible that the ease with which the warning reaches the summit of Assyrian power is purposely made to contrast with the rather complicated stages through which the sailors come to realize God's omnipotence. Nevertheless, I am obliged to record here that this fluidity in the movement of information in an Assyrian capital goes counter to what we know about the wide gulf separating Assyrian rulers from their people. Realism, after all, may not always serve the storyteller best.

wayyiggaʿ haddābār ʾel-melek nîneweh. Because *dābār* can mean "message" as well as "event," it is a minor issue whether it is the divine command itself or the popular reaction to it that reaches the king. Either one is possible, perhaps even both. Jeremiah 51:9 offers the idiom controlling this clause (*nāgaʿ* [something] *ʾel-*) in an interesting context: "We would cure Babylon, but she is be-

[12] Similarly, Kleinert, as cited by Bewer 1912: 56.

yond cure. Let her be, and let each of us depart to his own homeland: for her sentence has reached heaven (*ki-nāgaʿ ʾel-haššāmayim mišpāṭāh*); it is lifted toward the clouds." In this last passage, it is obvious that Jeremiah is exploiting an idiom that can also have the meaning "to touch (something)." The "touching," however, is tactile rather than emotional (which would require *nāgaʿ be-*). Therefore, we should reject the translation offered by Stuart (1987: 484), "The word touched even the King of Nineveh."

The way the king is addressed, "king of Nineveh," has elicited much interest because cuneiform documents never use this phrasing for the reigning Assyrian monarch and because Scripture elsewhere cites him as "king of Assyria." The matter of a proper title would be trifling had some scholars not made opposite, but equally insupportable, decisions on its basis. Lawrence (1986) reconstructs the careers of powerful Assyrian governors of the early ninth century B.C.E. to claim that an Assyrian monarch with shrunken authority could have been termed "king of Nineveh." For Bewer (1912: 13), the title was invented only after the fall of Nineveh, when the proper way to address the Assyrian monarch was forgotten. Bewer does not explain why a narrator made such a glaring error when Scripture was available from which to pick an impeccably historical title.

Most modern commentators, however, consider this singular title to be good evidence that Jonah does not treat a historical event. If such a judgment implies that Hebrew narrators *unwittingly* confer historicity on a document of no historical value, we need to oppose it, for it demands too much historical precision from them. Consider the term "Pharaoh" as illustration. In Egypt's own literature, the term "pharaoh" is based on an excellent Egyptian etymology, *pr ʿ3*, "Big House," which, before the first millennium (B.C.E.), is used mostly as a circumlocution for the palace; afterward, however, it becomes just an epithet for the reigning ruler. Egyptian literature does not use it, however, as a substitute for the royal name; nor does it make it serve as equivalent to the Egyptian king's five personal names. Despite this fact, Hebrew literature (even in contexts that are certainly "historical") uses "pharaoh" frequently, citing it mostly by itself, but sometimes as an epithet just before the real name of a king (for example, Pharaoh Necho). This relative freedom in developing labels for rulers obtains even when Hebrew editors certainly must have known better. Thus, the phrase "king of Samaria" occurs twice (1 Kgs 21:1; 2 Kgs 1:3), where the more common formulary is "king of Israel." This occasional laxity as regards titles is not at all limited to Hebrew literature, for Mesopotamian sources can be inaccurate in recording a proper label for foreign leaders. For example, the Mari records speak of "kings" of the Benyaminites, when referring to tribal leaders who, strictly speaking, are not holders of crowns.

It is also possible that the narrator *purposely* formulated a bogus designation in order to alert a knowledgeable audience to the fictional aspect of the Nineveh episode. This device is not unknown to biblical lore. For example, in the otherwise literarily accomplished book of Judith we meet with a Nebuchadnezzar, king of *Assyria* (a mistake that anyone familiar with Kings and Chronicles would hardly make). It is possible that the references to "Belshazzar, the son (!) of Nebuchadnezzar" in Daniel and Baruch (less likely, "king of Assyria" in Ezra 6:22) belong to this category of attention-gathering devices. Variations on this technique include (1) inventing nonexistent locales, for example Judith's Bethulia and Jeremiah's Merathaim ("Double Rebellion," Jer 50:21); the same may obtain in the case of Uz (especially Job's), applied also as eponym, which seems to move about in biblical geography; (2) promoting nonexistent rulers for a period otherwise Scripturally well documented, for example, Darius the Mede of Dan 6:1 (etc.); and (3) formulating patently moralizing royal names, which no proud parents would bestow on a crown prince, for example, the names Genesis 14 assigns to the kings of Sodom, Gomorrah, and their allies; the rhyming name Judg 3:8–10 invents for the king of Aram-Naharaim ("Double-Streamed Aram"), Cushan-Rishathaim ("Doubly-Wicked Kushite"). These patterns by which fictionality is conferred on narratives are by no means restricted to the Hebrew imagination, but can be found in the writings of its neighbors.

The king of Nineveh has no name, which is not at all unusual for a book that names only Jonah; later traditions nevertheless try to fix the problem. A midrash picks for him the name Osnappar (Assurbanipal?), obviously from Ezra 4:10; another tradition identifies him with the Pharaoh of the Exodus who, having learned his lesson at first hand, readily believes in God and in his latest prophet. (Never mind the chronological difference.) Ibn Ezra equates him with Sennacherib, who likewise had firsthand knowledge of God's power (2 Kgs 19:36–37). (See Zlotowitz 1980: 124.) Church fathers argued whether the king was Satan (or his avatar, Nebuchadnezzar!), whose conversion foreshadows the final days; but Jerome was particularly displeased with this interpretation; see Duval 1973: 52, 424 n. 104. Islamic lore calls him Thaʿlab ibn Sharid, a rather sinister name ("Fox, son of Wanderer"), perfectly corresponding to a temper that recognizes God's power only after it is demonstrated from above; Thackston 1978: 322–23. Modern authorities who are wont to think that Jonah's visit to Nineveh really happened likewise try to pin a name on the king of Nineveh (Vaccari, cited by Burrows 1970: 83–84). Wiseman (1979) offers by far the most elaborate case. Erudite though it may seem, his evidence eventually proves superfluous because, having identified Jonah with the namesake of Jeroboam's time, his choices of contemporaneous Assyrian kings are rather limited; and he opts for Assur-dan III as the most likely monarch who would listen to the warnings of a Hebrew prophet. Relying on Wiseman, Stuart (1987: 490–92) gives authority to the choice by heaping on more facts from Assyrian history; but the foundation is pretty rickety. Stuart chooses Assur-dan because he had a reign (allegedly) full of natural disasters and therefore "would be the sort of king (among others) who might well have been predisposed to receive Jonah's message sincerely as a chance for respite from his trouble." This argument is not very convincing. In fact, I would have liked the opposite to be true; a change of heart in, say, an

Assurbanipal or an Esarhaddon would certainly be better testimony of God's greatness! Needless to say, nothing in Assyrian documents directly supports the preceding conjectures. Assur-dan and his son, Assur-nirari (V), continue to accommodate and serve the Assyrian god their names honor.

wayyāqom mikkisʾô wayyaʿabēr ʾaddartô mēʿālāyw wayyekas śaq wayyēšeb ʿal-hāʾēper. This is how Esarhaddon of Assyria acts when he hears news that his older brothers are plotting against his rise to power: "But I, Esarhaddon, who never turns around in a battle, trusting in the great gods, his lords, soon heard of these sorry happenings and I cried 'Woe!' rent my princely robe and began to lament loudly."[13] Esarhaddon did not arrive at this schedule without first consulting the gods. What Jonah says about events at the king's court, therefore, seems plausible for Israel no less than for Assyria. We are told that, upon hearing the news, the king of Nineveh silently prepares himself, bodily and spiritually as well, before decreeing national penitence. The program he follows is intricately staged, with its first scene presented in four clearly defined stages of one sweeping act. Between rising from his throne and sitting on the ground, the king exchanges a precious robe for a pauper's garb. For all that, we note that the king's authority is never diminished by these pious acts. On the contrary, he is able to speak for himself as well as for the nobles of the realm. This ability to retain control despite acting in full humility contrasts well with the ignominious responses predicted for those who hear of Tyre's fate, "All those ruling in the sea will come down from their thrones; they will remove their robes and strip off their brocade garments. Clothed in trembling, they will sit on the ground, shuddering at every moment, stunned by your fate" (Ezek 26:16).

It is interesting to note how the Masoretes punctuate the verse. They place an *atnah,* a strong disjunctive accent, under *mēʿālāyw* and assign a series of *zaqeph qaṭons*, a lesser disjunction, to each of the remaining phrases (at *nînewēh, mikkisʾô,* and *śaq*). These disjunctions impede the flow of motion; but by making it halting, they also allow the reader to focus on the king's movements, one by one, as if dependent on snapshots. This particularizing of the king's activities could have encouraged the Targum to expand on the narratives of the first two scenes by inserting appropriate qualifiers, "He arose from his *royal* seat (*mkrsy mlkwtyh*) and removed his *costly* garb (*lbwš-yqryh*). . . ." In the place of *ʾaddartô,* the Peshitta offers *tgh,* "crown," while the LXX gives *stolēn,* which for the New Testament is a "festal robe"; but it is a "leather cloak" according to most classical texts. The remaining versions translate the rest of the verse literally, choosing words deemed equivalent to the Hebrew.

In Scripture, *ʾadderet* (in two cases, *ʾeder*) is most commonly a cloak of skin (*śēʿār*), not necessarily precious, often worn by the prophet Elijah. Once, we are told of an *ʾadderet šinʿār ṭôbâ,* "a quality Mesopotamian cloak" that Achan stole

[13] In *ANET*³ 289. Different renderings for the first two lines are also plausible.

from among proscribed objects (Josh 7:21, 24[14]). Because there is nothing "royal" about this garment, many medieval Jewish commentators on Jonah derive the word from the root *ʾdr, which connotes breadth and magnificence. It is only the context, therefore, that invests splendor in this garment.

The present phrasing, *heʿebîr ʾadderet min-*, is unique to Scripture. The idiom *heʿebîr* [something] *min* operates in two distinct spheres. The first is mundane and alludes to possessions (rings, clothing, persons) that are "removed" from their location. (If such objects are immediately moved to another spot [for example, at 2 Sam 3:10], "to transfer" may be a better rendering for the idiom.) The other sphere is theological, with evil or sin as object; see BDB 719(Hiph. 4). It is therefore probable that the penitential context of Jonah inspired its narrator to choose an idiom with a twofold application.

In annotating v 3, I have already noted that the innocuous verb *lābē/aš*, "to wear, be clothed," controls the first appearance of "sackcloth." At v 8, "sackcloth" will be governed by the verb *kāsâ* in a reflexive conjugation (*HtD*), "to cover oneself," thus yielding a dynamic image of persons wrapping themselves in coarse garments.[15] In this verse, however, *kāsâ* is in the *piʿel* conjugation (*D* stem), which normally requires that a preposition be added to the object that is being worn, as in "she wrapped herself with a veil," *wattekas baṣṣāʿîp* (Gen 38:14); it may also require double accusatives, as in "I wrapped you with silk," *waʾakassēk mešî*" (for example, Ezek 16:10). The present construction, therefore, is anomalous, and some have suggested either emending the verbal form (see BDB 491[Pi. 1]), or simply consigning the whole phrase to a later (presumably less elegant) Hebrew style; Ehrlich 1912: 269–70. But *wayyekas* is particularly appropriate in the verse because it fosters a pun with *mikkisʾô*, "his throne," of a few words past. More importantly, the *D* stem of the verb (*kissâ*) is found in many passages featuring a vocabulary of redemption or grace, for example, transgression, righteousness, guilt, and iniquity (BDB 491[Pi. 2]). Because Jonah elsewhere employs more idiomatic language (at vv 5 and 8), it is probable that its narrator has chosen deliberately this unusual verbal form, to indulge a taste for a diction with multiple levels of meaning.

What the king sits upon is usually rendered "ashes." I avoid it here lest the reader imagine that the burning of a sacrifice accompanied the king's activities. This would be a minor concern but for the vows of sacrifice that the sailors and Jonah made in each of the preceding chapters. In fact, sacrifice is conspicuously absent from the king's edict as an avenue by which to obtain's God's mercy. The word *ʾēper* (as also its near homophone *ʿāpār*) is precise only in referring to soil, whatever its ingredients; the same can be said of Greek *spodos*, which the LXX uses in its translation. Scriptural references gravitate toward the meaning

[14] If the *nun* is removed from the middle word (*šnʿr*), we would have the commonly cited "leather cloak" (*śʿr*); but of a finer quality material.

[15] This verbal form most commonly requires the preposition *be;* but see Gen 24:65.

"ashes" for *ʾēper* when sacrifice is the context, just as the citations for *ʿāpār* lean toward the meaning "soil," but occasionally also mean "ashes" (BDB 779[2]). The two words can also be paired as a unit without the composition of the soil becoming a factor. A simpler Hebrew formulation, "to sit on the ground (*ʾereṣ*)," achieves the same sense.[16]

3:7. *wayyazʿēq wayyōʾmer benînewēh miṭṭaʿam hammelek ûgdōlāyw lēʾmōr hāʾādām wehabbehēmâ habbāqār wehaṣṣōʾn ʾal-yiṭʿamû meʾûmâ ʾal-yirʿû ûmayim ʾal-yištû.* This verse initiates the king's proclamation, which, in the Hebrew text, will be quoted through v 9. Because the first seven words of v 7 contain two verbal forms (*wayyōʾmer . . . lēʾmōr*) that commonly introduce quotations, there is no universal agreement on where to begin citing the edict. Moreover, the Masoretic punctuation of this segment has disjunctive accents on the first and third words, then a major caesura on the seventh word, suggesting at least two choices for the proclamation's starting point. Old Latin squeezes the initial verbal forms into one, *et praedicatum est,* "it was proclaimed," then ignores the noun *ṭaʿam* that follows. The LXX does not begin the quotation until *lēʾmōr* and then uses passive voices to introduce the edict's stipulations, *kai ekēruchthē kai errethē . . . para tou basileōs . . . legōn,* "and it was proclaimed and was commanded . . . by the king . . . saying." The Vulgate begins at the same point, but introduces it rather impersonally, *et clamavit et dixit in Nineve . . . dicens,* "One [the king?] proclaimed and told in Nineveh . . . saying. . . ." A few modern scholars offer a similar phrasing before reaching the body of the proclamation, for example, Wolff 1986: 144. To do so, however, Wolff distorts the text twice, first by ignoring the initial occurrence of the verb *ʾāmar,* and then by peculiarly treating the preposition *min,* "Then [the king] had proclaimed in Nineveh as an edict of the king and of the great men. . . ." Most modern exegetes follow a medieval Jewish exegetical tradition that locates the edict's beginning with *miṭṭaʿam.* This approach is more defensible than the previous one; nevertheless I shall propose a third possibility.

The two verbal forms *wayyazʿēq wayyōʾmer* do not belong to the body of the edict. The *H* stem of *zāʿaq* (likewise, *ṣāʿaq*) is commonly used when troops and people are summoned. In one instance, however, it is a prophet who is called to attention (Zech 6:8). The way it is used in Jonah, therefore, is unique and invites speculation that the narrator may have resorted to this verb because in the *G* stem it is commonly employed when seeking God's help (see at 1:5). Generally speaking, unless there is a need to specify the person(s) addressed (usually done by means of *le-/ʾel, ʾet*), the quoted statement follows directly upon the verb *ʾāmar.* In 1:14, 2:3, and 4:2 we find the conversive imperfect of

[16] For a more elaborate demonstration of the preceding points, see Gruber 1980: 401–79. The definite article in the Jonah phrase has nothing to do with collectives (so Trible 1963: 44); the idiom is construed with or without it.

ʾāmar directly opening into quoted statements. Note how Hezekiah broadcasts news regarding the Passover celebrations (2 Chr 30:6), "Couriers went out with communications (*ʾiggerôt*) from the king and his officers (*miyyad hammelek weśārāyw*), throughout Israel and Judah (*bekol-yiśrāʾēl wîhûdâ*), by order of the king (*ûkmiṣwat hammelek*), to wit (*lēʾmōr*): [proclamation follows]."

This evidence leads me to suspect that in our verse too, the edict begins right after *wayyōʾmer* and not after *benînewēh*, "in Nineveh," as it is universally given in modern translations, for example, NEB, "Then he had a proclamation made in Nineveh"; NJPS, "And he had the word cried through Nineveh."[17] The edict, therefore, is registering an address for its place of formulation. As far as I can tell, only Trible has offered a similar solution, albeit without discussion (1963: 227).

The proclamation informs us next on whose authority it is being issued: *miṭṭaʿam hammelek ûgdōlāyw*. There seems to be some discomfort among two of the versions over the way to treat the first word in the statement, for the Old Latin and the LXX simply ignore it. Symmachus, however, has *dogmatos,* which Greek commonly gives for Hebrew *dāt,* "law, regulation"; see Trible 1963: 44. The Targum also recognizes *ṭaʿam*'s import but offers *gzyrtʾ*, "ordinance, decree," a noun that cannot be confused with the verb *ṭāʿam,* which comes up presently; Levine 1978: 87–88.

In Hebrew usage, *ṭaʿam* has a range of meanings, "taste (savor), judgment, reason"; BDB 381. Rabbinic Hebrew duplicates this range but includes a technical meaning for *ṭaʿam,* referring to the "signs, accents, and punctuations" necessary to arrive at a correct reading of Scripture; see Jastrow 1950: 543. In biblical Aramaic, the word *ṭeʿēm* (in its various vocalizations) adds the following senses to this roster: "(official) report" and "(royal or divine) command, order, authority"; BDB 1094.[18] To the last definition belongs a number of scriptural passages wherein kings order that specific measures be taken. Such orders are not necessarily public, but are addressed to officials who will execute the royal will. Rabbinic Aramaic and Empire Aramaic reflect a similar, though slightly narrower, range of meanings; *DISO* 102.

Most Jonah translations give *ṭaʿam* a meaning unattested elsewhere in Scripture: a "decree" especially meant for public hearing. For this reason, some scholars seek support from Akkadian, where *ṭēmum* allegedly offers the necessary meaning. But while Akkadian *ṭēmum* includes a range of meanings similar to what obtains in Aramaic, to my knowledge neither *ṭēmum* nor the many idioms that include it refers to a publicly advertised "proclamation" or "announce-

[17] Moreover, I think that a Hebrew writer would probably have inserted *benînewēh* between *wayyazʿēq* and *wayyōʾmer* to arrive at such a rendering.

[18] Rabbinic Aramaic adds the notion of "(legal) argument"; Jastrow 1950: 543.

ment."[19] In fact, we know that a proclamation is being broadcast throughout Nineveh not because of *ṭaʿam,* but because of the verbal form *wayyazʿēq,* which I have just annotated. Therefore, the normally attested Hebrew meaning for *ṭaʿam,* "will, judgment," should suit the context. If a more refined meaning be sought, then biblical Aramaic has an excellent equivalent in Ezra 6:14, where the building of the temple progresses nicely "by authority of Israel's god, and by authority of Cyrus, Darius, and Artaxexes king of Persia," *min-ṭaʿam ʾelāh yiśrāʾēl ûmiṭṭeʿēm kôreš wedāreyāweš weʾartaḥšaśtʾ melek pārās.*[20]

The decree is on authority of the king and of his *gedôlîm,* "grandees." The term is well displayed in Hebrew when referring to the highest echelon of power around the king (BDB 153[6.b]). Even if the nearest phrasing is in the Aramaic of Dan 5:2–3, 10 (*malkāʾ werabrebānôhî*), it is not necessary to invoke Aramaism or Assyrianism to explain it better; see Landes 1982: 167* n. 93.

The words *hāʾādām wehabbehēmâ habbāqār wehaṣṣōʾn* tell us whom the injunction affects. The repetition of *hāʾādām wehabbehēmâ* in the next verse hints that we are dealing here with a merismus, a unified expression made up of two (or more) constituents, commonly opposite words. Such a construction is obvious when Scripture offers either an expanded formulation for the same notion, *meʾādām weʿad (hab)behēmâ* (other prepositions are also possible), or repeats the same noun before each of the two words (for example, *zeraʿ ʾādām zeraʿ behēmâ,* Jer 31:26). Because Hebrews apparently distinguished only between animates and inanimates (the latter includes plants), the edict could potentially apply to all living creatures. The order therefore follows with another merismus that restricts animal participation to a specific group.[21] Such movement from general to particular is common to Scripture and follows a principle that rabbinic biblical interpretation labeled *kelal u-perat.* Thus, a literal rendering (for example, KJV) of a passage such as Lev 1:2 obscures the main point of the rule, which is, "When among you an individual offers a sacrifice to the Lord, the animal must come from herd or flock only."[22] As a generic unit, *habbāqār*

[19] Landes has recently studied the word *ṭaʿam* in connection with Jonah, and his paper is rich in philological notes on the term; 1982: 156*–57*. See also Schüpphaus, in *ThWAT* 3.369–71. I do not address the suggestion that *ṭaʿam* be derived from Persian *framānā* (see Almbladh 1986: 34), because it is farfetched and because it seems to me offered mostly to confer a "late" date on Jonah.

[20] Note the different vocalizations of *ṭʿm* in this verse. It is possible that when referring to God's command (also at Ezra 7:23), Hebrew rather than Aramaic vocalization *ṭeʿēm* is followed.

[21] Some non-Semitic translations spoil this effect by attaching a conjunction to *bāqār;* Trible 1963: 45.

[22] The KJV translates *min-habbēhemâ min-habbāqār ûmin-haṣṣōʾn taqrîbû ʾet-qorbankem* as "Speak unto the children of Israel, and say unto them, If any man of you bring an offering unto the Lord, ye shall bring your offering of the cattle, *even* of the herd, and of the flock" (similarly, the LXX).

wehaṣṣōʾn (with reversed pairing or diverse formulation), thus refers especially to animals available for sacrifice and human consumption. If we recall that in Israel animals were apparently not kept as pets and that (officially at least) Hebrews shunned the raising of pigs, only equids and camels remain as the other domesticated mammals within the town. It may be trivial for the narrator so to limit *behēmâ,* but it does spare us from imagining Ninevites draping camels in sackcloth, let alone lions and elephants.

That animals are to join human beings in certain penitential acts has piqued the curiosity of not a few commentators, who commonly turn to Jdt 4:10–12 for another scriptural example (see below) and occasionally cull classical literature for similar scenes (Herodotus 9.24; Vergil, *Eclogues* 5.24–28; more citations in Keil and Delitzsch 1900: 408 n.1; Gaster 1969: 655–56). Some find in it satire or humor (Wolff 1977: 152–53); others regard it as deadly serious (Bewer 1912: 54). Of course, the book of Jonah has already prepared us well for such an encounter with the animal world when at 2:1 we met a fish with extraordinary responsibility. On this occasion, however, the participation of animals in penitential activities is meant neither to test our credulity nor to challenge the veracity of the Hebrew narrator; rather, it provides a background for the great confrontation between God and his prophet, where animals are conspicuous in a parting shot (4:11) that testifies to God's benevolence, compassion, and forgiveness.

As already seen by Trible (1963: 227), the edict's language follows a two-part program: banned actions are recorded first; required activities are listed next (see COMMENTS for a chart). Because the edict considers opposite types of activities, the narrator lists the participants twice. We should not follow, therefore, the many commentators who urge excision of *behēmâ* from v 7, from v 8, or from both (for example, Bewer 1912: 56). The remaining portion of v 7 details the proscribed program. The verbal forms in *ʾal-yiṭʿamû meʾûmâ ʾal-yirʿû ûmayim ʾal-yištû* are all negated jussives. The first two are chosen with care to fulfill a double service: they clarify what each segment of the population must avoid doing and offer an obvious display of wit. The verb *ṭāʿam,* "to taste, eat," is well represented in Scripture; but it is always used in connection with human beings. By contrast, when it has no direct object (that is, when intransitive) and when it is not used figuratively (regarding idolaters, fools), the verb *rāʿâ,* "to feed, graze," always has animals as subjects. The first two verbs in this particular clause of v 7, therefore, respectively address human beings and beasts, in the exact order given in the preceding phrase. This perception is reinforced by the way these two activities—people, dining; beasts, feeding—lack any conjunction to unite them into one sequence. We should not, therefore, regard the passage as a hyperbaton, a diction in which words are given in a confused order (Becker 1973: 257–63); nor should we regard it as hyperbole, in which the narrator is indulging in overblown and satiric illustrations of life among the pious Ninevites (Wolff 1977: 152). Nevertheless the third clause, *ûmayim ʾal yištû,* does have a conjunction; but it is a moot argument whether it refers just to the animals or to citizens as well.

The wit that is shown here depends on how many connections an audience makes among the verbs within the clause we have just discussed. That with full authority (noun: *ṭaʿam*) the king and his grandees order the Ninevites to partake (verb: *ṭāʿam*) of nothing is a pun immediately recognizable to past audiences (as it is also to many contemporary scholars). That the vocabulary is binding "sense" and "wisdom, perception" (all secondary meanings for the root *ṭʿm*) to the denial of worldly pleasures demanded of everyone could also occur to those reflecting on the verse. But it may require a bit more musing to realize that the regime imposed on innocent and dumb animals features a verb, *rāʿâ*, "to graze," which reminds the ear of *rāʿaʿ*, "to be evil." The latter verb and the word sharing its root are, as we have seen, well represented in Jonah; but it cannot be forgotten that Nineveh's own salvation begins when its citizens' wickedness (*rāʿātām*, 1:2) finally provokes God into action.

For the LXX and the Old Latin, the edict ends here, at the close of v 7. Instead of treating the verbal forms of the next verse as does our vocalized Hebrew text, these versions regard them as conversive imperfects (**wayyitkassû*, etc.). In the Greek and Old Latin renderings, therefore, the next verse (v 8) tells how the population reacts to the king's terse request. At the end of v 8, they add "saying" (Greek *legontes;* Latin *et dixerunt,* normally *lēʾmōr* in Hebrew), thus turning the contents of v 9 into expressions of the Ninevites' hopes. The appropriate lines read,

> 7Proclamation was made, and it was commanded in Nineveh by the king and by his great men, saying, "Let not men, or cattle, or oxen, or sheep, taste anything, nor feed, nor drink water." 8Therefore, men and cattle were clothed in sackcloth, and cried earnestly to God; and they turned every one from their evil way, and from the iniquity that was in their hands, *saying,* 9"Who knows if God will repent, and turn from his fierce anger, and so we may not perish."[23]

This ancient reading of Jonah does have its merits, and they will be rehearsed in the COMMENTS. In the remaining NOTES, I treat almost exclusively the Hebrew version.

[23] There is consistency in the way these two accounts are reflected in the Semitic and Indo-European languages. The Murabbaʿât Hebrew scroll does not have *lēʾmōr,* and therefore matches what we have in Hebrew. But we have enough of the Greek from Naḥal Ḥever to find it affirming the LXX's interpretation, albeit with a slightly different vocabulary. The Arabic version is eclectic here. It gives the edict's formulation as in the Hebrew, but opens v 9 with *waqālû,* "and they said," which it must have taken from the Greek.

3:8. *weyitkassû śaqqim hāʾādām wehabbehēmâ weyiqreʾû ʾel-ʾelōhîm beḥozqâ weyāšubû ʾîš middarkô hārāʿâ ûmin-heḥāmās ʾašer bekappêhem.* The edict turns to positive acts that must now be undertaken, and a series of jussives are there to encourage Nineveh's whole population to perform the appropriate rituals. That animals should be clothed in sackcloth (*HtD* of *kāsâ,* see above) during penance or mourning is itself not an absurdist touch. L. C. Allen (1976: 224 n. 23) reminds us of our own practice whereby horses and the catafalques they pull are dressed in the same color as those bereaved. Whether the language also forces us to imagine them praying to God (*weyiqreʾû ʾel-ʾelōhîm beḥozqâ*), however, is for each of us to decide. We may turn to Job 38:41, where hungry ravens appeal to God to provide for their chicks. Or we may look into the book of Judith (4:10–12), another "historical" narrative, that sharply distinguishes between wearing sackcloth and praying: everyone within town—animals included—put on sackcloth; but only Jews prayed:

> [When the men of Israel heard about Holofernes's march toward Jerusalem,] they, their wives, their children, their cattle, and all their resident aliens, hired or slave, wrapped sackcloth around their loins. All the Israelites in Jerusalem, including the women and children, lay prone in front of the Temple, and with ashes on their heads, stretched out their hands [Greek, Vulgate: sackcloth] before the Lord. (*Jerusalem Bible*)

In a previous comment on the use of the idiom *qārāʾ ʾel-* (at 1:2), I have noted that its verb is in the imperfect (conversive; jussive) on the two occasions that the subjects are foreigners: sailors (1:14) and Ninevites (here).[24] What is interesting, however, is that the king and his counselors needed to state that intense commitment must accompany prayers. While other scriptural contexts demand fervor when praying, it is striking that of five references to the idiom found in Jonah, 3:8 is unique in adding a qualification: it must be done *beḥozqâ.*[25] The noun, albeit seldom used in Scripture, is clear enough, and the versions are true to its intent even if, to do so, some among them resort to adverbs (Trible 1963: 45). I think it is placed here for a purpose. Heretofore, the Ninevites participate in acts of penitence that are fairly conventional as far as human beings are concerned (bizarre though they may be to us when they involve animals). The supplications, the wearing of sackcloth, the wallowing in

[24] Practical rather than textual reasons may therefore have guided the Syriac into translating with *bḥngtʾ,* "with a groan": one may assess the intensity of worshipers more sensibly by listening to their groans.

[25] Murabbaʿât reads in v 8 *[w]yqrʾw ʿl ʾlhym;* Milik 1961: 191. As an idiom for "to pray," *qrʾ ʿl* would be very unusual. It may well be due to scribal laxity, for it occurs only here; in any case, the reading of the consonant *ʿayin* is not certain.

dust, the fasting and the thirsting all are customary functions. Moreover, the individuals who fulfill them can also monitor whether their neighbors are similarly occupied, for communal activity must also be communally enforced. But how can the king ever ascertain that the Ninevites are conforming to the remaining program? Because *beḥozqâ* serves as a device by which to gauge the depth of a worshiper's *conviction,* it readies us well for a radical shift in the edict's demands.[26]

One verb, *šûb,* "to return," controls the twofold activities that come next, *weyāšubû ʾîš middarkô hārāʿâ ûmin-heḥāmās ʾašer bekappêhem;* for clarity, however, I use two English verbs in the translation. It is not at all unusual for Hebrew to particularize a verbal form given in the plural (*yāšubû,* "they must return") by inserting a noun in singular (*ʾîš,* "a man"); we have already seen examples of this phenomenon in 1:5 and 7. As vocalized, *weyāšubû* is a jussive, thus furthering the edict's instructions. (See above on the LXX's interpretation.) I have already alluded to the theological prominence this verb attains in matters of redemption and penitence. Basically meaning "to return, turn back" in the G stem, the verb *šûb* may also join with another verb to promote an extension or reconsideration of the thought or activity defined by that verb, "Isaac *dug anew* the wells (near Beersheba)," Gen 26:18; "[God] will *renew* compassion for us (and will trample our iniquities)," Mic 7:19; more examples in Joüon 1923: 533 (177.b). When construed with the preposition *min,* however, *šûb* yields the sense of "withdrawing, turning, retreating, recanting" from previous activities and thoughts. What is most impressive is that all of Jonah's four mentions of *šûb*—once in the former, but three times in the latter usage—occur in three verses within this chapter (3:8–10).[27] As much as anything else in Jonah, this sudden burgeoning of a theological idiom, when it is conspicuously absent everywhere else, focuses our attention on the major issue raised by Nineveh's dilemma.

Because *derek* is regarded as both a masculine and a feminine noun (see Ratner 1987), it can have adjectives of both genders. The phrase *derek raʿ* or *derek raʿâ* is quite common to Scripture, where it is figurative for "evil practices" as well as for "evil intentions" (BDB 203 [6.d]; citing other adjectives as well). Jeremiah and Ezekiel contain phrasings that are closest to Jonah's (Vanoni 1978: 136–37, gives the relevant references). As illustration, I cite Jer 18:11, a verse that follows immediately after the quotation I give in this chapter's heading: "Now therefore, tell whoever is in Judah and inform the citizens of Jerusalem, 'The Lord says this: I am now crafting a disaster just for you and devising a plan

[26] On the problem Jewish exegetes had in assessing the meaning of *beḥozqâ,* see Silberman (in press).

[27] The verb also occurs in the *H* stem; see the comments on 1:14. The verb *šûb* and its derivatives are heavily studied in biblical literature; see the comments and bibliography of Soggin, in *THAT* 2.884–91.

against you. Forsake, each of you, evil conduct (*šûbû nāʾ ʾîš middarkô hārāʿâ*) and correct your behavior and your actions.' "

(*weyašubû . . .*) *min-heḥāmās ʾašer bekappēhêm.* The word *ḥāmās* refers to the physical violence that issues from wicked design and purpose, and the Ninevites are being urged away from such deeds. Scripture has many phrasings and idioms with *ḥāmās,* and they tell of human provocations that lead God to punish mankind (Gen 6:11–13; Mic 6:12; Zeph 1:9 and others) as well as to save the innocent (Ps 18:49; 72:14; and others). Therefore, the term fits nicely within theological discourse (see H. J. Stoebe, in *THAT* 1.583–87). Of more interest to us is how *ḥāmās* is affected by the addition of *ʾašer bekappêhem.* We note first that the last word is in the dual, yet it has a plural genitive suffix. This construction encourages the mind to imagine a whole series of paired hands; consequently, it particularizes and individualizes the bearers of violence even as it distributes their culpability upon and among the whole community. The violence to which the king is alluding is internal to Nineveh's citizenry and need not, therefore, pertain to Nineveh's predatory activities against its foreign nations; see Bewer 1912: 53.

Following the Targum, medieval commentators are rather literal in understanding the phrase, suggesting that the Ninevites were hoarding goods acquired through battery (Silberman, in press; Zlotowitz 1980: 127–28). Somewhat similar are the opinions of some modern commentators: Wolff offers "deed of violence which clings to their hands" (1977: 144, 153); Stuart gives "frequent violence" and explains that the language is "connoting regularity and frequency" (1987: 484). This may well be the intent of the clause in Jonah. Nevertheless, I am minded of occasions on which *ḥāmās bekappayim* refers not to a specific brutal act, but rather to an ethical or moral stance. (Isa 59:6 uses the terminology to bridge physical and ethical abuses.) Such is the case when Job laments (16:17), "my face turns blotchy from weeping, and deepest shadow blackens my eyelids, because I indulge in no-violence (*ʿal lōʾ-ḥāmās bekappāy*), because my prayer is guileless." We have a similar abstraction in 1 Chr 12:18, where David tells delegates from Benjamin and Judah, "If you come here peacefully to be my allies, I am ready to make common cause with you; but if it is to betray me to my enemies—when I myself indulge in no-violence (*belōʾ ḥāmās bekappay*)—the God of our fathers can realize it and can make judgment." I think that this specialized meaning is applicable to Jon 3:8, and I am reminded of a Near Eastern notion that spiritual renewal is made more concrete by the cessation of violence. In a recently published Mari prophetic text (ARM XXVI:206), the god Dagan warns the king that "there will be a 'consumption' [i.e. plague]. Demand from each town that they return tabooed objects. A man who has done a violent act must be ejected from town." As a somewhat hyperbolic example, I cite a Sumerian passage from the cylinder inscription of Gudea of Lagash (about 2000 B.C.E.). Gudea has just awakened from a dream that communicates to him the god Ningirsu's wish for a new temple:

> [Gudea] gave instructions to his city as to one single man, and Lagash land became of one accord for him as children of one mother: (digging) sticks it took in hand, weeded up the thorns, stacked the cut grass. (Harsh) words from all mouths he barred, barred from that house (all) offense. Prick and whiplash he undid from goad and whip, and wool of mother sheep he put into (the overseer's) hands. No mother with her child had words, no child spoke to its mother saucily. The master of the slave who had obtained rent for the heddle, frowned not at him, and the mistress of the slave girl naughtily acting to rival her with the master, slapped not her face with anything. Before the ruler building the Eninnu[-temple], Gudea, no man let ominously words fall. (Jacobsen 1987: 403–4)

With the preceding remarks in mind, I can suggest that in the last clause of v 8 the verb *šûb* controls two separate but mutually reinforcing spheres of activities. The first is long-range, urging each and every Ninevite to a spiritual reassessment; the second is short-range, enjoined on all, and requires the community to manifest peaceful coexistence as sign of ethical regeneration.

3:9. *mî-yôdēaʿ yāšûb weniḥam hāʾelōhîm wešāb mēḥarôn ʾappô welōʾ nōbēd.* The interrogative pronoun *mî*, "who," readily binds with verbal forms to create a variety of rhetorical expressions (BDB 566–67 [f]). When it is followed by an imperfect it can be used to express a desire, and hence comes to fulfill the same function as the adverb *ʾûlay*, "perhaps," which I annotate at 1:6. In 3:9, *mî* is followed by a participle; such expressions are purely exclamative, as in "who is listening?" (Ps 59:8) and the present "who can tell?" (see GKC 476–77 [§ 151.a–d]). But such interjections, when placed at the heads of sentences (but not when at their end) can introduce the same type of wishful utterances as those with *ʾûlay*. Crenshaw's article has recently offered a contextual treatment of *mî-yôdēaʿ* (1986), from which I extract two citations for comparison with the constructions obtaining in 1:6 and 3:9.[28]

Jon 1:6	*Jon 3:9*	*2 Sam 12:22*	*Joel 2:14*
ʾûlay	*mî-yôdēaʿ*	*mî-yôdēaʿ*	*mî-yôdēaʿ*
yitʿaššēt hāʾelōhîm lānû	*yašûb weniḥam hāʾelōhîm wešāb mēḥarôn ʾappô*	*yeḥannanî YHWH*	*yašûb weniḥām*
welōʾ nōʾbēd	*welōʾ nōbēd*	*weḥay hayyāled*	*wehišʾîr ʾaḥarāyw berākâ*

[28] See 2 Sam 12:22, "Who can tell? The Lord may have pity on me, and the child may yet live"; and Joel 2:14, "Who can tell? [God] may reconsider and relent, leaving a blessing in the wake."

The adverb or the exclamation introduces sentences that then divide into two segments, the first of which sets a condition that has to be met if the wish expressed in the second segment is to occur. All of the above conditions have sentences with imperfects (in 2 Sam, I read the *ketib*), while the wishes they express are either phrased as cohortatives (Jon 1:16, 3:9) or as perfects with *waw*-conversives. Jonah 3:9 is unusual in that it sets up a double condition, one opening into the other, with the imperfect form *yāšûb* acting as auxiliary for two perfects with *waw*-conversives (*weniḥam* . . . *wešāb*). Because of its centered position, *hā'elōhîm*, "*the* God," serves as subject for both verbal forms just cited. I have gone to some lengths to explain the grammar of such constructions because it allows us to steer away from the Masoretic punctuation of this verse, which placed a disjunctive accent on the third word, *yašûb* (perhaps encouraged to do so by the Masoretic punctuation of *weyāšubû* in the previous verse). This punctuation forces a translation, "He who knows will turn back, then *the* God will have pity. . . ." Thus, for the Masoretes, the condition is set in the first three Hebrew words, while the rest of v 9 is now given over to a series of hoped-for goals. This reading is probably based on (late?) Hellenistic exegesis, for the Targum arrives at a similar notion: "He who knows that he has guilt in his hands must turn from them" (Levine 1978: 88–89). Nevertheless, it is not supported elsewhere by the Masoretes themselves, for they divide the first four words when duplicated in Joel 2:14 differently and correctly (see above). Moreover, the LXX also has "who can tell?" (*tis oiden*) for the context of Jon 3:9, albeit it assigns the question to the Ninevite citizenry rather than to the king.

Although I do not follow the Masoretes' punctuation and apportionment of statements within 3:9, it is nevertheless important to keep them in mind because they will help us reconstruct a major exegesis of the events transpiring in Nineveh (see the COMMENTS). Medieval Jewish exegetes generally adopted the received text and interpreted accordingly; but Ibn Ezra and Kimḥi do recognize the possibility I have adopted (Zlotowitz 1980: 128–29).

With regard to *weniḥam hā'elōhîm*, in my translation I capitalize the second word as "God," while in the quasi-parallel statement attributed to the helmsman (1:6), I treat it as a common noun. (See there too why I give "god himself" for *hā'elōhîm*.) It is possible to differ on this distinction; but I reason that on board ship the helmsman was not yet informed about Jonah's God. The edict's context, however, is quite different. It will not do for the king to make vague appeals to some powerful deity. In fact, because of what we read immediately afterward (v 10), the king could have only the Hebrew God in his mind (*contra* Stuart 1987: 484). I may note here that the Targum avoids an ambiguous mention of the deity involved, and therefore gives *YHWH* where Hebrew has *'elōhîm*.

Depending on the conjugation, the root *nḥm* realizes different meanings. In the *D* stem, *niḥam* means "to comfort," and the like, while in the *N* stem, *niḥam* (same spelling for the third-person singular perfect), the verb is about "repenting," "regretting," but also simply about "changing one's mind" (Stoebe, in *THAT* 2.59–63; Barr 1961: 116–18). When applied to God, *niḥam* can refer to divine activities that have already occurred (for example, at Gen 6:6–7; 1 Sam 15:11; 2 Sam 24:16; Jer 42:10); hence it is better expressed as "regret." The verb can also refer to divine actions that are contemplated but are never fulfilled; hence it is better reproduced as "changing one's mind; relenting" (Andersen and Freedman 1989: 639–79). All three occurrences of *niḥam* in Jonah (3:9, 10; 4:2) belong to the latter meaning. We may note here that the Naḥal Ḥever Greek fragments and the LXX differ on how to treat this same section. Greek normally uses a verbal form from *parakaleō* to render both the *D* and *N* stems of **nāḥam.* Nahal Ḥever Greek approximates the Hebrew well by having two verbal forms Barthélemy reconstructs as *epistrepsei kai paraklēthēsetai* (1963: 171). The LXX collapses the two verbal forms into one, *metanoēsei,* from a verb that elsewhere almost always translates the *N* stem **nāḥam;* it thus drops *yašûb,* probably because it would compromise its interpretation of events; see COMMENTS.[29] In offering "there will be compassion on us from God's part," the Targum (and the Syriac) parsed **nāḥam* as a *D* stem ("to have pity") and therefore resorted to the Aramaic *ethpael* of *reḥēm* in order to parallel the Hebrew meaning (*wytrḥm ʿlnʾ mn qdm YHWH*).

The second segment of the twofold condition is concerned that God draw back from anger. The expression *ḥarôn ʾap,* "heating up of the nose/nostrils/face" (occasionally, simply *ʾap*) is a metaphor for "anger," and this expression (unlike *ḥorî ʾap*) is always about God's anger. This does not mean (as is occasionally stated) that the Hebrews thought the nose a seat for the emotions; rather, they did make an obvious connection between anger and turning red, and between turning red and a raised temperature; see the excellent pages of Gruber 1980: 491–502. Syriac expands, *wmhpk mnn ḥmtʾ drwgzh,* "He turns away the heat of his anger," while the Targum strives for the same notion with *wytwb mtqwp rwgzyh,* "and turn away from the vehemence of his anger."[30] The LXX (*eks orgēs thumou autou*) and Naḥal Ḥever Greek (reversing the order of substantives), as well as Latin versions, avoid anthropomorphisms and compensate by joining two words for anger into one concept. This is unnecessarily followed in some translations that give, for example, "burning anger."

The wish itself can differ in construction. Both Jonah passages have prohibitives, *welōʾ nōʾbēd* (see discussion at 1:6); the remaining examples have perfects with *waw*-conversives.

[29] To translate Hebrew *šûb,* the LXX has *apostrephō* throughout, while Naḥal Ḥever uses *epistrephō.* The break at the end of v 8 may have contained *legontes.* For the vocabulary used in Greek to render the Hebrew repentance terminology, see G. F. Snyder in *IDBSup* 738–39.

[30] On the theology of the Syriac and Targum passages, see Gelston 1987: 152–53.

3:10. *wayyarʾ hāʾelōhîm ʾet-maʿaśêhem kî-šābû middarkām hārāʿâ wayyinnāḥem hāʾelōhîm ʿal-hārāʿâ ʾašer-dibber laʿaśôt-lāhem welōʾ ʿāśâ.* The verse replays previous vocabulary and constructions in order to reinforce the connection between cause (the Ninevites' plan of actions) and effect (God's change of mind). In sequence and language, the account of God's change in mind parallels what obtains in Exod 32:12–14. Moses uses imperatives as he urges God not to retaliate against Israel's worship of the Golden Calf, *šûb mēḥarôn ʾappekā wehinnāḥēm ʿal-hārāʿâ leʿammekā,* "Turn away from your anger and renounce plans for a disaster against your people." (Freedman reminds me that the same direct request is in Ps 90:13, itself attributed to Moses.) We are then told (v 14) that "The Lord renounced plans for the disaster he had threatened against his folk," *wayyinnāḥem YHWH ʿal-hārāʿâ ʾašer dibber laʿaśôt leʿammô.* Similar sentiments (though by no means the same responses) are common to Jeremiah, where *ḥāšab* occasionally replaces the (*D* stem) verb *dibber;* see Vanoni 1978: 138, 144–45. Targum once more avoids attributing human senses directly to God and therefore has "Their deeds became manifest to the Lord," *wgln qdm YY ʿwbdyhwn.*

Verse 10 contains a complex chain of five clauses:

1. *wayyarʾ hāʾelōhîm ʾet-maʿaśêhem*
2. *kî-šābû middarkām hārāʿâ*
3. *wayyinnāḥem hāʾelōhîm ʿal-hārāʿâ*
4. *ʾašer-dibber laʿaśôt-lāhem*
5. *welōʾ ʿāśâ*

The syntax of the first two clauses is of interest. The LXX and Naḥal Ḥever Greek fragments render 1 + 2 as "And God saw their works, that they turned from their evil ways"; it therefore handles 2 as an object clause, and this reading is followed by most modern translators. There is elegance to this approach in that the syntax of 1 + 2 now parallels that of 3 + 4, where "[that] he had threatened against them" is also an object clause.[31] It seems to me, however, that "they turned from their evil ways" may well be a causal clause, functioning in much the same way as *kî higgîd lāhem* of 1:10. When treated as such, *kî-šābû middarkām hārāʿâ* can then serve as the only testimony (in the Hebrew version) that Nineveh did indeed respond to its king's appeal. Laconic though it may be, this statement reassures us that God's mercy is not showered prematurely on undeserving folk.

In this verse derivatives of the root **ʿāśâ* are repeated three times. God

[31] Wishing to integrate v 10 better within the Greek scenario for events in Nineveh, Aquila, Theodotion, and Symmachus repeat a word found in v 8 (*ekastos*), "and they turned *everyone* from their evil ways"; Trible 1963: 47.

watches the Ninevites' deeds (*maʿaśêhem*), reconsiders what is planned for them (*laʿaśôt-lāhem*), and immediately withholds punishment (*welōʾ ʿāśâ*). Whether intentional or not, this dense repetition anchors an important reflection: deeds —and not just good intentions—are necessary for forgiveness. We also notice that the verse's last clause, *welōʾ ʿāśâ,* matches the crispness of the Ninevites' own wish as expressed at the end of v 9, *welōʾ nōʾbēd.* The narrator could have found no more effective way to comment on the relationship among divine anger, human repentance, and divine forgiveness: God judges Nineveh to be at fault before summoning Jonah as a messenger; Nineveh remains in peril throughout the prophet's experiences, on board ship and in the fish's belly; yet once the Ninevites unquestioningly repent of their faults, God's forgiveness is there to be had by all.

COMMENTS

> But God, being merciful, absolves sin. Reluctant to destroy, God constantly restrains his anger, never releasing it fullforce; for God keeps in mind that [mortals] are but flesh, a breath that vanishes once it leaves (the body). (Ps 78:38–39)

What convinces the Ninevites of the truth behind Jonah's words is beyond philology to recover; but convinced they obviously were, for they react sharply and quickly to his message. Of the measures taken in the Assyrian capital, we have two separate accounts from antiquity; one is preserved in the received Hebrew text, the other in the various Greek renderings. In the former the verbal forms in v 8 are jussives, while in the latter they are indicative aorists. We presume that these two accounts diverge because the Hebrew underlying the Greek translation was understood and interpreted differently by the Greek translator. In the NOTES, I give relevant philological and grammatical descriptions of the differences between these two accounts; here, I look at them comparatively.

CHANGES OF HEART, CHANGE OF MIND (3:5–10)

ANALYSIS OF 3:5–10

[Both Versions]

A. *Reaction in Nineveh.* Citizens from all walks of life:
   1. Believe in God
   2. Fast
   3. Wear sackcloth

B. *The King's action.*
   1. Moves from throne to sit on dirt
   2. Removes his robes to wear sackcloth

[Hebrew Version]	**[Greek Version]**
3. King promulgates edict:	
C. *The Edict. Introduction:* 1. Place: In Nineveh 2. From: King and Grandees 3. To: People and animals (domesticated).	C. *Edict promulgated,* in Nineveh, to people, beasts, cattle, and sheep.
D. *The Edict. Provisions:* 1. Negative orders: a. People: eat nothing b. Animals: no pasture or water.	
2. Positive orders: a. People and animals: i. Wear sackcloth b. People: i. Pray fervently ii. Cease violence.	D. *The Edict. Provisions:* 1. Negative orders: a. People: eat nothing b. Animals: no pasture or water.
3. Expectation: a. [MT punctuation: recognition] b. God will reconsider c. We will be spared.	
E. *Nineveh reacts to edict:* [retrojection; see below]	E. *Nineveh reacts to edict:* 1. People and animals: a. Wore sackcloth 2. People: a. Prayed fervently b. Ceased violence 3. Expectations: a. God will reconsider b. We will be spared.
F. *God's response:* 1. Recognizes their deeds [retrojection] 2. Reconsiders decision 3. Revokes decision.	F. *God's response:* 1. Recognizes their deeds [amplification] 2. Reconsiders decision 3. Revokes plans.

A most striking difference between the two accounts is the amount of attention they each give to two components of the narrative. The Greek version assigns the edict only a few words of v 7, "Let not men, or cattle, or oxen, or sheep, taste (anything), nor feed, nor drink water." This terse injunction, therefore, hardly requires more of Nineveh's inhabitants than what they were already doing *before* their king and grandees produced their *ukase;* in fact, it just adds animals to the list of those who are already fasting. We are therefore left with a program whereby the king, coming to repentance later than his people, can think of very little to sharpen repentance and contrition within his own land. In this respect, the king's role compares nicely with the part assigned to the helmsman in the first chapter of Jonah (1:6). Both of them are there to make pronouncements, authoritative yet not very consequential for the development of the narrative. (But see the INTERPRETATIONS section, on allegory in Jonah.)

The Greek account, however, expands the role of Nineveh's citizenry. As in the Hebrew report, they are the first to react to Jonah's message. They wait for their leaders' response to the challenge; yet, when the proclamation is published, they can find in it no urging that requires them appreciably to modify their current practices. The citizens therefore improvise: after throwing sackcloth on their animals, they begin to pray. More, each of them begins to alter daily behavior and to rethink the merits of violence. It is this deeply felt, yet totally *ad hoc,* individual reaction to Jonah's message that persuades God to rescind a planned punishment.

In the Hebrew text, it is the edict that holds the most attention, with the narrator allotting to it two full verses (8 and 9) and most of a third (v 7). Because of the large space allocated to it, the edict dominates this section's narrative, leaving any report on the way Ninevites react to an afterthought (v 10b).

Actually, the Hebrew text allows for two distinct positions on how God's change of mind is secured. The difference hinges on whether we sustain the disjunctive accent on the third word in v 9 (as it is given in the Masoretic text) or chose to move it back one word (perhaps even to disregard it completely). If we stay with the Masoretic punctuation (reflected already by the Targum), the king would actually be making a veiled statement, "He who knows, will turn back" (*mî-yôdēaʿ yāšûb*), rather than posing the rhetorical "Who can tell?" that I give in the translation. The Masoretes, therefore, may be proposing an esoteric interpretation of how Nineveh eventually survives, for its fate rests on a portion of the population that, realizing its perversion of moral behavior, reforms its ways. The few bring salvation to the many.

In the NOTES, however, I have defended shifting this accent from the third to the second word of v 9 and I thereby obtain a second Hebrew explanation for God's mercy: the piety of the Ninevites is measured by the king's sincere desire to move his people toward a more virtuous mode of behavior. The king remains center-stage throughout as he broadcasts various guidelines for behavior. Of the Ninevites' reaction to this enforced piety, we have only a laconic statement, inserted almost as an afterthought in v 10. The merit for Nineveh's survival is accorded, therefore, to the community's leadership, for in time of stress it quickly takes charge, rallying the population to public piety.

We cannot tell how far into the past to push any of these three readings. We may favor one reading over another; yet we cannot label one interpretation more correct or better founded than another for, as elsewhere in Jonah, we simply have different perceptions of the way God's word is obeyed by penitents. In the INTRODUCTORY REMARKS to this section, I collect scriptural testimony that shows that averting divine punishment may be due to the merit of the community when it fervently reacts to its own moral defects, to the virtue of the few who are not corrupted by their contemporaries, or to the penitence of Israel's king or leaders. These three avenues to salvation may therefore have informed, respectively, the Greek, the Masoretic, and my own reading of the miraculous survival of Nineveh.

We have yet to deal with a major issue left open by the COMMENTS of section VIII. From these pages, we have come to understand the reason behind Jonah's displeasure with God's response. Jonah may not have been surprised by the feverish activity in Nineveh; he may have even been moved by the energy and fervor that accompanied the Ninevites' anguished moves; for which of Israel's prophets is not beyond empathy with fellow human beings in despair? But what eventually pains Jonah most may not be the Ninevites' success, but God's behavior to him. Had God not pursued him to the gates of Sheol just so he could saddle him with an apparently frivolous errand?

In the COMMENTS to Jon 3:1–4, I focus on the way that Jonah understands the divine message he carries into Nineveh, *ʿôd ʾarbāʿîm yôm wenîneweh nehpāket*, "Forty more days, and Nineveh overturns." Jonah believes it to be neither an ultimatum nor a warning, but a *declaration of doom.* It is essential to the narrative that the Ninevites share the same understanding of the phrase, for their quick and desperate reaction must be motivated by belief, fear, despair, resignation, but also hope. When their piety and sincere pleas lengthen their city's life—not for long, at any rate, for Nineveh eventually falls to foreign weapons—the Ninevites may well have come to realize the power of mercy.

Even so, the Ninevites cannot have realized what the philological dissection of the phrase *wenîneweh nehpāket* has revealed (see annotations to 3:4): that Jonah's message allows it to bear an entirely different meaning. "Forty more days, Nineveh will turn over (that is, re[-]form)" can therefore also be predictive: of Nineveh's conversion to a better conduct, but also of the surcease God grants it. The narrator is ascribing this understanding of the verbal form neither to Jonah nor to the Ninevites, but to an omniscient God. In doing so, the narrator gives good reason why the survival of Nineveh should not be attributed to a capricious or erratic deity. God knew all along that Nineveh was destined, in the end, to earn divine forgiveness . . . at least for the time being (but see at 4:2).

In recognizing the amphibolic nature of *nehpāket,* we do more than perceive

Jonah's limitations or justify God's behavior; we unlock a major element of the plot. Jonah's failure to understand his own God's subtlety will lead to the great confrontation featured in the fourth chapter. Moreover, when we realize that the message carried into Nineveh bore a twofold meaning, we become better equipped for the marked shift in the tone the narrator adopts for the last chapter. Heretofore, we had only seen an angry God—against the Ninevites, against Jonah—relentlessly pursuing one goal, namely, that Nineveh must hear about its crimes. We had a rebellious prophet who learned, first through a humiliating then through an ennobling experience, that God's wishes cannot be circumvented. By the end of the third chapter (in fact, as soon as v 5 tells us that the Ninevites "believed in God"), God becomes more playful with Jonah, more tolerant of his caustic responses, more willing to indulge his stubbornness. As we shall also see, the narrative itself becomes more whimsical; more indulgent, I may say, in that it veers from attacking issues frontally. As we observe this shift in character, mood, and temper, we begin to wonder whether God's great deeds at sea, below waters, and within Nineveh are but mere exhibits for a prophet's education. All these modifications will be necessary because, to the last, the narrator needs to keep Jonah oblivious of the little games that Hebrew words can play.[32]

In the pages of the INTERPRETATIONS, I shall speculate on when and why narratives are made to carry such ambiguous and equivocal meanings.

[32] Scripture plays on words on many other occasions, and sometimes with even more pivotal consequences; see *IDBSup* 970 (3: Extended Wordplay).

X. Move/Countermove (Jonah 4:1–6)

I have sat lonely because of Your hand upon me, For You have filled me with gloom. (Jer 15:17; NJPS)

If you wonder, "How can we recognize a message the Lord has not said?": Whatever the prophet says in the Lord's name, which does not come to be, this is something the Lord has not said. The prophet has said it presumptuously; don't be afraid of it. (Deut 18:21–22)

Jonah argued with himself, saying, I know that the nations are nigh to repentance, now they will repent and the Holy One, blessed be He, will direct His anger against Israel. And is it not enough for me that Israel should call me a lying prophet; but shall also the nations of the world (do likewise)?[1]

[Jonah] connected his own ministry with the glory of God, and rightly, because it depended on His authority. Jonah, when he entered Nineveh, did not utter his cry as a private individual, but professed himself to be sent by God. Now if the proclamation of Jonah is found to be false, the disgrace will fall upon the author of the call himself, namely on God. There is no doubt, that Jonah took it ill that the name of God was exposed to the revilings of the heathen, as though He terrified without cause.[2]

[1] *Pirkei de-Rabbi Eliezer* X; Friedlander, 1981: 65–66. This aggadic work appears to date to the ninth century C.E.

[2] John Calvin, as cited disapprovingly by Perowne 1905: 84. Perowne's own opinion, unfortunately shared by many interpreters, is that "Jonah was displeased that the mercy of God should extend to heathen, and especially to heathen who were the enemies and future oppressors of his own people, and that he himself should be the messenger of that mercy. This view falls in entirely with the exclusive spirit which marks the Old Testa-

X. MOVE/COUNTERMOVE (4:1–6)

4 [1]This *outcome* was so terribly upsetting to Jonah that he was dejected.
[2]Praying to the Lord, he said,

> Please, Lord, this certainly was my opinion, while yet in my own homeland; accordingly, I planned to flee toward Tarshish because I realized then that you are a gracious and compassionate God, very patient and abundantly benevolent, who would also relent from bringing disaster.
> [3]Now then, Lord, take away life from me, because for me death is better than life.

[4]The Lord said, "Are you utterly dejected?"

[5]Jonah then left the city, but remained just east of it. He made himself a
shelter there and, sitting beneath it in the shade, he waited to see what would
happen to the city. [6]In order to deliver him from his distress, Lord God directed
a *qiqayon* plant, that then rose above Jonah to form a shade over his head. Jonah
was absolutely delighted over the *qiqayon* plant.

APPORTIONING JONAH 4: INTRODUCTORY REMARKS

How we apportion Jonah into integral units is more critical on this occasion than previously; for it can influence our very understanding of Jonah's denouement. In turn, what transpires between God and Jonah in this, their last meeting, controls our grasp of the whole book.

The division of Jonah into four chapters cannot be dated earlier than the Middle Ages. Above, in the comments appended to 2:10, I have observed that our oldest Hebrew copy of Jonah, found at Wadi Murabbaʿāt (second century C.E.), leaves an empty line at the end of the psalm and begins a new unit at 2:11. The scribe allows but a short gap to distance 2:11 from 3:1. Thereafter, the scribe copies continuously until completing 4:3. At that point, he stops the line in its middle; then, skipping another empty line, the scribe begins copying the remaining verses of Jonah (4:4–11).[3] There is no demarcation between the end

---

ment dispensation, while it brings out into bold relief the liberal and Catholic [*sic*] spirit of the New Testament, which is the object of this book to inculcate."

[3] Milik 1961: 190–92. I cannot explain two smaller gaps in the Murabbaʿāt scroll located in 4:2 (after *qdmty* and *hrʿh*), and two even smaller gaps at 1:13 (after *hym*) and 1:14 (after *YHWH*).

of chapter 3 (the Nineveh episode) and the beginning of chapter 4 (the Jonah–God confrontation).

Although for other biblical books the Masoretic division of texts does not always agree with what obtains at Qumran, what we now have of Jonah duplicates what is found at Murabbaᶜāt. The only difference is that in our editions, there are *setumôt* (closed units [of Scripture readings]) where each of the above units ends and a *petûḥāʾ* (an open unit) between 2:11 and 3:1. In its threefold division of Jonah's narrative, therefore, our Hebrew text perpetuates a textual tradition that could well antedate Qumran. It consists of (1) 1:1–2:10, from Jonah's attempted escape to Tarshish through his vow of thanksgiving sacrifices; (2) 2:11–4:3, from God renewing Jonah's life through Jonah's request that God end it; (3) 4:4–11, from God's response to Jonah's soliloquy through God's explanation for redeeming Nineveh. This tradition is also exegetical, as it plots Jonah's behavior along two trajectories. In the first (1:1–2:10), the direction is downward, with Jonah inexorably descending into Sheol's gullet. The truth of God's authority, however, veers him sharply from insubordination and toward reconciliation. In the second path (2:11–4:3), the move is horizontal, but opposite in direction. Jonah begins by accepting God's will, but is eventually dismayed by God's reaction to Nineveh's pleas. There remains a brief third segment with no spatial movement (4:4–11), given over to proving how Jonah wrongly evaluates the drama he had witnessed. Because it is compelling, many commentators espouse this assessment.

So far, I have adopted the Masoretic organization of Jonah narratives and have apportioned the commentary into subdivisions that remain true to it; but I think it is useful to depart from it now.[4] Chapter 4 gives us many opportunities to establish boundaries for the units. One method is by narrative changes: in *protagonists,* for example, when God begins talking, at v 4; in *scene,* for example, when Jonah moves out of the city, at v 5; in *countermove,* for example, when God arranges the first of three marvels, at v 6; in *narrative tone,* for example, when God defends Nineveh's redemption, at v 10. For some scholars, the change is a *temporal dislocation,* where v 5 is said to fit an earlier setting better (see below). Another method is by idioms and motifs: for *questions repeated,* for example, *hāhêṭēb ḥārâ lāk,* at v 4, then again at v 9 (twice); for *wishes repeated,* for example, at 4, then again at v 8; for *marvels reintroduced,* for example, at 6, then again at v 10. This procedure makes it more attractive to define three units for this chapter instead of just two.

I have chosen to follow a third possibility, which is to recognize the *reversal*

[4] As far as chapter 4 is concerned, modern commentaries either give it as one unit (Wolff 1977; Rudolph 1971) or subdivide it into units, the first of which ends at v 3 (Allen 1976); v 4 (Stuart 1987; Keller 1982; Maillot 1977); or v 5 (Bewer 1912). It is clear from these examples that the Murabbaᶜāt/Masoretic division is rarely followed.

of Jonah's mood as a mechanism for establishing two units: 4:1–6 (this section) and 4:7–11 (next section). I do not discriminate between these two segments to satisfy a purely mechanical urge to subdivide, but because it will permit me better to resolve the rift between Jonah and God. That conspicuously paired plays on words accomplish this reversal of mood is yet another clue for me that the narrator is investing much in this reversal.

NOTES

4:1. *wayyēraʿ ʾel-yônâ rāʿâ gedôlâ wayyiḥar lô.* Brief as it is, the verse affords us Janus vision by which to observe both sides of the narrative. It continues to feature *rāʿâ,* which, once removed from Nineveh, comes to lodge in Jonah himself (4:6). We recognize at once, however, that its meaning has shifted; for Jonah is not beset by "sin" or "iniquity," but by distress and misery, of mind, but soon also of body (v 6). Much called upon in Jonah, *rāʿâ* scores a number of firsts for this verse: the *verb rāʿaʿ* makes its only appearance in Jonah here; both verb and noun are uniquely linked in the same verse; and *rāʿâ* is qualified as "great" for the only time in Jonah.

Hebrew readily turns to constructions such as *wayyēraʿ . . . rāʿâ gedôlâ,* where verbs and their direct objects are created from the same root; they are natural to the language and allow their creators to play on sounds and occasionally also on concepts. These constructions hardly get their full due in English, where such repetition normally betrays improper diction. In Jonah, we have already experienced the use of such "cognate accusatives": at 1:10 and 16 when the sailors "were filled with dreadful fear" (*wayyîreʾû . . . yirʾâ gedôlâ*); twice at 1:16, when they "offered sacrifices" (*wayyizbeḥû-zebaḥ*) and when they "made solemn promises" (*wayyidderû nedārîm*). We have also found God instructing Jonah to transmit a message to the Ninevites (*qerāʾ ʾēlêhā ʾet-haqqerîʾâ,* 3:2). Something of the sort (a compound preposition rather than a noun) also occurs at 4:6, when Jonah is shaded by a plant (*wayyaʿal mēʿal*). Trible (1963: 241) rightfully stresses that the vocabulary chosen for paronomastic treatment actually rehearses major Jonah themes: evil, fear, divine message, vow, sacrifice.

At 4:1, however, we meet with a cognate accusative with a much more ambitious purpose than its predecessors. This one, *wayyēraʿ . . . rāʿâ gedôlâ,* actually opens brackets that will not close until the end of v 6, where we find yet another example of the same construction, but with an opposite sense, *wayyiśmaḥ . . . śimḥâ gedôlâ,* "[Jonah] was absolutely delighted." The resulting chiastic structure is so compelling that it leads me to place the contents of verses 1 through 6 within one unit. I shall soon note, however, that from Jonah's perspectives, these brackets must be taken ironically; for when he feels very badly, events will seem to go his way; but when he feels very good, they will deteriorate precipitously.[5]

The expression *yēraʿ ʾel-* is unique to Scripture. Hebrew, however, is well acquainted with *yēraʿ le-*, turning to it both in preexilic and postexilic literatures; Landes 1982: 160*–61*. The subject of the latter idiom can be an explicitly stated person (2 Sam 20:6); or it can be a succeeding clause (Neh 2:10). It can also be a preceding clause (Ps 106:32). Occasionally a demonstrative pronoun serves to focus what had preceded; for example, in 2 Sam 19:8, Joab rebukes David for risking his supporters' allegiance by endlessly lamenting Absalom's death, "*this* will hurt you more than all previous trouble (*zōʾt rāʿâ lekā mikkol hārāʿâ*) that befell you from your youth until now."

In some cases, however, Hebrew leaves it to the readers to realize that this unhappiness results from previously detailed circumstances. An example is Neh 13:8, where an insolent use of Temple space displeases Nehemiah; and the same also obtains in Jonah. Therefore, in order to locate the cause of Jonah's irritation, we must hark back to 3:10. (On this subject see G. I. Davies 1977.)

What an analysis of the idiom in 4:1 clarifies can easily be lost in a literal translation (for example, NEB's "Jonah was greatly displeased and angry"). In order to bring to the fore what the Hebrew of 4:1 is making implicit, I have had to make two adjustments. I first insert "This *outcome*" to remind readers that the turn of events at Nineveh is the real "subject" of *wayyēraʿ ʾel-yônâ.* Such a liberty is commonly taken in other renderings (for example, NJPS's "This displeased Jonah greatly, and he was grieved."). The second modification is to make "Jonah" depend on a preposition.[6] I do so because I suppose that the unique *yēraʿ ʾel-* should differ from the better attested *yēraʿ le-*. I have a scriptural justification for this strategy. In Ps 106:32, the preposition *le-* makes Moses an indirect object within the clause: "(The Hebrews provoked God's anger at Meribah,) so that it brought trouble *to* Moses on their account" (*wayyēraʿ lemōšeh baʿabûrām;* see Num 20:1–13, where Moses forfeits his hopes of entering the promised land). By this second adjustment, I mean to emphasize that Jonah *endures* rather than *initiates* this feeling of unhappiness. This is not a trivial point, because the fourth chapter will continue to feature this aspect of Jonah's character instead of the forceful and determinate personality we first meet somewhere near Jaffa.

wayyiḥar lô. It is important to assess what kind of emotion Jonah is experiencing as he is about to blurt out his thoughts. Most renderings have him angry, a passion that is thought to dominate his future encounters with God. Such a

[5] Contrast the way *wayyēraʿ . . . rāʿâ gedôlâ* is used in Jonah with its only other appearance (Neh 2:10), where, beyond helping to shape that specific verse, it has no paronomastic role.

[6] Ehrlich may have had the same feeling about the function of *ʾel-* when he refers to Eccl 9:13 (1912: 270).

perspective on Jonah is not without its consequences, for it colors our appreciation of his character; indeed a Jonah fulminating against an act of mercy is a frequent component in many assessments of the entire book. On its merit, Jonah is viewed as a "narrow little man," "dour" and "unlovely" (Neil 1962; see also Stuart 1987: 502), and the Hebrews who first told his story are judged "narrow" and "fanatic" (Bewer 1912: 64, whose notions are offensive). Therefore, much rides on the way we render the idiom in the last clause, *ḥārâ le-*.[7]

It is a fact that this idiom does not yield a single meaning, and this point is acknowledged already by Jerome, who comments as follows on 4:4: "The Hebrew word *hadra* [sic] *lach* can be translated, 'are you angry' and 'are you aggrieved.' Either one is appropriate to the prophet as well as the Lord: either he is angry because he dreaded seeming a liar to the Ninevites, or he is aggrieved, realizing that Israel will be hurt." (Note here that these two possibilities are preserved in the *Pirkei* passage I quote as epigraph to this section.)

In my comments on *ḥarôn ʾappô* of 3:9, I mention that *ḥārâ* (*qal*) refers to a heating sensation that we all experience when caught by emotion. When the "nose" is "heated" (*ḥārâ ʾap*), or when "heat" is "in the eyes of [someone]" (*ḥārâ beʿênê*), the idiom does indeed denote anger. (But see Gen 45:5, where it must mean something like NJPS's "reproach oneself.") By contrast, when the subject of *ḥārâ* remains impersonal or unstated, but the resulting "heat" is yet attached to (*le-*) someone, only parallelism or context can guide us to an appropriate rendering. It can mean "to be angered" (for example, Gen 18:30, 32; 31:36; 1 Sam 20:7; Neh 3:33; 4:1); it can also denote depression, chagrin, annoyance (for example, Gen 4:5–6; Num 16:15 [see Rashi's "Moses was very hurt"]; 1 Sam 6:8; 19:43; 2 Sam 13:21).[8] Worth considering is 1 Sam 18:8, which holds parallel vocabulary to 4:1, albeit in reverse order. Saul has just heard the refrains extolling David's prowess above his own. Between hearing the inflammatory couplets and raving against David, Saul "was very depressed (or distressed) and this matter was upsetting to him" (*wayyiḥar lešāʾûl meʾōd wayyēraʿ beʿênāyw haddābār hazzeh*). To render as does the RSV ("Saul was very angry, and this

[7] Jonah's alleged incapacity to share God's love with anyone who is not a Hebrew has unfortunately become a metaphor by which to censure Judaism and Jewish attributes. Therefore, it is important to stress how fragile are its foundations. While most heavy-handed manifestations of this repugnant disposition are behind us, it occasionally resurfaces, even in our time, as the recent book of the Ruethers (1989) indicates. I shall soon show, moreover, that whatever his emotional state, Jonah is not necessarily reacting to Nineveh's good fortune.

[8] Gruber (1980: 371–78) discusses individual renderings, citing Orlinsky's opinion that *ḥārâ* without *ʾap* may mean "to be distressed" or the like. But Gruber needlessly forces the same meaning on every citation of the idiom. See also Muraoka (1985: xiv), who muses about the failure to realize that Hebrew "can employ the same verb *ḥārâ* to indicate sorrow . . . and anger." C. Cohen (1972), analyzes Jonah 4 from this perspective.

saying displeased him") is psychologically not very cogent, for anger is a relatively healthy emotion, much less corrosive than dejection, despair, or depression. Moreover, because it is usually highly public, anger normally dissipates quickly. Not so is depression, when it transforms into self-deprecation and laceration. Thus, whenever Saul comes out of his brooding long enough to vent his frustration, he turns unattractively whiny and meek.

As to Jonah, although he is certainly shaken by God's treatment of the Ninevites, he is not necessarily angry. In fact, it would be very incongruous to have an angry Jonah open his mouth in prayer because, as far as I know, there are no instances in Scripture of *angry* individuals rising to praise or beseech God. It is simply not suited to the occasion.[9] The last time Jonah prayed (at 2:3) came after the prophet had surrendered his will to God. The last time the word *tepillâ* occurred, a penitent Jonah pleaded for God to accept his prayer (see at 2:8).

The versions render this phrase as it makes best sense to them. It is worth noting that, despite Jerome's sensitivity to the Hebrew of Jonah, the Vulgate alone unequivocally attributes "anger" to Jonah, rendering the second clause as *iratus est.* The LXX is closest to what I offer above: "Jonah was terribly saddened, and was confused/shaken up," *kai elupēthē Iōnas lupēn megalēn kai sunechuthē.* The LXX approximates the Hebrew paronomasia in the first clause by choosing like-sounding words: *lupeō,* normally used to speak of distress, and *lupē,* normally equivalent to Hebrew *ʿeṣeb,* "pain" or "sorrow." For the second clause, Symmachus and Naḥal Ḥever Greek offer *ēthumēsen,* where the LXX has *sunechuthē,* suggesting that Jonah became disheartened; Barthélemy 1963: 171; discussion: 233, 240 n. 1.[10] Arabic follows suit with *watakarraha min d̲ālika jiddan,* "he was very much grieved by all this"; Wright 1857: 113. The Targum focuses on the extreme displeasure of Jonah: "Jonah felt extremely bad and it affected him severely" *wbʾyš ʿl-ywnh byšʾ rbʾ wtqyp lyh.* For the last clause, Syriac has *wʿqt lh ṭb,* "it distressed him exceedingly."

4:2–3. *wayyitpallēl ʾel-YHWH wayyōʾmar ʾānnâ YHWH halôʾ-zeh debārî ʿad-heyôtî ʿal-ʾadmātî ʿal-kēn qiddamtî librōaḥ taršîšâ kî yādaʿtî kî ʾattā ʾēl-ḥannûn weraḥûm ʾerek ʾappayim werab-ḥesed weniḥām ʿal-hārāʿâ weʿattâ YHWH qaḥ-nāʾ ʾet-napšî mimmennî kî ṭôb môtî mēḥayyāy.* Jonah's monologue covers two verses,

[9] In 1 Sam 15:11, a *dejected* Samuel (note 16:1) appeals to God all night in favor of Saul.

The Jewish Renaissance rabbi Sforno (sixteenth century C.E.) actually suggests that Jonah's prayer is lost; Zlotowitz 1980: 133. Calvin finds here a Jonah who, "carried away by a blind and vicious impulse, is nevertheless prepared to submit himself to God" (quoted in Keil and Delitzsch 1900: 410 n. 1). Sievers (cited by Bewer 1912: 59) treats this clause as a gloss, "intended to soften the effect of [his] ill-temper."

[10] See the Syro-Palestinian version of Jonah, which has here an equivalent reading, *wʾštpyk;* Goshen-Gottstein 1973: 103.

and it is best to treat them both as a single unit here. This unit's introduction parallels what obtains in the sailors' supplication of 1:14: *wayyitpallēl ʾel-YHWH wayyōʾmar* versus *wayyiqreʾû ʾel-YHWH wayyōʾmerû.* Aside from the expected difference in conjugating the verbal forms (singular versus plural), the narrator relies on different verbs, both of which have been amply annotated already. The narrator may well have intentionally achieved this duplication in order to encourage comparison of the two prayers. To illustrate these differences best, it is useful to break down their elements:

	1:14	*4:2–3*
1. *Address*	Please, Lord;	Please, Lord;
2. *Justification* (*details*)		Is this not what I said: a. when still at home, b. therefore I fled;
3. *Testimony*		I realized then: (divine attributes);
4. *Petition*	a. We may not die; b. We may not incur guilt;	Take away my life;
5. *Motivation*	God is responsible.	Death is sweeter than life.

We should first differentiate between the contexts for the prayers. With the tempest becoming increasingly dangerous and with every available evidence forcing upon them God's wish, the sailors finally turn to God. They beg for their own survival and plead innocence in the crime they are about to commit. Only after the waves are stilled do the sailors consecrate themselves to worshiping God (1:16). In the context of 4:2–3 the latter step is never truly an element, for Jonah does not need to experience a "conversion." We have already heard him make a full confession of his attachment to that God in 1:10, as he explains to them why the lots single him out. Everything since then, whether it be his stay within the fish or his observation of events in Nineveh, merely bolsters God's omnipotence in his sight. This being so, therefore, we must wonder about Jonah's real goal when he addresses heaven in 4:2–3 (see COMMENTS).

1. The *Address*'s vocabulary (*ʾānnâ YHWH*) needs no elaboration here, for it merely emulates its equivalent in the sailors' prayer. This correspondence—elsewhere in Scripture addresses can vary in vocabulary and length—heightens the false sense that Jonah's prayer will beg for a similar dispensation. We are quickly disabused of that notion, however, for Jonah presently launches into a harangue.

2. The *Justification* is very elaborate, consisting of two major statements that are introduced by a strongly worded assertion. The Masoretes liberally assign

them disjunctive accents, thus imposing jerky starts for each of the three asyndetic clauses. As a result, Jonah's first thoughts seem to come out haltingly, by blocks, as if he were fully aware of the temerity of his response. The remaining segments of Jonah's discourse, which rely heavily on familiar sentiments, will flow more smoothly. This sputtering then steady pace by which we follow Jonah's address allows us access into his mind as he increasingly asserts himself and gains confidence, perhaps because God gives him unfettered moments in which to complete his soliloquy.

Jonah first states *halôʾ-zeh debārî.* As stressed by Brongers (1981), the thrust of the particle *halôʾ* (interrogative *he-* + negative adverb *lôʾ,* here written "full") must be grasped from the context. Some of the instances in which it is attached to *zeh/zōʾt* are obviously particularizing a fact, especially when no clarifying or expanding relative clauses follow (for example, at Gen 44:5; Judg 9:38).[11] Brongers cites 2 Sam 11:3 where, having inquired about a stunning woman he spied bathing, David is told, *halôʾ-zōʾt bat-šebaʿ,* "This can only be Bathsheba!" (See also 1 Sam 21:12; 29:3; Zech 3:2.)

With this vocabulary, Jonah draws God's attention to his *dābār,* a term that in Scripture refers to "word, statement" when bound with a first-person genitive pronoun.[12] The narrator might be playful in assigning *dābār* this time to Jonah when, in all of its previous occurrences, the word had always referred to God's order (1:1; 3:1, 3). In the Comments, I shall discuss God's knowledge of Jonah's excuse. In the Interpretations, I will address the narrator's purpose in withholding this piece of information until now.

The phrase *ʿad-heyôtî ʿal-ʾadmātî* informs us when and where Jonah had the thought he wants now to communicate. The construction *ʿad-heyôt* is by no means unusual. As a conjunction meaning "while," *ʿad* readily binds with finite verbal forms (BDB 725[II.2]); as a preposition with the meaning "during," it binds with construct infinitives (BDB 724[I.2.b]); and it operates in this way here. There is no merit, therefore, to the suggestion that, because LXX has *eti ontos mou,* we should read *be/weʿôd-heyôtî* (which in any case is not idiomatic to Hebrew; see Almbladh 1986: 36).

In Jonah's opening remarks, we find an impressive series of words ending in the syllable ***-tî:*** *heyô**tî**, ʾadmā**tî**, qiddam**tî**, yādaʿ**tî**.* There is reason to believe that the rhyme is intentional, so much so that it probably guides the choice of *ʾadmātî,* "my homeland." We recall that when needing to refer to Jonah's home-

[11] Here belongs Exod 14:12, which commentators frequently (but also mistakenly) cite as containing a good parallel (*halôʾ-zeh haddābār* . . .) to the formulation in Jonah. With the Egyptian cavalry at their heels, Israel actually ends up quoting to Moses a statement he allegedly made while they were in Egypt.

[12] Thus, *debārî* cannot imply "what has happened to me." Greek and Latin versions, but not the Naḥal Ḥever Greek fragments, give *debārî* as plural, *hoi logoi,* "words." They could be translating idiomatically instead of vocalizing the word **debāray.*

land earlier (at 1:8), the narrator had used *ʾereṣ* (but *yabbāšâ* when wishing to speak of "dry land," at 1:9, 13; 2:11). Moreover, by selecting *ʾadmātî*, rather than other synonyms for "land," the narrator makes an oral link between *ʾādām* of the edict (3:7) and *ʾādām* in God's closing comment (4:11).[13]

This rhyming assonance has another effect on this chapter's narrative. Because it features either first-person genitive pronouns (the first two instances) or first-person verbal endings (the last two), this series of four *-tî*s in eleven words decisively brings Jonah to the fore, a position that he had lost ever since the fish disgorged him on dry land. Having captured center stage, Jonah can begin to justify his past and present actions.

ʿal-kēn qiddamtî librōaḥ taršîšâ. An adverb introduces us to Jonah's *apologia.* The syntax of *ʿal-ken* is clarified by R. Frankena's study of 1966. Applicable to the present situation are occasions on which *ʿal-ken* establishes a causal relation between one clause and a dependent *kî* clause. The narrator could easily have had Jonah tell God, **ʿal-ken baraḥtî taršîšâ,* "This is why I fled to Tarshish"; instead, we find an unusual construction, in which the verb *qiddēm* (*D* stem) functions as auxiliary to an infinitive construct of the verb *bāraḥ;* GKC 350 n. 1 (114 n.). Again, there is good reason to believe that the narrator coined it expressly for this context. The verbal form *librōaḥ* instantly takes us back to that precise moment that Jonah moved in a direction opposite to his intended itinerary, *wayyāqom yônâ librōaḥ taršîšâ* (1:3). The verb *qiddamtî,* by contrast, looks ahead not only to the moment in which Jonah makes another unilateral move, this time choosing to sit *miqqedem lāʿîr,* but also to God's countermove as an "east wind" (*rûaḥ qādîm*) is listed among the weapons used to bring sense to Jonah.

Normally, *qiddēm* tells of making something come in front of another, whether in terms of time or in terms of space. To incorporate the sense of *qiddamtî,* it is best to rely on a translation that conveys the idea of motion while not losing sight of *librōaḥ*'s primacy. The versions are unanimous in resolving the problem in this way. Thus Greek (followed partly by Arabic and Syriac) has "This is why I anticipated fleeing" (*proephthasa tou phugein*); Latin offers "For this reason, I was concerned to flee" (*praeoccupavi ut fugerem*); Targum gives "Therefore, I hastened to flee on the sea [*sic*]" (*ʾwḥyty lmʿrq bymʾ*). (See Trible 1963: 48; Levine 1978: 90–92; Wright 1857: 4, 50, 113.) Such resolutions are not always available to English translations, some of which reduce the force of *qiddamtî* by turning it into either an adverb (NJPS's "[fled] beforehand"; Stuart 1987: 498, "earlier") or an adverbial phrase (Wolff 1977: 159, "the first time"). Truer to the Hebrew's intent are the RSV's "hastened to flee" or the Jerusalem Bible's "went to flee"; but not the NEB's "tried to flee," for its phrasing sug-

[13] Note that the versions also try to keep the terminology distinct: LXX *choras* (1:8) versus *gē* in 4:2; Targum, *mdynʾ* (1:8) versus *ʾrʿʾ* (4:2). The Vulgate, however, has *terra* in both instances.

gests that Jonah is admitting his failure. My own rendering has Jonah claiming that his escape toward Tarshish is premeditated; and this declaration opens a vast window into Jonah's mind, forcing us to consider a whole series of questions regarding the prophet's motives for sharing this detail with his God. (See COMMENTS and INTERPRETATIONS.)

3. The *Testimony* is introduced by a verb in the perfect, (*kî*) *yādaʿtî*, "because I realized (at that time)," underscoring that this illumination was Jonah's before his adventure began.[14] It contrasts well with 1:12, where Jonah uses the participle when he admits to knowing why a storm is raging. These two confessions of Jonah, as well as the sailors' decipherment of his guilt (at 1:10), follow a construction common to Hebrew, where a *kî* clause featuring the verb *yādaʿ* introduces an object clause headed by *kî* (Schoors 1981: 254). It is a mistake, however, to assess Jonah's remark as a quotation (as do NEB and Allen 1976) for, as already discussed at 1:2, *kî* does not introduce citations. In fact, when translators place this segment of Jonah's statement within quotation marks, they do so mostly because they have judged it to be imported into Jonah from other books of Scripture.

The Masoretes divide the testimony into three segments: *kî ʾattâ ʾēl-ḥannûn werahûm; ʾerek ʾappayim werab-ḥesed;* and *weniḥām ʿal-hārāʿâ*. By this punctuation, they could be encouraging us to regard the first phrase as introducing the remaining statements ("For you, O compassionate and kind God, are patient. . . ."). It is more natural, however, to consider everything that follows upon "For you are" as attributes of God. Continuing on a pattern familiar to us from surveying the sailors' prayers of 1:10 and Jonah's psalm of the second chapter, the narrator draws on familiar phrasing to create Jonah's testimony. The language that this testimony contains proves to be much loved in ancient Israel; so much so, in fact, that Hebrew historiographers have ascribed its "original" articulation to God himself (Exod 34:6–7):

> The Lord passed by [Moses], calling out, "The Lord, The Lord! A god compassionate and gracious; full of patience, abounding in benevolence, and trustworthy; who prolongs benevolence for millennia; who forgives iniquity, transgression, and offense; who, while not acquitting the guilty, assigns the iniquity of fathers upon their children, grandchildren, even upon descendants three and four generations removed."[15]

[14] Midrash Yona, however, has the prophet realizing God's compassion only after the miracle at Nineveh. See the COMMENTS to section XI and its last note.

[15] That Moses rather than God is speaking has been debated for a long time, despite the testimony of Num 14:18. In that case, read (from v 5), "The Lord descended in a cloud and after taking a stand next to him there, [Moses] invoked the Lord's name. As the Lord passed by him, he called out, 'The Lord, The Lord!'." The birth of this formulation (known to Jewish liturgy as the "Thirteen Attributes" [*middôt*]) and the manifold scrip-

Vanoni (1978: 144) locates constitutive elements of Jonah's testimony on a chart in order to compare them with selected analogues drawn from Scripture. It is useful to adapt and further develop his chart here, for it will illumine future discussion of the testimony (Jonah components and formulations are boldface).

a.	[col i–ii]	**kî** (*1a*); **ʾattâ** (*1b*);
b.	[col iii–iv]	**ʾēl** (*2a*); *YHWH* (*2b*); *ʾelōhîm* (*2c*)/*ʾelôah selîḥôt* (*2c′*)/ *ʾelōhê*+ suffix (*2c″*); *hûʾ* (*2d*); *ʾadōnāy* (*2e*);
c.	[col v–vi]	**ḥannûn** (*3*); **raḥûm** (*4*); misc. attributes (*4′*);
d.	[col vii–viii]	Alternate placement for a and b elements
e.	[col ix]	**ʾerek ʾappayim** (*5*)
f.	[col x]	**rab-ḥesed** (*6a*); var. *gedol-ḥesed* (*6b*); *gedol-kōaḥ* (*6b′*)
g.	[col xi]	*ʾemet* (*7*) [not in Jonah]
h.	[col xii]	**niḥām ʿal-hārāʿâ** (*8a*); miscellaneous equivalents (*8b*) and/or expansions (*8b+*).

		i	*ii*	*iii*	*iv*	*v*	*vi*	*vii*	*viii*	*ix*	*x*	*xi*	*xii*
A.	Exod 34:6–7			*2b*	*2a*	*4*	*3*			*5*	*6a*	*7*	*8b+*
A′.	Num 14:18				*2b*					*5*	*6a*		*8b+*
B.	Ps 86:15		*1b*	*2e*	*2a*	*4*	*3*			*5*	*6a*	*7*	
B′.	Ps 86:5	*1a*	*1b*		*2e*			*4′*			*6a*		
C.	Ps 103:8					*4*	*3*	*2b*		*5*	*6a*		
D.	Joel 2:13	*1a*				*3*	*4*	*2d*		*5*	*6a*		*8a*
E.	**Jon 4:2**	***1a***	***1b***		***2a***	***3***	***4***			***5***	***6a***		***8a***
F.	Neh 9:17		*1b*	*2c′*		*3*	*4*			*5*	*6a*		*8b*
G.	Neh 9:31	*1a*			*2a*	*3*	*4*	*1b*					
H.	Ps 145:8					*3*	*4*	*2b*		*5*	*6b*		
I.	2 Chr 30:9	*1a*				*3*	*4*	*2b*	*2c″*				
J.	Ps 111:4					*3*	*4*	*2b*					
K.	Ps 112:4					*3*	*4*						*4′*
L.	Ps 116:5					*3*	*2b*						*4′+*
M.	Deut 4:31	*1a*			*2a*		*4*	*2b*	*2c″*				*8b+*
N.	Ps 78:38				*2d*		*4*						*8b+*
O.	Nah 1:3				*2b*					*5*	*6b′*		*8b*

tural variations upon it cannot be securely set in Israel's past, and it is natural that scholars continue to issue radically differing opinions on them. There is some agreement, however, that Exodus gives it in its authoritative version; see most recently the comments and bibliographies of Durham 1987: 449–53, Fishbane 1985: 335–50, and Schneider 1979: 101–3; for Rabbinic elaboration, see Montefiore and Loewe 1974: 43–44; 324–25.

Column i shows that while less than half of our examples use *kî* to link the testimony to a previous statement, all of them have penance at issue. Urging acts of penance, Joel (D) cites God's manifold kindness and poses a rhetorical question about a change in divine reaction (see already at 3:9). In item G, *kî* allows Nehemiah to introduce testimony to God's mercy. The vocabulary duplicates what Nehemiah says in F except that the independent pronoun *ʾattâ* is set at opposite ends of the formulations, thus allowing Nehemiah to bracket a harangue on Israel's recalcitrance (9:16–31). Hezekiah (I) concludes a proclamation that urges Israel to a centralized celebration of the Passover, "for gracious and merciful is the Lord, your God; he will not turn away from you if you turn back to him." Moses reminds Israel of God's forgiveness when it repents (M). The psalmist alludes to God's forgiveness (B′) when recalling God's "abounding benevolence."

Column ii demonstrates that addressing God directly with testimonial is not very common. An instructive case is (H), where the psalmist sandwiches third-person glorification of God (vv 8–9) within second-person addresses.

Columns iii and iv should be examined along with columns vii and viii because they show how versatile narrators can be in treating the mention of God. It can be God's personal name (*YHWH*), an epithet, or a combination of both. Singly or doubled, in apposition or syncretistically, the name of God can head the full statement or end it; it can flank single or paired attributes, or be sandwiched within two such traits. No doubt, wordsmiths found certain combinations more appropriate to some contexts than to others. There is a preference for citing *YHWH* in one of these positions, in marked contrast to *ʾelōhîm;* but when *YHWH* is not listed in the chart above, it is often because the Tetragrammaton is in close proximity (for example, in Jonah [E], Joel [D]).

Columns v and vi reveal how much Scripture favors pairing *ḥannûn* and *raḥûm*, though occasionally some phraseologies will have one or the other. Two formulas seem to be favored: one in which *ʾēl* precedes the pair (as in Jonah); the other in which *YHWH* follows it. In the former case, *ʾēl* should most likely be regarded as the common noun "god" rather than "God," for it is often in apposition to the divine name or to a distinctive epithet. This may be the reason why the LXX and the Old Latin omit it from their Jonah renderings (Trible 1963: 48–49). If I do not have "god" in my translation, it is only because the context makes it a trifling point.

Commonly stated is that the pairing with *raḥûm* coming before *ḥannûn* is "earlier" than the other way around. Landes (1982: 160*) recognizes that assigning historical dates to certain psalms (let alone to segments from within them) is a difficult undertaking; yet he is willing to entertain the possibility for this particular case. I continue to be skeptical that Israel's wordsmiths would have reversed familiar sentiments once they entered a new era and would have rigidly adhered to the new formulations even as they kept older patterns undisturbed; see above, the notes on *miggedôlām weʿad-qeṭannām* of 3:5.

Columns ix and x may likewise benefit from a joint inspection because when *ʾerek ʾappayim* and *rab-ḥesed* are found together (in all but [B′]), the first always comes in front of the second (or its analogues). The Targum paraphrases these attributes, giving them as "delayer of anger" (*mrḥyq rgz*) and "who multiplies doing good" (*wmsgy lmʿbd ṭbwn*). The expression *ʾerek ʾappayim* means "long of 'nostrils' " (meaning: face), a disposition that in English we attribute to the sullen or morose. In Hebrew, however, it alludes to an exactly opposite temper, to a personality that is open, warm, and generous (Gruber 1980: 485–86, 502–10). The first element in *rab-ḥesed* is an adjective behaving as a noun in construct (GKC 418 [§ 128.w]), which is common enough in Hebrew. The phrase differs from another, *rōb ḥesed/ḥasādîm,* which has a noun in construct with another. The two expressions differ subtly, in that the former accents the never-ending outpouring of God's benevolence while the latter asserts its plenitude.

While column xii shows that other formularies could be found in this slot, Joel and Jonah give *niḥām ʿal-hārāʿâ* as part of the testimony. In these two passages, the verbal form is a participle (instead of the perfects we met in chapter 3). I have resorted to the subjunctive when translating this form because I want to bring out an interesting detail: as he ends his testimony, Jonah is not referring to the goings on in Nineveh—though the events are certainly on his mind—but is reasserting what seems a commonplace to him, that if given the slightest opportunity to do so, God customarily chooses not to punish evildoers. The same participial construction is found in Jer 8:6 where, however, the tone is ironic: "I [God] have strained to hear—yet they will deny it—but there is not one person who regrets his wickedness (*niḥām ʿal-rāʿātô*) by asking, 'What did I do?' Each is moving in set courses, like a horse plunging into combat." The Targum, once more, avoids anthropopathism by rendering, "who draws back his divine presence from allowing evil to happen" (*mtyb mymryh mlʾytʾh byšʾ*).

Jonah and Joel share the closest accumulation of the sentiments recorded on the chart above. When the parallel vocabulary in Joel 2:14 and Jonah 3:9 are taken into account, the connection between the two is striking enough to require attention. In older European scholarship, when the issues of origins and development of traditions were foremost on the minds of most scholars, the path of the testimony invariably was set from Joel to Jonah because Jonah was thought to come from a later period of Hebrew literature than Joel. We now believe that prophetic books are not likely to have survived unscathed from their time of origin and that later phraseology could have been imposed on the works of the earliest prophets. Moreover, expressions dear to an earlier prophet could find their way into much later books (see the INTRODUCTION). On the issue at hand, a few commentators are still willing to give Joel credit for notions expressed by Jonah (Day 1988: 49–50). Even so, G. H. Cohn (1969: 99 n. 2) and J. D. Magonet (1983: 77–79) find it possible to champion the opposite direction, especially because some forceful exegetes have dated the whole book of Jonah to the period of Jeroboam II (see the INTRODUCTION). It is not surprising therefore to find the most recent scholars neatly straddling the fence on the matter.

I cannot improve on this last posture; but if the issue is seen to go beyond which of the formulations has historical precedence over the other, it can be said that the narrator in Jonah exploited it to fuller advantage. In Joel, the vocabulary is assigned to the prophet and is integrated within a section that explores the same issue from diverse angles. But by setting the testimony within a complaint, by playing on language that is assigned first to the king of Nineveh, Jonah intensifies the dramatic potential of the material, raising the stakes in the confrontation that is about to occur.

4. Coming after a paean to God's mercy, Jonah's *Petition, weʿattâ YHWH qaḥ-nāʾ eet-napšî mimmennî kî ṭôb môtî mēḥayyāy*, seems stunningly incongruous. Does Jonah really expect God to bring him death when the Ninevites, wickedest of men, have just experienced divine mercy? Has Jonah so easily forgotten what it was like to taste death when the sailors fulfilled his wish for it (1:12)? For contrast, compare Jeremiah's prose prayer of 32:16–25, which shares the spirit of Jonah's invocation and testimony, yet ends with a petition and motivation that is fitting to the context.

Jonah introduces his request with *ʿattâ*, an adverb that, when succeeded by an imperative, implies that the time to discuss a matter is over and there is not much to do now but to fulfill what is being asked (BDB 774 [1.e]). The *motivation* is given immediately after the request.

The language, *qaḥ-nāʾ eet-napšî*, is pretty strong, made even more striking by the context. As the annotations to Jonah's psalm amply demonstrate, Scripture contains numerous appeals for longer, healthier, or renewed lives and includes repeated pleas that death be frustrated and Sheol, its realm, be distanced. Here is an example that evokes Jonah's vocabulary but has a more hopeful expectation (Ps 49:16): "But God reclaims my life from Sheol; indeed he retrieves me."[3] In contrast, Hebrew literature cites very few occasions on which individuals ask God to shorten their lives.[4] The examples we do have, however, are interesting in that each suits different aspects of Jonah's own request.

[3] *ʾak-ʾelōhîm yipdeh napšî miyyad-šeʾôl kî yiqqāḥēnî.* The verse comes at the end of another reference to the shades of nobles taken into the underworld (see above, at 2:7, notes to Ps 22:30). It is possible to break the line differently and translate, "Yet God reclaims my life; from Sheol, he indeed retrieves me."

[4] D. Daube (1962) has discussed the evidence. The theme relevant to Jonah is not to be confused with (1) suicide: Ahitophel, 2 Sam 17:23; Judas, Matt 27:5; (2) vindication through death: Samson, Judg 16:20; Razis's atrocious *hara-kiri*, 2 Macc 14:37–46; or (3) immolation to avoid falling into enemy hands: Saul and his armor bearer, 1 Sam 31:4–5; Abimelech, Judg 9:53–54; Zimri, 1 Kgs 16:18; and the infamous Masada self-massacre that only Josephus records (and probably heavily embellishes), *Wars* 7.320ff. For further remarks on the topic, see below, NOTES to 4:8, *wayyišʾal ʾet-napšô lāmût*.

a. *Testimonial.* The blinded Tobit and his much-widowed niece Sarah, miles apart but simultaneously, ask God to end their lives; Tobit 2–3. Like Jonah, Tobit locates his plea within a testimonial to God's justice, but exaggerates his own shortcomings. In effect he asks God either to heal him or kill him. Sarah, more desperate, even thinks of hanging herself, but ends up begging God to take her life.

b. *Grievance.* Job, who opens his indictment cursing his birth (chap. 3), catalogs the physical ailments that embitter his life and asks God to shorten it (6:9–14). As in Jonah, his plea arises from a need to protest his circumstances.

More tantalizing is Jeremiah's biting lament about his fate (20:14–18), sharing the sentiments expressed in Job 3 (scholars debate the direction of the inspiration), but ending in a motif (destruction of cities, incongruously attached to the fate of an individual) and vocabulary (*ʿāmal*, see below at Jon 4:10) that are highly evocative of Jonah's problems:

> Curses on the day that I was born; the day my mother bore me should lack blessings. Curses on the man who increased my father's joy with the news, "A son, a male, is born to you!" May this man be like the cities the Lord has overturned without relenting. May he hear screams in the morning and battle alarms by noon; because he did not kill me in the womb, with my mother, forever swollen with me, becoming my grave. Why did I issue from the womb only to see toil and anguish, to end my life in shame?[18]

c. *Depression.* Elijah asks God to end his life when he suffers privation and fierce heat (1 Kgs 19:2–4):

> Jezebel sent a messenger to Elijah with the following, "May the gods strike me anytime with afflictions if by this time tomorrow, I do not make your life like that of one among [the Baal prophets you massacred]. Realizing it,[19] Elijah fled at once for his life. He reached Beersheba, which is in Judah, and left his servant there. Having gone into the desert a day's journey, he moved to sit beneath a single broom brush (*rōtem*), and wished death on himself. "Enough already," said he, "Lord, take my life, for I am not as good as my ancestors" (*rab ʿattâ YHWH qaḥ napšî kî lōʾ-ṭôb ʾanōkî mēʾabōtāy*).

d. *Frustration.* Moses twice asks God to end his life. In the first case (Exod 32:32), Moses intercedes for the worshipers of the Golden Calf once it is clear that executing a few thousand persons will not be enough punishment: "Now

[18] For a good discussion of issues and difficulties, see McKane 1986: 482–90.
[19] The vowels of this verb are commonly emended to yield "frightened."

then, you may rescind their sentence; otherwise, blot me out from the record you have compiled" (*meḥēnî nāʾ missipreka ʾašer kātābtā*). This request is blustery and can be regarded as a cry from the heart, a category to which belong a few other appeals for death: Rebekah anguishes twice, once when carrying bellicose twins (Gen 25:22) and once when displeased with her daughters-in-law (Gen 27:46); Rachel wants to die, if childless (Gen 30:1); Samson can take no more of Delilah's gripes (Judg 16:16); and so forth.

Much more relevant to us is Moses' bitter diatribe against being misused. When the Israelites whine about the quality of their board (Num 11:10–15),

> Moses heard the people wailing, clan after clan, individually and publicly —making the Lord very angry and Moses outraged. So Moses said to the Lord, "Why are you making it difficult for your servant, and why have I pleased you so little as to place the onus for this people on me? Is it I who conceived this whole people? Did I give birth to it that you should tell me, 'Carry it at your breast, as a nurse carries an infant,' *until* reaching the land that you have pledged to their fathers? Where can I get meat to give all this people when they sob before me, 'Give us meat to eat!' I can't do this alone, carrying this whole people, for it is too heavy for me. But if this is how you are treating me, then just kill me (*horgēnî nāʾ hārōg*), to show that you favor me. I don't want to endure this outrage of mine."

It is obvious that this example and the incident of Elijah at Beersheba are the most reminiscent of Jonah's post-Nineveh experience. Elijah's case combines motifs that are distributed over two successive episodes in Jonah 4. Elijah had just recently demonstrated his zeal for Israel's God; yet he must escape Jezebel's wrath. In the desert, he finds a bush that, because it stands alone (the text insists awkwardly on this), cannot give proper shade from the sun's full blast. The ignominious run for life and the merciless heat combine to haunt Elijah: Should he have awaited God's order, as in past ventures (17:2–4)? Did he overestimate God's support for his own endeavors? Has he earned God's confidence and esteem as fully as did his ancestors? For Elijah, fortunately, this *crise de confiance* ends because, at Horeb, he soon shares the same experience as his ancestor Moses.

Whereas Elijah's self-doubts make him despair, Moses reacts to an abuse of his capacity as leader and prophet. Responsibility and duty are ennobling virtues when judiciously assigned; they can destroy the self-esteem of individuals, however, if they are beyond their capacity to undertake. Called upon once too often to bear the brunt of a very difficult situation, Moses finally breaks down. He complains with such forceful passion and with such an incredibly pungent vocabulary that, to soothe his bruised feelings, God finds it prudent to give ground. In fact, Moses' outburst does result in a major shift in God's policy.

These incidents, therefore, illustrate the problem of a God who occasionally slights the humanity of prophets (and patriarchs, for that matter); but they also demonstrate that God can alter plans to accommodate the yearnings of a deserving individual.

The versions slightly modify what we have in the Hebrew of Jon 4:3. The LXX (followed by the Old Latin) enlarges on the vocative by giving *despota Kurie,* "sovereign Lord." Both versions (and Syriac as well) turn the nouns in the motivation into infinitives, "It is better for me to die than to live." Targum employs final verbal forms to arrive at more precision: "it is better that I should die than I should live" *ṭb dʾymwt mdʾḥy* (see Trible 1963: 49; Levine 1978: 93).

With regard to the *setûmâ* that occurs at this point, see the INTRODUCTORY REMARKS.

4:4. *wayyōʾmer YHWH haḥêṭēb ḥārâ lāk.* God's only response is to pose a question. We need to know not only what this question means, but also why it satisfied Jonah enough that he does not give an answer. We shall raise the same twofold issue at 4:9, where the same query, lengthened by two words at the end, prompts Jonah to a briefer, but no less bitter complaint.

It is obvious that God is referring to Jonah's melancholic state, for there is repeat of *ḥārâ le-,* the idiom found at the end of v 1. (Possibly influenced by "to Jonah" in 4:9, some of the versions modify the Hebrew by inserting "to him" or the like; Trible 1963: 49.) The first syllable of *haḥêṭēb* is the interrogative adverb that we have just met at the beginning of Jonah's grievance (*halôʾ-zeh debārî*), and it is fitting to find it now in God's response. The particle can convey an exclamation; possibly because the text has God "telling" (*wayyōʾmer*) rather than "asking" (**wayyišʾal*) Jonah, therefore, the grammarian Joüon gives the whole as a declaration, "You really are angry!" (1923: 495 [§ 161.b]; also Brekelmans 1970: 175–76). The distinction may be negligible, especially to a listening audience, for reciters can modulate their voice toward a precise intent. A reading audience, however, needs to find the text less equivocal.

The versions themselves struggled with the problem of God's intent, leaving us with diverse renderings. The Targum takes it as a question: "Are you powerfully affected?" (*hlḥdʾ tqyp lk*); Levine 1978: 93. Arabic offers it as a statement: "How very grieved you are, Jonah!" (*mā ʾašaddan mā ḥazinta yā yūnān*); Wright 1857: 113. The Syro-Palestinian translation even adds here an answer derived from v 9; Goshen-Gottstein 1973: 103. Greek translations adopt a number of solutions: the LXX (followed by Old Latin) has "Are you very aggrieved?" while Aquila and Theodotion give "Are you really aggrieved?" (see Vulgate, "Do you really believe that you do well to be angry?"). Symmachus has recourse to the sharp interrogative *ara,* "Are you justly aggrieved?" (On all of these readings, see Trible 1963: 50.)

We have these disparate renderings because the versions handled *haḥêṭēb* differently. In the *H* stem *hêṭîb* can mean "to do well, act ethically to/toward someone"; but also "to do [an act] thoroughly, skillfully." Here and in v 9, the forms are infinitives absolute (spelled *hyṭyb* [*hêṭêb*] in v 9 of the Murabbaʿât scroll). In Scripture this infinitive absolute has three applications: (1) as subject, for example, in Jer 10:5, "[Idols cannot harm you], nor is benefit within their power"; (2) as emphasis for the verb *yāṭab,* for example, in Jer 7:5, "if you firmly correct your ways"; and (3) as an adverb that is best translated by "thoroughly" or "frequently" (clearest listing in Even-Shoshan 1982: 294; Isa 1:17 probably belongs here). Although one traditional exegete, sensitive to the Masoretic punctuation of v 4, treats the form as subject ("To do good grieves you?"), our *hêṭēb* is most likely an adverb. It is important, therefore, to consider God's response as addressing the depth of Jonah's gloom, and *not* as questioning its motivation, sincerity, or justification. The last is an alternative understanding common in Scripture, for example, "Have you any right to be angry?" (Allen 1976: 230) or "Does it do any good to be angry?" (Stuart 1987: 498–99).

From the preceding overview, we may conclude that God is not being churlish, spiteful, or even teasing. On the contrary, at this point there is the feeling that God sympathizes with Jonah's despair, perhaps even wishes to relieve his pain. Jonah's reaction in the next verse and his sharp retort to a similarly phrased question later on (at v 9) give us reason to presume that Jonah finds comfort in the measured words from on high, for the time being at least.

4:5. *wayyēṣēʾ yônâ min-hāʿîr wayyēšeb miqqedem lāʿîr wayyaʿaś lô šām sukkâ wayyēšeb taḥtêhā baṣṣēl ʿad ʾašer yirʾeh mah-yyihyeh bāʿîr.* This is a rather belabored verse: Jonah exits, sits, builds, sits, then stares at the city. The effect is once more (see at 4:2) of movements coming in spurts, as if Jonah is taking his time or is not sure how best to proceed. Contrast this nervous activity with the purposeful movement reported in 3:4, *wayyāḥel yônâ lābôʾ bāʿîr,* "Hardly had Jonah gone into town a day's journey when he called out. . . ." We also notice that in the present verse (4:5) the word "city" is mentioned three times; and although in each instance a different preposition is prefixed to it, this is altogether a surfeit of attestations for such a modest-sized verse. The narrator obviously wants to keep us aware of what is on Jonah's mind.

We are told that Jonah "left the city," a move that to many readers seems delayed for much too long. Are we to believe that Jonah remained in the city while the Ninevites grieved and prayed, fasted and clothed themselves and their animals in sack? Does Jonah share in this public piety? Does he keep on issuing the same warning throughout the vigil? If so, for how long? Moreover, how could Jonah be waiting to see what happens to the city, when whatever is to happen already has? To many exegetes, therefore, this statement betrays a confused chronology. Accordingly they try to solve it by one of the following methods (overview and distribution of opinions in Trible, 1963: 96–102 and Weimar 1982a).

1. *Textual reconstruction.* The text of Jonah is deemed to have been incor-

rectly transmitted, and the goal is to readjust what we have into what must have been. Finely tuning a proposal by Budde to strike out 4:5 (1904; himself relying on Böhme 1887), Bewer conjectures a series of misreadings and miscues on the part of ancient scribes that can be reversed simply by deleting from v 5 "He made himself a shelter there and, sitting beneath it in the shade, waited to see what would happen to the city"; 1912: 58–59. To Bewer, "the author lets Jonah stay there not because Jonah was uncertain about the result of the repentance of Nineveh but in order to teach him the great lesson he so much needed to learn." Bewer, therefore, turns a potentially charged confrontation into a didactic pastoral.

H. Winckler (1900) championed a medieval proposal (Bickerman 1976: 40 n. 24) whereby 4:5 is inserted right after 3:4. This transposition gives Jonah a presence in the Nineveh episode, voyeuristic though it may seem, as he observes the spiritual upheaval within the town; but it leaves chapter 4 without much tension and leaves us to wonder how and why an ancient scribe could commit such a lapse in transmitting the text. Trible, who partially follows Winckler, lamely suggests that the scribe moved 4:5 to its present position in response to God's query of 4:4 (1963: 101–2).[20]

2. *Grammatical readjustment.* Keeping the text as is but translating the verbal forms in 4:5 as pluperfects allows some scholars to treat 4:5 (even the whole of vv 5–11) as a "flashback." Already Ibn Ezra's solution, and periodically espoused since then, this course is widely adopted nowadays ever since Lohfink featured it in an influential study (1961). In some recent efforts (Wolff; Weimar), in fact, Jonah's story sustains a veritable "flashback" epidemic. It must be kept in mind, however, that recourse to pluperfect is not always dictated by grammar; rather, it can be a method by which to resolve chronological cruxes without subjecting the text to emendations or manipulation; see the criticism I offer at 1:5 and 3:6. In any case, the construction here (imperfect with *waw*-conversive) does not suit well a pluperfect condition, whether to have an act fit before, or to have it synchronize with, a preceding event.

Another way to resolve the problem grammatically is to focus on the clause *ʿad ʾăšer yirʾeh mah-yyihyeh bāʿîr* and to judge the first verb as a rare example of the imperfect bearing a past tense, "He sat [under the booth] until he saw what happened in the town"; BDB 725 (II.a.[b]); Joüon 1923: 304 (113.k).

3. A few exegetes explain the sequence of events as given in the text. Magonet (1976: 58–60) thinks that the way the book is organized gives a solu-

[20] Nielsen (1979) proves that committing major textual surgery on Jonah to realize its "original" form is still in vogue. He strips the story down to one-fifth of its present size and, in the process, turns the Hebrews into the dullest of storytellers. Nielsen's "Ur-Jonah" lacks all of the scenes with which we are familiar: on board ship, within the fish, the king of Nineveh's edict, even God instructing Jonah about heaven's way. See also Schmidt 1976: 47.

tion to the problem of 4:5. Following one of Lohfink's opinions that Jonah's exit from the city is a response to God's query, Magonet regards it as a structural parallel to his flight to Tarshish when God commands him to go to Nineveh. According to Magonet, the logic of this move and countermove becomes plain only when these activities turn into the game that both protagonists end up playing. Magonet's explanation (adopted by Almbladh 1986: 37), however, can satisfy only if Jonah is given no mind of his own, but kept hostage to God's diversionary tactics.

Traditional interpretations also try to justify Jonah's activity as given in our received text. A prophet, Jonah knows that Nineveh's repentance will not last long. He therefore just awaits its inhabitants' turnabout, which is sure to come and which, just as surely, will prompt God into retaliation. This is the Targum's opinion, for it expands the last clause to read, "[Jonah sat] in order to see what *finally* would happen to the city" (*ʿd yḥzy mh-yhy bṣwp qrtʾ*); Levine 1978: 93; see Trible 1963: 98. And this is also the interpretation underlying some readings of Tobit 14:3–4, which I cite in the COMMENTS to section I (1:1–3). I shall come back to another line of inquiry in the COMMENTS to this section.

wayyēšeb miqqedem lāʿîr. This *ʿîr* is Nineveh. We notice that the narrator does not mention Nineveh in the speeches of Jonah and does not refer to it in activities attributed to him (see COMMENTS). It is only when God wants to deliver his lesson, at 4:11, that the name is invoked once more. Yet *ʿîr,* which is repeated twice in this verse, links this chapter to its predecessor, even to chapter 1.

Why tell us where Jonah decides to sit in observation? It could be that the narrator is teasing us to recall (and perhaps contrast) the king of Nineveh's movements as he sits contrite on the ground (3:6). It might be that the storyteller wishes to give the scene a touch of *realismo*, perhaps aware that Nineveh was flanked to the west and north by the Tigris and the Khoser and that there were a few hills on the town's remaining sides (nice geographical detail in Parrot 1961: 2). Lacocque and Lacocque (1981: 86) think the narrator is playing on the other meaning of *qedem*, "past," wishing us to contemplate Nineveh's past. The versions themselves find no puns here: the LXX simply gives "over against the city" (*apenanti tēs poleōs*); the Old Latin has *contra*, "opposite"; the Arabic says simply, "beyond the city," *kharija lmadina.*

More likely at stake here, however, is the purely literary function of this information. Above, I have noted that this *qedem* is flanked by two other cognates, *qiddamtî* of v 2 and *qādîm* of v 8. Beyond serving paronomasia, *qedem* can also place Jonah to the east of Nineveh so that, when the easterly winds of v 8 come, he will be there to take their blows. Because of his location, Jonah also is first to feel the heat when the sun rises. These are minor suggestions; what may be more to the point, however, is that Hebrew narrators have a strong preference for the east over other cardinal points.

wayyaʿaś lô šām sukkâ. There is no problem in rendering this clause: Jonah built for himself a makeshift shed. Occasionally (Isa 4:6), *sukkâ* could be used figuratively for a divinely produced protection; but most commonly the term refers to any shelter that is temporary. Isaiah 1:8 likens Israel to a "shelter in a vineyard, a shed in a cucumber patch": therefore, a forlorn and temporary abode. Job 27:18 uses the term to epitomize fleeting endeavors. The clause following, "sitting beneath it in the shade" (*wayyēšeb taḥtêhā baṣṣēl*), may seem unnecessary in view of the function of such structures; but it does prepare us for Jonah's reaction to the plant God will raise presently. What have puzzled scholars, however, are the purpose and eventual fate of this *sukkâ:* if it functioned properly, why would God need to raise a plant over Jonah's head? And why would Jonah lament the desiccation of the plant when there was a *sukkâ* to shield him from the hot sun? Here too, a grammatical resolution is invoked by Lettinga 1980: 169 (§ 72.d.1), who cites the clause as another example of the conversive imperfect bearing "conative-voluntative" nuances: "There, [Jonah] wished to build for himself a hut [but presumably did not]." This is much too convenient a way to get rid of a problem that I will consider presently (v 8). Likewise facile is the opinion that the *sukkâ* is symbolic, making it ill suited for such profane usage as giving shade; Lacocque and Lacocque 1981: 87–88. This is fine as interpretation (Jungian or otherwise) of the incident; but not very good narratology or philology.

We are told that Jonah sat beneath his booth, *ʿad ʾăšer yirʾeh mah-yyihyeh bāʿîr.* This phrase could also be rendered, "Jonah waited to see what would happen within town." The text does not tell us what Jonah expected to find happening to or in the city, and this is a major reason why some scholars either insert this verse (or parts of it) after 3:4, or grammatically weaken its implication (see above). The few scriptural attestations of *hāyâ bāʿîr* speak of something/someone that can be found within a city. In one case, however, we are told that God's hand "struck against the city" (*hāyetâ yad YHWH bāʿîr*), bringing horrors on Ekron (1 Sam 5:9).

4:6. *wayyeman YHWH-ʾelōhîm qîqāyôn wayyaʿal mēʿal leyônâ liheyôt ṣēl ʿal-rōʾšô lehaṣṣîl lô mērāʿātô wayyiśmaḥ yônâ ʿal-haqqîqāyôn śimḥâ gedôlâ.* Jonah gives up center stage to witness the second of God's marvels on his behalf, the first being the appearance of a fish to save him from drowning. On that occasion, Jonah does not share with us his immediate reaction to the miracle; but the psalm serves as ample testimony of Jonah's gratitude for God's action. Here, however, the impact is instantaneous. The verse divides into two areas of concerns. The second tells us how Jonah greeted the plant. The first deals with the plant, its creation and purpose. To serve this latter program, four clauses are laid out into an *A a : b B* pattern: the outside sections, *A* and *B,* have God as their subject; sandwiched within them are *a* and *b,* which have the *qîqāyôn* as subject. Each of these sets of clauses consists of a verbal and an infinitive clause. This artful pattern is furthered by a playful desire to run two infinitive clauses together without a separating conjunction, so that the ear can hear repetitions of the consonants *ṣl* (*ṣēl . . . lehaṣṣîl*). This playfulness is lost on some critics, who urge deletion of one of the two infinitive clauses; see Bewer 1912: 61; Trible 1963: 102–3. In my translation, I could not easily duplicate this effect, and I have had to move the fourth clause (*B*) to the head of the English sentence.

wayyeman YHWH-ʾelōhîm qîqāyôn. The Murabbaʿāt scroll and the versions support the antiquity of the combination *YHWH-ʾelōhîm;* however, a few Hebrew manuscripts (as well as some Greek renderings) either drop the second name or give *ʾadōnay-YHWH;* Trible 1963: 51. As I have discussed it in 2:1, the narrator accords individual attention to each of *wayyeman*'s four attestations. I review here the subject in each occurrence: at 2:1 it is *YHWH;* at 4:6, *YHWH-ʾelōhîm;* at 4:7, *hāʾelōhîm;* and at 4:8, *ʾelōhîm.* It may be accidental that the narrator reaches this particular progression or scheme; but we can nevertheless observe a move from the most (*YHWH*) to the least (*ʾelōhîm*) personal of God's names. Verse 6 contains a syncretism that serves as transition. Moreover, we notice that the first two examples (with *YHWH*) result in miracles that are beneficial to Jonah, whereas the last two turn out badly for him. At any rate, it is not prudent to depend on this shift in nomenclature when elaborating theories on the growth of the Jonah narrative.[21]

What kind of plant is the *qîqāyôn?* Because the search for its modern name is not usually regarded as a test case for biblical inerrancy (as is the fish of chapter 2), already in the medieval period some rabbis judged it unnecessary to identify the plant botanically.[22] The recent article of Robinson on the *qîqāyôn* (1985) relieves me from reviewing the various identifications and justifications. Particularly useful is his chart of page 403, where he gives an exhaustive catalog of the term *qîqāyôn* as rendered in ancient and modern translations. Two plants are most commonly cited in recent renderings: the "(climbing) gourd" (*Cucurbita*) and the "castor bean" (*Ricinus communis*). Nonetheless, arriving at a decision can also be complicated by the bewildering physical differences in contemporary (let alone ancient) species. More distressing, perhaps, are the radically disparate descriptions for the same plants; thus a respected biblical botanist can describe one particular candidate (the *Ricinus*) as perfect for Jonah's comfort while another can dismiss it as worthless for the same purpose (ibid. 399–400).

I am no botanist; but having once combed the literature on botanical history to identify the fruits and condiments recorded in Mari's administrative archives, I have developed a healthy skepticism about the pronouncements of specialists

[21] Trible (1963: 82–87) offers an excellent overview and critique of various theories. Wolff (1977: 78–80, 169–70) refers gingerly to Schmidt's newer proposal.

[22] Jerome is very humorous in reporting how much trouble he got into when translating *qîqāyôn* as "ivy"; Antin 1956: 109–13.

as far as ancient specimens are concerned.[23] It does not help that the *qîqāyôn* occurs only this once in Scripture and that, like the fish, this plant is displayed with minimal realism: In less than a full day, the *qîqāyôn* grows to remarkable stature and then withers. Altogether, this description cannot apply to the average shrub or tree—be it a gourd, an ivy, or a castor bean. I may be permitted, therefore, not to attach a specific label to *qîqāyôn;* instead, I shall follow Aquila and Theodotion who, with their *kikeōna,* found it prudent just to approximate a transcription of the Hebrew, possibly also to pun on Jonah's name (*yônâ*) as well.

In order to learn God's own reason for creating the *qîqāyôn,* we skip to *lehaṣṣîl lô mērāʿātô.* Although *rāʿâ* has slipped from addressing a mental anguish to marking a physical distress, it is obvious that the narrator nevertheless wants this clause to reverse Jonah's condition reported in v 1, "This *outcome* was so terribly upsetting to Jonah that he was dejected." The verbal form here is perfectly suited to the goal, for *hiṣṣîl (H* stem of *nāṣal) min-* is fine theological language, referring to God's rescue of individuals from enemy, guilt, or death. It is worth observing also that because inanimates do not control this verbal form, the *qîqāyôn* cannot be responsible for rescuing Jonah from his misery. It is true, however, that we have no scriptural equivalent for construing this verbal form with the preposition *le-* and that dittography may obtain here (for **lehaṣṣîlô;* see Exod 18:9, *hiṣṣîlô*). If so, the dittography is very old, for Murabbaʿāt also has *lô* and the versions saw one there too. Because of the artful design of this verse, however, the narrator may have purposely inserted *lô* to emulate (*wayyiḥar*) *lô,* again of v 1. At any rate, there is no reason to follow Ehrlich (1912: 270), who replaces the whole verbal phrase with *lehāqēl.*

There are other proposals for this verbal form. Because in the LXX this clause reads *tou skiazein autō apo tōn kakōn autou,* "to shade him from his calamity," some commentators propose to read the Hebrew **lehāṣēl lô,* deriving it from an obscurely attested *H* stem of *ṣālal* (III, BDB 853; Jastrow 1950: 1284, reflexive or doubtful). In fact, it may be better to assume that the LXX (as well as the versions that depend on the LXX) is influenced by the preceding clause. Similarly affected by the context is the Targum's *lʾgnʾ lyh/ʿlyh,* "to cover, protect" (from *gnn*). The Vulgate inserts here, "for Jonah was very distressed" (*laboraverat enim*); I do not know why.

We can now turn to the first of two clauses under the control of the *qîqāyôn: wayyaʿal mēʿal leyônâ.* The verb *ʿālâ* in the *G* stem commonly refers to the growth of plants, and it cannot be correct to treat the verbal form as an *H* stem, as do many renderings, for example RSV's, "And the Lord God appointed a

[23] The best articles on the subject are published in the recent *Bulletin on Sumerian Agriculture,* and their cautious authors repeatedly stress how difficult it is to juggle ancient testimony, archaeological discoveries, and modern botany. M. Stol (1987) has a fine discussion on what we know of the gourd family (where he locates Jonah's *qîqāyôn*) in ancient times.

plant, and made it come up over Jonah" or TEV's "The Lord God made a plant grow up over Jonah." Were God the subject of the second clause, *qîqāyôn* or its equivalent would need to be inserted in it: **wayyaʿal (ʾet-)haqqîqāyôn mēʿal yônâ.* The versions uniformly give the plant as subject.

Alternatively, the narrator may well be teasing our memory here, for the form does recall *wattaʿal* (albeit an *H* stem there), which we met in v 7 of Jonah's psalm: "but you lift me up from the Pit alive, Lord, my god." Moreover, on both occasions, the idioms are construed with the preposition *min* (at 4:6, paronomastically compounded into *mēʿal le-*); further, we meet with a double reference to God on both occasions: *YHWH ʾelōhây* in 2:7; *YHWH-ʾelōhîm* in 4:6. All of this may yet be coincidental; what is less likely to be so, however, is the presence of the root **ʿly*—antithesis to another crucial root **yrd*—at important moments in Jonah's narrative: at 1:2, to launch the narrative; at 2:7, to initiate Jonah's restoration to favor, and at 4:6, to set him up for his final test.

The infinitive clause that follows, *liheyôt ṣēl ʿal-rōʾšô,* prepares us for the misery that Jonah will soon encounter when the *qîqāyôn* withers. It conspicuously repeats the word *ṣēl,* "shade," which, in the preceding verse, was produced by Jonah's *sukkâ.*

With *wayyiśmaḥ yônâ . . . śimḥâ gedôlâ,* we have come to a full reversal of Jonah's mood. Hebrew is rich in vocabulary expressing cheer and happiness; the midrash on the Song of Songs (at 1:4) lists ten such substantives, some of which have verbal cognates of their own. As far as I know there has not been a systematic study of the Hebrew vocabulary to differentiate among such categories as pleasure (a gratification), happiness (a state or condition), or joy (an emotion). Most commonly cited in Scripture are the present verb *śāmaḥ* and its derivatives, and the few references I have overviewed seem to cut across the various categories just cited. The actual language used in 4:6 is surprisingly infrequent in Scripture. Attaching a cognate accusative to the *G* stem of *śāmaḥ* occurs elsewhere only a couple of times (1 Kgs 1:40; 1 Chr 29:9); while construing the verb with *ʿal* is found a handful of times, each with its own shade of meaning: Isa 9:16 (rejoice *over* persons); 39:2 (rejoice *by* arrival of delegates—but cf. 2 Kgs 20:13); 1 Chr 29:9 (rejoice *because* of sacrifice); 2 Chr 15:15 (rejoice *because* of oath). While these two features can be found in the same verse (1 Chr 29:9), their combination into the same clause is unique to Jonah and may well be due to its narrator's creativity.

In the INTRODUCTORY REMARKS to this section, I indicate why this allusion to Jonah's delight with the *qîqāyôn* proves to be an excellent demarcation for Jonah's commerce with God. In the COMMENTS, I will presently consider why Jonah is so pleased with the *qîqāyôn* when his own *sukkâ* was available for shade.

COMMENTS

> Once during his reign, when Hezekiah fell mortally ill, the prophet Isaiah son of Amoz came to tell him, "This is what the Lord says, 'Settle your own business, you are dying and cannot recover.' " Hezekiah turned his face to the wall and prayed to the Lord, "Please recall, Lord, how I communed with you, sincerely and wholeheartedly, and have fulfilled what you have wished." Hezekiah broke into incessant weeping.
>
> Isaiah had not yet crossed the inner court when the Lord's order came to him, "Turn back and tell the leader of my people Hezekiah, 'The Lord, God of your ancestor David says, I have heard your prayer, seen your tears, and I am healing you. After tomorrow, you must go up to the temple. I will add fifteen years to your life, and will rescue you and this city as well from the grip of the Assyrian king. I will protect this city for my own sake, and for the sake of David my servant.' "

Reported in 2 Kgs 20:1–6 (with a slightly divergent account in Isa 38:1–8), this incident gives us an excellent instance in which a prophet is entrusted with a message that God soon rescinds.[24] It may be useful to compare it with what obtains in Jonah. Isaiah carries a notice of doom to a seriously ill Hezekiah. While his message may not be as pithy as Jonah's statement to the Ninevites, it is just as categorical and final. Upon hearing the news, both Nineveh and Hezekiah immediately believe in their truths. Hoping against hope, they quickly take measures to confront their sentence: the Ninevites by following a stern prescription; Hezekiah simply by turning to the wall (a sign of utter despair) to pray and weep.

God modifies Hezekiah's fate as readily as Nineveh's. There is a deliciously realistic touch at the beginning of 2 Kgs 20:4 that is lacking from the Isaian

[24] See also 2 Chr 12:5–8, cited in the INTERPRETATIONS section. Berlin 1976: 231 n. 14 gives two other examples of unfulfilled prophecies, the first better than the second: Ezekiel's predictions on the destruction of Tyre (reported in 26–28) are later tabled (29:17–20); and Jeremiah's prediction of a humiliating burial for Jehoiakim (22:19) is not supported by 2 Kgs 24:6. In the INTRODUCTORY REMARKS to section IX, I cite a third example regarding the prophet Micah's unfulfilled (!) prediction of Jerusalem's (immediate) downfall.

Possibly inspired by Jehoash's breaching of fortifications in Jerusalem (2 Kgs 14:11–14), rabbinic traditions claim that Jonah is once charged with predicting Jerusalem's fall. Because its inhabitants repent, Jerusalem is spared; but Jonah's reputation does not fare as well, for he is deemed a "false prophet." When God asks him to go to Nineveh, Jonah, who knows that God will relent, is loath to be judged harshly by the Ninevites and therefore heads toward Tarshish. On this tradition, see Ginzberg 1947: 246–47.

parallel account. We are told in Kings that Isaiah had not yet reached the palace's gate when God asked him to turn back with news of a reprieve. From this detail, we learn that the amount of time spent in penance is not what really sways God; rather, the sincerity of the repentance is what matters most. We also notice no hesitation on Isaiah's part to fulfill this sudden turnabout. In fact, Hezekiah alone seems surprised by it; so much so that he, as had others worthier than he (Exod 4:1–9; Judg 6:17–22, 36–40), asks that a concrete sign confirm his recovery.

It could have been far easier on Isaiah than on Jonah to serve God so submissively. Isaiah did not have to trek hundreds of miles to deliver God's messages. Moreover, while Hezekiah may be slightly selfish ("après moi le deluge," he once thinks—2 Kgs 20:19), he is basically a decent, God-fearing king. Nevertheless, no less than Nineveh, which is soon destroyed by foreign powers, his kingdom's salvation proves temporary and ephemeral.

For our purpose, however, the sharpest contrast between the two episodes is in the way the prophets react to God's change of mind. Isaiah accepts it without question; Jonah finds in it an occasion to revert to his earlier character. When God had first contacted him, Jonah—perhaps never the most docile of prophets—had nevertheless proved to be a quick learner. He had given in to God's wishes as soon as he had spotted stormy clouds over his Tarshish-bound ship. Jonah may have had his doubts about his survival when the sailors dumped him into turbulent waters; it would have been fitting punishment for disobeying God. Yet (he could have reasoned), if death had overtaken him then and there, because of his efforts a whole shipload of men had come to acknowledge the Hebrew God. Fortunately, survival within a fish had strengthened his bonds to that God and his resolve to abide by God's will.

We all know what happens from that point on, how Jonah finds himself once more on the same errand. Jonah broadcasts God's message, and it affects the Ninevites powerfully. Now in the COMMENTS for the previous two sections, I have argued that the message Jonah carries into Nineveh includes a construction, unique to Jonah in usage (*nehpāket*, at 3:4), that bears contrary meanings: Nineveh will soon be destroyed *or* Nineveh will undergo a (spiritual) change. I have also proposed that only the first of these two meanings is deemed relevant, by the Ninevites and Jonah alike. In the case of the Ninevites, it drives them toward penitence; in the case of Jonah, toward dejection. One question instantly looms: why is God treating Jonah differently from Isaiah? Why not share with him reconsideration of the Ninevites' fate and commission him to bring this good news to them? Communicating cheerful tidings is, after all, also a job for prophets.

To suggest an explanation, I go back one more time to those same COMMENTS sections and bring into the discussion the second potential meaning for *nehpāket*. In the narrative of chapter 3, only God can be conscious of the possibilities that Nineveh will either change its ways or be destroyed. Accordingly, when the Ninevites do repent, Jonah's words find confirmation no less than if Nineveh had been destroyed for its sins. Hence, in this instance (contrary to what happens in the matter of Hezekiah's illness) *there is no other message to convey,* and there is no occasion for Jonah to participate once more as message-bearing prophet. This is obvious to God; but not so to Jonah.

This may explain to us why Jonah's prophetic role ends with his first and only announcement to the Ninevites: he is simply kept out of God's two-edged reasoning (in itself, a feature not unknown to the Bible, if we recall that God never reveals to Job why his life turned miserable or tells Cain why his brother's offering was more attractive). Jonah's behavior, as related in 4:1, is of shock and dismay. It may well be that his *apologia* of 4:2 is a particularly clever way for the narrator to give constancy to the prophet's character, perhaps even to impose upon the complete narrative a continuous if not a cyclical form (Duval 1973: 595). For us, this confession also gives access to a statement or thought the prophet made long ago, in either case available to an omniscient God. Jonah claims that even as he was entrusted with a mission, he already knew that God is vulnerable to human entreaties and that, given the slightest opportunity to extend or to end life, God would invariably choose the first of the alternatives.

We naturally presume that Jonah has Nineveh in mind when delivering his audacious lines, even if Jonah is never quoted as wishing harm to the city; indeed, Jonah himself never directly mentions that city in his soliloquy and God alone brings it back by name into the dialogue, at 4:11. But if Jonah is referring to Nineveh, then we must question the relevance, if not the veracity, of certain elements in this speech. Is it true, for instance, that Jonah had such thoughts 'way back then? If so, it is remarkable that we hear nothing about any of them until this moment, either from God, who might be expected to squash such effrontery, or from Jonah, who had the opportunity to flash them once more at 3:2. Or could it be that Jonah, perhaps due to his depressed and irked state, is consoling himself by inventing an "I told you so" to soothe his wounded heart? In either case, we must also wonder, what good does it do Nineveh (or Jonah) to refresh God's memory in such a crass way? Once Jonah recognizes that Nineveh survives its ordeal, why throw such provocative testimony before God? Jonah cannot seriously expect (as some medieval and modern exegetes do) that God would change directions once more and strike Nineveh down, especially not after Jonah had just finished praising his maker for nurturing precisely the divine virtues that gave Nineveh new life.

We must also consider how Jonah's keen awareness of God's immense compassion integrates with his entreaty that God kill him. It is not easy to offer a good reason for Jonah's feeling that only his own murder would adequately compensate for Nineveh's survival. Indeed, Jonah's radical solution does not seem to me emotionally cogent: if we deem him angry because of God's mercy on Nineveh, should we not expect him to vent his rage on God rather than on himself? If we imagine him depressed, would it not be more likely that Jonah should take his own life?

Instead of confronting this catalog of queries and suspicions, I might introduce an alternative exposition of Jonah's confession. Proceeding from the narrator's remarks (4:1) about Jonah's unhappiness and dismay (or anger if one prefers it), let us suppose that Jonah delivers this speech not only to address God's generosity to a great (albeit despicable) Assyrian city, but also to debate God's responsibility to a prophet. Any person, whether commissioned by God or not, can frighten a city into repentance, and the consequences will be good for all concerned, for one cannot mislead when moving people toward the good. But when a prophet carries a message of doom, especially to a great city such as Nineveh, and God revokes it without giving his prophet a role to play in the reversal, how could that prophet trust in his own calling? How will Jonah know that he remains God's prophet?[25]

Jonah's message, therefore, would be serving double duty: we may think it is about Nineveh, but Jonah above all means it to be about himself. This ambiguity would be a fitting response to God's clever commission of 3:4. "Even as you were sending me to this god-awful city," Jonah is asserting, "I planned my escape to Tarshish; and I put this plan into effect because I have always known the truth about you: that when it comes right down to it, you will forgive and you will not punish: not Nineveh for its sins; not me for disobeying you. Even as the seas were raging, even as I was falling into the gaping mouth of a fish, I knew you to be full of bluster; when eyeball to eyeball, as usual you blinked first!" And now comes the challenge, whether delivered from an irked or from a dejected mind, "God, now that you know how I really feel about this whole experience, you can go ahead and kill me; erase, if you dare, that miracle you performed in the sea for me."

Victim of a particularly human illusion, that his own imagination and responses cannot be different from God's, Jonah is turning the table on God, forcing him to acknowledge that the dignity of one individual is as precious as the salvation of a whole community. By gently inquiring into Jonah's state of mind, however, God seemingly avoids challenging his complaints.

It will not do, of course, to end on this note. Happiness for Nineveh cannot be replaced by dissatisfaction for Jonah, no matter how we react to his petulance. As Jonah delivers his appeal for God to kill him, however, a resolution to the confrontation is already incubating; for with this line, Jonah whittles down the concerns his book addresses from the metaphysical to the purely personal.

[25] This point is nicely made in Berlin's fine article, 1976: 232–35. See already Feuillet 1949: 1125–26. Fáj (1974: 316) cites (disapprovingly) a "Hymn to Nineveh" by the Byzantine hymnographer Romanos Melodos (probably fifth to sixth century C.E.), in which Jonah criticizes God for giving him a doom message without entrusting him with glad tidings.

Until God chooses to revive them as central concerns, in 4:10–11, sin, penitence, and redemption no longer hold center stage. In their place stands, as in Job, the one issue of an individual's private complaint against God.

This reduction of a major theological issue to a skirmish between unequal powers is abetted by Jonah's moves reported in 4:4. We are told that, desiring to observe what is going on in the city, Jonah sets up a shelter east of Nineveh. Now it is difficult to know what Jonah expects to find happening in and to the city, and I have discussed some opinions in the preceding comments. As *interpreters* rather than as *textual critics,* we should reject placing this verse after 3:4 at least because it would not be reasonable to hold that for more than two thousand years people never recovered sight of what really happens in the story. Suffice it to say that a major shift in the story occurs at this point, as Jonah sits still and allows unnatural occurrences once more to affect his well-being.

Jonah is supposed to crawl under the *sukkâ* that he builds in order to benefit from its shade. Soon, however, God directs the *qîqāyôn* to shade him from above his head. The pun is directional, depending on a contrasting location for this *ṣēl,* but it is also protean: through this divine act meant "to deliver him from his distress," Jonah acquires a satisfying response to his complaint. This plant, marvelously rising above his head, is a sign of a new equilibrium between him and God, of a renewed understanding between the two. It is important, therefore, not to compare this *qîqāyôn* to the "broom bush" under which Elijah sits (1 Kgs 19:4, quoted in the NOTES above), for the bush plays a relatively benign role in that particular episode. Far closer to the *qîqāyôn,* as a manifestation of God's grace and as a symbol of reconciliation, is Elijah's encounter with God at Horeb, coming as it does immediately after he bitterly protests being abandoned (1 Kgs 19:9–18).

From Jonah's perspective, the story can end now on this happy note: Nineveh and its fate are no longer central to Jonah; his difference with God is now resolved. From God's standpoint, however, there is still the matter of educating a prophet on divine mercy.[26] Now that Jonah has turned the issue into a personal, if not physical, problem; now that he has come out from his deep funk, God will readily turn to pedagogic instruments that are too obvious to be misunderstood by Jonah, and by us as well.

[26] This perspective is commonly adopted in traditional Jewish exegesis. See now Sternberg 1987: 318–20.

XI. Heat and Light (Jonah 4:7–11)

◆

Who equals you as a god, in removing iniquity and disregarding transgression from what remains of his bequest [Israel]? God does not perpetuate anger endlessly, for he is indeed a lover of benevolence. Once again God will be compassionate with us, containing our sins. You will hurl into the deepest sea all their trespasses. You will be steadfast with Jacob, benevolent with Abraham, as you vowed it to our ancestors from time immemorial. (Micah 7:18–20)[1]

For they are not a people with sense; therefore their maker will not pity them, their creator will not favor them. (Isa 27:11)

I reclaim them from Sheol; from Death I redeem them. Where are your plagues, Death? Sheol, where is your scourge? Is compassion concealed from my sight? Though he thrives among reeds, comes an east wind—the Lord's wind—from the wasteland rising, desiccating his well, scorching his spring, plundering, hoards, every valued object. (Hos 13:14–15).

Do I enjoy seeking death for the wicked—says the Lord God? Would he not live on, just by repudiating his ways? (Ezek 18:23; see also 33:11)

For the fate of people and the fate of beasts is one and the same: as the one dies so dies the other, and all have the same life-breath. People have no superiority over beasts, because they all amount to nothing: they all

[1] These last verses of the book of Micah (which comes right after Jonah among the Minor Prophets) are traditionally appended to the reading of Jonah on the Day of Atonement (Yom Kippur; see Introduction). Because Micah comes after Jonah in Hebrew Scripture and because Micah, like Jonah, takes up themes developed in Exod 34:6–7 (see Fishbane 1985: 349–50), it would not be wholly incongruous for readers to attribute these verses to a chastened Jonah.

go to just one place. Having come from dust, they all return to dust. (Eccl 3:19–20)

Que la terre est petite à qui la voit des cieux. (J. Delille)

XI. HEAT AND LIGHT (4:7–11)

4 [7]God himself[a] directed a worm, at the break of dawn, on the morrow; it
attacked the *qiqayon* plant so that it withered. [8]With the rising sun, God directed a *fierce* east wind. As the sun pounded on Jonah's head, he swooned and,
longing to die, he thought, "Death is better for me than life."
[9]God asked Jonah, "Are you utterly dejected over the *qiqayon* plant?" "Dejected enough to want death," he answered. [10]The Lord then said, "You yourself
were fretting[b] over the *qiqayon* plant, on which you did not labor, nor did you
cultivate it, a plant that came up one night and perished the next; [11]yet I myself
am not to have compassion[b] on Nineveh, that large city, where there are more
than twelve myriads of human beings, who cannot discern between their right
and left hands, and animals galore?"

[a] Or: "The God"; see NOTES to 1:6.
[b] Same verb in Hebrew; see NOTES.

NOTES

4:7. *wayyeman hāʾelōhîm tôlaʿat baʿalôt haššaḥar lammaḥorāt wattak ʾet-haqqîqāyôn wayyîbaš.* By now we are most familiar with the verb *mānâ,* having met it twice earlier (see NOTES to 2:1 and 4:6). In these examples, construct infinitives are called upon to develop the purpose of God's commands: at 2:1, a fish is to swallow Jonah (*liblōaʿ*); at 4:6, a plant is to deliver him (*lehaṣṣîl lô*) from his distress. In contrast, no infinitives follow on *wayyeman* on this (v 7) or on the following occasion (at v 8); rather, we only have clauses that twice mention the verbal form *wattak.* Yet, while at 4:7 the subject of *wattak* is the worm that God had readied, at 4:8 the subject is the sun, and not the "east wind" that God had prepared. Modern renderings that ignore Hebrew syntax and merge two clauses into one at 4:7 (for example, NEB's "God ordained that a worm should attack the gourd") do not recognize how the narrator plots the four appearances of *wayyeman:* when God commissions operations that would hurt Jonah (at 4:7 and 8) rather than activities helpful to him (at 2:1 and 4:6), God no longer *directly* moves them into action. Jonah may need to know that a divine power is bringing fish and plant to his aid; but he does not need to discover why he is suddenly without protection. (In fact, Jonah mercifully sleeps through the early manifestations of these harmful events; see below.) There is a distance now between God and the instruments of Jonah's misery, and the condition will work nicely in a coda that emphasizes object lessons rather than harsh punishments.

While Hebrew has other names for crawling invertebrates (*rimmâ;* perhaps also *sās,* "caterpillar?" or "moth"), Scripture mentions most commonly *tôlaʿ, tôlēʿâ,* or, as we have it here, *tôlaʿat.* Some scholars give "larva," "maggot," "weevil," "beetle," or "centipede" for its occurrence in Jonah. Considering its miraculous function in this episode (see the next paragraphs), however, there is no reason to be more precise than the narrator about the true biological classification of this *tôlaʿat.* We should just keep in mind that elsewhere it is cited as an instrument of God's disfavor (Deut 28:39) and as a voracious consumer of human remains (Isa 14:11, 66:24). More worthy of attention is the activity assigned to the worm: it *attacks* the plant. The narrator has two purposes in mind when choosing the verb *nākâ* (*H* stem), where elsewhere such varmints "feed" (*ʾākal*) on their targets (see Deut 28:39 and BDB 37 [2]): (1) to parallel the worm's activity with the sun's (v 8), especially because the sun is better attested as subject of the *H* of *nākâ* (Isa 49:10; Ps 121:6); and (2) to dramatize the contact between the worm and the plant, thus intangibly contributing tension to the confrontation between God and Jonah. The Targum, however, does not appreciate these goals, for it renders these forms respectively as *mḥṭ,* "it bit (the plant)," and *ṭpḥt,* "it slapped (Jonah)"; Levine 1978: 95–96. The Syriac makes the worm the subject of *wqṭmth,* "and it cut it [the plant] off"; Almbladh 1986: 38.

The worm attacks the *qiqayon* plant precisely *baʿalôt haššaḥar lammaḥorāt.* This concern to pinpoint when something occurs is in marked contrast to previous episodes in which time is served up as a formula, if it is given at all. The worm begins gnawing or sucking on the plant "at the break of dawn, on the morrow." (Greek and Vulgate offer idiomatic equivalents.) We presume that the assault occurs while Jonah sleeps (so too, Byzantine artistic depictions of the occasion, Ovadiah 1974) because *lammaḥorāt* (more fully *lammaḥorat hayyôm,* 1 Chr 29:21), refers to a day that immediately follows the present one. The Syriac version, in fact, places "on the next day" (*wlywmʾ ʾḥrnʾ*), the beginning of the verse. If so, it nicely counterbalances an earlier occasion when God interferes in Jonah's life as he lies sleeping (1:5–6). The phrase's vocabulary is itself rich in paronomastic potential. The first word, *baʿalôt,* echoes previous references to the root *ʿālâ,* most immediately when the plant is said to "rise" over Jonah's head (v 6). It also reverses the sequence of consonants in the preceding *tôlaʿat* (see also under 2:1). Moreover, repetition of the consonants *ḥet* and *resh* in *haššaḥar lammaḥorāt* keeps us minded of Jonah's dejection (verb: *ḥārâ*).

The narrator eagerly limits the time it took the worm to destroy the plant fully. Before the sun rises, we are told, the *qîqāyôn* shrivels and dies (verb: *yābaš,* reminiscent of cognate *yabbāšâ* of 1:9, 13 and 2:11). It is difficult to estimate (if it is at all necessary) how long the rampage lasts. The "break of dawn" can be a prelude to a day's activities (Josh 6:15); but enough darkness (same root as "dawn") remains to prevent individuals from recognizing each other (Ruth 3:14). A "man," who wrestles with Jacob through the night, seeks to retreat at dawn with his anonymity still intact. Sunrise, coming next, finds Jacob limping toward Penuel (Gen 32:23–33; similar sequence in Gen 19:15–26). A slightly more calibrated progression is reported in the sordid incident of Judges 19. A concubine is gang-raped throughout the night (*kol-hallaylâ ʿad-habbōqer*), but is abandoned when "dawn breaks" (*ketib: baʿalôt haššaḥar*). By daybreak, she manages to drag herself to the doorpost of her master's host (*lipnôt habbōqer . . . ʿad-hāʾôr*), where she is found in the morning (*babbōqer*).

4:8. *way(ye)hî kizrōaḥ haššemeš wayyeman ʾelōhîm rûaḥ qādîm ḥarîšît wattak haššemeš ʿal-rōʾš yônâ wayyitʿallāp wayyišʾal ʾet-napšô lāmût wayyōʾmer ṭôb môtî mēḥayyay.* This verse contains the final example of a *wayyeman.* Unlike all of its previous occurrences, however, this formulation is preceded by an introductory *way(ye)hî kizrōaḥ haššemeš.* One way for Hebrew writers to synchronize two activities reported in successive clauses is to have *way(ye)hî* plus an infinitive construct with *ke-*, usually in the first clause (BDB 224 [2.a]). This situation is what obtains here, for the narrator wants to tell us that God stirs the wind just as the sun rises. It is not clear to me whether we should know this in order to limit how long it takes for the plant to dry up, or simply to recognize that the sun cannot begin to hurt Jonah until this wind completes what it is ordained to do. If the latter, it sharpens the problem we face when inspecting *wayyeman ʾelōhîm rûaḥ qādîm ḥarîšît,* because this statement seems to have no future in the subsequent narrative.

The word *ḥarîšît* is one of five that are unique to the book of Jonah.[2] It does appear in a Qumran hymn, where it is said that the poet's bowels heave like "a ship in a *ḥarîšît* tempest" (7:5). But this vocabulary is without doubt taken from Jonah, as its parallel passage in 6:23 demonstrates.[3] So far, the term has eluded clear-cut explanation, first because the root **ḥrš,* despite its rich assortment of meanings, is not easily applicable to "wind"; second because *ḥarîšît* follows a pattern that best suits feminine ordinals, and therefore modifies "wind" incongruously (Landes 1982: 165 n. 49).

This combination of difficulties leads ancient and modern exegetes to offer diverse suggestions. Some scholars defend meanings available to the Hebrew root **ḥrš* (hence, either "sultry" or "cutting"); some emend various consonants

[2] The others are *sepînâ* [1:5]; *yitʿaššēt* [1:6], *qerîʾâ* (3:2), and *qîqāyôn* (4:6ff.). There are also many constructions that are unique to Jonah.

[3] The parallel passage merely speaks of *bzʿp ymym,* "furious seas." I cite this parallel passage (7:23) in the COMMENTS to Jonah's psalm (section VI). Note also that this phrase is balanced by *rwḥ ʿwʿyym* in both Qumran passages (manifestly the *rûaḥ ʿiwʿîm,* "distorting spirit," of Isa 19:14).

in *ḥarîšît* (hence, *ḥarîsît*, "sunny," *ḥarîrît*, "glowing"); some offer completely different words (*maḥarebet*, "scorching," *mašḥît*, "destroying," *baššaḥar*, "at dawn"). It would not be very productive to record what is found in the ancient versions or to offer more suggestions, for they too are just shots in the dark.[4]

The phrase *rûaḥ qādîm ḥarîšît* consists of a feminine noun (*rûaḥ*) separated from its feminine adjective (*ḥarîšît*) by a masculine noun with which it is in construct (*qādîm*). Scripture has only one other equivalent phrase, at Exod 14:21, "The Lord pushed the sea with a powerful east wind" (*berûaḥ qādîm ʿazzâ*). *Rûaḥ (haq)qādîm* (without an adjective) occurs a dozen times and is cited as one of four winds God summons from the four quarters of the Earth.[5] Blowing all night, this east wind can carry locusts into Egypt (Exod 10:13); it can shatter a Tarshish fleet (Ps 48:8; see Ezek 27:24–26); it can dry up vegetation (Hos 13:5 [quoted above]; Ezek 17:10; 19:12). These attestations clearly indicate that whenever Hebrew narrators call upon the east wind, they are alerting readers to God's controlling presence.[6]

[4] Long lists of proposals and their champions can be found in Trible 1963: 53–54; Bewer 1912: 61–62; and Snaith 1945: 39. The Babylonian Talmud expresses puzzlement over the meaning of the word (*Giṭṭin* 31b; quoted from Soncino Talmud 1936b: 129): "What is the meaning of *ḥarishith?*—Rab Judah said: When it blows it makes furrows in the sea. Said Rabbah: [what it means is that] when it blows it stills all other winds."

[5] Any of these four winds can bring ill as well as good to human beings. The remaining three are *ṣāpôn, dārôm*, and *yām*, respectively, the north, south, and west winds. *1 Enoch* 76:1–6 has this to say about the "east wind" (cited from Charlesworth 1983: 55): "And I saw the twelve wide openings in all the directions through which the winds come out and blow over the earth. . . . The first (group of) winds goes out from those openings called easterly. Out of the first gate, which is in the direction of the east and inclines toward the south, proceed extirpation, drought, pestilence, and destruction. Out of the second gate, (located) directly in the center, proceed rain and fruitfulness together with dew. Out of the third gate, which is in the direction of the northeast, proceed (both) cold and drought."

[6] It may be worth noting that the "east wind" is ecologically vital only along the Mediterranean shoreline and is much less operative in Assyria. Modern climatologists tell us that in wintertime the east wind can flip around depressions over the Mediterranean, bringing heavy rains to the coastal region. During the same period, it can also draw sultry winds from high-pressure cells in Iraq and Syria, developing a hot, dry, but also stagnant condition, which not only dries up budding plants, but also plays havoc with the human cooling mechanism. During this period, however, the sun's rays do not effectively penetrate the resulting haze, so that the combination of sun and sirocco presumed to have devastated Jonah's body is not likely to have obtained (see *Enc Jud* 9.189–94). Near Nineveh, southwesterly winds from the Arabian deserts are responsible for the hottest temperatures. (South-)easterly winds, known today as *sharqi* (whence our own "sirocco"), usually come in wintertime and bring much-needed rains; Godfrey 1944: 166–81. This pattern is reflected in cuneiform literature, in which the *šadûm*, "east wind," is rather benign, nothing like the *šūtū*, "south wind," or the *imhullum*, "evil wind." (For other

Readers of Jonah, however, already know about winds and their significance, ever since God cast a "mighty" one upon the sea (1:4). In that account we simply have the feminine noun *rûaḥ* and its adjective *gedôlâ*. I am inclined to believe that the mysterious *ḥarîšît* is probably just another synonym for "big, powerful," not the least because the only other adjective Scripture attaches to "east wind" (Exod 14:21, cited above) is likewise about power (*ʿazzâ*). In view of the unusual density of puns in this particular section of Jonah, I would not be surprised if the narrator chose this unfamiliar word because its consonants (*ḥet, resh, shin*) echo the preceding verse's (*baʿalôt*) *haššaḥar* (*shin, ḥet, resh*). We may further notice how the repetition of the consonants *ḥet* and *shin* in vv 7 and 8 mimics the sounds of rushing winds. I offer one more argument why the wind's strength is relevant here.

It is possible that the east wind works in tandem with the sun against poor Jonah (some scholars speak of a *khamsin* or a sirocco); but this is not what the Hebrew text tells us. Rather, it makes it clear that Jonah suffers only when the sun begins mercilessly to beat on him (*wattak haššemeš ʿal-rōʾš yônâ*). We have noticed that elsewhere in Scripture (Isa 49:10; Ps 121:6), those struck by the sun are direct objects of the verb. Here, however, the preposition *ʿal* modifies the action, doubtless to bring us back to the plant's express mission, which is (v 6), "to be a shade *over his head*" (*lihyôt ṣēl ʿal-rōʾšô*). By now we know that even as the east wind begins to stir, the *qiqayon* plant has already withered and can no longer be of help. Does this leave Jonah with any other protective device? I would like to revive a venerable suggestion, offered by the eleventh-century Jewish exegete Joseph Kara, that the purpose of the wind is to sweep away the hut (*sukkâ*) that Jonah himself had built outside of Nineveh (v 5); Zlotowitz 1980: 138–39. Winckler comes to the same conclusion.[7]

When Elijah begs for death in the wilderness of Beersheba, there is no verb that describes his physical condition; we are only told that Elijah goes to sleep right after uttering his words of despair (see above, at 4:3). Joseph Kara and Ibn Ezra are troubled by Jonah's sensitivity to the sun and propose that the fish's gastric juices destroyed his hair and damaged his skin. But the Hebrew only states that when the sun "strikes against" his head, Jonah *yitʿallāp*. The ancient versions find this verbal form difficult, and they paraphrase to avoid a literal rendering. Among their proposals, I list only the following: the LXX's *kai ōligopsuchēse*, "he was faint, discouraged" (same verb used for the idiom *qāṣar nepeš* of Num 21:4 and Judg 16:16); Aquila's *kai apeskarize*, "he convulsed" (also used for *wehûʾ-nirdām*, said of Sisera in Judg 4:21); Symmachus's *kai*

winds [*šārum*] consult the Akkadian dictionaries under *ištānum*, "north wind," *amurrûm*, "west wind," *mehûm*, and *imsuhhum*.)

7 1900: 264–65; cited favorably by Budde 1904: 228. Among other major surgical procedures upon the text of Jonah, Winckler emends *ḥarîšît* into *wattaharōs ʾet-sukkātô*, "it threw down his shelter."

pareluthe, "he was incapacitated"; Theodotion's *kai ekseluthē,* "he became faint"; the Vulgate's *et aestuabat,* "he seethed"; the Targum's *w'štlhy,* "he was faint"; the Syro-Palestinian version's *wzʿrt npšh,* "he was bothered"; the Syriac's *w'ʿṭrq,* "he was vexed" (see Trible 1963: 55; Goshen-Gottstein 1973: 104). While these proposals are generally faithful to the context, it may nevertheless prove useful to inspect the Hebrew form, *wayyitʿallāp.*

The BDB entry (763) collapses two separate roots, bearing different meanings, into a single entry, *ʿālap:* "to wrap oneself" (Cant 5:14, Gen 38:14[8]) and "to weaken, feel faint" (Isa 51:20, Amos 8:13; see Ezek 31:15). The latter is the sense that seems most appropriate to Jonah. The verb *wayyitʿallāp* is an *HtD* imperfect, occurring elsewhere only in Amos 8:13, where adolescents are said "to swoon" when deprived of water. (Interestingly enough, the LXX for Amos gives here *ekleipsousin,* from a verb that is different from those cited above.) Now "to cover oneself" and "to feel faint" are two meanings the root **ʿlp* shares with the aurally proximate **ʿṭp,* the *HtD* of which had occurred in Jonah's psalm (2:8): "Even as my life ebbs away, it is the Lord whom I recall." To my mind it is not a coincidence that we have in Jonah two *HtD* conjugations of verbs that share two of their three consonants. Moreover, both these verbal forms have the word *nepeš* in close proximity. (See COMMENTS.)

Unlike the previous occasion, when dejection leads Jonah to challenge God into shortening his life, this time Jonah wishes death upon himself. The LXX translates freely, "he despaired of his life" (*kai apelegeto tēn psuchēn autou*); but the Vulgate is closer to the Hebrew, *et petivit animae suae ut moreretur,* "he requested his soul, that it should perish." Syriac obtrusively imports Elijah's explanation about not being equal to his fathers. The phrase *šāʾal ('et) nepeš,* which occurs four times in Scripture, incorporates two separate idioms lumped together in the dictionaries (BDB 981 [1.a]). The first (without *'et*) is equivalent to *biqqēš nepeš* and has someone "seeking" another's life: Job protests that he never exacted another person's life through a curse (31:30); God praises Solomon for not seeking an enemy's life (1 Kgs 3:11). In the second idiom (with *'et*), a person addresses the soul with a query that comes after the verb *'āmar,* "to say"; it therefore belongs under BDB 981 (2.a) (with *šāʾal* [*'et-*]*pî,* literally, "to ask the mouth"; that is, "to consult"). This is what we have in Jonah and in Elijah's Beersheba episode (1 Kgs 19:4).

Now, when people discuss death with their own souls, we could take it as a fanciful way of asking God to take their life. This may be the case when Elijah voices his distress and perhaps also in Jon 4:3 (minus the idiom), when Jonah

[8] A meaning "to rouge oneself" for Gen 38:14 is suggested by some recent commentators on the basis of Ugaritic *ġlp;* conveniently, for a summary, see Sasson 1972: 435 (#93). This sense is not likely, if only because Judah is not supposed to see Tamar's features (facial or otherwise). Like his father's first experience of his mother, Leah, Judah is in the dark and being duped when enjoying Tamar's favors.

asks God to end it all for him. It is certainly not what we have in Jon 4:8. In fact, the contrast between the two occasions in which death attracts Jonah itself generates interesting queries regarding his states of mind before and after the creation of the *qiqayon* plant; see the COMMENTS that follow. I am, therefore, reminded of a category of literature in Egypt, exemplified by the famous "Debate of a Man with his Soul (*ba*)," wherein poets hold extensive dialogues with their own souls regarding the advantages of taking their own lives (*ANET*³ 405–7; Lichtheim 1973: 163–69).[9] From Lichtheim, I select a few of the many bitter assertions that might also have occurred to poor Jonah as the sun fries his head:

Lo, my name reeks
Lo, more than carrion smell
On summer days of burning sky.
. . .
To whom shall I speak today?
I am burdened with grief
For lack of an intimate.

Death is before me today
Like the fragrance of myrrh,
Like sitting under sail on breeze [*sic*] day.

4:9. *wayyōʾmer ʾelōhîm ʾel-yônâ hahêṭeb ḥārâ-lekā ʿal-haqqîqāyôn wayyōʾmer hêṭēb ḥārâ-lî ʿad-māwet.* Portions of this verse strongly recall information in v 4. While the Masoretes divided the segments that are duplicated in vv 4 and 9 into three parts, they punctuated them differently:

v 4 (The Lord)	*v 9 (God)*	*v 9 (Jonah)*
1. *wayyōʾmer YHWH*	*wayyōʾmer ʾelōhîm ʾel-yônâ*	*wayyōʾmer*
2. *hahêṭēb*	*hahêṭēb ḥārâ-lekā*	*hêṭēb ḥārâ-lî*
3. *ḥārâ-lāk*	*ʿal-haqqîqāyôn*	*ʿad-māwet*

In v 9, the introduction has "God" rather than v 4's "the Lord"; we cannot tell why. Because this is not a dialogue, the narrator specifies to whom God is

[9] Marti (cited by Bewer 1912: 62) may have been on the same track, but unduly influenced by Job 31:30, when he suggested that the idiom be rendered, "he cursed himself." Note also Landes 1967a: 27–28, "Feeling totally helpless and alone . . . [Jonah] directs his last request, not to Yahweh, but to himself: he asks his *nephesh* ('life principle, self') to die." Vanoni 1978: 206, wrongly criticizes Landes for this assertion.

posing a question. The inquiry itself is "felt" differently by the Masoretes. In v 4, God's words linger on the adverb "utterly" before getting on to the main verbal phrase. Here, however, the previously heard question is stated quickly—note the linkage created by the conjunctive/disjunctive accents—so that all attention can gather on the new piece of information, *ʿal-haqqîqāyôn,* "regarding the *qiqayon* plant."

In the overheated atmosphere in which Jonah suffers, it could well be that God's query means to be more pungent this time around than when first formulated in v 4; for the root *ḥārâ* can remind of *ḥārar,* "to scorch, burn." Jonah answers with the same vocabulary as God's, and the Masoretes underlined the connection by reproducing the same punctuation as in the previous section. In this way, too, they sharpened the contrast between *ʿal-haqqîqāyôn* and *ʿad-māwet,* "until death." It used to be thought that *ʿad-māwet,* which does not occur elsewhere in Scripture, turns Jonah's answer into a hyperbole and thus underscores his essentially petulant character; König even favors understanding the whole episode as comic (1906: 750). Ever since Thomas proposed that this phrase is colloquial for "very much" (or some such superlative, 1953: 220), many recent translations have adopted this suggestion, for example NEB's clever "mortally angry." Although such a solution softens the fractious personality frequently assigned to Jonah, it also derails proper assessment of an important element in Jonah's response to God's miracle; see COMMENTS.

The versions themselves are unanimous in maintaining the actual allusion to death; and this connection is reflected in Matt 26:38 (also Mark 14:33), where Jesus is obviously thinking of his own death when he appropriates the language of Jonah (and of Ps 42:6–7 [Engl. 42:5–6]), "My soul is very sorrowful, even to death" (*heōs thanatou*).[10] Moreover, when the phrase in Jonah is taken concretely, we can once more hark back to 2:6, where Jonah's life is about to end as sea waters are engulfing him *ʿad-nepeš,* "up to the neck."

4:10–11. It has been observed by some commentators (for example, Almbladh 1986: 39–40) that God's monologue strikes out from a minor premise (v 10) in order to arrive at a major one (v 11). This hermeneutic principle, which eventually acquires the name *qal wāḥōmer,* is well known in the rabbinic tradition; but it probably obtained too in biblical times, for a number of passages clearly adopt this method of argumentation. I give two examples: first, Gen 44:8, where Joseph's brothers are arguing their innocence: "Here we brought back to you from the land of Canaan the money we found in the mouths of our bags. How then could we have stolen any silver or gold from your master's house!" (NJPS); and, second, Ezek 15:1–6: "The word of the Lord came to me: O mortal, how is wood of the grapevine better than the wood of any branch to be found among

[10] See also Ps 42:12 [Engl. 42:11] and 43:5. In the Greek Bible, the psalms are, respectively, 41 and 42.

the trees of the forest? Can wood be taken from it for use in any work? . . . Even when it was whole it could not be used for anything; how much less when fire has consumed it and it is charred! Can it still be used for anything?" (NJPS).[11] In annotating the last two verses of Jonah, it may therefore prove useful to place in parallel the two segments of God's arguments and then to compare them. We need to keep in mind, however, that this method is risky, for it presumes congruity or contrast that might well be beyond the narrator's intent.

4:10	*4:11*
wayyōʾmer YHWH	
a. ʾattâ ḥastā ʿal-haqqîqāyôn	*a′. waʾanî lōʾ ʾāḥûs ʿal-nînewēh hāʿîr haggedōlâ*
b. ʾašer lōʾ-ʿāmaltā bô welōʾ giddaltô	*b′. ʾašer yeš-bāh harbēh mištêm-ʿeśrēh ribbô ʾādām*
c. šebin-laylâ hāyâ ûbin-laylâ ʾābād	*c′. ʾašer lōʾ-yādaʿ bên-yemînô liśmōʾlô*
	d. ûbhēmâ rabbâ

In *ʾattâ ḥastā ʿal-haqqîqāyôn* (*a*) and in *waʾanî lōʾ ʾāḥûs ʿal-nînewēh hāʿîr haggedōlâ* (*a′*), opposing personal pronouns serve as entry headings, under which are cataloged the contrasting postures adopted by God and by Jonah (at least as God formulates them). The opposition between *ʾattâ,* "you (Jonah)," and *ʾanî,* "I (God)," is evocative of (legal) disputations wherein individuals contrast their own situations to those of their opponents. A disjunctive *waw* widens the gulf

[11] An excellent example is found in 2 Kgs 5:13, "If the prophet gave you [Naaman] demanding instruction, would you not follow it? How much more when he said, 'bathe and become pure!' " Ezekiel 14:12–23 is an extended section that depends on this interpretive principle (see especially v 21). Other passages already cited by Rabbi Ishmael are listed in two articles ("Hermeneutics"; "Interpretations") of the *Enc Jud* 8.367, 1421. See also Fishbane 1985: 250 n. 50; 420, 526 n. 2 (with bibliographies).

As a rhetorical principle, this method of formulating an argument is very ancient, and an example can be found in a Mari letter, ARM(T) X:43, written by a daughter (perhaps sister) of King Zimri-Lim of Mari. This letter, which she writes "to Beltum, my mother," is made clearer by the remarks of Veenhof 1982: 133–34: "May my Lord (Shamash) and my Lady (Aya) keep you well as a favor to me. Why have you not worn my garb, but returned it (to me instead), thus heaping insult and curse on me? I am a princess and you are a queen. How much (more of an affront) is this to me—whom you and your husband have made enter the convent—when even common soldiers treat well their share of the booty! Therefore, do well by me yourself, and my Lord (Shamash) and Lady (Aya) will surely treat you well in the eye of the town and its inhabitants." For more Akkadian examples, see *CAD,* volume E, under *ezib.* In Latin terminology this form of a fortiori inference may argue either *a minori ad maius* or *a maiori ad minus.*

separating the two perspectives. The plant, which is Jonah's concern, is mirrored by "Nineveh," which is God's. In this verse, the narrator brings out *hāʿîr haggedōlâ* a final time, and it serves a number of functions beyond readying us for more information about Nineveh's immense population (*b′–c′*): it promotes a contrast between a mere plant and a major city; it sets up a play on words between *haggedōlâ* and *giddaltô* of *b;* most importantly, it brings us back to the beginning of the saga, to 1:2, when Jonah chooses to err and when God prepares for him an elaborate lesson.

In *a* and *a′*, the conjugated forms belong to the same verb, *ḥûs;* but they too help to develop the contrast. Applied to Jonah, the perfect is used (*ḥastā*); applied to God a negated imperfect is called upon (*ʾāḥûs*). To translate this verb the LXX uniformly uses *pheidomai,* "to spare" (which serves the LXX also to render Hebrew *ḥāmal* and *ḥāśak*). But Jerome employs different Latin verbs: in *a,* he gives *tu doles,* "you grieve over (the plant)" while in *a′* he has *ego non parcam,* "I should not spare (Nineveh)." Jerome might have done so because he sensed that to credit Jonah with an emotive feeling about a plant would not be convincing. In fact, Jonah welcomes death because of his own suffering and not out of passion for the plant's demise. To evaluate Jerome's decision, we need to inspect the way Scripture uses *ḥûs.*[12]

This word often supports a metaphor in which the eye, as subject, "feels" favorably about (*ʿal*) an object. It is about feeling compassion and mercy and therefore easily associates with other verbs of similar implication (*rāḥam* and *ḥāmal*). In most cases, the real subjects (God or various highly placed individuals) demonstrate sympathy to human beings (or groups) of lesser status. In Gen 45:20, however, the object is not a human being, but possessions. In welcoming Israel into Goshen, Pharaoh (obviously foreshadowing Exod 12:33–36) bids Joseph's brothers to "take from the land of Egypt wagons for your children and your wives, and bring your father here. And never mind your belongings (*ʿênekem ʾal-tāḥōs ʿal-kelêkem*), for the best of all the land of Egypt shall be yours." This translation is from the NJPS, which nicely recognizes that, for Pharaoh, the Hebrews cannot be harboring compassion or pity regarding their baggage.

Jonah's plant is likewise not a human being, and scholars who are aware of the issue strive to make an adjustment in the way *ḥûs* operates in 4:10–11. Most scholars treat it as associated with animates. But, in order to maintain a consistent translation for this verb in both of its appearances (vv 10 and 11), Wolff posits that the narrator, purposely striving for irony, is saying the opposite of what he means (1977: 173). Butterworth, who rightly criticizes Wolff's premise ("no valid argument can be based on an ironical premise"), opts instead to treat

[12] On *ḥûs,* see BDB 299; *ThWAT* 2.811–19; Fretheim 1978: 230–33; Wolff 1977: 173. Landes (1982: 151*) effectively disproves that Aramaic influences this verb's presence in Jonah.

the verb as controlling nonanimates (1978). He therefore renders the two contexts as follows: "you are sorry to lose the plant" and "should I not be sorry to lose Nineveh" (see also NEB). In order to retain a consistent English rendering for both occurrences of *ḥûs,* however, Butterworth considers Nineveh to be a nonhuman object, while in fact cities (Jer 13:14; Ezek 24:14) and nations (Joel 2:17), no less than individuals (Neh 13:22), are metonymically said to enjoy or lose God's compassion.

Here Jerome's insight can be useful. He obviously realized that Latin cannot match the Hebrew as it attains two distinct meanings by using the same verb, *ḥûs.* Had Jerome emulated the Hebrew and given the same Latin verb in both verses, he might have compromised the meaning for one of the contexts. By the same token, had he chosen a bland verb for both contexts (as does NJPS ["to care about"] or Stuart 1987: 499 ["be concerned about"]), Jerome could have satisfied neither situation. Therefore, Jerome decided to sacrifice balanced vocabulary in order to realize idiomatic precision. I follow Jerome's approach, but in a note I alert readers to the phenomenon at stake.

ʾăšer lōʾ-ʿāmaltā bô welōʾ giddaltô (*b*) and *ʾăšer yeš-bāh harbēh mišštêm-ʿeśrēh ribbô ʾādām* (*b'*) are relative clauses introduced by the particle *ʾăšer* in order to give us more information, respectively, about the plant and about Nineveh. The former twice calls upon the negative adverb *lōʾ,* "not," in order to accentuate Jonah's lack of involvement with the life cycle of the plant. This nonparticipation is given in two stages, though it is possible that they may refer to one continuous single act (hendiadys, that is, "upon which you have not labored to cultivate"). In the first phase, Jonah is said not to have *ʿāmal be-* the plant. While the verb *ʿāmal* and its derivatives are found in all phases of Hebrew (*contra* BDB 765), the present idiom occurs elsewhere only in wisdom literature, where it is used to comment (also negatively) on the construction of a building (Ps 127:1) and on the accumulation of unearned fortunes (Eccl 2:21). The LXX is much more pungent here, turning to the verb *kakopatheo,* which is about an enduring affliction ("for which you have not suffered").

Jonah is next charged with not *giddal* the plant. In the *D* stem, this second verb refers to the raising of plants elsewhere only in highly literary contexts: Isa 44:14 and Ezek 31:4, the latter being metaphoric about Assyria. Normally, the verb refers to the raising of children or to enhancing the status of individuals. It is very likely therefore that its choice in Jonah means to further the parallelism with what is said about Nineveh, that *great* (*gedôlâ*) city.

In my observations at 3:3, I give reasons why the phrase *ʿîr-gedôlâ lēʾlōhîm* addresses God's dominion over Nineveh instead of conveying information about its size ("an exceedingly large city"), and it is possible that *ʾăšer yeš-bāh harbēh mišštêm-ʿeśrēh ribbô ʾādām* serves as a comment on the earlier phrase. The accent in this clause is on multitudes and crowds, not so much to give us one more piece of information about Nineveh's magnitude, but to explain why God should be concerned with it at all.[13] We are invited, therefore, to contrast the positive description of God caring for thousands of living souls to the negative image of Jonah remaining unmoved by the demise of just one plant.

The population count given in *b′* is somewhat labored. The narrator invokes the numeral *ribbô,* "10,000," citing for it a figure that, exceptionally for Scripture, requires two digits (roughly, "two" and "ten").[14] A more prosaic equivalent of the formula is available in Scripture (note *mēʾâ weʿeśrîm ʾelep,* "120,000," in Judg 8:10 and 1 Kgs 8:63). By using the adverb *harbēh min-,* "more than," however, the narrator steers away from providing an accurate population count. Consequently, if we desire to know how close the narrator comes to assessing Nineveh's real population, we are left to our own devices.

A. T. Olmstead long ago guessed that 300,000 persons lived in early seventh-century (B.C.E.) Nineveh during Sennacherib's reign (cited by Wolff 1977: 175). On the basis of an Assurnasirpal (II) stone slab found in 1951, Wiseman and Mallowan once claimed that about 70,000 persons lived in Calah (itself supposedly about half the size of Nineveh).[15] The assertion depended on a misunderstanding of the document's phrasing, and Wiseman has radically scaled down this estimate since then (1979: 39–42). Because this is an issue that surfaces often in Jonah scholarship, I sought the opinion of Simo Parpola, chief editor of the State Archives of Assyria project, who kindly allowed me to present his response here (Bitnet note of January 24, 1989):

13 The LXX has *katoikousi* where Hebrew has *yeš-bāh,* suggesting that it is rendering Hebrew **yšbw;* Trible 1963: 57.

14 The noun also occurs in the spelling *ribbôʾ* (so also in some Hebrew manuscripts of Jonah; Trible 1963: 57), the latter sometimes being regarded as Aramaic (but see Dan 7:10). It also has an equivalent in *rebābâ,* which is generally regarded as preexilic and therefore older than our word. A quick look at BDB 914 (where both words are treated) shows that both words break the confines within which scholars assign them. Sometimes *ribbô* is assigned to a Northern Israelite dialect because it occurs in a difficult phrase in Hosea (8:12). To my mind all of this is hypothetical and, luckily enough, in no way affects our passage. See Landes (1982: 154*) who collects the relevant information. I might add that the West Semitic form of the noun (*ribbatum*) now occurs at Mari and possibly also at Ebla; see Durand 1984.

15 The text itself reads (translation, Grayson 1976: 176), "when I consecrated the palace of Kalach, 47,074 men (and) women who were invited from every part of my land, 5,000 dignitaries (and) envoys of the people of the lands Suhu, Hindanu, Patinu, Hatti, Tyre, Sidon, Gurgumu, Malidu, Hubushkia, Gilzanu, Kumu, (and) Musasiru, 16,000 people of Kalach, (and) 1,500 *zarīqū* of my palace, all of them—altogether 69,574 (including) those summoned from all lands and the people of Kalach—for ten days I gave them food, I gave them drink, I had them bathed, I had them anointed. (Thus) did I honour them (and) send them back to their lands in peace and joy."

As far as I know, there is no serious study of the matter and estimates I have seen vary greatly, but here are a few basic facts to start with. The area of the walled city, less the citadels, is 5.2 km^2 [= 2 square miles]. We know from real-estate purchase documents that many houses had a second floor. After the construction of the city walls (around 700 B.C.E.), the city had 80 more years in which to grow as an imperial capital, and it can thus be reasonably supposed that the entire walled area was more or less built-up by the 620's. This is confirmed by post-canonical purchase documents showing that the population had spread over the city walls. Applying the population density of 1917 Baghdad (358 persons/hectare [= 2.5 acres]) to Nineveh, which seems reasonable, gives a figure like 278,684 to the walled area in the citadels alone. With the palace personnel and the garrisons on the citadels included, one would come close to 300,000; but one would still have to include the population outside the city walls and the suburbs. . . .

Even an estimate like 300,000 could be too low rather than too high. The archives found in a small (0.5 hectare [= 1.25 acres]) area in Assur indicate that even small households occupying 30 m^2 [= 18 × 16 square feet] in this area possessed slaves, and therefore the average family size was more than the "nuclear" four attested in the Harran census. My preliminary estimate for the population density in the area is 630/hectare. Applied to Nineveh, it suggests 327,600 for the walled city area less the citadels.

Let me stress that the figures I have cited are just rough estimates and they can and must be calibrated in various ways, a task that remains to be done. But I feel confident that if 300,000 is given as a round figure for the population of Nineveh during its heyday, the estimate cannot be terribly far off the mark.

"More than 120,000 individuals," therefore, is a tally that is not at all implausible for Nineveh even before its heyday. (On its population, see the NOTES to 3:3.) Modest though it be, this estimate nevertheless must have been beyond the comprehension of a Jerusalem citizen, whose city expanded to 24,000 souls after the fall of Samaria (Broshi 1974: 23–24), but shrank to a fraction of that amount during and just after the Exile. In adopting a relatively quaint phrasing, however, the narrator might be wishing to let the audience calculate the population of Nineveh, compelling it to grasp the massive outpouring of God's redemptive grace. Moreover, this formulation allowed the narrator to advance a play among shared consonants in the words *ribbô,* "myriad," and *harbēh,* "more than" (Almbladh 1986: 40). In turn, when this play on the consonants *resh* and *beth* is extended to the last word of v 11 (*rabbâ*), linkage is achieved between clauses *b'* and *d* (see also below). I follow the narrator's style of wording; and instead of deciphering the amount into a conventional sum (for example, NEB's "one hundred and twenty thousand"), I duplicate the Hebrew even if "twelve myriads" is slightly archaic for our taste.

Interpretatively pregnant is the narrator's choice of *ʾādām*, "human being" (always a collective), in place of *ʾîš/ʾanāšîm*, more commonly used when citing large numbers of persons. Above, at 3:7 and 3:8, we met twice with *ʾādām*, each time bound with the word *behēmâ*, "beasts." There, the king of Nineveh directs *hāʾādām wehabbehēmâ*, that is, every living being within town, to participate in penitential acts. The narrator brings this pairing once more to our attention (*ʾādām . . . ûbhēmâ*), despite the fact that a relative clause (*c′*) separates the two components. (This pairing was recognized already in the Talmud, *Babylonian Keritot* 6b; Soncino Talmud 1948b: 46.) It is possible that, to weaken the effects of this distancing, the narrator enters the adjective *rabbâ* (attached to *behēmâ*, uniquely in Jonah), thus allowing a play on the same consonants *resh* and *beth* obtaining in *b′*.

The plant has lived without Jonah's involvement; but *šebin-laylâ hāyâ ûbin-laylâ ʾābād* (*c*) details how precarious is this existence.[16] Thanks to God, Nineveh is rich in human life; but *ʾašer lōʾ-yādaʿ bên-yemînô lišmōʾlô* (*c′*) rehearses the consequences. We note that each segment relies on its own mode of balancing between two entities: *c* has *bin- . . . bin-*; *c′* gives *bên . . . le-*. Therefore, while the phrasings are by no means lexically equivalent, they are aurally reminiscent of each other.

The relative clause *šebin-laylâ hāyâ ûbin-laylâ ʾābād* (*c*) is introduced by the particle *še*(ˑ), giving us more detail about the plant. Very much as in the preceding clause (*b*), *c* allocates its information to two segments, but calls upon duplicated *bin-* to bind them into one unit. The verbs *hāyâ*, "to be(come)," and *ʾābad*, "to perish," are semantically opposite. The latter is especially meaningful to Jonah, because it is placed in the mouths of prayerful sailors (1:6, 14) and Ninevites (3:9). The gap between life and death is measured by an interval separating one evening from another. Albeit a lovely notion, *bin-laylâ*, "son of a night," is itself a very unusual phrase, unique to Jonah, and it may not be beyond our narrator to have coined it as yet another way to recall how our hero was introduced in 1:1, *yônâ ben-ʾamittay*. Because in Hebrew the word "son," whether attached to a name or (even figuratively) to another noun, is normally written *bēn*,[17] it is also possible that this peculiar formulation aims at providing balance to a detail about humankind (*bên-yemînô lišmōʾlô*) given in *c′*. It could also be an incorrectly transmitted *bên . . . bên*. Many Hebrew manuscripts have the latter reading (Trible 1963: 56–57), which is possibly reflected in

[16] Trible rightly rejects turn-of-the-century arguments to delete this clause (1963: 103).
[17] The word *bin* occurs (1) when followed by the names Nun (Joshua's father) and Yakeh (Agur's father); (2) once also before an infinitive (Deut 25:2). For figurative usage, see BDB 121 (6); GKC 418 (v).

Philo's treatment of Jonah (Levine 1978: 98). At any rate, only exceptionally are the versions slavish in translating it.[18]

A large number of past and present commentators contend that *c′* (*ʾašer lōʾ-yādaʿ bên-yemînô liśmōʾlô*) is about either children or the mentally deficient, presuming that v 11 is classifying three branches of Nineveh's population: adults, persons who "do not know right from left," and animals; Levine 1978: 98; Zlotowitz 1980: 141–42. (The TEV renders this passage, "After all, it has more than 120,000 children in it, as well as many animals!") I doubt that children are of concern here, for *c′* is a relative clause that is delivering more information on *ʾādām*. Now the noun *ʾādām* may collectively refer to a whole population and thus include women and children; it may also be linked with or contrasted to animals as well as to inanimates; it may even denote mortality, weakness, or the like, when set opposite divinity. But *ʾādām* cannot refer just to children.[19]

The verb *yādaʿ*, "to know," can allude to both practical and gnomic knowledge. The only other biblical statement to duplicate Jonah's *yādaʿ bên- . . . le-* seems to be about human senses rather than moral discrimination. It occurs in 2 Sam 19:36, when Barzillai blames old age for his no longer enjoying good food and pleasant music. In most other cases, when the object of various "perception" verbs is set between the pair of prepositions *bên . . . le-*, this knowledge is comparative and discriminative, where the obvious choice is set between clear-cut opposites: "good" and "bad" (Lev 27:33 [*biqqēr*]; 1 Kgs 3:9 [*hēbîn*]); "sacred" and "profane" (Ezek 22:26; 44:23 [*H* stem of *yādaʿ*]); "many" and "few" (Num 26:56 [*N* of *ḥālaq*]); "upright" and "base" (Mal 3:18 [*rāʾâ*]); "sanctified" or otherwise (for example, Ezek 42:20 [*hibdîl*]). Sometimes, however, the choice between two options is not as obvious. Such is the case in the present clause, where individuals are to "discern between their right and left hands," a formulation that is unique to Jonah.

Although in Hebrew, as in many other tongues, to be on the "right" implies gaining protection or favor, there is only one instance in Scripture wherein "right" explicitly equals "good," while "left" equals "bad": "A wise man's heart

[18] Syriac has *dbr llyh yʿʾ* ("grow out") *wbr lly ybš* ("dry up"). Similarly, the Syro-Palestinian version gives *dbrt lylyʾh ʾtʿbdt w brt lylh ʾbdt;* Goshen-Gottstein 1973: 104. I do not know why Calvin, who is more literal than the Vulgate, nevertheless has *filia,* "daughter," where Hebrew has *bin,* "son" (1847: 515). A. Bok suggests that it is because the moon (and the night) is commonly personified as female (private communication).

[19] So also Wolff 1977: 175. The detail regarding the child Immanuel and his ability to choose good over evil (Isa 7:15–16) differs in context, language, and purpose. Occasionally cited also is 1 Kgs 3:5–9, where Solomon asks God for wisdom because he is a young lad, "not knowing which way to move." This statement illustrates Solomon's modesty in recognizing human limitation, and it obviously pleased God (see v 10).

is on his right; the fool's, on his left" declares Eccl 10:2.[20] "Right" and "left" are frequently paired in Scripture, more commonly in this sequence than in the reverse (and especially so, when with suffixed pronouns). The pair most often is benignly connected with opposite directions or sides; it alludes to moral deviation only when Hebrews are enjoined not to swerve "right or left" from God and the law. (On this subject, see *ThWAT* 3.658–63; *Enc Jud* 14.177–80.) Therefore, whether Jonah's phrasing is figurative for a mental or even a moral handicap is difficult to establish. We may decide that God changes the Ninevites' sentence because they are deemed incapable of making the correct decision (Stuart 1987: 507); if so, we will need to decide whether it contrasts with the statement about Nineveh's population made in chapter 3. There the Ninevites seem profoundly capable of recognizing their limitations. Moreover, we need to show that such an explanation makes sense to a Hebrew audience who remembers Nineveh's conniving minds no less than its bitter weapons. I have an impression, which I cannot prove readily, that "human beings, who cannot discern between their right and left hands," is amplifying on what the previous clause had just said about Nineveh's density. We are now being informed that this city is so teeming with life that Ninevites do not know who their neighbors are. If understood so, then not only is the narrator returning one final time to a motif repeated in all but the second chapter of Jonah, but we might also be gaining another perspective on God's reaction to events in Nineveh. God would be skeptical about the effectiveness or duration of one stipulation in the king's edict that urged everyone to "turn away from the violence they plan against others" (3:8).

I have already offered grammatical reasons why *ûbhēmâ rabbâ* stands at the end of v 11, seemingly as a coda to God's arguments: syntax has distorted a desired link between the vocabulary of God's lesson and that of the king's edict; paronomasia has led to a scripturally unique formulation.[21] Yet the words "and animals galore" seem perfectly suited as an ending to Jonah and his tale. In the COMMENTS, I offer a few reasons why.

COMMENTS

A man who saw a ship sink with all hands protested against the injustice of the gods: because there was one impious person on board, he said,

[20] The notion may explain Gen 48:12–20, though the NJPS comments that it has to do with luck. See also Matt 25:31–46. That "right" equals "good" or "correct" (the opposite equation is not necessarily applicable to "left") is a function of the way the word is defined in English and in other Indo-European languages. In Hebrew and other Semitic languages, the word for "right" does not immediately yield such an equivalence.
[21] One manuscript (Eb 88) reads *wbhm'*; Peiro and Castro 1977: 36.

> they had destroyed the innocent as well. As he spoke he was bitten by one of a swarm of ants which happened to be there; and, though only one had attacked him, he trampled on them all. At this, Hermes appeared and smote him with his staff, saying: "Will you not allow the gods to judge men as you judge ants?"
>
> [Moral:] Let not a man blaspheme against God in the day of calamity, but let him rather examine his own faults.[22]

When we took our leave of Jonah, he believed that he had come to a satisfying resolution of his disagreement with God. For him, the reason for God's mercy to the Ninevites was certainly shrouded in mystery; but when unexpectedly and miraculously God raised a *qîqāyôn* to shade his head, Jonah decided that, after all, God cared deeply about him; he therefore became "absolutely delighted over the *qiqayon* plant." Let us keep in mind how easily God reversed Jonah's mood, for it makes us doubt a prevalent opinion that Jonah sulked because Nineveh escaped punishment. For God, however, there remained the burden of making Jonah understand that justice and mercy are not necessarily synonymous in God's lexicon and that no issue can be framed solely in terms of a prophet's personal satisfaction.

This section opens with a series of divine interferences that seriously affect Jonah's physical well-being. Unlike the spectacular sprouting of the *qiqayon* plant, which apparently took place within the prophet's sight, its ruin is accomplished while the prophet sleeps. The narrator seems keen to make this point, possibly to magnify the reversal of fortune: for Jonah, only a night's sleep separates full happiness from abject misery.

The only verb to describe Jonah's perilous physical condition, the *HtD* of *ʿālap* in 4:8, is so suspiciously reminiscent of the *HtD* of *ʿāṭap* in 2:8 that we might find it instructive to compare their contexts. When in the fish's belly Jonah had declared, "Even as my life *ebbs away,* it is the Lord whom I recall." This declaration came just as Jonah recognized God's saving measures, and it was followed by a yearning that his prayers might reach God. How different is Jonah's present reaction, now that he nears the end of his mission! Jonah forgets the miracles God had done for him, in the sea and in Nineveh's outskirts alike.

[22] This fable, attributed to Aesop, is widely quoted. I give it here in an accessible translation, that of Handford 1954: 152–53 (#148). It cannot be dated precisely. Stith Thompson 1955–58: vol. 6 classifies it under motif *U* 21.3. H. Schwartzbaum (1966) refers to it in considering a wide variety of midrashic and Muslim narratives in which shipwrecks are grounds to discuss theodicy. While the differences in detail between this fable and Jonah are numerous, they stand parallel in their common exploration of issues regarding arbitrary gods. The fable's affinity to the sequence of events in Jonah is also arresting. Moreover, its moral is two-stranded: one is delivered by a deity and is uncannily reminiscent of God's apothegm in 4:10–11; the other is appended to the fable's end, and its message cannot be totally alien to the many pregnant lessons that Jonah seeks to teach. See further the INTERPRETATIONS (under "The Audience").

Only physical discomfort is on his mind now. When he looks for release from his misery, it is not God whom he addresses, but his own soul; it is not continuity of life that he craves, but its end.

Jonah twice seeks death. The first time he asks it of God (v 3), who naturally does not satisfy his wish. This instance compares nicely with Elijah's similar request (1 Kings 19), for both Jonah and Elijah invite death when they feel abandoned by God. By contrast, the second time Jonah courts death (v 9), he wishes it upon himself. While the reasons Jonah gives for so drastic a measure are the same in both circumstances, "for me death is better than life," it is striking that when the sun tortures him, Jonah never thinks of turning to the God who, by means of a *qiqayon* plant, has just demonstrated ample solicitude for him. For someone who has recently affirmed that "rescue is from the Lord" (2:10), Jonah seems to forget that death, no less than life, is God's to dispense.

When this plant dies, God uses the occasion to develop an argument (vv 10–11) that so readily draws us into its inner logic that we may easily neglect to question its basic premise. God forces Jonah to focus on the *qiqayon* plant as the source of his dejection, when his despair actually comes from a combination of circumstances, the withering of the plant being only one of them. The hot sun would certainly qualify as another reason, and the east wind too, even if we cannot easily assign it a function. True, Jonah does admit to being "dejected enough to want death"; but is this answer evidence that Jonah accepts the premise as God narrowly draws it? The plant certainly gives Jonah a welcome shade from the sun when a booth may not have been enough; but he also derives pleasure from it because the plant is symbolic of God's care when, once, he felt forlorn and abandoned. Its demise, no less miraculous than its birth, brings Jonah's self-doubts back to full force, and he again turns to death as a solution to his psychological impasse. It is in this sense, then, that Jonah answers God's question affirmatively.[23]

Two features may enhance our appreciation of God's speech. The first has to do with the way direct speech is allotted to both protagonists, which can immediately be noticed when given as a table:

vv 2–3	Jonah's monologue	39 words
v 4	God's query (unanswered)	3 words
v 8	Jonah's query (sotto voce)	3 words
v 9	dialogue: God	5 words
	dialogue: Jonah	5 words
vv 10–11	God's monologue	39 words

[23] To Fretheim (1978; followed by Wolff 1986: 172–73) God is forcing Jonah into untenable positions whether he answers "yes" or "no." Their discussion, however, depends on translating the phrase *hahêṭēb ḥārâ l-*, "is it right for [Jonah] to be angry?" See my objections in the NOTES to 4:4.

This symmetry in apportioning words is much too developed and obvious to be accidental. Because it can be appreciated best by the reading eye rather than the hearing ear, we may regard this accord as a studied maneuver on the part of a *writer* (rather than a *teller*). The goal or purpose of such an elaborate enterprise, however, is open to speculation. I can suggest that this balance and harmony are intended to keep us aware that God's responses are countermoves to Jonah's utterances. If so, we are encouraged to *limit* the application of the lesson we derive from Jonah's last chapter to the unusual conditions that forced the confrontation between God and a displeased prophet. In other words, we are invited to perceive Nineveh's good fortune as uncommon and not easily reproducible; on future occasions, when populations sin badly enough to deserve divine punishment, God might not prove as charitable.

The second feature has to do with the *qiqayon* plant and the way it is used as a peg upon which God's thesis hangs. As we read about its cycle of life, we are alerted first not just to the lack of human involvement in its growth ("on which you did not labor, nor did you cultivate it"), but also to the reverse, to the divine investment in its miraculous rise. We are then told of the plant's brief life ("a plant that came up one night and perished the next"). As it happens, these three characteristics are also cited in metaphors Hebrew poets construct regarding the fragility of human existence. I only quote from the NJPS Pss 144:3–4 and 90:5–6:

> O Lord, what is man that You should care about him,
>   mortal man, that You should think of him?
> Man is like a breath;
>   his days are like a passing shadow.
>
> You engulf men in sleep;
>   at daybreak they are like grass that renews itself;
>   at daybreak it flourishes anew;
>   by dusk it withers and dries up.

What is said about the fate of the *qiqayon* plant, therefore, is also about the fate of human beings; Jonah's indifference to its existence is also about the neglect with which human beings can treat each other; its death due to a "worm" is also about the destiny that awaits us all. It is in failing to grasp this analogy, then, that Jonah also deserves God's censure.

In 3:10, the narrator has shared with us how and why Nineveh is given reprieve. It is not necessarily manifest that Jonah was privy to God's deliberations or that he understood what motivated the stunning reversal. It is telling of the vast gulf that distances Jonah from true knowledge of events that in 4:10–11 God uses none of the vocabulary crucial to chapter three (*šûb, niḥam, rāʿâ*). This neglect is particularly striking because Jonah's own confession alludes to some of them, and all God needs to say to alleviate Jonah's bewilderment is something like, "Yes, Jonah, what you say is correct as far as it goes; but there is more."

It is obvious, therefore, that God has chosen to deny Jonah the simple and perhaps even natural explanation for containing divine wrath: the sincere penitence of the Ninevites and the extraordinary measures their king adopts. This is not the first time that Jonah is kept in the dark when a simple clarification would have been most appropriate (see COMMENTS on sections VIII and IX). Instead, the second part of God's monologue dwells on Nineveh and its huge population.

Elsewhere in Scripture, there is featured a discussion between God and Abraham about the minimal number of righteous persons necessary to deflect divine anger from a monstrous people (Genesis 18; see COMMENTS on section VIII). Here, however, the argument about the redemption of sinners dwells on how large is the population that would perish. If God gives Jonah any direct reason for divine clemency, it is incorporated in the enigmatic sentence "human beings, who cannot discern between their right and left hands." At most, this explanation may be figurative for moral deficiency on the Ninevites' part (see NOTES). But we may be justified in finding the contention a trifle too trite; after all, is ignorance of true human values or of fair play reason enough to save the corrupt from a just desert? Had Isaiah (27:11, quoted above) not censured Jacob's oppressor (Assyria?) for its lack of judgment (*bînût*)?

God catches Jonah's (and our) ear by a seemingly incongruous afterthought regarding the beasts of Nineveh. In the NOTES I offer syntactic reasons why God's argument (and the book of Jonah for that matter) ends with "and animals galore" (4:11). By virtue of its peculiar placement, however, this phrase attracts extraordinary attention. As the *qiqayon* plant has led us to probe theological and universal issues, so now through the lot accorded dumb creatures we are invited to speculate about humanity and its creator. Calvin finds the mention of their rescue an excellent counterargument to Jonah's grief over the *qiqayon* plant (cited in Keil and Delitzsch 1900: 417; see also Stuart 1987: 508). No doubt following what is expressed in Eccl 3:19–20 (quoted above), Rashi thinks that the animals are figurative of human beings with beastlike sensibilities (Zlotowitz 1980: 142). Somewhat similar is Freedman's assessment (personal communication) that the animals serve to comment on the Ninevites' morals and on their intelligence, "in terms of behavior there is not much to choose between them." But most modern commentators, for example Wolff (1977: 175), consider the animals to be a link between the plant and human realms. Whether we are convinced by these suggestions or prefer to advance different explanations, we may nevertheless agree that ending on such a phrase is perfectly suited to Jonah, a small book of no more than 689 words, in which one can nevertheless read about storms over the seas and hot winds over distant lands, take a tour of Sheol and learn how to avoid its clutches, discover vast-bellied fish and miraculously generated plants, even meet humane pagans and penitent Ninevites.

Most comforting, however, are the book's final images of a kindly God who will find time to teach the mysteries even to initially unpromising learners.

The book begins with God having the first words and ends with God having the last say. Jonah's attempted escape toward Tarshish and the flashback in 4:2 give us fair information about how Jonah responds to those first words. We are told nothing, however, about his reaction to God's monologue. Is he skeptical about its logic? Does it drive him to further dejection? Or, on the contrary, does it restore his faith in God's justice? Pages of speculations can be written on this score; but it may be best to end these COMMENTS by revealing what took place according to a medieval Jewish homily: "At that very moment, [Jonah] fell flat on his face saying, 'Direct your world according to the attribute of mercy, as is written, "Mercy and forgiveness belong to the Lord our God." ' "[24]

[24] Midrash Yona, quoted from Jellinek 1938: 102 (Wünsche 1907: 51). The quotation is from Dan 9:9, which, when fully cited, proves even more perfectly appropriate as Jonah's response: "for we rebelled against him, and did not obey the Lord our God by following his teachings that he set before us through his servants the prophets." The midrash to Jonah is not alone in taking the story a few more steps beyond the account in Scripture. In 3 Macc 6:8 (early first century B.C.E.) we find God restoring Jonah "to his household." Josephus laconically states, "when he had published [God's message to Nineveh], he returned (home)" (*Jewish Antiquities* 9.10.2). Other traditions speak of his wife's pilgrimage to Jerusalem and imagine Jonah as entering Paradise without dying first; Ginzberg 1947: 253; 1946: 351–52 n.38–40. Most elaborate on Jonah's career after he completes his mission to Nineveh is the *Lives of the Prophets:* "Jonah was from the district of Kariathmos near the Greek city of Azotus by the sea. And when he had been cast forth by the sea monster and had gone away to Nineveh and had returned, he did not remain in his district, but taking his mother along he sojourned in Sour [Tyre?] a territory (inhabited by) foreign nations; for he said, 'So I shall remove my reproach, for I spoke falsely in prophesying against the great city of Nineveh.' At that time Elijah was rebuking the house of Ahab, and when he invoked famine upon the land he fled. And he went and found the widow with her son [that is, Jonah], for he could not stay with uncircumcised people; and he blessed her. And when her son died, God raised him again from the dead through Elijah, for he wanted to show him that it is not possible to run away from God. And after the famine he arose and went to the land of Judah. And when his mother died along the way, he buried her near Deborah's Oak. And after sojourning in the land of Saraar [Seʾir] he died and was buried in the cave of Kenaz, who became judge of one tribe in the days of anarchy. And he gave a portent concerning Jerusalem and the whole land, that whenever they should see a stone crying out piteously the end was at hand. And whenever they should see all the gentiles in Jerusalem, the entire city would be razed to the ground." (Quoted from *Lives of the Prophets,* 10.1–11, in D. R. A. Hare's rendering [Charlesworth 1985: 392–93].) Although Hare places it much earlier, this Jewish-influenced Christian text probably dates to the third or fourth century C.E. The Jonah material pulls together information from 1 Kings 17, Genesis 35, Judges 3, and Habakkuk 2. Muslim traditions give Sadaqa as the widow's name. They expand on the birth and miraculous childhood of Jonah with anecdotes reminiscent of legends regarding Muḥammad. Jonah marries Anak, the daughter of the prophet Zachariah. It is at this point that God asks him to go to Nineveh. See Thackston 1978: 321–22.

INTERPRETATIONS

Jeremiah sought the honor of [God] and the honor of [Israel]; . . . Elijah sought the honor of [God] and not the honor of [Israel]; . . . Jonah sought the honor of [Israel] and not the honor of [God].[1]

"Oppressing (yonah) *city"*: ought [Zion] not have learnt from the city of Jonah, viz. Nineveh? One prophet I sent to Nineveh and she turned in penitence; but to Israel in Jerusalem I sent many prophets; and so it is written, *Yet the Lord forewarned Israel, and Judah, by the hand of every prophet, and of every seer, saying: Turn ye from your evil ways, and keep My commandments and My statutes,* etc. (II Kings XVII, 13).[2]

In the story of Jonah we have a representation of the whole of a man's career in this world. Jonah descending into the ship is symbolic of man's soul that descends into this world to enter into his body. Why is Jonah ([*yōnâ,*] lit. aggrieved)? Because as soon as [the soul] becomes partner with the body in this world she finds herself full of vexation. Man, then, is in this world as in a ship that is traversing the great ocean and is like to be broken, as it says, "so that the ship was like to be broken" (Jonah 1,4).[3]

[1] Adapted from *Mekilta, Pisḥa;* cited from Halperin 1980: 90.

[2] *Lamentation rabbah* 31; quoted from A. Cohen 1939: 57. This exegesis of *hāʿîr hayyônâ* (Zeph 3:1) also cites Jer 7:25. It is interesting that the Syriac for this phrase renders "city of Jonah." The NJPS suggests emending the last word to *hazzônâ,* thus, "the harlot city." Many other emendations are also proposed.

[3] The Zohar (*wayyaqhēl* 199); Simon and Levertoff 1949: 173. On this allegorical reading of Jonah 1–2, see the note to an adjacent passage I cite in section VII. The Zohar treats the name of the prophet as a participle of *yānâ,* "to oppress, maltreat"; hence it calls him the "aggrieved." See the quotation from *Lamentation rabbah* and *ḥārôn hayyônâ,* "the anger of oppressors," in Jer 25:38.

JONAH

[The book aims] to teach that God should be praised for sparing the penitents whatever their nation and even more so when they are many in number.[4]

Let us learn by the example of Jonah not to measure God's judgments by our own wisdom, but to wait until he turns darkness into light. (Calvin 1847: 121)

. . . and as the book of Jonah, so far from treating of the affairs of the Jews, says nothing upon [the book's authorship], but treats altogether of the Gentiles, it is more probable that it is a book of the Gentiles than of the Jews; and that it has been written as a fable, to expose the nonsense and satirise the vicious and malignant character of a Bible prophet, or a predicting priest. (Paine 1834: 119)

[This short story is directed] against the impatience of the Jewish believers, who are fretting because, notwithstanding all predictions, the antitheocratic world-empire has not yet been destroyed; —because YHWH is still postponing His judgment of the heathen, giving them further time for repentance. (J. Wellhausen, quoted by Budde 1904: 229)

The fundamental purpose of the book of Jonah is not found in its missionary or universalistic teaching. It is rather to show that Jonah being cast in the depths of Sheol and yet brought out alive is an illustration of the death of the Messiah for sins not His own and of the Messiah's resurrection.[5]

The story sounds in fact like an allegory of a nervous breakdown and subsequent spiritual conversion. (A. Koestler, quoted in Preminger and Greenstein 1986: 473)

The alternative to Jonah's absurdity is the absurdity of God. (Good 1981: 55)

[4] D. Kimḥi, cited from König 1911: 752. R. E. Clements (1975: 28) offers a similar judgment: "The theme of Jonah is the possibility of man's repentance, and its purpose is to show that where this occurs among men then it elicits a related change of purpose on the part of God."

[5] E. J. Young 1960: 263. So already Calvin, cited from the 1847 edition (21).

INTERPRETATIONS

The Biblical story of the prophet Jonah bears out the tragic hopelessness of activity and at the same time the need for a life of action. In an immense struggle the prophet overcomes the desire for comfort common to us all, a longing which deems any commitment and championship abortive and superfluous.[6]

The Book of Jonah is an expression of what may be called "la condition prophétique." The prophet cannot escape his mission and is bound to suffer when he attempts to fulfill it. (Berlin 1976: 234–35)

The story of Jonah is not only a religious manifesto but also a psychological tableau of the human condition. Jonah is not just a Jew from Palestine called out of anonymity by a commissioning voice from without. He is a human being, every person. . . . He is also a paradigm of our resistance to election by God, for nothing is more repulsive to us than to be so designated (elected, chosen) by the Outer Voice for a self-transcending task, when we would rather follow our inner voice and our biological dictates ("what feels good") for our self-satisfaction and our self-aggrandizement. (Lacocque and Lacocque 1981: 126–27)

The book of Jonah—considered by some theologians to be the most important text of the Old Testament—brilliantly illustrates the revalorization (one is tempted to say re-creation) of some archaic and universally distributed symbols of mythico-ritual scenarios. (Mircea Eliade, Preface to Lacocque and Lacocque 1981)

Beginning as a punitive affair between God and Nineveh, temporarily interrupted by the go-between's recalcitrance, Jonah evolves before our eyes into a story of a prophet's education. (Sternberg 1987: 320)

Show me a text that speaks of God's unbounded mercy and images of the Holocaust appear before my eyes. It's not anything I can help. *Theology* doesn't help. This is visceral. (Rosen 1987: 222)

Jonah, as we have discovered it by now, is a rather strange book. It is very short, but it shifts scenes readily and radically; it features a prophet, but hardly

[6] E. Petrovics 1966; from the jacket notes to the Hungaroton recording (LPX 11420) of his 1966 oratorio, *The Book of Jonah.* Petrovics, a Hungarian composer of Yugoslavian origin, adapted M. Babits' famous Hungarian poem of 1939 that urges individuals to assume responsibility for the fate of others.

gives him a message to convey; it remembers the names of places, but has practically no memory for those of persons; it relishes confrontations, but uses baroque devices by which to resolve them. Yet, the book has gripped audiences for hundreds of years, in sermons, folklore, literature, art, and music. Jonah is remembered along with his whale: to some because he is avatar for the resurrected; to others because he lived the lesson learned by sinners; to yet more because he glimpsed, albeit with little appreciation, a playful God.

It is common for biblical scholars to locate Jonah within a known genre of literature, hoping that the traditions and affinities it shares with comparable material will permit better insight into Jonah's many interpretive problems. But because scholars are normally reluctant to admit more than one possible literary classification for a single piece of literature, there is a tendency to force Jonah into one category or another, be it myth, fable, folktale, allegory, midrash, legend, parable, satire, parody, theodicy, or the like. This condition is reflected in the sampling of opinions with which I preface this section. Needless to say, each position appeals fully only to a small fraction in scholarship.

In all major Jonah publications—be they commentaries or specialized studies—authors review and evaluate the literary categories to which the book belongs. Until recently, this was a practical exercise.[7] Because of present interest in literary aspects of Scripture, however, Jonah typology has mushroomed alarmingly, and the procedure is not economical or even useful. To begin with, proposals are not always well argued or clearly expressed (see already Burrows 1970: 85). Their advocates sometimes confuse the task of establishing a literary category with that of clarifying the tale's characters, discussing its narrative style, exposing its author's intent, or reconstructing its audience's reaction. Moreover, in proposing new categories, many authors falsely imagine that new labels imply inventive interpretation and attach fashionable terminology to barely redrawn older classifications.

In this chapter, I examine selected attempts at classifying Jonah. By doing so, I hope to make it evident that there are many reasonable readings and interpretations of the book as a whole. The demonstration should not surprise us because Jonah, a book of uncertain origin and purpose, could not have survived the test of time without satisfying diverse tastes and expectations. While in the INTRODUCTION I readily concede that various independent units were spliced into each other to form Jonah, in this section I shall presume that the book has come to possess coherence and integrity nonetheless.

[7] Among recent studies, I mention only Feuillet 1949: 1110–21; Bickerman 1976; Trible 1963: 126–84; Allen 1976: 175–81; Wolff 1986: 83–85; Burrows 1970; Alexander 1985; and É. Levine 1984. Each one of these works contains fairly large bibliographies on the debate.

Jonah as History or Fiction[8]

Historicity and how to confirm it are problems that in biblical studies are by no means confined to Jonah, though the prophet's case is indeed more conspicuous because his activities sometimes test the limits of human credulity. The truth of the matter is that most of what is recorded as history in Scripture (including many events placed in the postexilic period) has yet to find independent confirmation. Moreover, what Israel wants most to communicate through its literature—its discovery of God, its adoption of a superior code of behavior, and its call to exemplify divinely inspired verities—is given us in forms and constructs that are largely impervious to historical appraisal. We may eventually discover a document that says on it, "Abram son of Terah"; but can we ever find means by which to substantiate the revelations God conveyed to him? (Stated conversely, knowing that Hammurabi or Sennacherib existed does not affirm the verities they attribute to their gods Marduk and Assur.) Can we ever evaluate how divine providence orchestrates Joseph's alienation from his brothers? Moses' many bouts with his people in Sinai? Saul's brooding over David? Elijah's struggles against Jezebel?

Most scholars who label Jonah as "history" are nevertheless aware of the circumstantial nature of their evidence: once they seek attestations of Jonah's existence beyond Scripture, they meet with none; once they try to verify what occurred in Nineveh, they do not succeed. Therefore, they must be satisfied just to recreate *historically plausible* scenarios. Not surprisingly, such scholars turn to the documents from Assyria to show that what Jonah tells us about Nineveh is conceivable during the ninth (or any other) century B.C.E., when Assyria (allegedly) was weak. In sections VIII and IX and in the INTRODUCTION, I have had occasion to critique this approach; here I want to point out that scholars who insist that Jonah is recording history risk equating what is plausible with what really has happened in the past. This approach ignores the fact that plausibility and verisimilitude are also goals for imaginative writing, resulting in "historical fiction" (in which historical personalities are placed within nonhistorical contexts) or "fictional history" (in which fictitious happenings are set within a historical event).

Many researchers call Jonah myth, (prophetic) legend, novella, short story, or folktale. By such labels, they mean to emphasize the nonhistorical aspect of Jonah's adventures. But in doing so some scholars sometimes confuse folkloric treatments of events with their lack of value as history. That such need not be the case is occasionally demonstrable when we inspect the richly decorated

[8] Overviews in Burrows 1970: 80–89; Feuillet 1949: 1111–19; Trible 1963: 127–43 and notes; and Alexander 1985: 36 n. 3.

material concerning Charlemagne and his court. There, deeds most uncommon (the battle at Roncevaux, for example) have proved to be based on authentic events. In the case of Jonah it needs to be asked (and is often not): how implausible must a piece of literature be for us to deny it that "kernel" of truth we lavish on so many other unauthenticated pieces from Scripture? As regards the Nineveh of Jonah, for example, can we be satisfied with turning up a record of it repenting? Or must we also prove that if it repented at all, it did so upon the visitation of a Hebrew? With regard to Jonah's undersea adventure, is it enough to prove that human beings cannot survive gastric juices? Or must it also be proved that Jonah himself never played Pinocchio (who, it may be recalled, survived inside a whale along with his crafter, Gepetto)?

I may sum up by observing that although Jonah is written in a style that impedes historical inquiry, it contains enough historicizing touches to encourage those who are not satisfied just to search Stith Thompson's *Motif-Index* for appropriate parallels. Whether Jonah is history or fiction, therefore, is likely to be debated as long as Jonah is read. In the meantime, we may seek to understand how Jonah works as a narrative with a prophet for its major character.

Narrative Art and Literary Typology in Jonah

In inspecting Jonah's narrative art, I find it economical to concentrate on diverse literary categories advanced by commentators when they treat the book beyond history. I divide my investigations into three sections, successively focusing on: (A) the narrator, in which I assess opinions holding that the narrator uses Jonah to criticize contemporaneous doctrines or institutions; (B) the audience, in which I discuss theories that Jonah is best appreciated figuratively, as a parable or allegory; and (C) character roles, in which I incorporate diverse perspectives on portraiture in Jonah.

The Narrator

Je tente de cacher l'art par l'art même. (Rameau)

The Location of Jonah's "Confession." As we read the story of Jonah, we are impressed by how much relevant information the narrator controls. The teller not only recounts what goes on aboard ship and in downtown Nineveh, hears what Jonah utters under water, and reports every word exchanged between God and Jonah, he is also aware of everyone's feelings as well as knows what God thinks of the Ninevites' repentance.

In assuming this omniscient posture, Jonah's narrator is well within known scriptural narrative conventions.[9] It comes as a jolt, therefore, when an early thought of Jonah's is sprung on us near the story's end. "Please, Lord," Jonah is quoted as saying in 4:2, "this certainly was my opinion (or my word), while yet in my own homeland; accordingly, I planned to flee toward Tarshish because I realized then that you are a gracious and compassionate God, very patient and abundantly benevolent, who would also relent from bringing disaster." Beyond containing Jonah's justification, this verse conveys sentiments of major importance to Israel's theology. We may be puzzled by the handling of this verse because it is unlike other occasions on which plot demands the withholding of information: Abraham and Isaac lie about their marriages; Esther's ancestry and religion are kept from Haman; Boaz's plans for Ruth are hidden from Mr. So-and-So. Here the narrator is concealing Jonah's thoughts from a God who, according to biblical convention, can only be omniscient.[10] By withholding Jonah's initial reaction to God's directive until after mercy is granted Nineveh, the narrator seriously interferes with the flow of the story. Our own reaction to Jonah, indeed to the whole tale, would surely be quite different had we read the first verses in chapter 1 as follows:

> When the Lord's command to Jonah the son of Amittay was, "Set out for Nineveh, that large city, and declare doom upon it; the wickedness of its citizens is obvious to me," Jonah prayed to the Lord saying, "Please, Lord, I realize that you are a gracious and compassionate God, very patient and abundantly benevolent, who will relent from bringing disaster." Thereupon, Jonah sought to escape the Lord by heading toward Tarshish. . . .

In such a reading Jonah, who knows that God will relent, is starkly condescending. When God does forgive Nineveh, however, it would not be because he chooses to do so, but because there is no other way for God to function. In other words, had Jonah's avowal been placed where it belongs chronologically, authorial omniscience would be more total, but at the expense of a severely compromised freedom for God to dispense mercy; and we might not as easily forgive the narrator for shuttling Jonah to the edge of Sheol, when all along he was the perfect foreteller!

In the NOTES to 4:2 and in the COMMENTS to section X, I treat this verse as

[9] See Sternberg's stimulating third chapter, "Ideology of Narration and Narration of Ideology," where the issue of omniscience is discussed.

[10] This observation is not beyond exceptions. In the narratives, there are a few occasions on which God asks questions of individuals (Gen 3:9; 4:9) or is said to seek information (Gen 11:6; 18:21). Some of them are purely rhetorical formulations (the first three examples); others are plainly more difficult to explain away (the last example).

organic to the plot and even test the possibility that Jonah invents the excuse just for the occasion. Here, however, I inspect the narrator's strategy in placing Jonah's confession in its present location.

It is always possible that the narrator is acting amateurishly on this occasion, squeezing in a much esteemed notion regarding God's compassion just after it was actively put to test. Nevertheless, while few would argue that all of Scripture is written with homogeneous perspective or equal skill (my own prize for infelicitous Hebrew goes to Esther), ascribing to the narrator such a lapse in judgment may create more problems than solutions; for we may begin to doubt his control over the tale and his reliability as a fair communicator of Jonah's behavior. (I think of how much more complicated would be the problem of locating 4:5!) It is more prudent, therefore, to imagine that the narrator has deliberately rearranged the information into the order we now have. Naturally, we wonder, "Why so?"

Let us once more turn to Jonah's affirmation of God's attributes and ask: would the confrontation between God and Jonah evolve differently if 4:2 were cut from its present location? If we excise this doctrinal affirmation from its present location, we obtain the following sequence at the beginning of chapter 4: "This *outcome* was so terribly upsetting to Jonah that he was dejected. Praying to the Lord, Jonah said, '[Now then,] Lord, take away life from me, because for me death is better than life.' " We note that this abbreviated statement still tells of a depressed Jonah who is pining for death. The remaining verses can also stay their course: Jonah pitches camp east of town; God provides him with a miraculous shade; instruments of God's devising unsettle Jonah, preparing him for the same lesson that is now drawn in our text. In sum, to move Jonah's confession to its chronologically natural location (after 1:2) may jeopardize God's autonomy, distort the portrayal of Jonah, and undermine the story's major turnabout (Nineveh's survival). Remarkably enough, however, to remove it from the story hardly affects narrative sequence and coherence. The only loss would be our awareness of Jonah's opinion.

Yet Jonah's views are crucial; if not to the outcome of the story, certainly to the way readers and listeners assess Jonah and judge his relationship with God. We need to know Jonah's reasoned explanation of his own behavior not only because it turns him into a multidimensional personality, but also to let us assess the wisdom of his attempted escape and to let us ponder whether God treats him fairly. Consequently, the recording of Jonah's afterthought effectively sets him in conflict with the tale's other main character, God. This perceived cleaving of purposes and perspectives will prove useful in continuing to evaluate proposals on the literary category of Jonah. If this division is consciously developed, can we explore the benefits of creating opinions with which to disagree? Can we know whether the narrator favors one position over another? Because scholars who think Jonah is a satire, parody, burlesque, or farce usually answer "yes" to these two questions, it may be instructive to evaluate their conclusions.

Jonah as Satire, Parody, or Farce. Writers adopt satire as a literary vehicle by which to critique institutions, activities, or personalities, normally of their own time. If the satire mimics a specific victim, it may be termed a parody; if it ridicules hyperbolically, it can be called a burlesque or farce; if it entertains serious subjects comically or whimsically, it may be labeled a travesty.[11] Satires, parodies, burlesques, farces, and travesties rely on various levels and kinds of wit, humor, and irony when alerting an audience to unacceptable behavior. By definition, however, this class of literature must be deliberate and intentional. Therefore, while an audience may not always realize that what they are reading is a satire (or the like), satirists cannot pen their works unintentionally or accidentally.

Scholars who place Jonah in one of these categories generally agree that the narrator's position is also God's, and that the prophet's position is surrogate for the institutions or concepts deserving ridicule. To demonstrate the contrast in positions, they uncover the ironic or satiric tone the narrator adopts; to prove that Jonah is a satire, burlesque, or farce, they document various manifestations of the humor adopted in the book: incongruent behavior, exaggerations, fantastic settings, absurd postures. It is unfortunately true, however, that almost every author I am about to discuss adopts a contemptuous diction, a jocose style, or a burlesque tone when assessing specific episodes, investing Jonah with more humor and levity than the text supports.

In this age of literary appreciation of Scripture, it is no longer necessary to prove that satire, parody, perhaps even burlesque were known to Israel and its neighbors; likewise, it is not necessary to discuss here the comic in Hebrew literature.[12] Jonah has inspired comic routines ever since the Middle Ages; his story is retold in anthologies meant to amuse children; even his name has entered our dictionaries to describe a personality with farcical potential; see Michaels 1987. In the Notes and Comments, I have had occasions to cite various passages that I deemed funny.[13] But the issue here is not whether there is

[11] These are simplistic, but generally accepted definitions; see Pollard 1970 and Holman 1980. Needless to say, readers will readily find differing and even opposite explanations for this terminology.

[12] The works of Chotzner 1883 and 1905 (first chapter) are no longer serviceable. Stinespring has a short article ("Humor") in the *IDB.* Although very few scholars today doubt that examples of Hebrew humor are preserved in the Bible, the topic is still begging for a major treatment. One problem is that Bible readers differ in recognizing whether an episode means to be funny.

[13] For example: at 1:5, especially the LXX's "But Jonas was gone down into the hollow of the ship, and was asleep, and snored"; at 2:1, regarding Jonah's place within the fish; at 2:11, as regards the fish unceremoniously landing Jonah on dry ground; probably at 3:8, when animals are impressed into penitence; possibly at 4:9, in the bitterness of Jonah's response. I need not add that many puns, whether meant to display the author's virtuos-

humor, comedy, or buffoonery in this book, but whether the narrator *intentionally* derides Jonah when wishing to ridicule other targets. Can we recover the clues and signals that reveal how the narrator is rebuking, censuring, mocking, or even condemning certain institutions or ideas? The case for this intent so far made by scholars is weak. One reason that it is not convincing has to do with the fact that practically all of our knowledge of ancient Israel is tightly corseted within the confines of Scripture. If the ancient Hebrews satirized at all, they must surely have had a much wider choice of targets than meets our eye! Yet, even when scholars limit their rummaging to the pages of Scripture, they have still to agree on what is supposed to be the object of Jonah's satiric verses.

Already in 1793, Thomas Paine considered Jonah to be a satire on one prophet's malignant character (quoted above); he thought so, however, because he believed it to be written by Gentiles! D. F. Payne (1979) thinks Jonah is a skeptic's reaction to apocalyptic notions of doom. For Burrows (1970: 94–105, repeating arguments Good had presented more engagingly in 1965), the narrator of the book is attacking the narrow-mindedness of returning Exiles. As I have already suggested in the INTRODUCTION, however, what happened when the Exiles came back to Jerusalem does not seem to be of particular importance to Jonah. Jonah is no more "self-centered, self-righteous, and self-willed" (p. 97) for arguing with God about mercy than are Abraham, Moses, or Job when they too confront him. All of them know some truths about the Hebrew God and are reacting instinctively to occasions on which they feel that such truths are being distorted. Jonah, in fact, readily accepts his charge once mercy is shown the sailors and readily makes his peace with God when shown the slightest evidence of care for his feelings (see NOTES to 4:6 and COMMENTS to section X).

J. A. Miles suggests that Jonah is a parody, aimed at "those among [the returning Hebrew Exiles] who were serious in a new and, to some, unwelcome way about the religious writings of Israel" (1974–75: 169–70). For him, Jonah is an attack against a number of stereotypes and stock features in Scripture. This is much too vague an assignment, for by definition parody must target a specific institution or piece of writing. Moreover, Miles does not always correctly follow what goes on in the story. Jonah neither represents nor parodies the theme of prophets who are initially reluctant to accept their charge; Jonah dodges his charge not because he thinks himself inadequate for the task but because he thinks the errand is unnecessary; Jonah's success is not achieved despite his reluctance, but because his marine misadventure taught him to fulfill God's will. Other amendments to Miles' readings are already available in Berlin's critical paper (1976).

J. C. Holbert thinks that the book is an attack against prophetic hypocrisy (1981: 75). (Somewhat similar, but less pungently stated, is M. West's position,

---

ity or otherwise, belong to the world of wit; see most particularly Halpern and Friedman 1980.

1984.) Although Holbert wants "hypocrisy" to cover something other than false prophecy, he does not identify those prophets whose hypocrisy Jonah allegedly embodies. Moreover, he misreads Jonah's reactions, in particular to Nineveh's redemption. Jonah is not angry because Nineveh is saved, he is aggrieved because God has played him as a part-time prophet (see below). Jonah is no hypocrite when earlier he extols God before the sailors (1:9); to the contrary, he comes to accept his charge at that very moment (see the NOTES to that verse). There are many other unjustified assertions in Holbert's study, and they are made less attractive by a drive to kibitz ("At best, we have 'fox-hole' religion here, or perhaps better 'fish-belly' religion," p. 73 [about 2:8]).

Ackerman explains that Menippean satire offers the closest analogue to the form and style of Jonah. He thinks that the prophet is himself the object of derision (1981: 227–29; see also R. Payne 1989). Menippean satire, according to Ackerman, features individuals often reduced to caricature who are placed in preposterous situations and are prone to making illusory statements.[14] But Ackerman makes the symbolism of Jonah's psalm concrete and spills its images upon the remaining chapters (pp. 216–17). As a result, the activities of Jonah are read with distorting lenses and the language that reports them is often hyperbolic: Jonah's thanatic urge when on board ship leads him to seek death even at Nineveh's gate; the *qîqāyôn* recalls the tree of life, and the worm brings to mind Eden's serpent; ships are wombs, their holds become Mount Zion, as does also the *sukkâ* of 4:5; echoes of theomachy abound. Ackerman's vision, while stimulating, may better be termed a personal allegory of Jonah rather than a dissection of a satire.

J. Mather, a historian of ideas rather than a Bible specialist, begins with a series of ex-cathedra, unsubstantiated statements on the humorous in Jonah; but his essay (1982) eventually offers an intricate analysis of character interactions in Jonah. Mather treats the book as a comedy with just two actors, God and Jonah; all remaining personalities are but "props," behaving in a manner so exemplary as to deflect or minimize the attention of an audience. Mather identifies God as the farceur and Jonah as the straight man. An audience that is aware of the farce can focus on his activity while keeping emotionally distant from Jonah. Moreover, because an audience readily discriminates between the real and the unreal in a farce, it does not worry about historical consequences or aftereffects of certain events. It would therefore not pursue Nineveh's history as it becomes a murderous foe of Israel; nor would it care whether the sailors remain attached to the worship of God. Mather posits that by adopting the comic a narrator is

[14] That there is a vast gulf between the ways that classicists and students of literature understand the genre is not for me to discuss here; see E. P. Kirk's valuable introduction on the topic (1980). Ackerman does not refer to Menippean satire in his recent contribution on Jonah (1987). I learn from an *SBL* abstract that A. Lacocque (1986) also intends to treat Jonah as a Menippean satire.

able to engage an issue that is otherwise difficult to handle: if God is an omniscient and omnipotent lover of justice, how can there be leeway for the unexpected and miraculous event or hope for the remorseful and penitent human being?

For Mather, Jonah epitomizes the believer who is repeatedly surprised by God. But—and this is where Mather's discussion takes an interesting turn—because Jonah is resilient and durable, he comes to mirror God's character and activity: just as God troubles Jonah, repeatedly surprising him, Jonah troubles everybody and everything around him; just as Jonah is sensitive to the sailors' predicament, God proves sensitive to the Ninevites'. The two, in fact, prove equally surprising and unpredictable, in their activity and in their assessment of each other. Mather comes close to finding in each the other side of a doppelgänger:

> despite all the conflict between God and Jonah, the cross-purposes of these two figures are deeply intertwined. In spite of Jonah's truculence, God continues to keep after him. And Jonah's preferences and efforts notwithstanding, he repeatedly turns out to be agent of God's mercy and not just the object of God's unsettling attention. It is as if, through their durable persistence, God and Jonah have found worthy antagonists and friends in one another.[15]

Mather may have uncovered a reading the narrator deeply structured into the tale; but he can also be developing an interpretation that may never have occurred to Jonah's author.[16] Nevertheless, I think Mather is more successful in defending the case for Jonah as a satire (or the like) than are other attempts; this is so, possibly, because Mather conceives of a narrator who is reacting not against an issue specific to Israel's past but against a predicament endemic to monotheistic beliefs.

The Audience

(For more on this subject, see the discussion of D. F. Payne 1979.) A narrator may furnish Jonah and God with opposing perspectives without intending to satirize institutions or ideas; yet this contrast may prompt an audience to search for meanings hidden from a surface reading of the book. It may be useful, therefore, to examine the way that an audience augments or deepens its understanding of scriptural narratives by making equations with other writings. I will

[15] Page 290. Mather compares his own remarks to Elie Wiesel's meditation on Jonah; 1982: 129–55.

[16] When below I present Jonah as a "comic dupe/hero," I shall arrive at explanations that parallel Mather's findings without, however, attributing them to a satiric narrator.

therefore weigh diverse suggestions that the book be treated as a parable, a fable, a *mashal* (a Hebrew categorizing term), or an allegory.

Jonah as Parable, "Mashal," Fable, or Didactic Fiction. Scripture does not have specific labels with which to differentiate between parables or fables. Occasionally, however, Hebrew writers title such narratives *mashal,* a term that covers what for us is a broad literary typology (see below).[17] It follows also that the convention defining fables as parables with nonhuman characters can only be ours and not theirs.[18] Unlike allegories, in which information is transposed from one plane to another without necessarily relieving the text of its obscurity, parables and fables are didactic and mean to illumine and explain; they are also paradoxical, because they use fiction to convey long-held truths.

While we may doubt the historical worth of Jonah, we cannot presume that its narrator and early audiences found it much too fantastic to replay the past authentically. About the only potential indicator that the narrator meant us to treat Jonah as pseudo-historical is the use of anomalous title "king of Nineveh" (see NOTES to 3:6). In Scripture, the anecdotal segment of a parable or fable tended to be brief and was invariably followed by its own interpretation. Therefore, once listeners realized that they were hearing a code by which to interpret an immediately preceding account, they would recognize that a parable or fable had just been presented to them. If they chose to do so, they could then classify as fictional the account immediately preceding the interpretation.[19]

If Jonah were a parable or a fable, I assume that it would have duplicated the form of either composition: an anecdote followed by its own explanation. Although Jonah is beyond the size usual for a Hebrew parable or fable, the main obstacle in treating it as such is that its concluding verses (4:10–11) do not

[17] The most recent full assessment of *mashal* is Landes 1978. For etymology, see also C. Cohen 1982; for further discussion, see Rosenberg 1986: 33–46. While *māšāl* is applied to various categories of literature, it does not encompass stories about prophets.

[18] This observation is also applicable to classical literature, for a number of Aesopian fables feature human characters. Later in the classical period, pithy morals were grafted onto didactic anecdotes to achieve what we know as "fable." See also the Aesopian fable I cite in the COMMENTS to section XI.

[19] When explanations do not immediately follow such narratives, we usually label them allegories. I give a brief list here without segregating the parables from the fables. It can be easily modified depending on whether one includes a number of allegories commonly mislabeled as parables (for example, Ezek 19:1–9, 10–14): Judg 9:8–15, Jotham's fable of trees seeking a king; 2 Sam 12:1–4, Nathan's parable of the poor man's lamb; 2 Sam 14:4–11, woman of Tekoa's parable of two sons; 1 Kgs 20:39–43, prophet's parable of the escaped prisoner; 2 Kgs 14:9, Jehoash's fable of the thistle and cedar; Isa 5:1–6, parable of the vineyard; Isa 28:23–29, parable of the farmer; Jer 18:1–10, parable (?) of the potter (explained?); Ezek 17:3–10, fable of the two eagles and vine; Ezek 24:3–5, parable of the boiling pot; Ezek 34:1–10, parable of the dry bones.

function as interpretive keys in the way that other conclusions to parables normally do; for nothing in these verses suggests that the narrator is shifting into another sphere of comprehension: the plant remains a plant in v 10 and the Ninevites remain Ninevites in v 11 (*contra* Scott in *Enc Jud* 13.72).

In the modern period, however, a more elastic definition for both parable and fables has come to fore, and we find either or both terms applied to long poems (Eliot's *The Waste Land*, Auden's *Age of Anxiety*), to complex prose (Golding, *The Lord of the Flies*; much of Kafka's work) and to drama (Becket, *Waiting for Godot*), any of which may or may not include roles for animals or plants. It is clear to me that those who call Jonah a parable are actually adopting this expanded sense; in fact, some scholars are cautious enough to label them "parable like" (Childs) while others simply regard them as didactic fiction. I give in the following paragraphs a brief overview of some of the more recent opinions.[20]

Parable: C. Lewis (1972: 163) suggests that "In Jonah, then, the troubled conscience of the ancient world finds its lone protesting voice—he is truly a 'child of forthrightness.' " S. H. Blank (1974: 127–28) thinks Jonah is "a prophet as paradigm. He stands for the generation of Israel whom the author of Jonah knew as contemporaries. And the story calls the people back to their destined mission to the nations, the Ninevehs of the world." A. Maillot (1977), who adopts a very jocular idiom—he styles himself a humorist (p. 9)—nevertheless follows a fairly conventional exegesis, calling Jonah "une parabole de l'histoire du salut" (p. 10). A. Rofé (1982: 119–20, 135–44; 1988: 159–66) distinguishes between the *exemplum* and the prophetic parable on the basis of historical rather than fictive settings. Jonah, he believes, belongs to the latter category and means to teach about the quality of God's justice.

Fable: Coppens (cited by Trible 1963: 143) terms Jonah an "apologue" (a more learned term for "fable"), by which he means something not too different from what Rofé suggests.

Mashal: Landes (1978), who offers a rich discussion on whether the Hebrew word *māšāl* can be applied to Jonah, ends up with a qualified yes:

> Structurally arranged to depict comparisons between Jonah and the other protagonists in the story, with the overall purpose of presenting paradigmatic types of conduct or ways of thinking for the readers either to reject or embrace, the Book of Jonah seems designed to function as a *māšāl*, a *māšāl* in the form of an example story (*Beispielerzählung*), whether or not the author may have had this term in mind when he wrote. (148–49)

[20] Overviews and catalogs of earlier opinions are available in Burrows 1970: 91–92; Trible 1963: 158–61; Alexander 1985: 38–40.

Didactic fiction: Alexander (1985: 40) labels it "didactic fiction." Stuart regards Jonah as a "sensational [emotionally stimulating], didactic, prophetic narrative" (1987: 435–37). L. Schmidt (1976: 113) calls it an *erzählte Dogmatik.* Wolff roams widely, finding satire in Jonah 1, caricature in Jonah 2 and heavy irony in Jonah 4. He suggests that the book is an "ironically didactic novella" (1986: 84–85). É. Levine (1984) thinks Jonah is a philosophical tractate in which a narrator lets us choose between two equally cogent positions: that of Jonah, which is that evil must be punished, and that of God, which is that penitents might be forgiven. And Fáj (1974: see 328, 345) locates Jonah within Stoic philosophy and turns to its logic to resolve "the paradox of the 'false' divine message."

Allegory and Jonah.

You are laughing? If the name is changed, the story told is about YOU. (Horace, *Satires* 1.1.69)

An allegory—wherein information is given meanings imported from other sources—can be read into any literary work, with only common sense and good taste to control the imagination.[21] Nonetheless, we must distinguish between an allegory, *originally structured* as such by its writer—Spenser's *Faerie Queene* or Bunyan's *Pilgrim's Progress*—and one that is merely *read as such* by its interpreters. Moreover, a piece of literature may include allegorical passages, whether they are originally so conceived or may only be plausibly read as such.[22]

Especially during the past century, many Jonah scholars have favored reading the whole book as an allegory of Israel's postexilic tribulation. They have failed to convince primarily because they assume that the complete tale was originally conceived as such, and secondarily because their interpretations are singularly bound to Israel's historical experience. By matching characters and details in Jonah consistently with what they regard as being the prevailing historical context, they came up with eccentric readings in which even the *qiqayon* plant had a human analogue (in this case, Zerubbabel). To my mind it is an

[21] There are almost as many definitions, elaborations, classifications, and subdivisions of allegory as there are literary critics willing to tackle the problem of figurative language. J. Rosenberg's recent volume (1986) adopts a particularly elastic definition of allegory; yet his first chapter, "The Question of Biblical Allegory," is itself a rewarding reflection on the value of reading a single text on many levels. Bruns 1987 is a fine overview, which distinguishes among allegory, *symbolon,* and *hyponoia.*

[22] The history of Song of Songs interpretation is an excellent biblical example of the last category. I have elsewhere argued that almost every major explanation of this text has depended on the venerable allegorical readings of the rabbis and church fathers (1979; 1985a).

unreasonable assumption that the perspective of the Jonah allegorist has to be limited to history, and, at that, the little *we* know of Israel's postexilic history.[23]

Such criticisms might be blunted were it conceded that Jonah is not an allegory, but that it gives opportunity to allegorize. If we were to operate under this assumption, it would be necessary neither to establish equivalences rigorously throughout the narrative nor to recreate historical conditions obtaining at the time of its composition; for the allegory would be operating on the interpretive, but not necessarily on the compositional, level. This is exactly what is at stake when the New Testament equates Jonah's three-day stay in the fish's belly with Christ's experience in the Netherworld (passages cited in section VII), and when the Zohar (quoted above) reads Jonah's first chapter as an allegory of the soul's trials and tribulations.

In the COMMENTS to section XI, I suggest that God's allusion to the fragility of the *qîqāyôn's* life cycle (4:10) mirrors the fleeting life allotted to human beings. In this sense the plant's destiny can be deemed an allegory of human existence. A more elaborate allegory may be also read into the fate of Jonah's storm-tossed ship. In the INTRODUCTORY REMARKS to section II, I showed that sea voyages, tempests, and shipwrecks inspired lessons linking the fate of nations to the delinquency of its leaders. They also provided materials for constructing allegories regarding the health of a state. The "Ship of State," as this manifestation of the allegory is labeled, was known widely and spanned millennia. It is tersely recalled in a simile of Abdu-Kheba, ruler of Jerusalem during the Amarna period (EA 288), "I have become like a ship in the midst of the sea!"[24] Israel, whose prophets Hosea, Amos, Isaiah, and Ezekiel knew how to use allegory well, found occasions to weave the "Ship of State" into its literature. Thus, we find Ezekiel embedding it in his famous oracle against Tyre (chapter 27). But it is most impressively recalled in Ps 107:23–30, a paean to the goodness of God's grace that I cite as epigraph to section III.

The "Ship of State" remained a favored literary device among the Jews of the Roman period, as is obvious from 4 Macc 7:1–3: "Like an outstanding pilot, indeed, [is] the reason of our father Eleazar, steering the vessel of piety on the sea of passions, though buffeted by the threats of the tyrant and swamped by the swelling waves of torture, in no way swerved the rudder of piety until he sailed

[23] These theories are carefully reviewed by Trible 1963: 153–58. See also Burrows 1970: 89–90. P. R. Ackroyd is in the minority among contemporary scholars in advocating an allegorical interpretation of Jonah (1968: 244–45): "The possibility that the book of Jonah contains an elaborate allegory of the exile—Jonah equals the people, the fish equals Babylon—appears in some respects to do violence to the directness with which the message of the book is given. Yet it is difficult to avoid the impression that the experience of the Jewish people in the exile was in part responsible for that particular representation of their true place in the purpose of God which this little book sets out."

[24] Quoted from *ANET*^{3} 488–89.

into the haven of deathless victory" (cited from Charlesworth 1985: 552). Church fathers read Jonah 1 as allegorizing the fate of humankind. A well-known manifestation typologized Jonah as Christ and the shipmates who cast him seaward as unreconstructed Jews. But the "Ship of State" allegory was most highly prized in classical literature, with the poet Alcaeus of Lesbos (sixth century B.C.E.) providing us with the earliest preserved example.[25] In its model version, the "Ship of State" required the following elements: a ship, representing the state; a helmsman, symbolizing its leader; and bad nautical conditions, giving occasion for the poet's observations and warnings. Sailors, who symbolized the people, might react in chorus, alerting or responding to specific national crises. It is worth noting here that the "Ship of State" allegory was not commonly read as a *roman à clef;* that is, readers did not find it necessary to make specific equations with living prototypes in order fully to appreciate its symbolism and implication (W. S. Anderson 1966: 89–90).[26]

[25] On christological readings of Jonah 1 featuring the "Ship of State" allegory, see Duval 1973, 2: 602–9. On Greek manifestations of the allegory, consult the succinct overview of Page, 1955: 179–97; with bibliography. The major study of the topic is J. Kahlmeyer's, 1934, especially pp. 39ff.

[26] To illustrate the pervasive, ubiquitous, and ageless power of the "Ship of State" imagery, I cite here "Arion," a brief poem by Pushkin taken from p. 59 of *The Bronze Horseman: Selected Poems of Alexander Pushkin* (translated and introduced by D. M. Thomas, New York: Viking Press, 1982):

> There were many of us on the ship;
> Some were tightening the sail,
> Others were plunging the powerful
> Oars into the deep
> Waters. Leaning calmly on the tiller,
> Our skilful helmsman steered the loaded bark
> In silence; and I—full of carefree faith—
> I sang to the sailors . . . Billows
> Were suddenly whipped up by a storm . . .
> Both helmsman and sailor perished!
> —Only I, the mysterious singer,
> Cast ashore by the storm,
> Still sing my former hymns, and dry
> My wet clothes in the sun, beneath a rock.

Readers of many backgrounds and interests can enjoy this poem: they can easily deem it an allegory of Pushkin's perception of his own intellectual (or spiritual) growth; they can value it as a clever adaptation of the classical legend of Arion, a legendary muse who similarly survived the cold seas; they can read it biographically, as testimony of relief upon surviving the failed Decembrist coup in which Pushkin was heavily implicated. If the last interpretation is favored, the "Helmsman," "sailor," even "bark" could be de-

Because storms were commonly used as settings for political allegory, the one in Jonah readily invites a similar inspection. It must be stated that what follows is but one possible reading of the allegory and that the episode in Jonah 1 would begin at v 4, when God creates such obvious difficulties that the ship itself—personified, as is common to "Ship of State" accounts—expects to crack up. Allegorists would not need to frame a specific time period to equate the ship with Israel as a corporate identity; for it would be enough to evoke any troubled period in order to make the allegory meaningful. The sailors and their behavior would be typical of Hebrews who turn to every resort but the correct one when trouble hits home. In such circumstances, the prophets among them would be approached only as a last measure.

I am especially encouraged to develop such a reading when inspecting the role of the helmsman. It can be noted that his appearance in Jonah 1 is restricted to a line (v 6) that, while seemingly superfluous to the development of the narrative, is crucial to the requirements of the "Ship of State" concept. The helmsman, therefore, is any leader who approaches a prophet because he is at a loss to discover the real reason behind God's anger. Because this leader leaves it up to the prophet to remedy the situation, the prophet becomes central in this negotiation between God and his people. When the prophet reveals the correct procedure, however, Israel and its leaders may judge it to be outlandish, and at first they may refuse to accept the painful consequences. When, after much soul searching, the Hebrews (in the guise of sailors in chorus) accept their burden, they will be able to declare, "Indeed you are the Lord, and whatever you desire, you accomplish" (v 14), for then they will have found God ready to be merciful. It is a rather comforting lesson, all in all.

Character Roles

Sailors and Ninevites. Although the sailors and the Ninevites are not the prime focus of the narrator and can therefore exist nameless in the tale, they nevertheless receive a surprisingly nuanced portrayal. This is especially so when we recognize that the representation of the sailors mutually complements and reciprocally reinforces the portraiture of the Ninevites. A few illustrations are in order.

From the tempest's onslaught until its sudden cessation, the sailors remain on stage. The scene aboard ship is pandemonium, from heaven shifting to the sea, to the ship (personified), to the sailors, to Jonah. In consonance with commonly shared opinions regarding the onset of storms, the sailors know that divine ire is the cause. Still, they follow traditional and time-tested measures:

---

coded by reviewing the list of Pushkin's companions who were exterminated, jailed, or exiled.

they pray to the gods even as they follow pragmatic measures. At this stage, there is no reason to think them ready to acknowledge the presence of a guilty party among them. Within the confines of chapter 1, the helmsman's address to Jonah has no future; for Jonah does not do as asked. But his reflection on the prospects for divine salvation ("Up! invoke your god; perhaps god himself will intercede on our behalf so that we may not perish") proves justified and will be imitated by the king of Nineveh. While these sentiments expressed in extremis are familiar enough from Scripture, it does not hurt at all for Israel to read that foreigners in opposite corners of the earth arrive independently at this powerful truth. Even so, the narrator is not pleased just to hear venerable Hebrew convictions echo in the mouths of the helmsman and the king of Nineveh; rather, he uses the repetition of these beliefs as a psychological bridge between the events aboard ship and those at Nineveh. The trauma aboard ship becomes a subtext that clarifies and explains the Ninevites' behavior and thus serves to render slightly more persuasive their instant turn to God when a single foreigner utters the briefest of verdicts (see the COMMENTS to section VIII).

By casting lots, the sailors eventually discover that Jonah is the cause of their troubles. That in the midst of a tempest they would politely pose a series of questions (not all of which can be of immediate benefit to them) obviously retards the tale's thrust; that the sailors would ask Jonah, the designated guilty party, to instruct them on the way to behave, certainly tests our credulity. In the COMMENTS to section III, I suggest reasons why the narrative sustains well such flaws; here, I want it additionally recognized that these moments in which formalities triumph over terror are carried over into chapter 3, thus justifying to those who demand narrative realism why the Ninevites lack elemental curiosity about the visiting doomsayer.

The sailors' inability to accept Jonah's proposed solution—to pitch him overboard—leads them to lose their cunning: they try to row ashore when navigational experience over centuries has taught mariners to remain in open sea during a storm (see the COMMENTS in section IV). The narrator is being especially clever here, for centuries of prophetic experience should have also taught Jonah that escaping God's burden is beyond possibility. These two incidents, in which Jonah and the sailors try to avert unpleasant choices, reinforce each other and serve to bolster an important contribution of the book of Jonah: God's will is to be obeyed even when it is beyond human understanding.

When the sailors find peace of mind, they are so impressed by the remarkable turnabout that they make vows and offer sacrifices. This happy ending (as far as it concerns the sailors) is sufficient comment on divine mercy: even when they fail to fulfill divine will, individuals may yet be given a new opportunity to mend their ways. While this observation will serve us well when Jonah sinks into the fish's gullet, it is especially relevant to the Ninevites' own repentance. Their instantaneous turn toward piety does not come as a surprise to anyone, except perhaps Jonah. Impressive though they may seem, the Ninevites' ensuing penitential acts (supplications, wearing of sackcloth, wallowing in dust, fasting and thirsting) nevertheless omit at least one feature that seems justified under similar circumstances: the offering of sacrifice (possibly also the making of vows; see the NOTES to 3:5–6). The memory of readers, however, can rectify this omission by transporting precisely these operations from what is told in the last verse of chapter 1.

Jonah and "Third-Person" Prophets. In Jonah literature, it is common for scholars to wonder whether the Jonah son of Amittay of Kings is also featured in the book of Jonah. The issue needs to be drawn with more nuance. If, on the one hand, we ask whether the ancient Hebrews distinguished between two similarly named personalities, then "no!" must be the clear answer. "Jonah" and "Amittay" are singular names in the Hebrew Bible, and it is beyond probability that in Scripture two different individuals would bear the same names *and* patronyms.[27] While it is possible that 2 Kings 14 and the book of Jonah once circulated with main characters of different names, the fact that "Jonah ben Amittay" occurs in both contexts forces us to assume that Scripture knowingly chose to link the respective narratives. (See also above, p. 116.)

If, however, we ask whether contemporary scholarship needs to distinguish between the Kings and Jonah protagonists, then we quickly reach an impasse because there is no extrabiblical basis by which to argue the matter either way. Whereas most scholars today judge the Kings material to be earlier than what is found in the book of Jonah, H. Winckler (1900: 262) once championed the reverse: the Jonah of the Minor Prophets inspired an insertion into 2 Kings. In view of my remarks (see the INTRODUCTION) on the difficulty of dating the traditions about Jonah (as distinct from the equally vexing issue of dating the version now before us), we need not be dogmatic about the direction the influence took. We may instead inspect the roles played by a group of prophets who, like Jonah, have not left us their own written account of their prophecies.

Although the term *nābî*ʾ is never applied to Jonah in the book bearing his name, it would not be wise to deny him prophetic status, for other prophets, whose credentials are beyond dispute, are similarly treated (Micah is another example). But Jonah is not a first-person prophet, that is, one whose pronouncements are recorded (for example, Isaiah, Jeremiah, Hosea); rather, he belongs to the category of *named* prophets about whom stories are told. Here is a brief list of such prophets, divided into four categories:[28] (1) Prophets whose narratives

[27] But see 1 Esdr 9:23, which substitutes *Iō(a)nas* where Ezra 10:23 has Eliezer. For another link between the two Jonahs, see the NOTES to 1:9.

[28] This is not an exhaustive list; I give only the prophets whose names are recalled in scripture, and I do not deal with those mentioned in the Pentateuch (for example, Abraham [Gen 20:7], Aaron [Exod 7:1], Miriam [Exod 15:20], Moses [Deut 18:15, 34:10

are integrated into the biographies of United Monarchy rulers; (2) prophets about whom at most two activities are recorded, whether they lived in Israel or in Judah; (3) prophets whose activities are recalled in a series of episodes; and (4) prophets, seers, and "men of God" who are found in Chronicles but not in Kings.

Examples of the first category are Samuel, Gad, and Nathan.

Category 2 can be further divided into prophets of the Kingdom of Israel and those of the Kingdom of Judah. Among the former are (a) Ahijah of Shiloh, who, in a balanced diptych, predicts the inauguration and the demise of the Northern Kingdom (1 Kgs 11:29–39; 14:1–18); (b) Jehu son of Hanani, who foretells an evil end for the usurper Baasha of Israel (1 Kgs 16:7–12) and, in 2 Chr 19:2–3 (see also 20:34), berates Jehoshaphat of Judah. The chronological gap between the two events is large, but not impossible to surmount; (c) Micaiah son of Imlah, who, confronting the false prophet Zedekiah, predicts defeat for the allies Ahab and Jehoshaphat (1 Kgs 22:8–28 = 2 Chr 18:7–27). But v 28 implies that this Micaiah may have been identified with the prophet Micah; and, of course, (d) Jonah, son of Amittay, who lived during the reign of Jeroboam II (2 Kgs 14:25). Among the prophets of the Kingdom of Judah are (a) Shemaiah, the man of God, who early in the reign of Rehoboam warns him not to declare war against Israel (1 Kgs 11:21–23 = 2 Chr 11:1–4). In 2 Chr 12:5–8 an additional Shemaiah tradition is placed at the end of Rehoboam's reign, in which the prophet predicts Shishak's destruction of Jerusalem. Upon God's change of mind, however, Shemaiahu (*sic*) foretells a partial remission of the sentence; (b) Huldah, wife of Shallum, who predicts dire happenings to Judah, but kind treatment of Josiah's remains (2 Kgs 22:14–20 = 2 Chr 34:22–28); (c) Shemaiah, the Nehelamite, a false prophet who tries to frustrate Jeremiah's labors (Jer 29:24–32); (d) Uriah, son of Shemaiah, whom Jehoiakim has killed for prophesying against Jerusalem (Jer 26:20–24); and (e) Hananiah, son of Azzur, a false prophet who predicts rosy days for Jerusalem (Jeremiah 28, reign of Zedekiah).[29]

Included in the third category would be the tales about Elijah and Elisha, which occasionally duplicate each other, reporting supernatural events and feats (1 Kgs 17:8–24; 18:46; 2 Kgs 2:7–25; practically everything said about Elisha), encounters with God (1 Kings 19), and travels abroad to fulfill God's wishes (1 Kgs 19:15; 2 Kgs 8:7–15).

In the fourth category, the following prophets seem to appear and disappear

---

and see Num 11:25 and 27]. I may add that the only named prophet in the book of Judges is Deborah, *ʾēšet lappîdôt*, a designation that probably means "torch-bearing woman" (that is, a mantic; but see the designation of Huldah, 2 Kgs 22:14). On Balaam, see below.

[29] Noadiah, the prophetess, is mentioned as an opponent of Nehemiah (Neh 8:14).

at the convenience of the narrator:[30] (a) Azariah, son of Oded, in the reign of Asa (2 Chr 15:1–7, but not in 1 Kings 15). In 2 Chr 15:8 the same prophecy is assigned to "Oded the prophet"; (b) Hanani, a seer during the reign of Asa of Judah (2 Chr 16:7–10, but not in 1 Kings 16), whose activities are linked to those of his better known son, the prophet Jehu; (c) Jahaziel, son of Zechariah, during the reign of Jehoshaphat (2 Chr 20:14–19, but not in 1 Kings 22); (d) Eliezer, son of Dodavahu of Mareshah, during the time of Jehoshaphat (2 Chr 20:37, but not in 2 Kgs 22:47–49); (e) Zechariah, son of Jehoiada, the priest, murdered by Joash (2 Chr 24:20–22, but not in 2 Kings 12); and (f) Zechariah, "instructor in the *visions* of God," during the reign of Uzziah (2 Chr 26:5, but not in 2 Kings 15).

The Jonah of Kings fits nicely in the second category, where nonwriting prophets are introduced by names and patronyms to act out comparatively limited roles. But what distinguishes Jonah from them (indeed from the prophets in the other categories) is that he is assigned an unusual task: immediately after Jeroboam son of Joash is declared an evildoer in the sight of God, Jonah comes to predict for him the most glorious reign ever granted a king of Israel![31] This mission is deemed so startling that it was found necessary to enter an explanation that satisfactorily rationalizes Israel's survival but inadequately justifies Jeroboam's triumphs: God did not punish Israel as it deserved because "the Lord observed how very bitter was Israel's plight, with absolutely no ruler, no one to rescue Israel" (v 27). These two features are clues why Jonah is also a protagonist in the book by his name: there, too, Jonah is sent on a mission that eventually gives Nineveh a reprieve from destruction; and there, too, the reason God gives for being merciful (4:11) is not totally satisfying (see Clements 1975: 23–24 and the COMMENTS to section XI).

The remarkable missions assigned to the two Jonahs—one to go to Jeroboam II, the other to go to Nineveh—find arresting analogues also in the assignments given to the prophets I list in category 3. Elisha fulfills a forecast uttered to Elijah (1 Kgs 19:15–16) by traveling to Damascus (2 Kgs 8:7–15) and by encouraging Hazael to usurp the throne. Hazael becomes one of Israel's most savage oppressors, and Elisha sheds tears even as he fulfills God's order. Nineveh, too, eventually preyed on Israel and Judah; but only in rabbinic traditions does Jonah

[30] The examples gathered in this category suggest to me that Hebrew writers found it possible to go beyond their sources to sharpen certain points in the narratives. Because we do not have the sources used to compile the books of Kings, we cannot tell whether the same impulse obtained when prophets are mentioned once or twice (category 2).

[31] The passage is quoted in the COMMENTS to section I. As is noted by many commentators, Amos's harsher criticism of Jeroboam may be more appropriate to the context (7:9, 10–11).

lament his role in Nineveh's survival.[32] The potential link with the episodic tales about prophets of eighth-century Israel allows me to suggest that Jonah's many adventures may be informed by the same kind of creativity as produced the cycles of Elijah and Elisha. The respective narratives share an interest in reporting supernatural events and feats, direct encounters with God, and (involuntary) travels beyond Israel's frontiers to carry God's message.[33] It should therefore not be at all surprising when occasionally language and context in Jonah duplicate what we read about Elijah (see NOTES and COMMENTS to sections X and XI). But I cannot say whether the Jonah narratives share these affinities with the Elijah/Elisha cycles because they were written at the same time and under the same circumstances or because whoever "wrote" Jonah consciously imitated the Elijah/Elisha episodic style.

Jonah as "Comic Dupe."

> . . . mais les voraces ont complètement mangé et devoré les coriaces.
> (A. Jarry, *Ubu Roi* 5.1)

What distinguishes the various legends regarding "third-person" prophets is not merely the tasks they are assigned and the success with which they accomplish them, but also the way they interact with God. Jonah's own relationship with God undergoes subtle changes within the confines of a very few lines (see the COMMENTS to section IX). One feature remains constant, however: Jonah is never taken into God's confidence, not at the beginning of the book and not at its end. Rather, he is left to guess from events how to interpret God's motives and reasoning. This condition is most sharply realized in chapter 3, when Jonah is to tell Nineveh, "Forty days more, and Nineveh overturns" (*ʿôd ʾarbāʿîm yôm wenînewēh nehpāket*, 3:4). In the NOTES and COMMENTS to sections VIII–XI, I try to demonstrate that the ambiguity in the language is deliberate and, in fact, is a major plot element.[34]It may be opportune to summarize my observations

[32] This conjunction of undeserved augury and the naming of Jonah son of Amittay may have been in the mind of Budde (1904: 228) when he (mis)labeled the book of Jonah a midrash on 2 Kings 14. E. Nielsen (1979: 502) follows suit. Others have proposed to read Jonah as a midrash (see Alexander 1985: 37 n.5): on Exod 34:6 (focus on Jonah's confession); on Jer 18:8 (focus on God's change of mind); on Obadiah (answering why Edom survives; König 1906: 748); on Amos 7:9, 11 (R. Coote, cited by Stuart 1987: 433).

[33] Elisha's travel to Damascus and the role he played in Hazael's usurpation are no less remarkable than Jonah's accomplishment in Nineveh. Neither activity can be confirmed by independent sources. For the evidence about Damascus, see Pitard 1987: 132–38.

[34] In case one wonders why this ambiguity is never applied to the story of Sodom and Gomorrah, it is good to recall that Jonah 3:4 is unique in applying the *N* stem of the verb *hāpak* to cities. Hence, it alone permits mining the potential play on meaning which this

here: Jonah (and the Ninevites for that matter) regarded the phrase as predicting doom only; but God alone knew that it also forecast Nineveh's change of heart. This type of paronomasia is fairly common in non-Israelite narratives regarding oracles (recall those emanating from Delphi and Dodona), and it must have amused an audience to have a prophet who does not fully fathom his own predictions.[35]

From God's perspective, Jonah fulfills his mission whether Nineveh crumbles or finds spiritual renewal, which explains why God cannot be dissatisfied with Jonah's activities once the prophet reaches Nineveh. From Jonah's perspective, however, his charge was to declare doom only. When Nineveh survives and he is not commissioned to prophesy weal—as Isaiah had been (see the COMMENTS to section X)—Jonah sulks. Because he never grasps the double-edged meaning behind the message he communicates, Jonah perceives God's change of mind as a breach of proper etiquette obtaining between God and prophets, so he feels misused. I have sought to suggest that it is this perceived indignity, and not Nineveh's deliverance, that drives Jonah to grieve and complain.

As Jonah delivers his *apologia* (4:2), however, a major shift in narrative focus occurs. No longer is the debate about wicked cities and the messages that must be carried to them, but about human pride, divine freedom, and the breadth of God's mercy. The immediate consequence of the miraculously sprouting *qîqāyôn* is a reversal of Jonah's self-doubts, for it allows him to imagine that God still favors him; but the plant plays a yet more pivotal role in that God uses it to forge a subtly layered lesson about egoism and its frequent complement, indifference to others.

In all of this, God uses Jonah to make points beyond the prophet's immedi-

---

stem allows. Discussions about the destruction of Sodom and Gomorrah uniformly rely on the *G* stem and on derivative nouns.

[35] See also Bickerman 1976: 61 n. 89. I analyze a particularly striking example embedded in a Mari dream report (1984c: 286–87). Well known are the series of Delphic oracles with double-edged vocabulary that Croesus consistently misinterprets (Herodotus 1.23ff.; see Flacelière's handy volume on the subject). For biblical examples, see König 1900: 10–11; Bühlmann and Scherer 1973: 88–89. There is an interesting manifestation of this phenomenon in Huldah's prophecy regarding Josiah and his kingdom (2 Kgs 22:14–20; see above). She says that Judah shall be destroyed (vv 16–17), but that, because of his piety, Josiah is to be buried "in peace"; furthermore, he shall not witness his land's destruction (vv 19–20). This message may have so emboldened Josiah that he opposed Necho at Megiddo, where he was slain; 2 Kgs 23:29–30. (The Chronicler offers a pious explanation for Josiah's behavior.) As predicted, Josiah is buried in Jerusalem (possible pun on "peace"?), and he also never witnesses his kingdom's fall. With regard to ambiguity in biblical narratives, which is currently a favorite topic in biblical interpretation, see M. Sternberg, who offers a nuanced categorization of the many ways ambiguity enriches the reading of Scripture; 1987: index, s.v. "ambiguity."

ate fate. Jonah comes to be a tool by which to drive home profound ideas as well as homespun truths. As such, he represents the *comic dupe,* a character (by no means always humorous) that is still known to Middle Eastern folklore under the Turkish name Nasreddin Hodja or as Arabic Juha.[36] In Scripture this character role is assigned to at least two other nonwriting messengers of God: one of them is unnamed, but his tale occupies 1 Kings 13; the other is Balaam, son of Beor, whose experiences are recounted in Numbers 22–24.

In the first of these stories, 1 Kings 13 relates how a "man of God" comes to Bethel. He predicts the advent of Josiah and displays many proofs of his authentic powers. We later learn (v 8) that the "man of God" was operating under strict instruction on how to conduct himself. When a prophet from Israel, also unnamed, falsely cites new directives from God and persuades the "man of God" to alter his activities, the latter is killed by a lion, but his corpse miraculously is left whole to receive a proper burial. His deceiver asks to share the same tomb when he dies. The story is set at the beginning of the reign of Jeroboam I, but finds its completion at the tail end of Josiah's reign, about three centuries later (2 Kgs 23:16–18). When its two segments are brought together, the tale becomes a paradigm for the intertwined fates of Israel and Judah. When viewed by itself, 1 Kings 13 illustrates what happens when prophets modify a divine order (compare vv 9 and 17) or slacken in their zeal before thoroughly fulfilling their missions. The tale also warns against easy acceptance of contradictory prophecies, especially if conveyed by seemingly unimpeachable instruments. Yet, even as prophets fail, the story implies, God will continue to care for their dignity.[37]

Already in antiquity, Origen connected Jonah and Balaam, because both were reluctant prophets and because they were charged with messages to nations not their own.[38] The traditions about Balaam that are preserved in Hebrew

[36] Hodja/Juha tales range all over folklore typologies, predominantly, fitting into the trickster category. A holy man, Hodja can also be on the other side of the joke, and his example drives home a worthy lesson. There are examples in which heaven plays games with Hodja. Collections of such tales are found in Barnham 1924, but the most thorough treatment is still that of Wesselski 1911. Dundes gives a bibliography on the comic dupe in 1965: 400–2. Mather (see above) and Rauber (below, n. 41) are two scholars who arrive at similar formulations by taking dissimilar paths.

[37] On this tale and its contribution to the problem of false prophecy, see Crenshaw 1971: 41–46. Somewhat complementary is the lesson delivered by the tightly drawn narrative about the prophet who makes seemingly absurd demands of other prophets (1 Kgs 20:35–36). This incident is itself used as background for lambasting Ahab's peacemaking with Ben-Hadad of Damascus.

[38] Duval 1973: 194–97 n. 107. The *midrash rabbah* on Exod 4:3 assembles Moses, Balaam, Jeremiah, and Jonah in the category of reluctant prophets (ibid. 89 n. 95). Jonah and Balaam share a mixed evaluation from later traditional exegetes, Jewish and Chris-

Scripture are multiple and complex.[39] Those collected in Numbers 22–24 themselves are woven from segments of probably independent origins that link prose and poetry, realism and fancy. In Num 22:7–14, an enemy of Israel asks a Gentile prophet to go to a foreign land in order to prophesy against God's chosen. The prophet, consulting with the god of the enemy, refuses to accept his charge. Note how the *mise en scène* here is as unlikely as the opening verses in Jonah, where a prophet is commissioned to forewarn a nation that will bring an end to Israel. In Num 22:15–21, an enemy of Israel again asks a Gentile prophet to go to a foreign land in order to prophesy against God's chosen. The prophet consults with his enemy's god and is given leave to speak that god's message, *if he is approached by men once more.* In Num 22:22–35, without awaiting for a proper omen the prophet makes his way. An angel is ready to strike him, but he is saved by his wondrously talking donkey. *The prophet learns his lesson* and continues his mission. In Num 22:36 to 24:35, Balaam finally appears before Balak and, on two successive occasions, blesses Israel (involuntarily) using God's own words. When asked to curse Israel for the third time, Balaam comes to accept his fate. His subsequent responses are equally complimentary toward Israel, albeit drawn from his own inspiration. Balaam completes his mission and returns home, empty of the honors that Balak was to grant him; but he becomes a wiser prophet, having learned to recognize the greatness of Israel and of its God.

Jonah as "Comic Hero."

> The reasonable man adapts himself to the world: the unreasonable one persists in trying to adapt the world to himself. Therefore all progress depends on the unreasonable man.[40]

While Jonah serves nicely as a comic dupe by which to affirm God's omnipotence, his personality is by no means self-effacing. Jonah's character actually differs markedly from the better-known paradigm in which, after mild protests, a prophet succumbs to God's will. Although some prophets will sometimes feel abandoned by God or will occasionally denounce the grinding demands God

tian. On Balaam, much has been written recently because of the discoveries at Deir Alla of accounts that mention him in obscure contexts. An accessible evaluation with bibliography is Hackett 1986. The "first Combination" of the Deir Alla text receives an integrated treatment in V. Sasson 1985.

[39] Deuteronomy 23:5–6, Josh 24:9–10, and Mic 6:5 stress only Balaam's readiness to act as an anti-Israel hireling. Numbers 31:8 and Josh 13:22 record that he was executed at Midian.

[40] Bernard Shaw, *Man and Superman,* from "The Revolutionist's Handbook," s.v. "Reason."

makes on them, none but Jonah experiences as many emotional fluctuations within so brief a narrative. Jonah keeps on reacting to God's activities, quickly and pungently: he protests his mission with his feet (chapter 1) only to surrender totally when caught (chapter 1); he fulfills God's order with alacrity (chapter 3), but then reproaches God when feeling slighted; he rejoices when feeling justified, but becomes suicidal a few hours later (chapter 4). Yet, throughout these episodes in which Jonah's feelings ride a roller coaster, we do not sense that Jonah ever acts out of character, even if we do not always sympathize with his reactions. This consistency in portrayal no doubt serves to unify the story; but it also fixes in our mind a remarkable trait about Jonah: he simply will not allow heaven to dictate moves in total disregard of his own dignity, and it is for this reason that we may call him a "comic hero."[41] In this light, the way chapter 4 ends is particularly suggestive: Jonah does not answer God because the narrator cannot let him rip into the weaknesses of God's logic (see the COMMENTS in section XI).

Jonah has two other traits that are worth noting: wherever he goes, Jonah brings bedlam in his wake and raises clamor, while paradoxically, Jonah remains aloof from other human beings.[42] Despite the crowd scenes in chapters 3 and 4,

[41] R. M. Torrance has this to say about the comic hero (1978: viii): "In the resulting conflict, or *agôn,* he proves himself a hero by courageous perseverance, resourceful intelligence, and a more or less conscious acceptance of the inevitable risks that he chooses to run in his willfully comic challenge to the deadly seriousness of his world." D. F. Rauber (1970) treats Jonah as a travesty (in the category's original sense), in which important truths are disguised as high comedy. He views Jonah as a prophet who develops from *schlemiel* ("born loser") to *mensch,* an admiring term applied to solid persons: "[Jonah] has a kind of twisted independence of mind and a great integrity of spirit; he is well worth listening to." Rauber's study is marred (some might say enriched) by a penchant to "Yiddishize" Jonah into a Hasidic tale, replete with warm-hearted but gruff-voiced personalities. See already Paul Goodman's play, *Jonah* (1965).

[42] On the loneliness of Jonah, see Fisch 1986: 217–20. It is tempting to follow this line of inquiry and offer a full-fledged psychological evaluation of Jonah. I resist it, but mention studies by other scholars who are not as reticent. Erich Fromm reads the tale as symbolic of the hero's inner experiences. Fromm's analysis is repeated by many of the scholars I am about to mention; pp. 22–23 of *The Forgotten Language* (New York: Holt, Rinehart and Winston, 1951), cited in Preminger and Greenstein 1986: 469–70. H. H. Fingert (1954) offers a classic Freudian Oedipal reading, "This prayer of Jonah's appears to be a symbolic representation of the childhood fantasy of being in the mother's womb" (p. 59). J. More (1970: 7) also gives a Freudian interpretation, but accentuates another dimension of the problem: "I therefore believe that Jonah's wish to destroy the people of Nineveh may be viewed as being determined, at least in part, by infantile sibling rivalry. Nineveh would, in this context, be the 'bad' mother. . . . God, Jonah's father-figure, is the God of Nineveh too." A. D. Cohen (1972: 171) presents a clinical analysis of Jonah's mental state at the opening of the fourth chapter: "Jonah's behavior represents a clear

he remains easily distinguishable: on ship, by not participating in efforts to placate the gods; in Nineveh, by disappearing as soon as he announces God's message. He also keeps his distance from God. In the second chapter—when in the belly of the fish—and even in the fourth chapter—when alone with his maker—we never sense the ease in relationship and the intimate rapport which we know to obtain among God, patriarchs, and many prophets.[43] Although at one point Jonah eventually tries to excuse his earlier conduct, God never feels the need to do the same when Nineveh is spared. On neither side, therefore, is there introspection, candid reassessment of positions, or a willingness to narrow differences. Instead, baroque situations replace reasoned dialogues as arenas in which to air the issues that matter most to God and Jonah. Escape toward Tarshish becomes a plausible alternative to declaring doom upon Nineveh; the fish's belly becomes a proper atmosphere in which to learn penitence; mischievous divine tricks on nature become the best vehicles by which to teach enduring lessons; wicked cities are spared because of a vast and vastly ignorant population.

God. In Jonah, God is never the distant participant, providentially guiding and sustaining the destiny of human beings; rather, he actively shapes the development of events and readily enters into *tête à tête* with his prophet. He is there to begin the tale and initiate its action by sending Jonah to unworthy Nineveh; he is also there to end the book with an object sermon. Even as Jonah hies into the ship's bowel, it suits God's purpose to let him wallow in a false sense of security; and soon Jonah learns that there is no escaping a divinely imposed burden.

This readiness to toy with mortals is a conspicuous vision the narrator has about Jonah's God; the ship, the sailors, the fish, the Ninevites, even nature itself are all called upon to demonstrate this attribute. We perceive one side of this trait, hard-edged and harsh, as God relentlessly boosts terror on all but the guilty party aboard ship; we recover another of its facets, mocking, even sinister, as God repeats what once was a solicitous question ("Are you utterly dejected?") just after ruining the only joy he gives to Jonah. These examples of God's more

---

clinical picture of despair and, more fundamentally, of depression." The Lacocques (1981) are influenced by Fromm's reading (see the quotation prefacing this section). Ackerman (1981) flirts with Jungian archetypes that are less obvious in his latest discussion of Jonah (1987). And U. Steffen's book (1982) is an attractive and nicely illustrated introduction to Jonah symbolisms. It includes overviews of psychoanalytic readings of Jonah.

[43] I must quote from a letter of D. N. Freedman, "This intimacy that lies at the root of revealed religion defies and nullifies all attempts at philosophical theology and in the end makes biblical religion at once sublime and exceedingly primitive and anthropomorphic."

harmful manifestations (some have used the adjective "demonic") are by no means confined to Jonah, for we meet them under various guises throughout Scripture: in Genesis 4, when Cain is made jealous of his brother; in Exodus 4, when Moses is attacked on the road to Egypt; in Judges 9, when an "evil spirit" distances Abimelech from the Shechemites; in 1 Samuel 16 (and following chapters), when Saul helplessly witnesses his own disintegration; in 1 Kings 22, when a "lying spirit" steers Ahab and Jehosaphat to defeat; in Isaiah 37, when Sennacherib is sent home to be murdered; in Job, when its hero is crushed just so that God could win a bet.[44]

Yet, as the poet teaches, "the Lord does not reject forever; having punished harshly, he has compassion befitting his immense benevolence" (Lam 3:31–33). Accordingly, this toying trait is not constant throughout the narrative, but is interrupted by occasions on which God shows concern for those in terrible straits. Even as the sailors increasingly panic (see NOTES on *wayyîreʾû* of 1:5, 10, 16), signs abound that all will be well: the helmsman has an insight into the cause of the storm (v 6); Jonah is quickly singled out by cast lots, and through him God gives the sailors clues on how to behave. Two more wonders (vv 13 and 15) follow to demonstrate that God can be patient with individuals when they are groping for the truth. The remaining chapters contain similar evidence of God's concern: in dispatching a fish to save Jonah from drowning; in forewarning Nineveh; even in raising the plant as shade over a moody Jonah.

This kindly disposition to individuals is most sharply drawn in 4:7–11, where, after satisfying Jonah's personal insecurity with the role of a prophet, God brings back the issue of Nineveh's deliverance. It is not enough for Jonah to walk away from Nineveh having learned nothing that he did not know before (4:2); rather, Jonah's eyes must be opened to another dimension of God's mercy: whether people repent from sin is not the only criterion that God evaluates when granting forgiveness. God refuses to rehearse the vocabulary of mercy with which Jonah is armed and deliberately trivializes the causes that swayed him to pardon Nineveh's crime. As in Job, the relevant lesson is about the incapacity of mortals to understand, let alone to judge, their God.

[44] Crenshaw (1971: 77–90) discusses these and other occasions on which God either afflicts individuals or beguiles them toward their own destruction. One of his conclusions is that "in essence deception [on the part of God] is but a means of leading Israel to repentance or judgment, the purpose of which is salvation" (p. 90). Lindström offers the most recent full study of the relevant passages (1983). He finds scriptural arguments on the cause of evil to be complex and not always consistent. While the Hebrews did not blame God for all evil, they also did not ascribe it to powers beyond God.

LOOKING AHEAD

It is the nature of biblical scholarship that each generation of researchers draws upon issues vital to its own time and invests them in its reinterpretation of Hebraic culture and literature. In an age (such as ours) in which there are reassessments of inherited assumptions, some venerable opinions regarding Jonah will be deemed obsolete while many more will be molded to suit prevailing convictions. It should follow, therefore, that elucidating Jonah (indeed any biblical text) is a goal that can never be permanently or fully realized.

I believe that the fate to which I am assigning this gem from Scripture is appropriate to a book that disturbs the predictable roles and distinct beliefs with which the Bible has taught us to be comfortable. I make no claim that my present contributions deserve to endure longer than the proposals I have just criticized; accordingly, as I take leave of Jonah, I offer my best wishes to the next person who would pick up the many challenges of this occasionally irksome, but always provocative and tantalizing, little book.

INDEXES

N.B. Page numbering refers to beginning of discussion that may cover several succeeding pages.

INDEX of SUBJECTS

Address
  by God to Jonah, 286, 306, 308
  by Jonah to God, 276, 306
Allegory (in Scripture), 335 n19, 337
Anger
  Jonah's, 274, 297
Animals
  biblical narratives, 144
  gender, 155
  God's concern for, 314
  God speaking to, 219 n4, 220, 310
  near eastern lit., 144, 145
  repentance, 247, 254
  on ship, 139, 140

Constellations
  Cetus ("whale"), 222
  Columba ("dove"), 222

Dawn, 301, 302
Days, counting, 153, 157
  "3," 153
  "40," 233 n15, 234, 267
Distance (measure of), 230
Divine name
  foreigner's use, 104, 131, 261
  Jonah's use, 118, 138
  used by sailors, 98
  use in Jonah, 17, 93, 291
  with *ʾāman,* 243

Edict of king, 252, 256
  versions, 265

Fables, 335
Fish (in Jonah), 149
Forgiveness
  of gods, 242
  God's, 241, 296
  God's, of Nineveh, 235, 267
  God's, of Sodom, 235

God
  and the demonic, 350
  justice and mercy, 316–20

Idolatry, 197–99

Jaffa, 80
Jonah

  (*the person*)
  confession, 275, 296, 328
  death wish, 305, 317
  and forgiveness, 274 n7
  God's concern for, 316
  loneliness, 349 n42
  name, 68, 69, 86
  and prophecy, 15, 85, 126, 225, 235, 296, 342
  state of mind, 347, 349 n42, 350

  (*comparison with*)
  Balaam, 347
  Elijah, 285, 298
  Hodja/Juha, 347 n36
  Isaiah (narrative), 294
  Micah, 241 n6

  (*the book*)
  aramaisms, 22, 204
  audience, 334
  date, 27
  division criteria, 271
  English (trans.), 12, 13
  folklore, 151

genre, 16, 326
-allegory, 337 n21, 338, 340
-mashal, 336
-midrash, 345 n32
-parable, 335
-satire, 331, 333 n34, 334, 345, 346, 347
hapax legomena, 302 n3
humor, 331 n13
interpretations, 11, 12
narrator, 126, 328
"original" version, 116
placement in canon, 14
structure, 16, 191, 270, 276, 280, 290, 306, 317
style, 17
text, 288
texts and versions, 9, 14
theology, 24, 329, 332
unity, 19
use: in Church, 29
in Synagogue, 28, 225

(*the psalm*)
language, 202, 204
meter, 209
poetry, 161, 205, 207
and history, 203 n64
in prose, 205
relation to book, 17, 147, 165, 203, 206
relation to psalms, 207 n67
scholarly approaches, 209
structure, 168, 203, 208, 210
type, 202
use
in Qumran, 213
as talisman, 214

Lot (casting and function), 108

Netherworld. *See* Sheol
Nineveh
in dating Jonah, 21
geography, 289
and God's concern, 309, 315, 319
and God's judgement, 234, 236
history of, 71
kings, 242 n7, 246, 250
king in Jonah, 248
language, 232
name, 71
ninevites/sailors, 340
population, 311
repentance, 244, 257, 264, 266, 296, 315, 318, 346
size, 72, 228
times Jonah sent to N., 226

Oracles, 346 n35

Parables, 335 n19, 336
Plants, 291, 301, 307
Jonah's concern for, 317, 333, 338
Pluperfect (use of), 99, 148, 288
Poetry (Hebrew), 161
Prayer, 194
content of, 135
form of, 132, 134, 154
structure, 276
Prophets
false, 241 n6
varieties, 343

Qāl waḥōmēr, 217 n1

Repentance, 244
of God, 263, 294
national, 245
personal, 246
Right (and left), 314
Roles (of characters), 340

Sacrifice, 200
Sailors (and sailing), 340
ancient, 81
and God, 142, 157, 202
and Jonah, 141
lost at sea, 91
and Ninevites, 340
semitic words for, 97
Sheol, 188
rescue from, 191
"Ship of State," 229 n25–26, 338
Ships
cargo, 98
cargo, law of, 99
construction, 100
hierarchy aboard, 103
hired by Jonah, 83
Mediterranean, 81
sacrifice aboard, 139
sailing season, 82
size and variety, 81
storms, 91, 95, 98, 100
Sun, 303
Synesius's voyage, 81, 142 n20

Tarshish, 78
location, 79, 92
type of ship, 92
Tehom, 184
Time (passage of), 158, 226

Vows, 140

Wind, 303 n5–6, 304
Wordplay, 291, 301, 304, 312
onomatopoeia, 277
prosopopoeia, 96
visual, 318

Yom Kippur, 28, 82, 159 n1, 299 n1

INDEX of AUTHORS CITED

Modern and Contemporary
Aalders, G. C., 150
Ackerman, J. S., 155, 333
Ackroyd, P. R., 338 n23
Aejmelaeus, A., 194 n52
Alexander, T. D., 327 n8, 337, 345 n32
Allen, L. C., 17 n14, 22, 229 n8, 230, 257
Almbladh, K., 23, 83, *passim* in Commentary
Alter, R., 208
Andersen, F. I., 162
Antin, P., 10, 13 n7
Archer, G. L., 150
Auffret, P., 201

Barnett, R. D., 230
Barnham, H. D., 347 n36
Barthélemy, D., 10, *passim* in Commentary
Batto, B., 175 n15, 185
Benjamin, W., 12
Ben-Yosef, I. A., 151 n15
Bérard, V., 82 n7
Berlin, A., 294 n24, 297 n25, 325, 332
Bewer, J. A., 68, *passim* in Commentary
Bickerman, E. J., 234, 236
Blank, S. H., 336
Blenkinsopp, J., 26 n25, 121 n20, 170 n8, 232 n13
Bodine, W. R., 12 n6
Borger, R., 242 n7
Brongers, H. A., 277
Bruns, G. L., 337 n21
Budde, K., 10, 15, 227, 288, 345 n32
Burrows, M., 327 n8, 332
Butterworth, G., 309, 310

Casson, L., 82 n7
Charlesworth, J., 339
Charpin, D., *See* Durand, J.-M.
Chotzner, J., 331 n12
Christensen, D., 208
Clements, R. E., 324 n4, 344
Cohen, A. D., 349 n42
Cohen, C., 335 n17
Cohn, G. H., 19, 274 n8, 282
Cooper, A., 182 n24, 189 n41, 190
Cooper, J. S., 22 n20
Coot, R., 345 n32
Coppens, J., 336
Crenshaw, J. L., 347 n37, 351 n44
Cross, F. R., 175 n14, 179, 180, 187 n23, 210, 211

Dahood, M., 190 n45, 193
Delitzsch, F., *See* Keil, C. F.
Dundes, A., 347 n36
Durand, J.-M., 189 n39, 311 n14
Duval, Y.-M., 87, 246, 339 n25, 347 n38

Eliade, M., 325
Ellison, H. L., 180

Fáj, A., 337
Feuillet, A., 204, 327 n8
Fichman, J., 16
Field, F., 10
Fingert, H. H., 349 n42
Fisch, H., 349 n42
Fishbane, M., 308 n11
Frankena, R., 278
Freedman, D. N., 162, 175 n14, 208, 219 n4, 233 n15, 263, 319
Fretheim, T. E., 317 n23
Fromm, E., 349 n42

Garr, W. R., 209
Gaster, T. H., 188, 255
Gelston, A., 11
Ginzberg, L., 12, 244
Goitein, S. D., 76, 94
Good, E. M., 125, 127, 324
Goodman, P., 349 n41
Gordon, C. H., 225
Goshen-Gottstein, M., 11
Grayson, A. K., 311 n15
Greenberg, M., 131 n2, 142 n20, 190 n45, 194 n52
Grether, O., 67, 68
Gruber, M. I., 274 n18, 282

Halperin, D. J., 214 n74, 323 n1
Halpern, B., 235, 332 n13
Harviainen, T., 121 n20
Haupt, P., 221
Hauser, A., 69
Held, M., 190 n43, 191 n46
Hoglund, K. G., 26 n25
Holbert, J. C., 332, 333
Holman, C. H., 331 n11
Huxley, A., 143

Jacobsen, T., 260
Jarry, A., 345
Jepsen, A., 69
Jirku, A., 68
Johnson, A. R., 180, 181
Joslin, M. C., 224 n2
Joüon, P. P., 66, 103

Kaufmann, Y., 21
Keil, C. F., *passim* in Commentary
Kirk, E. P., 333 n14
Koehler, L., 66
Koestler, A., 324
Komlós, O., 151 n15
König, E., 69, 84, 345 n32
Krantz, E. S., 81, 100
Krasovec, J., 162

Lacocque A./P.-E., 289, 325, 333 n14
Lambdin, T. O., 220
Landes, G. M., 22, 23, 73, 74, *passim* in Commentary
Lawrence, P. J. N., 248
Levine, B., 189 n39
Levine, É., 11, 13 n7, 66, *passim* in Commentary
Lewis, C., 336
Licht, J., 16, 213
Lindblom, M., 108, 110 n3
Lohfink, N., 77, 288

McCarter, P. K., 110 n3, 176 n16
McKane, W., 188 n38, 189 n40
Magonet, J. D., 18 n15, 76, *passim* in Commentary
Maillot, A., 336
Masing, H., 68
Mather, J., 333, 334, 347 n36
Melville, H., 65
Meschonnic, H., 194
Michaels, L., 331
Miles, G. B., 332
Milik, J. T., 10
Miller, P. D., 76
Mitchell, S., 143 n1
More, J., 349 n42
Muraoka, T., 179, 274 n8

Nielsen, E., 288 n20, 345 n32

O'Connor, M., 208
Olmstead, A. T., 311
Oppenheim, A. L., 230 n10
Orlinsky, H. M., 24, 25 n24, 69, 274 n8

Paine, T., 324, 332
Parpola, S., 311, 312
Payne, D. F., 334
Perowne, T. T., 201, 269 n2
Pesch, R., 16
Petrovics, E., 325
Pollard, A., 331 n11
Porten, B., 74, 118
Pushkin, A., 339 n26

Rainey, A., 118
Rameau, J.-P., 198
Rauber, D. F., 244, 347 n36, 349 n41
Robinson, B. P., 291
Rofé, A., 336
Rosen, N., 325
Rosenberg, J., 193 n50, 335 n17, 337 n21
Rudolph, W., 9, 68, *passim* in Commentary
Ruether, R. and H., 274 n7

Schmidt, L., 68, 337
Schneider, D. A., 10 n2, 20
Shaw, G. B., 348
Silberman, L. H., 259
Simon, P., 143 n2
Snaith, N. H., 125
Sperber, A., 11, 133 n5
Sperling, S. D., 25 n24
Stamm, J. J., 68
Steffen, U., 350 n42
Sternberg, M., 325, 329 n9
Stol, M., 292 n2
Stuart, D., *passim* in Commentary
Stuhlmueller, C., 68

Talmon, S., 86, 155 n22, 187
Thomas, D. W., 228, 307
Thompson, S., 328
Torrance, R. M., 349 n41
Trible, P. L., 9, 19, 20, 27, 69, *passim* in Commentary
Tromp, N. J., 171 n11
Trumbull, H. C., 220
Tyrer, J. W., 29

Vanoni, G., 103 n6, 280
Vaux, R. de, 230
Vermes, G., 213

Watson, W. G. E., 161
Weidner, E., 245
Wellhausen, J., 324
Wesselski, A., 347 n36
Westermann, C., 184
Wilson, A. J., 150
Wilson, R. D., 149 n8
Winckler, H., 288, 304, 342
Wiseman, D. J., 230, 232, 246, 249, 311

INDEXES

Wolff, H. W., 9, 27, 83, *passim* in Commentary

Yadin, Y., 111
Young, E. J., 324

Ziegler, J., 10
Zlotowitz, M., 12, 69, *passim* in Commentary

Ancient, Medieval, and Renaissance
Adrian of Tyre, 96
Aesop, 315, 316 n22, 322 n18
Alcaeus of Lesbos, 339
Antiphon, 91, 100, 111
Aristotle, 231
Augustine, 221 n8, 234

Calvin, J., 79, 96, 115, 269, 275 n9, 314 n18, 319, 324
Cyril, 246

Donne, J., 159

Herodotus, 91, 92, 231, 251
Hipponax, 94
Homer, 91
Horace, 90

Ibn Ezra, 77, 78, *passim* in Commentary
Ibn Gabriol, 150 n13
Ibn Janah, 198

Jerome, 10, 11, 87, *passim* in Commentary
Jewel, J., 65
Josephus, 87, 90, 101, 103, 138 n13, 154, 221, 234, 283 n17, 320 n24
Justin Martyr, 234
Juvenal, 90

Kara (Joseph), 304
Kimḥi (Radak), 17, 113, 190 n45, 198, 201, 219, 228, 244, 261, 324
al-Kisaʾi, 17 n13, 320 n24

Luther, 244

Maimonides. *See* Rambam
Menippus, 333

Nahman ben Isaac, 226

Origen, 347

Phaedrus, 90
Philo, 28, 101, 233, 234, 314

Radak. *See* Kimḥi
Rambam, 220
Rashi, 79, 319
Rashbam, 229
Rogier de Lisle, 223, 224 n2

Sforno, 179, 198 n54, 275 n9
Sophocles, 100
Synesius, 81, 149 n20

Vegetius, 81
Vergil, 255

INDEX of SCRIPTURAL REFERENCES

HEBREW SCRIPTURE

Genesis
1 94
9–10 119
26–28 156
3:9 329 n10
14 219
14–19 205
4 351
5–6 274
8 121 n19
9 329 n10
14–16 78
6:6–7 262
11–13 259
7:16 190
10:8–12 70
9 229
11 72
11:6 329 n10
12 242
8 121 n18
14 249
21–24 235
23 104
15:6 243
18 75, 235
20 75 n5, 87 n12
21 329 n10
22–23 133, 243
30 274
19:15–26 302
21 234
25 234

29 234
20 242
21:16 230
22 234
15 226
24:12 80
25:22 285
26:18 258
27:46 285
29:4 114
35 137
30:1 285
9 137
36 230, 231
31:23 230
36 274
32:23–33 302
35:16 230
38:14 305
40:15 127
42:7 114 n7
17 153
44:1–5 225
44:8 307
45:5 274
20 309
47:3 114
48:7 230
49 161, 206
13 100
18 195

Exodus
3:6 181
18 230, 231
4 351
1–9 295
6:29 227
7:13 234
10:13 303
19 94
12:33–36 309
14:21 303, 304
31 243, 244
15 161
4–5 185
8 175
18:9 292
19:25 121 n19
26:22 100
32 75, 241
12–14 263
32 284, 285
34:6 345 n32
6–7 241, 279, 280

Leviticus
1:2 254
11:9 149
13:6–7 225
58 226
16:8 111
8–10 108
18:25 96
28 220
20:17 198
22:25 140
27:33 314

Numbers
5:21 172
10:33 230
11:1–3 241
10–15 285
31 230
12:8 181
13:22 228
14 75
10–28 241
11 243
18 280
16 241
15 274
19:11 133
20:1–13 273
12 243
21:4 304
4–9 241
9 181
22 347
7–14 348
22–35 145
23 161, 206
19 239
24 206
26:56 314
31:8 348 n39

Deuteronomy
1:1 185
4:31 280
8:18 194
14:9 149
15:9 74
18:21–22 269
21:1–9 134 n9
23:5–6 348 n39
28:39 301, 310
29:22 234
32 161, 206
21 195
33 161, 206

INDEXES

Joshua
1:1 66
5:2 226
6:15 302
7 109
9:8 114
10:2 72
13:22 348 n39
19:13 69
46 80
24:9–10 348 n39

Judges
1:1 66
3:8–10 249
4:15–22 206
21 304
5 161
24–31 206
6:17–22 295
36–40 295
8:10 311
34 194
9 351
11:24 104
14 145
4 234
16:16 285, 304
17:2 121 n19
9 114
19 302
17 114
20 108
9 108
14–37 245

1 Samuel
1:1–3 66
21–22 140
2:1–10 164, 165, 206
5:9 290
12 242
6:8 274
7 242
3–14 245
9 145
9 228
10:19 108
14 110
24 109
43–46 109
15:10 68
11 239 n2, 262, 275 n9
29 239
16 351
1 275 n9
18:8 274
19:43 274
20:7 274
21:12 277
29:3 277
30:12–15 153
26 110

2 Samuel
1:1 67
19–27 206
3:33–34 206
7:5 68
10:3 234
11:3 277
12:1–4 144
22 245, 260, 261
13:21 274
17:14 234
25 116 n9
19:8 273
36 314
20:6 273
22 162
24 245
11 68
16 262

1 Kings
1:40 293
3:9 314
11 305
6:25 18
7:37 187
8:41–43 140
63 311
9:3 225
11:21–23 343
29–39 343
12:24 68
13 146, 347
2 74
11–32 234
11–34 18
21 68
14:1–18 343
16:7–12 343
17:1–6 146
2 68
17:2–4 285
8 68
8–24 343
21 153
24 24, 86
18:1 68
46 343
19 23, 317, 343
2–4 284

4 305
5 102
7 226
9 103 n6
15–16 344
21 242
1 248
21:9 245
17 68
27 245
22 351
8–28 343
19–23 234
49–50 92

2 Kings
1:3 248
2:7–25 343
23–24 146
4:4–5 190
5:13 308 n11
17–18 25
19 230
8:7–15 343, 344
14 20, 27, 69, 345 n32
23–27 86
25 116, 181, 227, 343
17:6 246
18:11 246
19 241
36–37 249
20 206
1–6 294, 295
8 153
12–19 242
13 293
22 242
23 242
16–18 347
24:4 242

Isaiah
1:8 290
3:3 15
5:12 181
14 184
9:16 293
11:11 226
14:11 301
15 100
19:19–22 129, 140
21 200
24 229 n9
23:1 96
26:19 188
20 190
27:11 299
36:4–11 232
37 351
38:1–8 294
10 171
10–20 206
22 153
39:2 293
42:6 25 n24
44:3 221
14 310
17 154
45:20 154
49:6 25 n24
10 301, 304
50:2 156
51:20 305
58:1–7 245
59:6 259
65:1–2 239
66:19 79
24 301

Jeremiah
1:5 25 n24
13 226
5:28 104
8:19 196
10:5 287
13:3 226
14 310
14:11–12 245
15:7 189
17 269
17:12–13 188
18:7–10 239
8 345 n32
11 258, 259
20:14–18 284
16 234
22:8 72
25:12 242 n7
29 75
38 323 n3
26:15 134 n9
26:18–19 241
20–24 343
28 343
29:24–32 343
31:22 176 n17
26 254
33:1 226
36 247
39:3 102
42:10 262
48:20 227
49:14 15
29 74

50:21 249
51:9 247, 248
51:34 151, 152 n17

Ezekiel
1:4 95
3:4–7 232
8:8 130
12:5 130
27–28 223
14:12–23 308 n11
14:13 96
15:16 307, 308
17:3–10 144
10 303
18:2 103
23 299
19:12 303
22:26 314
30 235
24:14 310
26:19–21 182 n24
27 23
4 175
13 133
24–26 303
31:4 310
15 305
32:23 100
24 187
33:11 299
42:20 314
44:23 314
47:10 156

Hosea
4:10 196
7:11 69
11:11 69
13:5 303
14–15 299
14:3 138

Joel
2:13 245, 280
14 260, 261
15–17 243
17 310
4:19 133

Amos
3:6–7 223
4:11 234
7:9,11 345 n32
8:13 305
9:2 130

Obadiah 345 n32

Micah
1:2 181
3:12 241
6:5 348 n39
12 259
7:18–20 299
19 174, 258

Nahum
entire 22 n20
1:3 280
3:10 108

Habakkuk
1:2 173
2:20 181

Zephaniah
1:9 259
10 176
3:1 68

Haggai
2:6 233

Zechariah
1:1 67
7 67
3:2 277
4:12 226
6:8 252
7:4–7 245
9:14 95
10:2 195

Malachi
2:13 226
3:18 314

Psalms
3:3–9 200
5:8 181
9:14 189 n41
16:4 195
18 161
5 183
5–6 173, 174
6 171
7 168, 193
42 173
49 259
21:8 149
22:30 189
27–28 189 n39
24 189 n41

26:4–5 84
7 199
30:4 183
12 246
31:17 195
23 177, 178
34:16–17 178
35:13 245
37 195
39 200
40:13 184
42:18 174
46:3 175
48:8 303
49 195
16 171, 283
50:14 138
56:13 200
65:2 140
67 165
68:24 149 n8
69 202
2 183, 184
16 152 n17
71:9 196
20 189
73 195
76:7 102
77:4 192
78 206
38 280
79:1 181
86:5 280
15 280
88:2–14 171, 172
3 192
7 173
89:49 171
90:5–6 318
91:2 198
95:5 119
102:2 192
103:4 183
8 280
105:16 75
18 184
106 206
3 195
32 273
107 123 n22, 165
5–6 192
18 189 n41
23 114
30 122, 123
111:4 280
112:4 280
115:2–8 135
116:3 171
5 280
14–18 140
17–18, 19 199
119 165
6 181
120:1 168
121:6 301, 304
130:1–2 169
135:5–7 135
7 136 n10
138:2 181
139:7–10 78
141:7 171
142:4 192
143:4–5 192
144:1–2 198
3–4 318
145:8 280

Job
3 284
7:3 148
16:17 259
17:13–19 190 n42
16 171
19:7 173
20:15 151
23:12 108 n1
24:16 130
27:18 290
33:14–17 102 n5
36:26 185
38:1 95
8–10 190
41 257
42:10 110

Proverbs
7:7 171
9:18 171
10:5 102
14:16 97
34 198
16:33 108, 109
18:8 108
19:5 102
23:34 175
25:16 220
26:20 122
30:19 175

Ruth
1:1 67
16–17 24
2:3 80

3:14 302
4:7 228

Song of Songs
entire 337 n22
1:4 293
5:14 305

Qoheleth
3:21 189
8:17 113 n5
10:2 315

Lamentations
1:15 74
3:31–33 351
54 177, 178, 183
4:6 234
16 181

Esther
1:1 67
8 102
2:19 226
4:16 245

Daniel
1:3 102
5–10 148
5:2–3 254
25 233
6:1 249
4 104
11 153
24–28 146
7:9 134
9:9 320 n24
10:9 102
11 227

Ezra
4:10 249
6:14 254
22 249
8:21 245
21–23 243
9 25
10 242
10:23 342 n27

Nehemiah
1:14 245
2:6 230
10 273
3:33 274
4:1 274
9:1–5 25
17 280
31 280
10:35 108
11:1 108
13:8 273
22 310

1 Chronicles
5:26 246
2:17 116 n9
12:8 259
19:3 234
24 111
29:9 293

2 Chronicles
9:21 82, 83
11:1–4 343
12:5–8 294 n24
15:1–7 344
15 293
16:7–10 344
19:2–3 343
20:14–19 344
20 243
34 343
35–37 92
37 344
24:20–22 344
26:5 344
29 241
21 301
30 241
6 253
9 280
30:27 193
34:22–28 343

APOCRYPHA and PSEUDEPIGRAPHA

Sirach
16:19 187
48:22 14
51:1–12 213
19 189

Judith
1:11 72
2:21 153
4:9–15 245
10–12 255, 257

Tobit
2 284
3 284

6:2 150
14:3–4 87

3 Maccabees
6:8 218 n2

4 Maccabees
7:1–3 338

1 Esdras
9:23 342 n27

2 Esdras
14:1 153

4 Esdras
1:39–40 14 n8

Baruch
1:10–13 243

Martyrdom and Ascension of Isaiah
4:22 14 n8

Lives of the Prophets
10:1–11 320 n24

Pseudo-Philo 136

NEW TESTAMENT

Matthew
8:23–27 100
12:38–42 217
16:18 189 n41

Mark
8:11–13 217 n1

Luke
4:16–20 28
11:29–32 32

Acts
1:12 230
23–26 108
10:14 132 n3
13:15 28
27 81
1–28 91
15 99 n3

2 Corinthians
11:25–27 91

KORAN

10 160 n2
21:87–88 159
37:145–46 218
68:48–49 218

QUMRAN

Hodayot 213, 214

RABBINICS

Babylonian Talmud
Baba Bathra 21
14b–15a 20
38a–39a 82
Giṭṭin 31b 303 n4
Keritot 6b 313
Megillah 31a 28
Nedarim 38a 83
Roš Haššana 16b 240 n4
Sanhedrin 89b 234, 235
Taʿanit 17a 159 n1
Yebamot 98b 223

Jerusalem Talmud
Makkot 2:6 240 n5

Mishnah
Berakhot 9:1 137 n12
Taʿanit 2:1 240 n3

Midrashim

Tannaitic
Mekilta, Pisḥa 89, 323

Rabbah
Exod 347 n38
Numb 15 n11
Lam 323, 323 n3
Eccl 140
Esth 97

On Jonah 88 n13, 141, 320 n24

Rab. Eliezer 87, 88, 150 n12, 269

Zohar
wayyaqhēl 199b 228, 323

CUNEIFORM LITERATURE

Akkadian
ARM 2:106 156, 157
ARM 10:43 308 n11
ARM 14:1 156, 157

INDEXES

ARM 26:206 259
T. Halaf 13f 245
Esarhaddon 242 n7
Gudea Cyl. 260
El-Amarna 288, 338

(From Anet[3])
140 [Anat] 189 n40
289 [Esarhad.] 250
543 [Esarhad.] 118
561 [Adad-Guppi] 242

INDEX of WORDS

Hebrew (arranged by roots)
ʾābad 20, 104, 132
ʾādām 254, 313
  ʾadāmâ 278
ʾadderet 250
ʾak 179, 180
ʾel (prep.)
  (+ nînewēh) 70
ʾēl
  hāʾelōhîm 103
  lēʾlōhîm 228, 229, 230
  ʾēlōhê haššamayim 22, 118
  (+ *qōnēh ʾereṣ*) 119 n15
ʾûlay (adv) 103
ʾāman 69, 243, 291
  ʾemûnâ 69
  ʾamittay 69
  ben-ʾamittay 86
  ʾemet 69
ʾāmar 177,. 219, 253
  leʾmōr 252, 253
  wayyōʾmer 252
  (– quote) 121 n19
  (versus *higgîd*) 121
ʾonîyâ 80, 81, 101
ʾanî 308
ʾanōkî 117
ʾôṣār 94
ʾāpap 184
ʾereṣ 115, 119, 186, 187, 188, 189
ʾăšer 112, 113, 310
ʾattâ 308

bôʾ
  (re: ships) 82, 83
  (+ *ʾel*) 194
  (+ *ʿim*) 84
  (+ *hālak*) 83
  (*mēʾayin* +) 114
behēmâ 254
beṭen 172
bālaʿ 151, 152
bāqār 254
bāraḥ 77, 278
berîaḥ 190

gādal
  giddal 310
  gādôl 20, 246
gôzāl 69
gôrāl 109
gāraš 178

dābār 227, 247, 277
  (+ *ʾel*) 227
  debar-YHWH 67, 68, 86, 225, 227
debîr 181
dāg 155, 156, 221 n7
  (+ *gādôl*) 149, 150, 151, 220
dām 133
  dām nāqîʾ 133
  dam neqîyîm 134
derek (+ *raʿ*) 258

ha-
  halôʾ-zeh 277
  hablê-šāwʾ 197, 199
  hāyâ 313
  way(*ye*)*hî* 66 (begins narrative)
    95 (impersonal)
  (+ *debar-YHWH*) 85, 225
hêkāl 181
hālak 111, 123
  mahalak 230
hapak 94, 234
  nehpāket 234, 236, 237, 267, 295, 345 n34
  (G versus N) 345 n34
zābaḥ 138, 200
  (+ *nādar*) 140
zākar 193
  (+ *YHWH*) 193
zāʿap 137
zāʿaq 252
  zāʿaq ʾel 98, 154

ḥābaš 184
  ḥābûš 186
**ḥwb* 96
ḥûs 309, 310
ḥāzaq 94
  beḥozqâ 258
**ḥll* 231 n12
  wayyāḥēl 231
ḥāmas 259
ḥesed 198, 199
ḥāšâ 96

ḥāšab (D) 96
ḥāpēṣ 135
ḥôq 108 n1
ḥārâ 307
  wayyiḥar lô 273
  (+ *le-*) 274, 286
  (+ *ʾap*) 274
  ḥārôn ʾap 262, 274
ḥarîšît 302, 303 n4
**ḥtr* 130

**ṭwl* (H) 93, 174 n13
  (+ *ʾel*) 94
  (+ *ʿal*) 94
ṭāʿam 255
  ṭaʿam 253, 256

yabbāšâ 119, 221
yādaʿ 20, 279, 314
  (legal) 125
  mî-yōdeaʿ 260
yehûdâ 115
  yehûdî (*m*) 116
**yāṭab*
  hahêṭêb 286
yām 95, 119
yemîmâ 69
yāsap H
  (auxiliary) 180, 181
yārēʾ 97, 137, 243
  yārēʾ YHWH 118, 137
  yirʾat YHWH/
    ʾelōhîm 120
yārad 99, 182, 187, 188
yārēk 100
yiśrāʾēl
  yiśreʾeli 116
  benê yiśrāʾēl 115, 116
yešûʿātâ 201

kî 75, 279, 280
  ki ʾattâ YHWH 134
  kî yōdēaʿ ʾānî 125
kēlîm 98

**lʾk* 114
  melāʾkâ 114, 126
lēb/lēbāb 174
  (+ *yāmmîm*) 175
laylâ
  bin-laylâ 313
lûlāb 82

māh(-)
  mah-zzōʾt
    (*ʿaśîtā*) 120
  mah-llekā 103

māḥorāt
  lammāḥorāt 301
mallāḥ 97
mānâ (D: *minnâ*) 20, 147, 148, 149 n8, 300
min . . . ʿad 254
mēʿîm 152
māṣāʾ 81
meṣûlâ 74, 175
mišbārîm 176

nābîʾ 342
**nbṭ*
  hibbîṭ 181, 181 n22
nāgaʿ (*ʾel*) 247
nādar (+ *zābaḥ*) 140, 248
nāhār 175, 176
  parallel *tehôm* 182
nḥm (D *or* N) 261, 262
  niḥam 20
nāṭal (*H) 93
nākâ (H) 301
nāpal 111
nepeš 133
  (+ *ḥayyîm*) 183
  (+ *ʿāṭap*) 193
nāqîʾ 133 (*See also* dām)
nāṣal (H) 292
nāśāʾ 124
nātan
  (+ *ʿal*) 133

sābab 176, 176 n17
sôp/sûp 184
saʿar 95
sukkâ 290, 298, 333
sepînâ 80, 101

ʿābad 313
ʿibrî 115, 116, 117 n12, 127
ʿad
  (+ *heyôt*) 277
  (+ *māwet*) 307
  (+ *nepeš*) 307
ʿôd 233, 234
ʿāzab 198
**ʿāṭap* (HtD) 316
  hitʿaṭṭēp 20, 193
ʿayin 178, 179
ʿal
  (+ *kēn*) 278
ʿālâ (G or H) 292, 293
  wattaʿal 190
  heʿelâ 182, 183
  baʿalôt 301
  ʿalâ lipnê 76
ʿôlām
  leʿôlām 190

INDEXES

ʿālap (HtD) 316
yitʿallāp 20, 304
ʿam 115
ʿāmad 136, 137 n11
ʿāmal (be-) 310
ʿānâ 170
ʿîr
bāʿîr 231
(+ *haggedôlâ*) 309
ʿāpār 252, 257
ʿāśâ 118, 120, 263
ʿāśâ le- 122, 263
ʿasîta (*mah-zzōʾt*) 120
maʿaśeh 263
**ʿāšat* (HtD) 104
hitʿaššēt 20, 103
cattâ 283

**pll* (HtD)
hitpallēl
(+ *ʾel/lipnê*) 154, 155
tepillâ 194

ṣōʾn 254, 255
ṣwm/ṣôm 245
ṣālal (H) 292
**ṣrr*
miṣṣārâ lî 169, 170

qîʾ (G or H) 151 n16, 152, 220
qārāʾ 226, 257
(+ *ʿal/ʾel*) 72
(+ *ʾel*) 72, 154, 169, 255
(+ *ʾel YHWH*) 131
(+ *ʿal*) 72, 87, 174, 257 n25
(+ *wayyōmaʾr*) 232
qedem 289
**qādam* (D)
qiddēm 278
qōdeš 181
**qālal* (H)
hēqal meʿal 99
qûm
(auxiliary) 69
qînâ 209
qîqāyôn 291, 298, 301, 307, 317, 333, 338, 346
qerîʾâ 226
qeṣeb 187

**rbb*
rab haḥōbēl 102, 103
ribbô 311
**rābâ* (H)
harbeh 312
**rādam* (N) 101, 102 n5
reḥōbōt ʿir 72, 312

rûaḥ
(+ *gedōlâ*) 94
rāʿâ 255
rēaʿ 110
rāʿaʿ 255, 256
yeraʿ ʾel 273
raʿ 20
rāʿâ 76, 111, 112, 256, 272
rāʿātām 75
**ršš* 79

śākār 83, 84
śaq 246, 257

še- 313
bešel ʾašer 113 n5
bešellemî 112, 113
šāʾal
(+ *nepeš*) 305
šeʾôl 119 n14, 170, 171, 172
šûb 24, 130, 131
(auxiliary) 258
(+ min) 260
**šāwaʿ* (D)
šiwwaʿ 172, 173
šāḥat 191
šālaḥ 114
**šālēm* (D)
šillam 200
šelōšet yāmîm 152, 153, 154
šāmaʿ 173, 232
šāmar 196 n53
šāmayim 119
šēnît 225, 226
šātaq 122, 123

tôdâ 200
tehôm 184
tôlaʿat 310

tôr 69
taršîš(*â*) 78

ARAMAIC (ARRANGED ALPHABETICALLY)

ʾkryz 232
ʾelāh šemayyāʾ 118 n13

ʾrym 93

bdyl mn 112
bmymrʾ dYY 244
btwšbḥt ʾwdʾh 200

drʿwʾ ʿbdtʾ 135

gzr 245 n11

ḥwbt 133

wyhbʾ ʾgrh 83
yhwdʾh ʾnʾ 117
ymʾ 177

kʿn 132

mymrʾ 178

nbwʾtʾ 226
nḥšwl 177

ʾd mwtʾ 184

qbyl bʿwtnʾ 132
qdm YY 137, 229

rb spnyʾ 102

ṭeʿēm 253

AKKADIAN

arkat eleppi 100
idû 84
igrum 84
rašāšum 79
sapinatum 101 n4
**trš* 79

SUMERIAN

é.gal 181
giš.má 101 n4
má.lah$_4$ 97